DRUG ABUSE

Nelson-Hall Series in Law, Crime, and Justice

Howard Abadinsky, Series Consulting Editor
Saint Xavier University

DRUG ABUSE
An Introduction

Howard Abadinsky

THIRD EDITION

Nelson-Hall Publishers
Chicago

Senior Editor: Libby Rubenstein
Production/Design Manager: Tamra Phelps
Photo Researcher/Illustrator: Nicholas Communications
Typesetter: E.T. Lowe
Printer: The Maple-Vail Book Manufacturing Company
Cover Painting: "And Getting Well Again" by Tim Stegmaier

Library of Congress Cataloging-in-Publication Data

Abadinsky, Howard. 1941–
    Drug abuse : an introduction / Howard Abadinsky.   3rd. ed.
        p.   cm.
    Includes bibliographical references and indexes.
    ISBN 0–8304–1476–2
    1. Drug abuse—United States.   2. Drug abuse—United States—Prevention.   I. Title.
HV5825.A6325   1996
362.29'0973—dc20   96–28084
CIP

BRIEF CONTENTS

CONTENTS

Chapter Three: The Pharmacology of Drug Abuse   69

Chapter Four: The Psychology and Sociology of Drug Abuse   123

Chapter Five: Drug Abuse: Treatment and Prevention   161

Chapter Six: The Business of Drugs 217

Chapter Seven: Drug-Law Enforcement 263

Chapter Eight: Drug Abuse: Policy and Alternatives   307

PREFACE

While there are numerous texts on drug abuse, they focus on a particular aspect or aspects of the issue: pharmacology, psychology, sociology, treatment, the business of drugs, prevention, laws and law enforcement, policy. None are comprehensive. This book strives to provide the reader with a thorough understanding of drug abuse policy. To accomplish that goal, it is necessary to examine drug history, biological, psychological, and sociological explanations of drug abuse, the various types of treatment and prevention programs, the business of drugs, and drug laws and law enforcement. Without an understanding of these topics, an informed discussion of policy is not possible. Without an understanding of the dynamics of drug abuse, discussion of the problem becomes an exercise equivalent to the proverbial blind men attempting to describe an elephant; each can accurately portray only that part he can touch. Hence the logic behind the comprehensive nature of this book.

Because the subject of drug abuse transcends so many disciplines—history, law, neuropharmacology, political science, social work, counseling, psychology, and sociology—the literature is massive and diverse. Combining all aspects of drug abuse in a single book is a daunting task. This third edition continues the comprehensive approach of the first two editions, updating and adding information on pharmacology, inhalants, herbal stimulants, the changing nature of the drug business, and recent developments in policy, particularly the emerging approach of *harm reduction.*

The author welcomes correspondence about his work, and can be reached at Saint Xavier University, 3700 W. 103rd Street, Chicago, IL 60655.

ACKNOWLEDGMENTS

I would like to thank Mark Blagen, Patrick Allen, and Fred Andes for their careful reviews and suggestions for this edition. I also want to thank previous reviewers whose suggestions have made a third edition possible: Wayman C. Mullins, James Yenan, Bruce D. Johnson, Bryan J. Vila, Laura E. Nagy, and Rick Aniskewiscz. Special recognition goes to the library staff at Saint Xavier University, especially Rose Bennett. And thanks to Nelson-Hall President Steve Ferrara for his confidence in me, and to my editor, Libby Rubenstein, for her interest and careful attention to detail.

1

AN INTRODUCTION TO DRUG ABUSE

There is probably one thing, and one thing only, on which the leaders of all modern states agree; on which Catholics, Protestants, Jews, Mohammedans, and atheists agree; on which Democrats, Republicans, Socialists, Communists, Liberals, and Conservatives agree; on which medical and scientific authorities throughout the world agree. That thing is the "scientific fact" that certain substances that people like to ingest or inject are "dangerous" both to those who use them and to others; and that the use of such substances constitutes "drug abuse"or "drug addiction"—a disease whose control and eradication are the duty of the combined forces of the medical profession and the state. However, there is little agreement on which substances are acceptable and which substances are unacceptable.
—Thomas Szasz (1974: xi; edited)

The legal distinction between licit and illicit drugs is sometimes treated as if it had pharmacological significance. Vendors of licit drugs and proponents of a "drug-free society" share an interest in convincing tobacco smokers and alcohol drinkers that smoking and drinking are radically different than "drug abuse." But a nicotine addict can be just as hooked as a heroin addict, and the victim of an alcohol overdose is just as dead as the victim of a cocaine overdose.—Mark A.R. Kleiman (1992: 7)

With an estimated 2.7 million hardcore users on the streets, and with Americans spending $49 billion annually on illegal drugs, action must be taken.—Office of National Drug Control Policy (1994: 1)

This opening chapter will prepare readers for discussions in subsequent chapters. We will begin by describing the problems inherent in defining terms such as *drugs* and *drug abuse,* the dangers of legal drugs—nicotine and alcohol—the drug use continuum from abstinence to dependency, classes of psychoactive drugs, and the problem of polydrug use. We will briefly review the various ways of responding to the problem of drug abuse and the relationship between drugs, crime, and violence.

DRUGS

The term *drug* is derived from the fourteenth-century French word *drogue,* meaning a dry substance—most pharmaceuticals at that time were prepared from dried herbs (Palfai and Janiewicz 1991). There is no completely satisfy-

Teenagers smoking in Boston. Despite vigorous anti-cigarette campaigns, the proportion of adolescent smokers has remained the same for the last ten years.

ing way of delineating what is and what is not a drug—for example, the differences between water, vitamin supplements, and penicillin (Goode 1989). Thus, some feel it appropriate to refer to *chemical* or *substance* abuse. Imprecision in the use of the term *drug* has had serious social consequences.

Because alcohol is excluded from most people's definition of *drug*, the public is conditioned to regard a martini as something fundamentally different from a marijuana cigarette, a barbiturate capsule, or a bag of heroin. Similarly, because the meaning of the word *drug* differs so widely in therapeutic and social contexts, the public is conditioned to believe that "street" drugs act according to entirely different principles than "medical" drugs, alcohol, and nicotine with the result that the risks of the former are exaggerated and the risks of the latter are overlooked (Uelmen and Haddox 1983).

"In contemporary society the word *drug* has two connotations—one positive, explaining its crucial role in medicine, and one negative, reflecting, not the natural and synthetic makeup of these chemicals, but the self-destruction and socially deleterious patterns of misuse" (Jones, Shainberg, and Byer 1979: 1). In this book the term *drug* will refer to substances having mood-altering (psychotropic or psychoactive) effects. This definition includes caffeine, which produces dependence and withdrawal symptoms,[1] nicotine, and alcohol, as well as illegal chemicals such as marijuana, heroin, and cocaine.

DRUG ABUSE AND ADDICTION

Drug abuse implies the misuse of certain substances—it is a *moral,* not a scientific, term: "An unstandardized, value-laden, and highly relative term used with a great deal of imprecision and confusion, generally implying drug use that is excessive, dangerous, or undesirable to the individual or community and that ought to be modified" (Nelson et al. 1982: 33). Drug abuse "implies willful, improper use due to an underlying disorder or a quest for hedonistic or immoral pleasure" (N. Miller 1995: 10). Joseph Westermeyer and Ronald Krug (1991) suggest a distinction between *abuse* and *dependence,* the latter referring to chronic use. Abuse, therefore, should refer to *excessive* use short of dependence.

---

1. Caffeine, found in tea, coffee, many cola drinks, and cocoa products, is the most widely used psychoactive drug—about 90 percent of the adult North American population ingests caffeine regularly. After the ingestion of caffeine, the chemical's compounds dissolve in the bloodstream and travel to the brain. Caffeine molecules are almost identical to a brain chemical—the neurotransmitter adenosine—that serves to control the release of other chemicals that excite the central nervous system. Caffeine occupies adenosine receptor sites in the brain, neutralizing this control mechanism. The result is an elevation of mood and a decrease in fatigue; and, in high doses, insomnia and a racing heart. Abrupt withdrawal of caffeine can result in headaches, lethargy, and depression-like symptoms (Blakeslee 1991, 1994; Griffiths 1990; Griffiths et al. 1990; "Quitting Caffeine" 1991).

SUBSTANCE ABUSE

The American Psychiatric Association (1994: 182) refers to substance abuse as a "maladaptive pattern of substance use manifested by recurrent and significant adverse consequences related to the repeated use of substances," including "repeated failure to fulfill major role obligations, repeated use in situations in which it is physically hazardous, multiple legal problems, and recurrent social and interpersonal problems."

There are numerous definitions of drug abuse that reflect social values, not scientific insight: "One reason for the prevalence of definitions of drug abuse that are neither logical nor scientific is the strength of Puritan moralism in American culture which frowns on the pleasure and recreation provided by intoxicants" (Zinberg 1984: 33). Such definitions typically refer to: (1) the nonmedical use of a substance, (2) to alter the mental state, (3) in a manner that is detrimental to the individual or the community and/or, (4) that is illegal. For example, the American Social Health Association (1972: 1) defines drug abuse as the "use of mood modifying chemicals outside of medical supervision, and in a manner which is harmful to the person and the community." Other definitions, such as those offered by the World Health Organization and the American Medical Association, include references to physical and/or psychological dependency (Zinberg 1984).

In fact drug abuse may be defined from a number of perspectives:

The legal definition equates drug use with the mere act of using a proscribed drug or using a drug under proscribed conditions. The moral definition is similar, but greater emphasis is placed on the motivation or purpose for which the drug is used. The medical model opposes unsupervised usage but emphasizes the physical and mental consequences for the user, and the social definition stresses social responsibility and adverse effects on others. (Balter 1974: 5)

The use of psychoactive chemicals, licit or illicit, can objectively be labeled "abuse" only when the user becomes dysfunctional as a consequence; for example, is unable to maintain employment, has impaired social relationships, exhibits dangerous—reckless or aggressive—behavior; and/or significantly endangers his or her health. Drug use can be viewed as a continuum: At one end is the nonuser who has never used prohibited, or abused lawful, psychoactive drugs; at the other end is the drug-dependent, a compulsive user whose every aspect of life revolves around obtaining, maintaining, and using a supply of drugs. For the compulsive user, failure to secure an adequate supply of the desired drug results in psychological stress and discomfort and with some physical withdrawal symptoms. "While compulsive users constitute only a small proportion of the overall drug-using population, they consume a disproportionate share of drugs and contribute disproportionately to the society's drug problem" (*Drug Abuse and Drug Abuse Research* 1987: 14; hereafter "Drug Abuse").

What we know about those who use psychoactive drugs is skewed toward compulsive users. Between the two extremes of nonuse and compulsive use are the experimental and recreational or casual user.

> For the recreational user, intoxication is voluntary, and regardless of the duration of use, such people tend not to escalate their use to uncontrollable amounts. For example, long-term cocaine users have found that recreational patterns can be maintained for a decade or more without loss of control. Such use tends to occur in weekly or biweekly episodes, and users perceive that the effects facilitate social functioning. (Siegel 1989: 222–23)

Noncompulsive users have received very little research attention because they are hard to find:

> Much data on users are gathered from treatment, law enforcement, and correctional institutions, and from other institutions allied with them. Naturally these data sources provide a highly selected sample of users: those who have encountered significant personal, medical, social, or legal problems in conjunction with their drug use, and thus represent the pathological end of the using spectrum. (Zinberg et al. 1978: 13)

Such data "cannot be used to support a causal interpretation because of the absence of information on individuals who may have ingested a drug but had minimal or no negative consequences" (Newcomb and Bentler 1988: 13).

Despite the lack of information on noncompulsive drug use, government policy typically avoids distinctions: "The highest priority of our drug policy," stated former "Drug Czar" William J. Bennett (Office of National Drug Control Strategy 1989: 8), "is to reduce the overall level of drug use—experimental, first use, 'casual' use, regular use, and addiction alike." This is because the casual user is "a potential agent of infection for the nonusers in his personal ambit" (1989: 11).

DRUG USE CONTINUUM

nonuser → experimental → culturally endorsed* → recreational → compulsive

---

* This category would include the use of drugs—wine or peyote, for example—in religious ceremonies.

Secretaries of the Chancellor's Office at UCLA unwind on a Friday afternoon after work. Such weekly drinking traditions are an example of culturally endorsed drug use.

In this book, while recognizing the shortcomings of any definition, we will use the following:

Drug Abuse: Ingesting a psychoactive substance[2] that is illegal to possess and/or that is taken in quantities that impair the individual's ability to function in society.

Norman Miller (1995) eschews the use of term *drug abuse* and opts, instead, for *addiction*[3] characterized by:

1. *Preoccupation:* The addict assigns a high priority to acquiring drugs. Social relationships and employment are jeopardized in the quest for drugs and the consequences of use.
2. *Compulsion:* The addict continues to use drugs despite serious adverse consequences. He or she will often deny the connection between the adverse consequences and the use of drugs.

---

2. This excludes the abuse of steroids, a synthetic version of the male hormone testosterone. Anabolic (meaning that they promote growth) steroids are taken (illegally) by athletes. In conjunction with weight training, anabolic steroids will promote extraordinary weight gain and muscularity, with serious side effects. They are not taken for their mind-altering qualities.

3. *Addiction* is from the Latin verb *addicere:* to bind.

3. *Relapse*: In the face of adverse consequences, addicts discontinue drugs but subsequently return to abnormal use.

Dennis Donovan (1988: 6) conceives of addiction as

> a complex, progressive behavior pattern having biological, psychological, sociological, and behavioral components. What sets this behavior apart from others is the individual's overwhelmingly pathological involvement in or attachment to it, subjective compulsion to continue it, and reduced ability to exert personal control over it. . . . The behavior pattern continues despite its negative impact on the physical, psychological, and social function of the individual.

Distinctions between alcohol and other psychoactive drugs, Miller (1995: 84) points out, reflect neither reality nor science:

> There is an enormous overlap between addiction to alcohol and addiction to other drugs. Polydrug addiction is the norm, not the exception, and, except for specific pharmacologic issues and timelines, the processes of progression, treatment, recovery, and relapse are nearly identical for addiction to alcohol and other drugs. For these and other reasons, it is almost useless to discuss addiction to alcohol as a disease without also including addiction to other drugs as a disease. . . . The essential characteristics of the diseases are identical.

There is a variety of lawful substances that are addicting and that have been abused by any number of "respectable persons," including major gov-

---

TOBACCO AND TEENAGERS

Despite vigorous anti-cigarette campaigns, the proportion of adolescent smokers has remained the same for the last ten years (Bartecchi, MacKenzie, and Schrier 1995). On August 10, 1995, President Bill Clinton announced a major initiative to curb cigarette smoking by adolescents: "Cigarettes and smokeless tobacco are harmful, highly addictive and aggressively marketed to our young people." The $50 billion-a-year tobacco industry responded with a federal lawsuit.

CIGARETTES

In his deposition, the plaintiff admitted that despite his illness, he still craved cigarettes. "At one point in his examination, lawyers asked him to demonstrate how he had smoked his cigarettes, and after putting one to his lips he declared: 'God, it feels good' "—a fifty-six-year-old cancer patient who is suing a major cigarette company (Margolick 1991: B6).

ernment officials. Social expectations and definitions determine what kind of drug-taking is appropriate and the social situations that are approved and disapproved for drug use. The use of drugs is neither inherently bad nor inherently good—these are socially determined values (Goode 1989). Thus, Mormons and Christian Scientists consider any use of tea and coffee abusive, while Moslems and some Protestant denominations have the same view of alcohol, although they permit tobacco smoking. The National Commission on Marijuana and Drug Abuse (1973: 13) argues that drug abuse "must be deleted from official pronouncements and public policy dialogue" because the "term has no functional utility and has become no more than an arbitrary codeword for that drug use which is presently considered wrong." As the history of "drug abuse" in chapter 2 informs us, moderate use of a drug will be defined as "abuse"—and illegal—or it will be socially acceptable—and lawful—if society so determines, *regardless* of the relative danger inherent in the substance. These inconsistencies are highlighted by tobacco and alcohol. *How society defines drug abuse determines how society responds to drug abuse.*

TOBACCO/NICOTINE

Nicotine is a drug that meets the rigorous criteria for abuse liability and dependence potential: It strongly stimulates the central nervous system, heavy doses producing disturbed vision, confusion, convulsions, and eventual death.[4] Small doses of the drug cause irritation of the mouth, throat, and bronchi; high blood pressure; increased risk of heart disease and cancer; and possible harm to the fetus of pregnant women. Treatment for dependence on the drug is quite difficult, and relapses are frequent. Tolerance develops, producing withdrawal symptoms when the consumption of nicotine ceases—slowing of the EEG, (electroencephalogram, which measures electrical impulses of the brain), restless sleep, decreased heart rate and thyroid functioning, anxiety, and anger (Hughes 1990). There are an estimated 46 million adults who smoke (Bartecchi, MacKenzie, and Schrier 1995).

Cigarette smoking shares certain critical features with classic forms of drug dependence. Nicotine is a psychoactive substance that can function as a euphoriant, and it serves as a reinforcer for humans and animals (Henningfield 1986). In 1988 the U.S. Surgeon General declared that nicotine is as addicting as heroin and cocaine. The more we find out about cigarette smoking, the more we realize the similarities between nicotine, opium, and cocaine. For example, it appears that many smokers have a genetic predisposition to nicotine addiction; and while some people smoke to relax, others do it to avoid depression. As noted with respect to opium and cocaine (chapter 3), some people may be using nicotine to self-medicate, and when such persons discontinue use they

---

4. The manner in which nicotine produces behavioral and cognitive effects is quite complex. See, for example, McGehee et al. (1995).

> ## KILLER DRUG
>
> "Cigarettes are one of the major drugs of addiction in the United States and in the world and are responsible for more premature deaths than all of the other drugs of abuse combined" (Schuster 1993: 40).

suffer both physiological and psychological withdrawal symptoms including debilitating bouts of depression. Most smokers require at least ten cigarettes per day in order to avoid experiencing withdrawal symptoms (Blakeslee 1988). In fact, it was discovered that "crack"—cocaine in a potent form that permits it to be smoked (discussed in chapter 3)—is less addictive than nicotine (Kolata 1989c). wow!

The National Cancer Institute revealed that in 1991 cigarette smoking surpassed heart disease as the number one killer in the United States—more than 400,000 deaths annually are linked to smoking-related illnesses (Bartecchi, MacKenzie, and Schrier 1995). Preliminary research has also linked cigarette smoking by fathers with an increased risk of brain cancer and leukemia in their offspring, and children whose parents smoke are three to four times more likely to develop serious infectious diseases. An estimated 5,600 infant deaths are caused by smoking among pregnant women (Associated Press 1995). The financial cost of smoking-induced illness is staggering, accounting for about 20 percent of health care costs in the United States (whose annual total is between $350 and 400 billion). Cigarettes are a leading cause of fires, and their toxic fumes can cause heart and lung damage in nonsmokers, particularly children exposed to cigarette smoke (Altman 1990). Two studies released in 1991 revealed that cigarette smoking accelerates deterioration of arteries that supply the brain, multiplying the risk of a stroke ("Two Studies Disclose Dangers. . . ." 1991). Furthermore, cigarette use typically precedes the use of illegal substances—a "gateway drug"[5] (Clymer 1994).

ALCOHOL

Alcohol is a potentially dangerous drug used by mainstream religions such as Judaism and Catholicism (although prohibited by Islam and several Protestant denominations). Its recreational use in moderation is an accepted part of American culture—two out of every three Americans consume alcohol. Nevertheless, the social cost of alcohol abuse is twice that of all illegal drug abuse.

---

5. Major studies reveal a significant rise in smoking cigarettes among adolescents (Hilts 1995; Verhovek 1995, Feder 1996 (b)).

> ## "HAPPY" NEW YEAR
>
> The seventeen-year-old high school student in Lake County, Illinois, joined a group of friends celebrating New Year's Eve. Over a three-hour period he consumed almost a quart of vodka. He subsequently passed out and died before paramedics arrived (Santana 1996).

Alcohol is reputed to be the direct cause of 80,000 to 100,000 deaths annually, and alcohol-related auto accidents are the leading cause of death for teenagers (Wicker 1987; Li, Smith, and Baker 1994). Research has revealed that the pharmacological effects of alcohol can cause aggression in some persons, and alcohol is a factor in nearly half of America's murders, suicides, and accidental deaths ("Coming to Grips with Alcohol" 1987; Chermack and Taylor 1995).

Researchers have discovered that even moderate drinking by pregnant women can impair a child's intellectual ability in school (Goleman 1989), and has also been linked to a tenfold increased risk of developing leukemia during infancy ("New Hazard of Drinking in Pregnancy Is Found" 1996). And drinking among adolescents continues to be a serious "drug" problem: On June 6, 1991, the U.S. Surgeon General reported that more than half of the nation's 20.7 million students in the seventh through twelfth grades drink alcoholic beverages, 8 million on a weekly basis; almost half a million have five or more consecutive drinks at least once a week. Nearly half of U.S. college students are binge drinkers (Associated Press 1994), and the country has more than 13 million alcoholics (D. Smith 1986).

According to scientific and pharmacological data used to classify dangerous substances for the protection of society, alcohol should be a Class II narcotic, available only with a government narcotic registry number. But alcohol for recreational use is permitted to be legally manufactured, imported, sold, and possessed. Because of this reality, while it has been associated with a myriad of social problems, since the repeal of Prohibition in 1933 trafficking in alcohol has not been associated with rampant violence and corruption. Indeed, the repeal of Prohibition resulted in a dramatic decrease in the murder rate in the United States, which began to increase in the 1960s along with the prevalence of illicit drug use (Myers 1995).

DRUGS OF ABUSE

In chapter 3 we will detail the pharmacology of major drugs in each of five categories according to their effect on the central nervous system: depressants, stimulants, hallucinogens, cannabis, and inhalants. In this chapter we will provide a summary look at the most important substances in each category in order to examine some larger questions with respect to drug abuse. The Institute for the Study of Drug Dependence (1987: 1; hereafter ISDD) offers some cautions:

> Drug effects are strongly influenced by the amount taken, how much has been taken before, what the user wants and expects to happen, the surroundings in which it is taken, and the reactions of other people. All of these influences are themselves tied up with social and cultural attitudes and beliefs about drugs as well as more general social conditions. Even the same person will react differently at different times.

A drug can have at least three different names: chemical, generic, and trade. Drugs that have a legitimate medical use may be marketed under a variety of trade names. Trade names begin with a capital letter, while chemical or generic titles are in lowercase.

Depressants. These drugs depress the central nervous system (CNS) and reduce pain. The most frequently used drug in this category is alcohol; the most frequently used illegal drug is the opiate derivative heroin. Other depressants, all of which have some medical use, include morphine, codeine, methadone, barbiturates, methaqualone, and tranquilizers. These substances can cause physical and psychological dependence—a craving—and withdrawal results in physical and psychological stress. Opiate derivatives (heroin, morphine, codeine) and opiumlike drugs such as methadone are often referred to as *narcotics.*

Stimulants. These drugs elevate mood—produce feelings of well-being—by stimulating the central nervous system. The most frequently used drugs in this category are caffeine and nicotine; the most frequently used illegal stimulant is cocaine, while another type, amphetamines, have some limited medical use.

Hallucinogens. These drugs alter perceptual functions. The term *hallucinogen,* rather than, for example, *psychoactive* or *psychedelic,* is a value-laden one. The most frequently used hallucinogens are LSD (lysergic acid diethylamide) and PCP (phencyclidine). Both are produced chemically, and neither has any legitimate medical use. There are also organic hallucinogens such as mescaline, which is found in the peyote cactus. The lawful use of peyote is limited to the religious ceremonies of the Native American church, which some, but not all, states exempt from this aspect of their controlled substances statutes.

Cannabis. Frequently used in the form of marijuana, cannabis exhibits some of the characteristics of hallucinogens, depressants, and even stimulants. Its lawful use (in the liquid form of THC, its psychoactive ingredient) is limited to the treatment of glaucoma and to reduce some of the side effects of cancer chemotherapy.

Inhalants. Inhalants are a diverse group of chemicals that produce vapors that when inhaled can produce an intoxication similar to that of alcohol. They include a variety of readily available products routinely kept in the home, such as glue, paint thinner, hair spray, and nail polish remover.

POLYDRUG USE

Drug abuse is made more complicated by the phenomenon of polydrug use—abusers consuming more than one type of psychoactive chemical. "In contradiction to the public's view of narcotics addiction as existing discretely apart from other addictions, the heroin addict is a multiple drug user who is often an alcohol abuser" (Vaillant 1970: 492). In a study of heroin addicts in San Antonio, for example, it was discovered that 100 percent used alcohol, almost half on a daily basis (Maddux and Desmond 1981). The District of Columbia reports that alcohol is frequently used to moderate the effects of cocaine. And "long-term heroin addicts report long-term and continuing addiction to alcohol" (McFarland 1989: 4). In Colorado, more than 35 percent of cocaine users admitted for treatment report the use of alcohol (Mendelson and Harrison 1989). The New York State Division of Substance Abuse Services (1986: 14–15) reports that the

> use of more than one substance continues to be the predominant pattern of abuse. Both heroin and cocaine are commonly used with one drug ameliorating the undesired effects of the other; PCP is used by some heroin abusers to heighten the effect of heroin. Alcohol use is almost always involved.

In San Antonio, approximately two-thirds of substance-related deaths have involved both cocaine and heroin (Spence 1989). In Minnesota, polydrug use, which includes alcohol, is widespread among that state's chemical-abusing population (Minnesota Department of Human Services 1987). Almost 19 percent of the persons admitted for heroin abuse treatment in Colorado reported the use of cocaine (Colorado Alcohol and Drug Abuse Division 1987).

Bruce Johnson and his colleagues (1985) found that 90 percent of the heroin addicts they studied also abused alcohol and cocaine.

> Heroin and cocaine abusers do not limit their drug consumption to heroin or cocaine. Much evidence shows that heroin addicts and cocaine abusers are also heavy polydrug abusers; they frequently use marijuana, pills, and alcohol. Many such abusers consume large amounts of alcohol daily. (Johnson, Lipton, and Wish 1986b: 2)

Mark Gold and his colleagues (1986: 55) found that "most cocaine abusers are concurrently abusing alcohol or other sedative-hypnotics to alleviate the unpleasant side effects of cocaine." Crack users frequently "administer heroin because it enhances the euphoric effect while ameliorating the intense stimulant effects of cocaine" (*Trends in Heroin* 1994: 1). Drug abusers unable to secure their preferred substance, because of insufficient funds or connections when the supply is scarce often seek available substitutes.

RESPONDING TO THE PROBLEM OF DRUG ABUSE

In a single incisive statement, David Musto (1973: 244) provides a summary of the history of U.S. policy toward drug abuse:

> American concern with narcotics is more than a medical or legal problem—it is in the fullest sense a political problem. The energy that has given impetus to drug control and prohibition came from profound tensions among socioeconomic groups, ethnic minorities, and generations—as well as the psychological attraction of certain drugs. The form of this control has been shaped by the gradual evolution of federal police powers. The bad results of drug use and the number of drug users have often been exaggerated for partisan advantage. Public demand for action against drug abuse has led to regulative decisions that lack a true regard for the reality of drug use.

Statutory limitations make the manufacture or possession of certain dangerous substances a crime and empower specific public officials to enforce these statutes. Drug Enforcement Administration agents are among those entitled to arrest violators of drug laws.

Relations with foreign nations, often the sources of the drugs, have been a theme in the domestic scene from the beginning of the American antinarcotic movement. Narcotics addiction has proven to be one of the most intractable medical inquiries ever faced by American clinicians and scientists.

Out of this history there developed two basic models for responding to the abuse of dangerous substances. The first is a *disease* or *public health model:* The abuser is "helpless" and "blameless," analogous to the cancer or coronary patient. The model defines substance abuse as a disease to be prevented or treated, just like any other public health problem. The second is a *moral-legal model* that defines alcohol and other psychoactive drugs as either legal or illegal and attempts to control availability through penalties. The moral-legal model utilizes three methods to control potentially dangerous drugs in the United States:

1. *Regulation.* Certain substances that may be harmful to their consumers can be sold with only a minimum of restrictions. These substances are heavily taxed, providing government with an important source of revenue. Alcoholic beverages and tobacco products are subjected to disproportionate taxation, and their sale is restricted to those above a certain age. Special licenses are usually required for the manufacture, distribution, and sale of regulated substances.

2. *Medical Auspices.* The use of certain potentially harmful substances is permitted under medical supervision. John Kaplan (1983: 644) notes that "this model seems to be the preferred one for drugs having medical uses, in that taken under the direction of a physician, their value outweighs their danger." Under this model the medical profession is given control over legal access to specific substances. In this category would be barbiturates, amphetamines, certain opiates (morphine and codeine), and heroin substitutes such as methadone.

3. *Law Enforcement.* Statutory limitations make the manufacture or possession of certain dangerous substances a crime and empower specific public officials to enforce these statutes. Certain other substances are permitted under medical auspices, but punishment is specified for persons possessing these substances outside of accepted medical practice. Thus, heroin has no permissible use in the United States—an absolute prohibition—while other psychoactive substances, such as morphine and Seconal (secobarbital sodium), are permissible for medical use but illegal under any other circumstances.

The official response to a particular substance—regulation as opposed to law enforcement—determines the manner in which the abuser will be treated. Thus, the alcoholic is typically viewed according to the disease model, while the user of illegal drugs has the criminal label attached. From the Civil War until the 1920s the U.S. response to dangerous drugs moved from permissiveness to one of rigid law enforcement—from the public health model to the moral-legal model. The practical effect of this change was "to define the addict as a criminal offender" (Schur 1965: 130), leading to the creation of a vast black market in which drug entrepreneurs quickly filled the void left by the withdrawal of lawful sources:

> In the 1920s this country had a large number of addicts, but they were not regarded as criminals by the law; in general, they did not commit crimes and conducted their lives much the same way as the nonaddict population did. Clinics and private physicians were free to prescribe maintenance doses. It was the outlawing of the addictive drug that gave rise to an illegal market controlled by organized crime; and it is the exorbitant cost of the outlawed drug that has driven addicts into criminal activity to support their habit. (National Council on Crime and Delinquency 1974: 4)

"The social importance of drugs does not lie in their capacity to injure and reduce the capabilities of drug users, though when misused drugs can inflict psychological and physical harm. These casualties are a small minority, and in most cases they could be treated if less punitive legal policy were operating" (Zinberg and Robertson 1972: 11). In fact, drug policy in the United States has been guided by "commonly shared simplifications"—in particular, the belief that

> drug problems are largely attributable to morally compromised or pathological individuals who were not properly inculcated in childhood with normal American values such as self-control and respect for the law. These individuals must be disciplined and punished by authorities to deter them from involvement (for pleasure or profit) with inherently dangerous, addicting drugs. (Gerstein and Harwood 1990: 41)

Drug abuse, notes Gresham Sykes, "became defined as a fundamental affront, part of a larger pattern challenging society with an alternative view of a meaningful life." The wrongdoing of the drug abuser was "moved into the category of the most serious offense—treason—where the individual forsakes his society for an enemy allegiance" (Sykes 1967: 77). A "clearer case of misapplication of the criminal sanction," writes Herbert Packer (1968: 333), "would be difficult to imagine."

DRUGS, CRIME, AND VIOLENCE

While there is certainly concern about the negative consequences of drug use on the individual, the current importance of drugs as an issue in the United States is due primarily to the relationship between drugs and crime. Although a great deal of crime, aside from drunk driving, is committed under the influence of alcohol—"Over 60 percent of homicides involve alcohol use by both offender and victim, and 65 percent of aggressive sexual acts against women involve alcohol use by the offender" (Smith 1986: 118)—public interest in the relationship between illegal drug use and crime has clearly overshadowed the alcohol-crime nexus.[6]

The outlawing of certain drugs created criminal opportunity for those daring enough to enter this market. They become part of a business that has no mechanisms for resolving disputes except violence (the business of drugs will be discussed in chapter 6). The outlawing of certain drugs also makes those who use (actually the crime is "possession") these chemicals criminals while substantially inflating the cost of the substances to the consumer. In order to secure their preferred substance, abusers of illegal drugs typically target salable property, but some abusers will also commit robbery and/or sell drugs. There is a criminal population whose nondrug law violations are based only on their desire to secure drugs. However, it is also clear that an unknown percentage, perhaps a majority, of drug abusers, particularly those addicted to heroin, were criminals whose drug abuse is simply part of a pattern of hedonistic and antisocial behavior. George Vaillant (1970: 488) reports that no matter what their class origins, most persons who use narcotics "have a greater tendency than their socioeconomic peers to be delinquent," and even drug-abusing physicians "are relatively irresponsible before drug addiction."[7] In the nation's capital, the drug-personal violence nexus has made it difficult to determine the primary cause of death: "Determining the cause of death has been complicated by the fact that many of the deaths have also been associated with violent incidents where the victims' bodies contained potentially lethal dosages of illicit drugs at the time of a shooting or stabbing death" (McFarland 1989: 5).

There is undoubtedly a high correlation between heroin use and nondrug crime (e.g., Gandossey et al. 1980; Johnson et al. 1985; Nurco et al. 1985; Inciardi 1986; Wish and Johnson 1986). One study found that more than half of the men arrested in twelve major cities tested positive for recent use of illicit drugs (Kerr 1988b). "A strong consensus has emerged in the research literature that the most frequent, serious offenders are also the heaviest drug users" (Visher 1990: 330). However, is it drug use that leads to criminal behavior?

A study of male adolescent ninth- and tenth-graders in Washington, DC, found that for about half of those who used drugs (mostly marijuana), criminal behavior preceded use; for the other half, criminal behavior followed drug use. However, "Those both using and selling drugs were more than twice as likely to have started using drugs before committing crimes as were those

---

6. For an examination of the relationship between alcohol and homicide, see Wieczorek, Welte, and Abel (1990).

7. Concern over the abuse of morphine by medical doctors dates back to at least the latter part of the nineteenth century (Mattison 1883), and in 1964 Charles Winick wrote of the physician addict, a loner who does not knowingly associate with other addicts. In fact, drug abuse is a significant problem for the medical profession, with the addiction rate for physicians estimated at anywhere from 30 to 100 times that for the population at large (Grosswirth 1982). In more recent years the drug of choice for abuse by physicians tends to be the powerful synthetic opiate fentanyl (Kennedy 1995).

FIGURE 1.1
Relationship between Drugs and Crime: Three Possibilities

1. Drug Abuse ————————————————————→ Crime
2. Criminals ————————————————————→ Drug Abuse
3. Sociological/Psychological variables   +{ ———→ Crime
                                             ———→ Drug Abuse

using but not selling drugs" (Brounstein et al. 1990: 3–4). In fact, we cannot be sure whether drug abuse leads to crime or criminals tend to abuse drugs. Or perhaps the variables that lead to drug abuse and the variables that lead to crime are the same: "That is, the relationship is not due to any causal connection, but rather to the fact that both criminals and drug-using behavior are the result of the same variables" (McBride and McCoy 1981: 283; also Speckart and Anglin 1985, 1987). Indeed, areas with high levels of delinquency and crime also have high levels of drug usage, while the reverse is also true. In their study, Cheryl Carpenter and her colleagues (1988) found that the most seriously delinquent adolescents also abused drugs, but crime and drug use appeared to be independent of one another—both apparently related to other causal variables. In fact, extensive research informs us that a relatively small segment of youths commit a disproportionate amount of juvenile crime, and "the majority of serious crimes committed by youths are concentrated among serious delinquents who are also heavy users of alcohol and other drugs" (Johnson et al. 1991: 206). For these persons, *both* drug use and crime appear to be part of a troubled lifestyle.

The question of whether crime is a pre- or postdrug use phenomenon is actually an oversimplification, and James Inciardi (1981: 59) argues that "the pursuit of some simple cause-and-effect relationship may be futile." His data found, for example:

> Among the males, there seems to be a clear progression from alcohol to crime, to drug abuse, to arrest, and then to heroin use. But upon closer inspection, the pattern is not altogether clear. At one level, for example, criminal activity can be viewed as predating one's drug-using career, because the median point of the first crime is slightly below that of first drug abuse, and is considerably before the onset of heroin use. But, at the same time, if alcohol intoxication at a median age of 13.3 years were to be considered substance abuse, then crime is clearly a phenomenon that succeeds substance abuse. Among the females, the description is even more complex. In the population of female heroin users, criminal activity occurred after both alcohol and other drug abuse and marijuana use, but before involvement with the more debilitating barbiturates and heroin.

A study of heroin addicts in Wilmington, Delaware, revealed criminal and drug careers rather independent of one another, the two merging as the use of heroin become overarching (Faupel and Klockars 1987).

This issue has serious policy implications. If drug abusers simply continue in crime after they have given up drug abuse, efforts to reduce crime by reducing drug abuse are doomed to fail. As James Q. Wilson (1975: 137) points out, perhaps "some addicts who steal to support their habit come to regard crime as more profitable than normal employment. They would probably continue to steal to provide themselves with an income even after they no longer needed to use part of that income to buy heroin" or any other illegal substance. M. Douglas Anglin and George Speckart (1988: 223) found, however, "that levels of criminality after the addiction career [is over] are near zero, a finding that is compatible with data presented by other authors and is illustrative of the 'maturing out' phase of the addiction career 'life cycle.' "

In fact, the sequence of drug use and crime has produced contradictory finding (Huizinga, Menard, Elliott 1989). For example, James Vorenberg and Irving Lukoff (1973) found that the criminal careers of a substantial segment of the heroin addicts they studied antedated the onset of heroin use. Furthermore, they found that those whose criminality preceded heroin use tended to be more involved in violent criminal behavior. Anglin and Speckart (1988) report that between 60 and 75 percent of the addicts in their samples had arrest histories that preceded addiction. Paul Cushman (1974: 43) found, however, that the heroin addicts he studied were predominantly noncriminal before addiction and experienced "progressively increased rates of annual arrests after addiction started." (Of course, this finding could be the result of addicts being less adept at crime.) Whatever the relationship—drug abuse leading to crime

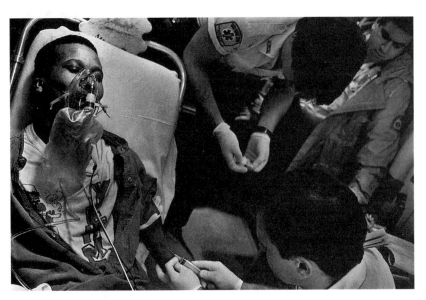

During the 1980s, crack replaced heroin as the "in" drug among young adults ages eighteen to twenty-five in the low-income areas of New York City. Here, New York Emergency Medical Service medics treat a teenager for a crack overdose.

or criminals becoming drug abusers—some researchers (McGlothlin, Anglin, Wilson 1978; Ball, Rosen, Friedman, and Nurco 1979; Johnson, Lipton, and Wish 1986) have found that the amount of criminality tends to be sharply reduced when persons who have been narcotic addicts are no longer addicted. Furthermore, Bruce Johnson and his colleagues (1985; 1989) and Anglin and Speckart (1988) found that the more frequent the drug use, the more serious the types of crime committed; for example, burglary and robbery instead of shoplifting and other larcenies. (For a summary of research findings on this issue, see Chaiken and Chaiken 1990.)

The issue of crime-drug abuse has typically been related to the abuse of heroin, not cocaine. During the time that this writer was a parole officer in New York (1964–1978), offenders who had used cocaine were rare, while studies by the New York State Division of Parole indicated that those who had used heroin were a substantial majority of parole clientele in the New York City area. Almost two decades ago, Troy Duster (1970: 42) was able to state that "cocaine usage is rare in the United States." However, during the 1980s there was a dramatic increase in the abuse of cocaine by the same populations that have traditionally been the major consumers of heroin. During these years cocaine use crossed social class lines, and the age of onset dropped considerably. Furthermore,

> Until recently it has been assumed that cocaine was not a criminogenic force toward income-generating crime because cocaine does not have the physiological addictive power of heroin and because cocaine users were viewed as unlikely to come from population groups with high crime rates. Cocaine was thought to be a drug of the middle and upper class. These assumptions appear to be unjustified. Weekly and daily cocaine use are associated with high levels of illegal income. (Collins, Hubbard, and Rachel 1985: 759)

During the 1980s, cocaine, however—in the form of crack—not heroin, became the "in" drug among young adults ages eighteeen to twenty-five in the low-income areas of New York City. This was a dramatic change from the drug scene of the late 1960s and early 1970s, when heroin was the major problem. Furthermore, heroin abusers typically use cocaine, many using it as frequently as they do heroin in a combination known as a "speedball." The use of these substances, David Smith (1986) notes, is part of a lifestyle that also includes abuse of alcohol, marijuana, barbiturates, and amphetamines—and crime. In one study of 105 drug abusers, cocaine was the primary drug of choice, and 50 percent also abused alcohol (Johnson, Anderson, Wish 1989). The crack phenomenon has apparently led to an increase in the popularity of cocaine in neighborhoods that traditionally had a problem with heroin. Observations in Harlem indicate that crack use, as was also the case with heroin, has become more stable: there are fewer new initiates and an older population making it a routine part of their life (Treaster 1991). And one study found that the business of crack is crime-intensive in that it "leads serious delinquents to become even more seriously involved in crime" (Inciardi and Pottieger 1991:

268). It appears that crack intensifies the criminal behaviors in which users were actively involved before initiation into crack use, except for women; they moved from property crimes to prostitution (Chin and Fagan 1990).

The National Institute of Justice concludes:

> Assessing the nature and extent of the influence of drugs on crime requires that reliable information about the offense and the offender be available, and that definitions be consistent. In the face of problematic evidence, it is impossible to say quantitatively how much drugs influence the occurrence of crime. (*Fact Sheet: Drug Related Crime 1994:* 3)

DRUGS AND VIOLENCE

More than two decades ago, Edwin Schur (1965) argued that narcotic addiction in the United States seems to reduce the inclination to engage in violent crime. However, a more recent research effort found that heroin abusers (not

Crack traffickers appear to be more violent than other kinds of drug abusers. The young man on the sidewalk shot himself while loading a pistol to fire at police during a car chase. The car he fled in was stolen and contained a machine gun, cocaine, and crack. Three others who were in the car were apprehended later that night.

necessarily addicts) are at least as violent as, and perhaps more violent than, their nondrug- or nonheroin-using criminal counterparts (Johnson, Lipton, Wish 1986), which is consistent with the writer's experience as a parole officer. In fact, the researchers report, "About half of the most violent criminals are heroin abusers" (1986b: 3). It is difficult to determine if this is simply a problem of changing definitions or a changing drug population. While there is no evidence that crime results from the direct effects of heroin itself—indeed, the substance appears to have a pacifying effect—the irritability resulting from withdrawal symptoms has been known to lead to violence (Goldstein 1985).

This writer dealt with heroin addicts for fourteen years and found many, if not most, to be quite capable of committing violent acts including homicide—they were frequently convicted of violent crimes. In addition, as we shall discuss in chapter 6, the heroin distribution subculture at every level—from wholesaling to street sale—is permeated with extreme levels of violence. And, as noted above, many drug abusers use more than one psychoactive chemical (polydrug abuse), thus expanding the possible behavioral effects of the different combinations. If the additional substance is alcohol, which is relatively inexpensive, the drug-crime nexus is mitigated (at least for income-generating crimes; as noted above, a great deal of violent noneconomic crime is known to be linked to alcohol intoxication). Crimes against persons and violence by drug users are often related to their use of alcohol (Dembo et al. 1991; P. Goldstein et al. 1991).

Other drugs (PCP and cocaine, for example) may involve otherwise "normal" persons in violent behavior. The Detroit medical examiner's office reports that 37 percent of that city's homicide victims had cocaine in their blood samples (Franklin 1987), indicating that cocaine users either engage in dangerous behavior or expose themselves to places and/or situations where violence is likely to occur. And persons intent on committing violent crimes, such as robbery, may ingest alcohol or stimulants for courage—alcohol in small doses acts as a stimulant (Hunt 1983). "The relationship between drugs and violence has been consistently documented in both the popular press and in social scientific research" (P. Goldstein 1985: 494).

Research has found that crack users are more likely to commit crimes against persons than against property. Crack sellers also appear to be more violent than other drug sellers, and their violence is not limited to drug transactions: "They are more often than other drug sellers involved in serious nondrug crime, including both property and violent offenses" (Belenko and Chin 1989: 25; also Fagan and Chin 1991). There has been a surge in children beaten and killed by their crack-abusing parents (Kerr 1988). However, a study in Kansas City, Missouri, of almost 1,500 arrestees, about half of whom abused cocaine, found that

> there is no reason to believe that drug-using offenders, especially those characterized by heavy or addictive use, are more likely to be arrested for serious or violent offenses than nondrug-using offenders. At the very least, it appears that

nondrug-using offenders commit relatively higher rates of violent and predatory crimes. (Whitlock, Collings, and Burnett 1990: 21)

In the next chapter we will look at the history that brought us to our present problem with drug abuse.

REVIEW QUESTIONS

1. Why is *drug abuse* not a scientific term?
2. What are the four variables that typically enter into a definition of drug abuse?
3. What factors determine whether the moderate use of a psychoactive substance will be defined as drug abuse?
4. With respect to dangerousness to the user, how does alcohol differ from narcotics?
5. What are the dangers of nicotine abuse?
6. What is the difference between drug abuse and drug addiction?
7. Why can't an individual's reaction to a measured amount of a drug be predetermined?
8. What are the essential differences between a depressant drug and a stimulant drug?
9. What are some examples of legal and illegal depressants and stimulants?
10. What is an hallucinogenic drug?
11. Why can't cannabis be classified as a stimulant, a depressant, or a hallucinogen?
12. With respect to drug abuse, what is an inhalant?
13. What are the essential differences between the disease/public health model and the moral/legal model of responding to the abuse of dangerous drugs?
14. What three methods does the moral-legal model use to control potentially dangerous drugs?
15. How does polydrug use make the issue of drug abuse more complicated?
16. What are the three possible relationships between drugs and criminal behavior?
17. What policy implications flow from the relationship between drugs and criminal behavior?

2

DRUG ABUSE: A HISTORY

The United States of America during the nineteenth century could quite properly be described as a "dope fiend's paradise."—Edward M. Brecher (1972: 3)

What we think about addiction very much depends on who is addicted.
—David T. Courtwright (1982: 3)

T he history of drug abuse and attempts at control provide insight into the complexity of more contemporary issues on this subject. As with many attempts at historical analyses, we are handicapped by the lack of adequate data on a number of items, particularly the extent of drug abuse at earlier periods in our history and of alcohol abuse during Prohibition. It is difficult to provide an empirically based analysis of changing policies with respect to drug abuse without the ability to measure the effect of these changes. In fact, we cannot provide such measurements. Even today the number of persons abusing various substances from alcohol to heroin is the subject of debate.

Policy decisions, as we shall see in this chapter, have frequently been based on perceptions, beliefs, and attitudes with little empirical foundation. They have often reflected popular prejudices against a variety of racial and ethnic groups, and sometimes they have concerned issues of international, rather than domestic, politics. Since the earliest drug prohibitions in the United States reflected a concern with alcohol, we will begin our examination with a history of that substance.

TEMPERANCE AND PROHIBITION

Drinking alcoholic beverages for recreational purposes has an ancient history, with records of such use dating back more than 5,000 years. The Bible records that Noah planted a vineyard and drank of the wine "and was drunken" (Genesis IX: 21). Later we are told that the daughters of Lot made their father drunk with wine in order that they might trick him into propagating the family line (Genesis XIX: 32–36). This unseemly use of alcohol could certainly serve as an object lesson against its use, but the practice of drinking alcoholic beverages appears near universal.

The United States has traditionally consumed large quantities of alcohol; in 1830, for example, the per capita intake was between five and ten gallons (Buchanan 1992). In 1785 Dr. Benjamin Rush, the Surgeon General of the Continental Army and a signer of the Declaration of Independence, authored a pamphlet decrying the use of alcohol; it helped fuel the move toward Prohibition and inspired the establishment in 1808 of the Union Temperance Society, the first of many such organizations. The Society was superseded by the American Temperance Union in 1836, and the work of the Union was supported by Protestant churches throughout the country.

U.S. opposition to alcohol was often intertwined with nativism, and efforts against alcohol and other psychoactive drugs were often a thinly veiled reaction to minority groups. As Joseph Gusfield (1963: 5) has noted, "The public support of one conception of morality at the expense of another enhances the prestige and self-esteem of the victors and degrades the culture of the losers." Prohibitionists were typically rural, white Protestants antagonistic to urban Roman Catholics, particularly the Irish, who used the social world of the saloon to gain political power in large cities such as New York and Chicago (Abadinsky 1994).

The temperance movement made great progress everywhere in the country, and it often rode, or coincided, with the anti-immigrant sentiment that swept over the United States during the late 1840s and early 1850s. In 1843 this led to the formation of the American Republican party in New York, which spread nationally as the Native American party, or the "Know-Nothings." (Many clubs were secret, and when outsiders inquired about the group, they were met with the response: "I know nothing.") Allied with a faction of the Whig party, the Know-Nothings almost captured New York in 1854, and succeeded in carrying Delaware and Massachusetts. They also won important victories in Pennsylvania, Rhode Island, New Hampshire, Connecticut, Maryland, Kentucky, and California. In 1855 the city of Chicago elected a Know-Nothing mayor and Prohibition legislation was enacted in the Illinois legislature (but was defeated in a public referendum that same year (Asbury 1950). Slavery and abolition, and the ensuing Civil War, subsequently took the place of temperance as the day's most pressing issues (Buchanan 1992).

In 1869 the Prohibition party attempted, with only limited success, to make alcohol a national issue. In 1874 the Women's Christian Temperance

Carrie Nation *(lower right)* of the Women's Christian Temperance Union leading her crusade into an Enterprise, Kansas, saloon in 1911.

Union was established. Issues of temperance and nativism arose again strongly during the 1880s, leading to the formation of the American Protective Association, a rural-based organization that was strongly anti-Catholic and anti-Semitic. (For an excellent history of nativism in the United States, see Bennett 1988.) In 1893 the Anti-Saloon League was organized. Around the turn of the century, these groups moved from efforts to change individual behavior to a campaign for national Prohibition. After a period of dormancy, the Prohibition movement was revived in the years 1907–1919 (Humphries and Greenberg 1981). By 1910 the Anti-Saloon League had become one of the most effective political action groups in U.S. history; it had mobilized Protestant churches behind a single purpose: to enact national prohibition (Tindall 1988). In 1915 nativism and prohibitionism fueled the rise of the Ku Klux Klan, and this time the KKK spread into northern states and exerted a great deal of political influence. During World War I an additional element, anti-German xenophobia, was added, because brewing and distilling were associated with German immigrants (Cashman 1981).

The acrimony between rural and urban America, between Protestants and Catholics, between Republicans and (non-southern) Democrats, between "native" Americans and more recent immigrants, and between business and labor reached a pinnacle with the ratification in 1919 of the Eighteenth Amendment. According to William Chambliss (1973: 10). Prohibition was ac-

Prohibition officers raiding Hammel's lunchroom, Washington, D.C., in 1923. Bureau agents were viewed as a public menace.

complished by the political efforts of an economically declining segment of the middle class: "By effort and some good luck this class was able to impose its will on the majority of the population through rather dramatic changes in the law." Andrew Sinclair (1962: 163) points out that "in fact, national Prohibition was a measure passed by village America against urban America." We could add, by much of Protestant America against Catholic (and, to a lesser extent, Jewish) America—"Thousands of Protestant churches held thanksgiving prayer meetings. To many of the people who attended, Prohibition represented the triumph of America's towns and rural districts over the sinful cities" (Coffey 1975: 7; Gusfield 1963).

Big business was also interested in Prohibition; alcohol contributed to industrial inefficiency, labor strife, and the saloon, which served the interests of machine politics:

> Around 1908, just as the Anti-Saloon League was preparing for a broad state-by-state drive toward national prohibition, a number of businessmen contributed the funds essential for an effective campaign. The series of quick successes that followed coincided with an equally impressive number of wealthy converts, so that as the movement entered its final stage after 1913, it employed not only ample financing but a sudden urban respectability as well. Substantial citizens now spoke about a new discipline with the disappearance of the saloon and the rampaging drunk. Significantly, prominent Southerners with one eye to the Negro and another to the poorer whites were using exactly the same arguments. (Wiebe 1967: 290–91)

Workers' compensation laws also helped stimulate business support for temperance. Between 1911 and 1920, forty-one states had enacted workmen's compensation laws, and Sean Cashman (1981: 6), points out: "By making employers compensate workers for industrial accidents the law obligated them to campaign for safety through sobriety. In 1914 the National Safety Council adopted a resolution condemning alcohol as a cause of industrial accidents."

The Eighteenth Amendment to the Constitution was ratified by the thirty-sixth state, Nebraska, on January 16, 1919. According to its own terms, the amendment became effective on January 16, 1920. Ten months after ratification, over a veto by President Woodrow Wilson, Congress passed the National Prohibition Act, usually referred to as the Volstead Act after its sponsor, Congressman Andrew Volstead of Minnesota. The Volstead Act strengthened the language of the amendment and defined as intoxicating all beverages containing more than 0.5 percent alcohol; it also provided for federal enforcement. Thus, the Prohibition Bureau, an arm of the Treasury Department, was created. The bureau soon became notorious for employing agents on the basis of political patronage.

In addition to being inept and corrupt, bureau agents were a public menace. By 1930, 86 federal agents and 200 civilians had been killed, many of them innocent women and children. Prohibition agents set up illegal roadblocks and searched cars; drivers who protested were in danger of being shot.

Agents who killed innocent civilians were rarely brought to justice—when they were indicted by local grand juries, the cases were simply transferred, and the agents escaped punishment (Woodiwiss 1988). The bureau was viewed as a training school for bootleggers because agents frequently left the service to join their wealthy adversaries.

Herbert Packer (1968: 263) reminds us that people do not necessarily acquiesce to new criminal prohibitions. He points out that resistance can be fatal to the new norm, and that moreover, when this happens "the effect is not confined to the immediate proscription but makes itself felt in the attitude that people take toward legal proscriptions in general." Thus, primary resistance or opposition to a new law such as Prohibition can result, secondarily, in disregard for laws in general: *negative contagion*. During Prohibition, notes Sinclair (1962: 292), a "general tolerance of the bootlegger and a disrespect for federal law were translated into a widespread contempt for the process and duties of democracy." This was exemplified by the general lawlessness that reigned in Chicago:

> Banks all over Chicago were robbed in broad daylight by bandits who scorned to wear masks. Desk sergeants at police stations grew weary of recording holdups—from one hundred to two hundred were reported every night. Burglars marked out sections of the city as their own and embarked upon a course of systematic plundering, going from house to house night after night without hindrance. . . . Payroll robberies were a weekly occurrence and necessitated the introduction of armored cars and armed guards for the delivery of money from banks to business houses. Automobiles were stolen by the thousands. Motorists were forced to the curbs on busy streets and boldly robbed. Women who displayed jewelry in night clubs or at the theater were followed and held up. Wealthy women seldom left their homes unless accompanied by armed escorts. (Asbury 1950: 339)

The murder rate in the United States rose from 6.8 per 100,000 persons in 1920 to 9.7 in 1933, the year Prohibition was repealed (Chapman 1991), after which it began to decline.

And while the United States had organized crime before Prohibition, it "was intimately associated with shabby local politics and corrupt police forces"; there was no organized crime activity "in the syndicate style" (King 1969: 23). The "Great Experiment" provided a catalyst of opportunity that caused organized crime, especially violent forms, to blossom into an important force. Prohibition acted as a catalyst for the mobilization of criminal elements in an unprecedented manner. Pre-Prohibition crime, insofar as it was organized, centered around corrupt political machines, vice-entrepreneurs, and, at the bottom, gangs. Prohibition unleashed an unparalleled level of competitive violence and served to reverse the order of power between the criminal gangs and the politicians. It also led to an unparalleled level of criminal organization (Abadinsky 1994). These criminal organizations would later become important in the drug trade.

OPIUM

The earliest "war against drugs" (other than alcohol) in the United States was in response to opium. Opium is a depressant and analgesic (a pain reliever). The ancient method of producing opium is to make incisions in the partially ripe seedpod of the *papaver somniferum* (the opium poppy, of which there are many species) just after the petals have fallen. A milky-white fluid oozes out and hardens on the surface into a dark brown gum—raw opium. There is some dispute as to when opium was first used. The young leaves of the plant have been used as a potherb and salad vegetable, and its small, oily seeds, which are high in nutritional value, can be eaten, pressed to make an edible oil, baked into poppyseed cakes, ground into poppy flour, or used as lamp oil. As a vegetal fat source, "the seed oil could have been a major factor attracting early human groups to the opium poppy" (Merlin 1984: 89).

There is no agreement on where the plant originated, and a great deal of debate surrounds its earliest use as a drug, which may date back to the Old Stone Age, about 2 million years ago (Merlin 1984). Opium was probably used medically and in religious ceremonies in western Asia and the eastern Mediterranean before the year 2000 B.C.E. (Before the Common Era). Some researchers believe that the opium poppy and its use were introduced into Europe from Asia during the late Bronze Age, 3500 B.C.E. (Merlin 1984). Archeologists have discovered ancient art relics that may depict opium use in Egyptian religious rituals as early as 3500 B.C.E. (Inverarity, Lauderdale, and Field 1983). By the sixteenth century B.C.E., the Egyptians had discovered the medical uses of opium, "listing it as an analgesic in the giant reference work called the Ebers Papyrus" (Burkholz 1987: 17). From Egypt its use spread to Greece (O'Brien and Cohen 1984).

Opium is discussed by Homer in the *Odyssey* (circa 700 B.C.E.), and the term *opium* is derived from the Greek word *opion*, meaning the juice of the poppy (Bresler 1980). Alexander the Great may have brought it to Persia and India about 330 B.C.E., although it "was through the spread of Mohammedanism by the Arabs that opium first reached Persia and later India" (Terry and Pellens 1928: 56). "Because Islam prohibits the use of alcohol, opium became widely used as a 'safer' recreational agent" (Synder 1989: 30). Opium was brought to eastern Asia by Arab merchants about the year 300 of the Common Era, although "its notorious endemic use in the Orient didn't begin until the 1700s, when industrious European mercantilists turned a modest native herb trade into the most profitable big business in the history of commerce up to that time" (Latimer and Goldberg 1981: 16). Wherever it was known, opium use was both medicinal and recreational. During the eighteenth and nineteenth centuries recreational use was popularized by English intellectuals such as Samuel Taylor Coleridge (1772–1834) and Thomas De Quincey (1952: 6), who in 1821 referred to the "divine luxuries" of opium eating and opium drinking.

In explaining the popularity of opium, Charles Terry and Mildred Pellens (1928: 58) state:

> When we realize that the chief end of medicine up to the beginning of the last century was to relieve pain, that therapeutic agents were directed at symptoms rather than cause, it is not difficult to understand the wide popularity of a drug which either singly or combined so eminently was suited to the needs of so many medical situations.

At a time when the practice of medicine was quite primitive, opium became the essential ingredient of innumerable remedies dispensed in Europe and America for the treatment of diarrhea, dysentery, asthma, rheumatism, diabetes, malaria, cholera, fevers, bronchitis, insomnia, and pain of any kind (Fay 1975). In the early sixteenth century the physician Paracelsus made a tincture of opium—powdered opium dissolved in alcohol—that he called laudanum, and until the end of the nineteenth century it proved to be a popular medication (O'Brien and Cohen 1984). De Quincey (1952) noted that opium was often cheaper than alcohol.

An "opium den" in New York City's Chinatown, 1925.

Opium is a labor-intensive product. To produce an appreciable quantity requires repeated incisions of a great number of poppy capsules: about 18,000 capsules—one acre—to yield twenty pounds of opium (Fay 1975). Accordingly, supplies of opium were rather limited in Europe until the eighteenth century when improvements in plantation farming impacted on opium production. Attempts to produce domestic opium in the United States were not successful. While the poppy could be grown in many sections of the United States, particularly the South, Southwest, and California, labor costs and an opium gum that was low in morphine led to a reliance on imported opium (Morgan 1981).

As the primary ingredient in many *patent medicines*—actually secret formulas that carried no patent at all—opiates were readily available in the United States until 1914, and quacks were adept at prescribing them for general symptoms as well as for specific diseases: "Patent medicine promoters listed dozens of such symptoms, some of which indeed might occur in a person not really sick at all. . . . All this had the most disastrous consequences. People who were not really sick were frightened into the medicine habit" (Young 1961: 68). The medicines often contained opium, which caused the patient, if actually sick, to gain the false impression that he or she was on the road to recovery. Of course, because scientific medical treatment was most often absent for even the mildest of diseases, a feeling of well-being was at least psychologically, and perhaps by extension physiologically, beneficial. However, babies born to opiate-using mothers were often small and experienced the distress of withdrawal. Harried mothers often responded by relieving them with infant remedies that contained opium.

The smoking of opium was popularized by Chinese immigrants, who brought the habit with them to the United States. During the latter part of the nineteenth and early twentieth centuries they also operated commercial "opium dens," which often attracted the attention of the police, "not because of the use of narcotics but because they became gathering places for thieves, footpads [highwaymen] and gangsters." In fact, "opium dens were regarded as in a class with saloons and, for many years, were no more illegal" (Katcher 1959: 287).

MORPHINE AND HEROIN

In 1799 (Latimer and Goldberg 1981) or 1803 (Merlin 1984; Nelson et al. 1982) or 1805 (Musto 1987) or 1806 (Bresler 1980), a German pharmacist poured liquid ammonia over opium and obtained an alkaloid, a white powder, that he found to be many times more powerful than opium. Frederich W. Serturner named the substance *morphium* after Morpheus, the Greek god of sleep and dreams; ten parts of opium can be refined into one part of morphine (Bresler 1980). It was not until 1817, however, that articles published in scientific journals popularized the new drug, resulting in widespread use by doctors. Quite incorrectly, as it turned out, the medical profession viewed morphine as an opiate without negative side effects.

By the 1850s morphine tablets and a variety of morphine products were readily available without prescription. In 1856 the hypodermic method of injecting morphine directly into the bloodstream was introduced to U.S. medicine. The popularity of morphine rose markedly during the Civil War, when the intravenous use of the drug to treat battlefield casualties was rather indiscriminate (Terry and Pellens 1928). Following the war, morphine use was so common among ex-soldiers as to give rise to the term *army disease.* "Medical journals were replete with glowing descriptions of the effectiveness of the drug during wartime and its obvious advantages for peacetime medical practice" (Cloyd 1982: 21). Hypodermic kits became widely available, and the use of unsterile needles by many doctors and laypersons led to abscesses or disease (Morgan 1981). David Musto (1973) argues, however, that the Civil War actually had very little impact on the popularity of opium. He notes that the importation of opium continued to increase from 1840 to the end of the century, per capita importation reaching a peak in 1896.

In the 1870s morphine was exceedingly cheap, cheaper than alcohol, with pharmacies and general stores carrying preparations that appealed to a wide segment of the population, whatever the individual emotional quirk or physical ailment. Anyone who visited nearly any physician for any complaint, from a toothache to consumption, would be prescribed morphine (Latimer and Goldberg 1981), and the substance was widely abused by physicians themselves. Until the late 1870s the concept of addiction was not widely known or understood (Morgan 1981). While it eventually became associated with the underworld elements of urban America, morphine abuse in the latter part of the nineteenth century was apparently widespread in rural America (Terry and Pellens 1928).

In 1874 a British chemist experimenting with morphine synthesized diacetyl-morphine, and the most powerful of opiates came into being:

> Commercial promotion of the new drug had to wait until 1898 when the highly respected German pharmaceutical combine Bayer, in perfectly good faith but perhaps without sufficient prior care, launched upon an unsuspecting world public this new substance, for which they coined the trade name "heroin" and which they marketed as—of all things—a "sedative for coughs." (Bresler 1980: 11)

Jack Nelson and his colleagues (1982) state that heroin was actually isolated in 1898 in Germany by Heinrich Dreser, who was searching for a non-habit-forming analgesic to take the place of morphine. Dreser named it after the German word *heroisch,* meaning large and powerful.

Opiates, including morphine and heroin, were readily available in the United States until 1914. In 1900 alone, 628,177 pounds of opiates were imported into the United States (Bonnie and Whitebread 1970). The President's Commission on Organized Crime (1986; hereafter PCOC) notes that between the Civil War and 1914 there was a substantial increase in the number of persons using opiates, the consequence of a number of factors including:

- The spread of opium smoking from Chinese immigrants into the wider community.
- An increase in morphine addiction as a result of its indiscriminate use to treat battlefield casualties during the Civil War.
- The widespread administration of morphine by hypodermic syringe.
- The widespread use of opium derivatives by the American patent medicine industry.
- Beginning in 1898, the marketing of heroin as a safe, powerful, and non-addictive substitute for the opium derivatives morphine and codeine.

Heroin was "put out as a safe preparation free from addiction-forming properties, possessing many of the virtues and none of the dangers of morphine and codeine, and recommended even as an agent of value in the treatment of chronic intoxication to these drugs" (Terry and Pellens 1928: 76).

THE PURE FOOD AND DRUG ACT

National efforts against opiates (and cocaine) were part of a larger campaign to regulate drugs and the contents of food substances; in 1879 a bill was introduced in Congress to accomplish national food and drug regulation. These efforts were opposed by the Proprietary Association of America, which represented the patent medicine industry. The medical profession was more interested in dealing with quacks within the profession than with quack medicines, and the American Pharmaceutical Association was of a mixed mind: Its members, in addition to being scientists, were merchants who found the sale of proprietary remedies bulking large in their gross incomes (Young 1961). Toward the end of the nineteenth century, the campaign for drug regulation was assisted by agricultural chemists, who decried the use of chemicals to defraud consumers into buying spoiled canned and packaged food. In 1884 state-employed chemists formed the Association of Official Agricultural Chemists to combat this widespread practice. They began to expand their efforts into non-foodstuffs, including patent medicines.

The nation's newspapers and magazines made a considerable amount of money from advertising patent medicines. Toward the turn of the century, however, a few periodicals, in particular *Ladies Home Journal* and *Collier's,* began vigorous investigations and denunciations of patent medicines. Eventually, the American Medical Association (AMA, founded in 1847), which was a rather weak organization at the close of the nineteenth century because the vast majority of doctors were not members (Musto 1973), began to campaign in earnest for drug regulation. The U.S. Senate hearings on the pure food issue gained a great deal of newspaper coverage and aroused the public (Young 1961). The most dramatic accomplishment, however, and the event that quickly led to the adoption of the Pure Food and Drug Act, was the 1906 publication of Upton Sinclair's *The Jungle*. Sinclair, in a novelistic description of the meat industry in Chicago, exposed the filthy, unsanitary, and unsafe conditions under which food reached the consumer. The sale of meat fell by almost 50 percent and President Theodore Roosevelt dispatched two investigators to Chicago to check on Sinclair's charges. Their "report not only confirmed Sinclair's allegations, but added additional ones. Congress was forced by public opinion to consider a strong bill" (Ihde 1982: 42). The result was the Pure Food and Drug Act passed later that same year, which required medicines to list certain drugs and their amounts, including alcohol and opiates.

CHINA AND THE OPIUM WARS

Because the U.S. response to drugs in the twentieth century is directly related to international affairs and trade with China, we need to review China's opium problem before returning to drugs as a domestic issue. China's historical experience with the West, particularly Britain, has generally been negative. The first British ship appeared off China in 1626, and its captain imposed his will on Canton with a bombardment. In response to the danger posed by British ships, the emperor opened the city of Canton to trade. (In the wake of the Napoleonic Wars, Great Britain possessed the most formidable naval fleet in the world, while the Chinese had virtually no national navy.)

The British East India Company enjoyed a government-granted monopoly over the China trade. Particularly important was the shipping of tea to England. By the 1820s the trade situation between England and China paralleled the current status of trade between the United States and Japan. While British consumers had an insatiable appetite for Chinese tea, few English goods were desired by the Chinese. The British attempted to introduce alcohol, but a large percentage of Asians have enzyme systems that make drinking alcohol extremely unpleasant. Opium was the exception (Beeching 1975). Poppy cultivation was an important source of revenue for the Moghul emperors (Muslim rulers of India between 1526 and 1857). When the Moghul empire fell apart, the British East India Company salvaged and improved upon the system of state control of opium. In addition to the domestic market, the British supplied Indian opium to China.

Opium was first prohibited by Peking in 1729, when only small amounts of the substance were reaching China. Ninety years earlier, tobacco had been similarly banned as a pernicious foreign article. Opium use was strongly condemned in China as a violation of Confucian principles, and for many years the imperial decree against opium was generally supported by the population (Beeching 1975). In 1782 an attempt by a British merchant ship to sell 1,601 chests of opium resulted in a total loss, as no purchasers could be found. By 1799, however, a growing traffic in opium led to an imperial decree condemning the trade. Dean Latimer and Jeff Goldberg (1981) doubt that opium addiction was extensive or particularly harmful to China as a whole. The poorer classes, the authors note, could afford only adulterated opium, which was unlikely to produce addiction. "Just why the Chinese chose to obtain their supplies from India," states Peter Fay (1975: 11–12), "is no clearer than why, having obtained it, they smoked it instead of ate it." In the end, he notes, the Chinese came to prefer the Indian product to their own. However, because the preference was to smoke opium, it had to be specially prepared by being boiled in water, filtered, and boiled again until it reached the consistency of molasses, thereby becoming "smoking opium."

Like the ban on tobacco, the one on opium was not successful (official corruption was endemic in China). As consumption of imported opium increased and the method of ingestion shifted from eating to smoking, official declarations against opium increased, and so did smuggling.

> When opium left Calcutta, stored in the holds of country ships and consigned to agents in Canton, it was an entirely legitimate article. It remained an entirely legitimate article all the way up to the China Sea. But the instant it reached the coast of China it became something different. It became contraband. (Fay 1975: 45)

In fact, the actual shipping of opium to China was accomplished by independent merchants, British or Parsee. Thus, notes Beeching, "The Honourable East India Company was able to wash its hands of all formal responsibility for the illegal drug trade" (1975: 26).

Opium furnished the British with the silver needed to buy tea. Because opium was illegal in China, however, its importation—smuggling—brought China no tariff revenue. Before 1830 opium was transported to the coast of China, where it was offloaded and smuggled by the Chinese themselves. The outlawing of opium by the Chinese government led to the development of an organized underworld. Gangs became secret societies—triads—that still move heroin out of Hong Kong and Singapore to destinations all over the world (Latimer and Goldberg 1981; this will be discussed in chapter 6). The armed opium ships were safe from Chinese government intervention, and the British were able to remain aloof from the smuggling itself.

In the 1830s the shippers grew bolder and entered Chinese territorial waters with their opium cargo. The British East India Company, now in competition with other opium merchants, sought to flood China with cheap opium and drive out the competition (Beeching 1975). In 1837 the emperor ordered his officials to move against opium smugglers, but the campaign was a failure and the smugglers grew even bolder. The following year the emperor changed his strategy and moved against Chinese traffickers and drug abusers, as only a total despot could do, helping to dry up the market for opium. As a result, the price fell significantly (Fay 1975).

In 1839, in dramatic fashion, Chinese authorities layed siege to the port city of Canton, confiscating and destroying all opium awaiting offloading from foreign ships. The merchantmen agreed to stop importing opium into China, and the siege was lifted. The British merchants petitioned the Crown for compensation and retribution. The reigning Parliamentary Whig majority, however, was very weak, and compensating the opium merchants was not politically or financially feasible. Instead, the cabinet, without Parliamentary approval, decided on a war that would result in the seizure of Chinese property (Fay 1975).

In 1840 a British expedition attacked the poorly armed and poorly organized Chinese forces. In the rout that followed, the emperor was forced to pay $6 million for the opium his officials had seized and $12 million as compensation for the war. Hong Kong became a Crown colony, and the ports of Canton, Amoy, Foochow, Ningpo, and Shanghai were opened to British trade. Opium was not mentioned in the peace (surrender) treaty, but the trade resumed with new vigor. In a remarkable reversal of the balance of trade, by the mid-1840s China had an opium debt of about 2 million pounds sterling (Latimer and Goldberg 1981). In the wake of the First Opium War, China was layed open to extensive missionary efforts by Protestant evangelicals who, although they opposed the opium trade, viewed saving souls as their primary goal. Christianity, they believed, would save China from opium (Fay 1975). Unfortunately, morphine, in the form of "antiopium pills," was actively promoted by Catholic and Protestant missionaries as an agent for detoxifying opium addicts (Latimer and Goldberg 1981).

The Second Opium War began in 1856, when the balance of payments once again favored China. In that year a minor incident between the British and Chinese governments was used as an excuse to force China into making further treaty concessions. And this time the foreign powers seeking to exploit a militarily weak China included Russia, the United States, and particularly France, which was jealous of the British success. Canton was sacked, and a combined fleet of British and French warships sailed right up the Grand Canal to Peking and proceeded to sack and burn the imperial summer palace. The emperor was forced to indemnify the British 20,000 pounds sterling, more than enough to offset the balance of trade, which was the real cause of the war. A commission was appointed to legalize and regulate the opium trade (Latimer and Goldberg 1981), which increased from less than 59,000 chests a year in 1860 to more than 105,000 by 1880 (Beeching 1975). Until 1946 the British permitted the use of opiates in its Crown colony of Hong Kong, first under an official monopoly and after 1913 directly by the government (Lamour and Lamberti 1974). Hong Kong continues to suffer with a large addict population.

THE "CHINESE PROBLEM" AND THE AMERICAN RESPONSE

Chinese were originally brought into the United States after 1848 to work in the gold fields, particularly in those aspects of mining that were most dangerous, because few white men were willing to engage in blasting shafts, placing beams, and laying track lines in the gold mines. Chinese immigrants also helped build the western railroad lines at "coolie wages"—pay few whites would accept. After their work was completed, the Chinese were often banned from the rural counties and by the 1860s were clustering in cities on the Pacific coast where they established Chinatowns—and smoked opium.

The British opium monopoly in China was challenged in the 1870s by opium imported from Persia and cultivated in China itself. In response, British colonial authorities, heavily dependent on a profitable opium trade, increased the output of Indian opium, causing a decline in prices that was aimed at driving the competition out of business. The resulting oversupply increased the amount of opium entering the United States for the Chinese population.

Beginning in 1875 there was an economic depression in California. As a result, the first significant piece of prohibitionary drug legislation in the United States was enacted by the city of San Francisco. "The primary event that precipitated the campaign against the Chinese and against opium was the sudden onset of economic depression, high unemployment levels, and the disintegration of working-class standards of living" (Helmer 1975: 32). The San Francisco ordinance prohibited the operation of opium dens, commercial establishments for the smoking of opium, "not because of health concerns as such, but because it was believed that the drug stimulated coolies into working harder than non-smoking whites" (Latimer and Goldberg 1981: 208).

Depressed economic conditions and xenophobia led one western state after another to follow San Francisco's lead and enact anti-Chinese legislation that often included prohibiting the smoking of opium. The anti-Chinese nature of the legislation was noted in some early court decisions. In 1886 an Oregon district court, responding to a petition for habeas corpus filed by Yung Jon, who had been convicted of opium violations, stated:

> Smoking opium is not our vice, and therefore it may be that this legislation proceeds more from a desire to vex and annoy the "Heathen Chinese" in this respect, than to protect the people from the evil habit. But the motives of legislators cannot be the subject of judicial investigation for the purpose of affecting the validity of their acts. (Bonnie and Whitebread 1970: 997)

"After 1870 a new type of addict began to emerge, the white opium smoker drawn primarily from the underworld of pimps and prostitutes, gamblers, and thieves" (Courtwright 1982: 64). In Chicago during the 1890s, Chinatown was located in the notorious First Ward, whose politicians grew powerful and wealthy by protecting almost every vice known to man. But First Ward alderman John "Bathhouse" Coughlin "couldn't stomach" opium smokers and threatened to raid the dens himself if necessary. There was constant police harassment, and in 1894 the city enacted an antiopium ordinance. By 1895 the last of the dens had been raided out of business (Sawyers 1988).

Anti-Chinese efforts were supported and advanced by Samuel Gompers (1850-1924) as part of his effort to establish the American Federation of

Labor. The Chinese served as scapegoats for organized labor, which depicted the "yellow devils" as undercutting wages and breaking strikes. Antiopium legislation was also fostered by stories of white women being seduced by Chinese white-slavers through the use of opium. In 1882 the Chinese Exclusion Act banned the entry of Chinese laborers into the United States. (It was not until 1943, when the United States was allied with China in a war against Japan, that citizenship rights were extended to Chinese immigrants and China was permitted an annual immigration of 105 persons.)

In 1883 Congress raised the tariff on the importation of smoking opium. In 1887, apparently in response to obligations imposed on the United States by a Chinese-American commercial treaty negotiated in 1880 and becoming effective in 1887, Congress banned the importation of smoking opium by Chinese subjects. Americans, however, were still permitted to import the substance and many did so, selling it to both Chinese and American citizens (PCOC 1986). The typical American opiate addict during the nineteenth century, notes Courtwright (1982), was a middle-aged white woman of the middle or upper class. As opposed to the Chinese, however, this addict did not smoke opium but was usually the victim of the poor medical practices prevalent at the time. The Tariff Act of 1890 increased the rate on smoking opium to twelve dollars per pound, resulting in a substantial increase in opium smuggling and the diversion of medicinal opium for manufacture into smoking opium. In response, in 1897 the tariff was reduced to six dollars per pound (PCOC 1986).

During the nineteenth century opiates were not associated with crime in the public mind. While opium use may have been frowned upon by some as immoral,

> employees were not fired for addiction. Wives did not divorce their addicted husbands, or husbands their addicted wives. Children were not taken from their homes and lodged in foster homes or institutions because one or both parents were addicted. Addicts continued to participate fully in the life of the community. Addicted children and young people continued to go to school, Sunday School, and college. Thus, the nineteenth century avoided one of the most disastrous effects of current narcotic laws and attitudes—the rise of a deviant addict subculture, cut off from respectable society and without a "road back" to respectability. (Brecher 1972: 6–7)

THE TWENTIETH CENTURY

In an effort to increase its influence in China, and thus improve its trade position, the United States supported the International Reform Bureau (IRB), a temperance organization representing over thirty missionary societies in the Far East, which was seeking a ban on opiates. As a result, in 1901 Congress enacted the Native Races Act, which prohibited the sale of alcohol and opium to "aboriginal tribes and uncivilized races." The provisions of the act were later expanded to include "uncivilized elements" in the United States proper: Indians, Eskimos, and Chinese (Latimer and Goldberg 1981).

As a result of the Spanish-American War in 1898, the Philippines were ceded to the United States. At the time of Spanish colonialism, opium smoking was widespread among Chinese workers on the islands. Canadian-born Reverend Charles Henry Brent (1862-1929), a supporter of the IRB, arrived in the Philippines as the Episcopal bishop during a cholera epidemic that began in 1902 and that reportedly had led to an increase in the use of opium. As a result of his efforts, in 1905 Congress enacted a ban against sales of opium to Filipino natives except for medicinal purposes: three years later the ban was extended to all residents of the Philippines. It appears that the legislation was ineffective, and smoking opium remained widely available (Musto 1973).

> Reformers attributed to drugs much of the appalling poverty, ignorance, and debilitation they encountered in the Orient. Opium was strongly identified with the problems afflicting an apparently moribund China. Eradication of drug abuse was part of America's white man's burden and a way to demonstrate the New World's superiority. (Morgan 1974: 32)

Bishop Brent also proposed the formation of an international opium commission, to meet in Shanghai in 1909. This plan was supported by President Roosevelt, who saw it as a way of assuaging Chinese anger at the passage of the Chinese Exclusionary Act (Latimer and Goldberg 1981). The International Opium Commission, chaired by Brent and consisting of representatives from thirteen nations, convened in Shanghai on February 1. Brent was successful in rallying the conferees around the U.S. position that opium was evil and had no nonmedical use. The commission unanimously adopted a number of vague resolutions, the most important being (Terry and Pellens 1928):

1. That each government take action to suppress the smoking of opium at home and in overseas possessions and settlements;
2. That opium has no use outside of medicine and, accordingly, that each country should move toward increasingly stringent regulations concerning opiates;
3. That measures should be taken to prevent the exporting of opium and its derivatives to countries which prohibit its importation.

Only the United States and China, however, were eager for future conferences, and legislative efforts against opium following the conference were generally unsuccessful. Southerners were distrustful of federal enforcement, and the drug industry was opposed. Efforts to gain southern support for antidrug legislation focused on the alleged abuse of cocaine by African Americans—the substance was reputed to make them uncontrollable. While there already existed tariff legislation with respect to opium, Terry and Pellens note that its purpose was to generate income. The first federal legislation to control the domestic use of opium was passed in 1909 as a result of the Shanghai conference. "An Act to prohibit the importation and use of opium for other than medicinal purposes" failed to regulate domestic opium production and manufacture, nor did it control the interstate shipment of opium products, which continued to be widely available through retail and mail order outlets (PCOC 1986).

A second conference was held in the Hague in 1912, with the United States, Turkey, Great Britain, France, Portugal, Japan, Russia, Italy, Germany, Persia, the Netherlands, and China in attendance. There were a number of problems standing in the way of an international agreement: Germany wished to protect her burgeoning pharmaceutical industry and insisted on a unanimous vote before any action could be agreed upon; Portugal insisted on retaining the Macao opium trade; the Dutch demanded to maintain their opium trade in the West Indies; and Persia and Russia wanted to keep on growing opium poppies. Righteous U.S. appeals to the delegates were rebuffed with allusions to domestic usage and the lack of laws in the United States (Latimer and Goldberg 1981). Nevertheless, the conference managed to put together a patchwork of agreements known as the International Opium Convention, which was ratified by Congress on October 18, 1913. The signatories committed themselves to enacting laws aimed at suppressing the abuse of opium, morphine, and cocaine, as well as drugs prepared or derived from these substances (PCOC 1986). On December 17, 1914, the Harrison Act, which represented this country's attempt to carry out the provisions of the Hague Convention, was approved by President Woodrow Wilson.

The Harrison Act

The Harrison Act provided that any person who was in the business of dealing in drugs covered by the act, including the opium derivatives morphine and heroin, as well as cocaine, was required to register annually and to pay a special annual tax of one dollar. The statute made it illegal to sell or give away opium or opium derivatives and coca or its derivatives without a written order on a form issued by the commissioner of revenue. Persons who were not registered were prohibited from engaging in interstate traffic in the drugs, and no one could possess any of the drugs who had not registered and paid the special tax, under a penalty of up to five years imprisonment and a fine of no more than $2,000. Rules promulgated by the Treasury Department permitted only medical professionals to register, and they had to maintain records of the drugs they dispensed. Within the first year more than 200,000 medical professionals registered, and the small staff of treasury agents could not scrutinize the prescription records that were generated (Musto 1973).

It was concern with federalism—constitutional limitations on the police powers of the central government—that led Congress to use the taxing authority of the federal government to control drugs. At the turn of the century, federal authority to regulate narcotics and the prescription practices of physicians was generally thought to be unconstitutional (Musto 1973). In 1919 the use of taxing authority to regulate drugs was upheld by the Supreme Court (*United States v. Doremus* 249 U.S. 86):

> If the legislation enacted has some reasonable relation to the exercise of the taxing authority conferred by the Constitution, it cannot be invalidated because of the supposed motives which induced it. . . . The Act may not be declared unconstitutional because its effect may be to accomplish another purpose as well as the raising of revenue. If the legislation is within the taxing authority of Congress—that is sufficient to sustain it.

The Harrison Act was enacted with the support of the AMA, which by that time "was well on its way to consolidation of American medical practitioners" (Musto 1973: 56), and of the American Pharmaceutical Association, which, like the AMA, had grown more powerful and influential in the first two decades of the twentieth century, the medical profession having been granted a monopoly over the dispensing of opiates and cocaine. The Harrison Act also had the effect of imposing a stamp of illegitimacy on the use of most narcotics, fostering an image of the immoral and degenerate "dope fiend" (Bonnie and Whitebread 1970). At this time, according to Courtwright's (1982) estimates, there were about 300,000 opiate addicts in the United States. But, he notes, the addict population was already changing. The medical profession had, by and large, abandoned its liberal use of opiates—imports of medicinal opiates declined dramatically during the first decade of the twentieth century—and the public mind came to associate heroin with urban vice and crime. Unlike the (often female and) "respectable" opiate addicts of the nineteenth century, opiate users of the twentieth century were increasingly male habitués of pool halls and bowling alleys, denizens of the underworld. As in the case of minority groups, this marginal population was an easy target of drug laws and drug-law enforcement.

The commissioner of the Internal Revenue Service was placed in charge of upholding the Harrison Act, and in 1915, 162 collectors and agents of the Miscellaneous Division of the Internal Revenue Service were given the responsibility for enforcing drug laws. In 1919 the Narcotics Division was created within the Bureau of Prohibition with a staff of 170 agents and an appropriation of $270,000. The Narcotics Division, however, was tainted by its association with the notoriously inept and corrupt Prohibition Bureau and suffered from a corruption scandal of its own: There was

> public dissatisfaction with the activities of the Narcotics Division, which was tainted by its association with the country's anti-liquor laws. The public dissatisfaction intensified because of a scandal involving falsification of arrest records and charges relating to payoffs by, and collusion with, drug dealers. (PCOC 1986: 204)

In response, in 1930 Congress removed drug enforcement from the Bureau of Prohibition and established the Federal Bureau of Narcotics (FBN) as a separate agency within the Department of the Treasury. "Although the FBN was primarily responsible for the enforcement of the Harrison Act and related drug laws, the task of preventing and interdicting the illegal importation and smuggling of drugs remained with the Bureau of Customs" (PCOC 1986: 205).

In 1916 the Court ruled in favor of a physician (Dr. Moy) who had provided maintenance doses of morphine to an addict (*United States v. Jin Fuey Moy* 241 U.S. 394). In 1919, however, the Court ruled (*Webb v. United States* 249 U.S. 96) that a prescription for morphine issued to an habitual user who was not under a physician's care, that was not intended to cure but to maintain the habit is not a prescription and thus violates the Harrison Act. However, private physicians found it impossible to handle the large drug clientele that was suddenly created: They could do nothing "more than sign prescriptions" (Duster 1970: 16). In *United States v. Behrman* (258 U.S. 280, 289, 1922) the Court ruled that a physician was not entitled to prescribe large doses of proscribed drugs for self-administration *even* if the addict was under the physician's care. The Court stated that "prescriptions in the regular course of practice did not include the indiscriminate doling out of narcotics in such quantity as charged in the indictments." In 1925 the Court limited the application of *Behrman* when it found that a physician who had prescribed small doses of drugs for the relief of an addict did not violate the Harrison Act (*Linder v. United States* 268 U.S. 5). In reversing the physician's conviction the Court distinguished between *Linder* and excesses shown in the case of *Behrman*:

> The enormous quantities of drugs ordered, considered in connection with the recipient's character, without explanation, seemed enough to show prohibited sales and to exclude the idea of *bona fide* professional activity. The opinion [in *Behrman*] cannot be accepted as authority for holding that a physician, who acts *fide bona* and according to fair medical standards, may never give an addict moderate amounts of drugs for self-administration in order to relieve conditions incident to addiction. Enforcement of the tax demands no such drastic rule, and if the Act had such scope it would certainly encounter grave constitutional guarantees.

In fact, the powers of the Narcotics Division were clear and limited to the enforcement of registration and recordkeeping regulations. "The large number of addicts who secured their drugs from physicians were excluded from the Division's jurisdiction. Furthermore, the public's attitude toward drug use," notes Donald Dickson (1977: 39), "had not much changed with the passage of the Act—there was some opposition to drug use, some support of it, and a great many who did not care one way or the other. The Harrison Act was actually passed with very little publicity or news coverage." Richard Bonnie and Charles Whitebread (1970: 976) note the similarities between the temperance and antinarcotics movements. "Both were first directed against the evils of large scale use and only later against all use. Most of the rhetoric was the same: These euphoriants produced crime, pauperism and insanity." However,

> the temperance movement was a matter of vigorous public debate; the anti-narcotics movement was not. Temperance legislation was the product of a highly

organized nationwide lobby; narcotics legislation was largely ad hoc. Temperance legislation was designed to eradicate known evils resulting from alcohol abuse; narcotics legislation was largely anticipatory.

In fact, notes Wayne Morgan (1981), comparisons between alcohol and opiates—until the nature of addiction became clear—were often favorable to opium. It was not public sentiment that led to antidrug legislation but, nevertheless, the result of such legislation was an increasing public perception of the dangerousness of certain drugs (Bonnie and Whitebread 1970). As we will see, this perception was fanned by officials of the federal drug enforcement agency.

Writing in 1916, Pearce Bailey (1974: 173–74) noted that the passage of the Act "spread dismay among the heroin takers":

> They saw in advance the increased difficulty and expense of obtaining heroin as a result of this law; then the drug stores shut down, and the purveyors who sell heroin on the street corners and in doorways became terrified, and for a time illicit trade in the drug almost ceased. . . . Once the law was established the traffic was resumed, but under very different circumstances. The price of heroin soared [900 percent, and was sold in adulterated form]. This put it beyond the easy reach of the majority of adherents, most of whom do not earn more than twelve or fourteen dollars a week. Being no longer able to procure it with any money that they could lay their hands on honestly, many were forced to apply for treatment for illness brought about by result of arrest for violation of the law.

Beginning in 1918 narcotic clinics opened in almost every major city. Information about them is sketchy (Duster 1970), and there is a great deal of controversy over their operations. While they were never very popular with the general public, most clinics were well run under medical supervision (Morgan 1981). While some clinics were guilty of a variety of abuses, the good ones enabled addicts to continue their normal lives without being drawn into the black market in drugs (Duster 1970). The troubled clinics, however, such as in New York, where the number of patients overwhelmed the medical staff, generated a great deal of newspaper coverage, resulting in an outraged public.

Following World War I and the Bolshevik Revolution, xenophobia and prohibitionism began to sweep the nation. The United States severely restricted foreign immigration, and alcohol and drug use were increasingly associated with an alien population. In 1922 federal narcotic agents closed the drug clinics and began to arrest physicians and pharmacists who provided drugs for maintenance. At issue was section 8 of the Harrison Act, which permitted the possession of controlled substances if prescribed "in good faith" by a registered physician, dentist, or veterinarian in accord with "professional practice." The law did not define "good faith" or "professional practice." Under a policy developed by the federal narcotic agency, thousands of persons, including many physicians, were charged with violations: "Whether conviction followed or not mattered little as the effects of press publicity dealing with what were supposedly willful violations of a beneficent law were most disastrous to those concerned" (Terry and Pellens 1928: 90). "After this initial burst of arrest activity directed against registrants, the Narcotics Division turned its attention to closing clinics that had been established to conduct research and treat large numbers of addicts who could not afford private care" (PCOC 1986: 202). They were declared illegal by the drug agency and closed (Terry and Pellens 1928).

The medical profession withdrew from dispensing drugs to addicts, forcing them to look to illicit sources and giving rise to an enormous illegal business in drugs. Persons addicted to opium smoking eventually found their favorite drug unavailable—the bulky smoking opium was difficult to smuggle—and they turned to the more readily available heroin, which was prepared for intravenous use (Courtwright 1982). The criminal syndicates that resulted from Prohibition added heroin trafficking to their business portfolios. When Prohibition was repealed in 1933, profits from bootlegging disappeared accordingly, but drug trafficking remained as an important source of revenue for organized criminal groups. (The business of drugs is discussed in chapter 6.) Law enforcement efforts against drugs have proven as ineffectual as efforts against alcohol during Prohibition, with similar problems of corruption.

The federal government shaped vague and conflicting court decisions into definitive pronouncements reflecting the drug enforcement agency's own version of its proper role: "American administrative regulations took on the force of ruling law" (Trebach 1982: 132). The drug agency also embarked on a vigorous campaign to convince the public and Congress of the dangers of drugs and, thereby, to justify its approach to the problem of drug abuse. According to Bonnie and Whitebread (1970: 990), the existence of a separate federal narcotics bureau "anxious to fulfill its role as crusader against the evils of narcotics" has been *the* single major factor in the legislative history of drug control in the United States since 1930.

The actions of the federal government toward drug use must be understood within the context of the times. The years immediately following World War I were characterized by pervasive attitudes of nationalism and nativism and by a fear of anarchy and communism. The Bolshevik Revolution in Russia, a police strike in Boston (see Russell 1975), and widespread labor unrest and violence were the backdrop for the infamous "Palmer Raids" of 1919, in which Attorney General A. Mitchel Palmer, disregarding a host of constitutional protections, ordered the arrest of thousands of "radicals." That same year the Prohibition Amendment was ratified, and soon legislation was enacted to stop the "huddled masses yearning to breathe free" from entering the United States. Large-scale (legal) immigration had ended. Drug addiction—morphinism/heroinism—was added to the un-American "isms" of alcoholism, anarchism, and communism (Musto 1973). In 1918 there were only 888 federal arrests for narcotic law violations; in 1920 there were 3,477. In 1925, the year the clinics closed, there were 10,297 (Cloyd 1982).

In 1923 legislation was introduced to curtail the importation of opium for the manufacture of heroin, resulting in a virtual ban on heroin in the United

States. (In 1956 Congress declared all heroin to be contraband.) Among the few witnesses who testified before Congress, all supported the legislation. The AMA had already condemned the use of heroin by physicians, and the substance was described as the most dangerous of all habit-forming drugs, some witnesses arguing that the psychological effects of heroin use serve as a stimulus to crime. Much of the medical testimony, in light of what is now known about heroin, was erroneous, but the law won easy passage in 1924 (Musto 1973). A pamphlet published the same year by the prestigious Foreign Policy Association summarized contemporary thinking about heroin (cited in Trebach 1982: 48): Heroin

- is unnecessary in the practice of medicine.
- destroys all sense of moral responsibility.
- is the drug of the criminal.
- recruits its army among youths.

The use of opiates, except for narrow medical purposes, was now thoroughly criminalized, both in law and in practice. The law defined drug users as criminals, and the public viewed heroin use as the behavior of a deviant criminal class.

The Uniform Drug Act

Until 1930 efforts against drugs were primarily federal. Only a few states had drug-control statutes, and these were generally ineffective (Musto 1973). At the urging of federal authorities, many states enacted their own antidrug legislation. By 1931 every state restricted the sale of cocaine, and all but two restricted the sale of opiates. There was, however, a considerable lack of uniformity among state statutes and a weakness in state enforcement procedures. As early as 1927 this, combined with the growing hysteria about dope fiends and criminality, resulted in several requests for a uniform state narcotic law (Bonnie and Whitebread 1970). The diversity of drug statutes was not an anachronism. A recognition of the need for greater uniformity in state statutes dates back to the first half of the nineteenth century, when a prominent New York attorney, David Dudley Field (1805–1894), campaigned for a uniform code of procedure for both civil and criminal matters. During the 1890s the American Bar Association set up the National Conference of Commissioners on Uniform State Laws, whose efforts resulted in a variety of uniform codes that were adopted by virtually all jurisdictions (Abadinsky 1995).

A uniform drug act for the states was the goal of the Committee on the Uniform Narcotic Act and representatives of the American Medical Association because doctors wanted uniformity of legal obligations. Their first two drafts copied a 1927 New York statute that listed coca, opium, and cannabis products as habit-forming drugs to be regulated or prohibited. Because of opposition to its inclusion on the habit-forming list, cannabis was dropped from later drafts with a note indicating that each state was free to include cannabis or not in its own legislation without affecting the rest of the act. The final draft also used the 1927 New York statute as a model and included suggestions from the newly appointed commissioner of the Federal Bureau of Narcotics (FBN), Harry Anslinger. It was adopted overwhelmingly by the National Conference of Commissioners on Uniform State Laws, to which each governor appointed two representatives. By 1937 thirty-five states had enacted the Uniform Act, and every state had enacted statutes relating to marijuana. Despite propagandizing efforts by the FBN, "The laws went unnoticed by legal commentators, the press and the public at large" (Bonnie and Whitebread 1970: 1034).

The lack of public concern is related to the demographics of drug abuse, which was concentrated in minority, lower-class areas and the criminal subculture. Before the Harrison Act, "Estimates of distribution reported considerable use of habit-forming drugs in rural areas" (Morgan 1981: 32). The South, where drugs often substituted for alcohol in dry areas, used more opiates than other parts of the country. After the Harrison Act, addicts in rural areas were attended to quietly by sympathetic doctors. Since the Harrison Act and its vigorous enforcement by the FBN, heroin use continues to be heavily concentrated in urban areas of poverty. For example, during the early decades of the twentieth century, heroin use in New York was heaviest in the Jewish and Italian areas of the Lower East Side. As these two groups climbed up the economic ladder and moved out, they were replaced by African Americans looking for affordable housing; this group then became the addict population (Helmer 1975). Demographics intensified the problem—African Americans had a higher number of births than Jews and Italians, and an extraordinary number of African American youngsters were at the age of highest risk for addiction, sixteen. It was the Vietnam War—fought in an area of the world noted for the production of opium—John Helmer (1975) argues, that changed the demographics of heroin use, with increasing numbers of white ex-servicemen found in the abuser population. (Vietnam and the Golden Triangle of Southeast Asia are discussed in chapter 6.)

Pointing to the similarities between the prohibition against alcohol and that against other drugs, David Courtwright (1982: 144) asks why, since both reform efforts ended in failure, did the public withdraw its support for one and increase its support for the other?

> One factor (in addition to economic and political considerations) must have been that alcohol use was relatively widespread and cut across class lines. It seemed unreasonable for the government to deny a broad spectrum of otherwise normal persons access to drink. By 1930 opiate addiction, by contrast, was perceived to be concentrated in a small criminal subculture; it did not seem unreasonable for that same government to deny the morbid cravings of a deviant group.

World War II impacted dramatically on the supply of heroin in the United States. The Japanese invasion of China interrupted supplies from that country, while the disruption of shipping routes by German submarines and attack battleships reduced the amount of heroin moving from Turkey to Marseilles to the United States. When the United States entered the war, security measures "designed to prevent infiltration of foreign spies and sabotage to naval installations made smuggling into the United States virtually impossible." As a result, "At the end of World War II, there was an excellent chance that heroin addiction could be eliminated in the United States" (McCoy 1972: 15). Obviously, this did not happen. The reasons will be discussed in chapter 6.

THE PROBLEM OF COCAINE

Cocaine is a stimulant, an alkaloid found in significant quantities only in the leaves of two species of coca shrub that are indigenous to certain sections of South America. People have been using cocaine for at least 5,000 years. To the Incas coca was a plant of divine origin reserved for those who believed themselves descendants of the gods. European experience with chewing coca coincided with Spanish exploration of the New World. While the early Spanish explorers, obsessed with gold, referred to coca-leaf chewing with scorn, later reports about the effects of coca on Indians were more enthusiastic. Nevertheless, the chewing of coca leaves was not adopted by Europeans until the nineteenth century (Grinspoon 1976). A "mixture of ignorance and moral hauteur played an important role in the long delay between the time Europeans first became acquainted with cocaine—in the form of coca—and the time they began to use it" (Ashley 1975: 3). The coca leaves tasted bitter and were favored by pagans—Peruvian Indians—"an obviously inferior lot who had allowed their great Inca Empire to be conquered by Pizarro and fewer than two hundred Spaniards." Early records indicate that the effects of coca—stamina and energy—were ascribed not to the drug but to a pact the Indians had made with the devil, or simply to delusion. The Indian is sustained by the *belief* that chewing coca gives him extra strength.

Who first isolated alkaloidal cocaine from the coca leaf is a matter of some dispute, as is the year in which it occurred. Richard Ashley (1975) favors the German chemist Frederich Gaedecke (whose name has been spelled in a variety of ways) and the year 1855. In any event, other scientists began experimenting with the substance, noting that it showed promise as a local anesthetic and had an effect opposite that caused by morphine. Indeed, at first cocaine was used to treat morphine addiction, but the result was often a morphine addict who was also dependent on cocaine (Van Dyke and Byck 1982). "Throughout the late nineteenth century, both coca itself (that is, an extract from the leaf including all its alkaloids) and the pure chemical cocaine were used as medicines and for pleasure—the distinction was not always made—in an enormous variety of ways" (Grinspoon 1976: 19). In 1884 Sigmund Freud began taking cocaine and soon afterward began to treat his friend Ernst von

THE BEST KNOWN "USER" OF COCAINE

"Save for the occasional use of cocaine, [Sherlock Holmes] had no vices, and he only turned to the drug as a protest against the monotony of existence when cases were scanty and the papers uninteresting." (Sir Arthur Conan Doyle 1899: 29)

Fleischl-Marxow, who had become a morphine addict, with cocaine. The following year, von Fleischl-Marxow suffered from toxic psychosis as a result of taking increasing amounts of cocaine, and Freud wrote that the misuse of the substance had hastened his friend's death. While Freud continued the recreational use of cocaine as late as 1895, his enthusiasm for its therapeutic value waned (Byck 1974). The usefulness of cocaine as a local anesthetic, however, led to the development of procaine, which in 1905 was introduced into medicine and continues to be used today, particularly in dentistry (Snyder 1986).

Enthusiasm for cocaine spread across the United States, and by the late 1880s a feel-good pharmacology based on the coca plant and its derivative cocaine emerged, as the substance was hawked for everything from headaches to hysteria. "Catarrh powders for sinus trouble and headaches—a few were nearly pure cocaine—introduced the concept of snorting" (Gomez 1984: 58). Cocaine was particularly popular in literary and intellectual circles (Grinspoon 1976). One very popular product was the coca wine *Vin Mariani,* which contained two ounces of fresh coca leaves in a pint of Bordeaux wine; it received the praise of such prominent persons as Sarah Bernhardt and John Philip Sousa as well as three popes and sixteen heads of state. Another beverage, Peruvian Wine of Coca, was available for one dollar a bottle through the 1902 Sears, Roebuck catalog.

The most famous beverage containing coca, however, was first bottled in 1894. According to Linda Gomez (1984), coca was removed from Coca-Cola in 1903, after a presidential commission criticized the use of habit-forming drugs in soft drinks. However, an advertisement for Coca-Cola in *Scientific American* in 1906 publicized the use of coca as an important tonic in this "healthful drink" (May 1988c: 29), and a 1908 government report listed over forty brands of soft drinks containing cocaine (Helmer 1975).

After the first flush of enthusiasm for cocaine in the 1880s, there was a decline in its use. While it continued to be used in a variety of potions and tonics, cocaine, unlike morphine and heroin, did not develop a separate appeal (Morgan 1981). Indeed, it gained a reputation for inducing bizarre and unpredictable behavior. After the turn of the century, cocaine, like heroin, became identified with the urban underworld and, in the South, with African Americans. "As with Chinese opium, southern blacks became a target for class conflict, and drug use became one point of tension in this larger sociopolitical struggle" (Cloyd 1982: 35). The campaign against cocaine took on bizarre aspects aimed at winning support for antidrug legislation among southern politicians, who traditionally resisted federal efforts that interfered with their concept of states' rights. Without any research support, a spate of articles alleged widespread abuse of cocaine by African Americans, often associating such abuse with violence and the rape of white women (Helmer 1975). Ultimately, notes Jerald Cloyd (1982: 54), "Southerners were more afraid of blacks than of increased federal power to regulate these drugs." At the time of the Harrison Act there was considerable discussion—but no evidence—of substantial cocaine use by African Americans in northern cities (Morgan 1981).

As with opiates, the legal use of cocaine was affected by the Pure Food and Drug Act of 1906 and finally by the Harrison Act in 1914. Before this many states passed laws restricting the sale of cocaine, beginning with Oregon in 1887. By 1914 forty-six states had such laws, while only twenty-nine had similar laws with respect to opiates (Grinspoon 1976). In 1922 Congress officially defined cocaine as a narcotic and prohibited the importation of most cocaine and coca leaves. This caused an increase in law enforcement efforts, and the price of cocaine increased accordingly. In 1932 amphetamines became available, and this cheap legal stimulant helped to further decrease user interest in cocaine (Cintron 1986).

From 1930 until the 1960s there was limited demand for cocaine and, accordingly, only limited supply. Cocaine use was associated with deviants at the fringes of society—jazz musicians and the denizens of the underworld— and sources were typically diverted from medical supplies. During the late 1960s and early 1970s, attitudes toward recreational drug use became more liberal because of the wide acceptance of marijuana. Cocaine was no longer associated with deviants. The media played a significant role in shaping public attitudes:

> By publicizing and glamorizing the lifestyle of affluent, upper-class drug dealers and the use of cocaine by celebrities and athletes, all forms of mass media created an effective advertising campaign for cocaine, and many people were taught to perceive cocaine as chic, exclusive, daring, and nonaddicting. In television specials about cocaine abuse, scientists talked about the intense euphoria produced by cocaine and the compulsive craving that people (and animals) develop for it. Thus, an image of cocaine as being extraordinarily powerful, and a (therefore desirable) euphoriant was promoted. (Wesson and Smith 1985: 193)

Cocaine soon became associated with a privileged elite, and the new demand was sufficient to generate new sources. Refining and marketing networks outside of medical channels (Grinspoon 1976) led to the development of the criminal organizations discussed in chapter 6.

During the 1980s a new form of cocaine—called *crack*—became popular in a number of cities, particularly New York. Its popularity dramatically altered the drug market at the consumer level: Both users and sellers were much younger than was typical in the heroin business. Younger retailers and a competitive market increased the level of violence associated with the drug busi-

DRUG HYSTERIA

According to Steven Belenko (1993: 24), ~~all drug scares have four common ele-~~ ~~ments:~~

1. The scope of the problem is never as great as originally portrayed in the media.
2. Despite the media portrayals, compulsive use and addiction are not inevitable consequences of using the drug.
3. The violent behavior associated with the use of the drug is not as common as initially believed, nor is it necessarily caused by the drug.
4. The popularity of the particular drug waxes and wanes over time, and prevalence rates do not continue to increase.

ness (discussed in chapter 6). The appearance of this new form of cocaine, which is smoked, set off a frenzy of media interest. Elected officials responded by increasing penalties for this form of the substance as opposed to the powdered form, which is sniffed.

By 1987 the rapid expansion of crack use stopped, and by 1989 its popularity began to diminish. The hysteria with which the media and public officials had greeted this "new scourge" was subjected to research and reflection: "Crack itself was never instantly addictive or totally devastating as asserted by the media, political speeches, and statements of public policy. In particular, it did not draw the naive and young in droves into this new and dangerous lifestyle." Indeed, crack use was centered in those populations in which drug abuse has always been endemic—the urban underclass (Johnson, Golub, and Fagan 1995: 291).

Cocaine has very limited medical use as a local anesthetic for ear, nose, and throat surgery. Synthetic drugs such as procaine (novacaine) have, for the most part, replaced cocaine as a local anesthetic. Coca leaves are legally imported into the United States by a single chemical company, which extracts the cocaine for pharmaceutical purposes. The remaining leaf material, which contains no psychoactive agents, is prepared as a flavoring for Coca-Cola.

MEXICANS AND THE PROBLEM OF CANNABIS (MARIJUANA/MARIHUANA)

Cannabis sativa L., the hemp plant from which marijuana and hashish are derived, grows wild throughout most tropical and temperate regions of the world. It has been cultivated for at least 5,000 years for a variety of purposes, including the manufacture of rope and paint. Its use as an intoxicant was brought to Africa by Arab traders, and the plant was introduced into Brazil through the slave trade in the 1600s. The word *marijuana* is derived from the Spanish term for any substance that produces intoxication: *maraguango*. Until the early 1900s recreational use of marijuana was popular chiefly among Mexican laborers in the Southwest and certain fringe groups such as jazz musicians (Weisheit 1990).

When the dried leaves of the marijuana plant are smoked like tobacco, perceptual changes occur that vary widely according to the strength of the substance, the person smoking the marijuana, and the environmental conditions. In the past most of the cannabis growing wild in the United States derived "from plants which were originally cultivated for their fiber, rather than drug content, so that they could be used in making rope and other nondrug products." Their psychoactive potency was therefore quite weak (Peterson 1980: 7). In more recent years this changed dramatically as entrepreneurial horticulturists in the United States began producing more powerful strains of the plant.

As already discussed in this chapter, race, religion, and ethnicity have been closely identified with the reaction to drug use in the United States: the Irish and alcohol; the Chinese and opium; African Americans and cocaine; and, finally, Mexicans and marijuana. Bonnie and Whitebread (1970) state that the strongest influence on marijuana legislation was racism: State laws against marijuana, they argue, were often part of a reaction to Mexican immigration. Before 1930 sixteen states with relatively large Mexican populations had enacted anti-marijuana legislation. "Chicanos in the Southwest were believed to be incited to violence by smoking it" (Musto 1973: 65). Jerome Himmelstein (1983: 29) argues, however, that the

> crucial link between Mexicans and federal marihuana policy was not locally based political pressure from the Southwest, but a specific image of marihuana that emerged from the context of marihuana use by Mexicans and was used to justify anti-marihuana legislation. Because Mexican laborers and other lower-class groups were identified as typical marihuana users, the drug was believed to cause the kinds of antisocial behavior associated with those groups, especially violent crime. (Himmelstein 1983: 29)

Because of marijuana's association with suspect marginal groups—Mexicans, artists and intellectuals, jazz musicians, bohemians, and petty criminals—it became an easy target for regulation (Morgan 1981). In the eastern United States marijuana was erroneously believed to be addictive and to serve as a substitute for narcotics that were outlawed by the Harrison Act.

In light of more contemporary research into marijuana (which will be reviewed in chapter 3), the hysterical anti-marijuana literature produced during the 1930s can often seem amusing. Earle and Robert Rowell (1939: 49) wrote, for example, that marijuana "seems to superimpose upon the user's character and personality a devilish form. He is one individual when normal, and an entirely different one after using marijuana." In fact, marijuana "has led to some of the most revolting cases of sadistic rape and murder of modern times." In 1936 the Federal Bureau of Narcotics presented a summary of cases that illustrate "the homicidal tendencies and the generally debasing effects which arise from the use of marijuana" (Uelmen and Haddox 1983: 1–11). The 1936 motion picture *Reefer Madness* presented a frightening portrait of the marijuana user. "It is clear," note Bonnie and Whitebread (1970: 1021–22), "that no state undertook any empirical or scientific study of the effects of the drug. Instead they relied on lurid and often unfounded accounts of marijuana's dangers as presented in what little newspaper coverage the drug received." By 1931 twenty-two states had marijuana legislation that was often part of a general-purpose statute against narcotics (Bonnie and Whitebread 1970). Despite its being outlawed, marijuana was never an important issue in the United States until the 1960s: "It hardly ever made headlines or became the subject of highly publicized hearings and reports. Few persons knew or cared about it, and marihuana laws were passed with minimal attention" (Himmelstein 1983: 38).

The Federal Bureau of Narcotics, operating on a Depression-era budget, was reluctant to take on the additional responsibilities that would result from outlawing marijuana at the federal level. It was the hope of Harry J. Anslinger, FBN commissioner from 1930 until his retirement in 1962, that the states would act against marijuana, leaving the bureau free to concentrate on heroin and cocaine. In order to get the states to act, the bureau dramatized the dan-

The 1930s low-budget movie *Reefer Madness* is considered hysterical propaganda today.

gers of marijuana. But in such trying economic times, the states were reluctant to take on added work, and the FBN's own propaganda campaign forced it to act (Himmelstein 1983).

At the urging of Anslinger, Congress passed the Marijuana Tax Act of 1937. Because of uncertainty over the federal government's ability to outlaw marijuana, the act placed a prohibitive tax on cannabis—$100 an ounce—rather than prohibit the substance outright. This tax act was a result of three days of congressional hearings that Bonnie and Whitebread (1970: 1054) characterize as "a case study in legislative carelessness." Commissioner Anslinger was able to orchestrate an undocumented and hysterical presentation before the House Ways and Means Committee on the dangers of marijuana, and the floor debate on the bill, they argue, represented a near-comic example of dereliction of legislative responsibility. Anslinger (with Tompkins 1953: 20–21) maintained that marijuana was "a scourge which undermines its victims and degrades them mentally, morally, and physically." The AMA's opposition to the bill was ridiculed by members of the Ways and Means Committee. Marijuana was being treated like just another narcotic (Bonnie and Whitebread 1970). The states followed the federal lead and increased their penalties for drug violations, including marijuana. In 1951 penalties for possession and trafficking in marijuana were substantially increased—along with those for other controlled substances—with the passage of the Boggs Act (discussed below).

"Veteran" hippies attending the Woodstock '94 concert in Sawgerties, New York, smoke marijuana.

During the 1960s public attitudes toward marijuana underwent considerable change. A noncomformist counterculture, whose members were often from the white middle class, emerged. The rebellious nature of the "hippies" encouraged greater experimentation with sex and drugs, marijuana in particular. In fact, note Charles Lidz and Andrew Walker (1980), marijuana use helped tie diverse interests—civil rights, antiwar, antiestablishment—together: Its primary import was as a membership ritual for an otherwise very diffuse and disorganized group. No longer confined to minority or subcultural groups—Chicanos, African Americans, Beatniks, musicians—marijuana soon found widespread acceptance among persons of the middle and upper classes. This led to significant scientific inquiry into the effects of marijuana, and toward the latter part of the 1960s it became clear that whatever its dangers might be, the substance was simply not in the same class as heroin or cocaine on any important pharmacological dimension. Young, white, middle-class users, however, like their ghetto counterparts, were being subjected to the significant penalties that obtained for heroin and cocaine.

The rise of middle-class marijuana use offered the public a new view of the phenomenon. Marijuana was the lead story in *Life* magazine's 31 October 1969 issue. The magazine presented photographs of white, middle-class persons enjoying marijuana in a variety of congenial social settings. Also included was an in-depth story of a young man from Nashville, Tennessee, a long-distance runner and prep school graduate attending the University of Virginia on an athletic scholarship. He was arrested for possession of three pounds of marijuana and in a Virginia state court received a sentence of twenty years. The same issue of *Life* contains an article by the former director of the U.S. Food and Drug Administration, James L. Goddard, who stated: "Our laws governing marijuana are a mixture of bad science and poor understanding of the role of law as a deterrent force. They are unenforceable, excessively severe, scientifically incorrect and revealing of our ignorance of human behavior" (p. 34). The following year Robert Kennedy, Jr.[1] and R. Sargent Shriver, III, juveniles at the time, were arrested for possession of marijuana. Public pressure soon caused legislators to reconsider state and federal penalties for offenses involving marijuana.

"As of 1965, marihuana laws still bore the mark of the harsh legislation of the 1950s. Simple possession carried penalties of two years for the first offense, five for the second, and ten for the third" (Himmelstein 1983: 103). By the end of the 1960s there was a significant reduction in penalties on the state level. However. the Comprehensive Drug Abuse Prevention and Control Act of 1970 established five schedules for controlled substances, and marijuana, along with heroin, was placed in the highest category, Schedule I:

1. The drug or other substance has a high potential for abuse.
2. The drug or other substance has no currently accepted medical use in treatment in the United States.

---

1. David Kennedy, twenty-eight, the son of the late Senator Robert F. Kennedy, died of a drug overdose in a Palm Beach, Florida, hotel in 1984.

3. There is a lack of accepted safety for the use of the drug or other substance under medical supervision.

While the penalties remained as high as imprisonment for five years for non-narcotic drugs, i.e., marijuana, such sentences are reserved for possession of large amounts with intent to sell—for wholesale traffickers, the only type of offender traditionally of interest to federal drug-law enforcement. Simple possession was made into a misdemeanor, a crime punishable by imprisonment for not more than one year. The major elements of the federal law were copied by most states.

In 1972 the (presidentially appointed) National Commission on Marijuana and Drug Abuse recommended that possession of marijuana for personal use or noncommercial distribution be decriminalized. The following year Oregon became the first state to abolish criminal penalties for the possession of one ounce or less of marijuana, replacing incarceration with relatively small fines. In 1975 California made possession of one ounce or less of marijuana a citable misdemeanor with a maximum penalty of $100, and there were no increased penalties for recidivists. By 1978 eleven states had decriminalized marijuana, a position supported by President Jimmy Carter (Himmelstein 1983) but opposed by the President's Commission on Organized Crime (1986), which was appointed by President Ronald Reagan. Since 1977 no additional jurisdictions have decriminalized marijuana (Weisheit 1990), and one, Alaska, after fifteen years has made it illegal again, the result of a ballot initiative in 1990.

In more recent years there has been some medical use of the active ingredient in marijuana—but not marijuana itself—to control the side effects of chemotherapy and to treat glaucoma.

AMPHETAMINES

Amphetamines are stimulants that were first synthesized in 1887. Manufactured under the trade name Benzedrine, in 1932 amphetamine was marketed as an inhalant for use as a nasal decongestant.

> Amphetamines were unique: never before had a powerful psychoactive drug been introduced in such quantities in so short a period of time, and never before had a drug with such a high addictive potential and capability of causing long-term or irreversible physical and psychological damage been so enthusiastically embraced by the medical profession as a panacea or so extravagantly promoted by the drug industry. (Grinspoon and Hedblom 1975: 13)

By the end of the decade, as its stimulating properties became widely known, amphetamines were used primarily as analeptics—stimulating drugs. Many amphetamine-based inhalants appeared on the market and were widely available without prescription. These quickly became the subject of widespread abuse. During World War II, the British, German, and Japanese governments issued amphetamines to soldiers to elevate mood and to counteract fatigue and pain, and American military personnel were exposed to their use through contact with the British military. During the Korean conflict the United States authorized the distribution of amphetamines to military personnel. The first major wave of abuse appeared when American servicemen in Korea and Japan mixed the substance with heroin to create "speedballs," which were used intravenously (Grinspoon and Hedblom 1975).

Dextro-amphetamine, a more potent version of Benzadrine, was marketed as Dexedrine; and methamphetamine, manufactured under the trade name Methadrine, is an even more potent analeptic. This is currently the drug of choice for street abusers, who refer to it by the brand name Methadrine, or "meth," "crank," "speed," or "ice." It is injected, snorted, or smoked. Reports of its abuse by businessmen and athletes appeared as early as 1940, and a black market in the substance—"pep pills"—began to develop. It was (is?) particularly popular among long-distance truck drivers and college students trying to stay awake. These substances were widely prescribed in the 1950s and 1960s as an aid in dieting, leading to abuse by housewives who took "diet pills." In the 1960s a widespread anti-amphetamine campaign with the slogan "Speed Kills" was launched by the Food and Drug Administration (O'Brien and Cohen 1984), and in 1971 federal laws restricted the conditions under which amphetamines could be prescribed. Widespread abuse continues, however, with the distribution of methamphetamine being an important source of income for outlaw motorcycle gangs (discussed in chapter 6).

During the late 1980s a new form of methamphetamine, a smokable crystal called ice, appeared on the drug scene. Media and political concern over the possible spread of this new form of drug led to what Philip Jenkins (1994: 7) refers to as a "drug scare":

> Drug scares generally follow broadly similar patterns in which it is suggested . . . that the drug in question is currently enjoying explosive growth in popularity; that it is extremely addictive . . . and that it is destructive to the user or to others, threatening health or encouraging bizarre and violent behavior.

In fact, Jenkins notes, the ice danger did not materialize as a national crisis, although it is popular in certain parts of the country.

BARBITURATES

Barbiturates are sedating drugs synthesized from barbituric acid. Barbituric acid was first synthesized in Germany in 1863 by Nobel Prize-winning chemist Adolph Baeyer. The first barbiturate was synthesized in 1882 but not marketed until 1903 (McKim 1991). Accounts vary as to how barbituric acid acquired its name. In 1903 it was released under the trade name Veronal, a name derived from the Italian city of Verona. It is known generically in the United States as barbital (Wesson and Smith 1977). Barbiturates were used to induce sleep, replacing other aids such as alcohol and opiates. Since the appearance of phenobarbital in 1912, thousands of barbituric acid derivatives have been synthesized, although only about a dozen are commonly used; these are marketed under a variety of brand names. Barbiturates were widely prescribed in the United States during the 1930s when their toxic effects were not fully understood. By 1942 there were campaigns against the nonmedical use of barbiturates, and by the 1950s it was one of the major drugs of abuse among adults in the United States. In the 1960s its abuse quickly spread to the youth population (O'Brien and Cohen 1984). Nonmedical abuse is usually the result of diverting licit supplies through theft or burglary, forged prescriptions, or illegal manufacture in other countries, particularly Mexico. Supplies diverted from licit sources may be repackaged in nondescript capsules, thus disguising their source (Wesson and Smith 1977).

TRANQUILIZERS AND SEDATIVES

Along with amphetamines and barbiturates, many doctors in the 1960s routinely prescribed a variety of substances to reduce anxiety. Tranquilizers or sedatives such as Miltown and Valium enabled millions of housewives to "get by with a little help from their friends." These substances were the subject of heavy advertising, much of it depicting women in need of relief from tension and anxiety, by drug companies who offered their products as aids in coping with the normal problems of life. Consumers often became so dependent on these substances that they could not function without them, having lost the ability to deal with normal levels of stress. As a result of unfavorable attention by health and consumer organizations, and a congressional hearing in 1979, the manufacturers of Valium and other manufacturers of tranquilizers shifted their focus but continued to promote these substances' ability to ease the stress of modern living. In 1980 the Food and Drug Administration required tranquilizers to be labeled as generally not appropriate for anxiety or tension associated with the stress of everyday life. Nevertheless, they continue to be widely prescribed for patients experiencing "troubling times": More than 3.7 billion tranquilizers are consumed by Americans each year (Shabecoff 1987: 12).

HALLUCINOGENS

Hallucinogens such as LSD became popular during the 1960s, particularly among rebellious college students and people who identified themselves as antiestablishment. Lester Grinspoon (1979: 57) states that "it is impossible to write an adequate history of such an amorphous phenomenon [LSD] without discussing the whole cultural rebellion of the 1960s." LSD was first synthesized in Switzerland in 1938, but its hallucinogenic qualities did not become apparent until its discoverer took his first "trip" in 1943. During the 1950s the army and the Central Intelligence Agency conducted LSD experiments on soldiers and civilians, without their knowledge or consent, to test its suitability for chemical warfare and its utility as a "truth serum" (Henderson 1994).

Although LSD arrived in America from Europe in 1949 for experimental use in treating psychiatric disorders (Stevens 1987), before 1962 it was virtually unknown except by a small number of psychiatrists and psychologists (Brecher 1972). Two psychologists, Timothy Leary and Richard Alpert of Harvard, were experimenting with the hallucinogenic mushroom psilocybin. While the "Psilocybin Project" began as a scientific endeavor, it ended as casual use of the drug by many friends and acquaintances, including a small clique of psychedelic enthusiasts such as the authors Aldous Huxley (*Brave New World*), and Ken Kesey (*One Flew Over the Cuckoo's Nest*), and the poet Allen Ginsberg. (See Wolfe 1968 for a look at Kesey and his "Merry Pranksters'" psychedelic world.) Experiments Leary and Alpert conducted on inmates at Concord State Prison suggested that aggressive and hardened inmates became introspective and caring under the influence of psilocybin. Leary began encouraging his psychology students to use psilocybin. Word of their activities spread beyond the Harvard community and was picked up by newspapers as a result of a story in the *Harvard Crimson*. Federal agencies began making inquiries. School officials were anxious to rid themselves of Leary and Alpert and their research, so control over psilocybin was placed under a faculty committee while the school waited the expiration of Leary and Alpert's teaching contracts. No matter, they had been introduced to LSD.

"In a major city like Los Angeles," notes Jay Stevens (1987: 171), "it was as easy to go on an LSD trip as it was to visit Disneyland. Interested parties could either contact the growing number of therapists who were using LSD in practice, or they could offer themselves as guinea pigs to any of the dozens of research projects that were under way at places like UCLA." Therapists were using LSD "to heighten the traditional psychotherapeutic values of recall, abreaction, and emotional release," in most cases with apparent success and without negative side effects (1987: 180). However, the reaction of mainstream, establishment medicine and psychiatry toward LSD was generally negative, particularly when it was utilized by nonphysicians such as psychologists. Stevens refers to the resulting conflict as a "turf war" between medically trained practitioners and all other therapists. There was also a great deal of LSD use that was not under the guise of any therapeutic milieu, such as at the "LSD colony" in Hollywood, where, according to Leary (Rosenbaum 1988: 135), "Cary Grant was the high cardinal."

In 1962 Congress enacted legislation that gave the Food and Drug Administration control over all new investigational drugs. Although aimed at amphetamines, the legislation also applied to LSD (Stevens 1987). That same year Leary, Alpert, and thirty-five disciples moved to Zihuatanejo, Mexico, where they used LSD freely. The two psychologists established the International Foundation for Internal Freedom and "Freedom Center" at a small hotel in Zihuatanejo. A second headquarters was opened in Newton, Massachusetts, just outside of Boston. Their goal was to "turn on America." Leary popularized the use of LSD, and as a result of his Harvard connection, LSD gained the attention of the mass media (Grinspoon 1979). As a self-appointed high priest of LSD (*High Priest* was also the title of his book), Leary traveled widely and lectured on the virtues of using acid to "turn on, tune in, and drop out." "Acid rock" songs such as "White Rabbit" by the Jefferson Airplane, "Sunshine Superman" by Donovan, and the Beatles' "Magical Mystery Tour" and "Lucy in the Sky with Diamonds," became top hits. The books of Nobel Prize-winner Hermann Hesse (1877-1962) were very popular among the youth of the sixties, and his work helped popularize the "psychedelic" experience (Engel 1974). Psychedelic jargon and colors became fashionable. The media reported on the activities, in New York's Greenwich Village and San Francisco's Haight-Ashbury district of the "hippies" who were part of the counterculture and antiwar movements.

In 1963 an editorial attacking LSD appeared in the *Journal of the American Medical Association,* and in 1965 LSD became illegal. In 1963 Leary and Alpert were discharged from Harvard; that same year the Mexican authorities closed down Freedom Center, and Leary was deported. In 1965 Leary was returning to the United States from a trip to Mexico with three other persons, one of whom had secreted marijuana in her undergarments. When the drug was discovered during a strip search. Leary blurted out, "I'll take responsibility for the marijuana." At the time possession of marijuana was a serious crime in Texas. Despite his defense that the use of drugs was part of his religious liberty, Leary was convicted and sentenced to thirty years in prison. Leary appealed; in the meantime his harassment by law enforcement agencies resulted in numerous arrests. In 1969 the U.S. Supreme Court ordered his marijuana case to be retried. In 1970 Leary was convicted again and sentenced to ten years. Leary appealed, but several weeks later he was convicted of another drug-related charge in California, where he received a one to ten-year sentence. He was immediately remanded to a minimum-security prison.

Facing further trials in other states, later that year the forty-nine-year-old Leary escaped from prison and subsequently reappeared in Algeria, where he found refuge with the Black Panthers. After being placed under house arrest for purposes of "revolutionary discipline," Leary fled again, this time to Switzerland. Eventually he made his way to Afghanistan, where he was captured by U.S. drug enforcement agents. Leary wound up in the maximum-security prison at Folsom, California. After reportedly agreeing to provide information to the government, Leary was released in 1976 (Rosenbaum 1988). For a number of years he was popular on the college lecture circuit, often appearing with G. Gordon Liddy, of Watergate fame, who was responsible for much of the harassment of Leary (Stevens 1987). In 1996, at age seventy-five, Leary died of prostate cancer (Mansrerus 1996).

GOVERNMENT ACTION IN THE POST WAR ERA

In the years immediately before World War II, the Federal Bureau of Narcotics seemed to have the drug problem well under control. Commissioner Anslinger released statistics indicating a significant drop in the addict population. Then came the war. Opiate smuggling dwindled, and those Americans of an age most susceptible to drug use were in Europe and Asia. Drug use was viewed as unpatriotic as well as illegal. Alcohol, barbiturates, and amphetamines were the substances most widely abused during the war years, when the price of opiates increased dramatically. The addict population appeared to reach an all-time low.

At the end of the war there was fear of an epidemic of drug use as U.S. soldiers began to return from Far Eastern locations where opiate use was endemic. The epidemic failed to materialize. The FBN became a victim of its own propaganda and apparent success, and Congress would not increase the drug-fighting budget (Morgan 1981). Then in 1950 and 1951 a spate of news stories on drug abuse reported that the use of heroin was spilling out of the ghetto and into middle-class environs, where it was poisoning the minds and bodies of America's (white) youth. Musto (1973) points out a parallel between the periods following World War I and World War II: Both were characterized by an atmosphere of hostility to radicals and Communists, and both led to punitive sanctions against drug addicts. Any expression of tolerance for radical political ideas or drug addicts was un-American. In a timely stroke of political genius, the Federal Bureau of Narcotics linked heroin trafficking to Red China.

Anslinger accused the People's Republic of selling opium and heroin to the free nations of the world in order to finance overseas ambitions (Cloyd 1982). As we shall see in chapter 6, Far Eastern heroin was, and continues to be, the business of Chinese Nationalists, Triads, Thais, and Burmese insurgents—not the People's Republic, which routinely executes drug traffickers. Indeed, "at the time of the Communist takeover in 1949, China was the world's largest producer and consumer of narcotic drugs" (Lee 1995: 194).

On the basis of statistics showing that between 1946 and 1950 there had been a 100 percent increase in the number of narcotics-related arrests, and that over a five-year period the average age of persons committed to a Public Health Service hospital had declined from 37.5 to 26.7 years, Congress concluded that drug addiction was increasing and that penalties for drug trafficking were inadequate. In 1951 Congress passed the Boggs Act, which increased penalties for violations of drug laws. Once again, using rather dubious statistical data, Congress concluded that the increased penalties of the Boggs Act had been quite successful in reducing drug trafficking. As a result, in 1956 Congress passed the Narcotic Control Act, which further increased the penalties for drug violations—for example, the sale of heroin to individuals under eighteen years of age was made a capital offense—and increased the authority of the Federal Bureau of Narcotics and agents of the Customs Bureau (PCOC 1986). State legislatures, responding to the federal initiative, significantly increased penalties for drug violations.

> Public concern over the problem of drug abuse, which had been relatively dormant during the 1940s and 1950s, flared again during the 1960s. The intensification of national concern resulted in increasing pressure for Federal initiatives in the area. In response to this development, a White House Conference on Narcotics and Drug Abuse was convened in 1962, which resulted in the establishment of the President's Advisory Commission on Narcotics and Drug Abuse (Prettyman Commission) on January 15, 1963. (PCOC 1986: 215)

The commission recommended that the antiquated legal notion that drugs could be controlled by taxation be discarded and they suggested that the responsibilities of the Federal Bureau of Narcotics be transferred to the Department of Justice. On the other hand, the commission recommended that the regulation of marijuana and lawful narcotic drugs be transferred from the FBN to the Department of Health, Education, and Welfare (HEW). It also recommended increasing the number of federal drug agents and enacting legislation for the strict control of nonnarcotic drugs capable of producing psychotoxic effects when abused.

In the 1960s concern increased over the diversion of dangerous drugs from licit sources. As a result, Congress passed the Drug Abuse Control Amendments of 1965, which, among other things, mandated recordkeeping and inspection requirements for depressant and stimulant drugs throughout the chain of distribution, from the basic manufacturer to (but not including) the consumer. Enforcement of the 1965 legislation was left to a newly created agency within HEW's Food and Drug Administration, the Bureau of Drug Abuse Control. The Treasury Department's monopoly over drug enforcement had ended (PCOC 1986).

A TURN TOWARD TREATMENT

During the 1960s the medical profession began to reassert itself on the issue of drug abuse in both treatment and research. Treating disciplines—psychology and social work—and researchers in sociology and public health began to focus on the drug issue as a social—not simply a law enforcement—problem. The social activism of the 1960s impacted on the problem of drug abuse (Morgan 1981), and a new strategic approach was implemented: reducing demand by rehabilitating large numbers of drug addicts. Arnold Trebach (1982: 226) argues that this approach was facilitated by the resignation of Harry Anslinger as commissioner of the FBN ("which had been accomplished with the active encouragement of the Kennedy brothers"). Anslinger was replaced by Harry Giordano, a pharmacist, and the pendulum of drug policy began to shift away from a law enforcement model toward a treatment model. The 1983 Prettyman Commission recommended the relaxation of mandatory prison sentences for drug convictions, greater research, and the dismantling of the Federal Bureau of Narcotics, whose functions were to be divided between the Department of Health, Education, and Welfare (prevention and treatment) and the Department of Justice (law enforcement).

In 1961 California established a civil commitment program in which drug addicts were taken into custody and committed—like mentally ill in need of hospitalization—to a nonpunitive period of confinement and drug treatment. Confinement was followed by a period of aftercare/parole supervision. In 1966 New York established the Narcotic Addiction Control Commission, a large-scale effort whose goal was to confine as many drug addicts as possible under civil commitment statutes. As in California, whose lead New York was following, confinement was followed by a period of parole supervision. (This writer was employed briefly as a senior narcotic parole officer for the Narcotic Addiction Control Commission. This agency, which expended billions of dollars, was dismantled during the 1970s as a very costly failure.) In 1966, Congress passed the Narcotic Addict Rehabilitation Act, which in lieu of prosecution authorized federal district courts to order the voluntary and involuntary civil commitment of certain defendants found to be drug addicts and mandated that the Surgeon General establish rehabilitation and post-hospitalization care programs for drug addicts. The legislation also authorized the financing of state efforts to treat addicts.

Between 1969 and 1974 there was a dramatic increase of federally funded drug rehabilitation programs, from 16 at the beginning of 1969 to 926 in 1974. Federal expenditures on drug treatment went from about $80 million to about $800 million during that period. About half of the 80,000 clients in these programs were being maintained on methadone (Moss 1977), a synthetic opiate. During the 1960s a pilot program of methadone maintenance was initiated at Rockefeller University in New York. The drug, which was taken orally, prevented withdrawal symptoms in heroin addicts who were maintained with daily doses. Trebach (1982: 227) refers to this approach to heroin addiction as the "greatest theoretical and practical departure in American rehabilitation strategies and clinical attitudes since the early 1920s." While the program was successful in aiding the rehabilitation of certain kinds of drug users, methadone when ingested intravenously produces a heroinlike euphoria, and by the early 1970s large quantities had been diverted to the illegal street market. In response, Congress passed the Narcotic Treatment Act in 1974, which required annual registration by practitioners dispensing narcotic drugs and imposed new standards for the legal dispensing of dangerous drugs (PCOC 1986).

The 1960s and 1970s also experienced a rise in the popularity of the "therapeutic-community" approach to treating addiction, the best-known communities being Synanon in California and Daytop Village in New York. Operated by recovered addicts, these drug-free centers use a variety of talking and confrontational therapies mixed with aspects of behavior modification.

(Methadone, therapeutic communities, and other approaches to the treatment of drug abusers will be discussed in chapter 5.)

63

Chapter Two:
Drug Abuse:
A History

COMPREHENSIVE DRUG ABUSE PREVENTION AND CONTROL ACT OF 1970

As the turn of the decade approached, alarming statistics (of dubious validity) about drug abuse were publicized. The drug problem was quickly becoming a major political issue. In 1968 President Lyndon Johnson decried the fragmented approach to drug-law enforcement. With congressional approval, the president abolished the Federal Bureau of Narcotics and the Bureau of Drug Abuse Control and transferred their responsibilities to a newly created agency, the Bureau of Narcotics and Dangerous Drugs (BNDD), in the Department of Justice. Revenue and importation aspects of drug trafficking remained within the Treasury Department's Internal Revenue Service and Bureau of Customs. In 1970 President Richard Nixon clarified the responsibilities of the federal agencies involved in drug control, announcing that BNDD "controls all investigations involving violations of the laws of the United States relating to narcotics, marijuana and dangerous drugs, both within the United States and beyond its borders." Several months later guidelines were promulgated that provided increased authority for Customs officials at ports and borders.

The two-pronged approach to dealing with drug abuse—investigating and prosecuting traffickers and reducing demand by preventing addiction and treating addicts—was now firm policy. Legislation in 1970 authorized HEW to increase its efforts at prevention and rehabilitation through a program of grants to special projects and made the HEW National Institute on Drug Abuse the agency with primary responsibility for drug education and prevention activities. The legislation also established five schedules into which all controlled substances could be placed according to their potential for abuse; imposed additional reporting requirements for manufacturers, distributors, and dispensers; promulgated new regulations for the importation of controlled substances; and established the Commission on Marijuana and Drug Abuse. BNDD was authorized to increase its strength by 300 agents.

The 1970 legislation represented a new legal approach to federal drug policy. It was predicated, not on the constitutional power to tax, but on federal authority over interstate commerce. The PCOC (1986: 228) notes that this shift had enormous implications for the way the federal government would approach drug enforcement in the future. The act

set the stage for an innovation in Federal drug law enforcement techniques. That innovation was the assigning of large numbers of Federal narcotic agents to work in local communities. No longer was it necessary to demonstrate interstate traffic to justify Federal participation in combatting illegal drug use.

The new approach was upheld by decisions of the Supreme Court, and the National Conference of Commissioners on Uniform State Laws drafted a model act based on the 1970 statutes, which has been adopted by most states.

A 1973 reorganization plan led to the creation of the Drug Enforcement Administration (DEA) within the Department of Justice. All drug-control investigative and enforcement responsibilities, except those related to ports of entry and borders, were given over to the new agency. In 1974 DEA adopted the Central Tactical Units (CENTAC) program to focus enforcement resources on major drug conspiracies (discussed in chapter 7). In 1982 the Federal Bureau of Investigation (FBI) was given concurrent jurisdiction with DEA for drug investigation and law enforcement. In addition, the DEA director was required to report to the director of the FBI, who was given responsibility for supervising drug-law enforcement efforts and policies. That same year the Department of Defense Authorization Act contained a provision outlining military cooperation with civilian authorities. This provision was aimed at improving the level of cooperation by delineating precisely what assistance military commanders could provide. It also permits military personnel to operate military equipment lent to civilian drug enforcement agencies (PCOC 1986). (In 1988 the military's role in drug-law enforcement was substantially increased; this is discussed in chapter 7.)

THE DRUG SCARE OF THE 1980S

As 1980 approached, the lack of public interest in and even tolerance of drug use began to shift as grass-roots parent groups began to influence the political landscape. A housewife

> who later presided over the National Federation of Parents for Drug-Free Youth, attended a rock concert in 1978 with her two young children and discovered rampant drug use all around them. Her anger, shared by others she contacted, apparently was a major factor in the defeat of her Congressman, . . . who had sponsored a bill favoring the decriminalization of an ounce of marijuana. That a broad base of parents were antagonistic to drugs and that they were now organizing their political power had been demonstrated. (Musto 1987b: 271)

With encouragement from Dr. Robert L. DuPont, then director of the National Institute on Drug Abuse, an "antipot" handbook for parents was published. The antidrug theme was soon picked up by the Reagan Administration.

The issue of drug abuse is politically safe and useful because no one is in favor of it. During the presidency of Ronald Reagan, drug abuse again became a major political issue. On 19 June 1986 Len Bias, a basketball star from the University of Maryland, died of a cocaine overdose; on 27 June Don Rogers, a defensive back for the Cleveland Browns, also died of a cocaine overdose. These widely reported incidents occurring within a short time of each other and less than five months before congressional elections led to an intensification of antidrug efforts, a widespread public relations effort utilizing sports and entertainment personalities whose message to television viewers was "Just Say No!" (to drugs). Not to be outdone, Congress responded with huge allocations to combat this scourge, and politicians scrambled for partisan advantage.

> Len Bias' death brought together the political and human aspects of drug abuse. His death accentuated that attention placed on drugs after the announcement of the "war on drugs." Although consensus about the need to "do something" was generally accepted, politicians continued to argue over the best approach. (Merriam 1989: 25)

With the elections over and Congress in the hands of the Democrats, the president significantly scaled back the allocations.

The fight against drugs and drug abuse was an important issue in the presidential campaign of 1988. The heat of the national campaign led to the enactment of an omnibus drug bill (Anti-Drug Abuse Act of 1988) in the final days of the 100th Congress. The legislation states, "It is the declared policy of the United States Government to create a Drug-Free America by 1995." The bipartisan measure, which was approved overwhelmingly, increased antidrug spending, earmarking 50 percent for treatment, a figure that is to increase to 60 percent over the next few years. On both federal and state levels, penalty distinctions between marijuana and drugs such as heroin and cocaine have been erased, resulting in "zero tolerance for drugs" (Pollan 1995).

The statute mandated greater controls over precursor chemicals and devices used to manufacture drugs, such as encapsulating machinery. It also created a complex and extensive body of civil penalties aimed at casual users. These include fines and ineligibility for federal benefits such as educational loans and mortgage guarantees, and/or the loss of a maritime, pilot, or stockbroker license for a number of years. There are enhanced penalties for selling drugs to minors, and a judge can impose the death penalty for murders committed as part of a continuing criminal enterprise or for the murder of a law enforcement officer during an arrest for a drug-related felony.

The legislation also established the Office of National Drug Control Policy headed by a director ("drug czar") appointed by the president. The director is charged with coordinating federal drug supply reduction efforts, including international control, intelligence, interdiction, domestic drug-law enforcement, treatment, education, and research, and also serves as a liaison between the federal government and state and local drug-control efforts. The first director was William J. Bennett, whose controversial statements as U.S. Secretary of Education under Ronald Reagan gained him a high public profile. Bennett served as drug czar for twenty-two months, during which time he used the position primarily as a rhetorical platform to focus attention on the issue of drug abuse as seen by the Bush administration. His approach attracted extensive media attention, but his actual powers as director were so circumscribed that he accomplished little else. Bennett resigned in 1990 and was replaced by Bob Martinez, a Republican governor of Florida who had been defeated in his bid for reelection. During his one term as governor, Martinez advocated stiffer penalties for drug traffickers and more extensive use of the military in fighting drugs.

In sum, this country moved from a century of permissiveness to Draconian sanctions as the result of foreign affairs, the policy of a single federal agency, and a volatile mix of racism and politics. This has led to two drug problems in the United States:

> One is the drug problem of the affluent. It is by no means insignificant, and it has caused more than its share of personal tragedies. But it is a *manageable* problem, and it has been steadily decreasing for several years, for reasons unrelated to the war on drugs. The other one is the drug problem of America's have-nots. That problem has grown malignantly in the face of the drug war—and it is much further from solution than it was when that war began. (Currie 1993: 3)

DRUG ABUSE IN THE 1990s

The 1990s were remarkable for the lack of political interest in drug abuse. Indeed, as officials began to recognize the extent of prison overcrowding resulting from our drug policies, statutory and administrative remedies were formulated that placed more drug offenders in diversion/drug treatment programs, probation, and on parole.[2] Laws providing significantly greater prison sentences for the sellers of crack cocaine than for sellers of powdered cocaine came under fire (the former is more likely to be used by minorities, the latter by middle-class whites). There is a mandatory five-year minimum for selling 5 grams of crack or 500 grams of powdered cocaine; and ten years for selling 50 grams of crack or 5,000 grams of powdered cocaine. There was general agreement that the number of casual drug users was down, although the number of hard-core users either remained the same or increased.

The cocaine market has been impacted by crack, and many crack users are purchasing the powdered form in large doses and converting it to crack themselves. This has reduced the demand for street-level crack, which many users believe inferior to what they can produce themselves from cocaine hydrochloride. The use of methamphetamine is increasing, with new supplies coming from Mexico. In some areas methamphetamine is almost as popular as

---

2. Ironically, the increase in the number of inmates having serious drug problems did not result in a substantial increase in prison-based drug treatment; only an estimated 2 percent are exposed to serious—not simply "Just Say No"—drug rehabilitation (Treaster 1995).

cocaine. Marijuana remains readily available, and both its use and sale transcend ethnic, racial, and gender boundaries. Users of marijuana tend to be under twenty years old (Office of National Drug Control Policy 1995b).

While cocaine remains the dominant (illegal) drug of abuse, heroin, prepared for smoking and snorting, has begun to make a comeback, particularly outside its typical core clientele of the urban poor (Kalogerakis 1995). This revival, which has been fueled by the availability of high-grade heroin, is following a pattern set by cocaine in the 1970s (Gabriel 1994). The abundance of heroin is reflected in the purity levels found at the retail level, which average almost 40 percent, as opposed to past street-level purity levels of 3–4 percent. In one five-day period in 1994, thirteen persons died of heroin overdoses. The drug, which had been purchased in one Manhattan neighborhood, had a purity level of about 90 percent (Holloway 1994). During 1995 the number of heroin addicts in the city jail on New York's Rikers Island increased by 23 percent, "providing substance abuse experts with some of the most solid evidence yet of the resurgence of heroin use" (Purdy 1995b: 24).

Now that we have completed our review of the evolution of the problem of drug abuse in the United States, in the next chapter we will examine the pharmacology of psychoactive substances.

REVIEW QUESTIONS

1. What was the relationship between nativism and Prohibition?
2. How can Prohibition be explained in terms of rural versus urban America?
3. Why did the end of Prohibition lead to an increase in drug trafficking?
4. Why can the United States during the nineteenth century be described as a "dope fiend's paradise"?
5. How was recreational use of opium popularized in Europe during the late eighteenth and early nineteenth centuries?
6. How did the primitive state of medicine explain the popularity of opium into the nineteenth century?
7. Why was the production of opium unsuccessful in the United States?
8. What was the "patent medicine" problem?
9. What was the relationship between the Civil War and the popularity of morphine?
10. What was the primary cause of the Opium Wars?
11. What was the relationship between the Chinese immigrants and legislation controlling opiates at state and local levels in the United States?
12. What international events led to the enactment of the Harrison Act?
13. What were the important events that led to the passage of the Pure Food and Drug Act?
14. How can the efforts of the temperance movement and the U.S.

response to drugs be explained, at least in part, in terms of racial prejudice?

15. What were the major provisions of the Harrison Act?
16. What was the relationship between the development of the Harrison Act and concern for federalism?
17. After the Harrison Act was passed, what was the Supreme Court's attitude toward physicians who dispensed opiates?
18. What was the role of federal drug enforcement officials in determining the U.S. policy toward drugs?
19. What was the relationship between prevailing political attitudes after World War I and our reaction to drug users?
20. What led to the development of the Uniform Drug Act?
21. What accounted for the general lack of public concern about drug abuse before World War II?
22. How did World War II affect drug use in the United States?
23. Why did Spanish explorers have a negative view of coca chewing?
24. What was the relationship between the campaign against cocaine and African Americans in the South?
25. What led to the sudden popularity of cocaine beginning in the 1960s?
26. Why has the domestic cannabis crop in the United States until recently been unattractive to potential smokers?
27. What has made domestic cannabis more appealing to potential smokers?
28. What was the relationship between racial and ethnic prejudice and efforts to outlaw marijuana?
29. What factors led to the significant decrease in U.S. penalties for possession of marijuana?
30. What was the relationship between the military and the promotion of amphetamines?
31. Why are amphetamines popular among some students and truck drivers?
32. What problem is inherent in prescribing sedatives to deal with stress?
33. What was the connection between Timothy Leary and the popularizing of LSD?
34. What was the relationship between public attitudes in the post-World War II era and the U.S. response to drugs?
35. What led to the "turn toward treatment" response to drug abuse during the 1960s?
36. What is the purpose of the Office of National Drug Control Policy (the "drug czar") ?
37. Why has the issue of drugs proven so popular with politicians?
38. What distinguishes the 1980s from the 1990s with respect to the problem of drug abuse?

3

THE PHARMACOLOGY OF DRUG ABUSE

In determination of a drug's status, more than abuse potential should be considered. What are the toxicities of the drug? What are the chances of becoming dependent on the drug? Is dependency on a drug necessarily bad? Sometimes these questions are difficult to answer. Certainly, two of the most toxic drugs we know are alcohol and tobacco (nicotine). These drugs are sold legally. . . . Dependency to both of these drugs develops, as it does to caffeine. . . . Why are we so concerned about dependency on opiates and not caffeine? Heroin, if given in pure form for long periods of time, has few toxic effects. Because of some apparent inconsistencies between a drug's pharmacology and its legal status, it is important to try to approach the pharmacology of drug abuse dispassionately.—Sidney H. Schnoll (1979: 255)

Drug abuse is often discussed in terms such as "overpowering desire," "compulsion," or even "enslavement," as if the substance had a power all its own to "hook" persons foolish enough to ingest it. These theories emphasize the involuntary nature of drug use—use based on a *craving*—that has found some support in laboratory experiments with animals. According to this approach, sometimes referred to as the *disease model,* the drug-dependent person is a victim of forces beyond his or her control. This theoretical approach has treatment implications. For example, it would be supportive of two very different approaches to substance abuse: (1) the use of methadone detoxification and maintenance; and (2) the Alcoholics Anonymous (AA) chemical-free approach, which emphasizes a need for total abstinence (methadone and AA will be discussed in chapter 5).

The pharmacology of drug use informs us that certain chemicals generate a strong physiological response in animals and humans. Indeed, with the exception of marijuana and hallucinogens, animals will abuse the same chemicals that humans do (Friedman 1993). More than a century ago those inclined toward a disease theory of addiction offered physiological explanations: The addict inherits a nervous system that has more energy or perhaps more actual nerve fiber. Drugs provide such nervous systems with a substance that is necessary but deficient. When a user finds that a drug satisfies this deficiency, repeated drug use naturally follows. A complementary theory views drug users as having an inherited predisposition to "nervous weakness" for which the use of drugs compensates. Other observers conceive of a lack of hereditary endowments that leaves some persons ill-equipped to deal with the fast pace of societal change, drug use providing chemical compensation.

In more recent times, scientists have argued that opiates alter the central nervous system by creating what appears to be a compulsion to use the drug to restore a sense of well-being. Heroin addicts themselves state they take the drug to "feel normal." Thus, to the heroin addict, notes John Irwin (1970: 19), "it is the fix that cures the sickness, and it is the fix that is central to the whole dope life." After a period of abstinence, an addict returning to heroin use is likely to state: "'It makes me feel normal again'—that is, it relieves the ex-addict's chronic triad of anxiety, depression, and craving" (Brecher 1972: 14). While drug use might begin through experimentation, dependence would be the inevitable result of these physiological changes. For example, some theories have described the opiate addict as a person whose body is malfunctioning with respect to the production of crucial neurotransmitters. According to this view, the user's choice of drug is the result of an interaction between its pharmacological properties and the primary feeling-state experienced.

Thus, according to *arousal theory,* those whose central nervous systems quickly habituate to incoming stimuli are most apt to be reinforced for engaging in antisocial behavior and less likely to learn alternative behavior patterns. Subjectively, such persons regard many ordinary environments as "boring" and "unpleasant" and would thus be more motivated than most people to seek novel and/or intense sensory stimulation. The behavior of such persons would

LIMITATIONS IN THE STUDY OF DRUG ABUSE

Our discussion of the pharmacology of drug abuse will necessarily have limitations because there is a great deal that is not known about how the drugs under discussion actually affect human physiology. There is evidence, for example, that the same substance can have a different impact on different people. The social context (the setting in which the drug is ingested) and the user's expectations can influence the drug's effects (Becker 1967, 1977; Schnoll 1979). A term such as "drug-induced euphoria" is misleading because it implies that "each psychoactive drug has some reliable, uniform effect on mental state." In fact, "Whether a person will interpret the effect of a drug like marijuana, LSD, or an opiate, especially the first few times he takes it, as euphoria or pleasure depended very much on set and setting and other complex psychological and social conditions" (Grinspoon and Hedblom 1975: 62). In other words, use of the substances discussed in this book is not *automatically* pleasurable. Many, if not most, people who have been exposed to morphine or heroin, for example, find the initial experience distinctly unpleasant: "Not everyone responds to the analgesic experience the same way. Some people find a narcosis tremendously alluring, while others report that the sensations of helplessness are disturbing and distinctly unappealing" (Peele 1980: 143). Thus, "One person's dysphoria may be another person's euphoria" (Schnoll 1979: 256). Some people get "high" from dangerous pursuits, others from chemicals, and still others seek to avoid both.

Laboratory studies, which form the basis for much of our knowledge of drugs of abuse, fail to reproduce social context, and their results are accordingly limited. Further, the dependence potential of various drugs is typically based on laboratory studies with monkeys and rats. However, in experimental environments these animals can also become addicted to stinging electric shocks delivered to the tail or the paws (Bennett 1988). Indeed, researchers have discovered that with animals "almost any environmental stimulus can serve as a reinforcer or punisher under the right environmental conditions" (Dworkin and Pitts 1994: 106).

Furthermore, studies do not actually replicate "street use," and any of the substances under discussion may be abused with alcohol or in some other combination. The effects of mixing drugs can be (Schnoll 1979):

1. *Additive:* Two drugs having similar actions are ingested, so the effect is cumulative. (1 + 1 = 2)
2. *Synergistic:* Two drugs having similar actions are ingested, but the effect of their joint action is more than cumulative. (1 + 1 = 3)
3. *Potentiating:* Two drugs have different actions, but when taken together one enhances the effects of the other. (1 + 1 = 4)
4. *Antagonistic:* Two or more drugs are taken together, and one counteracts the effects of the other(s). (1 + 1 = 0)

Drugs prepared for street sale are typically impure or a mixture of psychoactive chemicals. "The users of illegally purchased drugs are often totally unaware of the actual chemical substance, the dose being purchased, and the contaminants that may be present in the sample." Many of these contaminants can produce toxic reactions in their own right (Schnoll 1979: 257).

Distinctions between the pharmacology (discussed in this chapter) and the psychology and sociology of drug abuse (discussed in the next chapter) are quite artificial (Peele 1985). In other words, while the interaction of these three dimensions can explain drug use, the explanatory value of each by itself is limited. Their separation into different chapters in this book, therefore, is for pedagogical rather than scientific purposes. (The pharmacology of drug abuse also has important treatment and policy implications—topics of subsequent chapters.)

THE PHARMACOLOGY OF DRUG USE

Biology informs us that the body consists of cells organized into tissues and that specialized cells along the surface of the body receive information about the environment that is translated into electrochemical signals we experience as sight, sound, smell, and touch. Information is carried by neurotransmitters (chemical messengers released by neurons) across cells of the nervous system (neurons), which are separated by fluid-filled microscopic gaps (synapses). The neurotransmitters are received by receptor sites on the next neuron and finally by the brain, which processes the information and causes the body to respond. The drugs under discussion in this chapter affect the neurons of the central nervous system (brain and spinal cord), modifying the production, release, action, or breakdown of neurotransmitters, altering the chemistry of the brain, and disrupting the homeostatic functions of the body. Before we can begin our review of the physical dynamics of drug abuse, a number of terms need to be defined (presented here in alphabetical order).

KEY TERMS FOR CHAPTER 3

Agonists are substances that stimulate receptor sites.

Antagonists are substances that inhibit the action of a receptor site. They can counteract the effect of an agonist.

The **autonomic nervous system** (ANS) is a system of neurons primarily concerned with regulating involuntary bodily functions (such as heart, lungs, and digestion). It is divided into functions having opposite effects:

1. The *sympathetic* nervous system acts (actually reacts) to mobilize the organism for action—for example, for "fight" or "flight." The release of the neurotransmitter norepinephrine or noradrenalin (NE) into the blood system or of drugs that mimic NE (stimulants such as cocaine) activates the sympathetic nervous system.
2. The *parasympathetic* nervous system is concerned with the digestive system and acts to conserve bodily resources.

The **brain** is a dense mass weighing about three pounds and consisting of 10–50 billion anatomically independent but functionally interrelated neurons (brain cells). The brain contains areas that produce pleasurable sensations (reward pathways) when stimulated. All psychoactive chemicals exert their principal effects upon individual cells in the brain (Snyder 1986).

The **central nervous system** (CNS) consists of the brain and the spinal vertebrae, which carry information to the brain. The CNS receives information—stimuli—from the internal and external environment and responds by sending out information to muscles and glands. The CNS responds to stimuli through three processes:

1. *behavior processes,* which include voluntary movements such as walking and talking and involuntary (autonomic) movements such as breathing and heartbeat;
2. *affective processes,* which govern mood, feelings, and emotions; and
3. *thought processes,* which involve the ability to reason, categorize, organize, abstract, and pay attention.

Homeostasis is a state of equilibrium achieved through the self-adjusting characteristics of the body. Through homeostasis complex organisms adapt themselves to changes in the environment by means of, for example, body temperature, blood-sugar level, and heart rate. The physiology and biochemistry of the body change according to information received and processed by the nervous system, particularly the central nervous system, and the endocrine system (glands such as the thyroid and adrenal).

The **hypothalamus,** located near the bottom of the brain, integrates information from many sources and is the control center for the autonomic nervous system. It is also the primary point of contact between the nervous system and the endocrine system, sending messages in the form of impulses to appropriate con-

(continued)

KEY TERMS FOR CHAPTER 3 (con't.)

trol centers to restore normal levels of blood chemicals in line with the homeo-static needs of the body. Many drugs enter the brain in high concentrations at the blood-rich hypothalamus, creating initial autonomic effects on consciousness and mood.

Monoamine oxidases (MAO) are chemicals in the presynaptic terminals that control the level of neurotransmitters.

The **nervous system*** is a complex electrical-chemical coordinating system consisting of over 13 million specialized cells called *neurons* (see below) that receive stimuli and transmit information about environmental changes to a specific processing center. There are two basic nervous systems, the *central nervous system* (see above) and the *peripheral nervous system* (PNS), consisting of fibers and cells that connect the brain to the spinal cord and carry sensory information or muscle commands to the rest of the body. Functionally, the PNS is divided into the *somatic* (which carries information to the CNS from our conscious senses) and the *autonomic* (see above).

Neurons (or nerve cells) differ from other body cells in that they can conduct information in the form of electrical impulses over long distances. Neurons, which come in many sizes and shapes, form chains of specialized and excitable cells of the nervous system. There are over 100 billion neurons in the body, and across them, from neuron to neuron, move signals or impulses—information in the form of electrical activity. Neurons do not interlock but instead are separated by microscopic gaps called *synapses* (see below). The body of the neuron consists of three parts: dendrites, a cell body (soma), and an axon. Each neuron has multiple dendrites (short branches that give the cell a tentaclelike appearance), which form structural networks for receiving information from another neuron or from the environment in the form of light, sound, smell, etc., and convert it (through transduction) into electrical activity that is transmitted to the axon.

Axons may be long or short. Neurons in the brain stem have axons that extend into the spinal cord, where they divide into thousands of branches, making contact with different receiving neurons. The axon conducts ("fires") electrical impulses to terminals, which react by releasing neurotransmitters that are stored in synaptic buttons at the end of the axon. These move across the synaptic gap to receptor sites on the dendrites on the other side, triggering activity—the release of secondary messengers—in the next cell. Through this mechanism, an impulse is directed to the spinal cord and into the proper circuit for transmission to the brain.

Neurotransmitters are chemicals released from sacs (vesicles) clustered in the synaptic button at the end of axon terminals of neurons when a sufficient number of synapses are activated by electrical impulses. Some (such as dopamine) excite (speed "firing") and others (such as endorphins) inhibit (slow

---

    * It should be noted that the stomach has its own (secondary) nervous system with many of the neurotransmitters found in the CNS. The effects of various psychoactive drugs on the digestive system are apparently related to this secondary nervous system (Blakeslee 1996).

KEY TERMS FOR CHAPTER 3 (con't.)

"firing"). The body uses these chemicals to trigger such effects as anger or to regulate the operation of different organs. Each neurotransmitter has a receptor site (see below) designed to receive it, and the ensuing reaction may cause the stimulation or inhibition of a specific function. Drugs can mimic (agonists) or inhibit (antagonists) neurotransmitters.

Receptors are sites consisting of large molecules on the surface of cells where neurotransmitters attach, creating a lock-and-key effect and causing chemical substances to interact and produce pharmacological actions. Some receptor sites are sensitive to environmental stimuli; these receive information from the outside world and transmit it to neurons by way of electrochemical activity. Receptors are sensory-specific and distinguish between substances. Upon receiving the correct substance (creating a chemical fit), they transmit signals that bring about pharmacological action in the target tissue. Many psychoactive drugs (agonists) mimic the action of neurotransmitters and "fool" the receptor into accepting it (Palfai and Jankiewicz 1991). Competing drugs (antagonists) are able to occupy receptor sites without triggering activity, providing a basis for using chemicals to deal with drug abuse.

Synapses are fluid-filled microscopic gaps (.0002 mm) that provide a chemical bridge between the electrical activity from one neuron to another. A neuron may have over 10,000 synapses. There are two functional types of synapses: (1) excitatory synapses, which enhance electrical impulses, and (2) inhibitory synapses, which retard electrical impulses. Depressants reduce synaptic transmission by inhibiting nerve-impulse conduction at synapses; this causes a reduction in sensory pain signals received by the brain (Tortora 1983). Stimulants facilitate synaptic transmission.

DRUGS OF ABUSE

Psychoactive drugs are absorbed into the bloodstream and carried to the central nervous system. Eventually they pass the blood-brain barrier, causing the release of neurotransmitters in the brain. The barrier prevents certain substances from entering brain tissue (for example, penicillin, because it would cause convulsions) but readily admits psychoactive substances (and general anesthetics). Drugs enter the bloodstream in one of three ways:

1. *Oral ingestion:* The substance is swallowed and enters the bloodstream through the gastrointestinal tract.
2. *Inhalation:* The substance is sniffed and reaches the bloodstream through mucous membranes of the nose or sinus cavities, or it is smoked and is absorbed through the linings of the lungs.
3. *Injection:* The substance is injected into a vein (intravenous), and all of

the drug enters the bloodstream. Some is carried directly to the brain, producing an effect within seconds. Injecting a drug under the skin (subcutaneous) produces a delayed and reduced effect.

The amount of time it takes the substance to be eliminated from the body is measured in terms of *half-life,* the time it takes for one-half of the drug to be eliminated (through the liver and primarily into the kidneys for urination). The half-life of some drugs may be as short as a few minutes, while traces of other drugs may remain in the system for several weeks. The greater the half-life, the less severe the withdrawal symptoms after the use of the drug is discontinued.

Whatever the method of administration, the drug impacts on the dendrites of CNS neurons, which transmit the information across each cell body. At the end of the cell, dendrites release neurotransmitters that cross over the synapse to the dendrites of another neuron, where they seek out and lock into receptor sites. At the receptor sites the neurotransmitter inhibits or enhances the release of ions (electrical charges similar to those of a battery). The brain responds to the ions by sending out information to muscles and glands. All of the substances we are interested in affect the central nervous system and will be reviewed according to that effect. These drugs are depressants, stimulants, hallucinogens, and cannabis.

Depressants

This category of drugs includes alcohol, barbiturates, sedatives/tranquilizers, and the narcotics. The latter may be natural (opium derivatives such as morphine and codeine), semisynthetic (such as heroin), or synthetic (such as methadone and Demoral).[1] Depressants are typically addicting, and recent studies have indicated the possibility of a relationship between certain chemical deficiencies and the propensity for addiction to depressants.

Endorphins

During the 1970s a number of scientists, working independently, discovered in brain and body tissues three families of microscopic neurotransmitters (enkephalins, dynorphins, beta-endorphins) that have many of the characteristics of morphine. Scientists also discovered that the body contains receptor sites that have been programmed to receive these compounds (generally referred to as *endorphins,* a contraction of "endogenous morphine").

---

1. As opposed to depressants, which act centrally on the brain, analgesics such as acetaminophen (for example, Tylenol, Panadol, and Anacin-3), ibuprofen (for example, Nuprin, Mediprin, and Advil), and aspirin relieve pain via localized action. They are not addictive (Brody 1988).

When they reach the receptor sites in the CNS, endorphins relieve pain. Pain is the result of a trauma experienced by the body, information about which is detected by sensors that send impulses along the nervous system, through neurons and across synapses as they move toward the brain. The subsequent release of endorphins in the brain inhibits pain impulses.

When people stub a toe or injure a finger, they usually grit their teeth and clench their fists, activities that apparently cause the release of naturally occurring opiates that reduce sensations of pain. The athlete's ability to overcome pain during competition and the soldier's ability to perform heroic feats while severely wounded can be explained by the endorphin-receptor phenomenon, as can success in treating pain with acupuncture (Snyder 1977; 1989; Davis 1984; Goldberg 1988).[2] While these receptor sites are programmed to receive naturally occurring neurotransmitters (endorphins), they are also receptive to external chemicals such as opiates.

Endorphins also enable the organism (including many animals) to deal with psychological stress by curbing an autonomic overreaction and producing calm: They slow breathing, reduce blood pressure, and lower the level of motor activity (Davis 1984). A "deficiency in an endorphin system that ordinarily would support feelings of pleasure and reinforcement might lead to feelings of inadequacy and sadness" (Levinthal 1988: 149), a phenomenon that would render drug use essentially a form of self-medication.[3] As noted earlier in this chapter, the use of psychoactive substances does not automatically produce a pleasurable response. However, persons at risk for narcotic addiction may suffer from an endorphin deficiency. For such persons heroin addiction would be the result of a genetically acquired deficiency or of a temporary or permanent impairment of the body's ability to produce endorphins.

> This point of view would help account for the puzzling variability from individual to individual in the addictive power of opiate drugs. If an endorphin deficiency exists, however, the question would still remain as to what precipitating circumstances would lead to such a deficiency and whether these circumstances were environmental, inherited genetically, or a product of both. (Levinthal 1988: 154)

This has important policy implications.

The ingestion of large amounts of heroin or some other opiate may also cause this deficiency (Snyder 1977). Thus, an abstaining addict would be unusually sensitive to feelings of pain or stress and would be inclined to use narcotic drugs again. In other words, receptors become increasingly dependent on external depressants, which in turn further reduce the production of endorphins, leaving the receptors increasingly dependent on substances from the outside (Levinthal 1988: 156):

---

2. In one study, treating drug abusers with acupuncture was not found to be beneficial (Latessa and Moon 1992). Another study found it effective in detoxification treatment (Brewington, Smith, and Lipton 1994).

3. Mark Gold (1994) disputes the self-medication thesis.

As their endogenous source of supply is gradually lost, these receptors require an increasing amount of the drug to compensate, and a tolerance effect develops. If the opiate drug is later withdrawn, the receptors are now left without a supply from any source at all, and the symptoms of withdrawal are a consequence of this physiological dilemma.

However, many persons take heroin over long periods of time without becoming addicted, and hospital patients self-administering morphine for pain do not increase their intake over time nor do they suffer from a morphine craving when the pain subsides and they no longer have access to the drug (Peele 1985; Rosenthal 1993). Research has discovered that even tolerance and withdrawal symptoms in laboratory animals are affected by environmental cues (Hinson 1985; Bloom 1993). Indeed, "A person who has been removed from his drug-seeking environment in order to treat his addiction but then is returned to the same former drug-taking environment gets secondary associations from that environment that may in fact induce him to go back to using the drugs" (Bloom 1993: 22).[4]

Heroin

The opium poppy requires a hot, dry climate and very careful cultivation (Wishart 1974). Poppy seeds are scattered across the surface of freshly cultivated fields. Three months later when the poppy is mature, the green stem is topped by a brightly colored flower. Gradually the flower petals fall off, leaving a seedpod about the size of a small egg. Incisions are made in the seedpod just after the petals have fallen but before it is fully ripe. A milky-white fluid oozes out and hardens on the surface into a dark brown gum—raw opium. The raw opium is collected by scraping the pod with a flat, dull knife—a labor-intensive process. "Because the yield per acre is small and because laborious care is required in collecting the juice, it can only be grown profitably where both land and labor are cheap" (Ausubel 1978: 9). Lawfully produced morphine is usually harvested by the more modern industrial poppy straw process of extracting alkaloid from the mature dried plant. The extract may be either liquid, solid, or powder (*Drugs of Abuse* 1989). The Drug Enforcement Administration reports that more than 400 tons of opium or its equivalent in poppy straw concentrate are legally imported each year into the United States. Part of this quantity is used to extract codeine (an opiate alkaloid about 20 percent as potent as morphine), an ingredient used in many cough medicines.

The raw opium is dissolved in drums of hot water and lime (calcium oxide). Fertilizer is added, precipitating out organic wastes and leaving morphine suspended near the surface. After residual waste is removed, the morphine is transferred to other drums, where it is heated and mixed with concentrated ammonia. The morphine solidifies and falls to the bottom of the

---

4. In approximately two-thirds of cocaine-dependent subjects in a lab setting, drug cues increased craving for cocaine (Avants et al. 1995).

A Turkish woman collects seeds from a poppy plant.

drum, where it is filtered out in the form of chunky white kernels. In this dry form the morphine weighs about one-tenth as much as the original raw opium. To produce ten kilos of almost pure heroin the chemist mixes ten kilos of morphine and ten kilos of acetic anhydride and heats it at exactly 185 degrees for six hours, producing an impure form of heroin. While this step is not complex, it can be dangerous: "If the proportion of morphine to acetic acid is incorrect or the temperature too high or too low the laboratory may be blown up." Acetic acid is also highly corrosive, attacking both skin and lungs (Lamour and Lamberti 1974: 17).

Next, the solution is treated with water and chloroform until the impurities precipitate out. The heroin is drained off into another container, to which sodium carbonate is added until crude heroin particles begin to solidify and drop to the bottom. The particles are filtered out and purified in a solution of alcohol and activated charcoal. This mixture is heated until the alcohol begins to evaporate, leaving granules of almost pure heroin at the bottom. In the final step, the granules are dissolved in alcohol, and ether and hydrochloric acid are added to the solution. Tiny white flakes begin to form. These are filtered out under pressure and dried in a special process. The result is a powder between 80 and 99 percent pure known as *No. 4 heroin*. "In the hands of a careless chemist the volatile ether gas may ignite and produce a violent explosion that could level the clandestine laboratory" (McCoy 1972: 13).

For street sale, the white crystalline powder (the Mexican product contains impurities that give it a brown or "black tar" color) is diluted ("stepped on") with any powdery substance that dissolves when heated, such as lactose, quinine, flour, or cornstarch. Consumer-available heroin prepared for intravenous use usually has a purity of less than 10 percent, while the substance prepared for sniffing or smoking may contain 40 percent heroin.[5] In recent years, purity levels have been increasing. In equivalent doses, heroin is about 2½ times as potent as morphine because it more easily penetrates the blood-brain barrier. Once heroin reaches the brain, however, it is converted back into morphine (Royal College of Psychiatrists 1987; hereafter Royal College).

Heroin has analgesic and euphoric properties. While brief, sharp, localized (phasic) pain is poorly relieved by opiates, duller, more chronic, and less localized (tonic) pain is effectively relieved (Snyder 1977; Melzack 1990). As with all opiates, heroin

> acts chiefly on the central and autonomic nervous systems and, to some extent, directly on smooth muscles. Effects on the central nervous system are primarily depressant, although larger doses may bring out stimulant properties, especially at the spinal level of reaction. . . . The depressant actions include analgesia (relief of pain, sedation, freedom from anxiety, muscular relaxation, decreased motor activity), hypnosis (drowsiness and lethargy), and euphoria (a sense of well-being and contentment). (Ausubel 1978: 11)[6]

"Unlike anesthetics, opiates are able to produce marked analgesia without excessive drowsiness, muscular weakness, confusion, or loss of consciousness" (Ausubel 1978: 11). Exactly how morphine induces analgesia is not completely understood, although it appears to reduce the "emotional response to pain, to suffering, and to some extent also decreases knowledge of the pain stimulus." This may be physiological or psychological: Heroin appears to reduce anxiety and distress, creating a detachment from psychological pain (Ray 1978: 310).

> TOLERANCE. The continued use of heroin produces *tolerance:*

> a progressive increase in the ability of the body to adapt to the effects of a drug that is used at regular and frequent intervals. It is manifested in two ways: (1) progressively larger doses must be administered to produce the same effects; and (2) eventually as much as ten or more times the original lethal dose can be safely taken

as the metabolism adapts to the substance (Ausubel 1978: 14).

> Tolerance develops as the body becomes progressively immune to the chemical effects of the drug at the cellular level. Should usage continue, a physio-

---

5. Injection is the principal mode of ingestion in the United States. Very little heroin smoking has been reported, although snorting has been increasing in the eastern part of the United States. Most heroin in the western parts of the country is "black tar" from Mexico, which is suitable only for injection (*Trends in Heroin* 1994).

6. The effects of opiates vary with species; for instance, in cats and horses morphine produces intense stimulation and is sometimes used (illegally) to "dope" race horses for a better performance (Harris 1993).

logical dependence on the narcotic will occur as the affected tissues and cells accommodate the chemically induced processes that result from the introduction of the drug. The homeostatic processes of the body adjust to the narcotic and bring about a new physiological equilibrium. If the equilibrium and normal functioning are to be maintained at the physiological level, regular and stable amounts of the drug [or a similar drug—cross-tolerance] must be taken. (Biernacki 1986: 9)

It should be noted, however, that rapid physical tolerance does not develop in medical patients who take morphine for physical pain (Melzack 1990).

Tolerance to some aspects of heroin use, in particular the "high," requires an increase in the dosage in order to gain the same level of response. In other words, a maintenance dose of morphine or some other narcotic will prevent physical withdrawal symptoms. Those seeking the "high," however, must keep increasing the dosage until it is no longer feasible (that is, economically possible) to do so. They may then seek some way to reduce the level of tolerance, possibly by entering a drug rehabilitation program. With a lowered level of tolerance, the addict can resume low-dose usage and gain the sought-after response. There is also cross-tolerance; that is, tolerance to heroin carries over to other narcotic drugs, such as morphine and methadone (which will be discussed in chapter 5), but not to other depressants, such as alcohol or barbiturates. (Alcohol withdrawal symptoms—the delirium tremens or DTs, convulsions, and hallucinations—can be relieved, however, by barbiturates or sedatives because of cross-tolerance.)

Snorting a bag of heroin in the back of an abandoned truck.

EFFECTS OF HEROIN. Heroin is typically ingested intravenously, although some users inject it just under the skin—"skinpopping." Powdered heroin is placed in a "cooker"—a spoon or a bottle cap. A small amount of water is added, and the mixture is heated with a match or lighter until the heroin is dissolved. The mixture is drawn up into a hypodermic needle and inserted into a vein that has been distended by being tied with a tourniquet. The user may bring blood back into the hypodermic, where it can mix with the heroin, a process known as "booting." Heroin can also be sniffed like cocaine and even smoked. When smoked—"chasing the dragon"—heroin is heated and the fumes inhaled, usually through a small tube.

Michael Agar (1973) points out that the "junkie" can experience four different effects from ingesting heroin:

1. *The Rush:* Heroin produces euphoria, referred to as the "rush": "About 10 seconds after the beginning of an injection of heroin the subjects had a typical narcotic 'rush,' including a wave of euphoric feelings, visceral sensations, a facial flush and a deepening of the voice" (Dole 1980: 146). Addicts frequently describe the rush in sexual terms: "I felt like I died and went to heaven. My whole body was like one giant fucking incredible orgasm" (Inciardi 1986: 61). Indeed, heroin use substitutes for sex, in which the addict usually has little or no interest. Typically, the onset of heroin-using behavior coincides with adolescence, and remission usually occurs, with or without treatment, as the sex drive is reduced—there are few heroin addicts over forty years old. (Similar findings are reported with respect to crime and "aging out.") Agar (1973) notes that while heroin is usually believed to have no effect on an addict after his or her tolerance builds up, the heroin user actually experiences the rush no matter how addicted he or she is.

2. *The High:* Described by addicts as a feeling of general well-being, the high decreases with increased tolerance; thus, increasing dosages are required to achieve the high. While the rush is experienced over a period of seconds, the high can last for several hours.

3. *The Nod:* This is described by addicts as being "out of it," in a state of unawareness, oblivious to one's surroundings—an escape from reality. The nod ranges from a slight dropping of the eyelids and jaw to complete unconsciousness: "They become calm, contented, and detached. They appeared to be quite uninterested in external events." (Dole 1980: 146). One addict provides this description: "It just knocks you completely into another dimension. The nod is like—you know, it's not describable. There's not words to express the feeling. The feeling is *that* good. So good that once hooked you never really live the feeling down" (Rettig, Torres, and Garrett 1977: 35). Tolerance affects the nod dramatically, and doses greater than that required for the high are needed to sustain the nod.

4. *Being Straight:* This is how addicts describe their condition when they are not sick; that is, not suffering the onset of withdrawal symptoms—homeostatic. Unless an addict has been tricked into buying a "blank," he or she will

get a rush and get straight, although not necessarily experience a high or the nod (Agar 1973).

Heroin impairs homeostatic functions. There is a slight decrease in body temperature, although a dilation of blood vessels gives the user a feeling of warmth. The body retains fluids; there is also a decrease in the secretion of digestive fluids and a depression of bowel activity, so the user suffers from constipation. Heroin also causes a constriction of the pupils, which is why addicts frequently wear sunglasses. At relatively high doses the sedating effects cause a semistuperous, lethargic, and dreamy state—"nodding"—in which there is a feeling of extreme contentment. Unlike alcohol, heroin depresses aggression and also stimulates the brain area controlling nausea and vomiting. Instead of euphoria, some initial users experience nausea and vomiting: "I got such a bad pain in my head that I thought I was fucking brain damaged. I puked my guts out" (Inciardi 1986: 61).[7]

A very dangerous side effect of heroin is that it depresses the respiratory centers in the brain. Thus, an overdose can result in respiratory arrest and death from lack of oxygen to the brain. (Physicians use the antagonist Naloxone to undo the heroin-induced depressed respiration rate.) It is believed that there are millions of occasional users of heroin—*chippers* or *week-enders*—whose use parallels that of persons who drink heavily only on weekends or at parties; they appear to avoid addiction.

HEROIN WITHDRAWAL. The neuro-adaption we refer to as tolerance often results in *rebounding* when the substance is withdrawn. The withdrawal symptoms tend to be the opposite of the effects produced by the drug. "Thus, withdrawal from a depressant drug will give rise to brain excitation as adrenergic neurons that have been unnaturally inhibited by a drug such as heroin in its absence become hyperactive and cause anxiety, shaking, and cold sweat" (Royal College 1987: 34) and sometimes spontaneous orgasm. Heroin depresses the neurotransmitter dopamine (discussed below), and in withdrawal the dramatic increase in dopamine activity intensifies other unpleasant symptoms (Fishbein and Pease 1990). Clonidine, a nonaddicting drug (discussed in chapter 5), is often used by physicians to slow down these neurons and thereby relieve withdrawal symptoms (Davis 1984).

Withdrawal symptoms, David Ausubel (1978: 16) notes, while undoubtedly uncomfortable, "are seldom more severe than a bad case of gastrointestinal influenza." Symptoms subside in about a week, although the psychological symptoms may persist indefinitely. Children born to addicted mothers, in addition to having a host of other physical problems—small size, anemia, heart disease, hepatitis, pneumonia—also suffer from withdrawal symptoms (O'Brien and Cohen 1984), although this view is challenged by Stanton Peele

---

7. However, the vomiting caused by opiates "is not accompanied by the usual adverse feelings that nausea and vomiting produce in most people" (Harris 1993: 87).

SIGNS AND SYMPTOMS OF OPIOID WITHDRAWAL

In temporal order of appearance (Ginzburg 1986):

1. Several hours after last use:
   anxiety
   restlessness
   irritability
   drug craving
2. 8–15 hours after last use:
   lacrimation (running eyes)
   rhinorrhea (running nose)
   yawning
   perspiration

3. 16–24 hours after last use:
   sneezing
   sniffles
   anorexia (severe appetite loss)
   vomiting
   abdominal cramps
   bone pains
   tremors
   weakness
   insomnia
   goose flesh
   convulsions (very rarely)
   cardiovascular collapse

(1985). Peele argues that the symptoms exhibited by the newborn of heroin addicts—undue crying and ineffective feeding, followed cyclically by periods of restless sleep—do not result from heroin withdrawal but from the mother's unhealthy lifestyle. The National Institute on Drug Abuse reports that infants born to heroin-abusing mothers frequently suffer from Neonatal Abstinence Syndrome—withdrawal symptoms that may require medication.

MEDICAL USE. Since 1924 heroin has been virtually banned in the United States, even for medical use as an analgesic. The prohibition against the use of heroin under any circumstances, even to alleviate the intractable pain experienced by some cancer patients, is controversial. Arnold Trebach (1982: 79) argues that heroin should be made available under such circumstances. "For some patients, heroin is superior to other medicines for the control of pain, anxiety, and related conditions." Heroin, however, is not the most powerful of the narcotics. The synthetic chemical etorphine is 5,000 to 10,000 times more potent than morphine and "gives rise to euphoria and relieves pain in a dose as small as .0001 gram" (Snyder 1977: 44). Because of its potency, etorphine is usually used only by veterinarians to immobilize large wild animals (*Drugs of Abuse* 1989). John Kaplan (1983b) states that while most patients cannot tell the difference between heroin and morphine in equivalent doses, patients (in England where such use is legal) who take the drug intravenously tend to prefer heroin. The greater euphoric effect of intravenous heroin appears to provide some relief for terminal patients whose painful existence is often measured in weeks, days, or hours.

In an editorial, the *New York Times* (14 January 1988: 26) advocated support of legislation, "The Compassion Pain Relief Act," that would allow physicians to prescribe heroin to terminally ill patients in a hospital or hospice: "How many more Americans must suffer needlessly before Congress discovers its conscience?" Representative Charles Rangel (D-NY), former chair of the House Select Committee on Narcotic Abuse and Control, responds (1988: 18) that this legislation was strongly opposed by the major health care associations, including the American Medical Association and the National Hospice Organization, which cares for terminally ill patients. He argues that heroin is no better at treating cancer pain than other available painkillers.

> Why should Congress authorize medical use of this dangerous drug when the great majority of doctors and other medical professionals say they don't need it and don't want it? The risk of diversion and the risk of violence against hospital pharmacies by drug criminals seeking pure stocks of heroin are not worth taking for a drug that offers no unique therapeutic benefits.

DANGERS OF HEROIN USE. Ingesting heroin significantly more pure than the user's level of tolerance leads to overdose reactions that can include respiratory arrest and death. And because heroin is illegal, there is no way for the user to determine the level of purity. Indeed, the so-called "hot shot" is used as a relatively easy way of eliminating addicts who have become police informers. Another danger is that heroin cut for street sale may contain adulterants, or the user may mix the substance with other drugs, such as the stimulants cocaine and amphetamine, to enhance (potentiate) the euphoric reaction. This combination can be fatal to some abusers.

There are also the dangers associated with diseases that are transmitted by shared hypodermic needles, particularly hepatitis and AIDS. In New York City, where there are believed to be about 200,000 heroin addicts, as many as 60 percent may be infected with the AIDS virus, and addicts are the leading cause of the spread of AIDS. In addition to the threat of shared needles, infected addicts spread the disease through sexual relations with nonaddicts (Lambert 1988).

Barbiturates

There are about 2,500 derivatives of barbituric acid and dozens of brand names. Lawfully produced barbiturates are found in tablet or capsule form; illegal barbiturates may be found in liquid form for intravenous use because barbiturates are poorly soluble in water. "Barbiturates depress the sensory cortex, decrease motor activity, alter cerebrellar function, and produce drowsiness, sedation, and hypnosis" (*Physicians' Desk Reference* 1987: 1163; hereafter PDR). They inhibit seizure activity and can induce unconsciousness in the form of sleep or surgical anesthesia. Unlike opiates, barbiturates do not decrease, and may actually increase, reaction to pain. They can produce a variety of alterations in the central nervous system, ranging from mild sedation to hypnosis and deep coma. In high enough dosage they can induce anesthesia, and an overdose can be fatal. Barbiturates are used primarily as sedatives for the treatment of insomnia and as anticonvulsants (Mendelson 1980), although in some persons they produce excitation (PDR 1988). The user's expectations have a marked influence on the drug's effect.

> For instance, the person who takes 200 mg. of secobarbital and expects to fall asleep will usually sleep, if provided with a suitable environment. Another individual, who takes the same amount of secobarbital and expects to have a good time in a stimulating environment, may experience a state of paradoxical stimulation or disinhibition euphoria. (Wesson and Smith 1977: 28)

Barbiturates are classified according to the speed with which they are metabolized (broken down chemically) in the liver and eliminated by the kidneys: slow, intermediate, fast, and ultrafast. The latter—the best known being sodium pentothal—are used to induce unconsciousness in a few minutes. At relatively high dosage they are used as anesthetics for minor surgery and to induce anesthesia before the administration of slow-acting barbiturates. In low dosage, barbiturates may actually increase the reaction to painful stimuli. It is the fast-acting barbiturates, particularly Nembutal (sodium pentobarbital), Amytal (amobarbital sodium), Seconal (secobarbital sodium), and Tuinal (secobarbital sodium and amobarbital sodium combined) that are most likely to be abused (O'Brien and Cohen 1984). Exactly how barbiturates cause their neurophysiological effects is not fully understood, but the substance impairs the postsynaptic action of excitatory neurotransmitters (McKim 1991).

DANGERS OF BARBITURATE USE. Intoxication results in slurred speech, unsteady gait, confusion, poor judgment, and a marked impairment of motor skills. Like opiates, barbiturates are addicting; there is psychological and physiological dependence. Withdrawal symptoms range from the mild—muscle twitching, tremors, weakness, dizziness, visual distortion, nausea, vomiting, insomnia—to the major—delirium, convulsions, and possibly death (PDR 1987). It is the disinhibition euphoria that can follow barbiturate intake that makes them appealing as intoxicants (Wesson and Smith 1977). With continuous intoxication at high doses the user typically neglects his or her appearance, bathing infrequently and becoming unkempt and dirty as well as irritable and aggressive (McKim 1991). Barbiturates serve as a positive reinforcer for laboratory animals.

"Following a large overdose of secobarbital or phenobarbital (short-acting barbiturates), an individual may be in coma for several days" (Wesson and Smith 1977: 20). Unlike opiates, barbiturates impair motor skills and make it dangerous to operate motor vehicles. As with opiates, tolerance to barbiturates develops, but in contrast to opiates, there is a fatal dosage level, and the margin between an intoxicating dosage and a fatal dosage becomes smaller with continued use (PDR 1988: 537): "As tolerance to barbiturates develops, the amount needed to maintain the same level of intoxication increases; tolerance to a fatal dosage, however, does not increase more than two-fold. As this occurs, the margin between an intoxicating dosage and a fatal dosage becomes smaller." Drinking alcohol can further reduce that margin because alcohol "enhances the absorption and produces an additive CNS depression." Further, when under the influence of small amounts of barbiturates or a combination of alcohol and barbiturates, a "person may 'forget' that he has already taken barbiturates and continue to ingest them until he reaches a lethal dose." Such overdoses often appear, incorrectly, to be suicidal (Wesson and Smith 1977: 24). Barbiturate use during pregnancy has been associated with birth defects.

Methaqualone

Methaqualone was first synthesized in 1951 in India, where it was introduced as an antimalarial drug but proved to be ineffective. At the same time its sedating effects caused it to be introduced in Great Britain as a safe, non-barbiturate "sleeping pill." The substance subsequently found its way into street abuse, and similar patterns occurred in Germany and Japan. In 1965 methaqualone was introduced into the United States as the prescription drugs Sopors and Quaalude without any restrictions—it was not listed as a scheduled (controlled) drug. By the early 1970s "ludes" and "sopors" were part of the drug culture. Physicians were overprescribing the drug for anxiety and insomnia, believing that it was safer than barbiturates. Street sales were primarily diversions from legitimate sources.

Eight years after it was first introduced into the United States, the drug's serious dangers became evident, and in 1973 it was placed on the DEA's Schedule II list. Although chemically unrelated to barbiturates, methaqualone intoxication is similar to barbiturate intoxication. Addiction develops rapidly and an overdose can be fatal. However, while similar to barbiturates in its effect, methaqualone produces an even greater loss of motor coordination, which is why it is sometimes referred to as a "wallbanger." Methaqualone is now illegally manufactured in Colombia and smuggled into the United States.

Tranquilizers/Sedatives

Minor tranquilizers or sedatives—referred to pharmacologically as *sedative-hypnotics*—usually benzodiazepines, are among the most widely prescribed of all drugs—more than 70 million prescriptions for them are filled annually (McKim 1991). They are used medically to treat anxiety, insomnia, muscle spasms, and convulsions. The CNS contains benzodiazepine receptors that (through a complex process involving certain [GABA] receptors) inhibit the brain's limbic system, which regulates emotions (Smith and Wesson 1994). Although it has yet to be discovered, scientists believe that the body produces its own benzodiazepine-like substance that controls anxiety.

Some tranquilizers block dopamine (discussed below) receptors (which can lead to symptoms of Parkinson's disease). Sometimes referred to as "sleeping pills," these CNS depressants have largely replaced barbiturates, which reportedly have a significantly greater potential for abuse and risk for fatal overdose. Benzodiazepines have an upper limit of effectiveness—after a certain point, increasing the dosage will not increase the effect, and overdoses are rarely fatal (McKim 1991): "Even when a benzodiazepine is taken in an overdose of 50–100 times the usual therapeutic dose, fatalities from respiratory depression are rare" (Smith and Wesson 1994: 180). A life-endangering CNS depression can result, however, when benzodiazepines are used in conjunction with alcohol. Norman Miller and Mark Gold argue that the "potential for [benzodiazepine] abuse, addiction, tolerance, and dependence may be at least as great as with barbiturates and perhaps even greater" (1990: 71). The National Institute on Drug Abuse, however, reports that barbiturates have a significantly greater potential for abuse than benzodiazepines ("Drug Abuse" 1991).

The best-known benzodiazepines are Valium (diazepam), Librium (chlordiazepoxide), and Equanil and Miltown (meprobamate). (Some include Doriden—glutethimide—and even methaqualone in this category.) Valium is often prescribed to relieve stress because it produces a sense of calm and well-being. It is also addictive. Benzodiazepines are not effective for treating anxi-

A father mourns his nine-year-old daughter and six-year-old son shot by their mother a few weeks after she was released from a psychiatric ward. She was being treated with antidepressants and tranquilizers prior to the murders. Despite the inclination to think that the drug therapy was somehow responsible—either leading to the violence or failing to prevent it—such claims, especially applied to tranquilizers, have remained unproven.

ety beyond four months, and the drug can generate intense and severe secondary anxiety. Thus, if the underlying cause of the anxiety is not treated, benzodiazepines may worsen the condition and increase the risk of suicide (Miller and Gold 1990). The drug has a very long half-life (twenty-four to forty-eight hours), which means that even after it is discontinued, it stays in the system metabolizing slowly (Bluhm 1987).

A more recently marketed benzodiazepine, known as *Versed,* is four times more potent than Valium. It is used to induce "twilight sleep" for surgery patients who need to be relaxed but conscious. Yet another benzodiazepine, Rohypnol, is not approved for use in the United States but is prescribed in about sixty countries for severe insomnia. The substance induces muscle relaxation, short-term amnesia, and sleep. Rohypnol takes about fifteen to twenty minutes to affect the CNS, lasts more than eight hours, and leads to tolerance (Navarro 1995). The drug is popular in some adolescent/young adult crowds where it is known as "roofies" or "rope." It has also been implicated in cases of date rape—slipped into a woman's drink, causing the woman to blackout and have little if any memory of the assault. Rohypnol is often taken by cocaine addicts who want to come down more smoothly and by heroin addicts to offset withdrawal symptoms. When taken with other drugs such as alcohol, cocaine, or heroin, Rohypnol can cause respiratory depression and death (Navarro 1995; Seligmann and King 1996). In 1996 Rohypnol was reclassified as a Schedule I drug.

The full extent of the nonmedical use of sedatives is not known, although it appears that their abuse is often in combination with other controlled substances. They produce effects subjectively similar to alcohol and barbiturates, but unlike these other depressants, benzodiazepines have few effects outside the CNS (McKim 1991). Major or antipsychotic tranquilizers such as Thorazine (chlorpromazine) do not produce euphoria and thus are rarely used nonmedically (Nelson et al. 1982).

DANGERS OF TRANQUILIZER/SEDATIVE USE. As opposed to the barbiturates they have largely replaced, benzodiazepines produce sedation and little respiratory depression even in doses much higher than those used to treat anxiety or insomnia. However, repeated use leads to dependence, and discontinuing tranquilizers *can*—although it is unclear in what proportion of users—produce withdrawal symptoms that include anxiety, insomnia, agitation, anorexia, tremor, muscle twitching, nausea/vomiting, hypersensitivity to sensory stimuli and other perceptual disturbances, and depersonalization. Discontinuing use after prolonged exposure to high doses can produce hallucinations, delirium, grand mal convulsions, and, on rare occasions, death ("Drug Abuse" 1987; Smith and Wesson 1994). Valium withdrawal symptoms may first appear after seven to ten days and may be quite serious and even life threatening (Bluhm 1987). In the United States one out of four women and one out of ten men take benzodiazepines, and some researchers believe that "abuse, addiction, tolerance and dependence occur readily and frequently in general populations" (Miller and Gold 1990: 68). In some persons benzodiazepines can induce hostility and even aggression (McKim 1991). In laboratory animals benzodiazepines have proven to be less effective reinforcers than barbiturates ("Drug Abuse" 1991). Valium overdose is the second-leading cause of drug-related emergency room admissions in the United States (Bluhm 1987).

Alcohol

Alcohols are compounds used in perfumes, paints, and many other products. Ethyl alcohol (ethanol) is used as a beverage. A natural substance, ethyl alcohol is formed by the fermentation that occurs when sugar reacts with yeast. It can be made by distillation or by fermenting fruits, vegetables, or grains. In pure form the substance is colorless and has a bitter taste. While some persons apparently enjoy the taste of beverages containing alcohol, many others ingest the drug despite its taste. The substance can produce feelings of well-being, sedation, intoxication, or unconsciousness, depending on the amount and the manner in which it is consumed. There is extensive research indicating that alcohol taken in moderate amounts—more than five grams but not more than thirty grams—can help protect against heart disease by raising the level of high-density lipoproteins (so-called "good cholesterol"), which help cleanse the arteries of fatty deposits. A six-ounce glass of wine has about eleven grams of alcohol; a twelve-ounce can of beer about thirteen grams; and a one-ounce shot of liquor about fifteen grams (Angier 1991). (For a review of this issue, see the Spring 1994 edition of *Contemporary Drug Problems* 21.)

Alcohol is a *regulated* rather than *controlled* substance—it can be purchased and possessed with only a few restrictions. There are three major classes of alcoholic beverage:

1. *Beer:* Beer is produced by the fermentation of barley malt or other grains (brewing). It is usually flavored with hops or other aromatic bitters. In the United States beer generally contains no more than 5 percent alcohol (10 percent proof), although some co-called "ice" beers contain closer to 6 or (mostly foreign brews) 7 percent.[8] A variant of beer known as "malt liquor" can contain 8 percent alcohol (16 percent proof). There are also "light" beers (about 3 percent alcohol) and nonalcoholic (or "near") beers (about .05 percent alcohol).
2. *Wine:* Wine is obtained from the fermentation of the juice of grapes (and sometimes other fruits). It usually contains 6 to 14 percent alcohol (12 to 28 percent proof).
3. *Liquor:* When alcohol produced by fermentation (of corn, malt, grains, molasses, potatoes) reaches about 15 percent, it kills the alcohol-producing yeast cells. In order to obtain higher concentrations of alcohol, distillation is necessary. The mix is heated (alcohol has a

---

8. In 1935, fearing that beer manufacturers would attempt to lure customers by raising the amount of alcohol in their brews, Congress enacted legislation that prohibited the listing of alcohol content on beer labels. In 1995 the Supreme Court ruled that law unconstitutional.

lower boiling point than other liquids), and its cooling vapors are collected. After several distillations, nearly pure alcohol can be obtained. The colorless liquid is usually mixed with water, coloring, and flavoring. It contains at least 25 percent alcohol (50 percent proof) but may be as high as 50 percent alcohol (100 proof). This category includes whiskey (the Kentucky version known as bourbon; the Scottish version known as Scotch), brandy, rum, gin, and vodka.

Alcohol is a psychoactive/mind-altering chemical that, like heroin and tranquilizers, depresses the central nervous system. At low doses, however, it can act as a stimulant, and initially the user of alcohol often experiences it as a stimulant with euphoric effects (Bukstein, Brent, Kaminer 1989). This is apparently because of alcohol's ability to stimulate the release of dopamine (Dettling et al. 1995), which is discussed below. As with other drugs, the influence of alcohol is mediated through setting and expectations. Thus, for example, imbibers at a funeral will act differently under the influence than they would at a wedding or other happy occasion.

Alcohol is absorbed primarily through the small intestine. The rate of absorption depends on the type and amount of foods in the stomach—foods, especially solid and fatty foods, slow the absorption process. Body weight and gender also influence the effects of alcohol: Heavier persons have more bodily fluids and thus dilute more of the substance; females have less gastric acid and will absorb about 30 percent more alcohol than men. Once absorbed into the bloodstream, alcohol moves to wherever there is water in the body, including inside cells of the CNS. The chemical first affects the part of the brain that controls inhibitions—drinkers talk more and may get foolish or rowdy. Alcohol is an efficient tranquilizer, having the ability to reduce short-term anxiety (Willoughby 1988).

In the liver, alcohol is converted to acetaldehyde, which in high levels causes permanent liver damage. In the alcoholic—though not in persons not addicted to alcohol—acetaldehyde builds up and is transported through the blood-brain barrier, where it combines with neurotransmitters to produce TIQs (tetrahydroisoquinolines). TIQs attach to CNS receptors to produce a feeling of well-being similar to that produced by morphine. This activity causes brain cell membranes to become abnormally thickened and to require a constant supply of alcohol. Thus, the brain cells have become addicted to alcohol. In its absence, membranes function poorly, and the alcoholic experiences withdrawal symptoms (Catanzarite 1992).

Unlike other drugs of abuse, alcohol provides calories and is technically a food. Almost all alcohol is burned as fuel, with some eliminated through the lungs and in urine. Breathalyzer tests measure the BAL (blood alcohol level)—the amount of alcohol in the blood—because alcohol in the air exhaled closely parallels concentrations in the blood. In most states, a BAL of .10 is generally the legal standard for intoxication. Alcohol produces tolerance, and persons with high levels of alcohol tolerance can perform tasks with a BAL that would render a nontolerant person "a falling-down drunk." Alcohol has a

GENETICS AND ALCOHOLISM

"Substantial evidence indicates that genetic factors play a significant role in the development of at least some forms of alcoholism" (National Institute on Alcohol Abuse and Alcoholism 1992: 1).

cross-tolerance with barbiturates and benzodiazepines. It appears to act on the CNS in the same manner as benzodiazepines—that is, it acts on benzodiazepine receptors, which are inhibitory.

Genetics may play an important role in explaining why some persons abuse alcohol. Scientists report that hereditary factors overwhelmingly determine the condition of at least half of the nation's alcoholics.

> That alcoholism runs in families is a well-documented fact. Although it is highly probable that environmental variables contribute to this, evidence from clinical and animal research strongly suggests that alcoholism is a genetically influenced disorder. Exactly what is inherited, however, is not certain. (Schuckit 1983:42)

Studies have revealed that some persons with particular inherited characteristics are at greater risk for addiction than persons without these characteristics. "Researchers have identified as important influences such inherited characteristics as how an individual metabolizes alcohol, hormonal and behavioral effects of alcohol and tolerance of high levels of alcohol in the blood" (Brody 1987: 14; also see Tarter, Alterman, and Edwards (1985) and Tarter (1988) for a review of research on behavioral traits and predisposition to substance abuse). Studies have shown that first-degree relatives of alcoholics are more likely to be alcoholics than close blood relatives of nonalcoholics. Adopted children with alcoholic natural parents are more likely to become alcoholics than adopted children with nonalcoholic natural parents (Schuckit 1985).

Research (Blum et al. 1990) reveals that the genetic component of alcoholism appears to be related to an abnormality of a dopamine receptor gene. Persons having this defect are at potentially greater risk for the disease than the general population. While another study (Gelernter, Goldman, and Risch 1993) disputes the Blum et al. findings,[9] subsequent research identified a specific genetic (dopamine-related) abnormality associated with a susceptability for alcoholism (Dettling et al. 1995). It has been shown that serotonin (see below) neurotransmission also influences drinking behavior (Gulley et al. 1995), and a deficiency in serotonin or serotonin receptors has been linked to a predisposition to alcoholism (Goleman 1990). While a wide variety of studies clearly in-

---

9. "Individuals who become alcoholic or severely alcoholic probably do so for a variety of different reasons, and for the majority of alcoholics the causation may not even be primarily genetic" (Gelernter et al. 1993: 1677).

dicate that genetic factors influence the development of alcoholism, the studies differ in their estimate of the degree of genetic influence. While genes (segments of chromosomes that code for the production of specific proteins) are important in the control of behavior, they do not directly cause a person to become alcoholic or drug-dependent, although they are believed to produce a tendency or predisposition to respond to drugs (including alcohol) in a certain manner. "Thus, genes are not the sole determinant of alcoholism or drug dependence, but their presence (or absence) may increase the likelihood that a person will become alcoholic or drug dependent" (Pickens and Svikis 1988: 2).

> If you are the son of a male alcoholic who began his alcoholism in early adolescence or early adulthood, the chance of your becoming an alcoholic is seven to ten times greater than that of the average population. If you are the twin of a male alcoholic, the chance of your becoming an alcoholic is about 70 percent. This means there is some factor, or factors, passed to the male offspring that make them more vulnerable to the actions of alcoholism. (Bloom 1993: 24)

DANGERS OF ALCOHOL USE. Alcohol poses a number of potential dangers. The substance

- decreases the number of white blood cells,
- weakens the body's immune system,
- damages the liver, diminishing the body's ability to fight disease; in more extreme cases it causes cirrhosis, a scarring of the liver that is irreversible and often fatal,
- depletes the body of vitamins and minerals essential for growth and health,
- lowers hormone levels, leading to sexual dysfunction,
- makes the person more vulnerable to disease, particularly cancer in women and heart attacks in men,
- causes brain damage,
- can cause fetal alcohol syndrome (FAS), which results in birth defects, including mental retardation,
- is frequently a "gateway" drug for adolescents, who subsequently move on to illegal chemicals,
- when taken in conjunction with barbiturates or sedatives can lead to life-endangering central nervous system depression, and
- in some persons and in some situations can result (perhaps by lowering inhibitions) in physically aggressive and even violent behavior.

Using potentially dangerous instruments, such as automobiles, under the influence of alcohol can obviously be life-threatening to the user and others. Alcohol, like other depressants, is an addicting chemical, and like heroin, it produces tolerance and severe withdrawal symptoms including the "shakes," an increase in blood pressure and body temperature, nausea, diarrhea, and the dreaded DTs (delirium tremens). These are marked by confusion, anxiety, panic attacks, hallucinations, paranoia, trembling, and sometimes seizures. Withdrawal takes between three and five days to accomplish.

Inhalants

Inhalants are a diverse group of vapor-producing chemicals. When inhaled these vapors can cause an intoxication similar to that of alcohol. Inhalants include a variety of readily available products often kept in the home. They can be divided into four classes:

1. *Volatile solvents,* such as glue, paint thinner, cleaning fluid, nail polish remover, and gasoline.
2. *Aerosols,* such as hair spray, spray paint, and frying pan lubricants.
3. *Anesthetics,* such as nitrous oxide—"laughing gas"—used as a whipped cream propellant, and ether.
4. *Volatile nitrates,* such as amyl nitrate, a prescription drug used to treat angina, and butyl nitrate, used in room deodorizers.

With some exceptions, these products are usually not produced for their psychoactive qualities, but when used for mind-altering purposes they are *drugs.* In general, these chemicals are abused by young (preadolescent and adolescent) males, although some, such as the volatile nitrites, are popular among anal sex aficionados because they relax the sphincter muscles; they are also reputed to increase the intensity of orgasm. Inhalants are quickly absorbed into the bloodstream and carried directly to the brain, where they produce a rapid "high" whose effects subside in a few minutes to a few hours. Tolerance can develop, but withdrawal symptoms, if they exist, are mild (Hormes, Filley, and Rosenberg 1986).

Toluene (methyl benzene), a common ingredient of most solvents, has the greatest abuse potential, and some industries have added mustard oil to their toluene-rich products so that the nasal irritation it causes will deter abusers (Hormes, Filley, and Rosenberg 1986).

While the dangers of inhalants have often been exaggerated, chronic use can damage the brain, liver, and kidneys. Perception and coordination become impaired, and heavy use can cause unconsciousness. The "high" may be accompanied by sedation, hallucinations, and delusions. High dosage can result in vomiting, paralysis, and coma. A common method of use, placing it inside a plastic bag covering the head, can lead to unconsciousness and death by suffocation.

Stimulants

As the term indicates, substances in this category stimulate the CNS. In moderation they enhance mood, increase alertness, and relieve fatigue. Stimulants range from the mild, such as nicotine and caffeine, to the more powerful,

THE ALLURE OF STIMULANTS

Stimulants produce profound subjective well-being with alertness. Normal pleasures are magnified and anxiety is decreased. Self-confidence and self-perceptions of mastery increase. Social inhibitions are reduced and interpersonal communication is facilitated. All aspects of the personal environment take on intensified qualities but without hallucinatory perceptual distortions. Emotionality and sexual feelings are enhanced. (Gawin, Khalsa, and Ellinwood 1994: 113)

such as cocaine and amphetamine. It has been hypothesized (the *catecholamine theory of depression*) that stimulants such as cocaine and amphetamine may compensate for a deficiency in three (catecholamine) neurotransmitters—dopamine (DA), norepinephrine or noradrenalin (NE), and serotonin (SE)—that can otherwise result in apathy and depression (Khantzian 1985; Nunes and Rosecan 1987), bolstering the theory of drug use as self-medication. In fact, dopamine is necessary to sustain life. A DA deficiency is believed to cause Parkinson's disease[10]; an excess is believed to cause Tourette syndrome.[11] Their ability to block dopamine accounts for the therapeutic effects of antischizophrenic (neuroleptic) drugs (Snyder 1986), because the brains of schizophrenics are high in dopamine. Cocaine and the DA agonist amphetamine can cause schizophrenic symptoms because these substances interfere with the reuptake of dopamine, a process used to conserve neurotransmitters after release by bringing them back into the presynaptic terminal for storage so that the neurotransmitters can be used again (Palfai and Jankiewicz 1991; Bloom 1993). The failure of the reuptake system increases the concentration of dopamine in the brain, particularly within pleasure centers. (See Di Chiara [1995] for a further discussion of the role of dopamine in drug abuse.)

Norepinephrine (NE) governs arousal reactions and appears to play a role in elevating mood; NE agonists such as cocaine and amphetamine produce a high. Serotonin appears to play a role in visual sensory phenomena, cognition, sex, and aggression (Palfai and Jankiewicz 1991). The medically prescribed antidepressant Prozac (fluoxetine) inhibits the reuptake of serotonin.

In the presynaptic terminals of normal persons, chemicals called monoamine oxidases, or MAO, control the level of neurotransmitters. In some individuals an excess of MAO lowers the amount of dopamine, norepinephrine, and serotonin, which results in depression (Sunderwirth 1985). Indeed, MAO-

---

10. Clinical studies of cocaine users in their thirties show an increase in symptoms of Parkinson's—tremors or stiffness, apparently the result of a decrease of dopamine receptors (Hartel 1993). Flupentixol, a drug that blocks dopamine, reduces the effects of cocaine but cannot be used for drug treatment because it also produces symptoms of Parkinson's (Bloom 1993).

11. Tourette syndrome is an incurable genetic affliction whose symptoms can range from mild tics to coprolalia—periodic outbursts of foul language (Brody 1995).

MAO-B AND CIGARETTES

The MAO enzyme exists in forms A and B. Cigarette smokers have a 40 percent MAO-B deficiency, causing the dopamine triggered by nicotine to remain active and thus enhancing its impact. This characteristic of smoking cigarettes indicates that the cigarette may be a gateway drug that leads to addiction to other drugs of abuse (Glassman and Koob 1996).

inhibiting drugs such as Nardil (phenelzine) are medically prescribed to treat depression. The use of powerful stimulants by some persons and not others, given that both groups have equal access to these drugs, may be explained by physiological deficiencies, much as the use of insulin by diabetics can be explained—nondiabetics will not find the ingestion of insulin a positive experience. (This has important policy implications.) The users of stimulants, according to this view, are attempting to reduce inner tension and increase energy and activity levels (see, for example, Fishbein, Lozovsky, and Jaffe 1989). At the other extreme, in persons who are highly extroverted, perhaps even manic, stimulants make more dopamine available to the brain and are, thus, highly rewarding even in small doses, making such persons susceptible to addiction (Goleman 1990). In 1995, a variant of the dopamine receptor D^4 was found to be associated with "novelty seeking": persons with this genetic factor tend to be extroverted, quick-tempered, impulsive, and easily bored (Angier 1995).

Cocaine

Coca is a flowering bush or shrub *(Erythroxylon coca)* that stands three to six feet high and yields at most four ounces of waxy, elliptical leaves that are about 1 percent cocaine by weight. Pulverized leaves of the coca bush are soaked and shaken in a mixture of alcohol and benzene (a coal tar derivative). After the liquid is drained, sulfuric acid is added, and the solution is again shaken. Sodium carbonate is added, forming a precipitate, which is washed with kerosene and chilled, leaving behind crystals of crude cocaine known as coca paste.

It requires between 200 and 500 kilograms (one kilogram = 2.2046 pounds; hereafter kilo) of coca leaves to make one kilo of paste; 2½ kilos of coca paste are converted into one kilo of cocaine base—a malodorous, rough, greenish yellow powder of more than 66 percent purity—and finally into cocaine hydrochloride by being treated with ether, acetone, and hydrochloric acid. One kilo of cocaine base is synthesized into one kilo of cocaine hydrochloride, a white crystalline powder that is about 95 percent pure. Those who process the substance are exposed to noxious fumes and the real danger of an explosion.

INGREDIENTS FOR PRODUCING COCAINE HYDROCHLORIDE

- coca leaves
- acetone (paint and varnish solvent)
- benzene (common solvent)
- kerosene (available as a cleaning agent and as fuel for lamps and stoves)
- ammonia (commonly used to make cleaning agents, fertilizers, and synthetic fibers)
- lime (used to make bricks and mortar)
- sodium carbonate (used in glass, soap, and cleaners)
- potassium permanganate (used for purifying water and tanning leather)
- ethyl ether (a widely used solvent)
- hydrochloric acid (used for cleaning metal and preparing food products)

In 1989 the Drug Enforcement Administration was given the statutory responsibility for monitoring the sales of some of these precursor chemicals. Manufacturers are required to report their domestic sales of more than 50 gallons a month and foreign sales of more than 500 gallons a month.

Source: Browne (1989)

In the United States cocaine hydrochloride is "cut" (diluted) for street sale by adding sugars (such as lactose, inositol, and mannitol) or talcum powder, borax, or other neutral substances, as well as local anesthetics such as procaine hydrochloride (Novocain) or lidocaine hydrochloride. (Novocain is sometimes mixed with mannitol or lactose and sold as cocaine.) After cutting, cocaine typically has a consumer sale purity of less than 20 percent, although huge increases in the availability of cocaine can result in a level as high as 50 percent and a concomitant increase in the number of emergency room admissions for cocaine overdoses. The substance typically enters the bloodstream by being "snorted" into the nostrils through a straw or rolled paper or from a "coke spoon." Some abusers will take it intravenously, which is the only way to ingest 100 percent of the drug. Because this is a more efficient method, users with limited funds may buy and inject cocaine as a group. In Brazil the result of this practice has been a dramatic increase in the number of AIDS cases (Brooke 1991e). Inhaled, the drug's effects peak in fifteen to twenty minutes and disappear in sixty to ninety minutes. Intravenous use results in an intense feeling of euphoria that crests in three to five minutes and wanes in thirty to forty minutes. (Smoking crack cocaine is discussed below.)

In laboratory tests monkeys pressed a bar as many as 12,800 times for an infusion of 0.5 milligrams of cocaine. "No other drug, including opiates and amphetamine, has been reported to be more potent than cocaine in such tests"

(Geary 1987: 31). Cocaine short-circuits the reward pathways of the brain (Dunwiddie 1988), and in laboratory animals cocaine has usurped other rewards such as food and sex. The ultimate consequence of unlimited access to cocaine is death. Without unlimited access, however, monkeys are able to self-regulate their cocaine use (Siegel 1989).

Would monkeys in the wild succumb to the allure of unlimited amounts of cocaine? Laboratory conditions do not replicate the animals' natural environment, nor are the results of such experiments readily generalizable to humans, who have such species-exclusive traits as a sense of values and a desire for self-control (Peele 1985). Furthermore, noncocaine dopamine (discussed below) agonists are self-administered by and rewarding to animals while they do not produce euphoria in humans (Rothman 1994).

Cocaine causes the body to feel as if there were an impending threat, a response to stimuli that causes the release of stimulating neurotransmitters (dopamine and norepinephrine):

> In essence, the cocaine-stimulated reactions in the body are mimicking a natural physiological stress response; the generalized adrenergic discharge stimulates the energy-producing mechanisms to prepare the CNS and skeletal muscles for "fight" or "flight." The body feels the chemistry of fright, tension and anxiety, but the brain gives the message that everything is better than fine. (Gold et al. 1986: 38)

"At first, cocaine augments the action of naturally occurring chemicals, the neurotransmitters, that carry messages to the various reward or pleasure centers of the brain. Somehow, the brain is manipulated to provide the sought-

Coca leaves being harvested in Bolivia.

after pleasurable sensations until the neurotransmitters are too diminished in numbers to react to the cocaine" (Gold 1984: 5). The substance also acts on the hypothalamus to decrease appetite and reduces the need for sleep by inducing the release of stimulant neurotransmitters.

Precisely how cocaine affects the central nervous system is not clear, and there is no definitive model of cocaine neurobiology (Gold 1984; Nunes and Rosecan 1987). It is known that cocaine binds to specific receptor sites on brain membranes (Hanbauer 1988), and it is theorized that this triggers the release of dopamine and norepinephrine (Weiss and Mirin 1987). These neurotransmitters enhance mood and at high enough doses produce feelings of euphoria by activating the sympathetic nervous system, giving rise to increased heart rate, blood pressure, breathing rate, body temperature, and blood sugar (Washton 1989).

Normally produced dopamine, norepinephrine, and serotonin are reabsorbed by the discharging neurons, but in addition to stimulating their release, cocaine apparently blocks or inhibits this reuptake by preventing a reuptake transporter from performing its usual function.[12] As a result, neurotransmitters continue to bombard their receptor sites. The neurons remain in a state of excitement, the brain is stimulated accordingly, and euphoria increases (Holloway 1991; Sunderwirth 1985). Roy Wise reports that DA is the key to cocaine's euphoric qualities: "Cocaine also blocks noradrenaline and serotonin reuptake, but these actions and cocaine's well-known anesthetic effects appear to contribute little, if anything, to the rewarding effects of cocaine" (1994: 191). As the supply of dopamine depletes, however, depression sets in. And recent research has discovered that cocaine-dependent persons have fewer DA receptors than normal controls, which also helps explain why they feel depressed when not on cocaine (Holloway 1991).

In small doses, cocaine will bring about extreme euphoria and indifference to pain, along with illusions of increased mental and sensory alertness and physical strength:

> A few hundredths of a gram of cocaine hydrochloride, chopped finely and arranged on a smooth surface into several lines, or rows of powder, can be snorted into the nose through a rolled piece of paper in a few seconds. The inhalation shortly gives rise to feelings of elation and a sense of clarity or power of thought, feelings that pass away for most people in about half an hour. (Van Dyke and Byck 1982: 128)

At higher doses, however, the drug has the potential "to produce megalomania and feelings of omnipotence in most individuals" (Gold et al. 1986: 44).

Chemically similar substances such as lidocaine (Xylocaine) and procaine (Novocain)—as dental patients recognize—will eliminate all feeling when applied topically or subcutaneously. Single small doses of procaine, when taken intranasally or smoked, produce the same euphoric response, as

---

12. A strain of mice bred for the absence of the dopamine transporter are impervious to cocaine; they are also highly active, fail to eat, and often die from exhaustion (Grady 1996).

does cocaine in experienced cocaine users. Users cannot distinguish between the two substances, and tests indicate that laboratory animals will work as hard for procaine as they will for cocaine (Van Dyke and Byck 1982). In laboratory tests with animals, however, while procaine served as a reinforcer similar to cocaine, lidocaine did not (Balster 1988). There is evidence that it is the local-anesthetic properties of the "caines" that cause some of their stimulating effects (although this is disputed by Goeders [1988]), particularly the panic attacks reported by cocaine abusers (Post and Weiss 1988).

Crack

Then there is crack, the drug abuser's answer to fast food. Crack users are usually young men and women—according to one study (Frank et al. 1987), crack users in New York are primarily between seventeen and twenty-five years of age. The drug is relatively cheap, five to ten dollars a "rock" (although the per gram price, states Gold [1984], is twice that of cocaine hydrochloride). Despite the relatively low per-dose cost, those hooked on crack report spending between $100 and $200 a day on the substance. The nickname "crack" comes from the crackling sound the drug makes when it is smoked (Gold 1984). Crack is generally sold on the street in small glass vials or small plastic bags.[13]

While cocaine hydrochloride cannot easily be smoked—the melting and vaporization point is very high (195 degrees C)—freeing the alkaloid from the hydrochloride attachment will produce purified crystals of cocaine base that readily vaporize at 98 degrees C. Freebased cocaine can be crushed and smoked in a special glass pipe or sprinkled on a tobacco or marijuana product. Cocaine is converted into crack by cooking it in a mixture of sodium bicarbonate (baking soda) and water, which becomes hard when heat-dried. The soaplike substance is then cut into bars or chips (sometimes called quarter rocks) and smoked. Dennis Watlington (1987: 150), a former crack abuser, states that crack is typically smoked in a glass pipe about five inches long and a quarter-inch in diameter with a metal screen at the top to hold a small clump of the substance. When lit, the substance melts and clings to the screen. Some of it oozes down inside the stem, where it dries and forms a hard residue that can later be scraped off and smoked. "The most satisfying way to smoke crack," he notes, "is to insert this stem into a glass bowl the size of an espresso cup. Through a second pipe inserted into the side of the bowl, the smoker pulls the smoke after it collects in quantity in the bowl."

Because crack is inhaled directly into the lungs, bypassing much of the circulatory system en route to the brain, it takes about five seconds to impact—even faster than intravenous ingestion. When "crack is heated, the drug crosses the blood-brain barrier in only a few seconds, providing a virtually instantaneous 'high' and intense gratification, often described as a 'sexual eu-

---

13. Crack is frequently smoked in "crack houses." For a look at the social organization of crack houses, see Elifson and Elifson (1993).

"Crack can excite sexual desires while inhibiting the ability to achieve orgasm, creating sexual encounters that are prolonged and more conducive to the spread of AIDS" (Drug Enforcement Administration 1994a: 3).

First, the vapors produce a potent rush: "This 'rush' lasts a few seconds, and is replaced by a euphoric excitation that lasts for several minutes. A five- to twenty-minute period of less pleasurable hyperexcitability follows. Then the 'ultimate high' degenerates into the ultimate low" (National Institute on Drug Abuse 1986: 4).

> After smoking crack repeatedly, the user develops an intense craving for more. This craving is often uncontrollable, and the crack user will lie, steal, or even commit acts of violence in order to obtain more of the drug. Although it can take months or even years for a nasal cocaine user to progress from recreational to compulsive use, this can happen within days to weeks with crack. (Rosecan, Spitz, and Gross 1987: 299)

"Because of the large, concentrated doses that reach the brain, seizures are more likely to occur from smoking cocaine than from snorting it, and smoking can lead more easily to respiratory failure and/or cardiac arrest" (Washton 1989: 16).

Interviews with crack users in drug treatment programs revealed the apparent power of this substance (Frank et al. 1987: 12):

> Despite the many years of using other drugs, the experience with Crack was quite different. Most respondents had been in control of their drug use, even those who had been using very heavily. The majority (63 percent) had never needed treatment for their drug use before using Crack. The experience with Crack, however, was very much a jolt, for which these users were not prepared in spite of their past experience. For many it was a very frightening experience. Respondents remembered feelings and behaviors under the influence of Crack that they had never experienced before—the irritability, rage, and aggression. Most of the clients had held jobs and valued the money they earned. Now, in retrospect, the loss of so much spent on Crack was incomprehensible to them.

One review concluded that treatment programs that have shown success in treating other forms of drug abuse have found the crack habit nearly unbreakable (Kolata 1988). And children born to crack-abusing mothers exhibit serious emotional difficulties that may hinder psychological and social development (Blakeslee 1989). This is not necessarily a result of the pharmacology of cocaine but is more likely caused by poor prenatal nutrition and health.

While crack is admittedly a strongly dependence-producing substance, more recent research indicates that it is not an all-powerful drug for which treatment is not effective. In fact, it was discovered that crack is less addictive than nicotine although more addictive than alcohol (Kolata 1989c). A study of seventy-nine crack users in Toronto revealed a "lack of strong evidence to support the view that use of the drug is necessarily compulsive. Over half of the respondents had never or rarely experienced a craving to take crack" (Cheung, Erickson, and Landau 1991: 133).

Other versions of crack may contain any combination of freebase residue, concentrated caffeine, or different amphetamines. It was crack that led to the death of college basketball star Len Bias, twenty-two, and professional football player Don Rogers, twenty-three. The fact that crack is smoked rather than injected has increased its appeal. Indeed, it constitutes the first psychoactive drug experience of many young abusers, who try it even before alcohol and marijuana (Rosecan, Spitz, and Gross 1987). Reports—some would say hysteria—about the power of crack to produce dependence have subsided, and today it is rarely mentioned in the media.

WITHDRAWAL AND TOLERANCE. After frequent and high doses of cocaine, the failure to continue ingestion produces a withdrawal syndrome characterized by psychological depression, irritability, extreme fatigue, and prolonged periods of restless sleep. "Chronic users often find themselves caught in a futile, obsessive chase to recapture the original cocaine 'high,' but as dosages and frequency increase, so does the user's tolerance to the euphoric effects" (Washton, Stone, and Henrickson 1988: 367). Inciardi (1986: 79) states that this syndrome is not necessarily physiological—it may simply be the result of an emotional letdown that results when heavy abusers try to discontinue the drug—they *think* they have a physical need for cocaine. In any event, "Withdrawal in [cocaine-] dependent subjects is not characterized by the obvious physical signs like those observed with opiates or sedative-hypnotics" (Koob et al. 1994: 7). Indeed, "There is no withdrawal syndrome after abruptly stopping cocaine. That is, the body has never developed a need for cocaine to maintain homeostasis" (Washton and Washton 1993: 17).

> The absence of a clear-cut withdrawal syndrome and serious medical risk following abrupt cessation of the drug use obviates the need either for switching the cocaine-dependent patient to a substitute drug or for having to detoxify the patient by means of a gradual withdrawal procedure, as is routinely done in the treatment of heroin addicts and severe alcoholics. (Washton, Stone, and Henrickson 1988: 376)

Strong cravings for the substance and the malaise that follows cessation are possibly brain-mediated behavioral changes that could indicate physical dependence. The elevation in reward thresholds as a result of cocaine use could trigger a withdrawal effect after use is discontinued (Koob et al. 1994). "When the cocaine- or amphetamine-dependent person is not taking one of these drugs, dopamine release will be diminished to levels lower than normal, which could contribute to the anhedonia [inability to enjoy routine pleasures], dysphoria [chronic discontent], and other symptoms of withdrawal that motivate repeated drug taking" (Hyman and Nestler 1996:158). Despite the lack of signs of physical dependence, animals given free access to cocaine will continue to self-administer the drug until death, something they will not do for opiates (Geary 1987). The *Merck Manual* (Berkow 1982: 1427) refers to cocaine as "probably the best example of a drug to which neither tolerance nor physical dependence develops, but to which psychic dependence develops that can lead to addiction."

Tolerance, the homeostatic process by which the brain adjusts to the effects of a drug, means that ingesting the same amount will not produce the desired state of arousal. Inciardi (1986) states that the body does not develop any significant tolerance to cocaine, while Robert O'Brien and Sidney Cohen (1984: 65) argue "that the same dose frequently repeated will not produce similar symptoms over a period of time," and for that reason many cocaine abusers find a need to frequently increase the dosage. In an update of their 1976 book, Lester Grinspoon and James Bakalar (1985: 277) state that "contrary to what we and most other researchers once believed, it has now become clear that tolerance to cocaine can arise." Other researchers have reported that tolerance to the euphoric effects occurs with repeated administration (Zahniser et al. 1988), causing the abuser to increase the dosage. And "in face of dose escalation, one might eventually achieve blood levels of cocaine high enough to induce toxic local anesthetic effects" that include panic attacks and the risk of seizures (Post and Weiss 1988: 232). Other researchers report the development of tolerance under certain conditions and note that the "biological basis underlying sensitization or tolerance to cocaine is not yet fully understood" (Izenwasser and Unterwald 1994: 72). Roger Weiss and Steven Mirin report, however, a form of reverse tolerance: "Long-term users may experience more excitatory effects from the same, or even smaller, doses of the drug," a phenomenon referred to as *kindling* (1987: 48).

MEDICAL USE. In addition to its anesthetizing qualities, cocaine constricts blood vessels when applied topically. It is the only local anesthetic that has this effect, and cocaine was the anesthetic of choice for eye surgery because of this ability to limit the flow of blood. However, it was discovered that the reduced flow could damage the surface of the eye, so cocaine is no longer recommended for use in ophthalmology. It continues to be used in surgery of the mucous membranes of the ear, nose, and throat and for procedures that require passing a tube through the nose or throat (Van Dyke and Byck 1982) in about 200,000 operations a year (White 1989).

DANGERS OF COCAINE USE. In "very small and occasional doses," argues James Inciardi, "cocaine is no more harmful than equally moderate doses of alcohol or marijuana" (1986: 79). One research effort found that "experimental use of cocaine during adolescence has benign consequences over a one-year period," although the researchers could not deny the possibility of long-term negative consequences (Newcomb and Bentler 1986: 273). Large doses of cocaine, however, intensify each of the drug's reactions and can sometimes cause irrational behavior. In heavy abusers the euphoria is often accompanied by intensified heartbeat, sweating, dilation of pupils, and a rise in body temperature. After the initial euphoria, depression, irritability, insomnia, and, in more serious instances, paranoia may result. Extreme reactions, such as delirium, hallucinations, muscle spasms, and chest pain, may appear. Chronic users can also suffer from "cocaine bugs" (*formication*), a sensation similar to that of bugs crawling under the skin. In extreme cases, the sensation may become so great that the user will cut open his or her skin to get at "them." Less extreme reactions cause the user to scratch and pick at the "bugs," causing sores. "It is not clear why some cocaine users succumb to chronic abuse and psychosis when most do not" (Grinspoon and Bakalar 1976: 143).

Cocaine causes blood vessels to constrict and increases heart rate and blood pressure. As a result, the heart requires more oxygen-rich blood to nourish its muscle cells. In persons whose coronary arteries are narrowed by atherosclerosis, reactions can range from mild angina to a fatal heart attack. Even in persons with normal coronary arteries, the ingesting of cocaine has resulted in angina and heart attacks, believed to result from spasms reduce or shut off the flow of the oxygenated blood that nourishes the heart. There is also some evidence that cocaine can painlessly and permanently damage heart muscles. It cannot be determined with certainty if these reactions are caused by cocaine itself or by the mixing of street-sale cocaine with less expensive drugs such as amphetamine (Altman 1988). Cocaine use by pregnant women has been linked to various abnormalities in their infants because the substance reduces the supply of blood and oxygen to the fetus. (For a discussion of this issue, see Mayes 1992; Woods 1993.) Preschool children of crack cocaine-using mothers do not appear to suffer any language or cognitive development problems. However, in one controlled study they exhibited higher rates of emotional and behavioral problems than children from similar backgrounds whose mothers did not use cocaine. It was not determined if this is a function of the drug or the postnatal environment (Hawley et al. 1995).

Snorting cocaine will cause a runny nose and eczema around the nostrils, and gradual deterioration of the nasal cartilage can cause the nose to collapse. Injection of the drug quickly produces a powerful rush and may also cause abscesses on the skin. This form of ingestion "produces the more debilitating effects of psychoses and paranoid delusions" (Inciardi 1986: 81) and is also more likely than other forms of ingestion to have fatal results.

Although cocaine has the reputation of being an aphrodisiac, heavy use may cause male abusers to become impotent or incapable of ejaculation, and females can experience difficulty in reaching an orgasm. Freebasing and intravenous use increase sexual desire but not performance. In fact, cocaine may produce spontaneous ejaculation without sexual activity and can replace the sex partner of either gender (Gold et al. 1986).[14] Arnold and Nanette Washton (1993) report that cocaine produced hypersexuality and sexual compulsivity in

---

14. Cocaine has anesthetic properties, however, and is sometimes applied directly to the head of the penis or to the clitoris to anesthetize the tissues, prolonging intercourse by retarding orgasm.

COCAINE FOR RECREATIONAL USE

The justification for outlawing cocaine was mainly the supposed psychological and physiological consequences of prolonged use. But the law does not distinguish, as we must, between moderate and excessive doses. The more spectacular consequences of cocaine abuse are not typical of the drug's effects as it is normally used any more than the phenomena associated with alcoholism are typical of the ordinary consumption of that drug. (Grinspoon and Bakalar [1976: 119])

Our findings do not indicate that occasional cocaine use inevitably leads to severe drug dependency and major dysfunction. However, it also cannot be concluded that occasional or so-called "recreational cocaine" use is safe or harmless. (Gold et al. 1986: 49)

their patients, and "sexual feelings and fantasies often trigger powerful urges and cravings for cocaine."

In more recent years, versions of the drug other than cocaine hydrochloride have become popular among certain abusers in the United States. Coca paste, which is typically smoked with either tobacco or marijuana products, is used extensively in cocaine-processing countries. Because it requires less processing than cocaine, coca paste—called *bazuco* —is popular among low-income groups in these countries and has become a major abuse problem in Colombia (Riding 1986). In the latter part of the 1980s the substance made its way into the United States, where it became known as "bubble gum" to young abusers because of the phonetic association of *bazuco* with Bazooka bubble gum. The substance usually results from an error in the water/sulfuric acid ratio. The paste has at least traces of a host of dangerous chemicals used in its production, including kerosene, sulfuric acid, leaded gasoline, and potassium permanganate, which can cause irreversible damage to liver, lungs, and brain. Some intravenous abusers combine cocaine with heroin—a practice known as "speedballing." This was the combination that led to the death of comedian John Belushi in 1982. And many cocaine users appear to use heroin to soften and prolong the impact of cocaine (Treaster 1990g).

Amphetamines

"Among the commonly used psychoactive drugs," note Grinspoon and Peter Hedblom (1975: 258), "the amphetamines have one of the most formidable potentials for psychological, physical, and social harm." Unlike cocaine, amphetamines are products of the laboratory—synthetic drugs. Although their chemical structures are distinctly different (Snyder 1986) and amphetamine has no anesthetic properties, the effects of cocaine and amphetamines are similar. In fact, experienced intravenous cocaine users frequently identified amphetamine incorrectly as cocaine. In animal studies, cocaine and ampheta-mines often substitute for one another and have similar reinforcing patterns of self-administration (Balster 1988).

Amphetamine stimulates by triggering the release of dopamine, sero-tonin, and norepinephrine while inhibiting the reuptake of these cate-cholamines. Although some of the effects of amphetamine involve norapinephrine and serotonin mechanisms, dopamine appears to play a partic-ularly prominent role (Selden et al. 1993). Thus, like cocaine, amphetamine mimics naturally occurring substances and causes a biochemical arousal—a "turn on"—without the presence of sensory input requiring such arousal. The body becomes physiologically activated, but it is a "false alarm." Grinspoon and Hedblom (1975: 62) report that the "amphetamine user almost always considers the excitation of the central nervous system it produces a pleasant experience, at least at the beginning, and often he has a feeling of increased ef-ficiency, perseverance, endurance, and overall competence." Because reuptake of dopamine and serotonin is also blocked by amphetamine, there is a deple-tion of the neurotransmitters, which is believed responsible for the "crash" that results after the ingestion of high doses of amphetamine. (This reaction may be exacerbated by the fatigue associated with amphetamine overactivity and an unhealthy diet.)

First synthesized in 1887, amphetamine was introduced into clinical use in the 1930s (Smith 1979) and was eventually offered as a "cure-all" for just about every ailment. Between 1932 and 1946 there were thirty-nine generally accepted medical uses for amphetamine, including the treatment of schizo-phrenia, morphine addiction, low blood pressure, and caffeine and tobacco de-pendence. It was believed that the substance had no abuse potential ("Drug Abuse" 1987). Because amphetamines appear to act on the hypothalamus to suppress the appetite—although other CNS or metabolic effects may be in-volved—at one time they were widely prescribed to treat obesity. As opposed to more natural forms of dieting, however, the appetite returns with greater in-tensity after withdrawal from the drug, and it is only as a last resort that methamphetamine hydrochloride (Desoxyn) is used to treat obesity as one component of a weigh-reduction regimen. Even then the treatment is limited to only a few weeks.

As it became known that most of the benefits from treating many ail-ments with amphetamine were due to the drug's ability to elevate mood, med-ically accepted uses declined. Besides obesity, there are only two such uses in the United States: for treating narcolepsy, a rare sleeping disorder, and certain types of hyperactivity—hyperkinetic syndrome—in children with minimal brain damage or adolescent Attention Deficit Disorder (ADD), when other remedies have proven insufficient. "Amphetamine treatment of hyperkinesis," notes David Smith (1979: xx), "is not intended for use in children whose hy-peractivity is due to environmental factors or primary psychiatric disorders." Interestingly, tolerance does not develop in ADD children, and they pose no exceptional risk for drug abuse problems in later life ("Drug Abuse" 1987).

Legally produced amphetamine is taken in the form of tablets or capsules, while some abusers will crush the substance, dissolve it in water, and ingest it intravenously. There are three basic types of amphetamine, with the methyl-amphetamines having the greatest potential for abuse because they are fast-acting and produce a rush. Methamphetamine hydrochloride, which is from the methyl group, is a widely abused drug known on the street as "meth," "crank," "speed," or "ice."

Methamphetamine is usually available in powdered ("crystal meth") form and can be injected, snorted, or smoked, producing a two- to four-hour high. Ice, which is chemically the same as crystal meth but has a different structure, is a crystalline form of methamphetamine that is 90 to 100 percent pure. It is like rock salt in size and appearance, and produces a high reputed to last from seven to twenty-four hours. Because of its purity, ice exaggerates all of the effects of methamphetamine. Overdoses are more common with ice because it is difficult for smokers to control the amount of smoke being inhaled. Unlike crystal meth, which is produced domestically, ice usually originates in Asia, where it is manufactured by crime groups organized along ethnic lines. The substance could easily substitute for crack. A significant increase in illegal methamphetamine use is being experienced in California and the Southwest where the drug is cheaper than cocaine (Wren 1996).

As with cocaine, in small doses amphetamine will cause a rush, as well as illusions of increased mental and sensory alertness and physical strength and indifference to pain. Grinspoon and Hedblom (1975: 95) conclude:

> It appears that amphetamine can improve performance, mainly on simple and tedious tasks, by masking fatigue and increasing interest and confidence. It may increase the endurance of the athlete and enhance his performance in the short run, at the possible cost of overstraining his physical capacities. It does not help with more complicated intellectual work and may even make it more difficult by inducing anxiety, restlessness, or overestimation of one's capacities.

DANGERS OF AMPHETAMINE USE. Taken episodically and in low doses amphetamine can enhance sexual drive and performance; used habitually at high doses it may impair sexual functioning and in some abusers provide a substitute for sex (D. Smith 1979). Grinspoon and Hedblom (1975: 103) state that while some people experience improved sexual performance, which may be an important reason for its popularity, "Amphetamines are particularly dangerous in the hands of persons whose sexuality is abnormal or overtly perverse" because they appear to obliterate conventional restraints. The heightened feelings of energy, combined with a significant lowering of social restraints on unconventional or aggressive behavior, can, in some persons and/or in some situations, lead to extremely violent behavior:

> Under the influence of speed even the most normally lethargic person *must* do something, even if it is as boring and repetitive as stringing beads for hours. When such a deep and insistent need to do *something* is thought to be disapproved or blocked, the speed abuser may attack the perceived thwarter with murderous rage. (Grinspoon and Hedblom 1975: 204)

Unlike cocaine, tolerance develops to the stimulant effects of amphetamine, even with moderate use under medical auspices, and increased dosage can bring about toxic effects that include hallucinations, delusions, paranoia, and violent behavior. Herbert Meltzer (1979: 156) notes that "normal volunteers screened to exclude any subjects with schizophrenic symptoms will become psychotic within one day if given repeated doses of amphetamine totaling several hundred milligrams." Symptoms of psychosis at an abated level can persist for some time after the drug is discontinued (Institute for the Study of Drug Dependence 1987). Rhesus monkeys provided unlimited access to amphetamine will continually ingest the substance day and night, going almost completely without water, food, or sleep for six to eight days, until they collapse into exhausted sleep for two days. Upon waking they show an immediate interest in food and water. They then begin another week-long binge of amphetamine. When access to the drug is discontinued for a few weeks and the monkeys are returned to their cages, they will push the (now nonoperative) buttons for amphetamine an average of 4,000 times, indicating that a significant level of craving exists even in the absence of physiological dependence. When the substance is heroin, the monkeys will press the nonoperative buttons an average of 2,000 times, indicating that the craving for amphetamine is higher than that for heroin. Thus, "Amphetamines are much more likely to produce damaging drug dependence than opiates" (Grinspoon and Hedblom 1975: 178).

Interestingly, tolerance is not accompanied by a significant level of physical dependence, "and the withdrawal syndrome, if one exists, is not severe" (Berkow 1982: 1428). Withdrawal from amphetamines is less abrupt than for opiates because the drug stays in the system for considerably longer periods of time, and withdrawal symptoms are usually milder than for barbiturates (Grinspoon and Hedblom 1975). Withdrawal from high dosage over a prolonged period, however, results in extreme fatigue and lowered mood states, "sometimes with the intensity of severe depressions" during which the user is a suicide risk (Meltzer 1979: 155). John Morgan (1979) concludes that, as is the case with cocaine, even in the absence of physical dependence, chronic amphetamine habituation can lead to an overwhelming life involvement with the drug. Heavy dosage is also debilitating because it results in a lack of food intake and sleep: "Subjects who have self-administered large doses of amphetamines intravenously have been reported to go without sleep for 6 days" (Meltzer 1979: 155). Further, heavy dosage raises the blood pressure, which can lead to damaged blood vessels and heart failure. Although amphetamine may impair the ability to operate a motor vehicle, the substance is often abused by truck drivers to keep them awake during long hauls.

With $500 worth of chemicals and laboratory glassware and a rudimentary knowledge of chemistry, an outlaw chemist can easily produce a pound of meth or crack worth $20–30,000. As a result, hundreds of clandestine laboratories have sprouted up in remote regions throughout the United States. The main ingredient in methamphetamine—phenylacetic acid—produces a fetid, sickly sweet odor that can easily tip off law enforcement officials, which is

---

MORE DRUG-RELATED DEATHS

The children, ages one, two, and three, died screaming in the fire that critically burned their mother. The thirty-nine-year old woman and her children were victims of a fire caused by the explosion of the methamphetamine lab in their mobile home (parked on a California desert about sixty miles north of San Diego) ("Fire in Suspected Drug Factory Kills 3 Children" 1995).

why it is produced in rural areas. Outlaw chemists usually mix phenylacetic acid and acetic anhydride in a triple-necked flask with several other chemicals—a potentially explosive mix. It is then cooked for several hours, producing phenyl-2-propanone (P2P), which is distilled in order to purify the P2P from by-products. Mercuric chloride, a catalyst deadly to the touch, and other chemicals are used to turn P2P into methamphetamine. The mixture is cooked again for twelve hours and allowed to cool. The resulting oil is reduced to powder by using bleach or ether. The final product is a coarse crystal—the whiter the purer. Some chemists die as a result of the toxic fumes produced or from explosions that can easily be ignited by a tiny spark or even the flip of a light switch. Illegal methamphetamine production also poses a serious environmental problem, because outlaws dump the chemical wastes into local streams or lakes or bury it in ditches. Methamphetamine labs are so contaminated that they pose a risk to law enforcement officers who seize them (Weingarten 1989). The substance can also be easily synthesized using ephedrine, an ingredient common in over-the-counter cold remedies.

Hallucinogens

According to Erich Goode (1972) the term *hallucinogen* implies something undesirable and suggests being "crazy." Supporters of the use of such chemicals prefer the term *psychedelic,* which to Goode conveys a pro-drug bias. "A hallucinogen is a drug that changes a person's state of awareness by modifying sensory inputs, loosening cognitive and creative restraints, and providing access to material normally hidden in memory or material of an unconscious nature" (Jacob and Shulgin 1994: 74).

Hallucinogenic substances occur both naturally and synthetically. They excite the CNS, actually overwhelming its ability to modulate sensory input. Autonomic hyperactivity results in distortions of the perception of objective reality. These include:

1. *Depersonalization:* "Out-of-body" experiences or misperceptions of reality.

2. *Sensisthesia:* "Seeing" sound and "hearing" visual input.
3. *Hallucinations:* Perceiving sounds, odors, tactile sensations, or visual images that arise from within the person.

The sensory illusions produced by hallucinogens are often accompanied by mood alterations that are usually euphoric but sometimes severely depressive (*Drugs of Abuse* 1989) and that mimic severe mental illness ("Drug Abuse" 1987). There is marked impairment of judgment, which can lead to poor decision making and serious accidents (Berkow 1982). A number of hallucinogens produce cross-tolerance. Unlike depressants and stimulants, hallucinogens do not function as reinforcers in animals (Winter 1994). Hallucinogens apparently have their own receptors (5-HT$_2$) in the CNS (Lin and Glennon 1994).

Lysergic Acid Diethylamide (LSD)

LSD was synthesized in 1938. The first LSD "trip" was recorded by its discoverer, Albert Hofmann, a research chemist in Basel, Switzerland. In 1943 Hofmann accidentally ingested a minute quantity of the drug through the skin of his fingers (Grinspoon 1979). Hofmann relates:

> I had to leave my work in the laboratory and go home because I felt strangely restless and dizzy. Once there, I lay down and sank into a not unpleasant delirium which was marked by an extreme degree of fantasy. [While I was] in sort of a trance with closed eyes . . . fantastic visions of extraordinary vividness accompanied by a kaleidoscopic play of intense coloration continuously swirled around me. After two hours this condition subsided. (Quoted in Goode 1972: 98–99)

Three days later Hofmann experimented by swallowing 250 micrograms of LSD, not realizing that this was an extremely high dose; he soon became terrified, fearing that he would lose his mind or perhaps die (Grinspoon 1979).

LSD is produced from lysergic acid, a substance derived from the ergot fungus, which grows on wild rye or other grasses, or from lysergic acid amide, a chemical found in morning glory seeds. "Bread made from rye infected with the fungus causes a disease known as ergotism with hallucinatory as well as physiological symptoms" (Grinspoon 1979: 11). Although theoretically possible, manufacture of LSD from morning glory seeds is not economically feasible. Lysergic acid is a highly controlled chemical in the United States, and its precursor, ergotamine tartrate, is not readily available in this country. "Therefore, ergotamine tartrate used in clandestine LSD laboratories is believed to be acquired from sources abroad," and the difficulty in acquiring the chemical limits the number of independent manufacturers (Drug Enforcement Administration 1995b: 4). In 1949 LSD was introduced into the United States as an experimental drug for treating psychiatric illnesses, but until 1954 it remained relatively rare and expensive because the ergot fungus was difficult to culti-vate. That year the Eli Lily Company announced that it had succeeded in cre-ating a totally synthetic version of LSD (Stevens 1987).

Just how LSD works is not completely understood. "The molecular structure of LSD is similar to that of the neurotransmitter serotonin. LSD therefore has a high affinity for serotonin receptors and interferes with the normal functioning of these receptors" (Henderson 1994: 42). Stimulation of serotonin receptors by agonists such as LSD and the hallucinogen psilo-cybin inhibits the activity of a mechanism (a neural system called the *raphe*) that modulates sensory input into the brain stem. This mechanism would normally integrate sensory inflow and the emotional and ideational state of the organism and suppress irrelevant information. Serotonin ago-nists occupy serotonin receptor sites in the brain and thereby cause a backup of serotonin that exceeds the ability of MAO to control. Serotonin overloads the sensory input systems of the CNS so that normal stimuli take on distorted images—the size of the signal delivered to the cerebral cortex is greatly enlarged. This combination—inhibition of control mechanisms and increasing signal size—overload the brain (Ray 1978). The result is ac-tually a serotonin, rather than an LSD, trip and consists of intoxication for several hours (Palfai and Jankiewicz 1991).

We now know that effects of LSD range from blurred vision to a visual field filled with strange objects. Three-dimensional space appears to contract and enlarge, and light appears to fluctuate in intensity. Auditory effects also occur but to a lesser degree. All of these changes are episodic. Temperature sensitivity is altered, with the environment being perceived as abnormally cold or hot. Body images are altered—out-of-body-experiences—and body parts appear to float. Time is sometimes perceived as running fast forward or back-ward. "Perceptually," notes Grinspoon (1979: 12), "LSD produces an espe-cially brilliant and intense impact of sensory stimuli on consciousness. Normally unnoticed aspects of the environment capture the attention: ordinary objects are seen as if for the first time and with a sense of fascination or en-trancement, as though they had unimagined depths of significance."

There is apparently selective recall of some aspects of the LSD experi-ence: "During the period of drug activity the subject may report that he feels less friendly, more aggressive or agitated, or depressed. Much later, he will re-call the experience as illuminating and pleasurable. He will rarely recall psy-chotic symptoms" (Meltzer 1979: 162).

There are "good acid trips" and "bad acid trips." They appear to be con-trolled by the attitude, mood, and expectations of the user and often depend on suggestions of those around him or her at the time of the trip. Favorable ex-pectations produce good trips, while excessive apprehension is likely to pro-duce the opposite. Because the substance appears to intensify feelings, the user may feel a magnified sense of love, lust, and joy, or anger, terror, and despair: "The extraordinary sensations and feelings may bring on fear of losing con-trol, paranoia, and panic, or they may cause euphoria and even bliss" (Grin-spoon 1979: 13). According to James MacDonald and Michael Agar (1994:

A BAD TRIP

A bad trip is an acute anxiety or panic reaction following the ingestion of LSD. On a bad trip, painful or frightening feelings are intensified, just as pleasurable sensations are on a good trip. Distortion of the sense of time may cause this experience to seem almost unbearably long. The person may feel that he or she has lost control of the drug and that the trip will never end; he or she may exhibit paranoia or attempt to flee. A bad trip is an acute reaction to LSD, however, and dissipates as the effects of the drug wear off. (Henderson 1994b: 58)

12), a good trip, when everything is touched by magic but the user remains aware that reality will return when the drug wears off, turns into a bad trip when he or she "loses sight of this fact [that reality will return] for too long." The bad trip is the result of a failure to comprehend that reality has not changed, merely its perception while under the influence of LSD.

Ingesting LSD unknowingly can result in a highly traumatic experience, as the victim may feel that he or she has suddenly "gone crazy" (Brecher 1972). It only takes .01 milligram to have an effect. For those who knowingly ingest LSD, at this dose mild euphoria and a loosening of inhibitions usually occur (Grinspoon 1979). It should be noted that illegally produced LSD, like other similarly produced drugs, may contain any variety of additives, including amphetamines. Thus, laboratory studies utilizing laboratory produced (pure) drugs may not duplicate the experiences of many street users. Further, methamphetamine appears to increase the likelihood of a bad trip (Ray 1978). The physiological effects of LSD are as varied as the psychological and include dilation of the pupils (almost always); increased heart rate, blood pressure, and body temperature; mild dizziness or nausea; chills; trembling; slow, deep breathing; loss of appetite; and insomnia (Grinspoon 1979).

LSD is an odorless and tasteless white powder. It is relatively easy to produce; one ounce contains about 300,000 human doses (Ray 1978). Although LSD has been used experimentally to treat a variety of psychological illnesses, it currently has no accepted medical use. It may be taken orally or mixed with any number of substances or absorbed on paper ("blotter acid"), sugar, or gelatin sheets ("window panes"). A trip begins between thirty and sixty minutes after ingestion, peaks after two to six hours, and fades out after about twelve hours. There are no known physical dangers to long-term use, although psychosis has been reported in a few instances. A small number of users report recurring low-intensity trips—"flashbacks"—without ingesting the substance. Tolerance develops rapidly, with repeated doses becoming completely ineffective after a few days of continuous use, and there is cross-tolerance to other hallucinogens. LSD is not addicting—there are no physical withdrawal symptoms (ISDD 1987).

Phencyclidine (PCP)

Phencyclidine is reported to have received the name PCP—"peace pill"—on the streets of San Francisco, where the drug was reputed to give illusions of everlasting peace. Frequently referred to as "angel dust," PCP was first synthesized in 1956 and found to be an effective surgical anesthetic when tested on monkeys. As a *dissociative anesthetic,* it induces a lack of responsive awareness of both pain and the general environment without a corresponding depression of the autonomic nervous system (Dotson, Ackerman, and West 1995). Experiments on humans were carried out in 1957, and while PCP proved to work as an anesthetic, it had serious side effects. Some patients manifested agitation, excitement, and disorientation during the recovery period. Some male surgical patients became violent, while some females appeared to experience simple intoxication (Linder, Lerner, and Burns 1981). "When PCP was subsequently given to normal volunteers in smaller doses, it induced a psychotic-like state resembling schizophrenia. Volunteers experienced body image changes, depersonalization, and feelings of loneliness, isolation, and dependency. Their thinking was observed to become progressively disorganized" (Lerner 1980: 14).

PCP use does not seem to result in any significant tolerance or withdrawal symptoms ("Drug Abuse" 1991). "Generally, 24–48 hours are required until the person again feels completely normal" (Lerner 1980: 16). There is evidence of PCP receptors in the brain, suggesting that an "important relationship exists between the chemical structure of the 'phencyclidines' and receptors in the CNS related to neurotransmitters" (Burns and Done 1980: 100). Exactly how PCP acts upon the body, however, is not completely known, although it appears that the release of dopamine is a critical piece of the puzzle (French, Levenson, and Ceci 1990).

There are more than 100 variations (analogs) of the substance. As opposed to other anesthetics, PCP increases respiration, heart rate, and blood pressure, qualities that make it useful for patients endangered by a depressed heart rate or low blood pressure. In the 1960s PCP became commercially available for use in veterinary medicine as an analgesic and anesthetic, but diversion to street use led the manufacturer to discontinue production in 1978. It is now produced easily and cheaply in clandestine laboratories in tablet, capsule, powder, and liquid form and is sometimes sold as LSD. Its color varies, and there is no such item as a standard dose. Like any drug sold on the street, PCP is often mixed with other psychoactive substances. Most commonly, PCP is applied to a leafy vegetable, including marijuana, and smoked. "Street preparations of phencyclidine have continuously changed in name, physical form and purity" (Lerner 1980: 15). PCP is typically made by mixing ingredients in three buckets for several hours. This is often accomplished in the back of a moving van to disperse the fumes produced. The ingredients must be poured from one bucket to the other, leading to the term "bucket chemists."

DANGERS OF PCP USE. Within thirty to sixty minutes of ingesting a moderate amount of PCP, the user experiences a sense of detachment, distance, and estrangement from his or her surroundings. There is also numbness, slurred speech, and a loss of coordination. These symptoms, which last up to five hours, are often accompanied by feelings of invulnerability. "A blank stare, rapid and involuntary eye movements, and an exaggerated gait are among the more common observable effects" (*Drugs of Abuse* 1989: 50). Under laboratory conditions, a subject may experience feelings of "flying with angels" and "peace and tranquility" (Siegel 1989: 220). At the other extreme, there may be mood disorders, acute anxiety, paranoia, and violent behavior. Some reactions are similar to LSD intoxication: auditory hallucinations, image distortion—fun-house mirror images. "PCP is unique among popular drugs of abuse in its power to produce psychoses indistinguishable from schizophrenia" (*Drugs of Abuse* 1989: 50). As a result, "The phencyclidine-intoxicated patient is often improperly diagnosed and treated by well-meaning uninformed personnel" (Lerner 1980: 13). PCP-intoxicated persons can present severe management problems to treatment staff and law enforcement personnel.

Ketamine

Ketamine is an associative anesthetic that is similar to PCP but produces less confusion, irrationality, and violence. Developed in the 1960s, ketamine is used as a surgical anesthetic for children who are typically able to avoid unpleasant reactions, battlefield injuries in which rapid onset is critical, and repeated procedures such as chemotherapy and treatment of burns. Street users often refer to the drug as "K" or "special K." It is sold in powder, capsule, tablet, solutions, and some injectable forms. Its illegal use is associated with "acid house" music, which also makes references to other hallucinogens such as LSD and MDMA (discussed below). However, less is known about the extent of its abuse and dangers, although habituation can result in significant mental and emotional problems (Dotson, Ackerman, and West 1995).

Mushrooms and Cactus

In addition to the synthetic hallucinogens, some natural substances produce similar effects. Mescaline is the primary hallucinogenic ingredient of the fleshy part, or buttons, of the peyote cactus. It has been used by Indians in Northern Mexico as part of their religious rites since prehistoric times. The Native American church continues to use the cactus as part of religious ceremonies, having been exempted from certain provisions of the federal Controlled Substances Act. Twenty-three states also exempt the sacramental use of peyote from criminal penalties.[15] Peyote is usually ground into a powder and taken orally, although mescaline can also be produced synthetically. A typical

---

15. In 1990 the Supreme Court, in an Oregon case, ruled six to three that states can prohibit the use of peyote by members of the American Indian church, the First Amendment notwithstanding (Greenhouse 1990). In the wake of the Court decision, Congress enacted a statute providing a defense for people who use the substance "with good faith practice of a religious belief."

dose of 350 to 500 mg. produces illusions and hallucinations lasting anywhere from five to twelve hours (*Drugs of Abuse* 1989).

Psilocybe mushrooms have also been used for centuries in Native American religious ceremonies. The "sacred" or "magic mushroom" is typically eaten. Its active ingredients—psilocybin and psilocyn—are chemically similar to LSD and can be produced synthetically. Like mescaline and LSD, they affect perceptions and mood (*Drugs of Abuse* 1989), and users cannot distinguish between psilocybin and LSD.

Some other hallucinogens are dimethyltryptamine (DMT), which occurs naturally in many plants and is used by Caribbean and Latin American Indians, and Ololiuqui, the seeds of the morning glory plant, which are used by Indian priests in Latin America to produce delirium. Another hallucinogen is the magic mushroom of *Alice in Wonderland,* the *Amanita muscaria* of Russia and Scandinavia, where it was reputedly used by Vikings to increase their ferocity in battle (Ray 1978; although Blum 1969 disputes this).

Cannabis

Marijuana does not fit easily into any of the categories we have already discussed, so we will consider it separately. Its scientific name, *cannabis sativia,* Latin for "cultivated hemp," was given to it by the Swedish scientist Linnaeus, which accounts for the *L.* sometimes added to the term. The plant grows wild throughout most of the tropical and temperate regions of the world, including parts of the United States. It has been cultivated for the tough fiber of its stem. Its seed is used in feed mixtures and its oil in paint. The psychoactive part of the plant is an isomer of tetrahydrocannabinol (Delta9THC—hereafter THC), which is most highly concentrated in the leaves and resinous flowering tops.

The THC level of marijuana cigarettes varies considerably: Domestic marijuana has typically had less than 0.5 percent, although more recent plants have considerably higher levels. Indeed, the domestic cultivation of marijuana has spawned a significant market in horticultural equipment, suppliers of which advertise in *High Times,* a magazine devoted to marijuana use. Much of the cultivation in the United States is accomplished indoors:

> Care for these plants involves little more than watering during dry periods, light fertilizing, and weeding. The plants may grow to between sixteen and twenty feet tall. At harvest time these plants are cut at the base and hung upside down to dry so that they will not mold when packaged. The grower will sell both the leaves and any flowering tops, yielding as much as three pounds of marijuana per harvested plant. (Weisheit 1989: 7)

The plant grows best under the same conditions that favor corn. THC in Jamaican, Colombian, and Mexican marijuana ranges from 0.5 to 4 percent; and the most select product, sinsemilla (from the Spanish *sin semilla,* "without seed"), has been found to have as much as 8 percent. Male plants are killed so that the female plant, in seeking to trap pollen, produces more and more of the sticky resin that covers the buds. These buds grow as large as a man's arm from the fingertips to the elbow. Growers concentrate on sinsemilla, selling these flowering tops; indeed, nowadays the leaves of the cannabis plant—"shake"—are typically discarded. Indoor cultivation has been aided by miniaturization—"marijuana bonsai"—of plants with an abundance of THC-rich buds (Pollan 1995).

Hashish, usually from the Middle East, contains the drug-rich resinous secretions of the cannabis plant, which are collected, dried, and then compressed into a variety of forms—balls, cakes, or cookielike sheets. It has a potency as high as 10 percent. Hashish is usually mixed with tobacco and smoked in a pipe. Hashish oil—a misnomer—is the result of repeated extractions of cannabis plant materials to yield a dark, viscous liquid with a THC level as high as 20 percent. A drop or two on a cigarette has the effect of a single marijuana cigarette. Marijuana prepared for street sale may be diluted with oregano, catnip, or other ingredients and may also contain psychoactive substances such as LSD; marijuana from Vietnam often contained opium. In the United States marijuana is usually rolled in paper or inserted into a hollowed-out cigar ("blunting") and smoked, the user typically inhaling the smoke

Marijuana growers at work trimming leaves and flowers in a field drying shed. Note the plants hanging in the background.

deeply and holding it in the lungs for as long as possible. This tends to maximize the absorption of THC, about one-half of which is lost during smoking.

Exactly how marijuana affects the central nervous system is not entirely known. In 1990 researchers discovered cannabinoid receptors discretely located throughout the brain. These brain receptors are stimulated by the drug, indicating that there may be a naturally occurring THC neurotransmitter similar to the endorphins discussed earlier (Hilts 1990; Martin et al. 1994). THC appears to act as a dopamine agonist while also having an opiatelike effect on the brain's receptor system (Gold 1994). The psychoactive reaction occurs in one to ten minutes and peaks in about ten to thirty minutes, with a total duration of about three to four hours.

The most important variables with respect to the drug's impact are the individual's experiences and expectations and the strength of the marijuana. Thus, the first-time user may not experience any significant reaction. In general, low doses tend to induce restlessness, an increasing sense of well-being, and gregariousness, followed by a dreamy state of relaxation and frequently hunger, especially for sweets. Higher doses may induce changes in sensory perception resulting in a more vivid sense of smell, sight, hearing, and taste, which may be accompanied by subtle alterations in thought formation and expression. Cannabis preparations can also be eaten or drunk in mixtures of resin and water or milk, a form known in India as *bhang*.

Although the substance has some use in medicine—for example, to relieve the pressure on the eyes of glaucoma patients, to control the nausea and vomiting that accompany cancer chemotherapy, and to control the muscle spasms of multiple sclerosis patients—its use remains illegal. Since 1982, however, there has been a legally available pharmaceutical for ophthalmology and cancer treatment—Marinol (dronabinol), which is 98.8 percent pure THC. There is some dispute as to whether or not oral THC is as effective as smoking marijuana (see, for example, Grinspoon 1987 and a response from Jourbert 1987; also in opposition to smoking marijuana, see Nahas and Pace 1993). In 1989 an administrative law judge for the Drug Enforcement Administration recommended that marijuana be placed on a less restricted schedule, one that would make it available by medical prescription. The judge called marijuana "one of the safest therapeutically active substances known to man." The DEA rejected the judge's recommendation ("U.S. Resists Easing Curb on Marijuana" 1989).

Dangers of Marijuana Use

The negative short-term effects of marijuana seem quite limited: loss of inhibition, some users also experiencing a loss of self-confidence, aggressiveness, and even auditory hallucinations. High doses may affect short-term memory and reaction time and cause a significant increase in heart rate that is, however, no more dangerous than for those using caffeine and nicotine. Casual use results in the same impairments that one would expect from equal amounts of alcohol (Abel 1978). The long-range effects are more controversial, some claiming no significant physical or psychological damage and others finding the opposite.

ANALOGS AND DESIGNER DRUGS

There are many chemical variations, or analogs, of the drugs discussed in this chapter. These include semisynthetic opiates such as hydromorphine, oxycodone, etorphine, and diprenorphine and synthetic opiates such as pethidine, methadone, and propoxyphene (Darvon). The synthetic drug fentanyl citrate, which is often used intravenously in major surgery, works exactly like the opiates: It kills pain and produces euphoria and, if abused, leads to addiction. The substance is easily produced by persons skilled in chemistry. Fentanyl compounds are often sold as "China White," the street name for the finest Southeast Asian heroin, to addicts who cannot tell the difference. Those who know the difference may actually prefer fentanyl because it is usually cheaper than heroin and more readily available, and some users believe it contains fewer adulterants than heroin (Roberton 1986). However, fentanyl compounds are quite potent and difficult for street dealers to cut properly, a situation that can lead to overdose and death. One derivative, 3-methyl fentanyl, is extremely potent (approximately 3,000 times as potent as morphine) and is thought to be responsible for a number of overdose deaths in the San Francisco Bay area (Roberton 1986). In 1988, 3-methyl fentanyl led to the deaths of eighteen people in the Pittsburgh area. A local chemist without a criminal record was found to be the source—he apparently got the idea from a television news report. In 1991 the drug killed ten persons in one weekend in four northeastern cities (Nieves 1991). Fentanyl has been used (illegally) to "dope" race horses because the substance is very difficult to detect in urine or blood.

There is an emergent problem with analogs designed by underground chemists to mimic controlled substances.

> These chemists change the molecular structure of a drug and thus make the drug legally unrestricted. Since the passage of the Anti-Drug Abuse Act of 1986 all analogs of controlled substances have themselves become controlled substances. The changes in chemical structure may also change its potency, length of action, euphoric effects, and toxicity. ("Drug Abuse" 1987: 27).

MDMA

One analog, methylenedioxymethamphetamine (MDMA)—nicknamed "Ecstasy" or "Adam"—was patented in 1914 by a German firm (Nichols and

Oberlender 1989). It was not until its "rediscovery" in the late 1970s that the drug received a great deal of attention because of its purported ability to produce profound pleasurable effects. It proved popular among white professionals—earning its nickname as a "Yuppie drug"—and persons who consider themselves part of the "New Age" spiritual movement (Beck and Rosenbaum 1994). MDMA is reported to be popular on college campuses in the United States and at dance parties—"raves"—in Great Britain (Blakeslee 1995). An analog of methamphetamine, MDMA reportedly causes acute euphoria and long-lasting positive changes in attitude and self-confidence, with some symptoms resembling those caused by LSD but without the severe side effects typically associated with the amphetamines.

According to Jerome Beck and Marsha Rosenbaum (1994: 63):

> The effects of MDMA usually become apparent twenty to sixty minutes following oral ingestion of an average dose (100–125 milligrams) on an empty stomach. The sudden and intense onset of the high experienced by many users is commonly referred to as the "rush" (also the "wave" or "weird period"). This phase was often (particularly during initial use) experienced with a certain degree of trepidation, tension, stomach tightness, and/or mild nausea. This discomfort was generally transitory and melted away into a more relaxed state of being. Although novice users occasionally experienced some apprehension during this initial onset, anxiety levels typically decreased with subsequent use, allowing for increased enjoyment.

Dangers of MDMA

There is some evidence that MDMA may cause damage to nerve cells, especially serotonergic axons ("Drug Abuse" 1991), bringing on Parkinson's disease-like symptoms. In 1985 MDMA was placed on the DEA's Schedule I because of its high potential for abuse and lack of medically accepted use, although some medical supporters argue for its experimental use in psychotherapy. A recent research effort concluded that MDMA abuse could lead to chronic depression and other harmful effects. According to George Ricaurte (Blakeslee 1995), the drug destroys serotonin-carrying axons, which subsequently regenerate, making new connections to the brain. However, according to the researcher, in tests on monkeys and rats these new connections are markedly abnormal. In a letter to the *New York Times,* two other researchers (Goldsmith and Doblin 1995) challenged Ricaurte's findings, arguing that the drugs used in his experiments on monkeys and rats were forty-five times the usual recreational dosage.

Herbal Stimulants

The dynamic qualities of drug abuse are highlighted by the popluarity of so-called herbal stimulants, particularly *ephedra* (also known by its Chinese name *ma huang*). Ephedra is sold under a variety of brand names in the form of pills in many "health food" stores. It contains ephedrine, which is also laboratory-produced as a stimulant in nonprescription asthma medications, and some cold and allergy medicines. Sometimes caffeine is added to increase its stimulating properties. Within twenty minutes of taking the substance, there is a jump in the heart rate and blood pressure.

One popular brand is called Herbal Ecstasy, although it is not related to MDMA (discussed above). These substances are used by young people as a "safe" alternative to illegal drugs. Since it is classified as a dietary supplement—not a drug—ephedra is not subject to FDA regulation, although a number of states have passed restrictions on its sale because of reports of deaths believed related to herbal products containing the substance.[16] Adverse reactions include liver failure, elevated blood pressure, heart palpitations, and strokes (Crowley 1996; Lambert 1996; Burros and Jay 1996; Kolata 1996).

Now that we have examined the physiological impact of some drugs, in the next chapter we will look at the sociological and psychological aspects of drug abuse.

REVIEW QUESTIONS

1. What variables determine a drug's impact on an individual?
2. Why is laboratory testing of drugs on humans of limited value in determining the impact of these substances on actual substance abusers?
3. Why can't the findings of laboratory studies on animals be generalized to humans?
4. What effect do drugs have on the autonomic nervous system?
5. What is the relationship between homeostasis and tolerance?
6. What are receptor sites in the brain?
7. How can a deficiency in endorphins explain heroin use?
8. How does heroin affect the user?
9. How does the concept of tolerance help explain addiction?
10. Why would heroin addicts who do not intend to abandon the use of heroin enter a drug treatment program without being coerced?
11. For heroin users, what are:
    (a) the rush,
    (b) the high, and
    (c) the nod?
12. How does heroin impair homeostatic functions?
13. Why is a heroin overdose life-threatening?
14. What is the effect of barbiturates on the user?

16. The 1994 Dietary Supplement Health and Education Act was passed as the result of an effective lobbying campaign by the food supplement industry. The statute deregulated the industry and now permits the marketing of any supplement until the FDA is able to prove it unsafe. The law also enables companies to make unproven and unjustified health claims.

15. How are the different barbiturates classified?
16. How does methaqualone affect the user?
17. What are the medical uses of sedatives?
18. Why is alcohol considered a food?
19. What are the three classes of alcohol?
20. Why is alcohol referred to as a "regulated" drug?
21. How is alcohol similar to heroin?
22. What are the dangers of alcohol abuse?
23. What impact do stimulants have on a user?
24. How can dependence on cocaine be explained by a dopamine deficiency?
25. What naturally occurring phenomena does cocaine imitate?
26. What is the typical reaction to small doses of cocaine?
27. What are the possible negative reactions to heavy use of cocaine?
28. Why do some cocaine users prefer freebasing?
29. What are the possible effects of cocaine on sexual activity?
30. What are the differences between the effects of cocaine hydrochloride and crack?
31. What are inhalants and what are their dangers?
32. In what ways are the effects of amphetamine and cocaine similar?
33. Why is the use of amphetamine by certain persons dangerous?
34. How do hallucinogens affect the central nervous system?
35. What determines whether an acid trip will be good or bad?
36. How does PCP affect the user?
37. What are the dangers of PCP use?
38. What are the effects of smoking cannabis?
39. What are the analogs and designer drugs?
40. What is MDMA? What are its dangers?
41. What are herbal stimulants?

4

THE PSYCHOLOGY AND SOCIOLOGY OF DRUG ABUSE

Being a drug abuser becomes a lifestyle. It cannot be treated as an isolated biological or pharmacological problem.—Arnold W. Washton (PCOC 1984: 59)

Since the discovery of drugs as a social problem, attempts have been made to explain why some persons become dependent on chemicals while others, even those who use the same substances, do not. These explanations go beyond simply labeling abusers as "bad" or "weak" persons oriented toward a harmful vice.

There are many different interpretations of drug dependence.

> Some believe it is a medical disease,[1] while others believe it is a behavioral problem. Some consider it to have genetic origins; others consider it to be primarily environmentally determined. Some examine it within a cultural context, others consider it to be an individual adjustment reaction. Some view it as a personality disorder, while others view it as a psychosocial problem. It is probably true that there is no single correct interpretation of drug dependence. (Pickens and Thompson 1984: 53)

There is also a biopsychosocial model in which drug dependence "is seen as being determined by the interaction of psychological, environmental, and physiological factors" (Donovan 1988: 12).

Explanations of drug abuse often evolve from the particular discipline of the observer. While many of these explanations may seem competitive or even conflicting, our examination will emphasize their complementary nature, in that each provides a partial explanation for drug use. As we will see in chapters 5 and 8, these explanations have important treatment and policy implications. In this chapter, for pedagogical purposes explanations are placed into two broad categories: psychological and sociological. We will consider the major theoretical contributions in each category. But first, what is a theory?

THEORY

A theory helps us explain events. It organizes events so they can be placed in perspective, explains the causes of past events, and predicts when, where, and how future events will occur. According to Arnold Binder and Gilbert Geis (1983: 3), "A theory consists of a set of assumptions; concepts regarding events, situations, individuals, and groups; and propositions that describe the interrelationships among the various assumptions and concepts." Theory is the basic building block for the advancement of human knowledge. In the natural sciences, such as chemistry and biology, theory can usually be subjected to rigorous laboratory testing and replication, using rats and monkeys, for example. The social or behavioral sciences are concerned with behavior that is pecu-

---

1. "Moving etiological and rehabilitative issues from the context of morals to that of medicine offered many advantages. The legitimacy bestowed on substance abuse by treating it as a disease opened the way for more humane and effective treatment of patients. In addition, this view provided the impetus for scientific research into the condition" (Siegel et al. 1995: 67).

liarly human, and (ethically based) testing is limited accordingly. We can, for

125

Chapter Four:
Psychology
and Sociology
of Drug Abuse

example, subject rats to extreme levels of physical stress and then study their reaction to morphine. We could not, however, subject human beings to similar levels of stress, expose them to morphine, and then see if they become drug addicts. The social or behavioral sciences have to study the etiology of drug addiction in a more circuitous manner. We will review some of the theories that provide insight into these psychological and sociological dimensions.

PSYCHOLOGY OF DRUG ABUSE

Psychology examines individual (and clinicians attempt to treat "abnormal" or dysfunctional) human behavior. Some psychological theories of drug abuse are based on personality: "Drug addiction is primarily a personality disorder. It represents one type of abortive adjustment to life that individuals with certain personality predispositions may choose under appropriate conditions of availability and sociocultural attitudinal tolerance" (Ausubel 1978: 77). Robert Craig (1987: 31) notes that the psychological literature supports such a conclusion: "Drug addicts have a paucity of major psychiatric syndromes and neuroses and a plethora of personality disorders and character disorders." An extensive review of the literature on psychological testing of heroin addicts found them to be hostile, demanding, aggressive, rebellious, irresponsible, playful, and impulsive (Craig 1987). But many of these traits are also found in outstanding athletes. With respect to substance abusers in general, they "are characterized by disregard for established social customs, lack of control and

DRUG ABUSERS

Regardless of social class differences, substance abusers share important similarities. All reveal some problems in socialization, cognitive/emotional skills, and overall psychological development, which is evident in their immaturity, poor self-esteem, conduct and character disorders, or antisocial characteristics. Typical features include low tolerance for all forms of discomfort and delay of gratification; inability to manage feelings (particularly hostility, guilt, and anxiety); poor impulse control (particularly sexual or aggressive); poor judgment and reality testing concerning consequences of actions; unrealistic self-appraisal in terms of a discrepancy between personal resources and aspirations; prominence of lying, manipulation, and deception as coping behaviors; and problems with authority and personal and social irresponsibility (i.e., inconsistency or failures in completing expected obligations and persistent difficulties in managing guilt). (De Leon 1994: 19–20) foresight, inability to maintain lasting personal commitments, and the need for unusual and varied experiences" (Cox 1985: 233).

As part of the psychological explanation for drug abuse has been a presumed *addictive personality* that results from problematic family relationships, inappropriate reinforcement, the lack of healthy role models, contradictory parental expectations, and/or an absence of love and respect. The psychologically immature drug-dependent personality seeks gratification on a primitive level, or according to the pleasure principle finds drug use and its attendant behavior reinforcing. He or she ignores the long-term negative consequences of behavior and instead opts for the short-term positive reinforcement that drugs provide. Unfortunately, the search for the addictive personality—psychological variables that can predict future drug abuse—has not been fruitful (see Lang 1983). Peter Nathan (1988) points out that the search for predictors of drug dependence has discovered a variety of overt acts by prealcoholic and predrug abusers that reveal an unwillingness to accept societal rules. Beyond that, however, few consistent links have been found between other behaviors or personality factors and later abuse of alcohol and drugs. Furthermore, Nathan (1988) notes that large numbers of abusers have never demonstrated antisocial behavior in childhood and that a substantial number of antisocial or conduct-disordered children never develop alcohol or drug problems as adults.

Psychological theories can be broadly categorized into those following a Freudian or psychoanalytic strain and those following behaviorism or learning theory.

Psychoanalytic Theory and Drug Abuse

Psychoanalytic theory was fathered by Sigmund Freud (1856–1939). Although it has undergone change over the years, its basic proposition continues to be the influence of unconscious phenomena on human behavior. According to Freud there are three types of mental phenomena:

1. *Conscious:* what we are currently thinking about.
2. *Preconscious:* thoughts and memories that can easily be called into consciousness.
3. *Unconscious:* feelings and experiences that have been repressed and that can be made conscious only with a great deal of difficulty and that nevertheless exert a dominant influence over our behavior.

Stages of Psychological Development

Freud posited that unconscious feelings and thoughts relate to stages of psychosexual development from infancy to adulthood. Psychoanalytic theory conceives of the human being as a dynamic energy system consisting of basic drives and instincts which in interaction with the environment serve to organize and develop the personality through a series of developmental stages. Individuals from birth are pushed by these largely unconscious and irrational drives toward satisfaction of desires which are largely unconscious and irrational. (Compton and Galaway 1979: 90)

Although we lack conscious memory of these stages, in later life they serve as a source of anxiety and guilt, psychoneurosis and psychosis. The stages overlap, and transition from one to the other is gradual, the time spans noted below being approximate and dependent on individual and cultural differences.

ORAL STAGE (birth to eighteen months). During the oral stage the infant organizes his or her primitive impulses "around orality as a means of engaging the environment and achieving pleasure" (Greenspan 1978: 4). During this stage the mouth, lips, and tongue are the predominant sexual organs. Desires and gratifications are mainly oral—sucking and biting. The infant is unsocialized, devoid of all self-control, and narcissistic. In the normal infant, the source of pleasure becomes associated with the touch and warmth of the parent, who gratifies oral needs. When this is lacking, narcissism remains predominant, and in the narcissistically disturbed adult drugs become a substitute for maternal warmth and self-esteem.

The infant's physiological balance is precarious, so that any environmental change may cause distress. The anxiety experienced in the helpless state of infancy is ameliorated by the discovery of a maternal object capable of providing nurture. The absence of warm mother-infant interaction and sensory deprivation during this stage cause the adult to use drugs as a means of reducing anxiety; drugs serve as a substitute for maternal attachment, and drug abuse is a regression back to an unfulfilled oral stage. Experiments conducted on animals reveal that the young of many species experience separation anxiety that can be ameliorated by opiates. "For human species, the experience of social attachments and comfort becomes inevitably bound up with the euphoria of human affection, intimacy, and love." Opiates apparently provide a substitute, albeit an inadequate one, for the absent maternal object (Levinthal 1988: 145).

During this stage the infant attempts to reach a state of homeostatic peacefulness, and this requires a responsive and supportive maternal object. Because of trauma or deficiencies experienced during this stage of development, "The infant may fail to achieve homeostatic balance, in the context of an attachment to a maternal object," and this can lead to drug abuse in the adult. The "substance, be it heroin or some other narcotic or stimulant, works at a physiologic and psychological representational level to facilitate the attainment of this basic homeostatic experience" (Greenspan 1978: 74).

ANAL STAGE (eighteen months to three years). As the infant moves into his or her second year, the "instinctual organization is beginning to organize around the mental representations concerned with anality" (Greenspan 1978: 76). The anus becomes the center of sexual desire and gratification during this stage, with pleasure closely associated with the retention and expulsion of feces. Physiologically the child is now able to control eliminatory processes. He or she typically experiences toilet training and becomes partially socialized, the beginning of a parental internalizing process that is completed during the genital stage that follows. During the anal stage there may be an acting out of destructive urges such as breaking toys or even injuring insects or small animals. A great deal of adult psychopathology, including violent behavior and sociopathic personality disorders, is traced back to this stage. Depressants such as heroin, alcohol, barbiturates, and tranquilizers can provide a way of managing sadistic and masochistic impulses—self-medication—that were not successfully dealt with during the anal stage. Such persons do not take depressants for pleasure but to control internal rage. (The policy implications of this theory mitigate against our current response to drug use.)

If development is thwarted during this stage, the infant does not succeed in achieving "an internal sense of mastery and delineation of self from the primary other"—the maternal figure. Drugs are used in an effort to obtain a state of mastery and clear demarcation from the maternal figure that is necessary to manage the transition to the genital stage. In order to gain greater independence, the infant must relinquish the dependent attachment to the maternal object, and if successful he or she can then move into the genital stage. In those who fail to accomplish this transition, substance abuse "is a defense against separation anxiety and its accompanying depression" (Greenspan 1978: 78).

GENITAL STAGE (three to five years). In this stage, which anticipates adulthood, the main sexual interest is assumed by the genitals and in normal persons is maintained by them hereafter. During this period boys experience strong attachments to their mothers (*Oedipus complex*) and girls to their fathers (*Electra complex*); both have incestuous fantasies, although they do not fully understand the mechanics of adult sexual relations. The child must begin to relinquish the dependent maternal/paternal attachment despite feelings of sadness in doing so. Drugs provide solace to the adult who was unable to deal with the ensuing depression of separation.

As noted in chapter 3, psychoactive drugs often affect sexual performance by enhancing or depressing desire and/or performance. Drugs can provide a chemical means of dealing with disturbances experienced during the genital stage of development. Heroin, for example, may serve to suppress the sexual drive that is fixated in the genital stage; that is, the drug helps the person deal with unconscious (and guilt-provoking) incestuous wishes. Heroin causes a return to the oral stage, enabling the addict to avoid dealing with conflicts that were not adequately resolved during the genital stage. Drugs that stimulate sexual desire, on the other hand, may be necessary for the adult who has difficulty performing without them because of (unconscious and) unresolved incestuous feelings that are part of the genital stage.

LATENCY (five to adolescence). This stage is marked by a significant lessening of interest in sexual organs and by strong attachments and relationships with playmates of the same gender and age—it is difficult to get boys and girls to play together.

ADOLESCENCE/ADULTHOOD. The individual experiences a dramatic reawakening of genital interest and awareness. The incestuous wish, however, is repressed, and sexual interest is expressed in terms of mature (adult) sexuality. As noted above, drug use that substitutes for or enhances sexual activity allows the abuser to avoid or overcome the reawakening of incestuous sexual feelings that were never successfully reconciled during the genital stage.

While each stage is experienced and then left behind, it is never completely abandoned. Some amount of psychic energy (*cathexis*) remains attached to earlier objects of psychosexual development. If the strength of the cathexis is particularly strong, it is expressed as a *fixation*. For example, if instead of transferring his affection to another woman, the male remains fixated on his mother (or the female on her father), sexual problems—or, as noted above, drug use—will be manifested in adulthood. In any event, while the individual is experiencing each of these stages of development, corresponding psychic phenomena develop.

ID. Each person is born with a mass of powerful drives, wishes, urges, and psychic tensions that are energized in the form of the *libido*. These seek immediate discharge or gratification. These id impulses are asocial, operating on the primitive level of pleasure and pain (that is, they are hedonistic), and from about birth to seven months the id is the total psychic apparatus. Id drives are a central component of personality, impelling a person toward activity leading to cessation of the tension excitement it creates—satisfying the libido. For example, the hunger drive will result in activity that eventually satisfies (gratifies the id of) the person experiencing hunger. A craving for pleasure-producing chemicals will lead the id-driven person to seek drugs at considerable risk in order to satiate his or her desire, and the feelings of omnipotence that drugs can produce reinforce this drive.

EGO. Through the environment and training, infants learn to modify their expression of id drives and to delay immediate gratification. Ego development permits them to obtain maximum gratification with a minimum of difficulty—the ego tempers the id with reality and is the organism's contact with the real world. In normal development, the child learns to relinquish primitive id demands and to adapt behavior to social demands (Smart 1970). The stronger the ego, the stronger is the individual's ability to tolerate frustration. Poor ego functioning, manifested by an inability to tolerate the psychological discomfort of frustration, can lead to the abuse of chemicals that lower the discomfort and provide immediate gratification. Furthermore, note Henry Krystal and Herbert Raskin (1970: 31), in the ego-deficient personality, "Drugs are used to avoid impending psychic trauma in circumstances which would not be potentially traumatic to other persons"; in other words, drug use reflects a dysfunction in reality testing. Through drug use, notes Sandor Rado (1981), reality is avoided, but only temporarily; when the chemical reaction subsides, reality returns with renewed vigor, and the subject again seeks relief through drugs. However, the psyche now finds that the same dosage brings diminished relief—tolerance has developed—leading to increasing dosages.

As a result of disturbances in psychosexual development, a person may remain at the ego level of development; in other words,

> The child remains asocial or else behaves as if he had become social without having made actual adjustment to the demands of society. This means that he has not repudiated completely his instinctual wishes but has suppressed them so that they lurk in the background awaiting an opportunity to break through to satisfaction. (Aichhorn 1963: 4)

Drug use, a reversion to gratifications associated with the oral stage, is a symptom of such a disturbance. Drug use is also associated with the ego's need to be in control of the source of pleasurable feelings—it is narcissistic (Rado 1981). Edward Khantzian (1980) states that heroin use is caused by the ego's need to control feelings of rage and aggression, emotions that relate to the anal stage of development.

The choice of drugs is either ego-constricting or ego-expanding. The weak ego structure of heroin users causes them to seek quiet and lonely lives—a tranquility through ego constriction that is aided by narcotics. Cocaine and amphetamine users, on the other hand, often come from households with warm mothers and fathers who are strong and encouraging. For them, stimulant use grows out of a self-directed and intensely competitive personality: "They take cocaine to expand their egos and their self-confidence" (Spotts and Shontz 1980: 65). The user of stimulants is suffering from anxiety brought on by a lack of stimulation: The ego is disturbed by the absence of stimuli, and intense stimulation is preferred by those using amphetamines and cocaine to ward off boredom and depression (Krystal and Raskin 1970).

In the course of normal development, over time the child integrates outer (social) discipline and imposes it upon him- or herself. The instinctual impulses are brought under his or her own control, and we get the beginning of a superego (Smart 1970).

SUPEREGO. Oversimplified as the conscience, the superego is the counterforce to the id. It exercises a criticizing influence, a sense of morality that controls behavior. Tied to overcoming the incestuous feelings of the genital stage, the superego serves as an internalized parent, meaning that behavior is no longer exclusively dependent on external forces (the ego level of control). Failures in superego development may leave a person without strong internal controls over id and ego impulses and can result in behavior that is harmful or destructive. The sociopath lacks sufficient superego strength, and the ego is insufficient to control powerful id impulses.

PSYCHOSEXUAL DEVELOPMENT

oral stage	(birth to eighteen months)	id
anal stage	(eighteen months to three years)	ego
genital stage	(three to five years)	superego
latency	(five to twelve years)	
adulthood	(adolescence to death)	

At the other extreme is an overactive superego that cannot make distinctions between *thinking* bad and *doing* bad. Unresolved conflicts of earlier development (for example, an Oedipus complex) and id impulses that are normally repressed or dealt with through other less destructive processes (such as reaction formation, discussed below) create a severe sense of guilt. This guilt is experienced (unconsciously) as a compulsive need to be punished, to alleviate guilt the person commits acts for which punishment is virtually certain. August Aichhorn (1963) notes that such persons are victims of their own personalities. For them drugs accomplish a dual purpose: They reduce the anxiety caused by unresolved inner conflicts, while the deleterious aspects of drug abuse provide external punishment. According to Leon Wurmser (1978), society assists the drug abuser in this quest by imposing shame and punishment.

According to psychoanalytic theory, unconscious forces maintain a delicate balance as the person experiences life's various sociocultural and biological aspects. The balance is easily upset, crossing the very thin line between the normal and the neurotic or between the neurotic and the psychotic. In fact, there is only a difference of degree between the normal and the abnormal. When repressed material begins to overwhelm the psyche and threatens to enter one's consciousness, external defense mechanisms come into play in the form of psychoneuroses and, in more serious cases, psychosis. These responses may take the form of phobias—to heights, insects, or closed spaces, for example. In the paranoid reaction, the person projects his or her thoughts onto imagined enemies; in the reaction-formation, the destructive urges of the anal stage can be channeled into prosocial activities—becoming a surgeon, a veterinarian, or a butcher, for example. The degree to which defense mechanisms cause the person to become dysfunctional provides an objective measurement of abnormality. The psychoneuroses, or the primitive defense mechanism that is drug abuse, allow psychic energy to be discharged without having to confront unconscious material (Wurmser 1978). In his cocaine-abusing patients, Frederic Schiffer (1988) found that drug usage was a self-medication aimed at alleviating the pain of early trauma. Cocaine abuse represented an unconscious, symbolic repetition of childhood trauma. Old psychological injuries were reinflicted by the drug, which also allowed the patient to unconsciously gain a (false) sense of control over these early difficulties, providing an opportunity to struggle against them again.

DRUG USE AND ADOLESCENCE. Psychoanalytic theory views drug abuse as a symptom of neuroses that manifest themselves during adolescence. We recognize that adolescents typically undergo periods of boredom, anxiety, anger, frustration, and even short-lived depression. A defining feature of adolescence "is the rapid and far-reaching changes occurring in virtually all aspects of life and the resultant high-level stress" (Newcomb and Bentler 1988: 11). Research has identified these factors as well as the peer group as being associated with drug abuse. The typical adolescent has not had sufficient experience in dealing with feelings of psychosocial stress in a mature—that is, adult—fashion. Psychoactive drugs can be seen as a form of self-medication in response to the stressful conditions of adolescence. These frequently include affective disorders: "Drugs of abuse and medications prescribed for affective disorders have common neurochemical effects that presumably treat the abnormality" (Bukstein, Brent, and Kaminer 1989: 1139).

It is normal for an adolescent to grapple with the problems of physiological and psychological development. The struggle for identity through a progressive process of relationships and experiences enables him or her to manage the complexities of adolescence. He or she becomes more competent and eventually moves into young adulthood.

Fresno, California, youths light up outside a concert hall. Social patterns that develop during adolescence may encourage users to experiment with other drugs.

Adolescence is a period of development involving transitions in the major physical, intellectual, psychosocial, and moral processes that make up a person. Transitional stages of development are by definition periods of disequilibration and disruption and, therefore, [are] replete with opportunities for experiences that are both dangerous and growth-enhancing. (Baumrind 1987: 14)

The adolescent addict, however, sidesteps such growth by at first simply avoiding the situations in which he can gradually acquire competence or by passively going along with the whims and decisions of others and eventually by substituting the anxiety-reducing "normative" influence of the opiate drugs. (Chein et al. 1964: 202)

As Otto Fenichel (1945) points out, euphoric substances protect against painful mental states. However, because of this, the adolescent's reality-testing (an ego function) ability remains primitive, and his ability to tolerate stress and frustration remains at an infantile (oral) level. Like the infant during the oral stage, the addict is motivated only by a need to immediately gratify his or her perceived needs. This type of behavior is governed only by the primitive id impulses—the pleasure principle—without any real concern for the results. As a result of their extensive longitudinal research, Michael Newcomb and Peter Bentler (1988: 240) conclude that adolescent drug use, "particularly of cannabis and hard drugs, has measurably negative effects on several critical areas of life functioning as a young adult."

Heroin use typically begins during adolescence, with the drug serving as a means for avoiding psychologically demanding—but healthier—responses to developmental crisis, stress, deprivation, and other forms of emotional pain:

Their [addicts'] response has been to revert repeatedly to the use of opiates as an all-powerful device, thereby precluding other solutions that would normally develop and that might better sustain them. It is on this basis that addicts are probably so desperately dependent on their drugs and have so little confidence that they can endure without them. That is, the use of the drug *is* their characteristic or characterological way of adapting and dealing with their inner world and emotions and the real world around them. (Khantzian, Mack, Schatzberg 1974: 164)

Sociopsychological growth and maturity require grappling with reality—as exercise aficionados will recognize: "No pain, no gain." Drug use reduces social competence and adaptive behaviors. The therapeutic community, a particular approach to treating drug abusers discussed in chapter 5, responds to persons whose use of drugs is based on an inability to deal with the frustrations of reality.

According to Freud, "From the time of puberty onward the human individual must devote himself to the great task of freeing himself from the parents; and only after this detachment is accomplished can he cease to be a child and so become a member of the social community" (1961: 345–46). Freud points out that in neurotics, such as addicts, this detachment is not accomplished because the neurotic has a distorted pathological relationship with his or her parents. This relationship is characterized by overdependence and fear of being rejected. While there is an identification with the father (or father figure), it is "at best laden with hostility" (Frazier 1962: 97). Chein and his colleagues (1964) found that addicts, as opposed to controls from the same environment, came from either single-parent households or from families where the father was usually distant, presented immoral models of behavior, was primarily concerned with day-to-day gratification of appetites, and impulsive. As would be expected, the fathers had unstable work histories, pessimistic and fatalistic attitudes toward the future, and low aspirations for their sons. The level of interaction between father and son was minimal.

The addict's relationship with his mother includes a long history of emotional deprivation (Frazier 1962: 98):

> Frequently, a tense, dominant, autistic, unhappy mother forced the child into becoming an adjunct to herself rather than allowing him to develop as an independent person. The feeling of hostility toward the mother and the inability to form any close satisfactory relationships date back to these earliest years. The addict's conflicts reflect this oral deprivation in an infantile helplessness, and the drug helps him to regress to "happy" infancy that was never really happy. The effects of the drug handle his hostility and reduce tensions which are symptoms of these life-long conflicts. The hostility toward the mother generally remains unconscious, but it is expressed through the drug which not only "destroys" the user but also symbolically destroys the mother whom he has incorporated through identification.

According to Robert Savitt (1963: 45), it is not euphoria that the addict seeks in narcotics but the satiated feeling reminiscent of infancy: "When an infant's basic needs for sustenance and love are fulfilled, he falls asleep." Thus, the purported use of heroin for its euphoric properties is an exaggeration:

> It would appear that the elation which the heroin addict experiences has been stressed out of proportion to the sleep or stupor which often soon follows. . . . Like the infant who alternates between hunger and sleep, the addict alternates between hunger for a drug and narcotic stupor. (1963: 44).

The adolescent addict suffers from a narcissism (self-love), an infantile level of relating to others that retards the ability to form close, warm, emotional relationships. Other persons are simply instruments for his own purposes—even his own mother, whom he has not learned to differentiate as a portion of himself. Interpersonal relationships, even with peers, are shallow. Groups of "junkies" are tied together only by the one thing they share—drugs. It's an easy group, without demands, deliberate structure, or goals beyond those involving continued drug use. Stanley Greenspan (1978: 74) states that "substance abuse could emanate from the lack of this basic ability of attaching to the human object." A prominent feature of the family situation of the adolescent opiate addict "is the peculiarly close relationship between the addict and his mother. It is not a closeness of warmth or mutual regard so much as it is a clinging and feeling of being bound to-gether" (Chein et al. 1964: 212).

Drug-dependent adolescents suffer from severe ego inadequacies. They have been found to be relatively unresponsive/indifferent to opportunities for education, work, or recreation; they have limited interests and curiosity. They appear to suffer from gross disturbances in early life, leading to a restricted pattern of responsiveness. They have poor reality testing and an inability to delay gratification or accept frustration; they react to criticism by withdrawal, giving up easily in school or employment situations; they are unable to form realistic goal orientations. While recognizing all of the dangers inherent in heroin use, addicts are unable to exercise restraint. They use heroin to deal with frustrations and pain; they are retreatists for whom heroin relieves anxi-ety by changing feelings of tenseness and restlessness into feelings of comfort, relaxation, and peacefulness (Chein et al. 1964). Heroin helps overcome the usual tensions of adolescence. The heroin addict may also find heroin effec-tive in thwarting feelings of intense destructiveness and sadism associated with a disturbance in the anal stage of development. The drug pacifies such drives, and the negative and punishing results of heroin addiction satisfy the superego's need to punish such feelings (Yorke 1970).

As noted in chapter 3, there are significant sexual implications in drug use, particularly the intravenous use of heroin.

> Addicts are persons who have a disposition to react to the effects of alcohol, morphine, or other drugs in such a way that they try to use these effects to sat-isfy the archaic oral longings which is sexual longing, a need for security, and a need for the maintenance of self-esteem simultaneously. (Fenichel 1945: 376)

This pathology has its origins in infantile sexuality, both oral and genital. "The addict uses his addiction to express or act out repressed impulses and needs," and the discharge of psychic energy is pleasurable enough to replace other pleasurable activities, such as sex and eating (Chein et al. 1964: 235). The use of heroin is autoerotic, bypasses genital sex in favor of infantile or oral-stage eroticism (Yorke 1970).

Psychoanalytic theories of drug abuse have been criticized for their re-liance on retrospective self-reports and individual case studies—limited meth-ods lacking rigorous empirical grounding. This contrasts with the rigorous experimentation that underlies learning theory.

Behaviorism/Learning Theory

The second major school of psychological thought has its roots in the laboratory of experimental psychology with its dogs, pigeons, rats, monkeys, and mazes (see, for example, Rachlin 1991). Behaviorists typically reject psy-choanalytic theory as unscientific, that is, lacking the rigorous testing to which

CLASSICAL AND OPERANT CONDITIONING

Behavioral psychology recognizes two basic types of processes associated with learning (Tilson 1993: 2):

> *Classical conditioning* involves the pairing of two stimuli, one of which elicits a reflex and one of which is neutral [food and the sounding of a bell, for example]. With repeated pairing of the two stimuli, the previously neutral stimulus [bell] becomes a conditioned stimulus and elicits the response [salivating, for example] in absence of the original eliciting stimulus [food].
>
> *Operant conditioning* involves the repeated presentation or removal of a stimulus following a behavior to increase the probability of the behavior (i.e., reinforcement). A reinforcer is a stimulus that increases the probability of a behavior. If the probability of a behavior goes up following the presentation of some stimulus, then positive reinforcement has occurred. If the probability of a behavior goes up after the *removal* of a stimulus, then negative reinforcement has occurred.

learning theory has been subjected. Indeed, measurement of objective behavior is intrinsic to learning theory, which proceeds on the basis that all forms of behavior are conditioned: the result of learned responses to certain stimuli (S-R). Disturbed behavior such as drug abuse results from inappropriate conditioning (London 1964). To the behaviorist, a person is simply the sum product of his or her experience or learning, and learning is based on operant conditioning.

The behaviorist stresses—and has been able to prove—that animal behavior can be modified through the proper application of operant conditioning: positive and negative reinforcement. Behavior is "*strengthened* by its consequences, and for that reason the consequences themselves are called 'reinforcers.' " (Skinner 1974: 40). When some aspect of animal or human behavior is followed by a certain type of consequence—a reward—it is more likely to be repeated. The reward is called *positive reinforcement*. If the probability of a behavior goes up after the *removal* of a stimulus, then *negative reinforcement* has occurred. "A negative reinforcer strengthens any behavior that reduces or terminates it" (Skinner 1974: 47). For example, the negative reinforcement that occurs when a heroin addict fails to ingest enough heroin—withdrawal symptoms—strengthens drug-seeking behavior.

The noted behaviorist B. F. Skinner states that

> punishment is easily confused with negative reinforcement, sometimes called "aversive control." The same stimuli are used, and negative reinforcement might be defined as the punishment of not behaving, but punishment is designed to remove behavior from a repertoire, whereas negative reinforcement generates behavior. (1974: 63)

As noted in chapter 3, a particular psychoactive substance will be reinforcing to some persons or to most persons under certain conditions; for example, opiates when in pain. For most persons under ordinary circumstances, the same substance will not provide reinforcement—at least not reinforcement sufficiently positive to offset negative consequences—and they do not seek to repeat the behavior.

According to this view, drug use is merely the result of learning directly from others. Chein and his colleagues (1964) note that both the processes involved with the use of heroin (excitement) and the actions of the drug itself, become reinforcing, thus shaping—that is, molding—the behavior of the addict. Alfred Lindesmith (1968: 8) argues that a continuation of heroin use is based on negative reinforcement—"Persons become addicts when they recognize or perceive the significance of withdrawal distress which they are experiencing" when they cease to use heroin. Lindesmith argues that substances such as cocaine and marijuana, on the other hand, are positive reinforcers because they are taken to enhance mood rather than to stave off withdrawal. From the discussion in chapter 3, we know that Lindesmith's assertions are questionable: The physiological discomfort of heroin withdrawal is usually no greater than a bout with the flu; discontinuing the use of cocaine can produce depression; and sudden withdrawal from alcohol can be life-threatening.

The abuse of stimulants and depressants can be explained by learning theory. The use of cocaine, for example, can be quite rewarding: It elevates mood and provides a sense of well-being, strength, and energy, while discontinuing use provides negative reinforcement in the form of psychological depression or the "coke blues." Likewise, heroin use can be quite rewarding to the addict: It significantly reduces perceptions of physical and psychological pain, stress, and anxiety and provides a sense of euphoria, while discontinuing use provides negative reinforcement in the form of uncomfortable physical and psychological withdrawal symptoms. While initially chemicals such as cocaine or heroin may have been used for social reasons, these substances' ability to provide physiological and psychological rewards explains why addicts seek to continue use even in the face of considerable hardship—*drugs overcome competing reinforcers:*

> The balancing of pleasurable or rewarding experiences and punishing or unpleasant experiences that occurs during the early weeks or months of drug involvement may be of critical importance. If the net impact of those experiences is highly positive, the effect or memory of that "honeymoon" can remain remarkably strong over time, even as continuing reward diminishes and punishment increases, especially if alternative competitive behaviors are not exercised or reinforced as strongly. (Gerstein and Harwood 1990: 65)

Furthermore, while being known as a "junkie" or a "cokie" may have negative consequences in conventional society, it often provides positive reinforcement in that it allows entry and acceptance into a small clique that is the drug subculture. Daily activities can now be focused on a clearly identifiable goal—drugs. The sociological dimension of this concept appears below in a discussion of *anomie* and *retreatism.* Further, the illegal aspects of drug abuse provide a level of excitement that some persons may find quite rewarding. For drug users who must engage in criminality to support their habits, success in crime also provides an important source of reinforcement, particularly when they do not possess skills necessary to succeed in noncriminal endeavors that could offer a competing source of reinforcement.

Although a dose of intravenous methamphetamine would probably be physically pleasurable to anyone, Thomas Crowley (1981: 368) points out that not everyone who experiences the pleasure continues to use amphetamines. The person who continues use is more likely to be from an impoverished environment:

> Users in impoverished environments, with few other reinforcers available, will probably seek drug reinforcement more actively. This is likely the case with restrained, isolated, experimental monkeys; with heroin users in American black ghettos; and with cocaine users in the Andes. Similarly, long experience with disturbed, unloving parents seems to convince many young people that they can never achieve respect or love from others. These young people have not learned to expect reinforcement from their environment, and so they may more actively seek the predictable, regular reinforcement of drug abuse.

Most persons who find the intake of certain substances rewarding do not become compulsive about continued use. Thus, while some persons become obese because of their eating habits, most people do not become compulsive overeaters. While certain foods are pleasing to most people—chocolate or ice cream, for example—relatively few respond by compulsive intake. While large numbers of Americans use alcoholic beverages, most avoid dependence.

The adolescent drug user learns to deal with stress by using chemicals. Alternative coping mechanisms cannot provide reinforcement because they are not utilized. This leads to a deficiency in social competence, which causes further stress and, thus, increased drug use over time (Pentz 1985). This explanation provides the theoretical underpinnings for drug prevention programs that center on enhancing social competence.

Cognitive[2] Learning Theory

Many behaviorists recognize that human behavior is more complex than that of other species—that, for example, human behavior is often mediated by beliefs and symbols. The readiness to fight or die for a "cause"—the cross, the star of David, the crescent, the red star—illustrates the abstract complexities of human behavior. This recognition has led to *cognitive learning theory,* the major tenets of which are that

> human behavior is mediated by unobservables that intervene between a stimulus and a response to that stimulus. Beliefs, sets, strategies, attributions, and ex-

---

2. Cognition refers to learning and memory.

COGNITIVE LEARNING THEORY

An important distinction in learning theory is between observable and unobservable behavior. Many behaviorists use "behavior" only in reference to observable activity, but this is too restrictive. No matter what it is called, unobservable behavior, especially cognitive behavior, is important in people's lives. . . . A cognitive response is simply a thought or feeling, typically in reaction to some stimulus. But a thought or feeling may also serve as a stimulus for a subsequent response. So a cognitive event may act either as a stimulus or as a response, or as both, as these events often do. (Starkweather 1982: 37)

pectancies are examples of the types of mediating constructs currently considered crucial to an understanding of emotion and behavior. (Gold 1980: 8)

Furthermore, "The way an individual labels or evaluates a situation determines his or her emotional and behavioral responses to it." Thus, based on a past learning, a twisted cross (swastika) may have a different meaning to a Jew than to a Navaho (to whom it is a cosmic religious symbol). According to this approach, the drug abuser has difficulty in meeting societal demands or expectations, and this leads to anxiety. While anxiety is a universal experience, Steven Gold notes (1980: 9), drug abusers feel that "they cannot alter or control the situation; that they are powerless to affect their environment and decrease or eliminate the sources of stress."

Persons facing persistent difficulties and anxieties in their lives and who are not prepared to cope with them may resort to analgesic drugs for comfort. "While enabling them to forget their problems and stress, the pain-killing experience engendered by such drugs actually *decreases* the ability to cope. This is because such drugs depress the central nervous system and the individual's responsive capacity" (Peele 1980: 143). Heroin or alcohol provides relief from anxiety, and the user also attains temporary euphoria: "Under the influence of the drug the individual temporarily experiences an increased sense of power, control, and well-being." The drug acts as a powerful reinforcer—it can do for the abuser what he or she cannot do for him- or herself. However, these effects are short-lived, and after the drug wears off, the user finds that feelings of powerlessness return with full fury, which leads to further use of the drug and a cycle of continuing drug abuse.

The reliance on drugs to cope with stress therefore creates a vicious cycle; the more drugs are used, the more the individual believes they are necessary. Each drug experience serves to confirm for users the belief that they are powerless to function on their own. (Gold 1980: 9)

Behaviorists often refer to this state of thinking as "learned helplessness": Through inappropriate reinforcement, the drug abuser *learns* that he or she can neither escape nor avoid the stimulus leading to drug use.

PSYCHOANALYTIC LEARNING THEORY

Stanley Greenspan (1978: 80) explains drug abuse by integrating behaviorism and psychoanalytic theory into a model that defines external experiences in terms of stimuli and reinforcers derived from psychosexual stages of development and the organization of id, ego, and superego. He states, for example, that

> a substance abuser who achieves a basic and primitive homeostatic experience by using his addictive drug may be obtaining tremendous and potent reinforcement from the substance abuse. . . . Because of a lack of internalized control and the number of potent internal forces working from within, he tends to be vulnerable to environmental influences in rather dramatic ways and is sensitive to many potentially reinforcing events in his external environment [even though they may be destructive].

Stimulants such as amphetamine and cocaine provide not only primary reinforcement as a result of their impact on the central nervous system but also secondary reinforcement as the result of drug-induced behavioral change for those who wish to increase their assertiveness. Amphetamines, for example, can produce a sense of cleverness, clear-thinking, energy, alertness, and loquaciousness (Crowley 1981).

Learning theory is difficult to apply in the treatment of drug abusers. As noted above, drugs are so reinforcing—providing immediate gratification for those who have *learned* to enjoy their use—that finding appropriate reinforcers that can successfully compete is quite difficult.[3] Agonists and antagonists, discussed in chapter 5, can be used to thwart the reinforcing quality of psychoactive substances. That chapter will also examine treatment programs that apply behavior theory.

SOCIOLOGY OF DRUG ABUSE

Sociology is concerned with social structures and social behavior, so it examines drug use in its social context. A sociological perspective often views drug use as the product of social conditions and relationships that cause despair, frustration, hopelessness, and general feelings of alienation in the most disadvantaged segments of the population (Biernacki 1986). The National Institute on Drug Abuse ("Drug Abuse" 1987) outlines factors that are associated positively with adolescent substance abuse:

---

3. Relapse after treatment can also be explained by learning theory, i.e., the classical conditioned response: Certain clues associated with drug-taking behavior trigger a craving (Childress et al. 1993). These cues are discussed in chapter 5.

1. Families whose members have a history of alcohol abuse and/or histories of antisocial behavior or criminality;
2. Inconsistent parental supervision, with reactions that swing from permissiveness to severity;
3. Parental approval or use of dangerous substances;
4. Friends who abuse drugs;
5. Children who fail in school during late elementary years and who show a lack of interest in school during early adolescence;
6. Children who are alienated and rebellious; and
7. Antisocial behavior during early adolescence, particularly aggressive behavior.

Many sociological studies have found that drug use among adolescents is motivated by intermittent feelings of boredom and depression and that, like other aspects of adolescence, it is typically abandoned upon reaching adulthood. Furthermore, contrary to conventional wisdom, research has found that drug use is typically a group activity of socially *well-integrated youngsters* (Glassner and Loughlin 1989). That is, contrary to some psychological views,

Parents with a history of drug abuse may influence their children to become abusers—or their experiences may persuade them not to. This client of the Lutheran Medical Center's drug rehabilitation clinic in Brooklyn, New York, said in an interview, "There be times I'm smoking in the bathroom with one foot against the door so no one could come in. And when I come out, my son asked me was I sick. My face be so red and I have stuff around my mouth. But I be so far away I don't hear him none. . . . He know I need help to stay off the crack."

the adolescent drug user is socially competent (or ego sufficient). Sociological studies often challenge the conflicting views of the adolescent drug user as either a deviant isolate or a peer-driven conformist. Sociology also cautions us to separate drug use that is situational and transitional from drug dependence or addiction, which is compulsive and dysfunctional. This has important policy implications.

> Treatment approaches based on sociological (and any variety of social-psychological) theories usually stress resocialization, the adopting of prosocial values, and/or submission to a peer culture that is strongly opposed to drug use. For example, according to a social stress model, adolescents initiate substance use as a means of coping with a variety of stressors and influences that may arise from within the family, the school, the peer group, or the community. [And] adolescents will be more resilient and, as such, less likely to engage in problematic early usage as a means of coping with these stressors if they are members of prosocial, supportive social networks. (Rhodes and Jason 1990: 396)

A number of sociological studies have focused on the stages of alcohol, heroin, and cocaine addiction.

Stages of Drug Addiction

The alcoholic typically passes through several stages on the way to becoming addicted to alcohol (Catanzarite 1992):

- *Social Drinking:* In this initial pattern alcohol is used to enhance pleasant social situations. The drug is taken for relaxation and entertainment. For some individuals drinking alcohol has a ritualistic dimension—a glass of wine or beer or a drink with a meal and/or as part of a religious ritual. Others may have an alcoholic beverage after work with colleagues—"a beer with the boys." The social drinker imbibes small amounts and does not experience harmful effects such as loss of control or impaired judgment. While social drinkers view alcohol as generating positive feelings, they do not need the substance for enjoyment. The social drinker observes societal conventions about when, where, and how much to drink.
- *Heavy Drinking:* The heavy drinker uses alcohol to escape. For one type of drinker this critical step involves a circular problem—he or she experiences constantly high levels of stress and seeks relief by drinking alcohol, which creates additional stress that must be relieved by more alcohol. Another type resorts to heavy alcohol use when particular stressful problems are encountered and reduces drinking in their absence. By becoming intoxicated both types of drinkers violate social conventions about the use of alcohol and suffer negative side effects

with respect to family, friends, and employment. They become defensive about their drinking and deny the influence of alcohol on their lives.

- *Dependent Drinking:* The person is now addicted to alcohol and suffers from many consequences—an inability to function normally either socially, intellectually, or physically. He or she is not able to control drinking behavior and becomes obsessed and preoccupied with alcohol. Indeed, the person needs alcohol to "feel normal."

Heroin and cocaine addiction have been studied extensively, with two general conclusions (Gerstein and Harwood 1990):

1. Initial use is experimental in nature and begins during adolescence;
2. Very few persons *begin* using drugs after reaching age twenty-five (unless drugs were not previously available).

The pattern has a familiar sequence: from tobacco and alcohol to marijuana and then to other illegal psychoactive substances such as heroin and cocaine. While most new users do not progress very far, the earlier the onset of use the more likely is dependence. "Individuals who do not initiate the use of alcohol or tobacco tend not to initiate the use of marijuana. Similarly, those who do not initiate the use of marijuana tend not to progress to hard drug use" (Golub and Johnson 1994: 404).

The life of a heroin addict can be seen as a "career" with a number of "stages":

- *Experimentation:* The individual, usually an adolescent, experiments with a variety of substances, including alcohol, cigarettes, marijuana, and perhaps barbiturates and amphetamines, and may snort or use heroin subcutaneously.
- *Initiation:* The drug abuser is initiated into intravenous use of heroin. Although the first use is often accompanied by unpleasant side effects such as vomiting, he or she learns to enjoy subsequent injections. Heroin use begins to be a center of existence.
- *Commitment:* The user is now an addict and takes on the social identity associated with the drug subculture, orienting his or her life toward the maintenance of a heroin habit.
- *Disjunction:* The addict's life is now characterized by crime, arrest, and imprisonment interspersed with participation in drug-treatment programs in response to court direction (to avoid imprisonment), to reduce an expensive habit to manageable size, or to deal with severe physical ailments.
- *Maturation:* At some point, usually when the addict is closer to forty than to twenty, he or she typically begins to use only sporadically, or gives up drugs completely as a result of treatment, or simply experiences spontaneous remission—or he or she dies. There are relatively few elderly (over forty) addicts in the heroin-using population. This "aging

out" phenomenon is also found in other types of deviant behavior, such as crime in general.

"The addict lifestyle," notes Marsha Rosenbaum (1981: 14), "rotates around taking heroin for the purposes of alleviating withdrawal symptoms and/or getting high." Heroin is quite costly and too expensive for most addicts with only legitimate sources of income. Nevertheless, a habit requires intravenous use three, four, or five times daily, and the addict also requires funds for minimal life-support items such as food, clothing, and housing. "The addict's day," Rosenbaum (1981: 14–15) notes,

> often begins with withdrawal sickness . . . [discussed in chapter 3]. In order to alleviate these symptoms, the addict knows that s/he must use heroin. The symptoms become more intense with time. . . . Therefore, if possible, the addict is out the door with the goal of buying heroin in order to feel well.

If the addict is also a dealer, or is sufficiently organized, he or she is able to start the day with a fix. Few addicts, however, are able to plan even for the immediate future, so they rarely keep enough heroin in reserve to begin the day with a "wake-up fix." Without funds or drugs, the addict must begin the day "hustling" for money to get the first fix.

After a "connection" is made and the heroin is purchased, the drug must be ingested as part of an almost ritualistic process. A safe place must be found where the addict, often in the company of other addicts, can inject the substance with a hypodermic syringe into the exposed vein. The addict typically allows the solution to mix with blood by bringing blood back and forth into the syringe ("booting")—an act that some researchers see as analogous to sexual intercourse and that many users describe as more pleasurable and intense than sexual orgasm. In any event, as the short-term heightened feeling of euphoria that follows ingestion—the rush—subsides, the addict begins to experience the high, a feeling of general well-being that lasts about four hours. The cycle then needs to be repeated. Addicts often share their "works"—syringe and bottle cap—a practice that transmits diseases, particularly hepatitis and acquired immune deficiency syndrome (AIDS).[4] "This is the 'addict's cycle'— an existence almost literally from fix to fix—with the necessary heroin-related activities in between" (Rosenbaum 1981: 15).

In more recent years, heroin prepared for snorting or smoking has increased in availability and popularity. While heroin prepared for intravenous use typically is less than 10 percent pure, consumer doses of snorting or smoking heroin are often 40 to 45 percent pure. While injection is the only way to ensure that all of the substance reaches the bloodstream, the added purity of heroin prepared for snorting or smoking more than makes up for any loss

---

4. For an examination of the issue of AIDS and drug abuse, see the entire issues of the *Journal of Drug Issues* 19 (Winter) 1989 and 20 (Spring) 1990.

through less economical means of ingestion. And the user avoids the problems associated with the use of unsterile needles.

The heroin user recognizes the danger of addiction, but "it is typical of the early experience of the addict-to-be that he knows or knows of people who use narcotics and who get away with it" (Duster 1970: 192). He sees himself as indestructible: "the tendency of the ego to treat the self as exempt from the experience of personal disaster."

Here are some typical steps involved in becoming a cocaine abuser (based on Smith 1986):

- *Experimental Use:* The individual begins his or her initiation out of curiosity in a social situation in which some friends offer a "taste" of cocaine. Most of his or her friends are nonusers, and the subject uses cocaine only when it is offered to enhance feelings. Relationships remain normal, and no significant health or financial problems appear. There may even be an improvement in work performance and social functioning—gregariousness or extroversion.
- *Compulsive Use:* The subject begins to buy cocaine and increases the number of friends who are users. Solitary use of cocaine follows, and use to enhance moods and performance and to ward off depression associated with the "crash" of coming down off cocaine continues to increase. Social disruptions appear, particularly mood swings, as well as health problems due to a lack of proper nutrition and sleep. Work performance begins to steadily deteriorate, and the abuser avoids nondrug-using friends. He or she begins to encounter financial problems that result from supporting a growing cocaine habit.
- *Dysfunctional Use:* The abuser is preoccupied with drug use and associates only with cocaine-using friends. He or she may begin to deal in cocaine and/or to engage in other illegal or financially damaging activities to support the dependence on cocaine. Severe disruption of social life follows, including marital violence and divorce. Serious medical pathology appears, with a risk of seizure and toxic psychosis, paranoia, delusions, and hallucinations. The abuser has chronic sleep and nutritional problems as well. His or her physical appearance deteriorates; this is usually accompanied by a lack of concern with personal hygiene and dress. Compulsion, a loss of control, and an inability to stop despite adverse consequences lead the abuser to seek treatment, often because of pressure from family, friends, and/or employer and/or because of serious legal entanglements.

Early research (for example, Washton and Gold 1987) and journalistic sources reported that addiction to crack cocaine appeared to present a different progression because the speed with which this substance acts can lead to chronic habituation or addiction very quickly. In their research, however, Jeffrey Fagan and Ko-lin Chin (1991) found no significant difference between the addictive qualities of crack and powdered cocaine. Crack users, however, more often reported an inability to stop using it. For reasons that have not yet been determined, crack has proven to be more popular among women than heroin, leading to a significant increase in child neglect and abuse as well as to increasing numbers of newborn children with cocaine in their urine and syphilis resulting from the rampant sexual activity of their crack-abusing mothers (Kerr 1988f). A seller describes a crack house as "full of young girls—fourteen, fifteen, sixteen years old. Some of these girls stayed for days at a time, getting high and having sex with these guys," any guy who offered drugs (Williams 1989: 108). Smoking crack reduces inhibitions while creating a desire for more drugs, leading female users to unprotected sexual behavior and the risk of sexually transmitted diseases, including AIDS. In their research Fagan and Chin (1991: 327) found "no significant differences among those involved in crack, cocaine HCL [powdered cocaine], heroin or other drugs in the location, motivation or methods of introduction to their new drug." Most (90 percent) were introduced to the new drug by family or friends, and they (71 percent) got it free. In their study Andrew Golub and Bruce Johnson (1994) found that older crack users were nearly all former heroin injecters or cocaine snorters, while crack tended to be the first hard drug for younger users.

Let us examine some of the major sociological theories that help explain drug abuse.

Anomie

Derived from the Greek meaning "lack of law," *anomie* was used by the sociologist Emile Durkheim (1858–1917) to describe an abnormal social condition wherein the cohesion of society is weakened by some crisis, such as an economic depression, that causes each individual to pursue his or her own solitary interests without concern for the wider society. In 1938 Robert Merton "Americanized" the concept, arguing that no other society comes so close to viewing economic success as such an absolute value that the pressure to succeed tends to eliminate social constraint over the means employed to achieve success. In the United States, "good" (ambition) causes "evil" (deviance). According to Merton (1964: 218), anomie results when people, confronted by the contradiction between goals and means, "become estranged from a society that promises them in principle what they are denied in reality [economic opportunity]." This sense of strain is particularly strong among the disadvantaged segments of our population whose use of drugs is endemic.

Strain leads to anomie, to which people respond in one of four ways.

1. *Conformity:* Most scale down their aspirations and conform to conventional social norms.
2. *Rebellion:* Some rebel, rejecting the conventional social structure and seeking instead to establish a "new social order" through political action or alternative lifestyles.

3. *Innovation:* Some turn to innovation, which Merton defines as the use of illegitimate means to gain success, in particular professional and organized criminality, including drug trafficking.
4. *Retreatism:* The final response, retreatism, explains drug abuse: The individual abandons all attempts to reach conventional social goals in favor of a deviant adaptation.

The retreat into drug abuse allows the addict to expend time and energy to achieve an attainable goal—getting high. Dan Waldorf (1973: 10) notes:

> The need for heroin requires an active life. The addict *may* be, as psychologists have claimed, depressed, he may be psychopathic, and he may use drugs to escape some reality in his life, but he is active in pursuit of a demanding life that requires considerable skill and ability to sustain. Addiction is *not* some aberrant, part-time leisure activity that one indulges in from time to time but that never engages one's life. On the contrary, addiction does engage the addict in an active life that has a precise purpose and satisfies a specific physical need. Whatever the individual's motives for using heroin or the ways in which a specific addict approaches his heroin use, he most certainly experiences an absorbing or engrossing drive, lives an active life, and is very much part of a social group.

Edward Preble and John Casey (1995: 121) argue that the behavior of the heroin addict is anything but an escape:

> They are actively engaged in meaningful activities and relationships seven days a week. The brief moments of euphoria after each administration of a small amount of heroin constitute a small fraction of their daily lives. The rest of the time they are aggressively pursuing a career that is exacting, challenging, adventurous, and rewarding. They are always on the move and must be alert, flexible, and resourceful.

As a San Francisco addict explained to John Irwin (1970: 19), an addict's life is an adventure:

> Cowboys and Indians at the Saturday matinee didn't have a life that was any more exciting than this. The cops are the bad guys, you are the glorious bandit. . . . The chase is on all day long. You awaken in the morning to shoot the dope you saved to be well enough to go out and get some more. First you have to get some money. To steal you have to outwit those you steal from, plus the police. It is very exciting.

The typical heroin addict, note Bertram Sackman and his colleagues (1978: 433),

> exhibits as much pride in his heroin-getting skills as does the licit craftsman. He thinks about hustling and heroin, he talks about his exploits to other addicts, and his righteousness about heroin is rewarded by his women in the admiration and respect they accord him and his skills.

(Being "in the life," is reinforcing.) According to Richard Cloward and Lloyd Ohlin (1960), however, the heroin addict is actually a double failure, unsuccessful at both legitimate and illegitimate enterprises—his or her crimes are typically high-risk, low-yield activities. In this case, the first response to anomie is innovation; when that fails to reduce the anomic condition, the actor moves to retreatism.

Chein and his colleagues (1964) used a questionnaire to examine anomic attitudes. The questionnaires were administered to classes of eighth-grade male public school students in three neighborhoods with varying rates of delinquency—low, medium, and high (although even the "low" neighborhood had a relatively high rate of delinquency). Anomie was highly correlated with heroin use. But, as noted in chapter 1, the drug-crime sequence is not at all certain. According to the Cloward and Ohlin thesis, delinquency/crime precedes drug dependence, but research has not clearly supported this contention. In any event, the successful and skilled (innovative) criminal is so rare that the double failure thesis must be questioned (Lindesmith and Gagnon 1964).

And, of course, anomie does not explain cocaine use by persons who are not retreatists, and have achieved notable social and economic success in either criminal or noncriminal enterprises. Nor does it satisfactorily explain the relatively high rate of drug abuse among physicians, whose use of drugs is better explained by access than by anomie. Access, not anomie, is also put forth as an explanation for the high concentration of drug use in ghetto areas: Lack of viable economic opportunity induces more people to take the risks associated with drug trafficking, resulting in greater availability of illegal substances (Lindesmith and Gagnon 1964). Of course, greater access can be the result of anomie, drug trafficking being an innovative response to the anomic condition.

Bruce Alexander sees drug dependence (compulsive as opposed to casual or recreational use) as functional. The addict's behavior is an attempt to deal with a failure to integrate; that is, "failure to achieve the kinds of social acceptance, competence, self-confidence, and personal autonomy that are the minimal expectation of individuals and society" (1990: 39). In the *adaptive model,* as in the retreatist perspective, the addict perceives the identity and life of an addict with its attendant misery, ill-health, and social stigma to be less painful than the void of no identity at all. According to Alexander, persons who have not failed at integration and can form social strong bonds are not in danger of drug dependence. (This is an important part of social control theory, discussed below.)

Drug dependence serves "as a strategy to remove the individual [a retreat] from competitive situations in which defeat is almost certain" (Alexander 1990: 45). This model contrasts with the *disease model* of drug dependence because it sees the addict as a healthy person who is a social, not biological or psychological, failure. The addict is not under the control of a drug, nor is his or her drug use "out of control"; the behavior is self-directed and purposeful, although not necessarily on a conscious level.

Working from a psychoanalytical model, Schiffer (1988) found complementary factors motivating cocaine abuse in the patients he treated: cocaine taken because of a fear of failure—"retreatism"? "Unconsciously, despair seemed familiar and inevitable, and success seemed foreign and unattainable" (1988: 134). In contrast to these views, Erich Goode declares that "anomie theory seems to explain no significant feature of drug use, abuse, or addiction" (1989: 64). For Elliott Currie (1993: 145), however, the breeding conditions for anomie are connected to drug abuse, and these conditions have grown more severe: "It is not just that material prospects have dimmed for the relatively young and poor, but that they have dimmed just when there has been an explosion of affluence and a growing celebration of material consumption at the other end." This is exacerbated by the increasing gap between this country's wealthiest citizens and its poorest: Of the sixteen most industrialized nations, the United States has the widest gap between rich and poor, and its poor children are the worst off (Bradsher 1995).

Differential Association

As proposed by Edwin Sutherland (1973), differential association explains how criminal behavior is transmitted. Differential association complements learning theory: Criminal behavior is learned, and the principal learning occurs in intimate personal groups. The effectiveness of the learning depends on the intensity, frequency, and duration of the association. With respect to drug use, differential association can be conceived of as a scale in balance. On each side of the scale deviant and prosocial associations accumulate; at some theoretical point drug use will be initiated when there is an excess of deviant associations (drug abusers) over nondeviant or prosocial associations.

Robert Burgess and Ronald Akers (1969: 315) have reformulated Sutherland's central premise into a "differential association reinforcement theory":

> A person will become delinquent if the official norms or laws do not perform a discriminate function and thereby control "normative" or conforming behavior. We know from the law of differential reinforcement that the operant which produces the most reinforcement will become dominant. Thus, if lawful behavior did not result in reinforcement, the strength of the behavior would be weakened, and a state of deprivation would result. This, in turn, would increase the probability that other behaviors would be emitted which are reinforced and hence would be strengthened and, of course, these behaviors, although common to one or more groups, may be labeled as deviant by the larger society. Also, such behavior patterns themselves may acquire conditioned reinforcing value and subsequently be reinforced by the members of a group by making various forms of social reinforcement, such as social approval, esteem, and status, contingent upon that behavior.

In fact, initiation into drug use appears to be completely dependent on peer associations. "The first source of contact with the drug [heroin] was usually a friend," notes Troy Duster (1970: 180). The typical user receives his or her first "taste" free from new users who do not have expensive habits and will thus share their drugs. Most frequently he or she is introduced to heroin as a result of meeting a friend who was on his way to "cop" or was preparing a "fix": "He rarely sought out the drug the first time. Thus, initiation depended more on fortuitous circumstances than on a willful act by the new user" (Hughes 1977: 84).

In their study of heroin addicts in San Antonio, James Maddux and David Desmond (1981) found that only 4 percent obtained their first heroin directly from a dealer. Richard Rettig, Manual Torres, and Gerald Garrett (1977) report a similar scenario of heroin initiation in their book subtitled "A Criminal-Addict's Story." Chein and his colleagues (1964: 12) found that most addicts

> take their first dose of heroin free, in the company of one or more boys of their own age—in the home of one of the boys, on the street, on a roof, or in a cellar. . . . Frequently, the first occasion arises just before a dance or party, probably for the same reason that some of their peers and many adults brace themselves with one or more shots of alcohol, as a source of poise and courage.

Waldorf (1973: 31) found a similar pattern and notes that heroin use is a social, not solitary, phenomenon: "Persons are initiated in a group situation among friends and acquaintances." The first experience with drugs, notes Duster (1970: 183), "is usually in a group situation." In England the situation is the same: Geoffrey Pearson (1987: 9) found that "the first time someone is offered heroin it will be by a friend. Or maybe by a brother or a sister. But always by someone well known, liked and even loved." If the initiate becomes hooked, however, he or she is introduced into "an all-encompassing lifestyle that leaves little room for outside activities, except to the extent that these activities contribute directly to scoring and fixing heroin" (Rettig, Torres, and Garrett 1977: 210–11).

What of the relationship between parental use of psychoactive substances and the use of these substances by their children? (Peer relationships may simply serve as a mediating or intervening variable.) According to the theory of differential association, parental influence is responsible for generating the type of behavior that parents explicitly condemn in their children. "Use of legally prescribed drugs by adults," notes Denise Kandel (1974: 210), "would have as one unanticipated and clearly unwanted consequence the use of illegal, mood-changing drugs by their children." In her research, however, Kandel (1974: 235) found that "parental influence is relatively small, especially when compared with the influence of peers." Peers provide social acceptance or reinforcement for the rules governing acceptance or conforming behavior valued by the peer group. To the adolescent, this reinforcement is typically more relevant than that provided by parents. Kandel concludes, however, that parents can enhance differential association: "When their friends use illegal drugs, children of nondrug-using parents are somewhat less likely to use illegal drugs, whereas children of drug-using parents are more likely to use drugs."

According to Coryl Jones and Robert Battjes (1987: 15), the use of certain drugs allows adolescents to emulate adults while at the same time rebelling against parental standards:

> In emulation of their elders, adolescents use drugs to assuage immediate or anticipated discomfort, and, in rejection of their elders, they seize upon certain drugs of which their elders would disapprove. The use of illicit substances offers young adolescents the unique opportunity simultaneously to rebel against the rules their elders set down and to conform with the underlying attitudes which parental behavior manifests.

Anomie and differential association help explain what Patrick Hughes (1977: 88) calls a heroin epidemic. In a Chicago-based study he posits a theory of heroin contagion in the form of micro- and macroepidemics: "The multiple drug-using friendship group served as fertile soil for the growth of heroin addiction" into microepidemics, while

> macroepidemics generally occurred in neighborhoods that had recently undergone rapid population change, leading to a breakdown in community stability and established mechanisms of social control [anomie]. In other words, not only had heroin addiction become rampant in these neighborhoods, but so had other forms of deviance as well.

Hughes states that intensive treatment-outreach efforts can nip a new heroin-using network before it burgeons into an epidemic.

Identifying oneself as a "doper," "pothead," or "cokie" typically results from being enmeshed in a social network that includes others similarly situated. For some this becomes the primary reference group, and they may spend most of their time with other dopers, potheads, or cokies, withdrawing from nondrug-using social contacts. The substance becomes a symbol of group cohesion and unity and provides a sense of belonging, thus offering strong support for continued use (Roffman and George 1988).

Social Control Theory

If, as control theorists generally assume, most persons are sufficiently motivated by the potential rewards of engaging in deviant behavior such as crime and drug abuse, why do only a few engage in such behavior? According to control theorists, deviance "results when an individual's bond to society is weak or broken" (Hirschi 1969: 16). This category of person has difficulty forming social bonds, so his or her social relations are "cold and brittle" (Hirschi 1969: 141). The strength of this social bond is determined by internal and external restraints. In other words, internal and external restraints determine whether we move in the direction of deviance or law-abiding behavior.

Internal restraints include what psychoanalytic theory refers to as the *superego*—they provide a sense of *guilt*. As noted above, dysfunction during early stages of childhood development or parental influences that are not normative can result in an adult who is devoid of prosocial internal constraints. Some psychoanalysts refer to this as psycho- or sociopathology. (There is also evidence tying psychopathology to brain defects.) Criminal behavior devoid of any genuine remorse can be explained according to this theory. According to social control theory, deviants are poorly socialized, and the family is the basic unit for socialization. Thus, whether they are conceived of in terms of psychology or sociology, internal constraints are linked to the influence of the family (Hirschi 1969). Adolescent involvement with drugs and/or crime is therefore "highly correlated with family estrangement" (Brounstein et al. 1990: 10), an influence that can be supported or weakened by the presence or absence of significant external restraints.

External restraints include social disapproval linked to public shame and/or social ostracism and fear of punishment. In other words, people are typically deterred from criminal behavior by the possibility of being caught and the punishment that can result, ranging from public shame to imprisonment (and in extreme cases capital punishment). However, the strength of official deterrence—force of law—is measured according to two dimensions: risk versus reward. Risk involves the criminal justice system's ability to detect, apprehend, and convict the offender. The amount of risk is weighed against the potential rewards. Both risk and reward, however, are relative to one's socioeconomic situation. In other words, the less one has to lose, the greater the willingness to engage in risk. And the greater the reward, the greater the willingness to engage in risk. This theory explains why persons in deprived economic circumstances would be more willing to engage in certain criminal behavior. However, the potential rewards and a perception of relatively low risk can also explain why persons in more advantaged economic circumstances would engage in remunerative criminal behavior such as corporate crime.

Social control theory does not argue that only persons with weak societal ties will engage in drug use. Instead, it is the persistence of drug use that indicates a lack of societal bonds. Instead of conforming to conventional norms, through differential association some persons organize their behavior according to the norms of a delinquent or criminal group with which they identify or to which they belong. This is most likely to occur in environments characterized by relative social disorganization, where familial and communal controls are ineffective in exerting a conforming influence.

> A similar process also helps explain why drugs are sometimes rampant in more affluent communities. Just as strong families and cultures can shield the materially deprived from drugs, so weakened families, the absence of available or concerned adults, and the pervasiveness of an insistent consumer culture can make the affluent more vulnerable. (Currie 1993: 103)

In a longitudinal study designed to test social control theory, in particular that element relating poor interpersonal relations with deviance (in this case drug abuse), Denise Kandel and Mark Davies (1991: 459) found no relationship between integration failure and drug abuse. In fact, in contrast to psychoanalytic theory, they found illicit drug use to be

> positively associated with intimacy among members of male friendship networks, whether intimacy refers to confiding or to interacting with friends. Further, the structure of the networks of illicit users is similar to that of nonusers. To the extent that some differences occurred, they tended to indicate closer friendships for drug users than nonusers.

The researchers note that their findings tend to support subcultural (or cultural deviance) theory rather than control theory. George Vaillant (1983) found that culture plays an important role in the genesis of alcoholism and that family practices—drinking habits into which a child is socialized rather than a lack of social control (or even social distress)—are a dominant factor. The idea that drug abuse, in particular alcoholism, is the result of a habit learned in accord with the same principles that govern other learning experiences is consistent with the behavior/learning theory of drug abuse (Bandura 1969; 1977).

Subcultures/Cultural Deviance Theory

"Subcultures are patterns of values, norms, and behavior which have become traditional among certain groups." They are "important frames of reference through which individuals and groups see the world and interpret it" (Short 1968: 11). A person without important bonds to conventional society but with strong ties to a drug-using subculture would be more likely to abuse drugs. Members of a drug subculture promote its values and norms to persons who are attracted to "the life"—socialization. The person who joins must reorder his or her life in conformity with the new subculture in order to remain a member in good standing, to be accepted by other members. The subculture provides rewards and punishments along the lines proposed by operant conditioning in order to retain the member's loyalty.

Albert Cohen (1965) argues that certain lower-class subcultures negate middle-class values, and this negation is a severe handicap because middle-class cultural characteristics are necessary to succeed in our society. These characteristics include:

- ambition
- a sense of individual responsibility
- skills for achievement
- ability to postpone gratification
- industry and thrift

- rational planning, such as budgeting time and money
- cultivation of manners/politeness
- control of physical aggression
- respect for property
- a sense of wholesome recreation

The norms of some lower-class subcultures, according to James Short (1968) and Walter Miller (1958), are simply not conducive to conventional types of achievement. The members of an adolescent street group adhere to the norms of a lower-class subculture, whose focal concerns are (Miller 1958):

1. *Trouble:* law-violating behavior
2. *Toughness:* physical prowess, daring
3. *Smartness:* ability to con others, shrewdness
4. *Excitement:* thrills, risk, danger
5. *Fate:* being lucky
6. *Autonomy:* independence of external restraint

Trouble often involves fighting or sexual adventures while drinking; troublesome behavior for women frequently means sexual involvement with disadvantageous consequences. Trouble-producing behavior is a source of status. *Toughness* evolves out of the significant proportion of lower-class males reared in female-dominated households and the resulting concern over homosexuality, which Miller contends runs through lower-class culture. Gambling, also prevalent in lower-class culture, is rooted in the belief that life is subject to a set of forces over which there is little or no control—*fate. Autonomy* is often expressed in terms of "No one is going to push me around" and "I'm going to tell him to take this job and shove it." Such sentiments, however, often contrast with actual patterns of behavior; in other words, according to Miller, many lower-class persons desire highly restrictive social environments such as the armed forces, prison, and drug treatment programs: "Being controlled is equated with being cared for" (1958: 13).

Chein and his colleagues (1964: 13) note that "boys who become addicts are clearly related to the delinquent subculture. Even before they started using drugs regularly, most users have had friends who have been in jail, reformatory, or on probation" (1964: 13). Without exception, they found that addicts come from homes devoid of a father or a strong father figure—female-dominated households. They are identified with what others have dubbed the *criminal underclass subculture* (Johnson et al. 1990), of which the drug subculture is an important component.

The concept of a drug subculture, notes John O'Donnell (1969: 84), implies that addicts are in contact with each other.

In this contact, learning takes place. The learning can be of facts and techniques. For example, the neophyte can learn from more experienced addicts that his withdrawal symptoms are the result of not having his usual dose of narcotics, and will be relieved by a dose; that the intravenous route enhances the drug effect; how to obtain narcotics, or money for narcotics; new sources of narcotics; how to prepare narcotics for administration, and other knowledge of this kind. He will usually learn new attitudes too. He may learn to define himself as an addict, learn new justifications for his drug use, and new and negative attitudes toward the laws which try to prevent drug use.

As the drug user comes to define himself or herself as an addict, the wider society perceives him or her as such in a process known as *labeling*.

There are many different types of drug subcultures. Some are linked to the use of particular substances while others seem to be part of a larger subculture. Using participant observation, Patricia Adler (1985: 1) provides an insider's look at a marijuana- and cocaine-smuggling subculture centered in the middle- and upper-class environs of the coastal communities of Southern California. She states: "This subculture provides guidelines for their dealing and smuggling, outlining members' rules, roles, and reputation. Their social life is deviant as well, as evidenced by their abundant drug consumption, extravagant spending, uninhibited sexual mores, and focus on immediate gratification."

In general, cocaine abusers do not appear to present any clearly discernible subculture: Surveys of cocaine users have revealed that there is apparently no "typical" cocaine user (PCOC 1986).

Heavy cocaine users fit no easy stereotype of drug abuse:

A large proportion are successful, well-educated, upwardly mobile professionals in their early twenties and thirties. They are stockbrokers and lawyers and architects with sufficient disposable income to sink into a diversion that even at "social" use levels can cost $100 or more an evening. Many are, for the most part, otherwise law-abiding citizens who would cringe at being labeled criminals, even though they know what they are doing is illegal. A majority are men, but a growing number are women. And, as cocaine prices fall, more and more are teenagers and others for whom the drug's exorbitant cost once kept it out of reach. (National Institute on Drug Abuse 1986: 1)

Cocaine in the form of crack, however, seems to have produced a drug subculture in poor neighborhoods of urban areas.

The subcultural patterns include an argot of terms that describe the activities having to do with Crack, the various Crack combinations touted and paraphernalia needed for using, and the institution of base houses [where the substance is smoked] and Crack houses [where the substance is purchased]. (Frank et al. 1987: 6)

Blanche Frank and her colleagues (1987) point out that the development of this subculture is helping to glamorize and thereby spread the use of crack.

As opposed to heroin and cocaine hydrochloride, crack has proven particularly attractive to females, who are prominent among users and user-dealers. Young women quickly move from experimental to compulsive use. As a result, the female-dominated households typical of many ghetto neighbor-hoods are beginning to disintegrate. Mothers neglect or abandon their children, or worse—they encourage or direct them toward involvement in crack in an effort to support their own habits. The stimulation caused by crack creates high volatility; mothers lose control and child abuse results. The offspring of female crack abusers suffer from a host of serious impairments, and there are about 9,000 of these babies born every year. Young women, often adolescents, go on binges and engage in prostitution in order to secure the substance. Others become part of the crack subculture, acting as lookouts or filling other positions in drug networks whose leaders take on a parental role (Kolata 1989b). "Users typically smoke crack for as long as they have supplies of the drug or the resources to obtain more. For many women, a common way to finance a chronic crack habit is 'sex' " (McCoy, Miles, and Inciardi 1995: 172). The offspring of female crack abusers confront public school officials with a serious problem. As they reach school age, they enter a system that is unable to meet the needs of minority children in general. Add the special needs of crack children and the budgetary restraints imposed by a shortage of tax dollars and the results promise a continuation of the drug abuse cycle.

Harold Finestone (1964) drew a portrait of the black heroin subculture in Chicago at the beginning of the 1950s. He found that the stereotypical addict eschewed violence, used a deliberately colorful vocabulary, and disdained work. (This contrasted with a small number of white addicts interviewed by Finestone, whose type of adjustment stressed violence.) These addicts, whom Finestone (1964: 284) calls the "cats," had a lifestyle that centers on achieving "kicks." A kick is any act tabooed by conventional society "that heightens and intensifies the present moment of experience and differentiates it as much as possible from the humdrum routine of daily life." To the cat, heroin abuse provided the ultimate kick. A similar type of stereotypical heroin addict was found by Harvey Feldman (1977), who conducted his research in the late 1960s in a community pseudonymed "East Highland."

Symbolic Interactionism (Labeling)

Symbolic interactionism is a sociological approach that appears in such perspectives as labeling and societal reaction theory. Its central premise is that people make their own reality:

> Symbolic interactionists suggest that categories which individuals use to render the world meaningful, and even the experience of self, are structured by socially acquired definitions. They argue that individuals, in reaction to group rewards and sanctions, gradually internalize group expectations. These internalized social definitions allow people to evaluate their own behavior from the standpoint of the group and in doing so provide a lens through which to view oneself as a social object. (Quadagno and Antonio 1975: 33)

Symbolic interactionism does not explain drug abuse because its focus is not on the behavior of the social actor but on how the behavior or person is viewed by others—by society. Thus, Kai Erikson (1966: 6) states, "Deviance is not a property *inherent* in any particular kind of behavior; it is a property *conferred* upon that behavior by people who come into direct or indirect contact with it." In chapter 1 we noted that certain harmful substances—alcohol and tobacco—can be lawfully manufactured, distributed, and possessed while other chemicals are outlawed and the persons who choose to use them are labeled outlaws. In chapter 2 we noted that at one time the users of certain substances—opiates and cocaine—were not seen as outcasts or criminals. After the Harrison Act what had been lawful behavior became illegal, and a new class of criminals was created, as well as a lucrative new enterprise—drug trafficking. Using this perspective, Thomas Szasz (1974: 11) argues that "before 1914 [and the Harrison Act] there was no 'drug problem' in the United States." Thus, society is inclined to view those who abuse alcohol as suffering from a disease—alcoholism—while those who indulge in illegal chemicals are viewed—stigmatized—as deserving punishment. The societal interactionist view of drug use has important policy implications.

An example of positive labeling. Through participating in the community's Red Ribbon Campaign against drug and alcohol abuse, this group of Arizona high school students internalizes the message that being drug-free is good for them and society.

LABELING

Young offenders in particular must be confronted with penalties that both deter them from future drug use and embarrass them among their peers. Today, many young offenders boast about their lenient treatment in the hands of the authorities and wear it as a badge of pride; corrections officials must make sure that when juveniles are caught using or selling drugs, their punishment becomes a source of shame. We need a mix of sanctions for juvenile drug use that includes school suspension, parental notification, and postponement of driver's license eligibility, and extends to weekends of "community service" that involve arduous and unenviable public chores. (Office of National Drug Control Policy 1988: 25)

While those who abuse chemicals such as heroin and cocaine are labeled pejoratively, fired from employment, and subjected to law enforcement scrutiny, jail, and prison, the widespread acceptance of the traditional disease concept of alcoholism reduces the stigma associated with that problem. The disease model of alcoholism "provided a way for hundreds of thousands of alcoholics to make sense of their experience, to regain a measure of dignity and self-respect. And to begin to take control of and to rebuild their shattered lives" (Wallace 1993: 70).

Societal reaction labels—stigmatizes—certain actors, which causes a damaged self-image, deviant identity, and a host of negative social expectations. Furthermore, a damaged self-image can become a self-fulfilling prophecy. Edwin Schur (1973: 124) notes that "once an individual has been branded as a wrong-doer, it becomes extremely difficult for him to shed that new identity." During adolescence, "Many youths engage in socially disruptive and health-endangering behavior," although "most adolescents who experiment with drugs or other health-compromising and illicit practices do not escalate their worrisome behavior" (Baumrind 1987: 14). This should caution us against unnecessarily labeling persons, particularly young persons. "Zero tolerance" may be politically viable, but it can significantly limit a young person's social and economic options in a way that does not encourage conforming behavior as an adult.

According to Edwin Lemert (1951: 76), the labeled deviant reorganizes his or her behavior in accordance with the social reaction "and begins to employ his deviant behavior, or role based upon it, as a means of defense, attack, or adjustment to the overt and covert problems created by the subsequent societal reaction to him." This *secondary deviance* is best exemplified by drug abusers who are forced to associate with other drug abusers and, furthermore, must often resort to crime (secondary deviance) in order to support their primary deviance—drug habits.

Drug use has a sociopsychological dimension according to which the actor must *learn* that ingesting certain chemicals is desirable—intoxication, for example, is not inherently pleasurable. Expectations are based on learning and influence the direction of drug use. Thus, naive users such as hospitalized patients given doses of morphine to relieve pain do not experience euphoria and do not continue to seek out opiates when the pain subsides (Chein et al. 1964). Isidor Chein and his colleagues (1964: 348) go so far as to state that opiates "are not inherently attractive, euphoric, or stimulant substances. The danger of addiction to opiates resides in the person, not in the drug." Edward Brecher (1972: 13) notes that while there is "no doubt that the injection directly into a vein of a substantial dose of morphine or heroin produces a readily identifiable sensation," described by nonaddicts as a sudden flush of warmth and by addicts as a rush, few nonaddicts perceive the rush as particularly pleasurable. R. M. Gilbert (1981: 386) states that just because "a substance *can* have a pharmacological effect, it does not automatically follow that use of the substance is caused by or maintained by that effect." (See also Becker 1966: "Becoming a Marijuana User.") A sixteen-year-old cigarette smoker reports: "The first time I tried it, last year, I was like, 'This is totally gross.' I was coughing, and I turned green, and I thought I was going to throw up. So I had to *learn* to like it" (Verhovek 1995: 1; emphasis added).

People who believe they are drinking alcohol when actually they have been given nonalcoholic substitutes get more relaxed and outgoing, and a party atmosphere develops (Wood 1991). Indeed, levels of sexual arousal increase when people given a placebo believe they have imbibed alcohol, although alcohol reduces sexual performance (Mendelson and Mello 1995).

With these explanations in mind, in the next chapter we will examine the variety of methods used to treat drug abusers and prevent drug abuse.

REVIEW QUESTIONS

1. What are the components of a theory?
2. What is the major difference between testing theories in the natural sciences and in the behavioral sciences?
3. What is the theoretical basis for a physiological explanation of drug abuse?
4. What distinguishes psychological explanations of drug abuse from sociological explanations?
5. What is psychoanalytic theory's basic proposition?
6. How can problems experienced during the oral stage of development lead to drug abuse in the adult?

7. How can the use of depressants by an adult be connected to the anal stage of development?
8. What is the relationship between difficulty during the genital stage and drug abuse in adulthood?
9. How can drug abuse be explained by id drives?
10. How can drugs compensate for ego deficiencies?
11. How can a deficiency in superego development lead to drug abuse?
12. How can feelings of guilt generated by the superego lead to drug abuse?
13. How does psychoanalytic theory explain drug abuse during adolescence?
14. What basic belief underlies behaviorism/learning theory?
15. How does operant conditioning explain drug abuse?
16. According to the National Institute on Drug Abuse, what seven factors are associated with adolescent drug abuse?
17. What are the three stages to becoming an alcoholic?
18. What stages do heroin users and cocaine users go through on their way to addiction?
19. How does the theory of anomie explain drug abuse?
20. How does differential association explain the spread of drug abuse?
21. How does social control theory explain deviance, including drug abuse?
22. What is the connection between the delinquent subculture and drug abuse?
23. How does symbolic interactionism/labeling explain the "drug problem"?
24. How do expectations based on learning influence individual drug use?

5

DRUG ABUSE: TREATMENT AND PREVENTION

Many people are now implementing programs that comprise valid alternatives to the War on Drugs and are documenting their effectiveness. Although these approaches may seem tedious, they offer far more in the long run than the impossible promises of the drug warriors.—Bruce K. Alexander (1990: 2)

There are probably as many approaches to treating and preventing drug abuse as there are theories explaining the phenomenon. Unfortunately, drug abuse is unlike diseases whose etiology and thus treatment and prevention appear to be clearly physiological. In fact, considering drug dependence as a "disease," in the narrow sense of that term, is controversial (see, for example, Wilbanks 1990; Maltzman 1994). As with other chronic illnesses, the National Institute on Drug Abuse (NIDA) recommends speaking in terms of remission and improvement rather than "cure" when discussing the treatment of substance abuse ("Drug Abuse" 1987) because the problem has proven to be quite intractable.

Adding to the problem's complexity are the incongruities discussed in chapter 1: The moderate use of any variety of psychoactive substances—from nicotine to cocaine—may be the focus of a treatment response, not because of properties inherent in the chemicals themselves but because of the societal definition of "abuse." Thus, in the United States the moderate use of alcohol, tobacco, or coffee is seen as clearly within the mainstream of acceptable behavior, while even the occasional use of heroin or cocaine is often seen as requiring "treatment" (if not imprisonment). The difficulty is apparent: Patients who do not feel ill, do not want treatment, and are not dysfunctional are coerced into "treatment" by their families, their employers, or the criminal justice system. And, as Dean Gerstein and Henrick Harwood point out: "Drug treatment is not designed for the low-intensity user who is readily able to control his or her level of consumption and for whom functional consequences have not yet accumulated" (1990: 69–70).

This chapter examines the variety of treatment and prevention strategies for substance abuse. Typically, several treatment approaches are used simultaneously or sequentially, because drug abusers often suffer from a complex of medical and social problems. First we will examine approaches to treatment based on some of the theories discussed in chapter 4; then we will look at treatment programs that, although they appear under separate headings for pedagogical purposes, may in practice use a mix of psychological and sociological treatment modalities.

THE CURE INDUSTRY

Like the quest for an explanation of drug abuse, the search for a cure, particularly a "magic bullet" in the form of a chemical cure, has a history that cautions us to be skeptical. Opiates were once presented as a cure for alcohol dependence; morphine was offered as a cure for opiate addiction; cocaine was offered as a cure for morphine addiction (though patients became dependent on cocaine while remaining addicted to morphine); heroin was proposed as a cure for morphine addiction; and methadone was presented as a cure for heroin addiction. In fact, the "cure industry" has a long and often less than honorable history.

The medical profession "often shared the distaste for drug users that permeated the society" (Morgan 1981: 65). Furthermore, the problem of addiction was peripheral to the practice of most doctors, who typically sought to avoid association with the failure so common to treating drug dependence. This left a fertile field for the charlatan, and around the turn of the century the quest for a cure led to the development of an industry similar to that of patent medicines. Unregulated nostrums widely advertised as "cures" for drug dependence frequently contained alcohol, cocaine, and opiates. In 1906 these compounds came under regulation by the Pure Food and Drug Administration, which caused a significant decline in sales. In response, quacks began to portray themselves as outsiders feared by a medical establishment centered in the eastern United States. This approach had strong appeal, particularly in the South and Midwest, where anti-eastern feelings ran deep.

Any number of (self-proclaimed) doctors operated clinics for the drug dependent and grew quite wealthy from their "cures." The most famous was Charles B. Towns, a Georgia farm boy, insurance salesman, and stockbroker. David Musto (1973) refers to Towns as the king of the cure proclaimers. Arriving in New York City in 1901, Towns spent several years as a partner in a stock brokerage firm that failed in 1904. Shortly afterward he began advertising a "secret formula" that would cure drug addiction. The medical profession was skeptical, but Towns and his cure were widely accepted and promoted even by federal agencies; a 1909 article in the *Journal of the American Medical Association* was also favorable. The Charles B. Towns Hospital proclaimed a cure rate of between 75 and 90 percent. Determining "success" was rather simple—if the patient never returned, he or she was "cured." Eventually it was revealed that Towns' secret formula contained three ingredients: prickly ash bark, extract of hyoscyamus (henbane—a poisonous plant), and belladonna (deadly nightshade—a poisonous plant).

There were at the same time, however, sanitoriums whose approach to drug abuse was quite similar, if not identical, to that of many contemporary inpatient programs. The patient was withdrawn from drugs, sometimes with the aid of nonaddicting drugs. (Before 1914 treating addiction was all the more difficult because morphine was usually available in a pure form that made withdrawal all the harder [Morgan 1981].) The patient was given frequent baths, and as soon as he or she began to function more normally, a regimen of nourishing food and exercise was instituted. The patient, now withdrawn from drugs, engaged in such tasks as reading and gardening and was given a great deal of reassurance. The extent of the treatment often depended on a patient's ability to pay (Morgan 1981). More recently the profit that can accrue from treating certain types of substance abusers—such as those with appropriate health insurance—has led to the expansion of a private cure industry often based in health/hospital settings (Freudenheim 1987). These will be discussed later in the chapter.

CHEMICAL TREATMENTS

A variety of treatments use chemicals, often as a supplement to or in conjunction with some other form of treatment.

Opioid Antagonists

As part of the search for a "magic bullet," scientists developed a number of heroin antagonists, substances that block or counteract the effects of opiates. These substances bind with opiate receptor sites, thereby preventing stimulation, or displace an opiate already at the site. Some antagonists, such as cyclazocine and naloxone, have significant side effects. While cyclazocine taken orally effectively blocks the effects of heroin for twelve to twenty-four hours, it also produces nausea, sweating, a feeling of intoxication, anxiety, and hallucinations. Users suffer withdrawal symptoms when the substance is discontinued, although they do not develop a craving for it. A dose as small as .25 mg. of naloxone will block the effects of heroin for ten hours, but it is effective only when administered intravenously. Neither of these substances reduces the "drug hunger" of heroin addicts (DeLong 1972). Naloxone is recommended for testing for opiate dependence (Narcon test) before admission to a methadone program (Judson and Goldstein 1986). It has no effect on the nondependent person but causes immediate signs of heroin withdrawal in the opiate-dependent. The substance is administered to persons seeking methadone because such persons may not be opioid-dependent or may have only minimal dependence: "Treatment of these addicts with methadone raises important ethical and legal questions in view of the likelihood of producing physical dependence in previously non-dependent persons" (Peachey and Lei 1988: 200). According to federal regulations, admission to methadone treatment is restricted to persons who have been addicted to heroin for at least one year. The antagonist nalorphine (Nalline) counters the depression of the central nervous system caused by opiates and is administered as an antidote for heroin overdose.

The National Institute on Drug Abuse was instrumental in developing naltrexone hydrochloride, a long-acting orally administered narcotic antagonist first synthesized in 1965 and marketed as Trexan[1] by DuPont. This non-addicting drug defeats the effects of opiates by occupying their receptor sites in the brain. It will also displace any agonists that are present, causing severe precipitated withdrawal in people who are opioid-dependent. With few side effects, a fifty-milligram tablet of Trexan taken once a day will block any euphoric response to opiates. Discontinuing naltrexone will not cause

---

1. Under the brand name Revia, naltrexone is being marketed for use in treating alcoholism (Leary 1995).

withdrawal symptoms. Like any antagonist, naltrexone is effective only with patients motivated to give up the feeling of euphoria that opiates can provide. The manufacturer clearly states that it is recommended as an *adjunct* in the treatment of opioid abusers (Ginzburg 1986: 5): "Treatment failure cannot be blamed on the failure of naltrexone to block opioids nor is treatment success likely to be the consequence of a use of naltrexone alone."

Buprenorphine, which has a mixture of agonist and antagonist qualities, has been used experimentally to treat opiate dependence. The substance "has some methadone-like effects, but the magnitude of those effects is limited. It also has some antagonistic properties that block the effects of supplemental opioids" ("Drug Abuse" 1991: 54). While it is a highly effective analgesic—twenty-five to forty times more potent than morphine—it produces only mild withdrawal symptoms and does not appear to have a serious abuse potential (Ling, Rawson, and Compton 1994).

Detoxification

As in the past, contemporary treatment programs typically begin with detoxification—"a term left over from an obsolete theory that addicts suffer from an accumulation of toxins" (Dole 1980: 138)—with or without the assistance of drugs. Antagonists are sometimes used as an aid in heroin detoxification. Because of its potency, withdrawal from licit maintenance doses of methadone is generally accomplished by decreasing dosages. The antihypertension drug clonidine has been used to relieve many of the symptoms of opioid withdrawal, particularly those involving autonomic nervous system hyperactivity. The substance is nonaddicting ("Drug Abuse" 1987). Clonidine has been recommended by some physicians for the detoxification of methadone patients being maintained on relatively low dosages. Whereas methadone can be found in the patient's system more than a week after the last dose, clonidine has a shorter life. Thus, a clonidine patient can be placed on naltrexone immediately upon detoxification, whereas a methadone patient would experience unpleasant withdrawal symptoms under similar treatment (Ginzburg 1986).

Cocaine detoxification presents a serious problem because of the patient's craving for the drug. This may be associated with the depletion of dopamine, which, as noted in chapter 3, is essential to maintain life. The extreme depression that occurs during the early days of abstinence, particularly with crack users, can lead to suicide. While withdrawal from opiates and cocaine can be accomplished without using other chemicals—although the patient may feel quite uncomfortable—detoxification from sedatives can lead to seizures and cardiac arrest and therefore must be accomplished by decreasing dosages.

The use of chemicals to facilitate drug withdrawal can serve to attract drug abusers into treatment and increases the probability that they will complete detoxification. However, at least with respect to heroin abusers, the use of chemicals has some troubling aspects. Addicts typically enter treatment when their habit is too expensive to support and they have to work quite hard simply to prevent the onset of withdrawal symptoms, while a high level of tolerance prevents achieving the high. Under such conditions addiction is no longer fun. "Then he enters a detoxification ward and is comfortably withdrawn from heroin. Detoxification is made so easy, compared to 'cold turkey,' that addicts are not confronted with negatively reinforcing pharmacological and physiological aspects of addition" (Bellis 1981: 139). Detoxification reduces the addict's tolerance so that the high can be enjoyed once again at an affordable price. Drug program staff "should not be surprised or miffed when addicts leave the detoxification ward and inject heroin within a few minutes or hours" (1981: 140).

Opioid Agonists

Certain synthetic substances have a chemical makeup similar to that of opioids. The most widely used agonist, *methadone*, a wholly synthetic narcotic, was developed in Germany (where it was named *Dolophine* in honor of Hitler) when access to morphine was cut off during World War II. While it produces virtually the same analgesic and sedative effects as heroin and is no less addictive, orally administered methadone lasts longer. As opposed to the shorter-acting opiates such as heroin, the high it produces is less dramatic. While the effects of heroin wear off in two to three hours, the effects of oral methadone continue for twelve to twenty-four hours. Methadone can be prepared in a way that makes it difficult to inject, rendering it less likely to be diverted into the black market. After the war methadone was typically used in hospitals to systematically detoxify persons addicted to opiates (Dole 1980; Gerstein and Harwood 1990).

The first clinical use of methadone to treat narcotic addiction occurred at the U.S. Public Health Hospital at Lexington, Kentucky, where it was substituted for morphine and heroin to help detoxify addicted patients. Withdrawal from heroin was made relatively painless by first administering doses equivalent to the patient's street use of heroin. The doses were then lowered until the patient was no longer addicted, a process that took seven to ten days (Blackmore 1979). During the early 1960s, when narcotic addiction once again emerged as a major national concern, Vincent Dole and Marie Nyswander of Rockefeller University reported on their successful use of methadone to treat heroin addicts in a dramatically new way—through maintenance.

In 1964 Doctors Dole and Nyswander gave twenty-two hospitalized heroin addicts increasing doses of methadone until they reached a "stabilized state," meaning that they had neither withdrawal symptoms nor a craving for further increases in the dosage. "With repeated administration of a fixed dose, methadone loses its sedative and analgesic powers. The subject becomes tolerant" (Dole 1980: 146). The patients were then released, but they returned each day for an oral dose of methadone. The following year a research report by Dole and Nyswander (1965) revealed extraordinary results from this approach, which they ascribed to methadone's ability to provide a "pharmacological block" against heroin. Furthermore, it was theorized, heroin abuse in certain addicts results in a metabolic disorder that requires the continued ingestion of narcotics if the person is to remain homeostatic. With such disorders, methadone acts like any prescribed medicine by normalizing the patient's functioning. Continuing research with additional patients provided further support for methadone maintenance—addict patients refrained from heroin use, secured employment, and avoided criminal activity. In 1966 Dole and Nyswander established a large outpatient methadone program at Beth Israel Hospital in New York City. Other programs followed. Dole and Nyswander (1966) intimated that they had discovered the "magic bullet": methadone provides a *blockade* to the effects of heroin. (See Chambers and Brill 1973 for a review of these early methadone experiments and treatment programs.)

The typical methadone program begins with a period of inpatient care during which low doses of methadone are substituted for heroin (the patient is not informed of the dosage he or she receives). The methadone is usually mixed with orange juice (which helps reduce its bitter taste) and consumed in front of a nurse. Slow increases in dosage reduce the high, which disappears once tolerance develops. Addicts subsequently report daily on an outpatient basis and are given take-home doses for weekends. As they progress, less than daily pickups are permitted. Patients usually provide a urine specimen before they are given methadone. DeLong outlines the dosage levels (1972: 215):

> The general rule of thumb is that a daily dose of 100 mg. will block any effect of heroin for almost all addicts. Most programs administer a minimum of 80 mg., although a few may go as high as 300 mg. in selected cases. A program that administers 80 mg. or more is probably aiming at a blockage dose. A lower dose will not block the effect of heroin—an addict can achieve euphoria if he tries. However, the lower dose will block the narcotic hunger and thus remove some of the pressure for heroin use. For most addicts, a dosage of 40 or 50 mg. is enough to eliminate this craving, but an even lower dose may be enough if the addict has a light habit.

"The actions of chronic methadone treatment are to prevent withdrawal symptoms, prevent so-called 'drug hunger,' whatever the basis of that is; chronic methadone treatment also 'blocks' by cross-tolerance the euphoric effects of other short-acting narcotics" (Kreek 1987: 53).

By the late 1960s there were a few thousand addicts being maintained on methadone; by early 1973 there were approximately 73,000 (Danaceau 1974). This change was brought about by the Nixon administration, which was convinced that methadone could help reduce the crime rate—a cornerstone of the "law-and-order" presidency of Richard Nixon. Experts who knew better, argues Edward Jay Epstein (1974: 22), "chose not to deflate the unrealistic claim that methadone would substantially reduce crime." They hoped that such programs would lure otherwise recalcitrant hard-core heroin addicts into treatment. Eventually, however, the "bad news" came out. Methadone was not the "magic bullet." Indeed, there was no blockage but simply cross-tolerance—the patient maintained at significantly high doses of methadone would not experience the high from heroin. But methadone did not affect the euphoric rush. In fact, it was discovered that methadone patients, even those at high daily doses, were often abusing heroin as well as other drugs. Furthermore, while methadone maintenance was designed for heroin addicts, the problem was often one of polydrug use. In fact, cocaine is a major drug of abuse among methadone patients (O'Brien et al. 1990).

It was further revealed that the figures given out by Dole and Nyswander were deceptive: The rate of "cure" attributed to methadone was better explained by the screening mechanisms used—older and more motivated addicts were preferred—and by the fact that unsuccessful cases were simply dropped from the program and the final tabulations. Methadone clinics came under severe attack by those associated with the drug-free therapeutic communities (discussed below) and by 1979 were operating at about 90 percent of capacity

Heroin users line up for their doses of methadone at Beth Israel in the early years of the hospital's outpatient program.

(Blackmore 1979). Robert Newman (1977: xx) states that "proponents of specific treatment approaches rarely missed an opportunity to make exaggerated claims for their own modality, and to vilify publicly other therapeutic efforts." Residents also strongly opposed the opening of methadone treatment centers in their communities—the NIMBY (not-in-my-backyard) syndrome.

This is not to say that methadone maintenance has no role in treating heroin addiction. Methadone maintenance appears to be quite beneficial to certain heroin abusers. It can act as a crutch for persons motivated to give up heroin. The programs also attract addicts seeking a chemical cure, although the counseling and job assistance provided may be the real "cure." Even without such services, notes James DeLong (1972), methadone may have a placebo effect—the addict who believes that methadone is beneficial will find it so. To the extent that heroin addiction is explained by physiology, as discussed in chapter 3—for example, that persons with abnormal endorphin levels compensate by ingesting heroin—methadone maintenance is the equivalent of providing insulin to diabetics. If psychoanalytic theory is accurate, methadone may serve as an anti-aggression chemical for those heroin addicts whose drug use is based on a need to control rage and aggressive tendencies originating in a problematic anal stage of development (Khantzian 1980). In a review of evaluations of methadone maintenance programs, M. Douglas Anglin and William McGlothlin (1985: 274) conclude that "methadone maintenance has been shown to effectively reduce drug use, dealing, and income-generating crime, and to a lesser extent to increase employment and family responsibility." Furthermore, they note, methadone maintenance "appeals to a portion of the addict population that has not been amenable to other social intervention strategies." And methadone has proven effective in suppressing the administration of opiates in laboratory experiments with animals (Winger 1988).

There is some concern that older addicts who might have gone into remission without any intervention are nevertheless maintained on methadone—addicted. On the other hand, "Patients who terminate before they have achieved stable social functioning are very unlikely to remain abstinent"; and "even patients who terminate under the best of circumstances still may have less than a 50 percent chance of remaining abstinent as long as 3 years" (Hargreaves 1986: 70). Mary Kreek (1987) reports that only 20 to 30 percent of former "hard-core" heroin addicts remain heroin-free for three years or more following discharge from a methadone maintenance program, which is about the same percentage generally reported for other treatment modalities, including residential drug-free or short-term methadone detoxification programs. Anglin and McGlothlin (1984: 274–75) state that while methadone maintenance has not produced the wonderful results anticipated by early researchers, it makes a "real and beneficial contribution to reducing the social and individual costs associated with addiction."

The methadone maintenance program established by Dole and Nyswander at Beth Israel Medical Center in New York continues to operate, treating more than 8,000 patients who make more than 1 million visits annually to the center's twenty-three outpatient clinics. Most patients have been in continuous treatment for more than two years, about one-half for more than five years. Treatment is voluntary—the program will not take coerced patients. Patients can remain on methadone for as long as they wish, or they can opt for detoxification. For the past decade the program has operated above capacity.

Levo-alpha-acetylmethadol, better known as LAMM (or "Long-Acting-Methadone"), is used as a methadone substitute because it has the advantage of lasting up to seventy-two hours. LAMM also acts more slowly than methadone and does not produce a quick high (Schecter 1980; General Accounting Office 1990). This is both an advantage and a disadvantage. While LAMM's slow onset makes it an unlikely candidate for street use, addicts may be unwilling to stay with LAMM because of this quality (Ling, Rawson, and Compton 1994).

Chemical Responses to Cocaine Abuse

In chapter 3 it was noted that the neurotransmitter dopamine appears to play an important role in cocaine abuse. Dopamine antagonists are available, but they "can produce serious and permanent motor disorders, unpleasant subjective effects, or increases rather than decreases in cocaine self-administration in experimental animals" (Winger 1988: 125). Medication may be used as an adjunct to treating cocaine abusers either to deal with the deleterious effects of cocaine use itself or to treat the underlying motivations for using cocaine. Medication may be needed by addicts who are suicide risks during the post-cocaine "crash" period characterized by a lack of energy and an inability to feel pleasure or by those who exhibit transient psychotic states. Severe delusional states and paranoid reactions from excessive cocaine require medication.

As noted in chapters 3 and 4, it has been hypothesized that cocaine use may be a form of self-medication for those suffering from certain chemical deficiencies, particularly neurotransmitters that affect mood and activity levels. In fact, note Henry Spitz and Jeffrey Rosecan (1987), some cocaine abusers have been successfully treated with prescribed antidepressants, although crack addicts appear to be less amenable to such treatment (Kolata 1989). Rosecan and Edward Nunes (1987) outline the drugs used in treating cocaine abusers, emphasizing that medication should be used only as an adjunct to a comprehensive cocaine-abuse treatment program:

Tricyclic Antidepressants. Introduced in the 1950s, tricyclic antidepressants (TCAs) such as Tofranil (imipramine) treat depression by manipulating the level of several neurotransmitters.[2] They are used to treat cocaine depression, particularly in patients whose cocaine use appears to be a form of self-

---

2. In many cases, TCAs have been replaced by Prozac (fluoxetine), which acts on a single neurotransmitter—serotonin. Fluoxetine has been used experimentally to treat cocaine abuse, but with minimal effect (Foltin and Fischman 1994).

medication to ward off depression: "[TCAs] appear to reverse some of the neurochemical effects of chronic cocaine administration" (1987: 260). It is believed that TCAs may act as cocaine antagonists by displacing or blocking cocaine receptors in the CNS and may help reduce the craving for cocaine.

In 1990, the National Institute of Mental Health won a patent for one TCA, *desipramine*, a cocaine substitute used to wean users off the drug. The substitute does not have any of the dangerous side effects of cocaine and is believed to reduce craving (Andrews 1990). In limited clinical trials, desipramine has shown some ability to decrease the reinforcing effects of cocaine and to reduce the craving for it ("Drug Abuse" 1991; Kosten 1993b).

Lithium. Lithium is a standard drug for psychotic disorders, particularly depressive states. It is used with patients whose cyclothymia (mild mood swings) or manic depression or bipolar disorder (extreme mood swings) preceded cocaine use.

Ritalin. In patients with a history of child or adolescent attention deficient disorder (ADD)—inattention, impulsivity, hyperactivity—cocaine may be a self-medicating effort to deal with a disorder that in a few victims continues into adulthood. Such patients respond very well to methylphenidate (Ritalin), a stimulant that in ADD patients has a calming effect. While some of the literature indicates that Ritalin does not have positive results with non-ADD cocaine abusers, Edward Khantzian, a psychiatrist at Harvard Medical School, found Ritalin effective with cocaine addicts, although it is itself addictive (Goleman 1990).

Bromocriptine. Marketed as Parodel, bromocriptine is a dopamine agonist used to treat Parkinson's disease. As noted in chapters 3 and 4, chronic cocaine use may deplete the neurotransmitter dopamine, causing a craving in dopamine receptors. Bromocriptine appears to bind to the dopamine receptors, thus reducing the craving for cocaine. It does, however, have serious side effects, including nausea, headaches, dizziness, abnormal involuntary movements, and psychosis. According to Rosecan and Nunes (1987), its use is justified only in treatment-resistant cases where recovery is hampered by severe craving. And while bromocriptine decreased cocaine use in laboratory monkeys, its chronic administration produced toxic effects including preconvulsive signs (Winger 1988). A study by Kathryn Eiler and her colleagues (1995) found little benefit using bromocriptine to treat cocaine withdrawal.

PSYCHOLOGICAL TREATMENTS

Treatment based on psychological theories can be broadly divided into those that are psychoanalytically oriented—sometimes referred to as dynamic or clinical—and those that utilize some form of behaviorism. Some programs mix the two approaches.

A Psychoanalytic Approach

To the psychoanalyst,[3] symptoms of neurotic behavior such as drug abuse are tied to repressed material from early life—the developmental stages examined in chapter 4. The symptoms will disappear when the repressed material is exposed under psychoanalytic treatment. Thus, the psychoanalyst seeks to make unconscious affect and memories available to the patient's consciousness (Holinger 1989). Psychoanalysis and the therapies based on it aim "at inducing the patient to give up the repressions belonging to his early life and to replace them by reactions of a sort that could correspond better to a psychically mature condition." To accomplish this a psychoanalyst uses *interpretation*—attempts to get the patient "to recollect certain experiences and emotions called up by them which he has at the moment forgotten" (or repressed) (Reiff 1963: 274). This is accomplished through *dream interpretation* and *free association*. While in a relaxed state, the patient is asked to say what comes to mind about any given element in a dream, or the therapist may ask the patient to let a proper name or even a number occur to him or her. The train of associations stirred up by the dream, the name, or the number becomes an entry point for the release of repressed material, which the analyst helps the patient interpret. In order to recreate the emotional state originally attached to these associations, the therapist takes advantage of *transference*, the development of an emotional attitude, positive or negative, by the patient toward the therapist. Thus, the psychoanalyst may be emotionally (and unconsciously) perceived by the patient as a paternal or maternal figure in a re-creation of the emotions tied to very early psychic development.

In fact, psychoanalysis is rarely used to treat substance abusers, and there is a paucity of literature on treating substance abusers using this approach (Forrest 1985). This method requires highly skilled therapists, articulate patients—because psychoanalysis and the therapies based on it are "talking therapies"—and a long period of costly treatment: Psychoanalysis typically involves three to five fifty-minute sessions a week for as long as seven years, at $75 to $150 per session. There are few published reports of successful psychoanalytic treatment of drug-dependent persons, and those that exist deal almost exclusively with heroin addiction. As Clifford Yorke (1970: 156) has pointed out with respect to heroin addicts, "The number of confirmed addicts seeking psychoanalytic treatment is almost certainly very small, the number of analysts prepared to accept them even smaller, and the number of addicts who pursue their treatment to conclusion smaller still." In fact, Freud himself doubted the usefulness of psychoanalysis for treating drug addicts (Byck 1974).

3. *Psychoanalyst* is not a restricted title like that enjoyed by psychiatrists, who must be physicians, or clinical psychologists, who must hold a doctorate in psychology. While there are certifying bodies for psychoanalysts, they do not enjoy a government-supported monopoly on the use of the title. There is a great deal of acrimony between psychologists and psychiatrists over who is qualified to practice psychoanalysis (Goleman 1988).

Frederic Schiffer used short-term therapy based on a psychoanalytic model to treat cocaine addicts in a hospital and subsequently on an outpatient basis. He found their pathology to be based on psychologically abusive conditions covertly carried out by one or both parents during childhood. Patients were filled with a long-standing rage and pain that they could not understand. Therapy allowed the patient to understand and appreciate the cause of his (all patients were male) feelings. Finally, patients were helped to master their traumatic pasts by "reliving, in effect through the patient's memories and transference, the early trauma" (1988: 133). Another psychoanalytically oriented therapist recommends that the focus of early sessions be

almost exclusively in the realm of the patient's childhood and early adolescent history . . . since for many addicted individuals this therapeutic procedure results in a tremendous sense of release and catharsis. Many addicts and substance abusers have never before discussed their personal historicity in an open, honest, and drug-free manner with another human being. (Forrest 1985: 323)

The goal is to foster insight and self-awareness, which help the patient come to grips with his or her narcissistic disturbance that plays out as drug abuse (narcissistic tranquility). Substance abusers chemically extinguish unpleasant feelings and conflicts; self-awareness enables the patient to understand these emotions and thus learn to use nonchemical responses to them. (Forrest 1985).

Psychology, notes James DeLong (1972: 224), has not found a consistent pathology among drug addicts: "No psychiatric diagnosis can be shown to apply to all heroin addicts or even to a majority of them." George E. Woody and his colleagues (1983: 639) argue, however, that "recent studies indicate that the types of psychiatric problems observed in addicts are similar to illnesses that are often treated with psychotherapy when they occur in nonaddicted populations." In practice, therapists, while they may be steeped in psychoanalytic theory, generally avoid the psychoanalytical goal of effecting personality changes in drug abusers. Instead, they focus on improving the ego level of functioning by trying to help the patient maintain constructive reality-based relationships, solve problems, and achieve adequate and satisfying social functioning within the existing personality structure. The focus of treatment is on the functions of the ego and its ability to adapt to stress and changes in the environment, *despite* inadequacies experienced during early stages of development. (For a comparison of the effectiveness of different forms of psychotherapy with opiate addicts, see Woody et al. 1983, For a discussion of the techniques of psychoanalytically based therapy with addicts, see Kaufman 1994). This is accomplished through encouragement and moral support, persuasion and suggestion, training and advice, reeducation and counseling—not psychoanalysis. The therapist maintains a substance-abuse orientation and typically focuses on identifying specific needs rather than intrapsychic processes. He or she will deal with impaired self-esteem and ability to form sound interpersonal relationships, characteristics that depend on healthy psychosocial development at early stages of life. While recognizing the unconscious etiology, the therapist focuses on the client's present and future reality. Abstinence, not intrapsychic change, is the goal. For example, at City Roads, a short-term drug treatment program in London,

> the aims of counselling are to clarify *needs* and to build up the residents' *motivation* to do something about their needs. The first phase involves getting to know the resident, building up confidence and trust in City Roads. The very fact of sitting down and talking to a staff member who takes an interest in the resident is in itself fruitful. The resident starts to feel that someone cares. This was for them a very positive experience, which many drug abusers are not used to.
>
> The next step is "getting to the root of the problem," exploring the personal strengths and weaknesses and their origin, and the needs or problems under investigation are seen as psychological ones. People are seen as being unable to take responsibility, unable to form relationships, depressed, bitter, angry, frustrated, and lacking in trust. The causes of these problems are thought to lie in past experiences, most commonly in an emotionally unstable childhood characterized by lack of parental care, alcoholism in the home, an institutional upbringing, which are thought to lead to deprivation of warmth, care, and stability. (Jamieson, Glanz, and MacGregor 1984: 116–17; *edited*)

Behavior Modification

The strength of psychoactive substances as positive reinforcers and the negative reinforcement associated with abstinence provide conditioned responses that can explain the key difficulty in treating drug abusers: finding reinforcers that can successfully compete with these substances. Methadone's success in treating some heroin abusers can be explained in terms of behaviorism (Stitzer, Bigelow, and McCaul 1985). Furthermore, according to operant conditioning, for behavior modification to be effective, reinforcement, negative or positive, must follow immediately after the behavior is exhibited; this—instant gratification—is what makes drug use so reinforcing and why it is difficult to use behavior modification techniques with chronic drug users.

Behavior modification can also attempt to shape behavior by applying punishment or aversive stimulation. Aversive control was depicted in Stanley Kubrick's motion picture *A Clockwork Orange*. In actual drug treatment, Anectine (succinycholine) a muscle relaxant that causes brief paralysis but leaves the patient conscious, is injected into the subject immediately following the heroin cook-up ritual. The addict-patient remains conscious but is unable to move or breath voluntarily, conditions that simulate the onset of death. The dangers of heroin use are recited while the patient remains paralyzed.

Drug antagonists can serve a similar function by rendering opiates or other substances ineffective—lacking positive reinforcement—or extremely unpleasant—negative reinforcement or punishment. Disulfiram (Antabuse), metronidazole, or chlorpropamide can serve this purpose for alcohol abusers. Antabuse, the best known of these substances, disrupts the liver's metabolism of alcohol, producing a severe reaction that includes stomach and head pain, extreme nausea, and vomiting. (Milder reactions can be triggered by any number of products that contain alcohol, such as cough medicine, mouthwash, or even skin creams.) (In 1990 a patent was granted for a substance that has the appearance and smell of cocaine and even produces a numbing effect but is not psychoactive. The substance is used in conjunction with an aversive chemical (Andrews 1990).

In voluntary patients electric shocks may be self-administered whenever a craving for the chemical arises. Some researchers report that the use of chemical or electrical stimuli has not proven effective in producing a conditioned aversion in drug abusers, while success has been reported with verbal aversion techniques in which "a patient is asked to *imagine* strongly aversive stimuli (usually vomiting) in association with imaginal drug-related cues, scenes, and/or behavior" (Childress, McLennan, and O'Brien 1985: 951). Thus, *imagined* aversive stimuli may be superior to *real* aversive stimuli with the drug-dependent (although this appears to run contrary to a great deal of research in operant conditioning). In any event, "Aversive counterconditioning is not a substitute for support for life-enhancing behavior, rather it suppresses the undesirable behavior while other modalities support positive alternatives" (Frawley and Smith 1990: 21).

In an experiment using both chemical and verbal aversive techniques, cocaine abusers were provided with a nonpsychoactive substitute that smelled like cocaine and numbed the nose. The white substance was set out with a razor blade, straw, and mirrors for the preparation of "lines." The patient received an injection of nausea-producing drugs. Just before the onset of nausea, he or she snorted the lines of "coke." During the three-hour recovery period, the patient was encouraged to dwell on the drug paraphernalia and pictures of cocaine and to pair the use of cocaine with negative consequences. After six months of in-hospital and outpatient booster treatments, the abstinence rate was 78 percent. Although a few patients had used cocaine again during the six-month period, the relapses were quite brief (Frawley and Smith 1990).

Other behavioral therapies use biofeedback and relaxation training, and sometimes assertiveness training, to prepare drug abusers to better cope with the stress and anxiety believed linked to drug use. Researchers have found that certain environmental cues can activate drug cravings (Dole 1980; O'Brien et al. 1993). These are countered by desensitization treatment: "Patients are usually first relaxed, then given repeated exposure to a graded hierarchy of anxiety-producing stimuli (real or imaginal)" in order to provide a form of immunity (Childress, McLennan, and O'Brien 1985: 957).

Social learning theory, a variant of behaviorism, focuses on cognitive mediational processes. According to this view, people are active participants in their operant conditioning processes—they determine what is and what is not reinforcing. For example, as noted in chapter 4, the actor must *learn* that ingesting certain chemicals is desirable. In other words, behavior is complex and reinforcement often abstract. Thus, notes Albert Bandura (1974: 862), "Human beings can cognitively bridge delays between behavior and subsequent reinforcement without impairing the efficacy of incentive operations." People have a unique capacity to use abstractions—symbols such as the medals and trophies dear to any amateur athlete—as important reinforcers.

The drug abuser is seen as lacking the level of social competence necessary to cope adequately with a variety of situational demands. In using operant conditioning with drug abusers, the social learning theorist stresses patient analysis in order to discover the variables that are reinforcing. The therapist attempts to discover the situational demands and their related negative emotions that are related to the patient's drug use. The treatment begins with an assessment of the positive and negative aspects of drug use and a self-report on the type, amount, and frequency of drugs used. The assessment includes a focus on the social, physical, and emotional environments in which drug use occurs. After the assessment, the role of the therapist is to enable the patient to deal with triggering behavior so that it does not lead to drug use, with the patient's own report of the negative aspects of drug use serving as a motivator for adopting more positive coping strategies (Donovan 1988).

A cognitive approach developed by Anna Rose Childress (1993) first conducts a study to develop a set of cues that trigger drug cravings. Patients are then taught methods of combatting the urges, including a planned delay before acting on a craving, having an alternative behavior planned for this delay period, and systematic relaxation to counter drug arousal. Other techniques include listening to a recording of positive/negative craving consequences that instructs the addict to list the three most negative consequences of relapsing into drugs and the three most positive consequences of not acting on cravings. Negative imagery is used to encourage patients to remember their worst period of addiction—a type of scare tactic. Fred Wright and his colleagues (1993) use the Socratic method—challenging questions and answers—to stimulate patients to examine and modify their drug-related beliefs. Patients are also taught to keep a log of their cravings; after each entry they write spontaneous negative thoughts.

Success in modifying behavior using learning theory has been experienced in the controlled setting of a total institution (Goffman 1961) such as a prison or hospital. In such environments important reinforcers can be manipulated by therapists, often in the form of contingency management and contingency contracting.

Contingency Management and Contingency Contracting

Sometimes referred to as the *token economy*, contingency management rewards residents for behavior classified as "therapeutic" by providing them with points or tokens that can be redeemed for items valued by the patient, such as snacks, television time, and weekend passes. Roy Pickens and Travis Thompson (1984) describe the program utilized in a drug-treatment ward at the University of Minnesota Hospital, where point transactions—added or subtracted—are recorded by staff members in a small booklet issued daily to each patient. Points can be earned for engaging in personal-care activities such as cleaning the room or washing clothes, for doing chores such as preparing meals, for participating in ward activities, for attending classes aimed at helping residents think rationally about themselves, and for assertiveness and problem-solving that improve interpersonal skills. Extra points can be earned for good-quality participation; these are given to the resident at the end of each activity: "At this time a staff person marks the points earned in the patients' point booklets and briefly describes how the quality of their participation earned them extra points, or how they might improve their participation in the class to earn extra points" (1984: 55). Points earned are exchangeable for various goods or services, such as snacks, soft drinks, cigarettes, or personal-care items. It is obvious that contingency management is not designed to directly impact on drug-using behavior but is a means of getting patients to participate in the therapeutic activities that have abstinence as a goal.

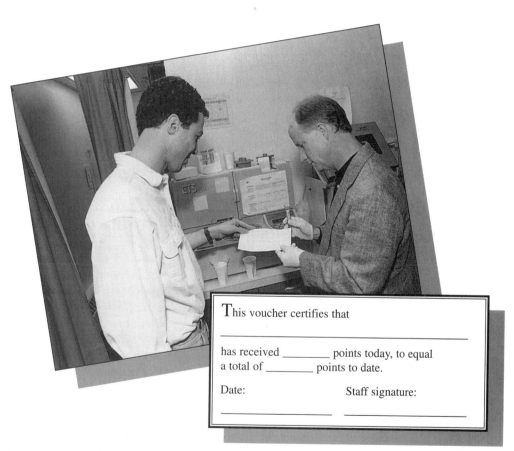

This voucher certifies that

_____

has received _____ points today, to equal
a total of _____ points to date.

Date: Staff signature:

_____   _____

An example of contingency management. In a program for cocaine abusers at the University of Vermont, a physician (right) gives a patient a voucher that can be exchanged for items that promote healthy living, such as YMCA passes and continuing education materials. The voucher, similar to the one shown here, is earned with urine specimens that test negative for cocaine.

Stephen Higgens and Alan Budney (1993) describe a contingency management program for outpatient cocaine abusers that provides points for drug-free urine samples: The number of points multiplies when consecutive negative samples are submitted. The points can be exchanged for a variety of gift items. At the end of three months, patients are shifted from points/gifts to lottery tickets.

Contingency management has been used by methadone clinics to treat patients who ingest opiates and other drugs while on methadone maintenance or methadone withdrawal programs. Rewards for a drug-free urine sample include a cash payment and methadone take-home privileges. Negative contingencies include the loss of cash payments or take-home privileges, daily urinalysis, and counseling (Stitzer et al. 1984; see also Magura et al. 1987; Kidorf and Stitzer 1996). Stephen Magura and his colleagues (1987: 117) report that contingency management utilizing take-home privileges did not have a significant effect on most methadone patients whose polydrug use included cocaine: Cocaine "seems especially attractive to patients and thus was resistant to behavioral modification."

The University of Minnesota Hospital utilizes contingency contracting in the form of "a formalized agreement between a staff person and the patient that specifies the manner in which learning principles are applied to the modification of the patient's behavior." The contingency contract is drafted and signed by the parties. The contract "details the specific behaviors to be changed, how such behaviors are to be monitored, and the contingencies [rewards or punishments] to be placed on the behaviors" (Pickens and Thompson 1984: 57). Contingency contracts are also used with patients during the first several weeks after discharge. The contracts are designed to allow for the implementation of behavioral contingencies in the patient's own home environment to reduce the likelihood of a return to drug use.

Contingency contracting with negative reinforcement has been used to ensure abstinence in cocaine treatment programs: "For example, a patient participating in such a contract will agree that, in the event of relapse, a previously drafted letter will be sent to his employer informing the latter of the patient's cocaine problem" (Kertzner 1987: 145). Robert Kertzner states that negative contingency contracting has been found to be very effective with patients who agreed to participate. However, one of the limitations of this strategy, he notes, is the large number of patients who decline to participate. "Others have modified this technique to include positive sanctions for continued abstinence, such as returning patients' money held in escrow" (1987: 146).

Opposition to Behavior Modification

There has been considerable opposition to both the theory and practice of behaviorism. Opponents argue that it views human beings as equivalent to animals—classical behaviorists refer to all species as organisms—and that the techniques used are reminiscent of animal training. It is sometimes described by opponents as "brainwashing." Behavior modification proceeds on the premise that whatever has been learned can be unlearned and replaced by a more suitable behavior. Drug use is therefore the result of inappropriate reinforcement that supports its continuance—drugs are obviously powerful reinforcers to those who enjoy them. The behavior modifier looks for the reinforcers that maintain the maladaptive behavior and designs strategies to change environmental conditions so that contingencies are placed on behavior patterns that are accepted by society. As opposed to other forms of therapy that require their subjects' cooperation, behavior modification can be accomplished without the patient's knowledge. In programs that use contingency management, failure to participate or conform results in punishment. Opponents have argued that the real purpose of such programs is to guarantee docile residents eager to earn things that while important in a total institution have no important reinforcing value in the outside world.

Behaviorists respond that they of course recognize the difference between animals and humans—the term *organism* simply being a semantic convenience. And while "brainwashing" does rely on many operant procedures, it involves more than changing behavior. Brainwashing seeks to change attitudes, opinions, and beliefs. Further, failing to inform patients that they are being treated by operant techniques would be both unethical and contrary to sound treatment practice: Change occurs more rapidly, behaviorists argue, when the patient knows the rules and what behavior is being targeted for modification.

Group Treatment

Treatment using psychotherapeutic techniques or behavior modification may utilize casework—one-to-one counseling—or group approaches. According to Helen Northern (1969: 52), "One of the advantages of the uses of the group approach is that stimulation toward improvement arises from a network of interpersonal influences in which all members participate." The basic theory underlying this approach is that peer interaction is more powerful than therapist-patient interactions within the one-to-one situation. In casework the relationship between therapist and patient may remain distant because the therapist typically lacks the all-important personal experience with drug abuse. In the group approach, the group, not the group leader-therapist, is the helping instrument, obviating the therapist's lack of personal experience with drugs. Furthermore, many critical interpersonal behaviors that may not emerge in the casework approach will emerge in a group (Flores 1988). "Group members are more likely to try new forms of behavior if these have been demonstrated effectively by others" (Kauffman, Dore, and Nelson-Zlupko 1995: 365).

Treatment groups are typically formed around one basic trait that all members share and from which the group derives its descriptive label. For example, they may be formed around cocaine abuse, with a subtrait being age or gender.[4] In general, notes Henry Spitz (1987), the more heterogeneous the group elements, the greater the intragroup tension, which promotes interaction. The more homogeneous the group elements, the greater the basis for intermember trust and group cohesion. Groups may also be organized at different points in the treatment process, such as intake, detoxification, inpatient, and outpatient. There may also be groups for parents, siblings, and spouses. No matter how the group is organized, commonalities "not only form the basis for group cohesiveness and support, but also facilitate the emergence of shared themes which serve as a focal point for group interaction" (Spitz 1987: 168). While group approaches have many advantages over casework, considerably fewer therapists are trained in the former than in the latter. Further, "patients whose motivation for change appears highly questionable should not be accepted into a group-oriented treatment program, because they usually have a negative, demoralizing impact on other patients who may be working hard to remain abstinent" (Washton, Stone, and Hendrickson 1988: 380).

While group approaches may vary,

> Most professionals who work with alcoholics and addicts on a sustained basis agree that group therapy offers the chemically dependent individual unique opportunities (1) to share and to identify with others who are going through similar problems; (2) to understand their own attitudes about addiction and their defenses against giving up alcohol and drugs by confronting similar attitudes and defenses in others; and (3) to learn to communicate needs and feelings more directly. (Flores 1988: 7)

Support provided by the group enables it to act as a catalyst for abstinence. (This has been the writer's experience working with groups of adolescent drug abusers.)

DRUG TREATMENT PROGRAMS

The treatment of drug-dependent people presents an obvious problem: If we don't know the cause, how can we offer the "cure"? This problem is exacerbated by programs that fail to develop theory-centered treatment responses or to incorporate the results of research into their approach to clients. While matching patient needs with specific treatments is the norm in medicine, this approach may be missing even in drug programs housed in medical settings (Hester and Miller 1988). The admissions policies of some inpatient programs depend more on financial status than on patient needs and program resources. Often these are relatively new programs looking for middle- and upper-class

---

4. For a discussion that favors women's therapy groups for drug addicts, see Kauffman, Morrison, and Nelson-Zlapko (1995).

patients, who are most likely to have third-party or insurance support. Assessment and intake are informal or based on available space. Mounting health-related costs have caused third-party payment organizations to "require treatment organizations to further document and better justify the need for treatment" (Winters and Henley 1988: 4). Indeed, the American Society of Addiction Medicine has established minimum criteria for inpatient drug and alcohol treatment for adults: Severe but manageable withdrawal risk; need for medical monitoring and a twenty-four-hour structured setting; high resistance despite negative consequences; inability of outpatient treatment to curtail drug use; home environment dangerous for recovery.

Treatment can be accomplished in a variety of settings—voluntary, involuntary, inpatient, and outpatient. The cost of these programs varies according to whether they are inpatient or outpatient, the qualifications of their staff, and the length of treatment. A particularly vexing problem is community opposition to drug-treatment programs. Attempts to open treatment centers in New York, New Jersey, Connecticut, and California have often been thwarted by vigorous community opposition (Kolbert 1989). In one incident the highly regarded Phoenix House (discussed below) had to abandon plans to open a treatment program on the site of a medical center in California's San Fernando Valley. The Nancy Reagan Center, as the facility was to be called, was enthusiastically supported by the former first lady, who was active in raising money for the project. Citing community opposition, she "just said no" and suddenly pulled out of the project, which led to its demise (Bennetts 1989).

Let us examine the settings and treatments offered by some drug programs.

Mandatory Treatment Programs

About half the states have statutory provisions for the civil commitment of drug abusers (Leukefeld and Tims 1988), although few make any regular use of them. Civil commitment, or the nonpunitive incarceration of addicts for purposes of treatment, dates back to 1935, when a federal narcotic "farm" was opened in Lexington, Kentucky. A second one was opened in 1938 in Fort Worth, Texas. Addict-patients who requested commitment and involuntary patients who had been prosecuted for criminal offenses spent six months at these facilities, which followed a standard course of withdrawal—physical restoration, psychological therapy in the form of individual and group counseling, and vocational counseling—after which patients returned to their communities. The physical structure of these facilities, however, resembled that of a modified prison, and security was strict (Morgan 1981). Reviews of the program were either mixed or inconclusive, and the federal government chose not to expand civil commitment. In 1961, however, California enacted a program built on the Lexington model.

California Civil Addict Program

In 1961 the California legislature established within the Department of Corrections the California Rehabilitation Center for the compulsory care of persons addicted to narcotics. In 1962 the U.S. Supreme Court ruled (in *Robinson v. California,* 370 U.S. 660) that drug addiction was an illness and that therefore a state could not make this status a crime. In that decision the Court also suggested that the Constitution would not be offended by involuntary civil commitment for the purpose of treating the illness of addiction. A later decision gave further support to the commitment-for-treatment approach, and in 1963 the legislature amended certain sections of the California Rehabilitation Act to emphasize treatment.

California statutes provide four methods of commitment (*All About the Civil Addict Program* 1994):

1. After a person has been convicted and sentenced to prison for a felony, the judge may suspend the sentence and order the district attorney to file for a narcotic petition. If the judge subsequently determines that the person is addicted or is in imminent danger of becoming addicted, the sentence can be suspended and the offender placed in the California Rehabilitation Center (CRC) at Norco. Most residents at the CRC fall into this category.

2. After conviction for a misdemeanor and before or after sentencing, the judge can certify the case to superior court for a commitment petition. After an examination, the offender may be sent to the CRC.

3. Any interested party may report to the district attorney under oath his or her belief that another person is addicted to narcotics or is in imminent danger of becoming addicted. If sufficient evidence (probable cause) is present, the district attorney may petition the superior court for a period of commitment not to exceed twelve months.

4. Any person who believes that he or she is addicted or about to become addicted may report such belief to the district attorney, who can then petition the superior court for a period of commitment not to exceed twelve months.

The California Rehabilitation Center, which has the capacity for about 4,000 males and 800 females, is a medium-security facility of the Department of Corrections with open dormitories, double fences, and armed officers at the perimeter. It has remedial and high school educational facilities, as well as vocational training. Various self-help groups such as Alcoholics and Narcotics Anonymous may be joined voluntarily. Leisure activities include organized and individual athletics. Following institutional care, civil commitments are released to aftercare/parole supervision, which includes regular testing for drug use. Patients who fail to live up to the terms of release can be returned to the CRC. Release to aftercare and return to the CRC are decided by the Narcotic Addict Evaluation Authority. Felony commitments on aftercare who remain drug-free for twelve or sixteen months (depending on the length of the commitment) may receive early discharge. Research into the performance of released patients indicates that they did no better than addicts who received drug therapy in California prisons.

Although the stated intent of the enabling legislation was, as noted above, nonpunitive, the program was placed under the Department of Corrections rather than a more appropriate treatment agency such as the Department of Mental Hygiene. As William McGlothlin, Douglas Anglin, and Bruce Wilson (1977: 5) note: "There is little doubt that the political climate in 1961 favored strong measures to suppress narcotic addiction and that the intent of the civil commitment legislation was at least equally as much for control as for treatment." Nevertheless, they report that the program clearly reduced daily narcotic use and related behavior among outpatient clients and that "to a lesser extent, the program also appeared to have had lasting benefits subsequent to discharge" (1977b: 198).

New York State Narcotic Addiction Control Commission

In 1966 New York adopted a program that incorporated most of the elements of the California program. But instead of placing its program in the Department of Corrections, New York established an independent agency, the Narcotic Addiction Control Commission (NACC), which was based on a mental health model. Addicts could be committed through the civil process—voluntarily or as a result of petitions initiated by family members—or through the criminal process in lieu of a prison term. Civil commitments and those based on misdemeanors were for a maximum of three years, with a five-year commitment for felonies. Addicts were required to reside in closed institutions—some were former prisons—where they received treatment for their addiction as well as educational opportunities and vocational training. Released to aftercare, they came under the supervision of a narcotic parole officer (as distinguished from a parole officer working for the Department of Corrections). Reverting to drug use could result in further institutional care, and urine tests were frequent. Unfortunately, so was absconding, because many addicts simply "jumped parole." The narcotic parole officers were unarmed and did not have peace-officer status, so absconders typically were not apprehended. A major factor in the demise of NACC was the constantly increasing cost of continuing a program for a supply of addicts that seemed unending.

Politics may have been another factor. The program had been established by Governor Nelson Rockefeller, who at the time was making a second bid for the Republican presidential nomination—he had been rejected in 1964 for being "too liberal" (the Republicans nominated Barry Goldwater). The drug problem, argues Edward Jay Epstein (1977), gave Rockefeller an issue that could attract conservative support without alienating liberal Republicans. In 1974 Rockefeller became vice president under Gerald Ford, and the program was dismantled. By 1979 all NACC commitment centers were closed, and a number of them were (re)converted into correctional institutions.

Federal Narcotic Rehabilitation Program

In 1966 Congress enacted the Narcotic Rehabilitation Act (NARA), which provides for the commitment of three groups:

1. Addicts choosing treatment as an alternative to criminal prosecution;
2. Addicts assigned after a criminal conviction; and
3. Addicts not criminally charged who volunteer for treatment or whose commitment is requested by a relative.

The act empowers a sentencing judge to commit drug-abusing defendants for a period of evaluation not to exceed ninety days. During that time the offender is evaluated by NARA staff from the Bureau of Prisons to ascertain his or her suitability for treatment. A report is then submitted to the judge, who can commit the defendant to the custody of the Surgeon General for treatment that may last up to thirty-six months; convicted offenders may be committed to the Bureau of Prisons for up to ten years of drug treatment (but not for more than the maximum sentence for their conviction) or placed on probation. Individuals who have not been charged with a federal crime can be committed by means of a petition submitted by the U.S. attorney on their behalf or on behalf of a relative. Involuntary patients have a right to a hearing with counsel to determine whether they are to be civilly committed. Treatment may last up to forty-two months, although the institutional phase may last only six months (Kay 1973). Upon release from institutional treatment, patients can be required to participate in an aftercare program under the Probation Division of the U.S. courts. A relapse can result in being reinstitutionalized (Eaglin 1986).

Other Mandatory Treatment Programs

Established as a result of court overcrowding, special "drug courts" have proven popular. In 1989 a special drug court was established by judicial order in Miami, Florida. This high-volume court expands on traditional drug-defendant diversion programs by offering a year or more of court-run treatment; defendants who complete this option have their criminal cases dismissed. Between 1991 and 1993 Miami influenced officials in more than twenty other jurisdictions to establish drug courts (*The Drug Court Movement* 1995).

In Maricopa (Phoenix) County, Arizona, the goal of drug court is considerably different—to increase the number of cases in the system. Using a catchy "do drugs, do time" slogan, law enforcement agencies target casual users to enforce a "zero tolerance" policy. Users are "held accountable" for their illegal drug use by a policy of arrest and threatened prosecution; those who accept the treatment option—which includes paying fees—avoid further court action. The program increases the number of persons remaining in the criminal justice system—"net-widening"—by reducing the number of petty

FIGURE 5.1
Diversion and Treatment Program Client Flow Chart

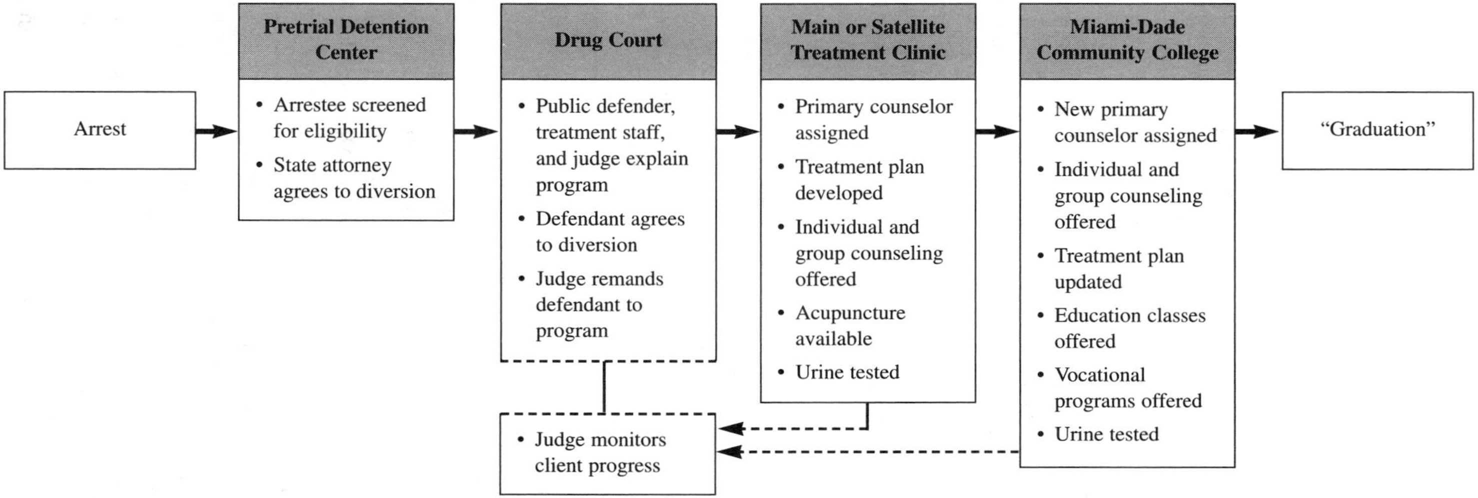

```
                    ┌──────────────────────┐
                    │ Pretrial Detention   │
                    │       Center         │
                    ├──────────────────────┤
┌─────────┐         │ • Arrestee screened  │
│ Arrest  │────────▶│   for eligibility    │
└─────────┘         │ • State attorney     │
                    │   agrees to diversion│
                    └──────────────────────┘
```

Pretrial Detention Center
- Arrestee screened for eligibility
- State attorney agrees to diversion

Drug Court
- Public defender, treatment staff, and judge explain program
- Defendant agrees to diversion
- Judge remands defendant to program

Main or Satellite Treatment Clinic
- Primary counselor assigned
- Treatment plan developed
- Individual and group counseling offered
- Acupuncture available
- Urine tested

Miami-Dade Community College
- New primary counselor assigned
- Individual and group counseling offered
- Treatment plan updated
- Education classes offered
- Vocational programs offered
- Urine tested

"Graduation"

- Judge monitors client progress

Source: Finn and Newlyn (1993).

PHILADELPHIA DRUG UNIT

The Pennsylvania Board of Probation and Parole operates a drug unit in Philadelphia that utilizes extensive urinalysis. Caseloads are limited to fifty, and all offenders referred for supervision must have been using drugs for at least three years. Parole agents assigned to the unit have undergone specialized training and are rotated every two to three years to regular units "to avoid burnout." All clients assigned to the unit are tested for drug use every ninety days, unless circumstances demand more frequent testing. Offenders who remain drug-free for nine months are reviewed for transfer to general supervision units. Immediately before transfer, however, there is a final urinalysis.

Clients whose test results are positive are tested weekly; two positive opiate urinalyses within a four-month period require that the client be placed in a withdrawal treatment program. If the parole agent believes that a client's pattern of drug abuse is disruptive to the reintegration and treatment process, or if the client's behavior constitutes a threat to the community or the client, the agent may place the offender in "protective custody" for forty-eight hours. If the agent believes that the client should be subjected to violation-of-parole procedures, the detention continues until the hearing is conducted (Abadinsky 1997).

drug cases that would typically be dismissed by the prosecutor (Hepburn, Johnston, and Rogers 1994).

Coercive supervision, civil or criminal, appears to have a positive outcome (Anglin 1988; Anglin and Hser 1990). Extensive research indicates that "coerced involvement in community-based programs and/or corrections-based treatment can have a substantial impact on the behavior of chronic drug-abusing offenders" (Anglin and Maugh 1992: 76). George Vaillant (1970: 494) found that while the most effective motivation for abstinence is that narcotics are illegal, "The most potent treatment was compulsory supervision. Thus, if the addict is followed over time, external coercion of some kind appears a critical variable in facilitating abstinence." This was the author's experience when as a parole officer (see Abadinsky 1997) he supervised heroin addicts in New York City. Close personal contact, unannounced home visits and searches, arm checks (for needle marks), and random urinalysis provided the ego and superego strengths for addicts to remain heroin free. "Besides offering addicts compulsory support and an 'external super-ego,' parole itself was probably a substitute for addiction in that it required ex-addicts to remain regularly employed" (Vaillant 1970: 495). The parole officer could redirect the considerable skills and energy required to be a successful heroin addict into seeking and maintaining legitimate employment (see also Eaglin 1986). From the behaviorist view, the probation or parole officer provides the basis for operant conditioning—applying positive reinforcement for abstinence and negative reinforcement for relapse.

While civil or criminal commitment can bring into treatment some drug users who would probably not enter voluntarily, it can neither overcome deficits in treatment services nor assure that patients will participate in treatment. (For a review of some difficulties with involuntary drug patients in clinical settings, see Schottenfeld [1989].)

Treatment Alternative to Street Crime (TASC)

The federally funded TASC program, initiated in 1972 to divert substance-abusing offenders out of the court system and into community treatment, stands somewhere between compulsory and voluntary treatment. Since its inception it has been expanded to include persons on probation and parole. TASC identifies, assesses, and refers appropriate drug- and/or alcohol-dependent offenders accused or convicted of nonviolent crimes to community-based substance abuse treatment, as an alternative to or supplement to existing criminal justice sanctions and procedures (Cook and Weinman 1988). TASC monitors the client's progress in drug treatment and reports back to the criminal justice agency that made the referral. Those who fail to conform to program requirements face further criminal justice processing.

Therapeutic Community

Therapeutic community (TC) is a generic term for residential, self-help, drug-free treatment programs that have some characteristics in common, including concepts adopted from Alcoholics Anonymous (AA) (DeLong 1972: 190-91):

> There is no such thing as an ex-addict, only an addict who is not using at the moment; the emphasis on mutual support and aid; the distrust of mental-health professionals; and the concept of continual confession and catharsis. However, the TC has extended these notions to include the concept of a live-in community with a rigid structure of day-to-day behavior and a complex system of punishment and rewards.

> A considerable number of [TC] clients never have acquired conventional lifestyles. Vocational and educational deficits are marked; mainstream values either are missing or unpursued. Most often, these clients emerge from a socially disadvantaged sector where drug abuse is more a social response than a psychological disturbance. Their TC experience can be termed *habilitation*—the development of a socially productive, conventional lifestyle for the first time in their lives. (De Leon 1994: 19)

THERAPEUTIC COMMUNITIES

"TC programs reflect a view of the drug abuse client as having a social deficit and requiring social treatment. This social treatment may be characterized as an organized effort to resocialize the client, with the community as an agent of personal change." (Tims, Jainchill, and De Leon 1994: 2)

The TC "views drug abuse as deviant behavior, reflecting impeded personality development and/or chronic deficits in social, educational and economic skills" (De Leon 1986: 5). The primary aims of the therapeutic community are

> a global change in lifestyle reflecting abstinence from illicit substances, elimination of antisocial activity, increased employability, and prosocial attitudes and values. A critical assumption in TCs is that stable recovery depends upon a successful integration of these social and psychological goals. The rehabilitative approach, therefore, requires multidimensional influences and training that, for most clients, can only occur after an extended period of living in a 24-hour residential setting. (De Leon 1986b: 69)

The therapeutic community becomes a surrogate family and a communal support group for dealing with alienation and the drug abuse that derives from it. Its purpose, notes Mitchell Rosenthal (1973), is to strengthen ego functioning. Therapy, except for the time spent asleep, is total. James DeLong (1972) notes that there is a quasi-evangelistic quality to the "TC movement." The residences are often similar to the communes that were popular during the late 1950s' and 1960s' counterculture movement, except that they generally have a strict hierarchy and insist on rigid adherence to norms even more stringent than those of the proverbial middle class. The model of all therapeutic communities, note Jerome Platt and Christina Labate (1976), is Synanon, founded in 1958 by Charles E. Dederich, a former alcoholic who was a participant in and advocate of the Alcoholics Anonymous (AA) approach to substance abuse. (AA is discussed later in this chapter.) The Synanon Foundation expanded rapidly into several states, with facilities run almost entirely by ex-addicts.

Therapeutic communities such as Odyssey House, however, have been more receptive to using professionals. The director of Phoenix House, which began in New York and now also operates in California, has psychiatrist Mitchell Rosenthal as its executive director. David Bellis (1981: 155) is quite critical of therapeutic communities that resist professional involvement and that use instead untrained staff and residents, "many hardly off heroin themselves," who, under no legal or professional oversight, unleash their own brand of "therapy" on addicts, many of whom are undergoing mandatory treatment because of a plea bargain, probation, or parole status. In his study of a failed therapeutic community, Robert Weppner (1983) points out that being a poorly educated ex-addict does not endow one with treatment skills. While Synanon requires a lifetime commitment, most TCs have abandoned or modified this aspect of the Synanon model. (Dederich eventually transformed Synanon into a cultlike phenomenon. In 1980 he pled guilty to plotting to murder one of his Synanon critics.) TCs frequently offer vocational training and education to prepare residents to live in the community without continuous help from the TC. Indeed, George De Leon describes the TC as "community as method": *"the purposive use of the peer community to facilitate social and psychological change in individuals"* (1995: 9; italics in original).

PHOENIX HOUSE

At Phoenix House in the Bronx, every day begins the same. After a 30-minute breakfast at 7:00 A.M., there is an hourlong meeting that includes inspirational songs and skits written and performed by the residents. The rest of the day consists of seminars, classes to prepare for the general equivalency diploma, rap sessions, job assignments, and more meals and meetings. There is little free time until 9 P.M. Lights are out at 11 P.M. The 185-word Phoenix House philosophy is recited from memory at least twice a day. The weekend schedule is slightly more relaxed, with rented videos available and highly supervised trips into New York. Most of the residents are between twenty and forty years old and on welfare, which helps pay for their stay at the program. They typically have lengthy criminal records (Marriott 1989).

ODYSSEY HOUSE

Odyssey House operates a TC for pregnant women and those with young children. Housed on New York's Wards' Island, residents include about two dozen women and children. Some of the women are pregnant, and most have been abusing crack. The facility is underfunded and must depend on private donations to make up for inadequate government support. As a result, children's clothing and nursery toys are in short supply. The residents

> participate in rigorous therapy, they are given parenting courses including such essentials as how to hold a baby and they must work at jobs. The overbearing and obnoxious scrape plates, while the shy and withdrawn are given pretty clothes and work as front-desk receptionists. But the most prized assignments are in the nursery. . . . Graduation requirements are stiff. Along with conquering addiction, women must complete the equivalent of high school, secure a driver's license and find a full-time job. (Martin 1990: 13)

Sixty-eight percent of the women complete the program.

A prominent feature of the TC has been the stiff entry requirement: a devastating initial interview that tests an applicant's motivation by focusing on his or her inadequacies and lack of success. Successful applicants must invest completely in the program, which encourages the resident to identify with the former addicts who run it, and become resocialized into a drug-free existence. The new resident is isolated from all outside contacts, including family and friends. The withdrawal process is accomplished without drugs but with the support of other residents. Once withdrawal has been accomplished, a program of positive and negative reinforcement is implemented. The resident is assigned menial work projects, such as cleaning toilets, but given an opportunity to earn more prestigious assignments and greater freedom through conformity with the program. Transgressions are punished by public humiliation—reprimands, shaved heads, wearing a sign indicating the nature of the violation. Those who leave, relapse, and return are required to wear a sign announcing their situation. Shame and guilt are constantly exploited to force the addict to conform and to change his or her view of drugs (Platt and Labate 1976). There is little privacy. Drug use, physical violence, and sexual activity between residents are punished with expulsion.

Residents are kept busy in a highly structured environment that offers little time for idleness or boredom. They are expected to be active in all aspects of the TC program. Failing to do so becomes the subject of criticism at the encounter session, a central feature of the therapeutic process. The encounter is a relatively unstructured, leaderless group session in which members focus on a particular resident (who occupies the "hot seat") and bombard him or her with criticisms about attitude and behavior. The target is encouraged to fight back—verbally—although the goal of such sessions is to destroy the rationalizations and defenses that help perpetuate irresponsible thought patterns and behavior—a resocialization process. "The style of the encounter, with its abrasive attacks and its permitted verbal violence . . . is designed to encourage the spewing out of pent-up hostility and anger, to force the patient to confront his maladaptive emotional response and behavior patterns" (Rosenthal 1973: 91).

Dan Waldorf (1973) points out that the TC is an exciting, friendly, and highly moral—almost utopian—environment. But, notes Mitchell Rosenthal (1984: 55), it is not for all abusers.

> Severe disturbances may be exacerbated by the TC regimen and may have an adverse effect not only on the disturbed client but also on the treatment environment and the progress of others in the treatment population. Also unsuitable for treatment are candidates whose drug involvement is of so limited a nature as to require a less rigorous intervention or who—despite the deleterious effects of drug abuse—are able to function with the help of a positive support network (e.g., family or significant others).

TCs have been established in prisons in New York, California, and a number of other states. These are called "Stay 'N Out" therapeutic communities. Inmates selected for the program are recruited at state correctional facili-

DAYTOP VILLAGE

Located on New York's Staten Island, Daytop Village (DV) consists of a large mansion built around the turn of the century. Superficially the facility resembles a college fraternity house. Persons entering or leaving must check in with the person seated at a desk near the entrance. Depending on the time of day, people may be busy cleaning, moving to and fro, or simply lounging, playing cards, checkers, or chess, and listening to music. Friends and relatives of the residents are not welcome, "as they are likely to undermine the progress that residents are making. Relatives are likely to upset a resident's progress more from misguided good intentions, but nonetheless, they are not free to visit except by special permission" (Sugarman 1974: 2). There is an "open house" on Saturday evenings, during which outsiders are encouraged to visit for a formal program. (This author has attended numerous open houses at Daytop Village.) It is explained to visitors that DV should not be considered a "program" but "a family of people helping each other to overcome their problems; that drugs themselves were not their real problem but only the symptom of underlying problems of personality, and especially the problem of not feeling good about oneself" (Sugarman 1974: 2).

A tour of the facility reveals that it is spotlessly clean—residents clean up after themselves immediately after smoking, drinking, or eating. Overall maintenance is assigned to new residents, who are responsible for the least desirable housekeeping tasks. Barry Sugarman (1974: 4) points out:

> One impression that may be formed in only a half an hour is of a well-ordered community where rules are generally respected and enforced when necessary, where people jump to carry out orders and do so quite cheerfully, and where people work hard. Considering the kind of people who live here and what they were like before, things seem to run with amazing smoothness. As one sees more, one discovers that this orderliness is only achieved at the price of constant pressure and surveillance, tough sanctions for deviance, and a high dropout rate.

As a parole officer, this author has had heroin addicts describe DV (and similar TCs) as being worse than prison; some refused to stay even when faced with the alternative of further incarceration.

The treatment approach at DV is almost an exact copy of Synanon's. It was put in place by David Deitch, who became director in 1964; Deitch had formerly been director of the Synanon house in Westport, Connecticut. Residents and staff reject the notion of a program and instead refer to the approach as "The Concept." The Concept begins when an abuser attempts to gain admittance and is told to call back at specified intervals for a number of days before being invited for an interview. Before the interview the prospect is left to sit for several hours in the living room and is required to ask permission to go to the washroom or for anything else he or she wants. The prospect is not permitted to talk to anyone except the specially assigned resident. This experience can be so nervewracking for some addicts that they leave before the interview. The interview itself is demanding and traumatic: The prospect is ridiculed and required to accept his or her situation for what it is—"Don't try to con us, we're dope fiends, too"—and to admit that drug

(continued)

DAYTOP VILLAGE

use is a symptom of being either stupid or a "baby." The prospect may be required to scream at the top of his or her lungs, "Help me" or "I need help."

Robert Brook and Paul Whitehead (1980: 33) report that, in contrast with the original intake/entry procedures, the atmosphere at DV is now less threatening. Admissions are now handled during a two-day period through the Screening, Induction, and Referral Unit.

> At this time, medical examinations are given and psychological, demographic, and drug history data are collected. After the interview the prospect is warmly welcomed into the community, given a tour, and introduced to the other residents. He or she is required to give up all personal possessions; telephone and letter-writing privileges must be earned. New residents undergoing withdrawal do so without medication and in the living room where he or she can interact with others, play cards, or listen to music. Exaggerations of suffering are ridiculed, while a "grin and bear it" attitude is supported by the other residents.

"This sharing of the experience lessens its wretchedness. We see here an interesting example of the way in which physical symptoms can be radically affected by the social context in which the person finds himself" (Sugarman 1974: 15). Novices are discouraged from talking to other new residents in order to avoid reinforcing negative behavior, and they soon begin to integrate into the continuing rounds of lectures and encounter sessions. Residents are to treat each other like brothers and sisters. Honesty, even if it is confrontational, is required, and drugs, violence, and sexual activity are strictly forbidden.

---

ties and housed in units segregated from the general population, although they eat and attend morning activities with other prisoners. The program, which lasts from six to nine months, is staffed by graduates of community TCs and by ex-offenders with prison experience, who act as role models demonstrating successful rehabilitation.

> During the early phase of treatment, the major clinical thrust involves observation and assessment of client needs and problem areas. Orientation to the prison TC procedures occurs through individual counseling, encounter sessions, and seminars. Clients are given low-level jobs and granted little status. During the later phase of treatment, residents are provided opportunities to earn higher-level positions and increased status through sincere involvement in the program and hard work. Encounter groups and counseling sessions are more in-depth and focus on the areas of self-discipline, self-worth, self-awareness, respect for authority, and acceptance of guidance for problem areas. Seminars take on a more intellectual nature. Debate is encouraged to enhance self-expression and to increase self-confidence. (Wexler and Williams 1986: 224)

Upon release, prison TC graduates are encouraged to become part of the extensive community-based TC network. Research into the effect of the prison TC on parole success found that "Stay 'N Out" reduced recidivism (Wexler, Douglas Lipton, and Kenneth Foster 1985; Wexler, Falkin, and Lipton 1990).[5]

There has been a great deal of controversy over the success rate of therapeutic communities, and most research has been inadequate or inconclusive (Brook and Whitehead 1980). Many TCs release statistics that cannot withstand scrutiny by disinterested researchers. The arduous screening process keeps out many drug abusers who would probably fail the program, and an abuser's graduation from a TC does not necessarily mean that the program has succeeded. A realistic portrayal would conclude that the TC provides some ex-drug abusers with a support system by enabling them to gain employment with a TC or similar program. Outside of the TC

> drug addicts, regardless of age, sex, or race, tend to occupy low status positions, rarely have legitimate sources of income, and are vulnerable to unemployment and general economic fluctuations. Impoverished educational backgrounds further limit their chances to better their positions. Within Synanon, addicts have positions that afford them a measure of self-respect and the opportunity to earn the respect of others. These factors help to account for the many who choose to remain in Synanon and make it a way of life. (Brook and Whitehead 1980: 29)

The TC insists on behavioral change that "is not away from antisocial behavior, that of the street addict, and toward the norms of the larger society, but toward norms accepted in the group alone" (Weppner 1983: xi). Those who need to manage in the community without the continuing support of the group are at risk, because they will return to the same environment that led to drug dependence in the first place, and they often bring with them all of the educational and vocational deficiencies they had upon entering. Those entering the TC with a greater degree of mental health, with limited or no attachment to a criminal subculture, and with employment skills are obviously better equipped to deal with post-TC existence.

Chemical Dependency (CD) Programs

As noted at the beginning of this chapter, during the last two decades the number of programs to treat substance abusers has increased. Some are profit-making and others are nonprofit; many call themselves "therapeutic communities," although they differ dramatically from the TCs discussed above. These programs typically share a number of variables: They do a great deal of out-

---

5. The severe problems that can be encountered when attempting to establish a prison-based drug treatment program are highlighted in a study by Mark Hamm (1991)

PRIVATE HOSPITAL DRUG TREATMENT

Parents are often frightened by media hype or hospital treatment center advertisements that they have seen on television. Insurance coverage and the parents' willingness to have someone else deal with the "abuser" are also factors. As a result, what may be experimental adolescent behavior becomes a reason to place an adolescent in an inpatient hospital treatment program. Such treatment programs are one of the few large-scale sources of profit for private hospitals. Managers of these programs have become desperate for adolescent admissions because of the vast overbuilding of these facilities that occurred during the 1980's. (G. Lawson 1992: 4)

reach—most employ a marketing person—and often advertise for clients likely to have health insurance, such as employed alcohol and cocaine abusers as opposed to heroin addicts, because the costs can run over $500 a day for inpatient care. Many CD programs are located in a health care facility, which typically increases the cost of treatment. Adding a chemical dependency program to a health care facility can help reduce the number of otherwise vacant beds that can be costly to any hospital. The treatment approach usually includes individual and group counseling, and the model tends to be eclectic rather than doctrinal.[6]

George De Leon (1995: 5) describes some of the common features of CD programs:

> Primarily they serve the more socially advantaged substance abusers whose fee for service is generally covered by insurance, in contrast to the major modalities whose costs are mostly tax subsidized. The treatment orientation of these programs is also varied, but mainly reflects a mix of traditional mental health and 12-Step perspectives [discussed below]. They offer a broad menu of services such as education, nutrition, relaxation training, recreation, counseling-psychotherapy, psychopharmacological adjuncts, and self-help groups.

"CD programs do not require patients to perform housekeeping duties. . . . [They] are especially attractive to patients with greater initial functional and social resources who can afford the better facilities and amenities" (Gerstein 1994: 56).

The typical program is a three- to six-week intensive and highly structured inpatient regimen:

> Clients begin with an in-depth psychiatric and psychosocial evaluation and then follow a general education-oriented program track of daily lectures plus two to three meetings per week in small task-oriented groups. Group education teaches

---

6. For a look at a theory-based approach to CD treatment, see Rawson et al. (1993); Washton (1989).

clients about the disease concept of dependence, focusing on the harmful medical and psychosocial effects of illicit drugs and excessive alcohol consumption. There is also an individual prescriptive track for each client, meetings once a week with a "focal counselor," and appointments with other professionals if medical, psychiatric, or family services are needed. (Gerstein and Harwood 1990: 171)

Harvey Siegel and his colleagues (1995: 69) are critical: "Since it is the treatment professional who retains all responsibility for prescribing and implementing the necessary therapeutic activity, patients may have difficulty achieving ownership of their recovery program."

Aftercare services are typically meager. "Aftercare is considered quite important in CD [twenty-eight-day] treatment, but relatively few program resources are devoted to it" (Gerstein 1994: 56). Patients are urged to participate in community twelve-step groups. In fact, virtually all of the many programs that this author has examined throughout the country utilize an Alcoholics Anonymous or Narcotics Anonymous (NA) twelve-step approach for both in- and outpatient treatment.

Alcoholics and Alcoholics Anonymous

Alcoholics Anonymous (AA) is a fellowship founded by William ("Bill W.") Wilson (1895–1971), a financial investigator and alcoholic, and Robert ("Dr. Bob") Holbrook Smith (1879–1950), a physician and alcoholic. (Nan Robertson [1988b] presents a rather unflattering view of the two, particularly of Wilson, whom she refers to as a Wall Street hustler and compulsive womanizer.) Bill W. had joined the Oxford Group (renamed Moral Re-Armament in 1939), an international religious movement, as the result of the influence of another alcoholic whose religious experience appeared to act as a "cure." Bill W. was influenced by the work of William James (1842–1910), a psychologist and philosopher, particularly his *Varieties of Religious Experience* (1902).[7] As part of the Oxford Group Bill W. began dedicating his activities to curing alcoholics, an effort that was quite unsuccessful until he met Dr. Bob, also a member of the Oxford Group, in 1935 while on a business trip to Akron, Ohio. He helped Dr. Bob become abstinent, and the two recognized that success in helping alcoholics was not to be found in preaching abstinence but rather in a fellowship where each alcoholic simply relates his or her story of drunkenness and conversion to a nonalcoholic lifestyle. The "listening" was as important as the "telling." "There could not have been just one founder of A.A.," notes Robertson (1988b: 34), "because the essence of the process is one person telling his story to another as honestly as he knows how." The group became

---

7. It is ironic that William James typically found his religious and philosophical insights while intoxicated from nitrous oxide (Tymoczo 1996).

AA ALTERNATIVES

The "spiritual" dimension of AA and its insistence on a disease model of alcoholism—alcoholics cannot help themselves—have encountered opposition and led to the establishment of alternative groups, such as Rational Recovery (RR) and Secular Organization for Sobriety (SOS). Although it is a voluntary self-help group in the AA mode, RR rejects the twelve-step approach as fostering dependency and instead argues that alcoholic participants are not powerless but fully capable of overcoming their addiction (Hall 1990). According to RR. alcoholism is not a disease but an individual shortcoming. Their approach emphasizes taking personal responsibility for behavior ("Clean and Sober—And Agnostic" 1991).

RR uses "The Big Plan," a commitment never to drink again. It focuses on planning to prevent relapses and attempting to gain insight into how self-defeating beliefs encourage drinking behavior. Various strategies are discussed to deal with "high-risk" situations where temptations may run high (Galaif and Sussman 1995). There are also groups that reject the total abstinence proviso of AA and instead emphasize sobriety—drinking in moderation—such as Moderation Management (Marriott 1995). MM is designed for persons who want to limit, rather than eliminate, their drinking (Foderaro 1995).

known as Alcoholics Anonymous after the title of Wilson's 1939 book, which AA members often refer to as "The Big Book" (it was quite bulky when originally published). Wilson, who died in 1971, was supported by the substantial royalties the book eventually generated. His wife, Lois Burnham, who died in 1988 at age ninety-seven, established Al-Anon for the family members of alcoholics. She was a nonalcoholic who patterned her organization on the AA model (Pace 1988). There are now similar groups for the family and friends of cocaine users—Co-Anon.

The AA program requires an act of surrender—an acknowledgment of being an alcoholic and of the destructiveness that results—a bearing of witness, and an acknowledgement of a higher power. While AA is nondenominational, there is a strong repent-of-your-sins revivalism—groups begin or end their meetings holding hands in a circle and reciting the Lord's Prayer (Robertson 1988b) or the Serenity Prayer: "God grant me the serenity to accept the things I cannot change; courage to change the things I can; and wisdom to know the difference" (DuPont and McGovern 1994: 27). As in Protestant revival meetings, the alcoholic/sinner seeks salvation through personal testimony, public contrition, and submission to a higher authority (Peele 1985; Delbanco and Delbanco 1995). AA also provides "an important social network through which members learn appropriate behavior and coping skills in drinking situations and become involved in various (nondrinking) leisure activities with other recovering alcoholics" (McElrath 1995: 314).

According to their publications, AA recognizes the potency of shared honesty and mutual vulnerability openly acknowledged. The AA group supports each member in his or her effort to remain alcohol-free. "Maintenance of sobriety depends on our sharing of our experiences, strength and hope with each other, thus helping to identify and understand the nature of our disease" (AA literature). The AA conceptual model is that alcoholism is a disease,[8] a controllable disability that cannot be cured—thus, there are no ex-alcoholics, merely recovering alcoholics. AA members are encouraged to accept the belief that they are powerless over alcohol, that they cannot control their intake, that total abstinence is required. New members are advised to obtain a sponsor who has remained abstinent and who will help the initiate work through the "twelve steps" (see below) that are the essence of the AA program. Those who are successful, "twelfth steppers," carry the AA message and program to other alcoholics—they become "missionaries" for AA. There are more than 50,000 registered AA groups in the United States (Delbanco and Delbanco 1995).

AA and groups based on the AA approach

> attempt to instill the substitution of more adaptive attitudes to replace habitual dysfunctional ones. The extreme use of denial and projection of responsibility for chemical dependency onto other people, circumstances, or conditions outside oneself is an example of a target behavior strongly challenged in the substance abuse self-help group. The familiar opening statement of "I'm an alcoholic and/or drug addict" epitomizes the concrete representation that defense mechanisms of projection and denial run counter to the group culture and norms. (Spitz 1987: 160)

"There is a minimum of formal organization, no power of punishment or exclusion in AA, and the only authority is shared experience" (Norris 1976: 737). The basic AA unit is the local group, which is autonomous except in matters affecting other AA groups or the fellowship as a whole. "No group has powers over its members and instead of officers with authority, groups rotate leadership" (AA literature). A secretary chosen by the members plans the meetings and sets the agenda. In most local groups the position is rotated every six months. Delegates to the General Service Conference serve two years. There are twenty-one trustees, of whom seven are nonalcoholics who are often helping professionals in social work or medicine and who may serve for up to nine years—alcoholic trustees may serve only four years. There are no entry requirements or dues—"the hat is passed" at most meetings to defray costs. Some of this money goes to support a local service committee and the General Service Office in New York. AA does not engage in fund raising, and no one person is permitted to contribute more than $1,000. The sale of publications generates considerable income. The financial affairs of the General Service Office are handled by nonalcoholics: "The reason is that Bill Wilson and the early AA's were afraid that if anybody running AA fell off the wagon, that

---

8. For a discussion of the model of alcoholism used in AA, see Miller and Kurtz (1994).

NARCOTICS ANONYMOUS

Nan Robertson (1988b) notes that some AA groups are less than accepting of persons addicted to substances other than alcohol—Bill Wilson was opposed to allowing heroin addicts to become part of AA. However, there are groups for drug abusers based on the twelve-step approach, such as Narcotics Anonymous (NA) and Cocaine Anonymous (CA).

THE TWELVE STEPS
OF NARCOTICS ANONYMOUS

1. We admitted that we were powerless over our addiction, that our lives had become unmanageable.
2. We came to believe that a Power greater than ourselves could restore us to sanity.
3. We made a decision to turn our will and our lives over to the care of God as we understood Him.
4. We made a searching and fearless moral inventory of ourselves.
5. We admitted to God, to ourselves, and to another human being the exact nature of our wrongs.
6. We were entirely ready to have God remove all these defects of character.
7. We humbly asked Him to remove our shortcomings.
8. We made a list of all persons we had harmed, and became willing to make amends to them all.
9. We made direct amends to such people whenever possible, except when to do so would injure them or others.
10. We continued to take personal inventory and when we were wrong promptly admitted it.
11. We sought through prayer and meditation to improve our conscious contact with God as we understood Him, praying only for knowledge of His will for us and the power to carry that out.
12. Having had a spiritual awakening as a result of these steps, we tried to carry this message to addicts, and practice these principles in all our affairs.

NA publishes a monthly journal, *The NA Way*, which is filled with brief personal stories, news, and opinion. (Narcotics Anonymous World Service Office, PO Box 9999, Van Nuys, CA 91409; telephone 818-780-3951.) Local AA chapters can be found in the telephone book.

would be bad enough, but if he were handling finances as well, the results could be disastrous" (Robertson 1988: 57).

Because of their fear of losing employment, recovering alcoholics were often unwilling to admit their problem in front of others—hence strict anonymity became part of the AA approach. AA never uses surnames at meetings or in its publications (Kurtz 1979). According to an AA publication: "Individual anonymity is paramount. No AA member has the right to divulge the identity or membership of any other member. We must always maintain personal anonymity at the level of press, radio, TV and film." (Hence the use of "Bill W." and "Dr. Bob.") AA members typically attend four meetings a week for about five years, after which attendance is less frequent, or they may drop out completely when capable of functioning comfortably without alcohol. "The movement works in quiet and simple ways. Members usually give of themselves without reservation; exchange telephone numbers with newcomers; come to help at any hour when a fellow member is in crisis; are free with tips on how to avoid that first drink" (Robertson 1988: 47).

The AA approach has been criticized because of its emphasis on total abstinence and its lack of research support:

> The erstwhile abstainer who, for whatever reason, takes a drink may in effect be induced to go on a spree by the belief that this is inevitable. Spree drinking could also be induced by the fact that status in A.A. is correlated with length of sobriety. Years of sobriety with their attendant symbols and status can be obliterated by one slip, so the social cost of a single drink is as great as the cost of an all-out binge. (Ogborne and Glaser 1985: 176)

Some twelve-step groups "do not consider members 'clean and sober' when they are using any psychoactive medication. Cases of adverse treatment consequences, even suicide, have resulted from well-meaning 12-step members dissuading individuals from taking prescribed medications" (DuPont and McGovern 1994: 56).

Evaluations of AA encounter definitional problems:

> First, there are no shared research definitions of recovery; that is, studies differ regarding the ways in which successes and failures are measured. Many investigators measure recovery in terms of whether or not the client is drinking. This definition may be too simplistic but is consistent with the AA goal of abstinence. Similarly, although the term "alcoholism" was first described in 1852, one review of the literature disclosed more than 200 definitions of the disorder. Lacking clear definitions of these terms, it is difficult to compare results across studies. (McElrath 1995: 316)

William R. Miller and Reid K. Hester (1980: 47), in a review of AA evaluation literature, state:

> Attempts to evaluate the effectiveness of AA have met with considerable, if not insurmountable, methodological problems, among them the very anonymity of

members, which precludes systematic follow-up evaluation. Most studies have failed to include control groups (a near impossibility because of the availability of AA to all who are interested), have relied almost entirely upon self-report (often via mailed questionnaires) and upon abstinence as the sole criteria for success, have been plagued by sizable attrition rates and large selection confounds, and have failed to use single-blind designs, thus remaining open to criticisms of interviewer bias (particularly when the investigators have been "insiders"—members of AA themselves). (See also Ogborne and Glaser 1985; Galaif and Sussman 1995.)

Nan Robertson (1988: 44), a Pulitzer Prize-winning reporter for the *New York Times* and a longtime member of Alcoholics Anonymous, writes: "About 60 percent of those coming to AA for the first time remain in AA after going to meetings and assiduously 'working the program' for months or even years. Usually, they stay sober for good. But about 40 percent drop out." On 22 February 1988 I wrote to Nan Robertson asking her to provide the basis for her statistics on the success of AA. She never responded.

THE MINNESOTA MODEL

"One of the best examples of 12-step program use is private inpatient chemical dependence treatment—the so-called Minnesota model, which integrates the 12-step fellowships into the medical treatment of addiction" (DuPont and McGovern 1994: xxii). The Hazelden Foundation in Center City, Minnesota, has inspired many similar programs in the United States and England.

Substance abuse is seen as an incurable but controllable disease. Total abstinence and "lifestyle" improvement are the treatment goals. The six- to eight-week program begins with an admissions assessment and detoxification, following medical protocol. Individual counseling is provided by abusers "in recovery" and professional staff, including physicians, social workers, nurses, and clergy. Therapy groups take various forms, all of which are present and future oriented, including problem solving, personal issues, and decision making related to substance use, family sessions, and confrontations similar to those of the therapeutic community. Rounding out the program are lectures and videos on a variety of related topics including AA/NA, the social and psychological aspects of substance abuse, and techniques for handling substance abuse problems, as well as reading and writing assignments. Aftercare usually involves attendance at AA or NA meetings (Cook 1988).

This treatment-rich private-sector approach to substance abuse is obviously quite expensive, and patients, who include such luminaries as Betty Ford and Elizabeth Taylor, are therefore representative of the economically successful. In a review of the Minnesota model research, Christopher Cook concludes: "Despite exaggerated claims of success, it appears to have a genuinely impressive 'track record' with as many as two-thirds of its patients achieving a 'good' outcome at one year after discharge" (Cook 1988b: 746).

In his careful research, Geary Alford (1980) found that a residential treatment program for alcoholics that used the AA approach was highly effective: "Approximately 50% of the patients completing inpatient treatment were essentially abstinent, employed or productively functioning, *and* exhibited stable, adaptive social relationships at two years post-discharge. This figure increases to 56% if very light-moderate drinking is allowed." Alford and his colleagues (1991: 122) report that an AA/NA model inpatient treatment program for adolescents whose drug use was primarily alcohol or marijuana was successful: "Some 71% of male treatment completers and 79% of female treatment completers were found to be chemically abstinent or essentially abstinent at six months after discharge." However, two years after treatment, the figure for men dropped to 40 percent, while 37 percent of those males who dropped out of the program were also found to be abstinent or essentially abstinent. Thirty percent of female noncompleters were abstinent or essentially abstinent after two years. As with the research reviewed by Miller and Hester (1980), Alford's (1980 and 1991) studies did not utilize a control group. In fact, AA successes appear to be concentrated among middle- and upper-class people with relatively stable lives before the onset of a drinking problem (Alexander 1990). As noted above, while treatment at most inpatient chemical-dependency programs in the United States is based on a disease model built around an AA/twelve-step approach, there is an almost total lack of relevant research data on effectiveness (Gerstein and Harwood 1990; Galaif and Sussman 1995). Furthermore, most of these programs provide no aftercare but refer patients to AA, which deals with the problems of drinking but not with related or contributing problems such as unemployment and interpersonal skills or with drug use as a form of self-medication (discussed in chapter 3).

Despite the paucity of research on its effectiveness, the twelve-step approach is very popular, some even arguing that it has become a fad. Groups such as Gamblers Anonymous, Overeaters Anonymous, Debtors Anonymous, and Sex Addicts Anonymous have been formed to address a host of social problems. While these groups claim inspiration from the AA twelve-step approach, critics see them as forums for whiners who want an audience to dwell on their injured selves (Delbanco and Delbanco 1995).

Evaluating Treatment Effectiveness

How well do drug treatment programs perform? A straightforward answer to this question is simply not possible.

> There are a variety of programs—hospitals, public health agencies, independent organizations—offering treatment; using an array of methodologies ranging from drug-free therapeutic communities to methadone maintenance; while the intensity of services and staff qualifications vary significantly. And the client population is similarly complex:

ON EVALUATING SUBSTANCE ABUSE PROGRAMS

Outcome evaluation can prove that treatment works and provides significant financial benefits. Outcome results can be powerful aids in marketing treatment services and persuading health care purchasers to continue to authorize such coverage. They can also be used to position an effective program in a highly competitive marketplace.

Source: From a publication of the American Hospital Association (Hoffman, Harrison, and Streed 1991: 138]). For an examination of the problems in evaluating drug treatment, see Moras (1993); De Leon, Inciardi, and Martin (1995).

They vary in age, social and economic background, number and types of drug abused, health status, and psychological well-being. Some have lengthy histories of addiction and treatment, while others are entering treatment for the first time in the early stages of dependence. Clients may be highly involved in criminal activity or may not have committed any crime other than drug possession. (Hubbard et al. 1989: 9)

Evaluation requires a measurement of success, such as being drug-free for a certain period of time. Tracking persons who complete treatment is often difficult if not impossible. Programs have different criteria for "completion." Some use length of time; others use number of visits or regularity of attendance. This makes it difficult to compare programs (Simpson 1989). Evaluating drug treatment requires a comparison with a similar population that is not being treated or with other programs treating similar populations. In fact, any research efforts that do not include a control group are suspect:

In the absence of a control group, it is difficult to determine whether unanticipated bias occurred in selecting the subjects for study, and whether the resulting experimental group is sufficiently representative for generalizations to be made about the outcome findings. Furthermore, without comparison groups, behavioral changes during and after treatment that result from the passage of time may wrongly be attributed to program activities. (Anglin and Hser 1990b: 408)

However, "there are ethical, political, and legal dilemmas in withholding treatment from control groups" (De Leon, Inciardi, and Martin 1995: 85).

Some private treatment programs are quite selective. Their patients are required to have financial resources or employment that provides third-party coverage, which are social indicators of a better prognosis. Other programs will accept persons with a host of social, psychological, and economic problems that are likely to impact upon prognosis. "In the real world of drug abuse treatment," note George De Leon, James Inciardi, and Steven Martin (1995: 88), "program staff choose the clients they feel are ready for treatment and are appropriate for a particular treatment modality." (For a review of drug treatment outcome research and its methodological shortcomings, see Anglin and Hser 1990b.)

It is also recognized that drug dependence is a career requiring treatment that is similarly oriented.

> Many researchers, practitioners, and clinicians have assumed that treatment should occur once and should result in a cure if it is to be termed effective. Substance abuse does not appear to be the kind of problem that makes this orientation pragmatic. When the community in which people live is so strongly pro-intoxication, it is not surprising that treated persons are recruited back into the drug lifestyle. [Therefore] while treatment does not need to be applied forever, repeated episodes of treatment are probably necessary for most who develop serious problems with intoxicants. (Senay 1986: 143)

Finally, many or most programs purporting to treat specific types of substance abuse are not based on a scientific approach to such problems. They are not organized and structured according to controlled studies with random assignment, and they are often not eager for independent evaluation.

Patrick Biernacki (1986: 191) notes that there are serious problems with gauging the success of drug-treatment programs. He asks, for example, what a 50 percent rate of success means: Would some, most, or all of the persons who were "successful" have abandoned drug addiction without treatment? In fact, he points out, drug-treatment programs may be successful only with those persons who have resolved to stop using drugs: "Once addicts voluntarily have resolved to stop using drugs, treatment programs may then be able to help them realize their resolutions to change."

One major study (Hubbard et al. 1989) involved 10,000 clients of forty-one long-term treatment programs who were admitted during 1979–1981. The longitudinal research involved three types of programs: methadone maintenance that included counseling services, therapeutic communities, and drug-free outpatient. While the methadone patients were primarily heroin users, the clients of the other programs were abusing heroin and other drugs such as cocaine and amphetamines. A majority had used marijuana and alcohol in the year before admission. The findings showed that while treatment results in substantial decreases in the abuse of both opioid and nonopioid drugs, relatively few clients achieve the goal of abstinence. There did not appear to be a significant difference in outcomes among the three modalities. The research found a significant decrease in criminal activity, suggesting that treatment is a viable alternative to incarceration for many criminal justice clients who are active drug users. The researchers conclude on an optimistic note: "Combined with results from other research, our findings provide comprehensive and convincing evidence that long-term treatment does work" (1989: 165).

One research effort in Philadelphia involved mostly employed African American military veterans who volunteered for a hospital-based twenty-eight-day treatment program. They had used cocaine for two to three years. Patients were randomly assigned to inpatient and outpatient programs in which participants attended daily group therapy, activities therapy, and individual counseling. Some also received psychoactive medication. The completion rate for outpatient treatment was 37 percent; for inpatient treatment it was 86 percent. Interviews conducted four months after treatment revealed that 76 percent had not used cocaine in the previous thirty days, while those who had averaged only 1.2 days of cocaine use per month. Limited urine tests supported the interview data. "Despite the significantly greater completion rate for the patients assigned to inpatient treatment, both groups showed equal levels of improvements at the four-month follow up point" (O'Brien et al. 1990: 83).

There is no clear research evidence on the effectiveness of short-term in- or outpatient treatment: "Given what is known about the importance of length of stay in treatment and the complexity of the recovery process in addiction, there is little likelihood that twenty-eight-day clinics or short-term modalities (one to six months) will yield positive outcomes" (De Leon 1990: 125).

In fact, it may be the availability of legitimate economic opportunity rather than the mode of treatment that predicts post-treatment success. Without such opportunity, clients in disadvantaged groups will remain enmeshed in the drug-abuse subculture and continue relying on income-generating crime (Anglin and Hser 1990b).

PREVENTION

Efforts at prevention attempt to reduce the supply or the demand for drugs of abuse. The former is the goal of drug-law enforcement (which will be examined in chapter 7); the latter has been the goal of coercive legislation and education. "Considering the difficulty and cost of treating individuals with substance abuse problems, the prospect of developing effective substance abuse prevention programs has long held a great deal of appeal" ("Drug Abuse" 1987: 35). Unfortunately, effective prevention has proven to be as elusive as effective treatment (and effective law enforcement).

Most efforts at prevention have focused on schools, and school-based antidrug programs are widespread. These have been dominated by three models (Ellickson 1995):

1. *Information Model:* Assuming that children and adolescents will avoid drugs when they understand their potential hazards, this model seeks to impart information. Furthermore, the model assumes that students will develop negative attitudes that will deter them from using drugs. "In short, the information model posits a causal sequence leading from knowledge (about drugs) to attitude change (negative) to behavior change (nonuse)" (1995: 100).
2. *Affective Model:* Shifting the focus away from education, this model instead seeks to affect personality. "The model assumes that

adolescents who turn to drugs do so because of problems within themselves—low self-esteem or inadequate personal skills in communication and decision making" (1995: 101). Affective model programs attempt to improve the affective skills (communication, decision making, self-assertion) believed related to drug use. In attempting to improve a student's self-image, ability to interact within a group, and problem-solving ability, the model focuses on feelings, values, and self-awareness and in some programs on personal values and choices.

3. *Social Influence Model:* Considered by many in the field to be the most promising of the models, the social influence (SI) model is centered on external influences that push students toward drug use, especially peer pressure, as well as internal influences, such as the desire to be accepted by "the crowd." In order to deal with adolescent vulnerabilities, SI seeks to familiarize students with the pressures to use drugs, enabling them to "develop counters [resistance skills] to

The information model of drug-abuse prevention is demonstrated by this rural health clinic worker's instruction in a small elementary school classroom in northern California.

JUST SAY NO TO DRUGS

In 1989 welterweight and middleweight boxing champion Sugar Ray Leonard appeared in nationally telecast antidrug announcements and made several school appearances urging students to "Say No to Drugs." In 1991, after stories appeared in the media, Leonard admitted that he had been a cocaine user.

pro-drug arguments and to teach them techniques for saying no in pressure situations" (1995: 102).

Educating persons, particularly elementary, high school, and college students (the primary population at risk) about the dangers of drug use would seem at first blush to be devoid of controversy and a sound response to the problem of drug abuse. After all, as Richard Brotman and Frederic Suffet (1975) point out, the thinking behind the idea appears to be quite rational: Provide valid information about the harmful consequences of drug abuse and most persons will avoid drugs. However, as Patricia Wald and Peter Hutt (1972: 18) note, "There is substantial uncertainty and confusion in the area of drug education and prevention" because "there is no real evidence that such educational efforts are successful." Indeed, as research by Isidor Chein and his colleagues (1964) revealed, youngsters with the greatest knowledge about drugs are the most susceptible to using drugs. Indeed, there is a substantial drug abuse problem among physicians, who presumably know a great deal about the dangers of drugs (Kennedy 1995).

Goodstadt (n.d.: 2) points out that informational programs typically suffer from major weaknesses that may actually encourage drug use: "The unfortunate result is that young people may become more rather than less likely to experiment with drugs." Providing greater knowledge about drugs may serve the unintended (or latent) function of piquing interest in and arousing curiosity about them and may possibly encourage more daring adolescents to seek out drugs. Dan Waldorf (1973) notes that in New York, heroin is seemingly everywhere in African-American and Puerto Rican ghettos, where young people are exposed to it at an early age. They know about heroin and drug addicts through first-hand exposure; they witness drugs being purchased and see addicts nodding on the streets and clustering in doorways, communal washrooms, and rooftops to "get off." They know addicts steal family belongings to sell for money to buy drugs. The real question, Waldorf states, is not why so many ghetto residents become drug abusers but why a majority avoid becoming addicted to a powerful substance that provides relief from an oppressive environment. However, while there is evidence that drug users know much more about drugs than nonusers, "There is no evidence that increases in such knowledge stimulate use" (Hanson 1980: 273). "Simply providing the child with information about substance abuse would primarily alter the behavior of well-socialized children from cohesive families rather than those most at risk" (Dishion, Patterson, and Reid 1988: 90).

The standard educational approach has been to present factual information concerning the dangers of substance abuse because it was assumed that increased knowledge would serve as an effective deterrent by enabling students to make rational decisions not to use drugs. "Such information has frequently been laden with ethical and moral judgments so that the 'proper' decision for the individual has been preordained" (Zinberg 1984: 204). An integral part of this approach has often been the "scare" lecture of physical education teachers or nonschool personnel such as police officers. While intended to frighten students away from dangerous substances, these lectures often contain so much misinformation or exaggeration that they raise students' skepticism and jeopardize all drug-education efforts. More recently the antidrug public-service message has often been delivered by well-known performers or athletes—a questionable approach given the level of substance abuse reported in these groups. A 1987 "Stop Substance Abuse" film featured athletes—including basketball star Orlando Woolridge of the New Jersey Nets—urging youngsters to avoid drugs; in 1988 the Nets announced that Woolridge was entering a drug rehabilitation program. The public schools are now turning away from the "scare'em" approach in favor of one that emphasizes the judgment and social skills necessary to avoid substance abuse (Berger 1989). Some research indicates that this approach shows promise, but only with those youngsters who were not likely to become problem drug users in the first place.

A D.A.R.E. classroom in Beverly Hills.

The American Social Health Association (1972: 5) states that drug education "must avoid overconcentration on 'the drug problem.' Many youngsters, knowing more about drugs than their parents and teachers, will not accept moralization but will respect realistic, valid information derived from a credible source." The dangers of exaggeration or misinformation in antidrug efforts are emphasized by Brotman and Suffet (1975: 60), who state that "if a program's audience disbelieves information on drugs which in their experience are not terribly dangerous, they may also discredit information on drugs whose dangers are more certain, and thus be induced to try them." A different approach to educating youngsters about certain dangerous chemicals avoids exaggeration and scare tactics, relying instead on a factual presentation about dangerous substances and the body's reaction to them, both good and bad. The goal is to provide information so that students can make informed decisions rather than to prevent drug use, which may be too much to expect from any educational program. Some problems with this approach are:

1. It may be opposed by public officials and/or parents who believe that schools should teach "proper" behavior, that is, "preach" on the evils of drug use;
2. A great deal is not known about drugs of abuse; and
3. Depending on their ages, students may not be able to understand the information.

"Some experts believe that giving specific factual knowledge reinforces the antidrug propensities of persons not likely to abuse drugs anyway but actually contributes to the 'seduction' of vulnerable high-risk groups by romanticizing the negativism that motivates their conduct" (Wald and Abrams 1972: 133). Research by Richard Stuart (1974) indicates that a fact-oriented drug curriculum may actually increase the danger of involvement with drugs. Furthermore, some research indicates that drug addicts are quite familiar with the effects and dangers of the substances they abuse, but they either discount the risks or view them as minor and part of the "game" (see, for example, Hendler and Stephens 1977). Troy Duster (1970: 192) reports that the prospective addict sees himself as an exception to the pattern of addiction he sees around him:

> It is typical of the early experience of the addict-to-be that he knows of people who use narcotics and who get away with it . . . [in that] they are neither addicted nor are they known to the police. This double victory is witnessed by probably every individual who knowingly used heroin illegally for the first time.

Goodstadt (n.d.: 3) suggests acknowledging the positive reinforcements of drug use:

> Drug-use consequences are not all negative; if they were, nobody would continue to use drugs. Moderate use of some drugs offers physical, psychological,

and social benefits for some people. Drug education programs that do not take into account this important aspect of the decision to start or continue using drugs diminish their credibility and effectiveness.

Norman Zinberg (1984: 207), a psychiatrist and well-known researcher on drug use, recommends educational programs that parallel the approach often used to deal with adolescent sexual behavior: "Although our society does not condone teenage sexual activity, it has decided that those who are un-

PROJECT DARE

The Los Angeles Police Department (LAPD) and the Los Angeles Unified School District jointly sponsor Project DARE (Drug Abuse Resistance Education), which is designed to equip fifth-, sixth-, and seventh-grade children with the skills and motivation they need to resist peer pressure to use drugs, alcohol, and tobacco. DARE's instructors are uniformed police officers on full-time duty with the project. All are veteran officers and volunteers carefully selected by DARE supervisory staff and fully trained by officers and specialists from the school district.

> A DARE police officer is assigned to teach in every elementary school under the LAPD's jurisdiction, offering the seventeen-session core curriculum to either fifth- or sixth-grade students. A junior-high program for seventh graders, which includes early intervention with students deemed at risk, is also at full implementation in fifty-eight junior high schools.
>
> In bringing the core curriculum to the elementary schools, DARE officers are assigned to five schools per semester, and they visit each classroom once a week. Beyond this, the officers conduct one-day visits at other schools for an assembly program and follow-up visits in individual classrooms; hold formal training sessions on drug abuse for teachers; and conduct evening parent meetings. (DeJong 1987: 4)

The use of uniformed police officers as instructors is seen as a key element in the program's success:

> Police have knowledge of the drug scene and its impact on both individuals and society as a whole that regular classroom teachers cannot match. Indeed, many classroom teachers frankly admit their discomfiture in teaching lessons on drug abuse. For children this age, police hold a mystique. Kids respond to them. (1987: 7)

Because the program "involves police officers in positive, nonpunitive roles, students are more likely to develop positive attitudes toward police officers and greater respect for the law" (1987: 17).

The DARE curriculum ends with a schoolwide assembly that includes the reading of the winning "DARE Pledges." Each student who completes the program receives a certificate of achievement signed by the chief of police and the superintendent of schools.

willing to follow its precepts should be given the basic information needed to avoid disease and unwanted pregnancy." Accordingly, drug education

> should provide information on how to avoid the effects of destructive drug combinations (for example, barbiturates and alcohol), the unpleasant consequences of using drugs of unknown purity, the hazards of using drugs with a high dependence liability, the dangers of certain modes of administration, and the unexpected effects of various dose levels and various settings.

Some people believe that responsible use of drugs is not an acceptable objective for education programs, especially for the young, but this position ignores the realities of drug use:

> First, use of alcohol and medications with parental supervision is usually neither harmful nor illegal. Second, it is unrealistic to talk to illegal drug users as if they do not, and would not, use drugs. Efforts to prevent drug abuse by reducing the most risky forms of drug use (for example, drinking and driving, cannabis use and gymnastics) need not condone illegal drug use. Third, it may be unrealistic to counsel immediate abstinence for chronic drug users; more responsible use of an illegal drug may be an appropriate intermediate objective for such a population. (Goodstadt n.d.: 3).

An eight-year study of adolescent drug use revealed that the vast majority of teen-agers who occasionally use drugs suffer no long-lasting negative effects and cannot in later years be distinguished from those who abstained from drug use (Blakeslee 1988).

A broad approach to prevention involves "affective" or "humanistic" education (although this term is likely to trigger negative responses in persons holding certain religious and social views). These efforts are designed to enhance self-esteem, to encourage responsible decision making, and to enrich students' personal and social development. The conceptual grounding for this approach was discussed in chapter 4 as part of behaviorist/learning theory: prevention through the enhancement of social competence. This approach has research support (Pentz 1985).

The bases of this approach are assumptions that ("Drug Abuse" 1987: 35):

1. Substance abuse programs should aim at developing prevention-oriented decision making concerning the use of licit or illicit drugs.
2. Such decisions should result in fewer negative consequences for the individuals.
3. The most effective way of achieving these goals is by increasing self-esteem, interpersonal skills, and participation in alternatives to substance use.

These assumptions are generally implemented through communication training, peer counseling, role playing, and assertiveness training. In the Los Angeles school system this approach has been implemented through Project DARE.

GIMMICKS, GADGETS, AND DRUGS

Television audiences have been exposed to a variety of antidrug messages geared to adolescents. Some are questionable; for example, drugs "fry your brain like an egg" (yet people use them and live quite well) or cause monkeys to give up food and sex (the stuff must be really great!). Now even cereal boxes, toys, and school notebooks contain antidrug messages.

Similar programs have focused on various areas of social functioning:

- The *social influence approach* attempts to "inoculate" students against using dangerous substances by making them aware of the social pressures they are likely to encounter and teaching skills that promote refusal.
- The *social learning approach* views chemical abuse from the perspective of learning theory; that is, like other behavior, it is learned through modeling and reinforcement. Through instruction, demonstration, feedback, reinforcement, behavioral rehearsal (classroom practice), and extended practice through homework assignments, the youngster is taught life-coping skills that have a rather broad range of applications, including drug resistance. There is considerable variation in age groups and length of program. Some groups are led by adults and others by peers.

Research has revealed that

simply giving information and training the child in self-control techniques would probably not be effective for the subset of children most at risk for later substance abuse. Even at age 10, this subset of most-at-risk children are already difficult to change, whether by family, teachers, or therapist. (Dishion, Patterson, and Reid 1988: 90).

In an extensive review of the research into drug education, David Hanson (1980: 273) concludes (emphasis added):

Research has demonstrated that while it is relatively easy to increase drug knowledge, it is more difficult to modify attitudes. A number of studies have reported greater changes in knowledge than in attitude, or have reported changes in knowledge unaccompanied by changes in attitude. Clearly the most rigorous test of educational effectiveness involves subsequent drug usage. By far the largest number of studies have found *no effects of drug education upon use.* A few have found drug usage to be reduced while others have found it to be increased following drug education. [For a more recent review, see Botvin 1990.]

HARM REDUCTION: A NEW APPROACH TO DRUG EDUCATION

Harm reduction is a new and controversial approach to drug education. Instead of focusing on preventing *use*, harm reduction attempts to prevent *abuse*. This paradigm recognizes that people will always use psychoactive substances whether they are legal or illegal and attempts to minimize the hazards of use—a more realistic goal (Duncan et al. 1994). (A policy of harm reduction is discussed in chapter 8.)

Harith Swadi and Harry Zeitlin (1987: 745) state: "It must be our conclusion that the available methods of drug education that aim at preventing drug abuse are at least ineffective, if not counterproductive." The National Institute on Drug Abuse ("Drug Abuse" 1987: 50) notes that "substance abuse prevention research remains in its infancy" and that "we are still far from having a range of prevention strategies whose long-term efficacy is in little doubt." The General Accounting Office (1987) reported to Congress that drug prevention efforts have been unevaluated or have shown little or no impact, and in 1990 William Bennett, the federal drug policy director, stated before a congressional committee that drug education was not effective and that children were more likely to respond to law enforcement efforts and punishment (Berke 1990b).

However, a well-designed research effort found Project ALERT to be effective in preventing or reducing adolescent use of cigarettes and marijuana. ALERT is based on a social influence model of prevention that seeks to motivate young people to resist drugs and helps them develop the skills to do so. Students develop reasons for not using drugs and responses to internal and external pressures to use them. The two-year research effort involved randomly selected seventh- and eight-grade students across geographic, racial, and socioeconomic lines. ALERT had clearly positive results with respect to cigarette and marijuana use among both low- and high-risk students. The impact on alcohol consumption was negligible, and a "boomerang effect"—increased use of tobacco—was found for confirmed smokers (Ellickson and Bell 1990). Positive results were reported in Kansas City, Kansas, and Indianapolis, Indiana, where, beginning in the sixth and seventh grades, students were exposed to information about the dangers of drug use at school, at home, and in the community. Parents were trained to reinforce the antidrug message at home, and public service announcements were carried by news organizations throughout the community. Of the high school students who participated in the program, 1.6 percent said they had used cocaine in the last month, while 3.7 percent of the control group did. With respect to marijuana, the figures were 14.2 percent and 20.2 percent; alcohol, 36 percent and 50 percent;

and cigarettes, 24 percent and 32 percent (Treaster 1990b; Johnson et al. 1990).[9]

Two short-term reviews of Project DARE (Nyre 1985; Aniskiewicz and Wysong 1990) have been positive: The program enhanced antidrug attitudes and knowledge while strengthening the social skills believed important in resisting drug use. A third evaluation (DeJong 1987b) contradicted these findings but, nevertheless, found that the DARE student showed significantly less drug use. A subsequent analysis by Earl Wysong, Richard Aniskiewicz, and David Wright (1994: 467), which tracked a DARE program for five years, found "no long-term effects for the program in preventing or reducing adolescent drug use." In their review of eight DARE studies, Susan Ennett and colleagues (1994) did not find encouraging results. They also questioned the use of law enforcement personnel as teachers in the program, noting that there are no studies on whether this is an effective use of police personnel. A convincing study of DARE will require longitudinal research over many years.

TECHNICAL PROBLEMS AND CRITICISMS

The difficulty in producing and implementing effective drug abuse prevention programs may be related to some of the technical aspects of these programs. It may be—and there is evidence to support such a hypothesis—that drug abuse prevention programs are too often "put together" and implemented by well-meaning but otherwise limited persons, which results in a "happy hands at home" approach to a complex problem. For example, Patricia Bush and Ronald Iannotti (1987: 70) note that programs designed to educate elementary school children about drug abuse often fail to consider *Cognitive Development Theory* (originally developed by Jean Piaget) and thus may be inappropriate to the children's developmental stage. "Health education programs which are produced by adults who are unaware of children's developmental stages, may be, while not necessarily counterproductive, a waste of resources." (The U.S. Department of Education has attempted to deal with this problem by preparing a curriculum model that is grade-level specific: *Learning to Live Drug-Free: A Curriculum Model for Prevention.*)

Furthermore:

> Strategies which are adequate for preventing experimentation among those at low risk of engaging in serious antisocial behaviors may be wholly inadequate for preventing initiation and use by those who exhibit a "deviance syndrome."

9. An evaluation of junior high school antidrug programs in the Kansas City, Missouri, area found that while school staff viewed the programs as beneficial and successful, outcome measurements did not support their optimism (Gilham, Lucas, Siverwright 1994).

On the other hand, well-founded strategies for preventing drug abuse among those at highest risk for abuse may be inappropriate for those at risk of only becoming experimental users. (Hawkins, Lishner, and Catalano 1987: 78)

Thus, a rational prevention program needs to establish and explicate its goals:

> If the goal of prevention is to prevent serious maladaptive behavior associated with drug abuse in adolescence, then it may be desirable from an etiological perspective to focus prevention efforts on those youth who manifest behavior problems, including aggressive and other antisocial behaviors during the elementary grades. On the other hand, if the goal is to prevent experimentation with drugs, or to delay the age of experimentation in the general population, such highly focused efforts may be inappropriate. (Hawkins, Lishner, and Catalano 1987: 80)

Diana Baumrind (1987: 32) offers a caution: "When socially deviant youths are required to participate in the school setting in peer-led denunciation activities they value, they are more likely to become alienated than converted." An eight-year study revealed that once an adolescent decides to use drugs in response to internal problems, peer-based prevention programs will not work (Blakeslee 1988).

Despite the lack of evidence supporting current drug-use prevention efforts, Michael Goodstadt (n.d.: 1–2) states that there is some promising evidence regarding the impact of educational programs based on smoking prevention studies that "offer approaches that can be applied to education about other drugs." In fact, "Americans are smoking and drinking less . . . not because the Army imprisoned North Carolina tobacco farmers or bombed stills in Scotland, but because attitudes have been changing with the help of education and treatment programs" (May 1988: 12). Increased public awareness of the dangers of alcohol abuse, coupled with an emphasis on physical fitness and nutrition, has dramatically reduced alcohol consumption in the United States. In an extensive review of prevention programs, Gilbert Botvin (1990: 512) concludes that while prevention efforts are in their infancy,

> the past decade has seen the development, for the first time in its history, of interventions that can actually reduce or prevent substance abuse. Greater emphasis has recently been placed on developing intervention models that are based on firm theoretical and empirical foundations. [For example, Kim, McLeod, and Shantizis 1990]

"At present it appears that the informational or rational approach has little systemic impact on behavior and alternative approaches, such as the developmental approach, have more promise for actually deterring drug use" (Bruvold 1990: 150). But Michael Newcomb and Peter Bentler (1989: 246) caution:

> Prevention and intervention should focus on the misuse, abuse, problem use, and heavy use of drugs to meet internal needs, cope with distress, and avoid respon-

sibility and important life decisions and difficulties. The youngsters facing these tasks are in need of help, education, and intervention. It is misleading to bask in the success of some peer programs that have reduced the number of youngsters who experiment with drugs (but would probably never have become regular users, let alone abusers) and ignore the tougher problems of those youngsters who are at high risk for drug abuse as well as other serious difficulties.

In fact, support for drug prevention programs, note Aniskiewicz and Earl Wysong (1990), may have more to do with politics than research. Such programs appear to rest less upon clear-cut evidence of effectiveness than upon their popularity as symbolic action against the "drug crisis." Being associated with such efforts can enhance the public standing of elected, police, and school officials.

In chapter 6 we will examine the large-scale industries that have developed around our inability to reduce demand for certain substances.

REVIEW QUESTIONS

1. Why has the medical profession historically avoided dealing with the problem of drug abuse?
2. What chemical "cures" have historically been offered to deal with drug abuse?
3. What are the drawbacks of using heroin antagonists?
4. What is an opioid agonist?
5. How have opioid agonists been used to deal with heroin addiction?
6. What are the advantages of using methadone maintenance rather than heroin maintenance?
7. What are the disadvantages of using methadone maintenance?
8. How does psychoanalytic theory explain drug abuse?
9. Why is it difficult if not impossible to use psychoanalysis to treat heroin addiction?
10. How is psychoanalytic theory usually operationalized in the treatment of drug abusers?
11. How does behavior/learning theory explain drug abuse?
12. Why is it difficult to apply behavior theory in the treatment of drug abuse?
13. How is contingency management/contracting used in the treatment of drug abuse?
14. What is meant by the civil commitment of drug abusers?
15. What is the therapeutic community (TC) approach to drug abuse?
16. What is the Alcoholics Anonymous twelve-step approach to dealing with substance abuse?
17. How does Rational Recovery differ from Alcoholics Anonymous?
18. Why is it difficult to determine the effectiveness of the AA approach?

19. Why are health care facilities often eager to include a drug rehabilitation program as part of their services?
20. Why is it difficult to determine the success of any drug treatment program?
21. What is the social learning approach to drug abuse prevention?
22. What drawbacks are inherent in educating youngsters about the dangers of drug abuse?
23. What is the "affective" or "humanistic" approach to drug education?
24. What general conclusion have researchers reached about the usefulness of drug education programs?

6

THE BUSINESS OF DRUGS

Regardless of what we think we are trying to do, when we make it illegal to traffic in commodities for which there is an inelastic demand, the effect is to secure a kind of monopoly profit to the entrepreneur who is willing to break the law. In effect, we say to him: "We will set up a barrier to entry into this line of commerce by making it illegal and, therefore, risky; if you are willing to take the risk, you will be sheltered from the competition of those who are unwilling to do so. Of course, if we catch you, you may possibly (although not necessarily) be put out of business; but meanwhile you are free to gather the fruits that grow in the hothouse atmosphere we are providing for you."
—Herbert L. Packer (1968: 279)

This chapter examines the international and domestic traffic in illegal drugs, which, by any estimate, is a multibillion-dollar-a-year industry. Because the product is illegal but nevertheless in great demand, drug trafficking is characterized by a level of free enterprise never envisioned by Adam Smith. It is a market totally devoid of legal constraints and one in which prices and profits are governed only by the law of supply and demand. As in any major industry, there are various functional levels: manufacturers, importers, wholesalers, distributors, retailers, and consumers. Workers in the drug business range from leaders of powerful international cartels to street dealers whose activities support a personal drug habit. At the manufacturing and importation levels, the drug business is usually concentrated among a relatively few persons who head major trafficking organizations; at the retail level it is filled with a large, fluctuating, and open-ended number of dealers and consumers. Because people at the highest levels of the drug trade are often connected by kinship and ethnicity, we will frequently refer to the ethnicity of criminal organizations in this chapter.

Drugs are smuggled into the United States from both source and transshipment countries. Traffickers may use circuitous routes to avoid the suspicion normally generated by shipments from source countries. For example, cocaine may be shipped from Colombia to the African continent; from there it is moved to the United States as part of legitimate maritime cargo. Pleasure crafts and fishing vessels blend in with normal maritime traffic, and low-profile vessels fabricated of wood or fiberglass and measuring up to forty feet in length are difficult to spot and do not readily appear on radar. Smugglers also use aircraft, landing on isolated runways and even highways or airdropping their cargo. Motor vehicles using land routes across Canada and Mexico and "mules" carrying drugs that they have put in condoms and swallowed round out the smuggling picture.

THE BUSINESS OF COCAINE: INTERNATIONAL TRAFFICKING

Cocaine is an alkaloid found in significant quantities only in the leaves of two species of coca shrub, one of which grows in the Andes of Ecuador, Peru, and Bolivia and the other in the mountainous regions of Columbia,[1] along the Caribbean coast of South America, on the northern coast of Peru, and in the dry valley of the Marañón River in northeastern Peru. Indians in Peru have been chewing coca leaves for at least twenty centuries. They also use the leaves as a poultice for wounds and to brew a tea, *mate de coca*, said to cure the headaches of tourists bothered by the 12,000-foot altitude of La Paz. While cash crops raised on the mountain slopes of Peru require a great deal of care (for example, the nutrient-poor soil needs continuous fertilization), coca is a hardy jungle plant that needs little or no fertilizer and produces abundant seeds. "Once a

---

1. Colombian coca is less potent than Peruvian or Bolivian.

coca field is planted, it will yield four to five crops a year for thirty to forty years, needing little in return but seasonal weeding" (Morales 1989: xvi).

Until the 1990s Peruvian traffickers were dependent on Colombians to process their coca paste into cocaine. Because the Colombian organizations have been weakened (for reasons discussed below), Peruvians now ship to Brazil and Ecuador, countries where precursor chemicals (discussed in chapter 3) are available, as well as to Colombia (Tullis 1995). In Bolivia, South America's poorest nation with a per capita annual income of $600, coca is grown legally, and its leaves are sold openly at street markets. Until the 1970s small amounts of coca paste were shipped from Bolivia to Argentina, Brazil, and Chile, where it was combined with tobacco to make *pitillos* (cigarettes). During the early 1970s, the industry changed dramatically when the demand for cocaine mushroomed in the United States, and numerous kitchen laboratories sprang up in response to the market. Later in the decade, wealthy and influential cattle ranchers in the Benji region, powerful ranchers, farmers, and businessmen in the Santa Cruz area, and some senior officers in the Bolivian military began to organize the industry on a large scale. Military involvement increased with the market, leading to a "cocaine coup" in 1980, after which a number of traffickers were freed from prison and the U.S. Drug Enforcement Agency pulled out of Bolivia (Henkel 1986). In 1982 the military junta was re-

A Colombian anti-drug helicopter sits in a field of coca plants discovered in a dense jungle near the Colombia-Ecuador border.

PRECURSOR CHEMICALS

Unable to account for the disposition of 6,000 metric tons of chemicals that could be used for manufacturing cocaine, in 1996 the United States imposed stringent controls on chemicals exported to Colombia. The sales of such chemicals had increased by 57 percent since 1990. Exporters now have to show that the chemicals have a legitimate use in Colombia, which includes identifying the company receiving the chemicals and its officers (Wren 1996c).

placed by a civilian government. Despite the change in government, the country has remained dependent on the income from its leading cash crop—coca.

Because of its bulk, coca leaves are usually processed into paste as close to their source as possible (usually Bolivia and Peru) and smuggled by small aircraft or boat into Colombia or Brazil. There it is refined into cocaine in jungle laboratories. In more recent years, laboratories have been relocating to cities far from cultivation sites in order to be closer to sources of precursor chemicals and because improved law enforcement methods enable the detection of jungle laboratories. The laboratories have, for example, increased their presence in northwestern Argentina and even in Buenos Aires. While precursor chemicals are usually manufactured in the United States and Germany, Panama and Mexico also serve as major transit sources. Colombian cartels using dummy companies and multiple suppliers pay up to ten times the normal prices for these chemicals (Rohter 1990).

For the most part, Bolivian traffickers make deliveries of cocaine in Bolivia, leaving the shipping and smuggling to other organizations—usually Colombians (Levine 1990). A new business–drug-trafficking elite that deals directly with European drug markets has emerged in the Santa Cruz area, and crackdowns in Colombia have induced some Colombians to settle in Bolivia (Lupsha 1990). These crackdowns have also caused traffickers to relocate their laboratories to Peru. As a result, the formerly primitive agricultural business of producing coca has been transformed: Cartels have formed and violence is increasing (Nash 1991b). In fact, increased law enforcement activity, the result of pressure from the United States, has caused the problem to expand throughout much of Latin America ("Widening Drug War" 1991).

According to then-President George Bush, the U.S. invasion of Panama in 1989 was "to combat drug trafficking." Since the ouster of Manuel Noriega, however, the drug problem has grown considerably worse. Panama has emerged as a major transshipment and laboratory source for cocaine; its geographic location, a long border with Colombia consisting of a dense, sparsely populated jungle province, and inadequate law enforcement allow the trafficking to thrive. Colombian traffickers have relocated to Panama, where they enjoy virtual immunity because of overworked, underfunded, and, by many accounts, corrupt law enforcement (Sheppard 1991). When they too became victims of the general lawlessness that has overtaken Panama, cartel gunmen hunted down and shot some armed robbers as an example to others (Sheppard 1991b; 1991c).

Pressure from law enforcement has also led to the "invasion" of Suriname, a Dutch protectorate in northern South America, by Colombian traffickers who are using it as a transshipment point to European and U.S. markets. Guatemala also serves as an important transshipment location. There the movement of drugs has been aided by top officers in that country's military. Greater surveillance of the Mexican-Southwest border and the Caribbean has led to increased use of Canada as a transshipment point. Aircraft originating in Colombia offload their cargo in Canada; from there it is transported by land across the border into Maine and subsequently into New York City. (See figure 6.1.)

THE CUBAN-COLOMBIAN CONNECTION

Until 1976 Cuban criminal organizations arranged for the importation and distribution of cocaine from Colombia. When Fidel Castro overthrew the corrupt dictatorial regime of Fulgencio Batista in 1959, he expelled American gangsters operating gambling casinos in Havana. Many of the gangsters' Cuban associates fled to the United States, along with the *narcotráficantes* who had distributed cocaine in Cuba. They settled primarily in the New York-New Jersey and Miami areas and began to look for new sources of income. Many Cubans who fled with or soon after the Batista loyalists were organized and trained by the Central Intelligence Agency (CIA) in an effort to dislodge Castro. After the Bay of Pigs debacle in 1961, members of the CIA-organized Cuban exile army were supposed to disband and go into lawful business. However, as Donald Goddard (1978: 44) points out, "They had no lawful business." Elements of these exile groups (they often overlapped) began to enter the cocaine business. At first they imported only enough cocaine to satisfy the needs of their own communities, but by the mid-1960s the market began to expand, and they began to import the substance in greater quantities.

Until the early 1970s the importation of marijuana, counterfeit Quaaludes, and cocaine into the United States was largely a Cuban operation, the sources of supply being Colombia. During the latter half of the 1960s, Colombians began migrating to the United States in numbers sufficient to establish communities in New York, Miami, Chicago, and Los Angeles. Many were illegal immigrants brought in through the Bahamas with false documents such as phony Puerto Rican birth certificates and forged immigration papers. The Colombian traffickers became highly organized both in the United States and at home. By 1973 independent foreign nationals could no longer deal drugs in Colombia. In 1976 the Colombians became dissatisfied with their Cuban agents in the United States—the latter were reportedly keeping most of the profits and shortchanging the Colombians. Enforcers, often young men from the Guajira Peninsula (Colombia's version of the Wild West), from Pereira, a

FIGURE 6.1
Countries of South America

Cocaine is derived from the leaves of two species of coca shrub. One species grows in the Andes of Ecuador, Peru, and Bolivia; the other, in the mountains of Colombia, along the Caribbean coast of South America, on the northern coast of Peru, and in the valley of the Marañón River in northeastern Peru. Refining takes place mainly in jungle laboratories, some far distant from cultivation sites, for example, northeastern Argentina.

crime-ridden little city between Cali and Medillín, or from *Barrio Antioquia* in the slums of Medillín, were sent in, and Cubans were systematically executed in Miami and New York. By 1978 Cubans remaining in the cocaine business had become subordinate to the Colombians. Then began the "cocaine wars" between rival Colombian gangs, which brought terror to South Florida.

Colombian Narcotráficantes

Colombia, with a population of about 26 million, is the only South American country with both Pacific and Caribbean coastlines. It has been torn by political strife that escalated into civil wars in 1902 and 1948. On 9 April 1948, the leftist mayor of Bogotá was assassinated in the street in front of thousands of his supporters. The assassin was immediately lynched. Three days of rioting ensued, setting the stage for a civil war. *La Violencia*, as the civil war of 1948–1958 is known, cost about three hundred thousand lives (Riding 1987a); it ended when liberals and the conservatives formed the National Front. But several Marxist insurgencies continued to threaten the stability of the central government. Kathleen Romoli (1941: 37) notes, "At the root of Colombia's easy violence is an extraordinary indifference toward death." The homicide rate is eight times higher than that of the United States, and murder is the leading cause of death for Colombian males aged fifteen to forty-four (Marx 1991c; Riding 1987a). In major cities such as Bogotá, a variety of vigilante groups routinely execute "undesirables"—left-wingers, vagrants, drug addicts, criminals ("Vigilantes in Colombia Kill Hundreds of 'Disposables'" 1994).

In Colombia, drug traffickers exemplify a lack of belief in the legitimacy of the country's political and economic institutions:

> Breaking the law—any law—is justified, and not just for the usual economic reasons that criminals favor. For traffickers, the law, law-enforcement officials, U.S. drug operatives, and drug-control organizations all represent the traditional elite, international imperialism, or other international competitive economic interests, none of which has any historical moral standing in their eyes. Therefore, moralistic arguments about restraining violent behavior do not capture these people's attention . . . [and] allows traffickers to garner enthusiastic support in some areas. (Tullis 1995: 66)

Romoli points out that because "death has small significance, human life has little importance" (1941: 37). In this sociopolitical atmosphere, bandits roamed freely, engaging in brigandage, terrorism, and revolution. In the northern cities of Barranquilla, Santa Marta, and the La Guajira Peninsula, smuggling (*contrabandista*) groups have operated for decades. Bandits, *contrabandistas*, and Guajiran Indians, often financed by Bogotá businessmen, emerged as crime "families," a *narcomafia*. Members are often related by blood, marriage, or *compadrazgo* (fictional kinship), and in many important respects the core groups resemble those of the Sicilian Mafia (discussed below).

The President's Commission on Organized Crime (1986: 78–79) points out that the Colombians have been able to control the cocaine market for a number of reasons:

> Geographically, Colombia is well-positioned both to receive coca from Peru and Bolivia and to export the processed drug to the United States by air or by sea. In addition, the country's vast central forests effectively conceal clandestine processing laboratories and air strips, which facilitate the traffic. Perhaps most importantly, the Colombians have a momentum by benefit of their early involvement in the cocaine trade. They have evolved from small, disassociated groups into compartmentalized organizations and are sophisticated and systematized in their approach to trafficking cocaine in the United States. Further, groups in the Colombian population in the U.S. provide traffickers access to this country and often serve as a distribution network for Colombian cocaine.

The economic modernization of Colombia failed to bring about a corresponding respect for government. Delegitimization of government and *La Violencia* "left legacies which have worked to permit, if not encourage, the development of the cocaine industry" (Thoumi 1995: 84). Delegitimization spurred the development of smuggling, particularly the export of products from Colombia to Venezuela and Ecuador—cattle, emeralds, coffee—providing experience in the trade of contraband and in money laundering. The cocaine traffickers' propensity for violence led to the domination of potential Bolivian and Peruvian rivals. LaMond Tullis (1995: 67) points out:

> Aside from their disdain for Colombian institutions and their long criminal records, Colombian traffickers share other characteristics. They appear to be great believers in fate and providence and seem unmoved by normal considerations of personal danger. It is a perspective unaltered by normal law-enforcement efforts and one that makes dealing with or trying to control them such a dangerous enterprise.

Colombia is a relatively large country, and many regions have only a weak federal presence. This has proved ideal for cocaine manufacture because it leaves areas where only local officials have to be bribed, a cheaper and less risky action. Speculative capitalism—the focus on very high short-term profits—a feature of Colombia's financial elite, provided the resources for the development of a cocaine industry (Thoumi 1995). The Colombian reputation for violence serves to maintain discipline and intimidates would-be competitors. Enforcers, well trained in their craft (Mowatt 1991), are known to torture and mutilate their targets—members of the victim's family, both women and children, and even pets are not spared.

The major Colombian trafficking organizations are structured to control each intermediate step in processing and exporting cocaine. Thus, "Each of the trafficking groups in Medellín, Bogotá, and Cali contain various sections, each with a separate function, such as manufacturing, transportation, distribution, finance and security." Not only does this bureaucratic structure promote greater efficiency, it also serves to protect the organization: "Few members of one section are aware of the others involved, and the loss of one member or even a whole section does not threaten the stability of the entire organization" (PCOC 1984: 562). At the lower levels, many workers move between one organization and another, often unaware of which organization they are working for at any given time. At the highest levels, members are well insulated from the physical operations of their organizations.

The PCOC (1986: 79–81) describes how Colombian operations are organized:

> Most laborers in the cultivation phase are Peruvian or Bolivian peasants who cultivate and harvest coca in remote areas of the Eastern Andes, then process the coca leaves to base in nearby villages. The growers are allied in small, independent groups, but are typically financed, overseen, and protected by members of a larger Colombian organization.
>
> Processed coca base is usually flown on light aircraft from the mountain villages to Colombian processing facilities by those members of the Colombian organization responsible for transportation. The planes land at clandestine airstrips, often simple mud runways, located near the processing laboratories. The laboratories vary widely in size, ranging from crude small-quantity operations to large, sophisticated complexes, and can be found both in Colombia's jungle and urban areas.
>
> Coca base is typically processed to cocaine hydrochloride in the laboratories, then bagged and taped into kilogram packages, which are sometimes coded to indicate a particular United States destination. The packages are loaded into duffel bags or burlap sacks, then removed by the transportation group to a "stash house," a large storage facility usually located near a seaport or a clandestine airstrip. The cocaine is held at the stash house until it is exported from Colombia, most often by private aircraft; the rest is shipped on ocean vessels or smuggled on commercial air carriers.

U.S. distribution is the responsibility of six-to-eight-person teams operating independently, selling cocaine to midlevel wholesalers. Team members are low-profile entrepreneurs who use legitimate businesses as fronts and employ lawyers and accountants.

> The money generated by the wholesale cocaine transaction is maintained for the organization by financial experts familiar with international banking and investing drug profits, and for assuring that a portion of the drug profit is returned to Colombia for reinvestment in the organization's cocaine enterprise. The cartel's own financial experts are supported by a complement of bankers, lawyers and other professionals in the United States who play a crucial role in facilitating these transactions. (PCOC 1986: 82)

The profits are enormous. When converted to a kilogram of cocaine hydrochloride, a $65 to $370 purchase of coca leaves increases in value to $1,900 to $5,000. At the wholesale level in Miami, a kilo of cocaine between 85 and

95 percent pure is sold for between $18,000 and $27,000. When it reaches the street-sale level, it can yield $300,000.

In the United States cocaine cartel representatives act as brokers to co-ordinate deliveries, usually 100 kilos at a time, to the various drug networks.

> The number of Colombian cocaine distribution networks is unknown because most are informally structured and operate in a fluid, transactional manner. Often a network will develop solely to distribute a single shipment of cocaine. The network may operate from six months to one year and then dissolve. (Comptroller General 1988: 13–14)

While structurally independent of the cartels, these distribution networks are symbiotic and in regular contact with their cartel sources:

> While the main organizers are handpicked by the Colombian traffickers, individual members of the same network seldom know one another and usually deal with one another on a single occasion. Each drug transaction is conducted separately and each part of the network is compartmentalized. Inventories are stored in hidden locations. After raids or arrests, the cartels conduct internal investigations to assure that their employees were loyal, security measures were followed, and lessons were learned to improve the operation. (Comptroller General 1988: 14)

However, the sheer volume of Colombian drug transactions makes them vulnerable to sophisticated law enforcement efforts:

> While most drug traffickers conduct financial transaction in cash, the volume of business conducted by the Colombian traffickers requires sophisticated record-keeping to track expenses and sales. Modern methods of monitoring inventories and deliveries are used; advanced communication centers arrange for the arrival of smuggled drugs, their distribution, the movement of cash proceeds, and other logistical matters. Distributors are instructed to keep accurate records, and many use facsimile machines to keep track of sales and to relay information to Colombia. (Comptroller General 1988: 19)

Infiltrating a Colombian group is near impossible:

> A prospective wholesale buyer must establish his bona fides at an audience with top management in Cali. If he is approved, he is not required to pay cash up front. He will send the cartel payment after he resells the drugs to middlemen. The wholesale buyer must put up collateral, cash or deeds to real property as insurance if he is caught. He must also provide human collateral in the form of his family in Colombia, who will pay with their lives if he ever turns informer. (Shannon 1991: 32)

Although they are commonly referred to as cartels, Colombian drug organizations are not tightly integrated monopolies. They "are in fact simply loose trade associations, assisting shifting coalitions of traffickers to more efficiently produce, market, transport, and distribute their products" (Lupsha 1990: 7). The most notorious have been those centered in Medellín and Cali.

Medellín, Colombia's second largest city, is a major Andean industrial and tourist center of about 1.5 million inhabitants located in the province of Antioquia. This province and neighboring ones bore the brunt of the civil violence of the 1948–1958 war. The city has a longstanding history of smuggling, a school for pickpockets, and a reputation as a place where assassins are trained in techniques like *asesino de la moto*: A passenger on a fast-moving motorbike uses an automatic weapon to spray the victim with bullets. The city's slum neighborhood of Palestino produces the *Palestinos*, hired killers who have been involved in dozens of murders in New York City. From the barrios of the Medellín hillside come the *sicarios* (from the Latin *sicarius*, meaning "hired killer"), young men often still in their teens who view contract murder as a career (Duzán 1994). The murder rate in Medellín is nearly nine times that in New York City. The city is virtually empty of any U.S. diplomatic personnel; the small U.S. Drug Enforcement Administration office was closed because of the danger (Uhlig 1989). Medellín is headquarters for several cocaine organizations known in Colombia as *Los Grandes Mafiosos* and in the United States as the Medellín cartel.

The origins of the cartel can be traced to the city's business class, which bankrolled cocaine deals with drug dealers of lower-class origins. When the latter became economically successful, they operated independently of their former patrons, sometimes even attacking business interests such as banks and forcing landowners to sell out at cut-rate prices (Duzán 1994). Political contributions and extensive bribery bought substantial immunity for the *narcotráficantes* of Colombia. When this failed, particularly for the Medellín groups, violence became the tool to neutralize enforcement. Officials are frequently offered a choice: *plata o plomo* ("silver or lead")—a bribe or a bullet.

The death of the cartel's most notorious trafficker, Carlos Escobar, in 1994 and the government crackdown on Medellín's cocaine organizations have left them in disarray and eclipsed by the drug organizations centered in Cali.

Cali Cartel

The drug boom in Colombia inspired a competing cartel in Cali, a city of 1.5 million about 250 miles south of Medellín. It is second only to Spain in the number of Spanish books it publishes each year, and advanced printing technology has made the city a center for counterfeiting, mostly of U.S. currency (Brooke 1991c). Members of the Cali cartel, a loose alliance of about fifteen trafficking groups with preeminence shared by two of the kinship-crime families, have typically favored bribery over violence. They take a percentage of the profits from shipments by smaller organizations and provide in return transportation, distribution, and enforcement services. While the Medellín cartel has generally used air transport, the Cali group prefers freighter cargo containers (Brooke 1991d).

The Cali cartel has avoided political entanglements and acts that could embarrass the government. Keeping a low profile, the Cali group uses violence to maintain internal discipline but has avoided attacks on public officials (Kraar 1988; Riding 1988).

> When blood is spilled at the hands of the Cali cartel, it was the result of internecine battles for supremacy in the business. Never did the violence reach out to the citizenry, never did it alienate the political establishment. The Cali cartel was not interested in buying up large tracts of land, joining with rightist forces to fight the guerrillas, or winning popular support among the peasantry by creating social welfare programs in the slums. Rather, it set about making money and doing so in the legitimate business world. (Duzán 1994: 138)

In 1995 it was revealed that the president of Colombia had sought and received campaign funding from the leaders of the Cali cartel. In 1995, on the heels of its success against the Medellín cartel and with increasing pressure from the United States, Colombian authorities moved vigorously against the major organizations in Cali. As a result, the price of cocaine in New York City soared almost 50 percent at the wholesale level (Krauss 1995). The level of Colombian violence in New York also increased:

Cali cocaine cartel member Jorge Rodriguez Orejuela arrested by police in Bogotà, Colombia, in March 1995.

Coming after the arrests of six of the top seven kingpins of the Cali drug cartel in Colombia, the surge in violent crime suggests that discipline is eroding in the upper levels of the Colombian distribution system that supplies . . . much of the Eastern Seaboard. (Krauss 1995b)

The crackdown has also had a negative impact on the Colombian economy, with a devaluation of the peso due to a shortage of dollars linked to the drug trade ("Drug Crackdown Said to Sap Colombia's Economy" 1995).

Ties between Colombian cocaine traffickers and Mexican heroin organizations increased dramatically during the 1990s (Lupsha 1995). Medellín and Cali organizations used smuggling networks established by Mexican drug organizations, and intermarriages between the groups have been reported. Mexican organizations either move the cocaine into the United States for the Colombians or purchase the drugs and deal them directly in the United States (Golden 1995b). It is estimated that the Mexicans are responsible for moving as much as 70 percent of Colombian cocaine into the United States (McMahon 1995). There is also evidence of a connection between the Colombians and Sicilian *mafiosi*.

Cocaine, Politics, Patronage, and Terrorism

The business of cocaine supports not only those directly involved in the trafficking but also their dependents and the legitimate businesses that depend on their patronage. U.S. dollars brought into poor Latin American countries help keep the *narcomafia* in luxury but also provide benefits for poorer elements of society. In the coca-growing regions of Peru and Bolivia, the *coqueros* provide a level of income that would otherwise be unavailable to the peasants who cultivate and process coca leaves for the illegal market. Government attempts to curtail coca cultivation always meet with opposition that is often violent.

The economics of coca in poor countries raises important policy issues. The Bolivian economy is dominated by coca, with an estimated three hundred thousand jobs generating annual economic activity worth billions, (Medina 1990). In Peru, any government that moves to eradicate coca, in addition to gaining the enmity of peasant voters and their elected representatives, risks strengthening the Marxist insurgencies. The Upper Huallaga River Valley, a dense jungle area about the size of West Virginia along the eastern slopes of the Andes is the world's most important source of coca; an estimated 250,000 acres are covered with the crop. The Revolutionary Armed Forces of Colombia (FARC) have been collecting taxes to permit the traffickers to operate in jungle areas and finally established more symbiotic ties: FARC guerrillas provide protection for cocaine-processing operations of the traffickers in the territory they share (Westrate 1985; "Drug Smugglers Used Cuban Base" 1988). At times the cooperation turned to violent conflict when the guerrillas raided cartel jungle headquarters for money and weapons (Duzán 1994).

MEXICAN-COLOMBIAN CONNECTION

In the early 1990s, the Mexicans struck a deal with the Colombians whose cocaine they were moving from Mexico into the United States on a contract basis: for every two kilograms of smuggled cocaine, the Mexicans would keep one kilogram as payment in kind (O'Brien and Greenberg 1996b; Wren 1996b). Both sides benefitted: the Colombians had an abundance of cocaine, and the Mexicans had a distribution network in the United States that they had previously used for heroin. The relationship with the Colombians also led to structural changes, some Mexican drug groups modeling their organizations along Colombian lines—compartmentalized units operating independently of each other but controlled hierarchically.

In the 1980s conflict in Colombia between leftist guerrillas and *narcotráficantes* intensified as the drug barons purchased huge tracts of land, an estimated 2.5 million fertile acres.

> In the process, they are also emerging as a powerful political force in the countryside where, backed by private armies of gunmen, they are trying to put an end to the kidnappings and extortion, traditionally carried out by rural guerilla groups. (Riding 1988b: 1)

For the traffickers, a Marxist government would bring an end to their lucrative business, if not to their lives. In fact, guerilla activity, particularly extortion from cattlemen, has left many eager to sell their ranches, often to the *narcotráficantes*, who are the most willing buyers and whose private armies can keep the guerrillas at bay (Weisman 1989). The rancher-traffickers invested their resources in turning organized peasant bands into fighting units. A U.S. congressional committee revealed that the private armies of a major cocaine trafficker had been trained by British and Israeli mercenaries, under the guise of helping Colombian ranchers fend off leftist guerrillas (Gerth 1991).

> Israeli, British, and Spanish mercenaries trained the death squads in terrorist techniques never before seen in Colombia. With their help, the private militias of the drug dealers learned how to make incendiary devices, the latest technology in bomb production, the use of plastic explosive and TNT. (Duzàn 1994: 136)

This relationship reportedly soured when Pablo Escobar began recruiting leftist guerrillas for his own use, while most of the rebel organizations reached a political accommodation with the Colombian government and ceased their military activity ("Why Did Gunmen Yield in Colombia?" 1991). Subsequently, right wing "death squads," also allied with the cartel, made their peace with the government and have engaged the traffickers in a bloody war.

The business of heroin originates in those areas of the world where the opium poppy thrives. Most of the heroin smuggled into the United States originates in areas of Asia known as the Golden Triangle and the Golden Crescent and in Mexico (see figure 6.2 below).

Golden Triangle

The Golden Triangle of Southeast Asia covers miles of forested highlands including the western fringe of Laos, the four northern provinces of

FIGURE 6.2
Major Asian Opium Regions

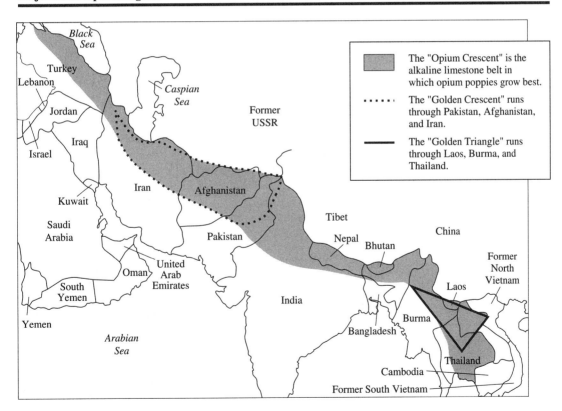

The "Opium Crescent" is the alkaline limestone belt in which opium poppies grow best.

The "Golden Crescent" runs through Pakistan, Afghanistan, and Iran.

The "Golden Triangle" runs through Laos, Burma, and Thailand.

Source: Abadinsky (1994), p. 200.

Thailand, and the northeastern parts of Burma, an area about the size of Nevada. These countries emerged from colonialism with relatively weak central governments and hinterlands inhabited by bandits and paramilitary organizations such as the Mong Tai Army and the Kuomintang. These organizations and indigenous tribal groups had been used by colonial officials, particularly the French, in their efforts against various insurgencies, particularly those with a Marxist ideology. As support for overseas colonies dwindled at home, French officials in this part of the world utilized the drug trade to continue financing their efforts. When the French withdrew from Southeast Asia, the United States took up the struggle against Marxist groups; the Vietnam War is part of this legacy. The Central Intelligence Agency waged its own clandestine war, and again heroin played a role in these efforts, because the indigenous tribal groups organized by the CIA cultivated opium. In Laos and South Vietnam, corrupt governments were heavily involved in heroin trafficking, making the substance easily available to American GIs (McCoy 1972). Thus, a longstanding and continuing tradition in this part of the world uses drugs to help finance military efforts.

Shan United/Mong Tai Army

The Shan States are somewhat larger than England and lie on a rugged, hilly plateau in east-central Burma, flanking the western border of China's Yunnan province. They comprise an array of tribal and linguistic groups, of which the largest are the Shans, who speak Thai and thus have more in common with their neighbors in Thailand than with those in Burma. The lowland Shans are rice cultivators, but on the mountain ridges around them, hill tribes cultivate opium. During the period of British colonialism (1886–1948), the Shan States were administered independently from Burma, and the Shan princes enjoyed a great deal of autonomy. With Burmese independence in 1948, the Shans, with great misgivings, agreed to join the Union of Burma in return for statehood and guarantees of a number of ministry posts. As a final incentive, the Shans were given the right to secede after 1957. Since a coup in 1962, Burma has been dominated by a repressive military. In 1989 the country changed its name to Myanmar, but brutality against its ethnic minorities continues.

The Burmese government's heavy-handed approach to the Shan States set the stage for revolution. Official Burmese financial policies were devastating to many hill farmers, who turned more and more to poppy cultivation as a cash crop outside central government control (Delaney 1977). Shan princes "had been encouraged to introduce the opium poppy to their fiefdoms by the British as far back as 1866 and opium shops had been opened throughout Burma to retail the narcotics to licensed addicts" (Bresler 1980: 67). Alfred McCoy (1972) notes, however, that in later years the British made a number of efforts to abolish opium cultivation in the Shan States, although these were never completely successful. In any event, many Shans blamed their princes for accommodating the central government. Traditional systems of authority deteriorated, and rebellion quickly followed.

Under the leadership of Chang Chifu, who is half-Chinese, half-Shan, and better known as Khun Sa, the Mong Tai Army, originally known as the Shan United Army (SUA), resorted to opium trafficking in order to purchase arms and support its independence movement (Delaney 1977). The SUA came to dominate the opium trade along the Thai-Burma border, where about four hundred thousand hill tribesmen have no source of income other than heroin (Permanent Subcommittee on Investigations 1981). The SUA was able to control both shipments of opium and the production of heroin in SUA laboratories.

In the 1980s the Thai government succeeded in driving the SUA out of Thailand and back into Burma, but the group continued to dominate the opium traffic, taxing drug caravans crossing their territory. In 1990 the Shans suffered significant setbacks. Khun Sa was indicted for drug trafficking by a federal grand jury in the United States, and his Mong Tai Army suffered defeats by organized Wa tribesmen (Schmetzer 1990). In 1995, in front of reporters from Thailand, the sixty-one-year-old Khun Sa submitted his resignation. He was retiring to raise chickens, he told them ("Asian Drug Lord Set to Retire" 1995). The 10,000-man Mong Tai Army continues to dominate the heroin trade in the Golden Triangle.

Khun Sa, indicted on drug charges in New York, addresses young recruits of his Shan United Army in 1994.

United Wa State Army

Until 1989 another formidable private army in the Golden Triangle served the Burmese Communist Party (BCP). The BCP force had in the past received support from the People's Republic of China. After Beijing cut off this aid in order to improve relations with Burma, the BCP, following a long-established precedent in the region, went into the opium business. The BCP controlled much of the poppy-producing area and received opium as a form of tax and tribute from local farmers, which it refined into heroin in its own laboratories.

In 1989 its ethnic rank and file, primitive Wa tribesmen, rebelled, and the BCP folded as an armed force (Haley 1990). Wa political groups reached an accommodation with the Mynamar ruling junta. One faction of the Wa, however, the United Wa State Army (UWSA), is headquartered on the border of China's Yunnan Province and uses heroin trafficking as a means of funding its efforts against Burmese control (Witkin and Griffin 1994).

The Kuomintang (KMT)

With the defeat of the Chinese Nationalist forces in 1949, the Third and Fifth Armies of Chiang Kai-shek stationed in the remote southern province of Yunnan[2] escaped over the mountainous frontier into the Shan States. While part of this army dispersed and became integrated with the local population, "More than six thousand of them remained together as a military entity, their numbers being swollen by indigenous tribesmen" (Lamour and Lamberti 1974: 94). By 1952 the KMT, numbering about twelve thousand, became the *de facto* power in the eastern part of the Shan States. In 1951 and 1952, with support from the United States, the KMT was rearmed and resupplied, and with additional troops from Taiwan and recruits from the Hmong hill tribesmen—poppy cultivators—attempted to invade China. When its attempts failed, U.S. interest and support waned, and the KMT settled permanently in Burma. For several years the Burmese military attempted to evict armed KMT intruders. It finally succeeded in 1954, forcibly escorting them to the Thai border, from which the Nationalist government evacuated about six thousand troops to Formosa. Nevertheless, the strength of the KMT grew through secret reinforcements from Taiwan and/or through recruitment among indigenous tribes to about ten thousand troops.

In 1961 a resentful government in Rangoon, perhaps with assistance from the People's Republic of China, finally drove the KMT into the Thai portion of the Golden Triangle (Lamour and Lamberti 1974), where it sold its military skills to a joint CIA-Thai army command fighting communist insurgents

---

2. Because it is located next to the Golden Triangle, China's Yunnan ("south of the clouds") province, with a population that includes twenty of the country's minority groups, has been a center for drug trafficking. High-quality heroin passes easily over borders that were opened for trade more than a decade ago, supported by rampant corruption among the police and other officials. The traffickers are well armed. Gunfights are frequent and the army has been used extensively to combat the drug gangs (Tyler 1995).

in the Shan States. This force tried to prevent the Laotian Pathet Lao from linking up with local insurgents. In 1961 and 1969, U.S.-backed airlifts of KMT troops to Taiwan were the last official contacts between the KMT remnants on the mainland and Chiang Kai-shek's government, but Lamour and Lamberti (1974) report that unofficial ties remained strong. The remaining troops, about four thousand strong, became known as the Chinese Irregular Forces (CIF). While the KMT had always dabbled in opium, it now became the sole support of the CIF. Despite this fact, the CIF has been tolerated on the Thai border as a barrier against communist insurgents.

In Mae Salong, Thailand, KMT General Tuan Whi-wen ruled a heroin empire, collected taxes, and drafted boys as young as thirteen into his army. The general died in 1980. In 1965 an opium war broke out between the SUA and the CIF, and the latter drove SUA leader Khun Sa into Laos. Khun Sa returned and in 1981 defeated the remnants of the CIF.

Dealing Heroin

Whether its source is the MTA, CIF, BCP, or UWSA, opium, in the form of morphine base or almost pure heroin, is usually brokered in Thailand. That nation of 50 million is almost as large as France and is a staunch anticommunist ally of the United States (Thailand sent troops to fight alongside American GIs in Korea and Vietnam). Thailand has been called "the world's biggest whorehouse." Its estimated 50,000 active brothels seem to provide the appropriate atmosphere for drug transactions. (Schmetzer 1991c)

At Mai Sai, the northernmost border town in Thailand,

> word of a potential customer spreads quickly around the dusty little town. A middleman sets up negotiations in an innocent-looking place, such as a bus station. The buyer pays in advance, depositing the money in a joint account with the seller at one of five local bank branches. Only then can the purchaser pick up the merchandise, often at a Burmese village a few hours away by foot. (Kraar 1988: 38)

In 1991 a military coup—one of seventeen since 1932—overthrew the democratically elected Thai government. Because of intensified action against heroin shipments through Thailand, traffickers have opened up routes through Cambodia, a country with a great deal of lawlessness and poor economic conditions (Atlas 1995).

At the center of much of this trade are ethnic Chinese organizations that have come to dominate a major part of the world heroin market. Bangkok has a large Chinese population, the result of heavy Chinese immigration during the early nineteenth century. Operating out of Bangkok, Yunnan Province (a major transhipment point where the Chinese government has not succeeded in wiping out the drug business), Hong Kong, Amsterdam, and British Columbia, Chinese criminal organizations have flooded their "China White" into major cities of Europe, Canada, and the United States. One group from Fujian has been reinforced by recent Chinese immigrants and dominates a large part of the drug trade in New York. Chinese criminal organizations overseas are often highly ritualized groups known as Triads; in the United States they are tongs with affiliated Chinatown street gangs.

Triads, Tongs, and Street Gangs

The term *Triad* refers to the societies' common symbol: an equilateral triangle representing the three basic Chinese concepts of heaven, earth, and man. The number three is very important to Triads, whose members are assigned numbers based on their positions (enforcers, or "Red Poles," are assigned number 426) or ranks (a leader, or "Hill Chief," is 489). The groups, based in Hong Kong and Taiwan, engage in highly ritualized dress and behavior, including secret hand signs, passwords, blood oaths, and an elaborate initiation ceremony. The Triad phenomenon is believed to have originated in opposition to the Ch'ing dynasty, established by the conquering Manchus in 1644 (Fong 1981). The Ch'ing dynasty ended in 1911 with the rise to power of Sun Yat-sen (1866-1925), who had been a Triad member. The fall of the dynasty eliminated the raison d'etre of the Triads, many of whose members turned to crime: gambling, loansharking, extortion, and trafficking in opium from the Golden Triangle.

Opium trade was strengthened considerably by the activities of Chinese Nationalist forces in the Golden Triangle. Chiang Kai-shek, himself a Triad member, is reputed to have used Triads in his war against communists and labor unions. Triads were, accordingly, sternly suppressed on the mainland by Mao Tse-tung when his communist forces defeated Chiang's Nationalist Army. Thousands of Triad members fled to the British colony of Hong Kong.

The drug-trafficking Triads expanded their operations during the Vietnam War, when thousands of GIs were attracted to the potent heroin of Southeast Asia. When the Americans withdrew from Vietnam, the Triads followed the market and internationalized their drug operations. With many soldiers stationed there, Europe became a major Triad marketplace, its operations headquartered in Amsterdam. Triad membership requires a sponsor who is a ranking official of the society, and many younger members are involved in the martial arts, because Triads control the training schools. Ko-Lin Chin (1990) reports that while Triads are rigidly structured, their business operations are not arranged along organizational lines, and there is often violent conflict between branches of the same Triad.

Fenton Bresler, testifying before the PCOC (1984b: 42–43), said:

> each specific organization operating within its own territory has its own flag. If I want to become a new Triad head, I have to ask the original guy back in Hong Kong or Taiwan to give me a flag, which means I can bring it over and that means this is my territory. The flag is a triangular flag. It authorizes for me to go to the new town and organize my branch.
>
> Theoretically, there is no control over me from the original base. Once I have my own flag, I become independent. I am a 789 [a symbolic number indi-

cating a boss] but really I am only semi-independent. Spiritually I am linked
with the old country.

In the United States, Triad members have been associated with tongs,
benevolent associations that bridge the worlds of legitimate business and
crime. (Chin states that "branches of the Triad societies in the United States
were historically called tongs" [1990: 9]; the term means "hall" or "meeting
place.") At the turn of the century "fighting tongs," who traced their origins to
Triads in China, controlled large-scale vice such as gambling, prostitution, and
opium dens, which operated in urban areas with significant Chinese populations. While most tongs were business, fraternal, or political in character, Ivan
Light (1977: 472) notes that the "fighting tongs" licensed illegal businesses
and were part of a tightly knit nationwide alliance. A purely local dispute between fighting tongs, therefore, "could and often did precipitate a fight between affiliates in every U.S. Chinatown." As the importance of gambling and
houses of prostitution in Chinatowns declined following World War I, vice entrepreneurs discovered the profitability of tourist enterprises, and restaurants
replaced the brothels and gambling halls.

Many contemporary tongs are national in scope, particularly the Hip
Sing, On Leong, and Tsung Tsin, and some are connected to Chinatown street
gangs such as the Ghost Shadows and the Flying Dragons in New York,
Chicago, Boston, and San Francisco. The gangs are typically used by the tongs
to provide security for their gambling operations: "The On Leong Merchants
Association utilizes the services of the Ghost Shadows street gang; the Hip
Sing Tong is allied with the Flying Dragons; and the Tsung Tsin Association
is connected to a gang called the 'Tung On Boys'" (Pennsylvania Crime Commission 1988: 22). The tongs have adopted the norms of the Triads, and tong
members are required to go through Triadlike ceremonies as part of their initiation (Chin 1990).

While these gangs draw upon the traditions of the Triads, particularly in
the ceremonial aspects of their initiations, they have many Vietnamese members (who are ethnically Chinese); these are apparently favored because of
their reputed skill with firearms. The gangs originated in 1965, the year new
immigration laws brought in a large influx of youths from Hong Kong. Their
arrival led to an upsurge of violent street crime in communities that heretofore
had been relatively crime-free, and gangs began to form and engage in robbery, kidnapping, extortion, prostitution, and loansharking. These Chinese
gangs have ties to Southeast Asian sources and have been involved in heroin
wholesaling (Chin 1990).

Golden Crescent

The Golden Crescent of southwestern Asia includes parts of Iran,
Afghanistan, and Pakistan. The region has limestone-rich soil, a climate and

altitude ideal for poppy cultivation, and, like the Golden Triangle, a ready abundance of cheap labor for the labor-intensive production of opium. The easy availability of low-grade smoking heroin known as "brown sugar" has resulted in an estimated 1.5 million addicts in Pakistan (Burns 1995). In Pakistan the typical poppy farmer resides in semiautonomous northern tribal areas outside the direct control of the central government in Karachi. "The Pakistani authorities have little control in these areas," notes Terry Atlas (1988: 6), and must appeal to tribal leaders to move against the region's dozens of illegal processing laboratories. In northwest Pakistan's Karakorum Mountains, one acre of poppies yields about a dozen kilos of opium gum; ten kilos of opium gum can be converted into a kilo of base morphine. The wholesaling is accomplished in lawless border towns such as Landi Kotal, which is about three miles from the Afghan border.

"In late 1979 the Soviets rolled their tanks into the opium provinces of Afghanistan's Pashtun and Baluchi peoples. Suddenly, the tribes that had spent the last decade maneuvering their heavily armed drug caravans past the increasingly troublesome patrols of the U.S. Drug Enforcement Administration's agents found themselves flung into the limelight as the new anticommunist 'crusaders' " (Levins 1980: 201). In 1991 U.S. officials announced that they would no longer provide military assistance to Afghan rebels, and the Soviet

Heroin is corrupting the Golden Crescent of southwest Asia, where addiction is eating into the fabric of community life. An addict for more than five years recovers from his addiction in the Abdul Sattar Edhi drug rehabilitation center outside Karachi, Pakistan.

Union agreed to stop aiding the Afghan government. On 24 April 1992 anti-communist *mujahedin* groups entered Kabul without resistance, and the rebellion officially ended. However, the conflict continues as various group vie for power. The Islamic Party, Afghanistan's best-armed group, uses heroin to further its political goals, which include imposing a radical Islamic regime on the country while helping similar groups reach the same goal in other countries (Weiner 1994).

For a while, the Soviet invasion of Afghanistan disrupted normal drug-trade routes into Iran and Turkey and, as a result, morphine base was moved through the Kyber Pass into Karachi or on to Delhi or Bombay. India became a major transshipment site for heroin entering Europe and the United States. Turkey continues to serve as a land bridge to Western markets for heroin from the Golden Crescent; Turkish criminal groups (*babas*), with important connections in the Western drug market, move heroin across the highways of Turkey and into Europe. From there other criminal organizations, in particular Sicilian Mafia and Neapolitan camorra groups, distribute the drug throughout the European market and into Canada and the United States. Since the collapse of the Soviet Union, republics that border on Afghanistan, such as Tajikistan and Kyrgystan, have become important drug laboratory and transshipment areas (Specter 1995). Morphine base is also delivered to mobile processing laboratories in Lebanon's Syrian-controlled Bekaa Valley, where along with domestic opium it is converted into heroin for shipment to Arab groups in Europe, Canada, and the United States. More than 30 percent of the farmers in the Bekaa cultivate the opium poppy (Kelly 1990). Also connected to this Middle Eastern traffic are a variety of terrorist groups (Ehrenfeld 1990; Sterling 1990) and Lebanese militias (Hijazi 1991), for whom drugs provide a source of funds or are exchanged for arms.

Mexico

Mexico is the source of "brown heroin," which got a foothold in the U.S. drug market after the demise of the French Connection (discussed below):

> In the five years after the collapse of the French connection, Mexico became the major source of U.S. heroin. Mexico's rise was logical: the country contains extensive regions suitable for both opium cultivation and refining and shares a lightly guarded 2,000-mile border with the United States. Mexicans could manufacture heroin and smuggle it into the United States with little risk of detection. This simplified trafficking system resulted in increased Mexican heroin availability in the United States. (PCOC 1986: 107)

In more recent years, Mexico has been the source of "black tar" heroin, a less refined but more potent—and very popular—form of the substance. Its widespread use has caused a sharp increase in heroin-related hospital emergencies (Comptroller General 1988).

BLACK TAR HEROIN

The conversion of the opium gum to black tar [No. 3] heroin is more convenient and requires only simple equipment which can be readily dismantled if law enforcement is detected in the area. In addition, almost anyone can be trained to perform the conversion process, making it unnecessary to pay the higher salary which would most certainly be demanded by legitimate chemists. The process is more rapid and more economical than that required to produce the higher purity [No. 4] heroin.

Source: Drug Enforcement Administration (1991): 11

The poppy is not native to Mexico but was brought into the country at the turn of the century by Chinese laborers working on the railroad. Chinese immigrants tended to dominate heroin trafficking until anti-Chinese pogroms and property confiscations during the 1930s caused the trade to pass into Mexican hands (Lupsha 1991). Roughly 90 percent of the Mexican poppy crop is harvested between September and April, with harvests peaking in November and March. The poppy fields are generally small and difficult to detect, although in some instances larger fields, cultivated by more sophisticated growers, have been discovered. In remote growing areas of the Sierra Madre states of Durango, Sinaloa, Chihuahua, and Sonora, the Mexican state just south of Arizona, opium gum is transported to nearby villages. *Acaparadores*, or gatherers, travel around the countryside buying large quantities of opium gum, which are flown to secret laboratories owned and operated by major heroin organizations. The conversion process for Mexican heroin takes about three days, although with special equipment and training it can be accomplished in one. While white heroin from the Golden Triangle and Golden Crescent can approach 100 percent purity, Mexican brown generally ranges from 65 to 85 percent pure. Once the chemists are finished, the heroin is moved to principal population centers (*Mexico: A Profile* 1995), and Mexican couriers transport the heroin to members of the trafficking organization in the United States.

The drug trade is big business in poverty-wracked Mexico, and large traffickers have traditionally received protection from the highest levels of government and law enforcement (Golden 1995). Indeed, some important traffickers have backgrounds in law enforcement. As Peter Lupsha notes, "For some of Mexico's top traffickers entrance into drug trafficking has simply been a lateral transfer" (1990: 12). This ugly facet of the drug trade was dramatized poignantly when several Mexican law enforcement officers were implicated in the torture-murder of a U.S. drug agent; they were acting on orders from drug kingpin Rafael Caro Quintero. When he was arrested, Quintero and other members of his Guadalajara cartel were found to be carrying credentials identifying them as agents of the *Dirección Federal de Seguridad*, the Mexican FBI. Sicilia Falcón, another leading Mexican trafficker, carried similar credentials (Lupsha 1991). In his hometown of Sinaloa, just south of Arizona, Rafael and other members of the Caro Quintero clan are revered in songs and legends (Bowden 1991).

The 1,933-mile border between Mexico and the United States has virtually no fences or barricades. The vast and remote border is difficult to patrol, facilitating the transportation of heroin into Texas, California, Arizona, and New Mexico. Heroin is also secreted in a variety of motor vehicles and smuggled past official border-entry points, while private aircraft move heroin north, making use of hundreds of small airstrips dotting the U.S.-Mexican border and dozens of larger airstrips on the Yucatán Peninsula.

FIGURE 6.3
The Border between Mexico and the United States Showing Significant Opium Poppy and Marijuana Cultivation Areas

The border between Mexico and the United States has virtually no fences or barricades, making it difficult to patrol. Heroin and other drugs are easily transported from Mexico into California, Texas, Arizona, and New Mexico.

Source: Adapted from Drug Enforcement Administration.

SHOTGUNNING

Mexican smuggling frequently relies on a technique known as shotgunning: a shipment of drugs will be divided into many smaller loads and secreted in automobiles in electronically controlled hidden compartments. Dozens of these vehicles will move across the border, overwhelming customs officials. If one or two of the cars are intercepted, that is a small price to pay for the others safely reaching distributors in the United States.

The major Mexican trafficking organizations supplying heroin to the United States

are generally extended familial organizations, but loyal workers sometimes are given the status of "quasi-family" [*compadres*] members of the groups. The organizations work to eliminate competition and to control as completely as possible all aspects of the heroin trade. Members act as opium cultivators, village middlemen, and heroin brokers and distributors. In the United States, the organization typically controls distribution from the wholesaler to the retail distributor, but has little or no involvement in street distribution. This is seen as an unnecessarily risky and low-profit aspect of the business, and is left to outsiders. (PCOC 1986: 108-109)

In 1995, it became apparent that Mexican drug trafficking was dominated by about a half-dozen *padrones* (bosses) who were sometimes allied, sometimes in competition, and sometimes in violent conflict, although gun battles have been infrequent. Indeed, the relative peace among major traffickers (low-level groups still tend to be violent) is seen as an indication of growing sophistication and hegemony in the drug business. While the padrones operate out of discrete sites in Mexico, their stature "comes not from controlling territory so much as from the international scope of their contacts and their ability to operate across Mexico with Government protection" (Golden 1995: 8).

In 1984 Mexican traffickers introduced poppy seeds into northwestern Guatemala; the final product is processed in Mexico for transport to the United States. Since then, several thousand acres in Guatemala have come under cultivation, and the poorly equipped police and armed forces, besieged by guerrilla insurgencies, usually avoid confronting the well-armed drug traffickers. Guatemala also serves as a transshipment point for cocaine, and many Colombian traffickers reside in the country (Gruson 1989; 1990). U.S. DEA agents and pilots under contract with the State Department have been searching out and spraying fields of opium poppies in Guatemala (Christian 1991). Since 1984 acres of poppy plants have also been discovered in Colombia. At the end of 1991, police raids in Colombia discovered thousands of acres of poppy

DRUG SMUGGLING INTERCEPTIONS

- a light gray spray-painted bust of Jesus composed of molded cocaine
- 5 pounds of cocaine packed in condoms surgically implanted in a sheep-dog
- 37 pounds of cocaine packed in condoms and inserted in the rectums of live boa constrictors
- 1,000 pounds of cocaine packed in hollow plaster shells shaped and painted to resemble yams
- 6,000 pounds of cocaine packed in kilo bricks inside ice-packed cases of broccoli
- 12,000 pounds of cocaine in the soles of a shipment of sneakers
- 16 tons of cocaine inside concrete fence posts

Source: Speart (1995)

plants, indicating that the cartels have moved beyond the experimental stage ("Colombian Heroin May Be Increasing" 1991).[3] As noted above, Mexican drug organizations have established close ties with Colombian cocaine organizations, in particular those from Cali, and now move cocaine, in addition to heroin, into the United States.

DOMESTIC TRAFFICKING

Importation is the highest level of the domestic traffic in cocaine and heroin. The actual smugglers ("mules") take the major risks, while the organizers who arrange for importation and distribution typically avoid physical possession of drugs. David Durk (1976: 49), the New York City detective partner of Frank Serpico, points out: "The key figures in the Italian heroin establishment never touched heroin. Guys who were in the business for twenty years and had made millions off it had never seen it. After all, does a commodities trader on Wall Street have to see hog bellies and platinum bars?" In fact, importation often entails little or no risk of arrest—cocaine or heroin can be secreted in any variety of imported goods, and possession cannot be proven. Furthermore, while a single shipment may be detected and confiscated,

3. Since 1991, poppy cultivation in Colombia has more than doubled; the country's climate permits year-round cultivation. The yield of opium gum, however, is relatively low compared to traditional source regions. Independent groups operating outside of the dominant cocaine cartels are trafficking in Colombian heroin. (Drug Enforcement Administration 1994b, 1995c)

A bizarre drug interception incident occurred in New York when condoms full of cocaine were found in this dog's abdomen.

smugglers often divide their supplies so that for every interception, other shipments arrive unimpeded. (Colombian cartels often insure their shipments through a joint arrangement. The cost of insurance is passed on to the import buyer, who is then financially protected in the event of interdiction by U.S. authorities.)

After importation, heroin is sold in ten- to fifty-kilo quantities to wholesalers—kilo connections—after which the heroin is "stepped on," or diluted, several times. The wholesaler, basically a facilitator, arranges for the cutting (diluting) of the almost-pure heroin. The actual physical work is often done by women. Between ten and twenty women cut from ten to fifty kilos in an apartment rented specifically for this purpose. Under guard and often working naked (as a precaution against theft of the precious powder) except for surgical masks, which they wear to avoid inhaling heroin dust, they mix the heroin with quinine, lactose, and dextrose, usually four or five parts of the dilutant to one part of heroin. They work through the night and are paid more than a thousand dollars each, making the risk and embarrassment worthwhile.

When the cutting is complete, jobbers—*weight dealers*—who have been waiting for a telephone call arrive with the necessary cash, which they exchange for two to five kilos of the cut heroin. The jobbers move the heroin to wholesalers, who cut it again. From there it moves to street wholesalers, then to street retailers, and finally to addicts. At each step of the process, profits accrue as the ounce of pure heroin increases in bulk as a result of additional cutting. A kilo of base morphine from the Shan States costs about $1,500. Converted to one kilo of between 70 and 95 percent pure heroin, it can sell for $11,000 in Bangkok. Upon entering the United States, it is sold for up to $200,000. Cut to a purity of between 20 to 60 percent, a kilo sells for about $250,000. When the original kilo reaches the street, its value has grown to more than $1 million (depending on how many times it has been stepped on).

The enormous profits in the drug business support a criminal underworld where violence is always an attendant reality. Transactions must be accomplished without recourse to the formal mechanisms of dispute resolution usually available in the world of legitimate business. This reality encourages the creation of private enforcement mechanisms, and the drug world is filled with heavily armed and dangerous persons employed by the larger cartels, although even street-level operatives are often armed. These private enforcement and protection resources limit market entry by warding off competitors and predatory criminals, thus maintaining the organization's internal discipline and security. In the drug business, terminating employment is often the same as terminating the employee.

The Mafia

At the upper levels of the domestic drug trade are a variety of ethnically based criminal organizations. Many, but not all, Italian-American organized crime groups ("Mafia Families" or *la Cosa Nostra*) have been involved in heroin trafficking. Their drug activities are aided by overseas contacts with the criminal organizations of southern Italy—Mafia groups in Sicily, 'Ndrangheta groups in Calabria, and Camorra groups in the Naples area—whose laboratories process the morphine base and arrange for shipment to the United States. (For a more detailed discussion of these groups, see Abadinsky 1994.)

The criminal organizations of Italy have grown wealthy from the drug trade. In the "Pizza Connection" case concluded in 1987, a Mafia group headed by Gaetano Badalamente of Cinisi, Sicily, was found to have supplied heroin valued at over $1.6 billion to a group headed by Salvatore Catalana, a captain in the Bonanno crime family of New York City. The Sicilian defendants purchased morphine base in Turkey and processed it in Sicily. Testimony in that case revealed that southern Italian criminal organizations, in addition to cooperating with their American counterparts, also engage in totally independent heroin operations.

Some Mafia groups in the United States entered the heroin business when the demise of Prohibition in 1933 created a need for new sources of profit to replace bootlegging and associated activities. The onset of World War II stifled this lucrative business. After 1945, however, these groups

BARBARIC VIOLENCE, RATIONAL VIOLENCE

Regular displays of violence are essential for preventing rip-offs by colleagues, customers, and professional holdup artists. Indeed, upward mobility in the underground economy of the street-dealing world requires a systematic and effective use of violence against one's colleagues, one's neighbors, and, to a certain extent, against oneself. Behavior that appears irrationally violent, "barbaric," and ultimately self-destructive to the outsider, can be reinterpreted according to the logic of the underground economy as judicious public relations and long-term investment in one's "human capital development." (Bourgois 1995: 24)

came to dominate the heroin trade by reestablishing lines of supply that had been disrupted by the war. They imported most of the substance from refineries controlled by Mafia groups in southern Italy and, later, from Corsicans in Marseilles. This was accomplished, argues Alfred McCoy (1972), with the assistance of the U.S. Office of Strategic Services (OSS) and later of its successor, the CIA. With the aid of the OSS/CIA, Mafia and Corsican criminal groups, badly weakened by the war, reasserted their authority in an effort to combat what the U.S. government perceived as a greater evil—the growth of communist political and leftist labor groups in Sicily and Marseilles.

According to the PCOC (1986: 106–107):

When the Italian government banned the manufacture of heroin in the early 1950s, *La Cosa Nostra* traffickers were forced to look for other sources. A new system was quickly devised, by which [the] Turkish morphine base was refined to heroin in Marseilles, then shipped to Montreal or Sicily. Organized crime groups located in these transshipment points then sent the heroin directly to the United States. This arrangement, popularly known as the "French Connection," allowed *La Cosa Nostra* to monopolize the heroin trade from the 1950s through the early 1970s. During the peak French Connection years, the LCN controlled an estimated 95 percent of all heroin entering New York City, as well as most of the heroin distributed throughout the United States.

The *Cosa Nostra* heroin monopoly lasted until 1972, when under diplomatic pressure from the United States, Turkey banned opium production and the French Connection collapsed. Amsterdam replaced Marseilles as the center of European heroin traffic, and Chicago, Los Angeles, and Miami joined New York City as major distribution centers. Other trafficking groups rose to compete with the LCN for heroin dollars in New York City and throughout the country.

FIGURE 6.4
Heroin Trafficking Organization

247

Chapter Six:
The Business
of Drugs

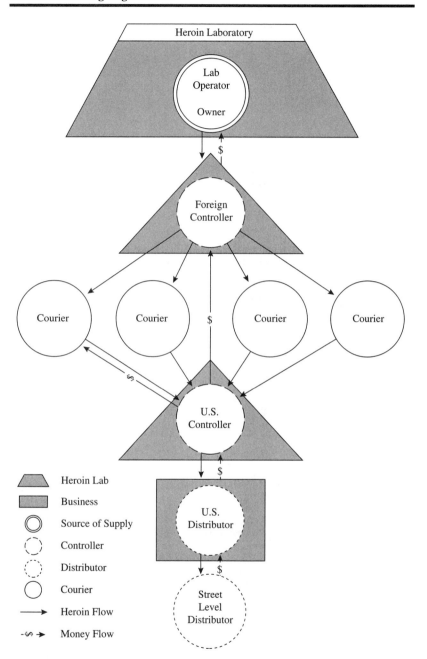

Source: Drug Enforcement, Summer 1994.

Black Drug-Trafficking Organizations[4]

There are important black criminal organizations in the heroin business, particularly in New York City, Detroit, Chicago, Philadelphia, and Washington, D.C. While African Americans have traditionally been locked out of many activities associated with organized crime (labor racketeering and loansharking, for example), dope is "an equal opportunity employer." Black criminal groups made strides in the heroin business when many African American soldiers became exposed to the heroin markets of the Golden Triangle during the Vietnam War. Until then African American groups were dependent on the Mafia families for their heroin. As a result of their overseas experiences, African American organizers were able to bypass the Mafia and buy directly from suppliers in Thailand. More recently, West African countries, Nigeria in particular, have become important transshipment centers for Golden Crescent heroin: "Nigerian couriers based in Lagos travel to Pakistan to obtain heroin, then continue on commercial flights to their final destinations, or return to Nigeria to repackage the narcotics into smaller amounts for smuggling to the West" (PCOC 1986: 124). Nigerian students or poor residents of Lagos are used as "mules"; they usually swallow heroin-filled condoms. The country is infamous for its official corruption. In the capital of Lagos, multimillionaire drug barons rule vast organizations, at the bottom of which are the drug couriers, who take most of the actual risks (Treaster 1992).

Customs officials use X-rays of the digestive tract to discover the drugs. In 1991 a Nigerian-Chicago connection was uncovered that used the Philippines as a transshipment point. Asian women transported heroin from Bangkok to Manila, where American Caucasian women received the drugs for transportation to the United States—all this in an effort to reduce the suspicion that Asian women flying from Thailand to the United States would attract. Couriers carried between 4.5 and 6.5 pounds of heroin and were paid $20,000 plus expenses (Schmetzer 1991d). In 1995 twelve members of a Nigerian ring that moved heroin from Bangkok to Chicago were arrested for drug operations that netted millions of dollars (O'Connor 1995).

As noted in chapter 2, the introduction of crack in the 1980s changed consumer demographics and subsequently the market itself. In Texas, crack distribution is reportedly controlled by Jamaican organizations commonly known as posses (after the western movies popular with Jamaicans) with a reputation for extreme violence—members are reluctant to travel without firearms. This limits their use of commercial airplanes, so they use cars, buses, and trains. The five-thousand-member "Shower posse," the most notorious of

---

4. Interestingly, although Jewish involvement in heroin trafficking is minimal today, it was important Jewish criminal entrepreneurs such as Arnold Rothstein and Waxey Gordon who paved the way for drug trafficking to become an important business in the United States soon after the passage of the Harrison Act (Katcher 1959: PCOC 1986). An exception is Herbert Sperling, leader of the so-called Jewish Mafia of heroin dealers in New York City. For his role in drug trafficking, Sperling has been serving a life sentence in federal prison since 1973.

the Jamaican groups, reportedly got its name for engaging in frenzied shootouts in which they shower gunfire (Witkin 1991). In Jamaica, the Shower posse has been linked to the Jamaica Labour Party and has engaged in bloody warfare with posses aligned with other political parties, including the ruling People's National Party (French 1992).

There are about forty Jamaican criminal groups with more than 20,000 members (Witkin 1991) operating in at least seventeen U.S. cities:

> The Jamaican posses currently active in the United States can be traced to specific neighborhoods in Jamaica. Key members formed their associations based on geographical and political ties in Jamaica. . . . The majority of posse members are convicted felons and/or illegal aliens. [They] differ from other narcotics trafficking cartels in that their members are importers, wholesalers and distributors. Therefore, their profit margin is higher than traffickers who utilize middlemen. A posse that controls 50 crack houses in one city can make $9 million a month. Other major importers of illegal narcotics, such as the Colombians and Cubans, are usually only wholesalers. They will turn profit on only one sale. The Jamaicans, on the other hand, never exchange any money until the narcotics are sold at the street level by members of the organization. The money is then funneled back up to the leaders. (McGuire 1988: 22)

Outlaw Motorcycle Clubs

The term *outlaw* is used by bikers belonging to any one of dozens of motorcycle clubs throughout the United States that are outside the organized mainstream represented by the American Motorcycle Association. These bikers view themselves as part of a fraternity whose lifestyle is the antithesis of that of the conventional world. Four of these outlaw clubs are sophisticated criminal organizations.

Toward the end of the 1940s, many World War II combat veterans, particularly in California, were seeking new outlets for pent-up feelings of hostility and alienation. They found excitement on their motorcycles and comradeship in association with other bikers. Their clubs became vehicles for continued quasi-military camaraderie. At the same time, the motorcycle became a symbol of freedom from accepted social responsibilities and restraints, and these new clubs came to be perceived as threats to local communities.

Shortly after World War II, a group of California veterans formed a motorcycle club called the "Pissed-Off Bastards of Bloomington" (POBOB). By some accounts, the POBOBs were dedicated to mocking conventional social values through acts of vandalism and rowdiness. In 1946, following the arrest of a POBOB member for fighting in Hollister, California, a reported 750 motorcyclists descended on the town and demanded his release. When local authorities refused, the bikers literally tore up the small community, a scene later depicted in the movie *The Wild One*, starring Marlon Brando. This film popularized the outlaw phenomenon. After the Hollister incident, the POBOBs developed into a more disciplined group and became the first outlaw motorcycle club to receive national notoriety—the Hells Angels.

From the fun-loving, hell-raising clubs of the immediate postwar era, a number of motorcycle gangs developed into structured, self-perpetuating, and disciplined organizations whose major source of income is from criminal activity. They have been particularly successful in exerting control over the methamphetamine market. George Wethern (1978), a former ranking member of the Hells Angels "Mother Club" in Oakland, California, states that because of their reputation for violence and anti-establishment attitudes, the Hells Angels were perfect middlemen for drug dealers. The wholesalers sold to the Angels, who then acted as distributors for street-level operators. Using violence, they restricted market entry and monopolized the trade in parts of California and elsewhere. Other outlaw clubs—particularly the Pagans, the Outlaws, and the Bandidos—have done the same in their areas of the country. Some of these clubs have chapters in Canada, Europe, and Australia.

Consistent with their founders' background as military veterans, the Hells Angels and other outlaw groups that have copied them exhibit a highly bureaucratic structure: a national organization headed by a president whose headquarters is known as the Mother Club. Surrounded by staff and bodyguards, the national president makes final decisions on all matters that local chapters cannot resolve. The Mother Club has the power to issue or cancel club charters. Admission to a chapter requires a probationary period during which candidates must prove themselves worthy of membership by following orders and committing felony crimes, which helps keep law enforcement agents from infiltrating the organization. When a man is admitted (there are no female members), he is allowed to wear the club's colors: the official emblem—such as the death's head and wings of the Hells Angels—on a sleeveless denim or leather jacket, along with the name of the club on top and the chapter name beneath. Because they are quite mobile and have connections

MEXICAN "SPEED"

While they are latecomers to the trade, Mexican drug organizations have become dominant in the manufacture and distribution of methamphetamine. They import precursor chemicals from Asia and Europe and convert them into "speed" in Mexican-based laboratories. The drugs are then smuggled into the United States (Dillon 1995). Mexican involvement with the substance apparently began when the Hells Angels turned to the Mexicans to avoid the hazards posed by methamphetamine manufacture: it is explosive, the chemicals are caustic, inhalation can be fatal, and the strong odor can alert law enforcement. Eventually, the Mexicans improved on the methods learned from the bikers and now it is the latter who typically buy for distribution from the Mexicans (Arax and Gorman 1995).

throughout the country, outlaw motorcycle clubs are excellent conduits for the distribution of illegal drugs. Club-connected chemists produce PCP and methamphetamine, which is distributed through the extensive networks that comprise the world of outlaw bikers.

Street-Level Drug Business

Below the wholesale level, cocaine or heroin is an easy-entry business, requiring only a source and funds. Any variety of groups can come together to deal heroin, such as street gangs in many urban areas. Jerome Skolnick and his colleagues (1990) distinguish between two types of street gangs. *Cultural gangs* are strongly grounded in a neighborhood identity; members may be involved in crime, including drug trafficking. Entrepreneurial gangs are organized for the express purpose of distributing drugs. The first type is maintained by loyalty to the gang and the neighborhood; the second is based on continuing economic opportunity. In the cultural gang, involvement in drug use and dealing can serve as membership requirements; stature in the group may be linked to success in the drug trade. Unlike the entrepreneurial gangs, these groups define themselves in terms of brotherhood, are highly protective of their turf, and engage in nonutilitarian violence with other gangs. While the cultural gang is not organized expressly to sell drugs, "the gang organization facilitates that activity" (1990: 7). This can also be said of the outlaw motorcycle clubs. However, the low level of cohesiveness, loose organization, high member turnover, and unstable leadership typical of most street gangs mitigate against their being effective drug entrepreneurs (Klein, Maxson, and Cunningham 1991).

In several areas of the country, particularly in New York City and Los Angeles, the relatively stable neighborhood criminal organizations who dominated the heroin and cocaine trade found new competitors: youthful crack dealers. Entry into the crack trade requires only a small investment: An ounce of cocaine converts to 2,500 milligrams of crack. Street gangs or groups of friends and relatives have entered the market, often resulting in competition that touches off explosive violence involving high-powered handguns and automatic weapons.

Jeffrey Fagan and Ko-lin Chin (1991: 25) state that violence was to be expected for two reasons:

> First, crack selling was concentrated in neighborhoods where social controls had been weakened by intensified social and economic dislocations in the decade preceding the emergence of crack. Second, the rapid development of new drug-selling groups following the introduction of crack brought with it competition. Accordingly, violence within new selling groups *internally* to maintain control and violence *externally* to maintain selling territory (product quality) was more likely to characterize the unstable crack markets than the more established drug markets and distribution systems.

SETTLING DRUG DISPUTES

"We don't see shootouts in the automobile business or even the liquor or the tobacco business. But if a drug dealer has a quarrel with another dealer, he can't sue" (Boaz 1990: 2).

Some street gangs have also been expanding their organizations and drug markets to other states. Los Angeles gangs, in particular the Crips, have moved into Seattle, Denver, Minneapolis, Oklahoma City, St. Louis, and Kansas City as well as smaller cities throughout California (Egan 1988). Along with their smaller rivals, the Bloods, they moved East with startling speed:

> Neither gang is rigidly hierarchical. Both are broken up into loosely affiliated neighborhood groups called "sets," each with 30 to 100 members. Many gang members initially left southern California to evade police. Others simply expanded the reach of crack by setting up branch operations in places where they visited friends or family members and discovered that the market was ripe. (Witken 1991: 51)

In 1992 it was reported that the Crips, or perhaps older former members of the gang, had developed direct ties with the Medellín cartel ("FBI Says Los Angeles Gang Has Drug Cartel Ties" 1992). Chicago's Gangster Disciples, a major drug-trafficking gang, is reputed to have branches in at least six states.

In New York City, Dominicans have demonstrated the necessary talent for moving large amounts of crack at the street level. They purchase directly from Colombian importers, with whom they share a common language and entrepreneurial values. Dominicans have apparently applied their well-known skills as tradesmen and merchants to becoming that city's top traffickers (Massing 1989). Known as Dominican-Yorks, the traffickers return their profits to such places as San Francisco de Macoris, a city conspicuous for its wealth in a country where the per capita income is less than $900 a year (French 1991). Dominicans reportedly control a significant portion of the cocaine traffic in New England (Drug Enforcement Administration 1991).

Thomas Mieczkowski (1986) studied the activities of a loosely organized retail heroin group in Detroit—The Young Boys, Inc. At the center of their activities is a *crew boss*, who receives his supply of heroin from a drug-syndicate lieutenant. The crew boss gives a consignment of heroin to each of his seven to twenty *runners*, young (sixteen to twenty-three years old) African American males whom he recruits. Afterward, each runner takes his station on a street adjacent to a public roadway to facilitate purchases from vehicles. To avoid rip-offs and robberies, each crew and crew boss is guarded by armed men. Runners reported earning about $160 for a 10½-hour workday.

Participants in these drug networks tend to be the most serious drug delinquents, who

> are frequently hired by adult or older adolescent street drug sellers as runners. Loosely organized into crews of three to twelve, each boy generally handles small quantities of drugs—for example, two or three packets or bags of heroin. They receive these units "on credit," "up front," or "on loan" from a supplier and are expected to return about 50 to 70 percent of the drug's street value.
>
> In addition to distributing drugs, these youngsters may act as lookouts, recruit customers, and guard street sellers from customer-robbers. They typically are users of marijuana and cocaine, but not heroin. Moreover, in some cities, dealers and suppliers prefer to hire distributors who do not "get high" during an operation. But their employment as runners is not generally steady; it is interspersed with other crimes including robbery, burglary, and theft.
>
> A relatively small number of youngsters who sell drugs develop excellent entrepreneurial skills. Their older contacts come to trust them, and they parlay this trust to advance in the drug business. By the time they are eighteen or nineteen they can have several years of experience in drug sales, be bosses of their own crews, and handle more than $500,000 a year. (Chaiken and Johnson 1988: 12)

The net profits in heroin for most participants at the street level, however, are rather modest. While dealers typically work long hours and subject themselves to substantial risk of violence and incarceration, their incomes generally range from $1,000 to $2,000 a month. Less successful participants eke

---

GANGSTER DISCIPLES (GDs)

The Gangster Disciples (GDs), with thousands of members, is headed by Larry Hoover, who has been serving a sentence for murder since 1973. The GDs are active in selling cocaine and heroin throughout Chicago, a number of suburban areas, and at least six states. They also extort money from other drug dealers for the right to sell in areas they control.

The size of the GDs requires a level of bureaucracy rarely seen in drug trafficking and it serves to make the organization vulnerable to prosecution. A list was kept of all persons dealing drugs in GD territory so they could be forced to pay "street taxes"—one day's profit per week. In a 1995 raid on a GD front group, federal agents found detailed records including an organizational chart, a list of GD officers and their rank, a list of opposing gang leaders, the gang's pledge of allegiance, and its "laws."

In 1995, Hoover and 38 GDs were indicted for 149 counts of criminal conduct involving their drug trafficking operations. (Authorities devised a prison visitor's pass with a hidden transmitter, and Hoover was recorded passing orders to lieutenants who visited him.) As a result of the imprisonment or indictment of virtually the GDs' entire hierarchy, the gang is having difficulties maintaining discipline and thwarting encroachments by rival groups.

out a living that rivals minimum wage. Many are involved to support their own drug habits, to supplement earnings from legitimate employment, or both. The sale of cocaine and crack is carried out by thousands of small-time operators who may dominate particular local markets—public housing complexes, city blocks, or simply street corners. Control is exercised through violence. Income is modest considering the dangers of death or imprisonment, and the sellers often work for less than minimum wage—for example, $30 a day for acting as a lookout or fifty cents for each vial of crack sold—$100 to $200 per week for long hours under unpleasant conditions without unemployment compensation, medical insurance, or any of the usual benefits of legitimate employment. A study in Washington, D.C., found that a majority of drug sellers in the sample did not sell drugs on a daily basis. Their median annual income was about $10,000; those who sold daily earned about $3,600 monthly (Reuter, Mac-Coun, and Murphy 1990).

The domestic business of cocaine requires only a connection to a Colombian (or Peruvian or Bolivian) source and sufficient financing to initiate the first buy. Any variety of persons several steps removed from the Colombian source are involved in the domestic cocaine business. Because the cocaine clientele is traditionally at least middle-income, distributors likewise tend to come from the (otherwise) respectable middle class. The popularity of crack, however, has dramatically altered the drug market at the consumer level, in particular the age of many retailers. James Inciardi and Anne Pottieger, experienced drug researchers, were shocked by the youthfulness of crack dealers compared with those involved in the heroin business: "While both patterns ensnare youth in their formative years, crack dealers are astonishingly more involved in a drug-crime lifestyle at an alarmingly younger age" (1991: 269).

Marcia Chaiken and Bruce Johnson (1988: 16) state that small drug sales are common among adult users; in fact, they point out, "Close to 10 percent of the young adults in this country sell drugs, mainly marijuana." They

---

NEW YORK CRACK SCENE

- After spotting him with a .357-caliber Magnum in his hand, police arrested Willie and found 300 vials of crack. They later found another 2,900 vials and more than $12,000 in small bills. It was the fifteen-year-old's second arrest. He was probably making about $350 a week working for a street distribution ring, a gang of teenagers known as the BDP.
- Nickie, from Wyandanch, Long Island, attempted to sell drugs to an undercover police officer. The ten-year-old was charged with possession of three vials of crack and sent to a children's services home for eighteen months.

Sources: Stone (1990); Roberts (1990).

COMMODITIES

On the floor of the Chicago Board of Trade (CBOT), the commodities typically bought and sold range from soybeans to pork bellies to platinum. Two CBOT clerks added a more exotic commodity—cocaine—which they placed in plastic sandwich bags tossed to customers during trading hours. The two were convicted of drug trafficking after they attempted to buy two kilos of cocaine from undercover officers (Crawford 1991; 1991b).

---

also note that some adolescents distribute drugs without being involved in more serious criminal activity. They sell drugs to adolescent friends and relatives less than once a month to support their own drug use, and "most of these adolescents do not consider these activities 'serious' crimes" (1988: 10). They rarely have contact with criminal justice agencies:

> Since these youths conceal their illicit behavior from most adults, and are likely to participate in many conventional activities with children their age, criminal justice practitioners can take little direct action to prevent occasional adolescent sellers from distributing drugs and recruiting new users. (1988: 11)

Like more conventional consumer items, drugs sold at the street level often carry a name and/or logo to promote "brand name" loyalty.

> Among the more important marketing techniques are attractive packaging (stamps), name recognition (brand names), and consumer involvement and camaraderie around drug-consuming activities (product name contests). Moreover, product names . . . that reflect strong, positive attributes and notions of success, strength, power, excitement, and wealth encourage consumers to make symbolic connections with these products. (Waterston 1993: 117)

As in other stages of the drug trade, the street-level business is filled with violence. Paul Goldstein (1985: 497) reports that violence in the drug trade is sometimes the result of brand deception.

> Dealers mark an inferior quality heroin with a currently popular brand name. Users purchase the good heroin, use it, then repackage the bag with milk sugar for resale. The popular brand is purchased, the bag is "tapped," and further diluted for resale.

> These practices get the real dealers of the popular brand very upset. Their heroin starts to get a bad reputation on the streets and they lose sales. Purchasers of the phony bags may accost the real dealers, complaining about the poor quality and demanding their money back. The real dealers then seek out the purveyors of the phony bags. Threats, assaults, and/or homicides may ensue.

In the drug business, Goldstein (1985) notes, norm violations—for example, a street-level dealer failing to return sufficient money to his superior in a drug network—often result in violence. Violence almost invariably results from the robbery of a drug dealer. No dealer who wishes to remain in the business can allow himself to be robbed without exacting vengeance. Death is also the punishment for a norm violation that although serious is nevertheless widespread in the drug business: informing. Informing may be the means of eliminating competition or exacting vengeance for the sale of poor-quality dope, but more often informing results from an attempt to gain leniency from the criminal justice system.

Occasionally, distinct patterns of injury can be recognized. For example, drug runners—teenagers who carry drugs and money between sellers and buyers—are seen in emergency rooms with gunshot wounds to the legs and knees. A more vicious drug-related injury has emerged in the western part of the United States. In this injury, known at "pithing," the victim's spinal cord is cut, and he or she is left alive but paraplegic (De La Rosa, Lambert, and Gropper 1990).

Methamphetamine and Marijuana Trafficking

The business of drugs involves substances other than cocaine and heroin. Most of these substances, such as PCP, LSD, amphetamines, and barbiturates, are produced in domestic laboratories; marijuana is also grown in the United States. Except in the case of methamphetamine trafficking by outlaw motorcycle clubs (discussed above), the persons and groups that manufacture and traffic in these substances are too varied for comprehensive coverage in this book. They fit into no particular ethnic pattern—white, rural, working- and middle-class persons are as likely to be involved as any identifiable racial or ethnic group. For example, there is little or no pattern to marijuana trafficking in the United States. It is an easy-entry business, and a number of relatives, friendship groups, and former military veterans have come together to "do marijuana." (For a journalistic look at one of the largest marijuana organizations in the United States, The Company, headed by Donald Steinberg, see Warner 1986; Mills 1986.)

Production of amphetamines, particularly methamphetamine, has blossomed in parts of rural America. In Texas, for example, authorities have been seizing more than 250 laboratories a year:

> Most of the labs are located in rural areas and are reportedly set up and run by local residents. The predominant pattern for methamphetamine lab operations in the plains of West Texas and in heavily wooded East Texas is similar to the operation of small-scale production and distribution of moonshine whiskey during the prohibition era; individually owned and operated, with networks of local

YUPPIE DRUG LORD

In 1976 William LaMorte, the son of a successful businessman and the holder of an MBA, owned a nineteen-room home in an exclusive New York village, a 110-foot yacht with a special deck to land his helicopter, and several supermarkets. His lavish lawn parties benefited police organizations and the local Republican party. LaMorte's multimillion-dollar income was based on marijuana and hashish. Between 1970 and 1985 he had smuggled an estimated 120 tons into the country from Colombia, Jamaica, Morocco, Lebanon, and Thailand, using small boats to offload the drugs from mother ships out at sea. Betrayed by his brother, who was seeking leniency for a cocaine conviction, in 1990 William LaMorte was convicted of drug trafficking and sentenced to a term of fifty years (Hays 1991).

users, but also with connections for export to urban population centers. (Spence 1989: 6)

In recent years there has been an increase in the involvement of Mexican gangs operating in southern California, where they produce methamphetamine in unpopulated desert areas.

Once the domain of outlaw biker gangs, the nation's meth trade has been taken over by Mexican drug families in the rural belt from San Diego County to Redding. Operating from Sinaloa and other states deep inside Mexico, these families oversee teams of cookers dispatched to orchards, cotton fields, chicken ranches, and abandoned dairies north of the border. (Arax and Goirman 1995: 1)

Until 1987 Garberville, California, a town of 1,400 located in Humboldt County, 200 miles north of San Francisco, was a boom town, the result of an economic miracle performed by a single crop—marijuana. In the early 1970s, hippie growers began cultivating marijuana for themselves and their friends. The business soon expanded, and marijuana became a major agricultural product for the three-county "Emerald Triangle." A quarter acre of plants could earn as much as $100,000 for its owner. At the same time, murders and other violent crimes soared, but so did the local economy. The growers in the valleys and hill slopes surrounding Garberville created an economic boom in this conservative rural town. Shopkeepers and motels catered to the traffickers; garden stores found new customers for irrigation equipment and organic fertilizer. In 1983 the Drug Enforcement Administration, the California Department of Justice, and local sheriffs began a successful campaign to eradicate the illegal harvest, to the chagrin of the local business owners (Schneider 1988).

But these successful efforts were short-lived, and federal authorities sent in the military. In 1990 U.S. army personnel, National Guardsmen, federal agents, and sheriffs' deputies spent two weeks raiding clandestine marijuana gardens in the rugged terrain of the King Range National Conservation Area in Humboldt County. There were local protests against the military deployment, and some residents filed a lawsuit to bar the use of the military. The National Guard spent $400,000 on the operation, which succeeded in destroying 1,200 plants. No growers were arrested (Bishop 1990b).

At the end of 1990, police officers discovered two elaborate underground marijuana farms in southern California. One was a 6,000-plant operation situated in a bunker under a home in Lancaster (sixty miles northeast of Los Angeles), and the other was a 4,000-plant farm under a house in Llano (about twenty miles from Lancaster). They were multimillion-dollar operations equipped with diesel-powered lights and ventilation systems.

In Kentucky, reputedly the second-largest marijuana-producing state in the nation, most cultivation takes place in the eastern region—mountainous and inaccessible Appalachia. The region is impoverished, with an unemployment rate of 25 percent. Gary Potter, Larry Gaines, and Beth Holbrook (1990: 98–99) state that "with its long-standing history of crime and violence, no one should be surprised that the Appalachian region of Kentucky is now one of the leading marijuana-producing areas." (For research into marijuana growers in Illinois, see Weisheit 1990).

The Cali cartel's second biggest industry is money laundering. The monthly gross for some New York operations, upwards of $7 million, translates into as much as 3,000 pounds of bills. This stash was confiscated in 1991.

Drug traffickers operating at the upper levels of the business have a serious problem: What to do with the large amounts of cash the business is continually generating? Further complicating the problem is that this cash is frequently in small denominations. To appreciate the amounts of money under discussion, we can look at one eight-month period in 1981 when twenty-nine Latin individuals, with no legitimate business in the United States, delivered $242,238,739 in cash to a single firm engaged in money laundering (Permanent Subcommittee on Investigation 1983). Envision, if you will, couriers delivering this sum in cardboard boxes, grocery bags, and suitcases in denominations of five, ten, and twenty dollars. In some cases "laundering" may simply be an effort to secure $100 bills so that the sums of money are more easily handled (500 bills weigh about one pound; $1 million in twenties weighs about one hundred pounds.) When customs agents raided a Houston house where money was stored before being laundered, they found the floor littered with one-, five-, and ten-dollar bills. Small bills are usually thrown in the trash or burned because they are not worth taking the time to count (Weingarten 1989b). In Los Angeles, federal agents discovered $10 million in cash and twenty tons of cocaine in an unguarded warehouse with a $6 padlock (Mydans 1989). In 1990 two Luxembourg-based banks controlled by Middle Eastern interests (and linked to the notorious Bank of Credit and Commerce International [BCCI]) with U.S. subsidiaries pleaded guilty to laundering $14 million in drug money (Gerth 1990). In 1991 several men from Lebanon and Argentina were convicted of laundering $1 billion in Colombian drug profits through the purchase and sale of gold, using jewelry companies in Houston, Miami, Los Angeles, and New York City as fronts.

Ever since Al Capone was imprisoned for income tax evasion, successful criminals have sought to launder their illegally secured money. Some use a "cash business" to mingle legitimate and illegitimate money on which they then pay income tax. In more elaborate schemes, large quantities of cash are converted into one or more cashier's checks, or small bills are changed into hundred-dollar bills and shipped out of the country or Telexed overseas. Cashier's checks or a suitcase filled with hundred-dollar bills can be taken out of the United States and deposited in the account of a company that may exist only on paper in a country with strict bank secrecy laws (e.g., Panama or offshore entities such as the Cayman Islands, the Bahamas, or the Dutch Antilles). The "paper" company returns the funds to the United States in the form of a loan to a "front" company controlled by the money's actual owner. The money has been laundered—freed from its connections to drug trafficking—because bank secrecy laws prohibit disclosing the identity of the person who actually holds the bank account.

In more recent years, currency exchanges have sprouted up along the Texas-Mexico border. These poorly regulated enterprises illegally accept large amounts of cash, which they then funnel into legitimate Texas banks. As a re-

MONEY LAUNDERING A LOT OF BULL

In 1990 customs officials in New York City seized over $6 million in suspected drug money that was being shipped to Colombia in containers of bull semen.

sult of this activity, the Federal Reserve Bank in San Antonio reported more than $2 billion in surplus cash surging through the banking system of south Texas; only Miami and Los Angeles have reported larger amounts (Weingarten 1989b). Drug money has changed the face of Starr County, Texas, where smuggling—historically cattle, liquor, and electronics equipment—has been a way of life. The area's remoteness and proximity to the Mexican border attract free-spending drug dealers. While very few of the more than 40,000 residents are involved in the drug business, many profit from it: Bank accounts and land values have soared, despite the county's having the lowest per capita income in the United States. In the town of Roma, population 8,058, inflated property taxes helped build a new sixty-acre, $11.5-million high school campus with an indoor pool and tennis courts—paid for in cash ("A Town That's Addicted to Illegal Drug Money" 1991).

Under the Bank Secrecy Act, financial institutions in the Untied States must identify the depositors and sources of money for cash transactions of $10,000 or more. (Some businesses that handle large amounts of cash, such as supermarkets, are legally entitled to an exemption.) These currency transactions must then be reported to the Internal Revenue Service (IRS). Persons planning to take $10,000 or more out of the United States must fill out a form disclosing this information to customs officials, who report it to the IRS. Failure to disclose such money to customs officials will, if discovered, result in permanent confiscation, in addition to criminal penalties. To overcome these disclosure requirements, money launderers need "cooperative" bank officials who (unlawfully) receive a percentage of the laundered money. An amendment to the Drug Abuse Act of 1988 requires offshore banks to record any U.S. cash transactions in excess of $10,000 and to permit U.S. officials to have access to the records. A failure to comply can result in a ban on the financial institution holding accounts in U.S. banks and denial of access to U.S. dollar-clearing and money-transfer systems (Egan 1991). (For a further discussion of drugs and money laundering, see Powis 1992.)

Our examination of the business of illegal drugs provides a framework for understanding the problems that confront law enforcement officials trying to constrain trafficking in dangerous drugs. This is the topic of the next chapter.

1. Why have cocaine-processing laboratories been relocating to cities far from cultivation sites?
2. What negative results have attended law enforcement pressure in Latin America brought on by the United States?
3. What was the role of Cubans in establishing the cocaine business?
4. Why do the Colombians dominate the cocaine business?
5. Why has it been impossible to permanently disrupt Colombian cocaine cartels?
6. Why have drug-producing nations in Latin America been unable or unwilling to curb production?
7. What are the political implications of U.S. reprisals against drug-producing nations?
8. How has the popularity of crack cocaine affected the business of drugs?
9. What are the three major heroin-producing areas of the world?
10. What is the link between politics and the production of heroin in the Golden Triangle?
11. What has been the traditional role of Chinese organizations in drug trafficking?
12. Why is it impossible to control the production of opium in the Golden Crescent?
13. How did the business of heroin change as a result of the demise of the French Connection?
14. How did Mafia groups come to dominate the heroin trade after World War II?
15. Why were African American heroin groups at one time dependent on Mafia groups, and why did this dependency end?
16. Why is the drug business typically violent?
17. Why is the street-level drug business an easy-entry enterprise?
18. Why have outlaw motorcycle gangs been able to dominate part of the amphetamine market?
19. What is the purpose of money laundering?
20. What are the various ways money laundering can be accomplished?

7

DRUG-LAW ENFORCEMENT

Drug laws reflect the decision of some persons that other persons who wish to consume certain substances should not be permitted to act on their preferences. Nor should anyone be permitted to satisfy the desires of drug consumers by making and selling the prohibited drug. . . . [The] most important characteristic of the legal approach to drug use is that these consumptive and commercial activities are being regulated by force.—Randy Barnett (1987: 73)

"The most important precipitating factor in narcotic addiction is degree of access to narcotic drugs" (Ausubel 1980: 4), an assertion supported by research into heroin consumption (Anglin 1988). This is why narcotic usage is higher in the inner city than in the suburbs and why the incidence of narcotic addiction in the United States approached the zero level during World War II.

> Thus, no matter how great the cultural attitudinal tolerance for addictive practices is, or how strong individual personality predispositions are, nobody can become addicted to narcotic drugs without access to them. Hence the logic of a law enforcement component in prevention. (Ausubel 1980: 4)

If drug abuse is seen as based on some combination of susceptibility and availability—"that drug abuse occurs when a prone individual is exposed to a high level of availability" (Smart 1980: 46)—it follows that a considerable reduction in availability can reduce drug abuse.[1] Availability also involves questions of cost—at some point the cost of purchasing a drug can reduce to near zero its availability to potential abusers, and law enforcement efforts can affect the cost of illegal drugs.

Before we can examine the strategies and techniques used by law enforcement agencies to deal with drug trafficking and to reduce the availability of drugs of abuse, we need to consider three issues that severely constrain law enforcement in general and drug-law enforcement in particular: constitutional limitations, jurisdictional limitations, and corruption.

CONSTITUTIONAL CONSTRAINTS

Law enforcement in the United States operates under significant constitutional constraints, generally referred to as *due process*—literally meaning the *process that is due* a person before something disadvantageous can be done to him or her. Due process restrains government from arbitrarily depriving a person of life, liberty, or property. There is an inherent tension between society's desire for security and safety and the value we place on liberty. Herbert Packer (1968) refers to this as a conflict between two conceptual models of criminal justice—crime control and due process. (A conceptual model is a way of representing an idea that facilitates discussion and understanding of the reality represented by the model.)

The *Crime Control Model* "is based on the proposition that the repression of criminal conduct is by far the most important function to be performed by the criminal justice process" (1968: 158). The stress is on achieving the greatest amount of societal security and safety. Effective crime control requires a high level of efficiency: The system must be able to investigate, ap-

---

1. That is, of course, if we discount the abuse of alcohol and the possibility/probability that persons unable to secure their preferred drug will switch to alcohol.

prehend, prosecute, and convict a large proportion of criminal offenders. However, the system must respond to these cases with only limited resources. Consequently, efficiency demands that cases be handled speedily, with a minimum of formality and without time-consuming challenges. This efficiency can be accomplished only by a presumption of guilt: "The supposition is that the screening processes operated by the police and prosecutors are reliable indicators of probable guilt" (p. 160). To maximize crime control after this screening, the system must move expeditiously to conviction and sentencing. The crime control model is characterized by a high level of confidence in the ability of police and prosecutors to separate the guilty from the innocent. It conflicts with the due process model.

The *Due Process Model* stresses the need for protecting individual freedoms. It assumes that the criminal justice system is deficient and stresses the possibility of error (p. 163):

> People are notoriously poor observers of disturbing events—the more emotion-arousing the context, the greater the possibility that recollection will be incorrect; confessions and admissions by persons in police custody may be induced by physical or psychological coercion so that the police end up hearing what the suspect thinks they want to hear rather than the truth; witnesses may be animated by a bias or interest that no one would trouble to discover except one specially charged with protecting the interests of the accused (as the police are not).

Due process confronts crime control and its need for efficiency and speed with an obstacle course of formalities, technicalities, and civil rights:

> Power is always subject to abuse—sometimes subtle, other times, as in the criminal justice process, open and ugly. Precisely because of its potency in subjecting the individual to the coercive power of the state, the criminal justice process must . . . be subjected to controls that prevent it from operating with maximal efficiency. (p. 166)

The due process model requires the system to slow down until it "resembles a factory that has to devote a substantial part of its input to quality control" (p. 165)—due process guarantees.

Due process, while it protects individual liberty, also benefits the criminal population by guaranteeing the right to remain silent (Fifth Amendment), the right to counsel (Sixth Amendment), the right to be tried speedily by an impartial jury (Sixth Amendment), and the right to confront witnesses (Sixth Amendment). The Fourth Amendment and the *exclusionary rule* are particularly important for drug-law enforcement.

The Fourth Amendment guarantees that

> the right of the people to be secure in their persons, houses, papers and effects, against unreasonable searches and seizures, shall not be violated, and no Warrants shall issue, but upon probable cause, supported by Oath or affirmation, and particularly describing the place to be searched, the persons or things to be seized.

In practice, information sufficient to justify a search warrant in drug cases is difficult to obtain; unlike such conventional crimes as robbery and burglary, there is an absence of innocent victims who will report the crime. The exclusionary rule is the court's way of enforcing the Fourth Amendment; it provides that evidence obtained in violation of the Fourth Amendment cannot be entered as evidence in a criminal trial (*Weeks v. United States,* 232 U.S. 383, 1914; *Mapp v. Ohio,* 357 U.S. 643, 1961), although there are a number of exceptions that are beyond the scope of this book to examine. The purpose of the exclusionary rule is to control the behavior of law enforcement agents by making enforcement efforts that violate the Constitution not worth the effort.

In order to respond effectively to drug trafficking, law enforcement officials require information about the activities of suspected traffickers. The Fourth Amendment and Title III of the Omnibus Crime Control and Safe Streets Act of 1968 (18 U.S.C. Section 2510–520) place restraints on how the government can secure this information. Thus, in order to surreptitiously intercept conversations by wiretapping telephones or using electronic devices ("bugging"), officials must secure a court order that, like a search warrant,

Legal control over drug-law enforcement agents is problematic, particularly with respect to covert operations. In Opa Locka, Florida, undercover officers posing as small-time street dealers sort out who bought what, while in the background an arrested customer is searched. This operation, known as a "reverse sting," has been declared legal in the courts, although many people arrested claim to have been entrapped. In one evening, often more than fifty people are arrested on felony charges because they purchased drugs from a police officer.

CRIME CONTROL VERSUS DUE PROCESS

The conflict between the crime control and due process models of criminal justice can be conceived of as a zero-sum continuum: court decisions or legislation that move criminal justice toward one model do so at the expense of the other. Exceptions to the exclusionary rule, for example, while they may increase the efficiency of law enforcement efforts against drug trafficking, also lessen the courts' ability to control police misconduct.

CRIME CONTROL   **DUE PROCESS**

←—————————————————————————————————→

    efficiency   *liberty*

must be based upon information sufficient to meet the legal standard of probable cause. When an order to intercept electronic communications is secured (generally referred to as a "Title III"), it is quite limited, requires extensive documentation, and demands that the persons intercepted be notified after the order expires. These requirements make electronic surveillance expensive, in terms of personnel hours expended, and difficult to properly accomplish.

The supervision of drug-law enforcement agents is also difficult, because they typically operate covertly, or undercover. This means that

> legal control over agents is problematic, and the circumstances of arrest are often such that there is a great temptation to perjury, violation of the exclusionary rule, misuse of informants, discretionary dropping, overlooking and altering charges, and other violations of procedural and/or legal rules. (Williams, Redlinger, and Manning 1979: 6)

The greater the pressure on law enforcement officers "to do something about drugs," the greater the temptation to avoid the significant constraints of due process and take unlawful (though often effective) shortcuts.

Jurisdictional Limitations

The Constitution provides for a form of government in which powers are diffused horizontally and vertically. This is accomplished by three branches—legislative, judicial, and executive—and four levels of government—federal, state, county, and municipal. Although each level of government has responsibilities for responding to drug abuse and drug trafficking, there is little or no coordination among them. Each level responds to the problem of drugs independently of the others. Federalism was part of a deliberate design to help protect us against tyranny; unfortunately, it also provides us with a level of inefficiency that significantly handicaps efforts to curtail drug trafficking.

On the federal level, a host of executive branch agencies (to be examined later), ranging from the military to the Federal Bureau of Investigation, are responsible for combatting drug trafficking. A separate federal judicial system is responsible for trying drug cases, and a legislative branch is responsible for enacting drug legislation and allocating funds for federal drug-law enforcement efforts. At the local level are about twenty thousand police agencies. Each state has drug-law enforcement agents, a state police or similar agency, and agencies that manage prisons and the parole system (if one exists). County government is usually responsible for prosecuting defendants, and a county-level agency, usually the sheriff, is responsible for operating jails. The county may also have a police department with drug-law enforcement responsibilities under, or independent of, the sheriff's office, and almost every municipality has a police department whose officers enforce drug laws. Each of these levels of government has taxing authority and allocates resources with little or no consultation with other levels of government. The sum total is a degree of inefficiency surpassing that of most democratic nations.

U.S. efforts against drug abuse are also limited by national boundaries: Cocaine and heroin originate where U.S. law enforcement has no jurisdiction. The Bureau of International Narcotics Matters within the Department of State has primary responsibility for coordinating international programs and gaining the cooperation of foreign governments in antidrug efforts. But the bureau has no authority to force governments to act in a manner beneficial to U.S. efforts in dealing with cocaine or heroin. Elaine Sciolino (1988: E3) reports that it "has little influence even within the department [of State]. Foreign Service officers," she states, "readily admit that they try to avoid drug-enforcement assignments because they generally do not result in promotions." The State Department also collects intelligence on policy-level international narcotics developments, while the CIA collects strategic narcotics intelligence and is responsible for coordinating foreign intelligence on narcotics. The CIA, however, has often protected drug traffickers who have provided useful foreign intelligence. U.S. efforts against drug trafficking are often sacrificed to foreign policy (Sciolino and Engelberg 1988).

In 1994 Bill Clinton signed legislation authorizing the president to provide assistance for the prevention and suppression of international drug trafficking and money laundering. While international law (multinational treaties) provides the basis for eradicating illicit poppy and coca cultivation, adherence to the treaty depends on a level of cooperation often sacrificed on the altar of domestic economic and political realities (discussed in chapter 6 and analyzed in chapter 8). Under the treaty, coca- and poppy-producing countries are to limit their cultivation acreage to a level in line with *legitimate* world needs. Strict controls over growers require them to deliver their crops to a government monopoly to prevent diversion to the black market. Crops growing wild are to be destroyed. The price paid by the government, however, is not com-

GOVERNMENTAL COMPLEXITY

Branches	Levels
Executive	Federal
Legislative	State
Judicial	County
	Municipal

petitive with that offered by traffickers, and the illegal diversion of coca or opium is the only significant source of cash for many peasant growers, whose standard of living is already marginal. Attempts to substitute other cash crops have met with only limited success, because such programs cannot challenge the reality of the marketplace. As noted in chapter 6, coca and poppy are grown in regions where governments often have only nominal control.

International Efforts

In 1990 President George Bush met with the leaders of cocaine-exporting countries in Cartagena, Colombia, to devise a plan to combat cocaine at its source with the emphasis on law enforcement. A second meeting was held in San Antonio, Texas, in 1992, during which it was revealed that U.S. assistance for antidrug efforts in Colombia would be shifted from the military to the police because the military used the money to combat guerilla groups, not drug traffickers.[2] Similar shifts were suggested for Peru and Bolivia. The latter countries requested more aid to create alternatives to coca trafficking, but this was rejected by the Bush administration because of budgetary constraints.

In 1988 the International Convention Against Illicit Traffic in Narcotic Drugs and Psychotropic Substances was adopted in Vienna, with two main purposes:

> First, to establish an internationally recognized set of offenses relating to drug trafficking that are to be criminalized under the domestic law of the parties to the convention; and second, to create a framework for international cooperation to enhance the prospect that traffickers and others who profit from trafficking will be brought to justice. . . .
>
> The Convention focuses on the eradication of drugs and drug-producing laboratories; the international transportation of precursor chemicals used to pro-

---

2. In 1996 President Bill Clinton declared that Colombia had failed to cooperate in the fight against drugs, making the country ineligible for most U.S. economic aid.

duce illegal drugs; the tracing of laundered drug trade profits back to the drug cartels; and the worldwide extradition of drug criminals so that they can have no safe havens. Significantly, the Convention obligates parties to make money laundering an extraditable offense, to afford the widest measure of international mutual legal assistance in judicial proceedings, and to cooperate closely to enhance the effectiveness of law enforcement actions to suppress narcotics trafficking and related offenses. (Thornburgh 1989: 59)

(Promoting cooperation in international drug-law enforcement is the role of INTERPOL, discussed below.)

Jurisdictional limitations, however, can sometimes overcome constitutional restrictions. For example, because the Bill of Rights applies only to actions of the U.S. government, the Fourth Amendment and exclusionary rule do not govern seizures in foreign countries by those nations' police. This holds even when the evidence seized is from U.S. citizens; thus it would be admissible in a U.S. court (Anderson 1992). Furthermore, the Supreme Court has held that constitutional protections do not obtain in U.S. government actions against foreign nationals on foreign soil. In *United States v. Verdugo-Urquidez* (110 S.Ct. 1056 1990), a Mexican national suspected in the 1985 torture-murder of a DEA agent was apprehended by Mexican police on a U.S. warrant and turned over to U.S. marshals at the California border. At the request of the DEA, Mexican police, without a warrant, searched the fugitive's two residences and seized incriminating documents, which were turned over to the DEA. The evidence was ruled admissible.

In a 1992 ruling on another case involving the DEA agent's murder, the Supreme Court ruled that kidnapping a suspect on foreign soil does not prevent the suspect from being tried in the United States. In this case (*United States v. Alvarez Machain,* 504 U.S.), Mexican bounty hunters kidnapped a medical doctor and took him to El Paso; they were paid $20,000 and given the right to settle with their families in the United States. The Mexican government reacted with outrage to the decision.

CORRUPTION

In the last chapter we examined the complex world of drug trafficking and the enormous profits that accrue to many of those involved. The easy availability of large sums of money and the clandestine nature of the business make drug-law enforcement vulnerable to corruption. There are two basic strategies available to law enforcement agencies—reactive and proactive—and many use a combination of both. *Reactive law enforcement* has its parallel in firefighting: Firefighters remain in their fire stations, equipment at the ready, until they get a call for service. Reactive law enforcement encourages citizens to report crimes; the agency will then respond to the reports. This type of law enforcement is used for dealing with such conventional criminal behavior as murder, rape, assault, robbery, burglary, and theft—all likely to be reported to the police. (It should be noted, however, that with the exception of murder and auto theft, studies indicate that most of these crimes are *not* reported to the police.) *Proactive law enforcement* requires officers/agents to seek out indications of criminal behavior, always a necessity when the criminal violation includes victim participation (e.g., gambling, prostitution, and drugs). These crimes are often described as consensual or "victimless," although they clearly have victims who are unlikely to report the crime to the police. The problem of corruption is in part tied to the proactive strategy.

In order to seek out criminal activity in the most efficient manner possible, proactive law enforcement officers must conceal their identities and otherwise deceive the criminals they are stalking. As James Q. Wilson (1978: 59) points out, both reactive and proactive law enforcement officers are exposed to opportunities for graft, but the latter are more severely tested: The reactive officer, "were he to accept money or favors to act other than as his duty required, would have to conceal or alter information about a crime already known to his organization." The proactive agent, however, "can easily agree to overlook offenses known to him but to no one else or to participate in illegal transactions (buying or selling drugs) for his own rather than for the organization's advantage." Undercover officers pretending to be criminals are difficult to supervise; the agency they work for often knows only what the agents tell it.

ON BEING SHOCKED

We should be shocked not that there are policemen on the take but that there are police officers not on the take. Making $35,000 a year, they arrest people who are driving cars worth several times that (Boaz 1990). The French Connection heroin case, the subject of a best-selling book and an Academy Award-winning movie (Best Picture and Best Actor of 1971), is an example. In 1962 Detectives Eddie "Popeye" Egan (played in the movie by Gene Hackman) and his partner Sonny Grosso (played by Roy Scheider) smashed an international drug ring that was smuggling Turkish heroin into New York from Marseilles. That same year, the drugs seized in connection with the case—fifty-seven pounds of almost pure heroin—were vouchered with the police property clerk by Detectives Egan and Grosso. In 1972 the Police Commissioner of the city of New York held a news conference: The French Connection heroin, he announced, had been stolen and replaced with white flour. Several days later, an inventory of the property clerk's office revealed that additional heroin was missing: A total of nearly four hundred pounds had been stolen—*by police officers* (Wallance 1981). In 1989 a DEA supervisory agent who had worked on the French Connection case was indicted for transporting more than sixty-two pounds of cocaine from Miami to Boston (Berke 1989).

CORRUPTION

- "12 Capital Officers Face Drug Charges." *New York Times* (December 16, 1993: 12)
- "2 Officers Charged in Drug Extortion." *Chicago Tribune* (November 8, 1994: Sec 2: 3)
- "Why Good Cops Go Bad. Corruption: A New Breed of Renegade Police Officer Can Be as Dangerous as the Gangs and Drug Dealers They Are Supposed to Control." *Newsweek* (December 19, 1994: 30–34)
- "9 New Orleans Police Officers Are Indicted in U.S. Drug Case." *New York Times* (December 8, 1994: 8)
- "Charges Filed Against Five Men in [Philadelphia] Drug Squad." *New York Times* (March 2, 1995: 10)
- "Officer Admits that He Sold Cocaine Taken from Dealers." *New York Times* (December 7, 1995:20)
- "Ex-Officer Sentenced in a [St. Louis] Drug-Ring Case." *New York Times* (March 27, 1996:11).

There is also corruption in foreign countries that grow, process, or serve as transshipment stations for illegal substances. "The corrupt official," notes the President's Commission on Organized Crime (1986: 178), "is the *sine qua non* of drug trafficking." The commission concluded that

> corruption linked to drug trafficking is a widespread phenomenon among political and military leaders, police and other authorities in virtually every country touched by the drug trade. The easily available and enormous amounts of money generated through drug transactions present a temptation too great for many in positions of authority to resist.

As if to emphasize this dimension of the drug business, in 1991 a federal judge in Florida sentenced the former Interior Minister of Bolivia, Luis Arce Gomez, to thirty years imprisonment for conspiring to import cocaine into the United States. While serving as interior minister in 1980 to 1981, Gomez protected drug dealers and sold cocaine, some from police vaults, to cooperative traffickers. He was extradited to the United States in 1989. In addition to corruption, there is the problem of brutality. The Peruvian military, for example, has earned widespread condemnation for violating basic human rights (Krauss 1991), and similar allegations have been made against the Colombian police and military. In Peru it is hard for an officer with a monthly salary of $80 to resist bribes that often range as high as $25,000. In fact, military officers often bribe superiors in order to secure a transfer to the coca-rich Huallaga Valley.

Then there is the problem of informants. Informants come in two basic categories—the "good citizen" and the "criminal." The former is such a rarity, particularly in drug-law enforcement, that we will deal only with the criminal informant, the individual who helps law enforcement in order to further his or her own personal ends. These include vengeance, efforts to drive competition out of business, and/or financial rewards, but most frequently the information is given to "work off a beef"—secure leniency for criminal activities that have become known to the authorities. Jerald Cloyd (1982: 188n) found that one federal district had a specified menu for every "beef": For each arrest resulting from informant assistance and yielding approximately the same amount of drugs that the defendant is being charged with, there is

INFORMING FOR PROFIT . . .

While the behavior of criminal of informants is usually motivated by a desire to avoid or ameliorate imprisonment, informing can also be quite profitable, as the case of Phillip Han reveals. Between 1987 and 1990, the stylishly dressed thirty-five-year-old member of the Ghost Shadows gang in New York's Chinatown received more than $400,000 for aiding the DEA. Before that, Han served a four-year term for murder conspiracy.

"DEA informants, working on commission, were kept so busy [during the 1980s] that at times the 300 registered informers outearned investigators, annually pulling down $50,000 to $75,000 in their constant quest to bring us information" (Stutman and Esposito 1992: 42).

. . . AND FOR FREEDOM

In an effort to convict Manual Noriega, federal prosecutors dropped three life terms and reduced the sentences of four convicted high-level drug traffickers by 546 years. The men testified against the former Panamanian strongman, and two were freed in 1991. Each had been given a new identity and government financial support worth hundreds of thousands of dollars. Some of the informants don't need government largesse; they have been permitted to keep the profits of their drug dealings—millions of dollars—in return for testifying against Noriega (Lubasch 1990; Richey 1991).

OTHER DANGERS

Special agents from the U.S. Customs Service and Drug Enforcement Agency used a battering ram to enter the posh California residence and responded with automatic weapons when fired upon by the occupant. The agents thought they were raiding the headquarters of a heavily armed drug gang that protected the house with vicious Rottweilers; the badly wounded computer executive thought he was defending his house against home invaders. No drugs, dogs, or weapons were found. Information leading to the raid was provided by a confidential informant who was subsequently convicted of perjury (Katel 1995).

a reduction of charges by one count. Being charged with two counts (one count of possession, one of possession with intent to sell), one arrest would get her a reduction of one count (felony possession) in exchange for an expedient plea of guilty. One good arrest and a guilty plea would reduce the charge to misdemeanor possession. Two good arrests would get her case dismissed.

Despite law enforcement agency regulations, often "While serving as informers, suspects are allowed to engage in illegal activity" notes Joseph Goldstein (1982: 37). "Continued use of narcotics is condoned; the narcotics detective generally is not concerned with the problem of informants who make buys and use some of the evidence themselves." Goldstein points out that although "informers are usually warned that their status does not give them a 'license to peddle,' possession of a substantial amount of narcotics may be excused" (1982: 37). Obviously, the more involved in criminal activity the informer—"snitch" or CI (confidential informant)—is, the more useful is his or her assistance. This raises serious ethical and policy questions. Should the informant be given immunity from lawful punishment in exchange for cooperation? If so, who is to make that determination? The agent who becomes aware of the informant's activities? His or her supervisor? The prosecutor who is informed of the situation? A trial judge? Should a murderer be permitted to remain free because he or she is valuable to law enforcement efforts in drug trafficking? Should a drug addict-informant be allowed to continue his or her abuse in order to keep in touch with traffickers? If so, doesn't this contradict the goal of drug statutes, which is to curtail drug abuse? Should the government encourage informants even if they face serious physical danger, and they usually do? Most drug agents would argue, however, that without informants there can be no effective drug-law enforcement. The issues are complex and without definitive answers.

There are other dangers. In South Florida, for example, given the number of law enforcement agencies and given their heavy dependence on intelligence, it is inevitable that there are informants who inform on other informants, who are probably informing on them. A consequence of that is selective prosecution: arbitrary decisions made by police officers and agents as to who will go to jail and who will be allowed to remain on the street. Given the vast amounts of money at stake in the drug business, selective prosecution raises the specter of corruption. (Eddy, Sabogal, and Walden 1988: 85)

Working closely with informants is potentially corrupting. The informant helps the agent enter an underworld filled with danger as well as great financial rewards. There is always concern that the law enforcement agent may become something else to the informer—a friend, an employee, an employer, a partner. The rewards can be considerable: Agents can confiscate money and drugs from other traffickers or receive payment for not arresting traffickers; at the same time they can improve their work record by arresting competing dealers. It is often only a small step from using drug traffickers as informants to going into business with them.

THE UNDERCOVER HOOK

D. had been a military policeman for two years and a police officer with Cheltenham Township in eastern Pennsylvania for fourteen years. He also worked undercover for the Narcotics Enforcement Team of the Montgomery County, Pennsylvania, District Attorney's Office for seven years. With more than 300 undercover buys that led to the convictions of more than 100 drug sellers, D. was considered an exemplary officer. In 1985, at age thirty-six, Detective D. suddenly resigned, telling his supervisors that he was suffering from depression. He then entered a drug rehabilitation program, hooked on free-base cocaine (Lewis 1988).

COCAINE CHIEF

The police chief of Brockton, Massachusetts, former head of the force's narcotics division, established a reputation for the fervor of his campaign against drugs and drug trafficking in this town of about 95,000, twenty-five miles south of Boston. He added undercover police officers to the narcotics squad and gave dozens of speeches on the evils of drug abuse. On 6 November 1989, the chief was indicted on charges of stealing cocaine from the police department's evidence room. After admitting a five-year daily cocaine habit, the chief resigned and entered a drug treatment program. In 1990, after pleading guilty to stealing cocaine, embezzling city funds, and intimidating one witness and suborning another to commit perjury, he was sentenced to seven to ten years in state prison (Hays 1989).

STATUES AND LEGAL REQUIREMENTS

The legal foundation for federal drug-law violations is Title II of the Comprehensive Drug Abuse Prevention and Control Act of 1970, as amended (usually referred to as the Controlled Substances Act [CSA]). Among the provisions of the CSA is a set of criteria for placing a substance in one of five schedules (see figure 7.1). Persons involved in the illegal drug business may be arrested and prosecuted for a number of different offenses: manufacture, importation, distribution, possession, sale; or conspiracy to manufacture, import, distribute, possess, or sell; or failure to pay the required income taxes on illegal income. Possession of drugs may be *actual*—for example, actually on the person, in pockets or in a package that he or she is holding; or *constructive*—not actually *on* the person, but under his or her control, directly or through other persons. Possession must be proven by a legal search, which usually requires a search warrant as per the Fourth Amendment (an important exception is at ports of entry). A search warrant requires the establishment of probable cause—providing a judge with sufficient evidence of a crime to justify a warrant. Drugs can easily be secreted in any variety of places, including inside the human body.

Conspiracy

Conspiracy is an agreement between two or more persons to commit a criminal act; the agreement becomes the *corpus* (body) of the crime. Conspiracy requires proof (beyond a reasonable doubt) that two or more persons planned to violate drug laws and that at least one overt act in furtherance of the conspiracy was made by a conspirator (for example, the purchase of materials to aid in the transportation or dilution of illicit drugs). Conspiracy statutes are valuable tools for prosecuting drug offenders because:

1. Intervention can occur before the commission of a substantive offense.
2. A conspirator cannot shield himself or herself from prosecution because of a lack of knowledge of the details of the conspiracy or the identity of co-conspirators and their contributions.
3. An act or declaration by one conspirator committed in furtherance of the conspiracy is admissible against each co-conspirator (an exception to the hearsay rule).
4. Each conspirator is responsible for the substantive crimes of co-conspirators; even late joiners can be held liable for prior acts of co-conspirators if the latecomer's agreement is given with full knowledge of the conspiracy's objective.

FIGURE 7.1
Substances of Abuse

277

Chapter Seven:
Drug-Law
Enforcement

Schedule I
A. The drug or other substance has a high potential for abuse.
B. The drug or other substance has no currently accepted medical use in treatment in the United States.
C. There is a lack of accepted safety for use of the drug or other substance under medical supervision.

Schedule II
A. The drug or other substance has a high potential for abuse.
B. The drug or other substance has a currently accepted medical use in treatment in the United States or a currently accepted medical use with severe restrictions.
C. Abuse of the drug or other substances may lead to severe psychological or physical dependence.

Schedule III
A. The drug or other substance has a potential for abuse less than the drugs or other substances in Schedules I and II.
B. The drug or other substance has a currently accepted medical use in treatment in the United States.
C. Abuse of the drug or other substance may lead to moderate or low physical dependence or high psychological dependence.

Schedule IV
A. The drug or other substance has a low potential for abuse relative to the drugs or other substances in Schedule III.
B. The drug or other substance has a currently accepted medical use in treatment in the United States.
C. Abuse of the drug or other substance may lead to limited physical dependence or psychological dependence relative to the drugs or other substances in Schedule III.

Schedule V
A. The drug or other substance has a low potential for abuse relative to the drugs or other substances in Schedule IV.
B. The drug or other substance has a currently accepted medical use in treatment in the United States.
C. Abuse of the drug or other substance may lead to limited physical dependence or psychological dependence relative to the drugs or other substances in Schedule IV.

Source: Drug Enforcement Administration.

FIGURE 7.2
Federal Trafficking Penalties: Narcotic Penalties and Enforcement Act of 1986

CSA Schedule	Drug	Quantity	Penalty — First Offense	Penalty — Second Offense	Drug	Quantity	Penalty — First Offense	Penalty — Second Offense
I and II	Heroin	1 kg mixture	Not less than 10 years. Not more than life. If death or serious injury, not less than 20 years, not more than life. Fine of not more than $4 million individual, $10 million other than individual.	Not less than 20 years. Not more than life. If death or serious injury, not less than life. Fine of not more than $8 million individual, $20 million other than individual.	Heroin	100 gm mixture	Not less than 5 years. Not more than 40 years. If death or serious injury, not less than 20 years, nor more than life. Fine of not more than $2 million individual, $5 million other than individual.	Not less than 10 years. Not more than life. If death or serious injury, not less than life. Fine of not more than $4 million individual, $10 million other than individual.
	Cocaine	5 kg mixture			Cocaine	500 gm mixture		
	Cocaine Base	50 gm mixture			Cocaine Base	5 gm mixture		
	PCP	100 gm or 1 kg mixture			PCP	10 gm or 100 gm mixture		
	LSD	10 gm mixture			LSD	1 gm mixture		
	Fentanyl	400 gm mixture			Fentanyl	40 gm mixture		
	Fentanyl Analog	100 gm mixture			Fentanyl Analog.	10 gm mixture		
	Others*	Any	First Offense — Not more than 20 years. If death or serious injury, not less than 20 years, not more than life. Fine $1 million individual, $5 million not individual.	Second Offense — Not more than 30 years. If death or serious injury, life. Fine $2 million individual, $10 million not individual.				
III	All	Any	Not more than 5 years, fine not more than $250,000 individual, $1 million not individual.	Not more than 10 years, fine $500,000 individual, $2 million not individual.				
IV	All	Any	Not more than 3 years, fine not more than $250,000 individual, $1 million not individual.	Not more than 6 years, fine not more than $500,000 individual, $2 million not individual.				
V	All	Any	Not more than 1 year, fine not more than $100,000 individual, $250,000 not individual.	Not more than 2 years, fine not more than $200,000 individual, $500,000 not individual.				

*Does not include marijuana, hashish, or hash oil.

Source: Drug Enforcement Administration.

FIGURE 7.3
Controlled Substances, Classified by Type and by Federal Schedule Number

	Drugs	Schedule	Trade or Other Names
NARCOTICS	Opium	II, III, V	Dover's Powder, Paregoric, Parepectolin
	Morphine	II, III, V	Morphine, Pectoral Syrup
	Codeine	II, III, V	Codeine, Empirin Compound with Codeine, Robitussin A-C
	Heroin	I	Diacetylmorphine, Horse, Smack
	Hydromorphone		Dilaudid
	Meperidine (Pethidine)	II	Demerol, Pethadol
	Methadone		Dolophine, Methadone, Metadose
	Other Narcotics	I, II, III, IV, V	LAAM, Leritine, Levo-Dromoran, Percodan, Tussionex, Fentanyl, Lomotil
DEPRESSANTS	Chloral Hydrate	IV	Noctec, Somnos
	Barbiturates	II, III, IV	Amobarbital, Phenobarbital, Butisol, Phenoxbarbital, Secobarbital, Tuinal
	Glutethimide	III	Doriden
	Methaqualone	I	Optimil, Parest, Quaalude, Somafac, Sopor
	Benzodiazepines	IV	Ativan, Azene, Clonopin, Dalmane, Diazepam, Librium, Serax, Tranxene, Valium, Verstran
	Other Depressants	III, IV	Equanil, Miltown, Noludar Placidyl, Valmid
STIMULANTS	Cocaine	II	Coke, Flake, Snow
	Amphetamines	II	Biphetamine, Desoxyn, Dexedrine
	Phenmetrazine		Preludin
	Methylphenidate	II	Ritalin
	Other Stimulants	III, IV	Anipex, Cylert, Didrex, Ionamin, Plegine, Pre-State, Sanorex, Tenuate, Tepanil, Voranil

FIGURE 7.3 *(con't.)*
Controlled Substances, Classified by Type and by Federal Schedule Number

	Drugs	*Schedule*	*Trade or Other Names*
HALLUCINOGENS	LSD		Acid, Microdot
	Mescaline and Peyote	I	Mesc. Buttons, Cactus
	Amphetamine Variants		2, 5-DMA, PMA, STP, MDA, MMDA, TMA, DOM, DOB
	Phencyclidine	II	PCP, Angel Dust, Hog
	Phencyclidine Analogs		PCE, PCPy, TCP
	Other Hallucinogens	I	Bufotenine, Ibogaine, DMT, DET, Psilocybin, Psilocyn
CANNABIS	Marihuana		Pot, Acapulco Gold, Grass, Reefer, Sinsemilla, Thai Sticks
	Tetrahydrocannabinol	I	THC*
	Hashish		Hash
	Hashish Oil		Hash Oil

*Synthetic THC, marketed under several trade names (e.g., Dronabinol, Maronal), is used medically for treatment of glaucoma and for alleviating side effects of chemotherapy for cancer.

Source: Drug Enforcement Administration.

There are three basic types of conspiracy:

1. *Wheel Conspiracies:* One person at the "hub" conspires individually with two or more persons, who make up the "spokes" of the wheel. For the conspiracy to be (legally) complete, the wheel needs a "rim": Each spoke must be aware of and agree with the others in pursuit of one objective.

2. *Chain Conspiracies:* Like the lights on a Christmas tree, each conspirator depends on the successful participation of every other member. Each member is a "link" who in order to complete the conspiracy must understand that the success of the scheme depends upon everyone in the chain.

3. *Enterprise Conspiracies:* Part of the RICO (Racketeer Influenced and Corrupt Organizations) statute of the Organized Crime Control Act of 1970, the enterprise conspiracy avoids the practical limitations inherent in proving wheel and chain conspiracies. The statute makes it a separate crime to conspire to violate drug laws as part of an agreement to participate in an enterprise by engaging in a pattern of racketeering activity. Members of the conspiracy need not know each other or even be aware of each other's criminal activities. All that needs to be shown is each member's agreement to participate in the organization—the "enterprise"—by committing two or more acts of racketeering, such as gambling or drug violations, within a ten-year period. The enterprise conspiracy facilitates mass trials, with each member of the enterprise subjected to the significant penalties—twenty years' imprisonment on each count—that can result from a conviction.

The Continuing Criminal Enterprise (CCE) statute is similar to RICO, but targets only illegal drug activity. The statute makes it a crime to commit or conspire to commit a continuing series of felony violations of the 1970 Drug Abuse Prevention and Control Act when the violations are committed in concert with five or more persons. The courts have ruled that a series requires three or more violations. "For conviction under this statute, the offender must have been an organizer, manager, or supervisor of the continuing operation and have obtained substantial income or resources from the drug violations" (Carlson and Finn 1993: 2).

Tax Violations

In 1927 the Supreme Court decided the case of *United States v. Sullivan* (274 U.S. 259), which denied the claim of self-incrimination as an excuse for failure to file income tax on illegally gained earnings. This decision enabled the federal government to successfully prosecute Al Capone and members of his organization. Drug entrepreneurs have devised ways to successfully evade taxes by, for example, dealing in cash, keeping minimal records, and setting up fronts. This is countered by the indirect methods known as the *net worth theory:* "The government establishes a taxpayer's net worth at the commencement of the taxing period [which requires substantial accuracy], deducts that from his or her net worth at the end of the period, and proves that the net gain in net worth exceeds the income reported by the taxpayer" (Johnson 1963: 17–18). In effect, the Internal Revenue Service reconstructs the total expenditures of the taxpayer by examining his or her standard of living and comparing it with reported income. The government can then maintain that the taxpayer did not report his or her entire income. The government does not have to show a probable source of the excess unreported gain in net worth.

The Attorney General of the United States has pointed out that "there is so much cash involved in large, illicit drug-trafficking operations that tracking the proceeds of such activities is often a more fruitful investigative endeavor than tracking the underlying criminal activities" (Thornburgh 1989: 17). Before the passage of the Money Laundering Control Act of 1986 (Title 18 U.S.C. sections 1956 and 1957), money laundering was not a federal crime, although the Department of Justice had used a variety of federal statutes to successfully prosecute money-laundering cases. The act consolidated these statutes with the goal of increasing prosecutions for this offense. Money laundering was made a separate federal offense punishable by a fine of $500,000 or twice the value of the property involved, whichever is greater, and twenty years' imprisonment. Title 18 U.S.C. Section 981 provides for the civil confiscation of any property related to a money-laundering scheme. Legislation enacted in 1988 allows the government to file a suit claiming ownership of all cash funneled through operations intended to disguise their illegal source. The courts can issue an order freezing all contested funds until the case is adjudicated (Weinstein 1988).

A person is guilty of money laundering if he or she, knowing that the property involved represents the proceeds of an illegal activity, attempts to conceal or disguise the nature, location, source, ownership, or control of the proceeds or attempts to avoid a transaction-reporting requirement. Furthermore, whoever transports or attempts to transport a monetary instrument or funds out of the United States in an attempt to conceal or disguise the nature, location, source, ownership, or control of the proceeds to avoid a transaction-reporting requirement with the intent to promote an unlawful activity or with the knowledge that the monetary instrument or funds represent the proceeds of an unlawful activity shall be guilty of money laundering. For a conviction under section 1957 the prosecutor must prove:

1. That the defendant engaged in a monetary transaction in excess of $10,000;
2. That the defendant knew the money to be the fruit of criminal activity; and
3. That the money was in fact the fruit of a specified unlawful activity (Weinstein 1988).

Until 1988 the act permitted the Department of Justice to prosecute attorneys and seize fees obtained from tainted sources. Defense attorneys argued that this created a situation "in which a defendant cannot retain an attorney because of the government's threat of criminal and civil sanctions against any attorney who takes the case" (Weinstein 1988: 381). The defendant is left without a free choice of attorneys and thus must depend upon a public defender who may not be familiar with the complexities of RICO prosecutions.

Supporters of this legislation argue that criminals who have grown wealthy from crime are not entitled to any greater consideration with respect to legal representation than their less-successful criminal colleagues, who are often represented by public defenders. On 18 November 1988, President Ronald Reagan signed the antidrug abuse bill, which contains an amendment to 18 U.S.C. Section 1957, effectively excepting defense attorneys' fees from the criminal money-laundering provisions. Thus, while criminal-defense fees could still be subject to forfeiture, the attorney who accepts tainted fees is exempt from criminal prosecution. In 1989 the Supreme Court, in a 5–4 decision, ruled that the government, under the Comprehensive Forfeiture Act, can freeze the assets of criminal defendants before trial (*Caplin and Drysdale v. United States,* 491 U.S. 616; *United States v. Monsanto,* 491 U.S. 600).

Seizure and Forfeiture of Assets

Federal and state statutes provide for the forfeiture of property used in criminal activity or secured with the fruits of criminal activity. Forfeiture has proved particularly useful in dealing with drug traffickers. There are four types of forfeitable items:

1. *Contraband,* such as controlled substances, are illegal to possess and may be seized and destroyed without a court order.
2. *Derivative contraband* includes conveyances used to transport contraband, such as aircraft, vessels, and motor vehicles. While not illegal in themselves, they are classified as contraband when used in furtherance of a criminal act.
3. *Direct proceeds* are usually cash.
4. *Derivative proceeds* include real estate and stock.

In practice, vehicles and cash are the most frequently seized assets, because the pursuit of real property requires extensive financial investigation. "The investigative expense may be cost effective," however, if "the property is valuable and the potential for disrupting the criminal organization is high" (Stellwagen 1985: 5).

There are two types of forfeiture proceedings: criminal and civil. *Criminal forfeiture* is applicable only as part of a successful criminal prosecution. "The defendant in the criminal case must be convicted of the crime involving the property, or the property cannot be subject to forfeiture" (Poethig 1988: 11). *Civil forfeiture* has certain advantages over criminal forfeiture: The level of evidence required is considerably less than than in a criminal action, and the considerable due process guarantees accruing to a criminal defendant are not applicable in a civil action. In fact, civil forfeiture can proceed even in the absence of a criminal prosecution.

Civil forfeiture proceedings are brought against property involved in a criminal offense instead of against a person. Possession of the property in and of itself may not be illegal, but the property may be subject to seizure and forfeiture because of the way it was used. No criminal charge or conviction need exist against the owner of the property for the civil case to occur. (Poethig 1988: 11)

RICO and the 1984 Comprehensive Forfeiture Act (CFA) provide for the seizure of assets under certain conditions. The CFA

creates a rebuttable presumption that any property of a person convicted of a drug felony is subject to forfeiture if the government establishes by a preponderance of evidence that the defendant acquired the property during the period of violation or within a reasonably short period thereafter, *and* there was no likely source for the property other than the violation. (PCOC 1986: 274)

Much of the money taken in forfeitures goes into state and local law enforcement efforts. To stop commuter customers from driving into New York City to purchase drugs, law enforcement officials have been seizing the cars of those making drug purchases. Some vehicles have been returned to their owners when the owners were not the ones arrested; hundreds of others have been auctioned off.

In any number of jurisdictions, disputes have arisen over how to allocate the fruits of seized assets. Because these funds do not incur a political cost—not being linked to taxes—they are highly valued. However, "Once the money reaches the local police, it often can become a political football with law enforcement and politicians squabbling over how to spend it" (Soble 1991: 23).

DEA-confiscated "hash" in Miami.

SNIFFING AND SEIZING

On 28 June 1988, federal agents swooped down on a Chicago businessman on the city's West Side, confiscating all of his property. Although no criminal charges had been filed against the man, a federal judge authorized the seizure of his suburban house (which was for sale for $280,000), an auto service station, two tow trucks, three autos, a beauty salon, a car wash, an apartment building, and $75,000 in cash from two bank accounts. A court order was requested to seize a third account. A civil complaint filed by the U.S. attorney stated that the businessman not only bought the properties with the proceeds of drug trafficking but also conducted his drug business from most of them, including his house, where he lived with his wife and four children. Although the businessman started out as a heroin dealer in 1978, federal officials state that he switched to cocaine when that substance became popular and had been selling the drug in kilo quanitites.

"Agents took dogs especially trained to detect narcotics to a West Side savings and loan in 1985 and let them sniff the thousands of dollars in cash that the businessman," Mexican-born Rene Villarreal, forty-six, and his brother "were depositing there. The dogs' reaction showed that the Villarreals' money literally smelled of cocaine" (Koziol 1988b: 1). The brothers had been dividing deposits and withdrawals of more than $10,000 in several transactions in order to avoid the currency reports that financial institutions are required to make to the IRS when a cash transaction exceeds $10,000.

On 20 July 1988, the body of Rene Villarreal was found in the bedroom of his home. His wife and children had been allowed to remain after the seizure, and Villarreal had simply moved back in with them. He had been shot once in the back of the head (Koziol 1988).

In several California communities, for example, police officials wanted to put the money into drug-law enforcement, but elected officials insisted instead on increasing the uniformed police force. There is also concern that pressure to produce revenue will encourage legally questionable activity and even alter the basic goal of drug-law enforcement.

Intertwined with this concern is that expressed over the seizure of property owned by innocent third parties. Three fraternity houses seized at the University of Virginia in 1991, for example, were owned by alumni, not the current occupants, some of whom were arrested for drug violations. (Two houses were returned before the 1991 school year began.) Innocent parties can be deprived of a residence, vehicle, business, or cash until they are able to prove they were not involved in law-violating activity—a reversal of the normal presumption of innocence. To get back seized property the owner needs an attorney, and litigation can take several months, without any guarantee of success. For persons who make the "mistake" of traveling with large amounts of cash—particularly if they are black, Hispanic, or Asian—

the results can be more than an inconvenience. A study by the *Pittsburgh Press* revealed several cases in which the cash of innocent persons was seized at airports and kept for years without any criminal charges being filed (Schneider and Flaherty 1991). In an editorial, the *Chicago Tribune* argued for "bringing sanity to seizure laws": "unchecked use of seizure power has, perhaps not surprisingly, led to unwarranted losses for innocent people—an inordinate number of them minorities, who are more likely to be stopped as approximating law-enforcement 'profiles' of drug couriers" (September 1, 1991: Sec. 4:2).

> Overcoming the burden of proof can be hard even for the most upright citizens. How does a mother prove she didn't know her son was using the family car to transport drugs? How does a landlord prove he didn't know a tenant was a drug dealer? . . . The effort is also expensive, and even if you win, you're still out the money to pay your lawyer, which can be more than the value of the property you've recovered. (Chapman 1992: 23)

In 1966 the Supreme Court determined that property could be seized even when the owner was innocent of any wrongdoing. (*Bennis v. Michigan* [No. 94-8729]).

Forfeiture has also been criticized as a plea bargaining device for drug kingpins who negotiate lighter sentences by promising to reveal hidden assets and by not challenging court seizure of these assets. Law enforcement agencies eager for additional funds promote leniency for those at the top of the drug trafficking ladder while imposing heavy penalties on those without substantial hidden assets at the bottom of the ladder (Navarro 1996).

Grand Jury

The grand jury is comprised of fifteen to twenty-three citizens selected to hear evidence against accused persons and to determine if sufficient evidence exists to bring these persons to trial—to *indict* them. While not all states use grand juries to indict defendants, all states and the federal government empower the grand jury to conduct investigations of criminal activity, usually pertaining to official corruption. The Organized Crime Control Act of 1970 requires that a *special grand jury* be convened at least every eighteen months in federal districts of more than 1 million persons; it may also be convened at the request of a federal prosecutor, and its life may be extended to thirty-six months. The special grand jury is often used to investigate drug-law violations.

The broad investigative powers of the grand jury permit jurors to consider tips and rumors as well as more substantial evidence offered by the prosecutor. Even illegally secured evidence may be used as a basis for questioning witnesses. A grand jury can issue subpoenas for documents and persons. Federal (and most state) grand juries do not permit witnesses to be accompanied by counsel (although defendants are free to leave the grand jury room to consult with their attorneys). Testimony before a grand jury is given under oath and recorded, although the proceedings are secret until released by the court. Witnesses who invoke their constitutional right to remain silent can be granted immunity, which requires that they testify or suffer summary incarceration for the remainder of the life of the grand jury.

LAW ENFORCEMENT AGENCIES

As noted above, local efforts against drug trafficking are usually directed at mid-level dealers, although most frequently it is the low-level street dealer who is arrested and prosecuted at the local level. Federal drug-law enforcement seeks to disrupt illicit trafficking organizations and to reduce the availability of drugs for illicit use. This is accomplished in three ways (Comptroller General 1983: 3):

1. Arrest, prosecution, and incarceration of traffickers and the immobilization of trafficking organizations eliminate some capacities for supplying illicit drugs.

LEVELS OF DRUG-LAW ENFORCEMENT

There are five levels of drug-law enforcement (Kleiman 1985):

1. *Source Control:* This comprises actions aimed at limiting cultivation and production of poppies and opium, coca and cocaine, and marijuana. Both the State Department and the Drug Enforcement Administration have agents assigned to foreign countries.
2. *Interdiction:* The interception of drugs being smuggled into the United States is primarily the role of the Coast Guard and Customs Service.
3. *Domestic Distribution:* The disruption of high-level trafficking is usually the responsibility of the Drug Enforcement Administration and the Federal Bureau of Investigation.
4. *Wholesaling:* The focus on mid-level dealing is usually the role of state and local law enforcement.
5. *Street Sales:* Low-level dealing, often by addicts supporting their own drug habits, is usually left to local law enforcement.

FEDERAL DRUG LAW ENFORCEMENT

Department of Justice
Drug Enforcement Administration
Federal Bureau of Investigation
Immigration and Naturalization
  Service
Marshals Service

Department of the Treasury
Bureau of Alcohol, Tobacco and
  Firearms
Customs Service
Internal Revenue Service

Department of Defense
Air Force
Army
Navy

Department of Transportation
Coast Guard

Postal Service
Postal Inspection Service

2. Removal of drugs from the distribution networks directly reduces supply.
3. Seizure of equipment and operating resources leaves the drug networks at least inconvenienced, at best crippled.

On the federal level, because the United States does not have a national police force, unlike most other democratic nations, the job of carrying out these objectives falls on a confusing number of agencies in several departments—Transportation, Justice, Treasury, Defense—whose responsibilities for enforcing drug laws often overlap. This fragmentation is the result of the ad hoc creation of law enforcement agencies at the national level—each time a particular problem arose, an agency was established without significant attention to the problem of coordination.

Bureau of Alcohol, Tobacco and Firearms (ATF)

ATF dates back to 1791, when a tax was placed on alcoholic spirits. It eventually evolved into the Prohibition Bureau, which with the repeal of Prohibition became known as the Alcohol Tax Unit. In 1942 the bureau was given jurisdiction over federal firearms statutes and in 1970 over arson and explosives. ATF agents often encounter drug traffickers during their investigation of firearms and explosives violations. They have been particularly active in efforts against outlaw motorcycle clubs, who typically traffic in firearms and drugs.

The Coast Guard, part of Department of Transportation, is responsible for drug interdiction at sea. Coast Guard personnel do not have to establish probable cause before boarding a vessel at sea.

> Responsible in large part for U.S. drug interdiction efforts, the Coast Guard's strategy has been mainly directed toward intercepting mother ships as they transit the major passes of the Caribbean. To effect this "choke point" strategy, the Coast Guard conducts both continuous surface patrols and frequent surveillance flights over waters of interest, and boards and inspects vessels at sea. In the past, major Coast Guard resources have been concentrated in the "choke points" traditionally transversed by traffickers. Cutters now more frequently patrol the Bahamas, the eastern passes of the Caribbean, and the Gulf, Atlantic and Pacific coastal areas. (PCOC 1986: 313)

Customs Service

The Customs Service was established in 1789 to collect duties on various imports. Customs inspectors examine cargoes and baggage, articles worn or carried by individuals, and vessels, vehicles, and aircraft entering or leaving the United States. Special teams of inspectors and canine enforcement officers concentrate on cargo and conveyances considered high-risk. In 1981 the Customs Service established the Office of Intelligence to better manage information and target suspects; it participates in several multiagency programs designed to combat organized criminal activities in drug trafficking. The service works with commercial carriers, often signing cooperative agreements, to enhance the carriers' ability to prevent their equipment from being used to smug-

---

(ALMOST) UNDETECTABLE COCAINE

In 1991 federal agents raided several houses in south Florida, where they discovered a rather unique method of disguising cocaine for smuggling purposes. Agents found hundreds of pounds of harmless-looking black plastic molds into which cocaine had been blended, making detection using routine methods impossible. In fact, only the discovery of chemicals used in cocaine processing alerted agents to the blend. The drug is extracted from the plastic in much the same way that it is removed from the coca plant. The plastic is about one-quarter cocaine and can be made into any shape, allowing cocaine to be smuggled in the form of toys, glasses, camera lenses, or any plastic product (Rhor 1991).

With more than 2,000 pounds of seized cocaine as a backdrop, U.S. Customs Commissioner George Weise and Puerto Rico Governor Pedro Rossello announce the antidrug initiative Operation Gateway on April 16, 1996.

gle drugs. Special agents of the Customs Service are responsible for carrying out investigations into drug smuggling and currency violations as part of money-laundering schemes.

The Customs Service is not hampered by Fourth Amendment protections that typically restrain domestic law enforcement. Customs agents do not need probable cause or warrants to engage in search and seizure at ports of entry; certain degrees of suspicion will suffice. The typical Customs case is a a "cold border bust," the result of an entry checkpoint search. Because it is impractical if not impossible to thoroughly search most vehicles and persons entering the United States, Customs agents have developed certain techniques for minimizing inconvenience to legitimate travelers and shippers while better targeting those most likely to be involved in smuggling activity. Besides being alert to various cues that act as tipoffs, the officials at border-crossing points have computers containing information such as license plate numbers and names of known or suspected smugglers. Persons arrested by the Customs Service become targets for offers of plea bargains in efforts to gain their cooperation in follow-up enforcement efforts by the Drug Enforcement Administration; they are pressured to become informants in return for some form of leniency.

The Coast Guard and Customs Service are hampered by the need to patrol more than 12,000 miles of international boundary, which more than 420 billion tons of goods and 270 million persons cross each year. About half the

DEA ANTECEDENT AGENCIES

- 1973–   : Drug Enforcement Administration
- 1968–1973: Bureau of Narcotics and Dangerous Drugs
- 1930–1968: Federal Bureau of Narcotics
- 1927–1930: Bureau of Prohibition
- 1915–1927: Bureau of Internal Revenue

drugs entering the United States come through commercial ports, where they are secreted in tightly sealed steel containers twenty or forty feet long, twelve feet high, and eight feet wide, millions of which enter the country every year. Customs officials can inspect only a small number (about 10 percent) of these containers, and without advance information, the drugs typically pass right through the ports. Drugs that are intercepted are easily replaced (Treaster 1990d).

Drug Enforcement Administration (DEA)

The DEA evolved out of several predecessor agencies, particularly the Federal Bureau of Narcotics (see chapter 2). It is a single-mission agency responsible for enforcing federal statutes dealing with controlled substances by investigating alleged or suspected major drug traffickers. The DEA is also responsible for regulating the legal trade in such controlled substances as morphine, methadone, and barbiturates. Diversion agents conduct accountability investigations of drug wholesalers, suppliers, and manufacturers. They inspect the records and facilities of major drug manufacturers and distributors, and special agents investigate instances in which drugs have been illegally diverted from legitimate sources. DEA special agents are also stationed in sixty-five countries (Thornburgh 1989), where their mission is to gain cooperation in international efforts against drug trafficking and to help train foreign enforcement officials. In 1990 the DEA deployed about thirty agents to operate from a Vietnam-style fire base at Santa Lucia, in Peru's Upper Huallaga Valley, in an effort to help police destroy clandestine cocaine-processing laboratories.

The basic approach to DEA drug-law enforcement is the *buy and bust,* or the *controlled buy.* Typically, a drug agent is introduced to a seller by an informant. The agent arranges to buy a relatively small amount of drugs and then attempts to move further up the organizational ladder by increasing the amount purchased. "The agent prefers to defer an arrest until he can seize a large amount of drugs or can implicate higher-ups in the distribution system or both" (Wilson 1978: 43). When arrests are made, DEA agents attempt to "flip" the suspect, convince him or her to become an informant, particularly if the person has knowledge of the entire operation, so that a conspiracy case can be effected. As discussed above, the use of informants is problematic.

Federal Bureau of Investigation (FBI)

The FBI is as close to a federal police force as exists in the United States. Its broad investigative mandate was expanded in 1982, when the FBI was given concurrent jurisdiction with the DEA for drug-law enforcement and investigation. In addition, the administrator of the DEA is now required to report to the director of the FBI, who has overall responsibility for supervising drug-law enforcement efforts and policies. Despite its increased mandate, the primary role of the FBI is to deal with espionage—it is the only law enforcement agency having jurisdiction over this activity. The dramatic changes in what was known as the Eastern (Communist) bloc have led to the reassignment of hundreds of FBI agents from counterespionage to more conventional criminal activity, such as drug trafficking.

Immigration and Naturalization Service (INS)

The primary role of the INS is to prevent illegal entry into the United States and to apprehend those who have entered illegally. Border Patrol officers check suspicious persons within 100 miles of border areas likely to be used as illegal crossing points, and they often arrest persons transporting drugs.

Internal Revenue Service (IRS)

The mission of the IRS is to encourage and achieve the highest possible degree of voluntary compliance with tax laws and regulations. When such compliance is not forthcoming or not feasible, as in the case of drug traffickers, the Criminal Investigation Division receives the case. Agents examine bank records, canceled checks, brokerage accounts, property transactions, and purchases, compiling a financial biography of the subject's lifestyle in order to prove that proper taxes have not been paid. As a result of the excesses revealed in the wake of the Watergate scandal, Congress enacted the Tax Reform Act of

"MULE SKINNING"

DEA special agents, working with state and local police agencies, monitor airports at key junctions for drugs entering the United States. In addition to such primary ports of entry as South Florida, Los Angeles, and New York City, they also cover such secondary locations as Atlanta and Chicago, where travelers frequently change planes. Using a *drug courier profile* developed over the past fifteen years, the agents look for specific clues—primary or secondary characteristics—that have been proven to characterize persons ("mules") most likely to be carrying wholesale quantities of illegal substances.

Seven primary characteristics:

1. Arrival from or departure to an identified foreign source country (such as Colombia) or domestic source city (such as Miami).
2. Carrying little or no luggage or empty suitcases.
3. Unusual travel patterns—for example, short turnaround times for lengthy airplane trips.
4. Use of an alias.
5. Possession of large amounts of currency.
6. Purchasing airline tickets using small bills.
7. Unusual nervousness.

Four secondary characteristics:

1. Exclusive use of public transportation, particularly cabs, to and from the airport.
2. Making phone calls immediately after deplaning.
3. Providing a phony telephone number when purchasing airline tickets.
4. Excessive travel to a source country or distribution city or cities.

While these primary and secondary characteristics may be consistent with lawful behavior, they also indicate a person who should be questioned. Passengers meeting enough profile characteristics may be approached and questioned—asked for identification and travel documentation. Agents are particularly interested in signs of excessive nervousness. If such signs are observed, agents will ask the passenger to consent to a drug search, which can include a cavity search. The rare refusal may result in detention and the securing of a drug-sniffing dog and/or a search warrant. At times, agents discover large amounts of cash that cannot be accounted for. This is seized until its "lawful" owner appears to claim it, a highly unlikely event. If a courier is arrested, efforts are made to "flip" the mule in order to implicate the person picking up the drugs.

Although its use is controversial, the "profile" permits drug agents to act in the absence of specific information (the sort usually provided by criminal informants). The use of the profile and the seizure of any evidence discovered have been upheld by the courts as legitimate law enforcement tools, the Fourth Amendment notwithstanding. In 1989 the Supreme Court, in a 7–2 decision, ruled that

(continued)

"MULE SKINNING" *(con't.)*

the profile provides a "reasonable basis" to suspect that a person is transporting drugs. The case involved Andrew Sokolow, who in July 1984 flew from Honolulu to Miami and returned to Hawaii forty-eight hours later. Sokolow, dressed in a black jumpsuit and gold jewelry, purchased two airline tickets in Miami for $2,100 in cash taken from a roll of twenty-dollar bills containing about twice that amount. He was traveling under a name that did not match his telephone listing. Sokolow did not check any luggage and appeared very nervous. After stopping him in Honolulu, drug agents used a drug-sniffing dog, which led them to 1,063 grams of cocaine in Sokolow's carry-on luggage. Writing for the Court, Chief Justice William H. Rehnquist stated that "while a trip from Honolulu to Miami, standing alone, is not a cause for any sort of suspicion, here there was more: surely few residents of Honolulu travel from that city for 20 hours to spend 48 hours in Miami during the month of July." The Court, however, did not base its decision on the existence or use of the DEA drug profile; according to the decision, agents must justify their decision to stop a suspect on the basis of their own observations and experience.

While the profile has proven useful in interdiction efforts, it is not without controversy because its use appears to relate to ethnicity and race; the darker a person's skin, the more likely it is that he or she will be targeted. A stop can involve several hours of detention and accompanying humiliation. Nevertheless, the practice has been extended to highways, where vehicles and their occupants, if they fit certain profiles, are subjected to a stop and interrogation.

Sources: Crank and Rehm (1992); Hedgepath (1989); Elsasser (1989); Greenhouse (1989); Belkin (1990).

1976, which reduced the law enforcement role of the IRS and made it difficult for law enforcement agencies (other than the IRS) to gain access to income tax returns. Amendments in 1982 reduced the requirements and permit the IRS to better cooperate with the efforts of other federal law enforcement agencies investigating drug traffickers.

Marshals Service

The Marshals Service is the oldest federal law enforcement agency, dating back to 1789. During the period of westward expansion, the U.S. marshal played a significant role in the "Wild West." Today marshals provide security for federal court facilities, transport federal prisoners, serve civil writs issued by federal courts, and investigate and apprehend certain federal fugitives. Marshals are responsible for seizing, managing, and disposing of forfeited properties and assets from major drug cases. The Marshals Service's most important task relative to drug trafficking is its responsibility for administering the Witness Protection Program.

Witness Protection Program

Because of the potentially undesirable consequences for a witness who testifies in a drug-trafficking case, efforts have been made to protect such witnesses from retribution. The Witness Protection Program was authorized by the Organized Crime Control Act of 1970:

> The Attorney General of the United States is authorized to rent, purchase, modify, or remodel protected housing facilities and to otherwise offer to provide for the health, safety, and welfare of witnesses and persons intended to be called as Government witnesses, and the families of witnesses and persons intended to be called as Government witnesses in legal proceedings instituted against any person alleged to have participated in an organized criminal activity whenever in his judgment testimony from, or a willingness to testify by, such a witness would place his life or person, or the life or person of a member of his family or household, in jeopardy. Any person availing himself of such an offer by the Attorney General to use such facilities may continue to use such facilities for as long as the Attorney General determines the jeopardy to his life or person continues.

The program was given over to the Marshals Service to administer. There was logic behind this arrangement (Permanent Subcommittee on Investigations 1981b: 54):

> Law enforcement officers wanted the protecting and relocating agency to be in the criminal justice system but to be as far removed as possible from both investigating agents and prosecution. That way the Government could more readily counter the charge that cooperating witnesses were being paid or otherwise unjustifiably compensated in return for their testimony.

The Military

The most controversial federal agency involved in drug-law enforcement is the Department of Defense (DOD). In 1878 congressional Democrats enacted the Posse Comitatus Act to stop Republican presidents from using the army to further Reconstruction in the states of the erstwhile Confederacy. The act provides that

> whoever, except in cases and under circumstances expressly authorized by the Constitution or Act of Congress, willfully uses any part of the Army or Air Force as a posse comitatus or otherwise to execute the laws shall be fined not more than $10,000 or imprisoned not more than two years or both (18 USCA sec. 1385 (1984).

DEPARTMENT OF DEFENSE

DOD has extraordinary technical capabilities developed from its long experience in monitoring the skies and the waters for incoming Soviet or other hostile military aircraft, warships, and missiles. DOD adds the ability to alert law enforcement agencies to the presence of suspected drug smugglers to an existing detection system along the southern U.S. border and in the Caribbean Basin (Mabry 1995).

In 1956 Congress added the air force to the Posse Comitatus Act, while the navy and marines promulgated administrative restrictions.

Until 1981 DOD limited its involvement to lending equipment and training civilian enforcement personnel in the use of military equipment. In that year, as part of a new "War on Drugs," Congress amended the Posse Comitatus Act, authorizing a greater level of military involvement in civilian drug enforcement, particularly the tracking of suspect ships and planes and the use of military pilots and naval ships to transport civilian enforcement personnel. As a result of this legislation, DOD provided surveillance and support services, using aircraft to search for smugglers and navy ships to tow or escort vessels seized by the Coast Guard to the nearest U.S. port. The legislation authorized the military services to share information collected during routine military operations with law enforcement officials and to make facilities and equipment available to law enforcement officials.

Further amendments to the 1981 legislation led to the use of military equipment and personnel in interdiction efforts against cocaine laboratories in Bolivia. These amendments permit the use of such personnel and equipment if the Secretary of State or the Secretary of Defense and the Attorney General jointly determine that an emergency exists in that the scope of specific criminal activity poses a serious threat to the interests of the United States. Combined operations involving U.S. Army Special Forces, DEA agents, U.S. Border Patrol officers, and Bolivian police and military officers have been successful in destroying hundreds of coca-paste laboratories in the coca-growing Champare region.

The 1981 statute and subsequent amendments maintain the prohibition against the involvement of U.S. military personnel in arrest and seizure activities. This prohibition was based on the fear that further DOD involvement in drug-law enforcement could:

1. compromise U.S. security by exposing military personnel to the potentially corrupting environment of drug trafficking (Sciolino and Engelberg 1988);
2. impair the strategic role of the military; and
3. present a threat to civil liberties.

CORRUPTING THE NAVY

In 1996, twenty-one American sailors were arrested in Italy by the Naval Criminal Investigation Service, whose agents were able to infiltrate a Nigerian drug ring that paid the defendants to carry bags of cocaine and heroin across European borders. A lieutenant commander was the highest ranking member of the group ("Navy Holds 21 Sailors in Italy Smuggling Case" 1996).

Despite this fear, in 1988 legislation was overwhelmingly approved to dramatically expand the role of the military and allow the arrest of civilians under certain circumstances.

The U.S. Department of State uses *former* military pilots to fly helicopter gunships, transport planes, and cropdusters used by U.S. and foreign drug agents in countries where U.S. military operations are barred. Early in 1990, hundreds of National Guardsmen, who as a *state* militia are not governed by the Posse Comitatus Act, were deployed to search for drugs along the border with Mexico and at ports of entry. Guardsmen routinely aid in California antidrug efforts. U.S. military officials have traditionally opposed the involvement of the armed forces in law enforcement. In 1989 and early 1990 their position was tempered by the reality of military budget cutbacks. The use of the military in the war on drugs justifies a level of funding that might otherwise be difficult to defend before Congress and the public. Nevertheless, the Pentagon continues to resist further military involvement in domestic law enforcement ("Military Doesn't Seek Big Role in Drug War, Pentagon Says" 1995).

Postal Inspection Service

The Postal Inspection Service, among its several responsibilities, investigates the use of the mails to transport drugs.

Strike/Task Forces

In order to overcome the inefficient competitive efforts and "turf-protecting" proclivities of enforcement agencies, since 1966 the federal government has utilized task forces in response to organized crime. That year the Department of Justice established the "Buffalo Project" in upstate New York, bringing together personnel from a number of federal enforcement agencies. The success of the project led to the establishment of a strike force in every city known to have organized crime (Mafia) groups. In his 1982 "War on Drugs" speech, President Ronald Reagan announced the creation of regional Organized Crime Drug Enforcement Task Forces (OCDETF), and by the end of 1983, twelve were located in such core cities as New York, Los Angeles, and Detroit. In 1984 a thirteenth, the Florida/Caribbean, was added. Law enforcement pressure in south Florida has led to an increase in drug smuggling across the Rio Grande in Presidio, Texas, former outlaw badlands that include Big Bend National Park. This has placed additional responsibilities on local sheriffs and U.S. Park Rangers (Suro 1992).

The Task Force Program relies largely on the Continuing Criminal Enterprise statutory provision and the Racketeer Influenced and Corrupt Organizations (RICO) statutes. The conviction rate in cases reaching disposition is

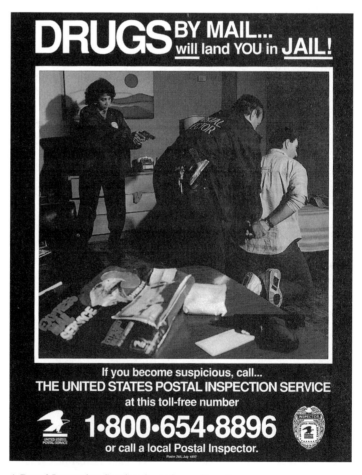

A Postal Inspection Service drugs-by-mail poster.

SKY HIGH

On 11 November 1989, officials seized sixty-six pounds of cocaine that had been flown into Doer Air Force Base, Delaware, from Panama. Officials arrested an army warrant officer and his brother, who were to pick up the drugs from the air force C-5 cargo plane.

---

approximately 95 percent. State and local officers participate in nearly one half of the Task Force investigations. (PCOC 1986: 319)

Local enforcement officers may be sworn in as special U.S. marshals, which allows them to enforce federal statutes and to cross jurisdictional boundaries typically inhibiting local enforcement agencies. Guidelines for the Organized Crime Drug Enforcement Task Force (1985) specify that a case is appropriate for Task Force adoption if it appears to:

- involve major drug trafficking figures;
- require the resources and expertise of another agency because of possible violations other than those involving narcotics;
- have serious investigative ramifications extending to other geographical jurisdictions; and/or
- require the assistance of an Assistant U.S. Attorney during the early stages of an investigation.

INTERPOL

The International Police Organization, known by its radio designation INTERPOL, assists law enforcement agencies with investigative activities that transcend international boundaries. Until 1968 "INTERPOL meant very little to the United States law enforcement community and was virtually unknown" (Fooner 1985: 19). In that year, Iran announced that it was going to end its ban on opium production; at the same time there appeared to be an epidemic of drug use in the United States. A U.S. (INTERPOL) National Central Bureau (NCB) was quickly activated in Washington.

There are about 150 INTERPOL members; a country becomes a member by merely announcing its intention to join. In each member country there is an NCB that acts as a point of contact and coordination with the General Secretariat in Lyons, France. INTERPOL has a headquarters staff of around 250, about 60 of whom are law enforcement officers from about 42 different countries. There is a large communications facility that links 72 member countries into a radio network; other nations use Telex or cable facilities. INTER-

POL is under the day-to-day direction of a secretary general; it is a coordinating body and has no investigators or law enforcement agents of its own.

The U.S. NCB receives about twelve thousand requests for assistance from federal, state, and local law enforcement agencies each year. These are checked and coded by technical staff and entered into the INTERPOL Case Tracking System (ICTS), a computer-controlled index of persons, organizations, and other crime information items. The ICTS conducts automatic searches of new entries, retrieving those that correlate with international crime. The requests are forwarded to senior staff members who serve as INTERPOL case investigators. These are usually veteran agents from a federal agency whose experience includes work with foreign police forces. Each investigator is on loan from his or her principal agency.

Requests for investigative assistance include a whole range of criminal activity—murder, drug violations, illicit firearms traffic—and often involve locating fugitives for arrest and extradition. The bureau also receives investigative requests for criminal histories, license checks, and other ID verifications (Fooner 1985). The Financial and Economic Crime Unit at INTERPOL headquarters facilitates the exchange of information about offshore banking and money-laundering schemes. Monitoring this type of activity can sometimes lead to identifying suspects involved in drug trafficking who had previously escaped detection.

ISSUES IN DRUG-LAW ENFORCEMENT

Besides those discussed at the beginning of this chapter, several perplexing issues complicate drug-law enforcement. The first involves measuring success: How can we determine if drug-law enforcement in general, or specific activities in particular, are successful? What criteria can provide a standard for measuring success? The number of persons arrested, convicted, imprisoned? The amount of drugs seized? The level of purity or price of the product sold on the streets? The number of persons admitted to hospital emergency rooms for drug overdoses? The number of persons seeking admission to drug treatment programs? In practice, we use all of these, with often confusing results. For example, *increased* arrests and drug seizures have often been accompanied by *declining* prices and greater levels of purity. A 1983 report by the Comptroller General points out that while enhanced federal resources increased the amount of illegal drugs seized, purity at the retail level increased while prices fell. The Comptroller General also revealed that some drug seizures are counted several times by different agencies eager to claim credit and increase their "stats." Sometimes there is triple-counting: The Coast Guard typically turns its interdicted drugs over to Customs, while the seizure may be the result of intelligence information developed by DEA, with all three agencies including the amount in their totals.

Successful law enforcement efforts, at least in theory, should reduce the available supply of drugs while driving up the price and reducing purity. When the level of purity dips below some hypothetical level but the price remains high, the abuser will no longer find it worth his or her while to make a purchase. Either the abuser will switch to a more readily available chemical—perhaps alcohol—or abandon drug use completely. In fact, successful law enforcement efforts may cause a switch from a less dangerous substance—for example, marijuana—to a more dangerous substance, such as heroin, a situation that apparently occurred when in 1969 Operation Intercept at the Mexican border effectively choked off supplies of marijuana. "There was an upsurge in heroin use among urban, white, middle-class high school students shortly after Operation Intercept" (Zinberg and Robertson 1972: 210). More recent successful campaigns against marijuana may be causing an increase in the use of alcohol, particularly among adolescents. Increases in law enforcement do not necessarily translate into reductions in supply: A widely heralded (by politicians) 1986 $1.7 billion federal antidrug law resulted in an increase in drug seizures and arrests with no discernible impact on supply (Johnson 1987).

The structure of the drug market, as noted in chapter 6, makes it the last refuge of laissez-faire capitalism: How does law enforcement affect the price of illegal drugs? Mark Kleiman (1985: 69) states that the key to analyzing this question "is the response of drug purchasers to increasing drug prices." If there is a reduction in supply and a corresponding increase in price, will the amount of drug consumption remain unchanged? Is demand relatively inelastic to price? If demand is relatively elastic, consumption will decrease as price goes up. This will cause a decrease in the profits of drug traffickers. If, however, demand is inelastic, drug-law enforcement may actually increase the profits of traffickers—those who elude arrest and prosecution will reap higher prices. With respect to heroin, Kleiman notes, consumption is likely to decrease in the long run as addicts, unable to keep up with the increase in price, enter drug treatment or find alternative drugs. The issue with respect to cocaine is more difficult. Cocaine has typically been relatively expensive, although the introduction of crack has altered the market. Nevertheless, Kleiman argues, an increase in price as a result of law enforcement efforts is likely to increase the profits of cocaine traffickers—it is a market relatively impervious to price.

At the domestic distribution level, successful law enforcement efforts whittle down the number of persons involved in drug trafficking. This may leave a void at certain levels of distribution that, in a seller's market, will simply attract new entrepreneurs. Furthermore, the better-organized groups resist and survive law enforcement efforts. Thus, the level of law enforcement vigor and ability determines whether or not certain groups will come to dominate the drug trade and bring a concomitant increase in profits by virtue of oligopolistic (scarcity of sellers) market circumstances. On the other hand, reduced law enforcement allows more groups to remain in business, with a corresponding reduction in profits resulting from a more competitive market. Under such conditions, organizations equipped with resources for violence may be tempted to use force to reduce competition.

Street-Level Law Enforcement

Efficient street-level enforcement, argues Mark Moore (1977), is a strategy worth pursuing, even if there is *displacement*—sellers moving to new locations and becoming more cautious. Jonathan Caulkins (1992) agrees that even when there is complete displacement, benefits to society accrue. Street-level enforcement makes sellers more cautious and thus more difficult to find. The buyer is forced to spend more time searching for a connection and less time searching for money (criminal opportunity) or actually using drugs. Under such conditions, many may be motivated to seek treatment, although there is often a shortage of available treatment programs. New users in particular will have difficulty "scoring." If this situation becomes widespread, profits from drug wholesaling will drop as if there were a drop in consumer demand.

In Lynn, Massachusetts, a drug task force made up of six state police officers and a city detective was deployed to decrease the flagrant selling of heroin in the city's High Rock area. Open drug dealing poses special threats.

> Some neighborhood residents, particularly children, may become users; and . . . the behavior of buyers and sellers will be disruptive or worse. In poor neighborhoods, the opportunity for quick money offered by the illicit market may compete with entry-level licit jobs and divert labor-market entrants from legitimate careers. When the drug sold is heroin, residents are likely to be bothered by users "nodding" in doorways and heroin-using prostitutes soliciting. (Kleiman 1988: 10)

The goal was achieved, and drugs were harder to purchase in the area. This led to an increase in the number of persons seeking treatment for drug abuse. A significant reduction in street crime was also reported for the area (Kleiman 1988). The drying up of immediate sources of heroin can potentially reduce experimentation, although long-term users ("junkies") will merely be inconvenienced. The time and energy required to establish new sources, however, might otherwise be spent on drug use and criminality. If treatment is available, the crackdown may serve as an incentive for entering a treatment program.

In New York City, a 1984 street-level enforcement effort known as Operation Pressure Point (OPP) was designed to improve the quality of life and reduce drug-related crime in an area of the city's Lower East Side. Drug trafficking in the area had become so open and blatant that the neighborhood took on the quality of an oriental bazaar, and residents and their political representatives demanded police action. OPP instituted aggressive patrolling by uniformed officers, cleared abandoned buildings and parks of drug users, and sent out detectives to make "buy-and-bust" arrests. The risk of arrest increased dramatically for both buyers and sellers, with the result that most abandoned the area and others resorted to low-profile trafficking. OPP followed up these activities with programs designed to strengthen the community and increase cooperation with and support for the police. The program achieved its goals, and

STREET-LEVEL DRUG ENFORCEMENT

Focused, saturation street enforcement will clean up an area, but it is costly and inefficient. It robs other areas of their fair share of scarce resources and it does not eliminate the intractable problem of drug dealing, but merely displaces it. It also focuses, inefficiently, on the lowest of the criminal chain and is sure to lead to abuses and repression, with sweeps and roundups.

Once installed, such operations are politically difficult to remove. By producing large numbers of arrests they create stresses on a frequently overloaded criminal justice system which then finds it more difficult to discriminate between the menaces that ought to be incapacitated and the casual dealer or seller; usually they all go free. (Bouza 1990: 47. Bouza is a former chief of police in Minneapolis.)

neighborhood residents reported being very satisfied. Similar operations in other parts of New York City, however, have not been as successful (Zimmer 1990).

Street-level enforcement is expensive and, if it is to be more than briefly effective, must be combined with sufficient prison space to accommodate the increase in population. In an attempt to stem the 1985 crack epidemic in New York City, police initiated a street-level crackdown with impressive results: Crack arrests and jailings reached record levels; felony drug arrests went up 21 percent the first year and 70 percent the next. Total jail sentences for drug felonies increased by 60 percent in 1987. Nevertheless, the street price of crack has dropped steadily since 1985. And in response to the stepped-up police activity, crack dealers began recruiting thousands of young addicts to make street sales; they are overwhelming a number of city neighborhoods as well as the city's overextended police force. "So intractable is the problem," say police officials, "that they [the police] have begun to focus instead on keeping some neighborhoods from descending into outlaw rule by drug dealers or gangs" (Wines 1988: 12). Placing unusually large resources in one area also raises the possibility that the problem will be displaced into areas where law enforcement efforts are less concentrated. Furthermore, the reduction of crime in Lynn, Massachusetts, discussed earlier, was short-lived, and a similar crackdown in Lawrence, Massachusetts, actually resulted in an increase in crime, particularly burglary and robbery (Barnett 1988). Despite the problems, increasing arrests for drug violations has become a national strategy, and it has led to severe prison overcrowding.

Street-level enforcement efforts bring with them the specter of corruption and related abuses: "Bribery, perjured testimony, faked evidence and abused rights in the past have accompanied street-level narcotics enforcement. Indeed, it was partly to avoid such abuses that many police departments began concentrating on higher-level traffickers and restricted drug efforts to special

CRACK PENALTIES AND RACE

Cocaine in the form of crack is most likely to be used and sold by African Americans, while powdered cocaine is often used and sold by whites. However, a cocaine dealer would have to sell $75,000 worth of the drug in powdered form to get the same mandatory five-year federal sentence that a crack dealer would receive for selling $750 worth. And "crack is the only drug that carries a mandatory prison term for possession, whether or not the intent is to distribute" (Jones 1995: 9).

units" (Moore and Kleiman 1989: 8). These special units have brought problems of their own; New York provides an example. In 1971, in order to centralize drugs, vice, and organized-crime enforcement and to prevent corruption through stricter supervision, the city established the Organized Crime Bureau. Early in 1992, the police department's chief of inspectional services submitted a confidential report citing recent cases in which the bureau's narcotic officers were accused of lying to strengthen cases and to obtain search warrants—there were no accusations of corruption. The report noted: "Of all units in the department, the greatest integrity hazards and vulnerability exist in narcotics" (Raab 1992).

CONCLUSION

Steven Wisotsky (1987) argues that, at least in theory, combatting cocaine abuse should be significantly easier than battling heroin abuse. There are only two main sources of cocaine—Peru and Bolivia—and the major traffickers operate out of Colombia with major supply lines more restrictive than those for heroin (which may come from several continents). As noted in chapter 3, however, there are analogs for many popular drugs of abuse. Successful interdiction may reduce the amount of heroin and cocaine entering the United States, but if demand remains unchanged, underground chemists will be inspired to greater creativity. As noted in chapter 3, experienced cocaine users cannot tell the difference between cocaine and synthetic substances that mimic cocaine; heroin addicts often prefer the synthetic opiate fentanyl to the greatly diluted heroin typically available on the streets.

Norman Zinberg and John Robertson (1972) argue that the substantial investment in drug-law enforcement not only increases criminality—drug abusers committing crimes to support habits—but also diverts resources that could be better utilized to deal with serious criminality. Not only are the police occupied with drug-law enforcement, but so are prosecutors and judges. There is a heavy burden on our jails and prisons and on our probation and parole systems. Our drug enforcement agents are exposed to great danger, both from a most violent class of criminals and from being around the drugs themselves.

Our "war" on drugs is really a fight against socioeconomic dynamics reputed to be unconquerable: the profit motive and the law of supply and demand. In the next chapter, we will examine the policy options available for responding to drug abuse.

REVIEW QUESTIONS

1. In terms of reducing drug use, how do "cost" and "availability" explain the purpose of drug-law enforcement?
2. What is the relationship between drug-law enforcement and the two models of criminal justice—crime control and due process?
3. How do constitutional and jurisdictional limitations constrain drug-law enforcement?
4. How does the exclusionary rule restrain drug-law enforcement agents?
5. Why is the supervision of law enforcement agents particularly difficult in drug-law enforcement?
6. What are the two main purposes of the 1988 (international) Convention Against Illicit Traffic in Narcotic Drugs and Psychotropic Substances?
7. Why is corruption more of a problem in drug-law enforcement than in other areas of law enforcement?
8. What problems arise in using criminal informants in drug-law enforcement?
9. What are the offenses for which persons involved in drug trafficking may be prosecuted?
10. What is the difference between *actual* and *constructive* possession of dangerous drugs?
11. What two legal elements are necessary to support a charge of conspiracy?
12. What is the advantage of using conspiracy statutes when dealing with drug-trafficking organizations?
13. What is the difference between criminal and civil forfeiture?
14. Why is civil forfeiture controversial?
15. What powers of a grand jury make it a useful tool in drug investigations?
16. Why is federal drug-law enforcement so fragmented in the United States?
17. Why is the use of the military in drug-law enforcement so controversial in the United States?
18. What are some of the latent unintended negative consequences of successful drug-law enforcement?

19. What are the advantages and disadvantages of concentrating drug-law enforcement efforts at the street level?
20. What are the responsibilities of each of these federal agencies with respect to drug-law enforcement?
    (a) Coast Guard
    (b) Customs Service
    (c) Drug Enforcement Administration
    (d) Federal Bureau of Investigation
    (e) Immigration and Naturalization Service
    (f) Internal Revenue Service
    (g) Military
21. What is a "controlled buy"?
22. What is the strike/task force concept, and what is its purpose?
23. Why is it difficult to measure success in drug-law enforcement?
24. How can drug-law enforcement actually increase the profits of some traffickers?

8

DRUG ABUSE: POLICY AND ALTERNATIVES

American drug policy has been predicated on one fundamental notion: that the societal objective is to eliminate "nonmedical" drug use. Inquiry has rarely been addressed to whether this goal is desirable or possible.—National Commission on Marijuana and Drug Abuse (1973: 20)

The discourse of anti-drug policy, as crystallized in certain key sloganised positions—such as "Just Say No" (personal choice) and "Stopping Supply at Source" (change the Third World, not our society)—simply does not articulate a reasonable range of policy options.—Nicholas Dorn and Nigel South (1988: 148)

This chapter examines the feasibility of altering our current approach to drugs of abuse. But before examining the possibility of changing our current policy, we need to return to the first chapter and recall some of the incongruities. Of the most widely used psychoactive drugs, heroin and cocaine (except for limited topical use) are banned; barbiturates, tranquilizers, and amphetamines are restricted; while alcohol, caffeine, and nicotine products are freely available. These inconsistencies make any response to the problem of substance abuse very difficult. How do you tell the progeny of cigarette-smoking, coffee- and alcohol-drinking, sedative-using parents that drugs should not be used for recreational purposes? Therefore:

> A major step toward developing sounder policy with respect to drugs would be to use that label for alcohol and nicotine (as the scientific literature already does), and to make an augmented Office of Drug Control Policy responsible for coordinating federal policy toward alcohol and nicotine as part of the overall national drug control strategy. (Reuter and Caulkins 1995: 1061)

To what extent does knowledge actually affect drug policy? While nicotine and alcohol are clearly dangerous psychoactive chemicals—*drugs*—semantic fiction portrays them otherwise: Statutory vocabulary and social folklore have established the fiction that alcohol and nicotine are not really drugs at all (National Commission on Marijuana and Drug Abuse 1973). Furthermore (the commission points out), to do otherwise would be inconsistent with our stated policy goal of eliminating drug abuse—an admission that we can never eliminate the drug-use problem. Joseph Gusfield (1975: 13) suggests that we distinguish between *scientific* knowledge and *political* knowledge:

> Scientific knowledge in the field of drug use is the body of facts and theories related to the uses of drugs. Political knowledge concerns public attitudes and organization toward drug use, including scientific knowledge. . . . Scientific knowledge can be only one of a number of factors which bear upon the symbolic and instrumental character of official public opinion.

Norman Zinberg (1984: 200) states that in the field of drug use, the truth will not necessarily set one free. In fact, he notes, the scientific truth is that not all psychoactive drug use is misuse; but because this contravenes formal social policy, those who present this message run the risk that "their work will be interpreted as condoning use."

Our response to easily abused substances is not based on the degree of danger inherent in their use. Indeed, measured on any dimension, alcohol is a more serious drug of abuse than marijuana, though this is not reflected in our legal system. Furthermore, many dangerous substances—amphetamines, barbiturates, and a variety of sedatives—were actively promoted for use in dealing with anxiety, stress, obesity, or insomnia. Famous abusers of these substances, such as Marilyn Monroe and Elvis Presley, are representative of a large abusing population not subjected to arrest and imprisonment. The pushers of these substances—the drug companies and their willing partners in the medical profession—are not arrested or prosecuted.

That some drugs are outlawed while others are legally and widely available is better understood in terms other than those of science or medicine—in terms of the tobacco industry, the alcoholic-beverage industry, the drug-manufacturing industry, and the media. (In fact, the public's knowledge of and response to the "drug problem" is mediated through newspapers and television). As Gusfield (1975: 5) notes, "The attention of public media to a problem gives it status as an issue. The attention of government and other public agents to a problem accentuates, in turn, its position on the public agenda." Leon Hunt (1977) points out that frightening news stories create pressure for more vigorous drug enforcement, which increases drug-fighting budgets, which yield more arrests. The resulting statistics are then viewed as proof of a growing drug problem. He concludes that public fear may not only be exaggerated but may also feed upon itself through media sensationalism.

The "volume of attention generated when the national press converges on a story, like drugs, virtually demands a political response. In their haste, these [politicians'] reactions may not always be carefully considered" (Merriam 1989: 31). "Convergence" occurs when media sources discover an issue and respond to each other "in a cycle of peaking coverage, before largely dismissing the issues" (Reese and Danielian 1989: 30n). In 1989 President George Bush made a major television address during which he "declared war" on drugs. For the next week, network news averaged four stories each evening on drugs, and an opinion poll indicated that 64 percent of the public viewed drugs as America's most important problem. A year later, that figure had fallen to 10 percent as new problems received presidential attention (Oreskes 1990).

Part of the difficulty in considering policy alternatives is a lack of definitive data on the scope of the drug problem.

ESTIMATES OF THE DRUG PROBLEM

Government efforts against drugs of abuse, with the exception of Prohibition (1920–33), have focused on those substances that are (except under medical auspices) illegal to possess. Success in the struggle against drug abuse is difficult if not impossible to measure. In the United States we cannot say with any degree of accuracy how many persons are abusing drugs or are addicted to any substance (including alcohol). This is a significant handicap in attempting to determine the effectiveness of any approach to drug abuse, whether it stresses law enforcement or seeks to reduce demand by treating abusers. This deficiency does provide the basis for important political posturing. For example, in his 1980 State of the Union message, President Jimmy Carter told Congress:

HALF FULL, HALF EMPTY

"Although considerable progress has been made in reducing the number of casual drug users, illicit drug use among adolescents is increasing." (Office of National Drug Control Policy 1995:5)

> At the beginning of my administration there were over a half million heroin addicts in the United States. Our continued emphasis on reducing the supply of heroin, as well as providing for the treatment and rehabilitation of its victims, has reduced the heroin population to 380,000.

Three years earlier, President Richard Nixon had proclaimed: "We have turned the corner on drug addiction in the United States" (both quoted in Trebach 1982). The Nixon administration referred to its achievements as *decreasing the rate of increase*, a measure that "allows bureaucrats and line programs (addiction treatment and drug-law enforcement deliverers) to claim victory in their fight against crime or addiction without threatening the continued funding of their organizations" (Bellis 1981: 79).

Information on the drug problem in the United States is actually derived from six indicators. Each indicator provides a different perspective on the problem, and they complement one another. Although the indicators have recognized limitations and deficiencies that affect the quality of information and make specific estimates uncertain, the agencies that prepare them believe the data can reliably portray general trends.

NNICC Narcotics Intelligence Estimates

The National Narcotics Intelligence Consumers Committee (NNICC) is a federal interagency mechanism for coordinating drug intelligence collection requirements and producing joint intelligence estimates. NNICC issues periodic reports on the worldwide illicit drug situation. The report contains estimates of illegal drug production and availability and discusses four major drug categories: marijuana, cocaine, opiates, and synthetic drugs. The report also contains information on drug-trafficking routes and methods and on the flow of drug-related money.

Estimates of illegal drug quantities are very difficult to make because little reliable data exist. NNICC obtains drug-production data for individual countries from host country records, local contacts, informants, and sophisticated intelligence-gathering techniques. It derives drug availability and consumption estimates from sample surveys, drug seizures, drug price and purity data, drug-related hospital emergencies, and other data.

311

Chapter Eight:
Drug Abuse:
Policy and
Alternatives

National Household Survey of Drug Abuse

The National Household Survey of Drug Abuse (NHSDA) is funded by the National Institute of Drug Abuse (NIDA). Between 1972 and 1990 it conducted a survey every two or three years and has conducted an annual survey since 1990. The survey provides data on incidence, prevalence, and trends of drug use for persons age twelve and older living in households. Results are based on about 9,000 interviews with persons randomly selected from the household population, who record their responses on self-administered answer sheets. In 1991 the NHSDA sample was increased to more than 30,000.

Household Survey data are used in conjunction with High School Senior Survey data (discussed below) to describe levels of drug use in specific segments of the population. Self-report surveys on drug use have been found to be reasonably trustworthy (Oetting and Beauvais 1990). Household Survey data may also be used in conjunction with DAWN data (discussed below) to describe long-term trends in drug abuse.

Survey limitations include the fact that the homeless and persons living in military installations, dormitories, and institutions such as jails, prisons, and hospitals are not covered, although the survey attempts to approximate these populations by using a controversial "imputation" procedure (General Accounting Office 1993). Also, some people refuse to participate. Because the survey is voluntary and the questionnaires are self-administered, the results may be biased (and probably understate the scope of the drug problem). Concern has also been expressed over privacy and comprehension issues. During the interviews of about 25–30 percent of respondents age twelve to seventeen at the time the survey was administered, there was a third person present. And any number of persons have difficulty with English or with understanding the drug-use jargon employed by the survey (General Accounting Office 1993).

High School Senior Survey

Since 1975 the NIDA has sponsored the High School Senior Survey (HSSS), an annual survey of drug use among high school seniors. Using a confidential questionnaire administered to students in their classrooms, information is collected from 15,000–19,000 respondents in approximately 135 public and private high schools. Primary uses of the data include: (1) assessing the prevalence and trends of drug use among high school seniors; and (2) gaining a better understanding of the lifestyles and value orientations associated with patterns of drug use and monitoring how these orientations are shifting over time. Follow-up surveys of representative subsamples of the original graduates that have been conducted for over a decade provide data on young adults and college students.

The survey has several limitations. High school dropouts (about 30 percent of students), who are associated with higher rates of drug use, are not part of the sampled universe. Chronic absentees, who may also have higher rates of abuse, are less likely to be surveyed (Liu 1994). In Texas, for example, youths entering that state's detention facilities are nearly twelve times as likely to have used cocaine as youngsters in school (Fredlund et al. 1990). Conscious or unconscious distortions in self-reporting information can also bias results. In addition, new trends in drug abuse, such as the use of crack may not be initially detected because the survey is designed to measure only drugs abused at significant levels. Questions about crack were asked for the first time in the 1986 survey. There is also concern over the lack of anonymity: The name, address, and telephone number of the respondent appears on the questionnaire's cover sheet in order to facilitate follow-up surveys.

Drug Abuse Warning Network (DAWN)

DAWN, which was initiated in 1972 and funded by NIDA, is a large-scale drug abuse data collection system designed as an early-warning indicator of the nation's drug abuse problem. An episode report is submitted for each drug abuse patient who visits the emergency room of a hospital participating in DAWN and for each drug abuse death encountered by a participating medical examiner or coroner. In a single emergency room "episode," a patient may "mention" having ingested more than one drug. DAWN records each drug a patient reports having used within four days before the hospital visit and relays the information to the Drug Enforcement Administration. Data are collected from a nonrandom sample in about twenty selected metropolitan areas throughout the country representing approximately one third of the U.S. population.

While standard definitions and data collection procedures exist, variations among individual reporters may occur. Incomplete reporting, turnover of reporting facilities and personnel, and reporting delays of up to one year (primarily for medical examiner data) are some of the system's limitations. For hospital emergencies, NNICC, in its last two publications, has used data from the DAWN Consistent Panel rather than from the Total Panel. The Consistent Panel includes only those hospitals reporting on a consistent basis (specifically, 90 percent or more each year). Data representing the total DAWN system were not used for trend analysis by NNICC because of reporting fluctuations. While medical examiner/coroner data are not subject to the same inconsistencies, reports are so small compared with the total DAWN system that it is not considered a valid trend indicator. (For a discussion of the uses and abuses of DAWN data, see Caulkins, Ebener, and McCaffrey 1995).

Retail Price/Purity

The price and purity levels of illegal drugs at the retail (consumer) level are key values in the NNICC estimating process. The DEA gathers these data, which are used as an indicator of drug availability. Drug prices are derived from a computerized database containing reports on purchases of, and negotiations to purchase, illegal drugs by undercover federal, state, and local law enforcement officers. Purity levels for heroin and cocaine are determined through laboratory analysis. (Purity levels are not applicable to marijuana and most synthetic drugs.) The limited number of reports and lack of randomness are problems that have plagued these indicators in the past (Comptroller General 1988). In addition, the price paid by undercover officers is affected by quantity discounts, thus underestimating the actual per-dose retail price; or the officers may pay a premium price because they are not known to their dealers, and new customers are typically charged more (Caulkins 1994).

Drug Use Forecasting

Drug Use Forecasting (DUF) began in New York City in 1987, and by 1990 twenty-five of the largest cities in the United States were involved. DUF data are collected in central police booking facilities in each city. For approximately fourteen consecutive evenings each quarter, staff obtain voluntary and anonymous urine specimens and interviews from a new sample of arrestees. In each site approximately 225 males are sampled. One hundred female arrestees are also interviewed in some of the sites. Responses are consistently high: Over 90 percent agree to be interviewed, and more than 80 percent of those interviewed provide urine specimens.

To obtain samples with a sufficient distribution of arrest charges, the number of male arrestees in each sample who are charged with drug-related offenses (sale or possession) is limited—one out of five; such persons are most likely to be using drugs at the time of their arrest and thus are undersampled. DUF statistics are minimum estimates of drug use of male arrestees. All female arrestees, regardless of charge, are included in the sample because of the small number of female arrestees available.

Urine samples are analyzed for ten drugs: cocaine, opiates, marijuana, PCP, methadone, benzodiazepine (Valium), methaqualone, propoxyphene

┌─────────────────────────────────────┐
│   **DRUG USE DATA**   │
└─────────────────────────────────────┘

Summing up the problem of drug use data and policy, Peter Reuter (1993: 179) states: "The apparently very discrepant figures that can be generated reasonably from different data sources and the transparent uncertainties of the whole exercise have undermined credibility. It has been easy for any group to reject estimates that do not suit its interests."*

* For a discussion of the problem of estimating drug use, see the entire issue of the *Journal of Drug Issues* 23 (Spring) 1993.

(Darvon), barbiturates, and amphetamines. Except for marijuana and PCP, which can be detected several weeks after use, urine tests detect use in the previous two to three days. The DUF reveals that cocaine continues to be the substance of choice of a majority of those arrested, with heroin remaining important but far less popular. Amphetamines were detected in less than 10 percent of the arrestees, who were most likely to be found in western states.

There are a number of validation issues with respect to the DUF. Central booking facilities, where the samples are selected, serve different areas of a city or county. This makes generalizing to the wider population of arrestees unreliable. The busy, if not frantic, pace of most central booking facilities makes respondent-selection procedures difficult, leading to questions about sampling techniques. And a study by the General Accounting Office (1993) revealed that DUF standards in the way arrestees are selected have not been applied uniformly across sites. Further, the nature of lockups in booking facilities makes confidentiality difficult to achieve.

POLICY ALTERNATIVES

What are the policy alternatives available to the United States? In chapter 2 we examined the history of the U.S. response to drug abuse. In order to consider alternatives, we need to look at the system adopted in England at about the same time that the Harrison Act was enacted in this country.

The British Response to Drug Abuse

British legislation controlling dangerous drugs dates back to the period when the United States was also considering such laws—both countries were responding to an international concern with drug addiction, particularly with the "Chinese problem." The first British drug-control laws (passed in 1916), however, dealt with cocaine, a substance being used by soldiers on leave from World War I. The Defence of the Realm Regulation prohibited the sale of cocaine without a doctor's prescription. In 1920, acting in accord with the Versailles Peace Treaty, Parliament enacted the Dangerous Drugs Act. This statute made it illegal to possess opiates and cocaine without a doctor's prescription, and the Home Office—a government ministry responsible for a number of public services, including police, prisons, and drug abuse treatment—limited doctors to dispensing drugs for "legitimate medical purposes." As with the Harrison Act in the United States, there was disagreement in England over the meaning of the legislation. The Home Office had difficulty translating the statute, and in response it persuaded the Ministry of Health to form a committee of physicians. The Departmental Committee on Morphine and Heroin Addiction was appointed in 1924, headed by Sir Humphrey Rolleston, chief of the Royal College of Physicians. The Home Office was inclined toward the U.S. approach—a *vice model*—but the appointment of a committee of physicians moved the problem of drug abuse toward a medical response (Stimson and Oppenheimer 1982).

Arnold Trebach (1982: 90) refers to the report of the Rolleston Committee as the best government report ever written on drug abuse. (It was produced at a cost of less than $320, including printing.) The report referred to the views of U.S. experts, particularly the strategy of abrupt withdrawal; the committee described this as impracticable and (incorrectly) possibly fatal. The committee noted that some medical experts favored a program of providing diminishing doses until the patient became drug-free. Other physicians argued, however, that some addicts will never be able to live drug-free, and for them, after all other treatment had proven unsuccessful, heroin maintenance was suggested—*if not cure, then care*. Most important, the committee report stated that drug abuse is a *disease*, not an indulgence. Addicts were not hedonistic criminals but sick persons (Trebach 1982).

The British system that resulted from the committee's report gave the medical profession almost unhindered freedom to treat narcotic (opiate and synthetic opiate) addicts by means of morphine and heroin. This approach continued virtually unchanged into the 1960s. There was a relatively small number (616 in 1936) of known addicts under medical treatment, and their names were voluntarily submitted by physicians to the Home Office. Patients were mostly older persons who had become addicted during medical treatment, often for chronic pain. These addicts did not use drugs for euphoria and did not belong to any drug subculture (Kaplan 1983b). By 1960 the number had fallen to 437, of whom 94 were heroin addicts. One year later, however, while the number of known heroin addicts in Britain remained minuscule by U.S. standards, it had increased by more than 40 percent. Most of the new addicts were young recreational users whose lifestyles were more deviant than those of the older class of addicts. The number continued to increase. By 1963 there were 222 known heroin addicts, and by 1968 there were 2,872 (Stimson 1988).

The 1961 report of a government committee headed by Sir Russell Brain indicated no significant increase in addicts and recommended no changes in policy (Stimson and Oppenheimer 1982). A second report by the same committee (Brain II) in 1965 found a significant increase in heroin addiction and concluded that it was caused by a handful of doctors who were overprescribing heroin, which was being diverted into a black market. The committee recommended that the use of narcotics and cocaine to treat addiction be restricted to specially licensed physicians and urged the establishment of drug treatment clinics. The committee also recommended that mandatory notification replace the voluntary method in use for decades.

> Following the lines of the Rolleston Committee, the Brain Committee regarded addiction as "an expression of mental disorder" rather than a form of "criminal behavior." The orthodox line was thus maintained, promoting a medical definition of the addict and the offer of treatment rather than a moralistic one leading to punishment. (Jamieson, Glanz, and MacGregor 1984: 5)

The recommendations of the Brain Committee were enacted in the Dangerous Drugs Act of 1967. Today specially licensed doctors can provide heroin or cocaine for drug treatment, but even this has become rare; most licensed physicians and clinics instead prescribe methadone (called Physeptone in England) for oral ingestion, although any medical doctor can provide these substances as analgesics for physical pain. As late as 1978, however, the government claimed that, in comparison with other countries, England had a relatively stable situation with respect to narcotic dependency. A few years later, it became obvious that the number of persons addicted to drugs was between 50,000 and 100,000 persons (out of a population of less than 47 million). In addition, "The casual use of drugs by young people now far outstrips the scale of the so-called 'drug problem' of the late sixties" (Jamieson, Glanz, and MacGregor 1984: xi).

The important changes in the British addict population reflected the social and political upheavals of the 1960s and 1970s, a phenomenon experienced on both sides of the Atlantic. Many of the "new addicts" in England were akin to the young American rebels who eschewed conventional society and flaunted their use of drugs (although not necessarily of heroin). The new British addict contrasted negatively with the traditional type, who was older and more conventional. The population of heroin addicts in Britain could be divided into two classes:

> There were some who lived the life of the junkie, spending much of their time in poverty, suffering from infections, and going the rounds of doctors, chemists, and Piccadilly Circus [in central London], and occasionally being arrested. But there were others who were more like the *stable* addict described in the early twentieth-century literature on addiction. These people, although addicted, led reasonably ordinary lives; they were inconspicuous in dress and manner, kept themselves apart from other addicts, and suffered few problems. Others were somewhere between these two extremes. (Stimson and Oppenheimer 1982: 1–2)

Rather than injecting the substance, many of the new addicts copied the Asian practice of smoking heroin, which "allowed the heroin habit to spread more widely than would otherwise have been possible" (Pearson 1987: 2). The Southwest Asian—Golden Crescent—heroin being smuggled into England has been prepared for smoking rather than injecting and is not water soluble. While in some parts of England over half of the users smoke heroin, in other parts intravenous use is predominant. (Smoking is a safer method of ingestion, but "only when the drug is relatively plentiful and cheap can the user contemplate letting some of it quite literally go up in smoke" [Auld, Dorn, and Smith 1986: 175]). The purity levels of heroin found in Britain far exceed those of heroin at the street level in the United States (Royal College 1987). The new addict population, not necessarily the increase in addict population, led to changes in the British approach to drugs: Trebach argues that physicians were not comfortable with maintaining drug addicts they perceived as undeserving young deviants. There was an additional problem, however—polydrug use. The new addict was frequently an abuser of substances other than heroin, for which the clinics did not have a treatment program.

Until the mid-1960s there was virtually no heroin smuggled into the country—black-market heroin was the result of pharmaceutical diversion. Major seizures began in 1971, with 1.14 kilos; in 1984 Customs seized 312 kilos and the police confiscated 49 kilos. The purity level of heroin prepared for street sale in 1984 ranged from 20 to 70 percent, and the price of British heroin has continued to drop (Stimson 1988). The current British response to drugs is quickly becoming that of the United States, with a primary emphasis on law enforcement (Dorn and South 1990). Penalties have been raised substantially, with life imprisonment the maximum sentence for trafficking in opiates, cocaine, and similar dangerous drugs (Turner 1991). However, while the role of the physician has been circumscribed, specialist doctors have a great deal more latitude than their American counterparts. "For example, several doctors are currently experimenting with providing cocaine- and heroin-laced cigarettes to their addicted patients, in the belief that doing so will reduce the incentive to enter the illegal drug market" (Reuter, Falco, and MacCoun 1993: 12).

What does the British system offer U.S. policy? To respond to that question, we must answer an antecedent query: Did the British system lead to a relatively low number of narcotic addicts, or did the relatively low number of addicts permit the use of a system of narcotic maintenance? Edwin Schur (1962) and Alfred Lindesmith (1968: 234) argue that it was the system that influenced the number of addicts. In England, states Lindesmith, where "doctors do prescribe for addicts, there is much less addiction than in the United States." Trebach (1982: 113), while sympathetic to the Schur-Lindesmith position—"that a humane and benign policy of treating addicts with kindness, and with licit supplies of drugs when necessary, contributes to keeping the total number of addicts in the society at a low level"—states that there is neither proof to support this conclusion, nor evidence to refute it.

Drug use did not become a major problem in Britain until the late 1950s, when "the British 'system' began to break down" (Stimson and Oppenheimer 1982: 31). John Kaplan (1983b: 161) concludes that "though the British experience with heroin maintenance provides us with a considerable amount of arguably relevant data, it is not very helpful in deciding whether the United States should attempt such a system." Stimson (1988: 41) argues that, contrary to Schur's statements (1962), "we can no longer accept the argument that the medicalisation of addiction prevents the development of drug cultures and markets."

POLICY ALTERNATIVES FOR THE UNITED STATES

Now that we have examined the British response, let us look at alternatives proposed for the United States, starting with the issue of drug maintenance and decriminalization.

Pros and Cons of Drug Maintenance and Decriminalization

John Kaplan (1983b: 101) poses the following policy question: "Could we not lower the total social costs of heroin use and the government response to it by allowing the drug to be freely and cheaply available in liquor stores, or as an over-the-counter drug?" Such policy would be consistent with the U.S. approach to other unhealthy habits such as cigarette smoking, drinking alcohol, and overeating, or to sports such as mountain climbing, skydiving, automobile and motorcycle racing, football, and boxing—an acknowledgment of an individual's freedom to enjoy him- or herself or to earn money, even through activities that may be injurious to that person's health. In fact, deliberately engaging in dangerous pursuits can be explained by their release of potentially reinforcing neurotransmitters such as endorphin or dopamine. Furthermore, as Edward Brecher (1972: 528) notes, most of the harmful aspects of heroin use are the result of its being illegal:

> Many American morphine and heroin addicts before 1914 led long, healthy, respectable, productive lives despite addiction—and so do a few addicts today. The sorry plight of most heroin addicts in the United States results primarily from the high price of heroin, the contamination and adulteration of the heroin available on the black market, the mainlining of the drug instead of safer modes of use, the laws against heroin and the ways in which they are enforced, the imprisonment of addicts, society's attitudes toward addicts, and other nonpharmacological factors.

"Our attempt to protect drug users from themselves," notes James Ostrowski (Committee on Law Reform 1987: 6), "has backfired, as it did during the prohibition of alcohol. We have only succeeded in making drug use much more dangerous and driving it underground, out of the reach of moderating social influences." Furthermore, imprisonment serves as a form of networking and recruitment for drug dealers and their clients (Currie 1993).

The Pros

The practical advantages of a drug maintenance/decriminalization policy are impressive.

1. There would be a reduction in the resources necessary for drug-law enforcement. According to Ethan Nadelmann, in 1988 federal, state, and local governments spent an estimated $8 billion a year on direct drug-law enforcement costs, not including such indirect, but nevertheless expensive, costs as imprisonment, probation, and parole (*Time* 30 May 1988: 14). These resources could be shifted to other areas of crime control and could be used for drug treatment and education.

Opposition to drug decriminalization is widespread and entrenched. San Francisco police carry a confiscated sign from a group wanting to legalize marijuana.

2. The low cost of psychoactive substances would curtail secondary criminality—that needed to support an expensive drug habit. It would obviate the need to trade sex for drugs, a practice that has spread AIDS.

3. Criminal organizations supported by drug trafficking would no longer remain viable, unless, of course, they moved into other criminal activities. (In Colombia, the government drive against major drug cartels left many henchmen and assassins scampering for other sources of income, leading to a dramatic increase in kidnappings. In 1990 there were 1,274 kidnappings, as opposed to 789 in 1989 [Brooke 1991]).

4. The aggressive marketing by traffickers aimed at expanding customer bases would no longer be operative; this marketing resulted in the widespread use of crack cocaine.

5. Those dependent on heroin, cocaine, or other currently illegal psychoactive substances could lead more normal lives, the time and energy needed to maintain the habit could be channeled into more constructive pursuits, and abusers would have an opportunity to become contributing members of society. For example, it is not the drug but the law that makes heroin hazardous to the addict. Opiates, like widely prescribed sedatives, provide relief from anxiety, distress, and insomnia to persons who would have difficulty functioning normally in the absence of such substances (Chein, Lee, and Rosenfeld 1964). Similar arguments can be made for cocaine and amphetamine.

6. The intravenous use of heroin would not necessarily involve the danger of hepatitis or AIDS because each user would have his or her own hypodermic kit. In the United States, while the incidence of AIDS among the homosexual population has stabilized, the disease is spreading quickly among drug addicts. Decriminalization would also make many drugs available in liquid form for oral ingestion. Under government oversight, drugs would be distributed in precisely measured doses, free of any dangerous contaminants. The chance of a drug overdose would thus be reduced.

7. Decriminalization would enable the use of social controls that inhibit antisocial, albeit lawful, behavior. Because drugs are illegal, users avoid detection and are shielded from social pressure. "Therefore, illicit drug users generally escape the potent forms of social control that are applied to smokers and drunk drivers" (Alexander 1990: 8).

The Cons

There are, of course, important disadvantages:

1. Cocaine, amphetamines, and heroin freely available to adults could be abused by youngsters as easily as cigarettes and alcohol are. Restrictions on these items have not proven effective in keeping the substances away from young people (see, for example, Feder 1996). And, as stated by Franklin Zimring and Gordon Hawkins (1992: 115), "If there is a universal proposition that is accepted by all parties to the debate on drugs, it is that children and youth should not have unregulated access to potentially harmful psychoactive sub-

BIPARTISAN INSANITY?

"If the drug war worked, I'd be all for it, but it doesn't. And when you look at what politicians say to get elected, you realize there's this bipartisan insanity. They say let's get tougher on drugs and more and more of what hasn't worked for the past 80 years." (Former police chief of San Diego, Joseph McNamara [Horowitz 1996: 28])

stances." Of course, it is unlikely that those adolescents motivated toward drug use will be thwarted by legislative acts and law enforcement efforts. Indeed, as noted in previous chapters, drug use typically begins during adolescence. Zimring and Hawkins (1992: 121) point out, however: "To the extent that prohibiton policies make drugs more difficult or more expensive for adults to acquire, the same policies will mean that young persons will encounter a prohibited drug less often and will often be unable to afford the purchase even when a source is located."

2. More people would be tempted to try legalized controlled substances, and abuse-related problems might increase accordingly. It was noted in chapter 1 that because of easier access, there is a higher rate of drug abuse among medical practitioners than among the general population. James Q. Wilson (1975: 142) argues that "all evidence suggests that the easy availability of heroin would lead to a sharp increase in its use." The PCOC (1986: 331) states that "legalization would almost certainly increase demand, and therefore spread this destruction." Robert Peterson (1991) argues that drug prohibiton, as contrasted with the devastation caused by a lack of similar controls over alcohol, saves billions of dollars and thousands of lives each year. Chanoch Jacobsen and Robert Hanneman (1992) state that the illegitimacy of drug abuse allows for the activation of informal social controls through families, peers, and community that restrain drug abuse.

Isidor Chein and his colleagues (1964: 348) argue, however, that "opiates are not inherently attractive, euphoric, or stimulant substances." That is, they are not seductive substances that "hook" the unsuspecting and the innocent. A study of 11,882 hospital patients treated with pain-killing drugs revealed that only four became addicted. A study of more than 10,000 burn victims who received injections of narcotics for weeks or months found not a single case of addiction attributed to this treatment (Melzak 1990). Russell Portnoy, M.D., director of analgesic studies in the Pain Service at Sloan-Kettering Memorial Hospital, points out, "Just as the vast majority of people who drink do not become alcoholics, those who are treated with opioid for pain do not become addicts" (Goleman 1987: 10). While two out of every three Americans consume alcohol, 10 percent of the drinkers account for half of all the alcohol consumed in the United States.

3. Legalizing all psychoactive substances would signal an acceptance of their use similar to the acceptance of alcohol and tobacco. Most users of alcohol do not become addicted, but Kaplan (1983b) argues that we do not know whether this would hold true for such drugs as heroin. Studies indicate that rats and monkeys perform considerable amounts of work to earn injections of heroin or cocaine but do not respond so eagerly to alcohol. However, as noted previously, many persons have used opiates without becoming addicted: hospital patients experiencing pain, "chippers" and "weekenders" who use heroin much as a social drinker uses alcohol, and soldiers returning to the United States who used high-quality heroin while in Vietnam but discontinued use when no longer confronted by the anxiety and depression of the Vietnam experience and when the cheap, high-quality heroin to which they had grown accustomed was no longer available (Robins 1973, 1974; Robins et al. 1980). The availability of cheap heroin in the United States, argues Wilson (1990), might have kept these veterans addicted. And the availability of cheap drugs may lead to greater use by pregnant women.

Kaplan (1983b) points out that several conventions have developed around alcohol use that limit its abuse potential, such as using it only at ceremonial occasions or when dining with the family, never drinking alone, and avoiding intoxication—being "a drunk." On the other hand, Kaplan (1983b) states, while conventions may develop around the use of heroin, the cultural model might turn out to be that of the "junkie." Kaplan fails to deal with the disease theory of addiction: What if some persons take heroin or cocaine to compensate for a physiological deficiency? Is this not analogous to the diabetic's use of insulin? Erich Goode (1972: 212) recommends abandoning efforts to eliminate or even drastically reduce drug abuse but, instead, to *live with it and make sure that drug users do not seriously harm themselves and others*" (original emphasis). If one accepts physiological theories (the disease model) of drug abuse or the concept of an "addictive personality," this is a reasonable suggestion.

Some researchers have found a strong correlation between poor mental health and drug abuse: Drugs are frequently self-prescribed by persons to deal with their mental problems "primarily to improve their level of affect and/or functioning." And psychoactive drugs do alleviate, at least temporarily, psychological discomfort, enabling the person to relax and/or function more effectively. To the "extent that drug use is, or is at least perceived as being, an effective strategy for improving one's mental health, there will be strong motivation for the user to persist in drug use" (Gove, Geerken, and Hughes 1979: 587).

4. The easy availability of legal heroin, cocaine, and other currently illegal psychoactive substances would reduce the incentive for those already addicted or habituated to enter drug treatment or otherwise to seek a drug-free existence. Of course, there is no reason to believe that a drug-free existence will facilitate a constructive, crime-free lifestyle in most persons currently using psychoactive substances. Most heroin addicts, for example, go right on using heroin despite the threat or actuality of imprisonment, and often despite efforts to cure the affliction.

The legal availability of heroin, however, could prolong heroin addiction beyond the age (thirty-five to forty) at which spontaneous remission typically occurs. Furthermore, as Zinberg (1984: 13) notes, the availability of cheap high-grade heroin in Vietnam helps explain its widespread use by U.S. servicemen.

> Heroin was so potent and inexpensive that smoking was an effective and economical method to use, and this no doubt made it more attractive than if injection had been the primary mode of administration. . . . The decreased availability of heroin in the United States (reflected in its high price) and its decreased potency (which made smoking wholly impractical) made it difficult for the returning veterans to continue use.

In order to develop a policy that answers these serious concerns, we need to understand the cause(s) of drug use. Are some persons more vulnerable than others? As we have seen in chapters 3 and 4, we do not know why some persons abuse drugs while others with similar access do not. We do not know why some persons who experiment with certain drugs become dependent while others do not. Any discussion of drug policy is conditioned on views of drug abuse and on the particular theory that one adopts:

1. Drug abuse is a disease with a physiological basis.
2. Drug abuse is a psychological condition or personality disorder.
3. Drug abuse is a response to oppressive social conditions.
4. Drug abuse is simply the pleasure-seeking activity of hedonistic persons.

What we do know is that currently there is a very high correlation between urban poverty and heroin and cocaine use. A great deal of drug use, it seems, feeds upon human misery. A serious effort to deal logically with drugs would require greater efforts to reduce the ills of urban America. Chein and his colleagues (1964: 381) extend this argument further: "Is a society which cannot or will not do anything to alleviate the miseries which are, at least subjectively, alleviated by drugs better off if it simply prevents the victims of these miseries from finding any relief?" Furthermore, Zinberg (1984) reminds us that much of the damage inflicted by drugs is the result of their illicit status and not their pharmacology. Post–Harrison Act efforts against certain psychoactive chemicals were based on their potential for harm. These efforts come full circle when the user is the target of vigorous enforcement efforts, as in the case of current drug policy: "We must focus responsibility and sanctions on illegal drug users" (White House Conference for a Drug Free America 1988: 9).

Kaplan (1983b) argues that our inability to predict the consequences of making heroin freely available mitigates against a policy of drug legalization. Ethan Nadelmann (1988: 91) points out, however, that "the case for legalization [of heroin, cocaine, and marijuana] is particularly convincing when the risks inherent in alcohol and tobacco use are compared with those associated with illicit drug use." Chein (et al. 1964) and Trebach (1982) recommend a more modest policy: placing greater trust in the medical profession and allowing physicians to treat addicts with a variety of drugs, including heroin. They recommend that clinics be established to implement this policy. (Such clinics have never been popular with community residents, and it would be difficult to open them in most neighborhoods.) Any person shown to be addicted to heroin could receive prescriptions for this drug. Determining whether or not a person is addicted and how much heroin he or she should be given would be left to the medical profession. Trebach notes that some drugs would be diverted into the black market, but there is already a considerable market in illegal heroin. Legalization would, of course, reduce the price of heroin, thereby reducing the incentive for dealing in the substance. This policy, Trebach argues, would attract heroin addicts in large numbers and cause significant decreases in crime. Such clinics would also offer a wide variety of social services, including help in becoming drug-free (which would be encouraged—but not imposed—by clinic staff). Trebach has not suggested a similar program with respect to cocaine, currently a major illicit drug of abuse.

Among those strongly opposed to drug decriminalization are many leaders of the African-American community. They have expressed the view that such programs are merely schemes designed to tranquilize members of the minority community who would be attracted by the availability of cheap drugs to alleviate their social and psychological frustrations. Some would abandon protest and political activity for the "easy fix," and such programs would saddle the minority community with lifelong abusers robbed of the incentive to give up drugs.

Congressman Charles B. Rangel of Harlem, while chairman of the House Select Committee on Narcotics Abuse and Control, vigorously opposed any type of drug maintenance program or decriminalization. He states that while "illegal drug-trafficking violence would end under decriminalization, a new crime source would be created by the influx of new addicts" and that "hyperactive reactions to such drugs as cocaine will spur criminal behavior" (1990: 14). The congressman outlined his opposition in a series of provocative questions (1988):

- Would we allow all drugs to be legally sold and used, or would we select only the most abused, such as cocaine, heroin, and marijuana?
- Who would administer the dosages—the state or the individual?
- What quantity of drugs would each individual be allowed? What about addicts? Wouldn't we have to give them more in order to satisfy their craving? Or would we give them just enough to whet their appetites?
- What do we do about those who are experimenting? Do we sell them the drugs, too, and encourage them to pick up the habit?
- Would the government establish tax-supported facilities to sell these drugs?
- Would we get supplies from the same foreign countries that support our habit now, or would we create our own internal sources and "dope fac-

tories," paying people minimum wage to churn out mounds of cocaine and bales of marijuana?

- Would there be an age limit on the purchase of drugs, as there is with alcohol? What would the market price be? Who would set it? Would private industry be allowed to get in on any of this?

The congressman's answers to these questions are as simple as his recommendation for dealing with drug abuse: "Let's see if we can get a coordinated battle plan that would include the deployment of military personnel to wipe out this foreign-based national security threat." Common sense, notes Ostrowski, "tells us that illegal drugs will always be readily available. Prison wardens cannot keep these drugs out of their own institutions—an important

---

THREE MODELS OF DRUG MAINTENANCE/DECRIMINALIZATION

1. Dangerous drugs can be dispensed only through government-controlled clinics or specially licensed medical personnel and only for short-term treatment purposes; unauthorized sale or possession entails criminal penalties. Long-term maintenance is limited to the use of methadone. This is basically the approach currently used in England.
2. Dangerous drugs can be prescribed by an authorized medical practitioner for treatment or maintenance; criminal penalties are imposed for sale or possession outside medical auspices. This is the old British system.
3. Dangerous drugs can be sold and used as tobacco and alcohol products are; that is, nonprescription use by adults is permitted. This was the case in the United States before the Harrison Act.

Pat O'Malley and Stephen Mugford (1991) argue for a more limited version:

1. Providing safer options, by, for example, making coca tea readily available, but significantly limiting cocaine and severely restricting crack, which, along with morphine and heroin, would be available only through prescription or licensing arrangements. There would be no incentives to attract new users.
2. Offering and encouraging safer ingestion. For example, smoking opium would be readily available but intravenous drug use severely restricted.
3. Permitting cultivation and possession of small amounts of marijuana and criminalizing large-scale operations.
4. Banning all pro-drug advertising—including for tobacco and alcohol products—while encouraging education and antidrug advertising, which would be financed through drug-related tax revenues.

lesson for those who would turn this country into a prison to stop drug use" (Committee on Law Reform 1987: 13; also Purdy 1995).

Until 1988 the debate over drug decriminalization remained basically academic—that is, discussed seriously only by a few university educators and liberal or libertarian political ideologues. In that year, drugs became a—possibly *the*—major political issue of the presidential campaign. In response to the obvious—that antidrug efforts have not had any significant effect—*Time* magazine (30 May 1988) presented a cover article on the issue: "Should Drugs Be Made Legal?" In a balanced presentation, *Time* outlined the benefits and disadvantages of such a proposal and concluded that

> even though corner drug shops are not going to pop up anytime soon, nor should they, the hot new debate over legalization is a significant one. It reflects the widespread and understandable dismay over antidrug efforts that have gone to such discomforting lengths as to call in the military without noticeably making a dent in the crime and abuse problem. And it could turn attention to the need for more effective treatment and education efforts, rather than merely more election-year frenzy and posturing.

The following year, the *New York Times* reported that while popular opinion still opposed decriminalization, debate over the issue had intensified: "It has become a staple of editorial pages, letters to the editor, talk shows on television and radio and public lectures. And many who do not go as far as advocating legalization show a new interest in the subject" (Corcoran 1989: 9). The discussion of decriminalization brought a hostile response from William Bennett, (then) the "drug czar" (actually, federal director of drug policy). He argued that public discussion of the issue only worsens the problem and undermines efforts to combat drug abuse (Sly 1989).

The discussion of British policy centered on the problem of heroin. The drug problem of the contemporary United States, however, extends well beyond that substance, with cocaine abuse a major problem. Although this may change, only Steven Wisotsky (1987) has presented a serious proposal to decriminalize cocaine. Edwin Schur (1962) is not much interested in it, and Alfred Lindesmith (1968), who mentions it only briefly, does not see cocaine as a serious problem because, according to him, cocaine is not addicting and does not cause withdrawal symptoms. Kaplan (1983b) notes that monkeys who become addicted to heroin will increase their dosage to a relatively high level and then stabilize the amount and work to earn food or other rewards; laboratory animals given unlimited access to cocaine, however, will continue to increase self-injected doses of the substance until the supply is cut off or they die from debilitation (see Dworkin et al. 1987). Of course, monkeys do many things that humans do not, and this may be one of them. Interestingly, Brecher (1972)—writing on behalf of Consumers Union—advocates legalizing heroin for addicts but takes no similar position with respect to cocaine (or amphetamines).

Wisotsky (1987) argues that we have continuously focused on the negatives of substances whose nonmedical use is subjected to criminal sanctions.

Yet these substances provide relief from anxiety, euphoria, a sense of enhanced well-being, and experiences that the user obviously finds pleasing. While these substances carry some dangers, so do a host of other substances such as tobacco, alcohol, and even certain foods whose abuse can lead to obesity and high blood pressure; not to mention firearms, skydiving, mountain climbing, motorcycle and automobile racing, and any number of dangerous pastimes that people find pleasurable—that produce a "high." Why pick on chemicals, or rather on the specific chemicals we have chosen to control with criminal sanctions? To the person whose appetite appears insatiable, certain food is addicting, yet we do not restrict the intake of potentially harmful foods that have little, if any, nutritional value.

"Most people," states Wisotsky, "will not *permit* themselves to become addicted, just as most people will not consistently overeat to the point of obesity." With respect to heroin and cocaine, the "dominant pattern consists of controlled recreational use or social use, not chronic, compulsive, or obsessive use" (1987: 207). Zinberg (1984) points out that our policies have failed to distinguish between the controlled user of psychoactive substances and the one for whom drug use has become dysfunctional. The use of drugs in the United States is widespread, and most of those ingesting psychoactive chemicals, from alcohol and marijuana to heroin and cocaine, do not become dysfunctional. However, the President's Commission on Organized Crime (1986: 483) recommended that "no Federal, State, or local government funds should go directly or indirectly to programs that counsel 'responsible' drug use or condone illicit drug use in any way."

It appears irrational to give the dysfunctional alcoholic a "legal pass" while subjecting the controlled user of marijuana, heroin, or cocaine to criminal sanctions—sanctions that can result in labeling that, in itself, may be socially, psychologically, and economically debilitating. In fact, much of what society decries about drug abuse is the result of our policy of criminal sanctions. With a redefinition of the problem, Wisotsky (1987: 214) asserts, "Drug abuse would become like any other health problem, managed by research, prevention, education and treatment," an approach that could be funded by the considerable amount of money now expended on drug-law enforcement. This approach would help destroy heroin and cocaine cartels that threaten the integrity and stability of a number of nations faced with Marxist insurgencies while reducing the everyday dangers to which we expose the public and our drug-law enforcement agents.

There has been some movement in this direction with respect to marijuana, the possession of which—for personal use, as noted in chapter 2—has been decriminalized in some states, and some authorities have proposed the legalization and taxation of the substance ("Which War on Drugs?" 1987). Although the state supreme court in Alaska decriminalized the possession of small amounts of marijuana in 1975, fifteen years later voters passed a ballot initiative making it illegal once again. (Marijuana was also recriminalized in Oregon.) There is no evidence to indicate that legal changes have resulted in a marijuana-abuse problem in these states. Such European countries as the Netherlands and Spain have similarly decriminalized the possession of mari-

PUNISH DRUG ABUSERS

"I called for stringent measures for drug users, especially the well-off who believe they can escape punishment." Newt Gingrich, Speaker of the House of Representatives (1996: 7).

juana for personal use. In the Netherlands, more than 2,000 coffee shops sell marijuana and hashish under government regulation. About half of the marijuana sold is grown locally (Kinzer 1992).

In the United States, the decriminalization of marijuana, however, appears to have considerable opposition. In a letter to the *New York Times* (1 December 1987: 26), Lee I. Dogoloff, executive director of the American Council for Drug Education, cites statistics indicating an overwhelming number of Americans (74 percent) oppose decriminalization. Dogoloff states that the adverse effects of alcohol and tobacco do not justify decriminalization of marijuana, which, he argues, also carries health risks. The President's Commission on Organized Crime (1986: 483) suggests that laws in certain states that decriminalized the possession of marijuana are equivalent to condoning the use of drugs and should be reconsidered. And in 1992 the U.S. Public Health Service rescinded approval of marijuana for a handful of carefully screened patients suffering from AIDS, cancer, or glaucoma. In an editorial, the *Chicago Tribune* argued that "apparently the federal government just wants to have nothing more to do with marijuana, no matter who might benefit." The reason: "It doesn't want to be embarrassed politically by having to admit that marijuana might not be all bad, that it may have some benign uses after all" (March 16, 1992: 20).

The noted economist Ludwig von Mises (1949: 728–29), a favorite of many political conservatives, argues:

> Opium and morphine are certainly dangerous, habit-forming drugs. But once the principle is admitted that it is the duty of government to protect the individual against his own foolishness, no serious objections can be advanced against further encroachments. A good case could be made out in favor of the prohibition of alcohol and nicotine. And why limit the government's benevolent providence to the protection of the individual's body only? Is not the harm a man can inflict on his mind and soul even more disastrous than any bodily evils? Why not prevent him from reading bad books and seeing bad plays? The mischief done by bad ideologies surely is much more pernicious, both for the individual and for the whole society, than that done by narcotic drugs.

Nadelmann (1988: 97) adds:

> There is little question that if the production, sale, and possession of alcohol and tobacco were criminalized, the health costs associated with their use and abuse

could be reduced. But most Americans do not believe that criminalizing the alcohol and tobacco markets would be a good idea. Their opposition stems largely from two beliefs: that adult Americans have the right to choose what substances they will consume and what risks they will take, and that the economic costs of trying to coerce so many Americans into abstaining from those substances would be enormous and the social costs disastrous.

For a detailed discussion of the legalization issue, see Krauss and Lazear (1991).

A somewhat ambiguous middle position was adopted in Zurich, Switzerland—a policy of containment. Vigorous police action drove hard-core users into a park near the heart of the city, where open drug sale and use were tolerated. "Needle Park" accommodated about four hundred hard-core users of heroin and cocaine and about three thousand others who passed through daily. An AIDS prevention program was established in the park, and free needles were distributed as part of the effort. Social workers attempted to guide users into treatment programs, and volunteers provided free lunches. Because of the number of drug overdoses—an average of twelve daily—five doctors had to be stationed in the park. Urination killed off all the trees and flowers. Drug users were drawn to the park from all over Europe, an important factor leading to the park's demise: In 1992 the park was shut; it remains sealed behind a ten-foot iron fence (Treaster 1990h; Cohen 1992). The drug market in Zurich did not end with the closing of the park; it moved a half-mile away to a little-used railway station. There a policy of tolerance again ensued until increasing violence,

Zurich's Needle Park in 1989.

including the murders of four dealers, led to a 1995 government crackdown and the area was closed off with razor wire and steel fencing (Cowell 1995).

Harm Reduction

David Turner (1991: 184–85) notes that the current British system involves two barely compatible policies operating at the same time:

> On one hand, there is a political policy. This is to a large extent led by the Home Office, which coordinates government drug policy. Its focus is on supply reduction and penal policies, in a belief that elimination of drug use is possible. On the other hand, there is the services policy, largely led by the Department of Health. Its focus is on local prevention campaigns, on providing a variety of local services including detached work, needle and syringe exchange schemes, advice and counseling services, diversion from custody, a variety of prescribing options for short-term out-patient detoxification to long-term prescribing and rehabilitation. At the heart of this approach is the view that drug use cannot be eliminated, but its most harmful consequences for the individual, society, and public health can be moderated.

England, among other European countries, has been exploring a third model of response to drug abuse, an alternative to the extremes of enforcement and treatment—*harm reduction.*

Harm reduction is offered as an alternative to the *supply reduction* strategy—aggressive law enforcement and pressure on producer nations—and the *demand reduction* strategy—treatment and prevention. This alternative recognizes that while abstinence is desirable, it is not a realistic goal. Instead, this approach examines harm from two points of view: harm to the community and harm to the drug user. The focus, then, is on lowering the amount of harm to each.

> Each policy or programmatic decision is assessed for its expected impact on society. If a policy or program is expected to reduce aggregate harm, it should be accepted; if it is expected to increase aggregate harm, it should be rejected. The prevalence of drug use should play no special and separate role. (Reuter and Caulkins 1995: 1060).

The harm reduction approach is more easily achieved in England, where controlled substances can be prescribed for those dependent upon them. In the province of Merseyside, a severely disadvantaged region whose largest city is Liverpool, vestiges of the "old British system" remain, with addicts taking home injectable opiates. Merseyside also introduced a needle-exchange program (in order to reduce transmission of HIV and hepatitis B transmission) that was user-friendly, designed by the addicts. The police cooperated by not

USE REDUCTION v. HARM REDUCTION

"By almost exclusively emphasizing use reduction as an indirect means of reducing harm, we forgo opportunities of directly intervening to reduce harm and we may even increase harm in the process" (Reuter and MacCoun 1995: 31).

placing drug services under surveillance and by referring drug users who had been arrested to drug treatment. "By no means soft on drugs, the Drug Squad of the Merseyside police force arrest and charge a greater number of people for drug offenses than all other provincial forces." Nevertheless, their focus on harm reduction means that first offenders found in possession of any drug are cautioned—harm reduction aims at "avoiding the amplification of a drug-using career that may stem from a first conviction" (O'Hare 1992: xiv). As part of a harm reduction approach, in Edinburgh, Scotland, physicians, in order to battle an alarming number of AIDS cases, are permitted to prescribe oral doses of nearly any drug craved by abusers. And there is indeed harm reduction: Great Britain has the lowest rate of AIDS in Europe (Schmidt 1993).

In the view of Alan Marlatt, Julian Somers, and Susan Tapert (1993), harm reduction seeks to avoid marginalizing drug users because more can be done to control the often destructive behavior of drug abusers when they are "normalized." While abstinence is an ultimate objective, in the continuum they posit *any* steps that decrease risk are worthwhile goals:

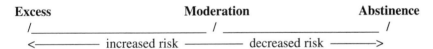

Excess   **Moderation**   **Abstinence**

/_____ / _____ /

<——————— increased risk ———— decreased risk ———>

The focus is on reducing the risky consequences of drug use rather than on reducing drug use per se. In place of the "war" analogy and "total victory" rhetoric, they support even small steps that reduce harm. For example, intravenous use would be made safer with needle-exchange programs. The next step would be to encourage safer methods of ingestion. Risk would be further reduced by substituting methadone for heroin or other legal substances for cocaine and then by moderating the use of drugs—including nicotine and alcohol—en route to abstinence, when this is possible. Related risk-taking behavior would also be targeted in an effort to deal with AIDS and other sexually transmitted diseases; in this case the focus of harm reduction would be on reducing the frequency of high-risk sexual activity and by promoting less risky sexual practices, monogamous sex, and the use of birth control. The country most identified with a policy of harm reduction is the Netherlands.

Dutch Drug Policy. In place of prohibitionism's "war on drugs" and "user accountability," the Dutch have implemented a pragmatic and non-moralistic approach to the problem of drug abuse. They distinguish between "soft" drugs and "hard" drugs. During the 1970s possession of small amounts of marijuana was virtually decriminalized, and the substance remains widely available in so-called "coffee shops" (de Kort 1994). Trafficking in hard drugs can bring a twelve-year sentence. While drug users are rarely arrested, those involved in secondary criminality are prosecuted, and drugs are not a mitigating circumstance (Silvis 1994). "Criminalization of the consumer is considered a harmful way of discouraging drug use" (Wever 1994: 64).

Extensive social services in the Netherlands provide aid to drug abusers that is not available in many other countries, including the United States. Nevertheless, in the early 1980s downtown areas of larger Dutch cities became increasingly dominated by a highly visible population of untreated drug users. This fostered a change in approach, which heretofore had focused almost exclusively on promoting abstinence. Treatment was expanded to deal with the host of social and physical problems experienced by abusers. Harm reduction became the focus: If abstinence is not possible, then safer use of drugs and safer sex practices (to deal with the problem of AIDS) should be the near-term goals. Drug abusers are now provided with health-related education, and there is a wide variety of treatment programs readily available, including methadone maintenance (Wever 1994).

Drug-abuse prevention efforts in the Netherlands treat alcohol and tobacco, as well as heroin and cocaine, as *dangerous* drugs—legal versus illegal is not considered a sound basis for differentiation. This avoids the double standard approach that raises cynicism in young people. The focus is on risky behavior, which also includes eating disorders. The policy seeks to deglamorize drugs and stresses individual responsibility for the consequences of substance abuse. Persons are cautioned against using dangerous substances while being provided with information on how to reduce the risks for those who insist on experimenting with drugs (Marshall and Marshall 1994). As noted above, there are extensive treatment programs for those who become drug dependent. Ineke and Chris Marshall point to differences between the Dutch and the American approach to drugs (1994: 226):

> The American mass media, public, politicians, and educators appear to devote considerably more resources and energy to issues related to drug prevention than is the case in Holland. Differences in intensity of prevention efforts reflect fundamental differences in the definition of drugs as a social problem in the US and Netherlands: In the US, drugs are viewed as a terrible evil to be fought with heavy arms (both in terms of prevention and repression); in the Netherlands, from a policymaker's viewpoint, drugs are viewed as a "normal" social and health risk controlled by minimal measures or even ignored (e.g., cannabis, XTC).

They (1994: 226) conclude that the "Dutch pragmatic approach has prevented the use of radical measures such as forced treatment, drug testing at the workplace, and fear-inducing information campaigns—'solutions' which may give the appearance of a tough approach, but which frequently cause more problems than they solve."

Now that we have reviewed the English experience, the pros and cons of drug maintenance/decriminalization, and the concept of harm reduction, let us examine U.S. policy in two broad categories: supply reduction and demand reduction.

NEEDLE-EXCHANGE PROGRAMS

Only six states allow the purchase of syringes without a prescription and do not have laws prohibiting their possession (G. Judson 1995), although addicts may be unwilling to absorb the cost of their purchase.* In an effort to reduce the spread of AIDS among intravenous drug users and to reduce AIDS among infants of addict mothers, a number of needle-exchange programs have been initiated. It was discovered that intravenous-drug abusers who are also diabetics do not get AIDS. At first this appeared connected to their diabetes, but it was subsequently explained by their legal access to hypodermic needles (Chapman 1991). A study by researchers from Yale University found that a needle-exchange program in New Haven, Connecticut, reduced new infections among intravenous drug users by more than 30 percent (Navarro 1991).

In 1988 a service agency in Portland, Oregon, became the first to distribute free needles as part of a pilot project involving 125 addicts. Oregon has no law restricting the distribution of hypodermic needles, but addicts frequently do not have the necessary funds to purchase them. Officials in a number of foreign cities have been distributing needles, but "proposals to hand out clean needles have touched off intense debate in cities from San Francisco to Boston. Opponents among law-enforcement, political, religious and drug treatment officials contend that free needles would promote drug use" (Lambert 1988b: 7).

Nevertheless, by 1992 eight U.S. cities had needle-exchange programs. Half of them are in the state of Washington (Navarro 1992). Switzerland and the Netherlands distribute hypodermic needles to reduce the spread of AIDS (Bollag 1989), as does almost every country in Western Europe. Australia has a needle-and-syringe-exchange program, which has been operating in the state of New South Wales since 1986. While Australia has a relatively high number of AIDS cases, there are very few intravenous drug users with AIDS (Wodak 1990). In 1995 a report by the National Academy of Sciences commissioned by Congress found that programs that encourage drug abusers to exchange used needles for new ones greatly reduce the spread of AIDS (Leary 1995b).

---

*In 1992 Connecticut changed its law to permit the purchase and possession of hypodermic needles without a prescription. As a result, the number of AIDS cases fell by 40 percent (G. Judson 1995).

ONE DEA AGENT'S LAMENT

"It is both sobering and painful to realize, after twenty-five years of undercover work, having personally accounted for at least three thousand criminals serving fifteen thousand years in jail, and having seized several tons of illegal substances, that my career was meaningless and had absolutely no effect whatsoever in the so-called war on drugs" (Levine 1990: 11).

Supply Reduction: Improving the Criminal Sanction

"In the criminal market, an increase in price," the result of improved law enforcement, "without a significant consumption decrease will raise total revenue." Under such conditions, the advantages accrue to better-organized firms that, are "able to wield violence and corruption effectively, because such firms are the most enforcement-resistant." And their profits will advance in proportion to the increase in price and the reduction of competition (Kleiman 1989: xvii).

As noted in chapter 7, focusing on domestic-level distribution organizations may actually lead to an increase in the profits of criminal organizations strong enough to survive in a reduced-competition market. In fact, there is not a single documented instance in which one or a succession of high-level drug cases coincided with a substantial reduction in consumption in a city (Kleiman and Smith 1990). On the other hand, Kleiman (1985: 80) argues, "A focus on lower-level dealers and users will reduce wholesale prices [fewer buyers]—which are the revenues of high-level dealers—and perhaps reduce the quantity sold." He (1985: 85) recognizes a political problem with this approach: "Going after small wrongdoers while largely ignoring big ones may be sensible regulation, but it is not visible justice" (1985: 85). There is a more practical concern: the cost of arresting, prosecuting, and imprisoning large numbers of persons.

This approach was the mainstay of the so-called (Governor) "Rockefeller Laws" in New York during the 1970s. As a result of the laws, the time needed to dispose of drug cases nearly doubled between 1973 and 1976, and by mid-1976 the system was approaching collapse. Research indicates that the use of drugs increased during this time, as did drug-related crimes such as burglary, robbery, and theft (Joint Committee on New York Drug Law Evaluation 1977). In 1987 the strategy recommended by Kleiman caused New York City to establish special courts to rapidly dispose of felony drug cases through plea bargaining because the regular criminal courts were being flooded with arrests of street-level drug dealers. Because of the volume, it was taking six to twelve months to dispose of a case, which created a chaotically overcrowded situa-

A RACIST DRUG WAR?

A study conducted by *USA Today* revealed that African Americans are four times as likely as whites to be arrested on drug charges, even though both groups use drugs at about the same rate; and African Americans are more likely to be imprisoned for drug charges than non-Hispanic whites (Meddis 1993).

tion on Riker's Island, the city jail for persons awaiting trial (Raab 1987). In the decade from 1981 to 1991, the average daily jail population in New York City increased 170 percent. The *New York Times* concluded that

> New York City's war on drugs has resulted in so many arrests that there are simply not enough prosecutors, judges, Legal Aid lawyers or probation officers to give adequate attention to each of the thousands of cases, let alone courtrooms to try the suspects in or jail cells to hold the convicts. ("Drug Arrests and the Courts' Pleas for Help" 1989: E6)

Other states followed New York's lead, with similar results. The number of people convicted of drug felonies in state courts increased almost 70 percent in the two-year period from 1988 to 1990. In Cook County (Chicago), Illinois, the chief criminal court judge stated that drug cases were overwhelming the county's court system ((O'Connor 1990). In the federal courts, the number of drug arrests has so backed up the system that judges are unable to attend to civil cases, increasing delays despite a drop in the number of civil filings in the past few years.

In New York, from 1976 to 1991 the prison population almost tripled: in 1991 it housed about 60,000 inmates; in 1995, more than 68,000—135 percent of capacity. A similar problem is being experienced in California, where the prison population went from 22,000 in 1982 to 102,000 in 1991; in 1994 the figure was about 125,000. The federal prison system is operating at more than 160 percent capacity. In Illinois in 1989 more than 21,000 inmates inhabited state correctional facilities designed for 16,492; by 1994 the number was above 37,000, 60 percent over capacity. Jails throughout the United States are already being operated severely over capacity, and any strategy causing a significant increase in the inmate population could be disastrous.

The General Accounting Office (1991) found that overcrowded jails and prisons, the result of increased drug arrests and prosecutions, resulted in more offenders being placed in probation and parole systems, which, in turn, has generally decreased the level of supervision of probationers and parolees. It has also led to emergency prison release programs and an increase in plea bargaining—a system that is spinning its wheels. Jails and prisons are scarce resources because of their exorbitant cost: The annual per-inmate cost of imprisonment ranges as high as $30,000, and the cost of building a prison is as high as $100,000 per cell. Are scarce tax dollars being spent wisely in the "war" on drugs?

With respect to local law enforcement efforts, Manhattan district attorney Robert M. Morgenthau (1988: 27) has stated: "We are putting more drug dealers in jail for longer terms than ever before." But not only have we not 'conquered drugs,' but drugs are more available on the streets of our cities than ever before."

What about a policy of incarceration for only the most serious criminal offenders, such as robbers, among the drug-abusing population? Unfortunately, this is not feasible: "Existing criminal justice practices would fail to detect most persons who actually are robber-dealers" (Johnson, Lipton, and Wish 1986a: 187). In their study, Bruce Johnson and his colleagues found that none of the high-rate addict-robbers were ever arrested for robbery. In fact, "Less than 1 percent of self-reported crimes by cocaine-heroin abusers result in an

---

WINNING THE WAR BY GETTING TOUGH

- On 15 August 1988, a thirty-two-year-old real estate attorney and Harvard Law School graduate was sentenced to fifteen years in prison for possession of cocaine. The police discovered thirty-six grams (28.35 grams equals one ounce) of diluted cocaine in a raid on the attorney's house in Hoffman Estates, Illinois. Authorities had been tipped off by a boarder seeking leniency for a drug conviction of his own.
- A forty-nine-year-old dockworker was flagged down by an acquaintance and for five dollars agreed to drive him to a hamburger stand. Once there, the friend was arrested by federal agents for dealing drugs. The dockworker, who had no criminal record, was convicted of conspiracy and received a ten-year sentence as mandated by the 1986 Anti-Drug Abuse Act. He will be eligible for release after serving 8.5 years.
- In St. Louis, a twenty-four-year-old mother of three young children received a mandatory 11.5-year federal prison sentence without possibility of parole for her minor role in a cocaine deal. It was her first offense, and evidence indicates that her involvement was a result of a combination of fear and ignorance.
- In California, a thirty-six-year-old Mexican-American field worker, the mother of five daughters, who does not speak English, was found guilty of transporting several hundred pounds of cocaine and heroin into the United States. Susana claimed that she did not know that the van, which was not hers, contained drugs; at trial it was not proven that she did know. Her ten-year sentence does not permit parole but does allow for about sixteen months off for good behavior.

Sources: "New Drug Law Leaves No Room for Mercy" (1989); Tackett (1990); "Minor Drug Players Are Paying Big Prices" (1990); Chapman (1991).

DRUG AVAILABILITY

"As far as drug availability is concerned, the drug war has been a total failure. Drugs are as widely available now as they ever have been " (Gazzaniga 1995: 50).

arrest; the higher the crime rate, the lower the possibility of arrest per thousand crimes" (1986b: 4).

In a report to the Ford Foundation, Patricia Wald and Peter Hutt (1972: 37) recommend reducing penalties to a fine or abolishing them completely for those possessing drugs for personal use.

> If this were done, drug users—but not drug traffickers—could then be handled on a public health and social-welfare basis. . . . Law-enforcement efforts would, and in our opinion should, continue, but they would be directed at illegal distribution. And illegal drugs would remain subject to confiscation wherever found.

In Switzerland and the Netherlands there has been an unofficial policy of tolerating small-time drug sellers and their customers, as long as they do not become public nuisances. At best, law enforcement efforts, states Kleiman, can prevent the "effective decriminalization" of drugs, the point at which trafficking "is so open and flagrant that demand increases because the apparent social disapproval is reduced" (1989: xviii).

Increasing penalties for drug trafficking seems an unrealistic strategy because sentences for trafficking are already high—forty years for a second offense—and because capital punishment (for drug transaction-related murders) has now become part of the federal effort against drugs. (Severe penalties encourage in traffickers the mindset that they have little or nothing to lose by using violence in their attempts to avoid arrest and prosecution.)

Some third world countries execute drug dealers but the impact of this policy is questionable. For example, while Malaysia imposes the death penalty for anyone found trafficking in heroin or marijuana, the substances are readily available even to foreigners traveling through that country. The Drug Enforcement Administration points out that "despite severe penalties, no significant diminution of trafficking or production occurred" (1991b: 9). Draconian attempts to deal with opium and heroin abuse in Iran have proven unsuccessful. Smugglers and traffickers have been hung at a rate of about six hundred a year since 1988 (Ghazi 1991). (The U.S. State Department has accused Iran of executing political prisoners under the guise of drug-trafficking cases [Tyler 1991].) Nevertheless, it is estimated that there are more than eight-hundred-thousand heroin addicts in the country (Ghazi 1991).

The People's Republic of China routinely executes drug traffickers found in possession of a pound or more of heroin; in 1994 more than 466 were killed in Yunnan province alone (Tyler 1995). A huge neon sign on a downtown street of the drug-impacted province graphically depicts the final moments of twenty-eight young men and women, drug traffickers who were executed on 5 February 1990: "A banner on the billboard explains that the 'drug criminals' were shot 'to protect the people's bodies, minds, health, and to assure social stability and economic development in the motherland' " (Schmetzer 1991: 14). In one six-week period in 1995, China executed 152 persons for drug violations (*Chicago Tribune* June 29: 15). Despite the executions, drug trafficking continues to thrive, particularly in Yunnan and Guangdong provinces in southern China (Tyler 1995), and the country has become a transshipment point for Golden Triangle and Golden Crescent heroin. Drug addiction in Yunnan province has brought with it the plague of AIDS (Tyler 1995b).

Increasing the government's drug-law enforcement ability—for example, by improving enforcement resources and centralizing the operational

THE MICHIGAN EXPERIENCE

Under a Michigan "get tough on drugs" law, the mandatory term for possession of more than 650 grams (about 23 ounces) of an illegal drug exceeds that for either rape or second-degree murder. By 1992 there were more than 160 persons serving life sentences without parole for drug offenses. One was Gary Fannon. Fannon had just completed high school and was planning a career as an auto mechanic when he was approached by an undercover Michigan police officer. The officer, who was later fired for drug use, paid Fannon to purchase drugs for him, the amounts getting larger and larger until he bought 2.2 pounds for $32,000. Although he had no prior criminal record, Fannon was sentenced to life without parole.

However, Michigan has a desperately overcrowded prison system combined with severe budgetary problems. In 1983 the legislature had to enact the "Prison Overcrowding Act" to allow for the automatic release of inmates as new commitments were received. While the Michigan law was upheld by the U.S. Supreme Court (*Harmelin v. Michigan,* 111 S.Ct. 2680, 1991), in 1992 the state supreme court ruled it unconstitutional: The justices found the denial of parole to be unconstitutionally harsh—it is the penalty for first-degree murder—and ordered those sentenced under the law to be considered for parole after ten years.

In 1991 the Minnesota Supreme Court found unconstitutional and discriminatory against African Americans a state law providing twenty years in prison for crack possession but only five years for possession of powdered cocaine. In 1988, of the persons charged with crack possession in Minnesota, 96.6 percent were black, while those charged with possessing cocaine hydrochloride were 79.6 percent white.

Sources: Cauchon (1992); Associated Press (June 15, 1992); Associated Press (December 13, 1991).

A STING HURTS

U.S. Drug Enforcement Agency (DEA) agents hid 100 pounds of cocaine on a Belize Air International Flight going from Miami to Honduras. Hoping to track and capture drug smugglers, the DEA did not inform the three crew members, the three passengers, or Honduran officials that the drugs were on board. In Honduras, the cocaine was discovered and the passengers and crew were detained and subjected to twelve days of electric shock and rubber hose beatings (they allege in a law suit). The six were released when U.S. officials acknowledged the sting ("Victims of Botched U.S. Sting Sue" 1995).

command structure of the executive branch—can bring its own dangers. These are stressed by Edward Jay Epstein (1977: 8), who argues that President Richard Nixon used "the war on heroin" to "set up a series of special units which, it was hoped, would conduct clandestine surveillance of both government officials and newsmen during his first administration." On the basis of an executive order, the Office of Drug Abuse Law Enforcement (ODALE) was established, with agents requisitioned from the Bureau of Narcotics and Dangerous Drugs, Customs, IRS, and the Bureau of Alcohol, Tobacco and Firearms. This strike force was funded by the executive branch (Law Enforcement Assistance Administration), thus bypassing the need for congressional approval. A special-action office was set up in the White House to work with ODALE; it included Watergate participants Egil Krogh, G. Gordon Liddy, and E. Howard Hunt (McWilliams 1992). Had the Watergate scandal not intervened, Epstein (1977: 252) argues, the drug superagency proposed by the administration "might have served as the strong investigative arm for domestic surveillance that President Nixon had long quested after." As noted in the last chapter, inefficient law enforcement is the price we pay for our constitutional form of government.

Successful eradication and interdiction efforts can impact on both availability and price. However, because of the pattern of price markups in the cocaine business, efforts to eradicate crops or supply routes that increase the cost of the coca leaf tenfold add only 5 percent to the retail consumer price, while doubling seizures from importers increases consumer cost by only 10 percent (Passell 1990). John DiNardo (1993: 63) failed to find "any significant effects of law enforcement on the price of the cocaine faced by users." (See also Caulkins, Crawford, and Reuter 1993). In theory, if at some point the price rises significantly and/or the amount available for consumption falls off considerably, abusers will seek treatment or give up their drug-using habits. Past experience also reveals that when drug abusers are unable to secure their preferred substance, they frequently switch to other substances that may be even more harmful. We have already seen that heroin and cocaine have analogs pro-

WINNING BATTLES, LOSING WARS

Reducing the market for illegal drugs can have unpleasant outcomes because:

> competition will increase among dealers, perhaps violently. In addition, because selling cocaine has been the primary source of earnings for poor adult males dependent on cocaine, these individuals may turn to other forms of crime to finance their continued consumption, relying more on muggings, burglary, and shoplifting for income, just as heroin users/dealers have done for many years.

Source: "Cocaine: The First Decade." *Drug Policy Research Center Issue Paper 1,* April 1992.

duced in the United States. As long as demand remains strong, we can anticipate that successful interdiction will encourage the production of domestic inorganic (agonists) depressants and stimulants.

Wisotsky (1987) argues that our law enforcement efforts have failed and will continue to do so. He certainly has the lessons of history and classical economics on his side. "Stop talking about winning drug wars," states Trebach (1987: 383). "In the broadest sense, there is no way to win because we cannot make the drugs or their abusers go away. They will always be with us. We have never run a successful drug war and never will." Nevertheless, more extreme measures are being considered, such as shooting down aircraft suspected of transporting drugs. Legislation to accomplish this was introduced into the Senate in 1989 but ran into a storm of opposition from pilots fearful of possible mistakes. The Mexican government reports, however, that they have been shooting down aircraft suspected of carrying drugs when the planes refuse to respond to warnings (Weiner 1989).

Richard Cowan (1986: 27) argues that federal efforts against cocaine led to the development of crack: *"The iron law of drug prohibition is that the more intense the law enforcement, the more potent the drug will become.* The latest stage of this cycle has brought us the crack epidemic." Free market conditions provide an incentive for traffickers to improve the attractiveness of their product. Jeffrey Fagan and Ko-Lin Chin (1991) point out that crack was the subject of an ingenious production and marketing strategy (see also Witkin 1991). A glut of cocaine forced prices down in 1983, but even lower prices did not increase sales enough to keep up with production:

> At this point, a new product was introduced which offered the chance to expand the market in ways never before possible: crack, packaged in small quantities and selling for $5 and sometimes even less—a fraction of the usual minimum for powder—allowed dealers to attract an entirely new class of consumers. Once it took hold this change was very swift and very sweeping. (Williams 1989: 7)

OOPS!

In 1991 the Peruvian government intensified its efforts against drug traffickers in the coca-growing region of the Amazon jungle. Firing automatic weapons, the national police succeeded in bringing down a commercial airliner that was en route to an Amazon city, killing all seventeen persons aboard.

Source: "Peruvian Plane Is Shot Down in Error" (1991: 11).

By 1990 there was evidence that the crack epidemic had peaked but that heroin use was on the increase. Because heroin had lost its dominant market position to cocaine, purity levels increased substantially, allowing new users to snort or smoke the substance instead of injecting it intravenously in the more traditional manner. These changes, however, may eventually lead to an increase in price and a decrease in purity, causing many addicts to shift to the more economic (and more dangerous) intravenous ingestion (Treaster 1990g).

Insofar as drug abuse is caused by societal deficiencies in education, housing, and other quality-of-life-variables, the more we expend on law enforcement, the less we have available to deal with these social ills, which continue to foster greater drug abuse. Not only are we spinning our wheels in the mud, but the faster we go, the deeper the hole becomes. Furthermore, "When criminals are the most successful people in a community, the effect on that community's natural order is devastating. The authority of parents, schools, religious leaders, and (legal) businesspeople is undermined, and violent criminals become role models" (Boaz 1990: 3).

We must recognize a troubling aspect of drug trafficking: It operates according to the powerful forces of free market capitalism. It is paradoxical that politicians who argue that capitalism defeated Communism in Eastern Europe also talk of defeating the business of drugs. They fail to recognize that these same forces are operating in the drug trade, and that government cannot compete effectively with the free market.

Supply Reduction: Controlling Drugs at Their Source

Our current policy of attempting to control drugs at their source has had unintended consequences. The successful effort to force Turkey to curtail its production of opium in the 1970s resulted in a concomitant rise in production in Mexico and Southeast Asia. In Southeast Asia, the United States has pro-

<table>
<tr><td>VOICE OF EXPERIENCE</td></tr>
</table>

"Economics has a natural law: Supply is determined by the demand. When cocaine stops being consumed, when there's no demand for it . . . that will be the end of the business" (Cali Cartel leader Gilberto Rodriguez Orejuela in Moody 1991: 36).

vided weaponry to the government of Burma (Myanmar) to deal with drug trafficking in its part of the Golden Triangle. These armaments enabled the brutal Burmese military to be more effective against indigenous populations fighting for independence from Rangoon. In response, the opium growers and drug traffickers controlled by the independence movements increased their drug-related activities in order to secure better weaponry such as ground-to-air missiles to use against U.S.-supplied helicopters. Most of the money given to Colombia to fight the cocaine cartels has been used instead by the military in its fight against Marxist insurgencies (de Lama 1989; Lane et al. 1992). A similar situation exists in Peru, where U.S. military assistance is used to fight leftist insurgents. At the end of 1991, the United States began withholding drug-fighting aid to Peru because of charges that the Peruvian military was aiding cocaine traffickers: Army units have reportedly fired on police helicopters engaged in antidrug missions (Krauss 1991b). U.S. advisors in Bolivia believe that many of the military conscripts they are training for antidrug enforcement will eventually be employed by the traffickers because their training makes them a valuable resource (Lane et al. 1992).

There is concern that the fight against drugs is simply a way for the United States to finance a sub-rosa war against leftist insurgents without incurring strong congressional opposition (Shenon 1990; Krauss 1991) that could focus attention on the excesses of government forces. In Peru, for example, the government response to terrorists has grown indiscriminate and sadistic. This was dramatized by a 1991 incident videotaped by a news reporter in which a medical student, on his way to a study session, and two unfortunate teenagers were arrested and shoved into the trunks of police cars. Their bodies were later found with multiple bullet wounds (Nash 1991). "Peru leads the world in documented cases of disappearances of people taken prisoner by security forces" (Brooke 1991g: 6). According to the Human Rights Watch-Americas, pressure on the government of Bolivia to deal with coca cultivation has led to widespread trampling of civil rights and physical abuse of citizens (Vivanco 1995).

U.S. criticism and threats against the government of Mexico for not doing enough against drug trafficking have caused a great deal of ill will south of the border. Mexican officials respond that their efforts have been extraordinary; they argue that the United States has failed to deal with the consumption end of the problem (Rohter 1988). Peter Smith (1987: 130) states that the "Mexican government has made a good faith effort to eradicate narcotic production and trade. Thousands of police and about 25,000 military troops have been assigned to this campaign; hundreds have been wounded or have lost their lives." Smith points out that the Mexican establishment has no reason to permit the consolidation of narcotic kingdoms, an empire within an empire, because "drug-trade patronage lies outside the control of the regime . . . and, in times of declining resources, it therefore threatens the regime."

The danger of using the military in efforts against drug trafficking is highlighted by one incident: On 11 April 1988, commandos from the Mexican military attacked a welding shop in a sedate residential neighborhood in Caborca, Mexico, a prosperous farming town sixty miles south of Arizona. The soldiers were apparently targeting the organization of Miguel Caro Quintero, brother of the imprisoned drug kingpin Rafael Caro Quintero, but instead killed four young apprentices with machine-gun fire. The Caro Quinteros do not own the welding shop, although they do own many legitimate businesses in the area. Under rising pressure from Washington to do something about drugs flowing into the United States from Mexico, "but burdened by limited budgets, training and intelligence-gathering capabilities," Larry Rohter (1988b: 7) notes, "they [the Mexican military] often end up antagonizing the very citizens they are charged with defending, and whose rights they are supposed to respect." In 1991 Mexican soldiers killed seven Mexican drug agents who were preparing to raid a Colombian plane that had landed on a rural air strip (Golden 1991b). In 1990 the Mexican government launched a media campaign in the United States to present its version of the fight against drugs. In fact, Mexican antidrug efforts have led to a rise in poppy production in neighboring Guatemala, whose government is ill equipped to respond to the problem (Sheppard 1990).

We have gotten macho with the government of Colombia, imposing customs restrictions on passengers and shipments that originate or stop there; Avianca Airlines has been fined millions of dollars by the U.S. government. But policymakers sitting safely in Washington do not have to deal with the reality that is Colombia:

> First drug traffickers murdered the security chief of Avianca, Colombia's largest privately owned airline, two days after he seized $5 million worth of cocaine that had been smuggled aboard a Miami-bound cargo jet. . . . Then several days later, two of the victim's colleagues received death threats, one in the form of a miniature casket delivered to his doorstep and the other a funeral mass card bearing his name. (Wiedrich 1988: Sec. 4: 1)

Both resigned. The cocaine business has been detrimental to the Colombian economy, in contrast to its effect on poorer countries. In Cartegena, for example, drug-inspired terrorism led to travelers' advisory warnings by U.S. and Canadian governments, causing a severe economic downturn in this tourist port city of about 500,000. (Government leniency for traffickers

HYPOCRISY?

What is the difference between exporting a pound of coke from a producer country and exporting an AR-15 and its ammunition from the U.S. to murder innocent people in developing countries? Why are countries such as Germany free to export materials used to refine cocaine? Why do countries like Switzerland, Panama and even the U.S. protect money whose origin is dubious? (Cali cocaine cartel leader Gilberto Rodriguez Orejuela in Moody 1991:36)

brought an end to this violence and tourism returned ["Colombian City Basks in Terror's End" 1991].) In addition to the cost of government efforts to fight the traffickers, the stigma on Colombian products and the associated security mechanisms add enormous costs to exporting Colombian products ("Colombian Growth Hurt by Cocaine" 1991). And, as noted in chapter 6, crackdowns, insofar as they have succeeded in Colombia, have had an unintended result—displacement. Ecuador and Brazil now have cocaine-processing laboratories; Argentina, Uruguay, and Chile have emerged as major money-laundering centers; drug-related corruption scandals have hit Argentina and Venezuela, which, along with Chile, serve as major cocaine transshipment centers (Nash 1992).

Colombian officials, like the Mexican government, criticize the United States for doing little to stem consumption. During the Colombian presidential election of 1990, campaign speeches frequently made angry references to Marion Barry, the mayor of Washington, D.C., who was videotaped by federal agents smoking crack. His misdemeanor conviction on only one of fourteen charges relating to drug use further inflamed Colombian public opinion (Brooke 1990h). After his release, Barry was reelected mayor of the nation's capital. To place the issue in perspective, Peter Bourne points out that "more Colombians die from the effects of U.S. tobacco products than the number of Americans who die from Colombian cocaine. Yet we are unwilling to lift even a twig to curb the trafficking of this drug whose cultivation is subsidized by U.S. taxpayers" (1990:11). Colombians can also justifiably complain about the smuggling of firearms from the United States into their country, a trade encouraged by weak U.S. gun control laws. In 1989 firearms purchased in Miami gun shops were used to assassinate three Colombian presidential candidates. The United States is a primary source of weapons for Latin American drug traffickers: Ships and planes with drug cargoes easily load up on firearms for the return trip (Rohter 1991).

In Peru and Bolivia inhabitants of coca-growing areas are strongly opposed to U.S.-inspired efforts to eradicate their most important cash crop, and both countries face Marxist insurgencies that are particularly strong in these remote regions. In 1987 thousands of coca growers blocked roads and staged demonstrations to express their opposition to the presence of fourteen military

COCA

Not only is coca fully integrated into Andean society but it is also an integral part of the region's ecosystem—a stubborn and dismaying biological fact impeding those who would like to make it disappear. As a cultivated plant, coca is nearly ideal. It has few predators and pests. . . . The plant will grow in soils too poor and on slopes too steep to support other crops, will live for forty years or more, and will tolerate many harvests a year. (Weil 1995: 72)

instructors from the United States who had been sent to help Bolivian authorities train members of their antidrug force. The growers were from a region where the soil is not considered good enough to grow anything *but* coca bush (Christian 1987). That same year, the United States cut aid to Bolivia in retaliation for that country's failure to curtail coca cultivation. Such action may do more harm than good, notes Peter Lupsha (1990): It may increase the influence of the rich drug-trafficking cartels over these governments. Unfortunately, in addition to providing a livelihood for Bolivian farmers, cocaine brings an estimated $600 million into Bolivia, more than all legal exports combined ("U.S. to Cut Bolivian Aid Over Drug-War Failure" 1987). In Peru's Upper Huallaga Valley, which extends for 200 miles along the Huallaga River, an estimated sixty thousand families depend on coca as a cash crop for their survival. Large-scale eradication, notes Alan Riding (1988b: 6), could "provoke a social convulsion, forcing thousands of families to leave the area" and creating deep resentment that Marxist guerrillas exploit. "Coca is Peru's largest export, earning more than one billion dollars a year. As many as one million of the country's twenty-one million citizens are involved in the trade" (Massing 1990: 26). Despite millions of dollars in U.S. aid to eradicate coca in Peru, the effort has not been successful: By the end of 1990 there had been a 25 percent increase in coca cultivation (Brooke 1991b). RAND analyst Peter Reuter points out an irony: "Increasing the risks of growing coca [and thereby reducing quantities] might raise the price needed to induce farmers to grow it" (Passell 1991: C2).

Wisotsky (1987: 57) states that:

> In both Peru and Bolivia, the failure of coca control is not a temporary aberration but a function of culture, tradition, and the weakness and poverty of underdevelopment. These basic social conditions render effective enforcement against coca impossible. Widespread corruption in the enforcement agencies, the judiciary, and elsewhere in government is endemic. Indeed, the central governments do not necessarily control major portions of the coca-growing countryside, where the traffickers rule like feudal lords.

Participation in the illicit cocaine economy, writes Edmundo Morales (1986: 157), "is inevitable. Not only is the natives' traditional way of life intertwined with coca, but their best cash crop is the underground economy for which no substitute has yet been provided."

Crop-substitution programs as part of our effort to control drugs at their source have met with only limited success. As long as demand remains high, the price offered for poppy or coca will be many times that received for conventional crops. There are other problems: In 1991 the leader of a Peruvian coca-growers association who had agreed to a crop-substitution program was murdered, reputedly by corrupt government officials earning money from the cocaine business (Strong 1992). Attempts to eradicate the crop by cutting or burning result in healthier and more bountiful growth, while uprooting coca plants causes the soil to become unproductive for as long as eight to ten years (Morales 1989). An eradication program in the Upper Huallaga Valley was established with U.S. funding in 1982, but since that time about forty of its workers have been murdered. The United States subsequently suspended the program (Massing 1990). An alternative is the use of aerial herbicides that are either sprayed or dropped as pellets and that melt into the soil when it rains. A major difficulty is finding environmentally safe herbicides: The United States has been conducting research on a variety of such substances. The most successful herbicides, however, kill many species of plants, including crop plants,

ROBERTO FERNANDEZ, BOLIVIAN FATHER AND COCA GROWER

Roberto Fernandez is a Bolivian who earns the equivalent of one dollar a day as a mine-entrance watchman. "Some days, if I don't have enough work, I can't buy each of my children a whole bread roll. I have to cut the breads in half. Or, if I eat one bread roll myself, my daughter Erica [age six] has no breakfast. I have to work 16 hours a day so that Erica can have her breakfast."

"When Roberto Fernandez considers whether to cultivate the coca plant," notes James North, "he does not visualize despairing crack addicts in far-off American cities that he will never be able to visit. . . . No, he sees his daughter Erica." (North 1988: 21)

IN THE UPPER HUALLAGA VALLEY

An old barefoot Indian man walked into one of the showrooms recently, carrying a large sack on his back. He looked around a moment, spotted a little blue pickup, and asked the price. The dealer named a sum, the equivalent in (1980) Peruvian soles of about U.S. $10,000. Fine, the old man said. He would take it. He opened his sack, took out a heap of crumpled bills and counted out the money. The dealer handed him the keys and the sale was over. (Morales 1989: xvi) and they remain in the soil, affecting future plantings. Environmentalists have raised objections to the use of herbicides, and the companies that produce them are concerned about potential liability and fear that their employees in South America may become targets of retribution by trafficking organizations (Riding 1988b).

Furthermore, Lee McIntosh (1988: 26) has found that a "single genetic mutation can give rise to complete resistance in a similar herbicide. This implies it may be necessary continually to spray different classes of herbicides in the future." The human and political dangers inherent in this approach to drug control should serve as a restraining influence.

While Mexico "was once considered as having one of the most successful crop eradication programs in the world," the Comptroller General (1988b: 8) notes that "it has been unable to significantly reduce illegal cultivation despite more than $118 million in U.S. and Mexican funding between 1984–87 to support a bilaterial aerial eradication program." Use of herbicides in Mexico has led growers to develop techniques to make aerial eradication more difficult:

> In 1977 when eradication of almost 10,000 hectares [hectare = 2.47 acres] of opium poppies was reported, fields were large and in open flat areas. Cultivators reacted to the aerial eradication program by decreasing the size of their fields and planting in more remote areas, often at higher altitudes and often on the sides of steep ravines, under trees, or otherwise camouflaged. Spraying the higher, more remote fields required greater aircraft capacity for fuel and herbicides. . . . [And] farmers were often able to wash off the herbicides sprayed on their plants. (Comptroller General 1988: 19)

In fact, notes Lupsha (1990), if all of the coca that the producing countries of Latin America have publicly committed themselves to eradicate over the next few years were actually eradicated, the effect in the United States would be minimal. It is likely that African, Middle Eastern, and southeast Asian areas would be able to cultivate enough to meet consumer demand in coca indefinitely (as they have done with opium). Epstein (1988: 25) points out that "the entire cocaine market in the United States can be supplied for a year by a single cargo plane." Furthermore, as noted in previous chapters, curtailing importation without affecting demand provides an incentive for greater domestic efforts: the production of synthetic analogs for cocaine and heroin and stronger strains of marijuana. The highly inventive marijuana horticulturists of California are using a new, faster-growing, highly potent strain that matures in three months (older strains require four months). The cultivation of this new strain has been discovered in the national forests of Northern California. (Growing marijuana on federal lands was made a felony in 1987, punishable by a prison term of up to ten years.)

In response to law enforcement efforts against imported marijuana, some innovative growers have established elaborate underground farms equipped with diesel-powered lights and ventilation systems. Their use of hy-

SUSPICIOUS GARDENING

DEA agents have issued subpoenas to dozens of garden-supply centers seeking the names of their customers. The super-sleuths think this is an effective way to find out who is secretly growing marijuana.

This is great news because it must mean that the DEA has finally corked the immense flow of cocaine, heroin, marijuana and other illegal drugs coming from abroad. . . . They must have shut down the narcotics traffic if they have enough time to subpoena garden centers for their lists of amateur gardeners so they can discover which ones are growing tomatoes and which ones are actually drug kingpins. . . .

It shows how ludicrous and futile the nation's interdiction efforts can get. U.S. drug policy would make a lot more sense if the government put a greater effort on reducing the demand for illegal drugs. (*Chicago Tribune* editorial, 23 October 1991)

droponic technology—growing plants in water to which nutrients have been added—has helped make marijuana the number one cash crop in the United States. In response, the DEA has been subpoenaing the records of businesses selling hydroponic equipment in order to discover indoor marijuana growers. These records contain the names of mostly legitimate growers paying by check or credit card—marijuana traffickers usually pay cash—who may be subjected to DEA inquiries (Bishop 1991).

There is evidence that U.S. efforts against drug trafficking are often secondary to foreign policy considerations. The Anti-Drug Abuse Act of 1986, for example, requires the president to "certify" to Congress that producer and transshipment nations have made adequate progress in attacking drug production and trafficking. Without certification, a country can lose aid, loans, and trade preferences. Elaine Sciolino (1988) reports that the law has numerous loopholes allowing several nations to be certified despite their failure to cooperate in the war against drugs. In 1990 of the twenty-four major drug-producing and drug-transiting countries only four—Afghanistan, Burma, Iran, and Syria—were denied certification. At the other extreme, the United States has turned to the military in Guatemala, a major producer of opium and a leading transshipment point for Colombian cocaine, to take the lead in efforts against trafficking. The Guatemalan military, however, has been responsible for human rights abuses that have plagued the country (Gruson 1990). For many years we tolerated the drug-trafficking activities of our Central American ally, General Manuel Noriega. When his politics took on a decidedly anti-U.S. tone, in 1988 the general was indicted and apprehended, following the "Operation Just Cause" invasion of Panama. (For a discussion of Noriega, his relationship with the United States, and drug dealing, see John Dinges 1990; Kempe 1990.)

Peter Andreas and his colleagues note that "after more than a decade of U.S. efforts to reduce the cocaine supply, more cocaine is produced in more places than ever before. Curiously, the U.S. response to failure has been to escalate rather than reevaluate." And they state:

> The logic of escalation in the drug war is in fact strikingly similar to the arguments advanced when U.S. coutnerinsurgency strategies, undercut by ineffective and uncommitted governments and security forces, were failing in Vietnam: "We've just begun to fight." "We're turning the corner."

Andreas and his colleagues argue that "since failure can so easily be used to justify further escalation, how do we know whether we are really turning the corner or simply running around in a vicious circle?" (1991–92: 107).

Demand Reduction: Drug Testing

The PCOC (1986), in what has become its most controversial recommendation, has suggested extensive drug testing as a device for reducing consumer demand. Public and private employers began testing new and old employees, generating criticism and lawsuits. Drug testing of prospective employees has become almost routine at many major corporations. The military has extended its program of drug testing, and various levels of govern-

A 1986 demonstration in Berkeley, California, opposing a plan for mandatory drug testing.

ment have initiated the testing of employees in critical areas involving public safety, particularly law enforcement and transportation. Some states have reacted to increasing protests about the practice by enacting legislation barring random testing of employees, and in a number of states the practice is thwarted by constitutional provisions guaranteeing individuals the right to privacy.

In such states, for an intrusive act such as mandatory drug testing to be constitutional, there must be a "compelling interest." In a 1987 case, a computer programmer dismissed from her job for refusing to take a drug test on the grounds of personal privacy was awarded $485,000—a San Francisco jury failed to find "compelling interest." That city has subsequently enacted an ordinance prohibiting mandatory testing except when an employer has reason to believe—"reasonable suspicion"—that an employee is impaired because of drug use (Bishop 1987). In 1989 the Supreme Court upheld the testing of railroad employees for drugs after an accident and ruled that personnel of the U.S. Customs Service in sensitive positions must submit to drug testing, even in the absence of "individualized suspicion" (*Skinner v. Railway Labor Executives' Association,* 109 S.Ct. 1402; *National Treasury Employees Union v. von Raab,* 109 S.Ct. 1384). In a six-month study completed in 1990, slightly more than 3 percent of 65,000 U.S. transportation workers tested positive for drugs—mostly marijuana and cocaine—as did 4.2 percent of applicants for such positions (Cawley 1990). Lower federal courts have rejected the testing of *public* employees suspected of using drugs in a manner that does not affect job performance; the U.S. Constitution does not similarly protect *private* employees. In an Oregon case, the U.S. Supreme Court (6–3) approved of the random urinalysis of public school athletes as a condition of their continued participation (*Vernonia School District v. Acton,* No. 94–590, 1995).

Drug testing can only determine that the subject has used a drug recently; it cannot determine when or how much. Tests cannot discern the casual user from a chronic one. There is concern over the inadequacy of testing—false positives that could destroy the careers of innocent employees. There is also some irony: An employer is interested in having a drug-free workplace because controlled substances are presumed to be detrimental to job performance. If this is so, then monitoring job performance—a rather routine managerial task—makes more sense than drug testing; there are persons who will perform quite well even though their urine reveals drugs. Nevertheless, drug testing has spawned a growth industry.

Primarily because of its low cost, about five dollars a test, the enzyme-multiplied immune test is the most frequently used urinalysis (Wish n.d.: 2):

> These tests depend on a chemical reaction between the specimen and an antibody designed to react to a specific drug. The chemical reaction causes a change in the specimen's transmission of light, which is measured by a machine. If the reading is higher than a given standard, the specimen is positive for the drug.

Eric Wish (n.d.: 2) notes that there have been complaints of relatively high rates of false positives using this test, sometimes as a result of commonly used licit drugs cross-reacting with the test's antibody. "Sloppy recording procedures by laboratory staff and failure to maintain careful controls over the chain of custody of the specimen can also produce serious test errors."

The most accurate test, gas chromatography/mass spectroscopy, notes Wish (n.d.), is relatively expensive, about $100 per specimen for screening and confirmation, but so is the cost of firing or not hiring someone because of a false positive. Drug-testing programs often use the enzyme-multiplied immune test for an initial screening and then submit all positives for gas chromatography/mass spectroscopy. Because of the legal implications of a false positive, new controls have been added, resulting in significant improvements over testing methods used during the 1980s. The National Institute of Drug Abuse (NIDA) certifies drug-testing firms, a necessity for securing federal contracts. NIDA has certified about fifty labs, which must maintain stringent standards in areas such as sample collection, storage, personnel, laboratory controls, and testing procedures and accuracy.

In more recent years there has been increasing interest in hair analysis for drugs of abuse. Collecting samples is easy and is not subject to evasive actions designed to produce false negatives—shampooing, for example, has no effect. Hair analysis has been used for some time to detect exposure to such toxic metals as mercury and lead. In a process similar to urinalysis, dissolved hair shafts reveal whether drugs are in the blood. Because of the unique qualities of hair growth—about one-half inch a month—it may be possible to determine the amount of drug use over a period of several months and whether it is increasing or decreasing. There are complications, however. The test can also be positive for those who come into contact with drugs via touching the skin or sweat of a user or through exposure to air where the substance has been smoked (Baumgartner, Hill, and Blahd 1989). Hair analysis has been suggested as an initial screening method for drug use. Positive results are corroborated by urinalysis (Magura, Kang, and Shapiro 1995; Mieczkowski 1995).

Security companies investigate drug residues in the workplace by using portable machines that can identify vapors from minuscule particles of heroin, cocaine, and methamphetamines. Samples are gathered at such critical areas as doorknobs or desktops by cloth or vacuum cleaners and analyzed through gas chromatography, a process that separates out compounds according to their boiling points. A readout indicates the type of substance detected ("Sniffing for Drugs by Testing Vapors" 1991).

The rationale behind drug testing is confused. The standard explanation is that impaired workers represent a workplace hazard. This may indeed be true, but drug testing does not reveal impairment, and impaired workers are most likely to be alcohol abusers. There is a lack of documentation proving that workers testing positive for illegal drugs have a higher rate of accidents (Noble 1992). Sound public relations may better explain workplace drug testing than sound public policy.

Demand Reduction: Criminal Prosecution for Fetal Liability

"The intractable nature of our narcotics problem," noted Russell Baker (1988: 15), "may be gauged from the absurdity of the ideas advanced to end it." The latest absurdity is the prosecution of drug-using pregnant women for fetal endangerment, delivering drugs to a minor, or child abuse. This novel use of the criminal sanction—"creating crime" (Maschke 1995)—dates back to the end of the 1980s, when drug abuse was high in the political consciousness of elected officials, and an increasing number of "drug babies" were being reported. It is estimated that about 350,000 infants annually are exposed prenatally to some form of illegal drug (Nolan 1990). Prosecution is sometimes used to coerce women into drug treatment, although drug treatment programs may not be readily available and those that are may be unwilling or unable to provide for pregnant clients. The first woman convicted for delivering a controlled substance to her fetus, in Florida in 1990, was sentenced to a year in a drug treatment program and fourteen years probation; her conviction was upheld by a state appeals court the following year but was later voided by the Florida Supreme Court (Lewin 1991; 1992). In 1991 the Michigan Court of Appeals ruled that a woman who took crack hours before giving birth could not be charged with delivering cocaine to her son through the umbilical cord. In response to the decision, the Muskegon County prosecutor defended his decision to charge the woman: "This is a major health care crisis and we must use whatever means we can to reach a solution" (Wilkerson 1991: 13). Health care officials who supported the woman expressed fear that prosecuting drug-using pregnant women will drive them away from prenatal care. Courts have dismissed similar cases in North Carolina, Ohio, and Pensacola, Florida (Lewin 1991).

It is difficult, if not impossible, to separate the effects of drugs from those of poverty and poor prenatal care. While we know that women who abuse heroin during pregnancy frequently give birth to infants suffering from Neonatal Abstinence Syndrome—the newborn suffers withdrawal symptoms—we do not know if there are long-range effects directly attributable to the use of drugs. Furthermore, the fetus can be endangered by any number of maternal behaviors not related to *illegal* drug use—for example, "too much or too little exercise, an inadequate or harmful diet, or use of cigarettes, alcohol [6,000 to 8,000 born annually with fetal alcohol syndrome], and other [lawful] drugs" (Nolan 1990: 13–14). Other risks include the general environment and specific workplace exposures. Research has revealed that infants (about 750,000 per year) exposed to a high level of cigarette smoke (one pack or more per day) suffer from decreased birth weight, head circumference, and body length; there are also increased rates of spontaneous abortions and bleeding during pregnancy. As noted in chapter 1, an estimated 5,600 infants die each year as a result of smoking by their pregnant mothers. A study in 1994 revealed that mothers who smoke as few as ten

RUSH TO JUDGMENT?

Despite considerable concern about the high rate of cocaine use among pregnant women, studies have failed to find a homogenous pattern of fetal effects, and there is little consensus on the adverse effects of the drug (Finnegan et al. 1994). An overwhelming majority of women using cocaine also ingest other drugs, including nicotine, alcohol, marijuana, and opiates. And many suffer from sexual and physical abuse (Finnegan 1993).

cigarettes a day cause their children under five to test positive for cancer-causing compounds (Hilts 1994). There is also concern about the long-range effects of fetal exposure to tobacco with respect to intellectual and behavioral development (Nolan 1990).

And what of the liability of the father who is using illegal drugs or alcohol or tobacco? Recent research suggests that psychoactive substances are hazardous to spermatozoa (Finnegan 1993). Furthermore, what about the societal responsibility to provide adequate prenatal care for all pregnant women? (For an examination of the legal aspects of the fetal liability issue, see the entire issue of *Criminal Justice Ethics* 9, Winter/Spring, 1990.) It would appear that the nonmedical use of controlled substances is only one facet of a significantly greater social problem that will not be resolved by a simplistic recourse to criminal law. Rocco D'Angelo and Rudolph Alexander (1991) favor compulsory drug treatment using civil statutes, although they recognize that adequate treatment facilities for pregnant women do not yet exist. There are only about 10,000 slots for the estimated 250,000 pregnant women who could benefit from them (Associated Press, 18 September 1991), and a national survey found a scarcity of treatment facilities for drug-abusing women with limited financial resources (Wellisch, Prendergast, Anglin 1994).

An equally pressing problem is the cost of providing for infants of drug-abusing mothers: Foster care for one child ranges from $15,000 to $20,000 a year. New York City has responded to this problem by permitting drug-abusing mothers to keep their children at home under the intensive supervision of a social worker (Treaster 1991). A study in Illinois found that while white and African-American women show similar rates of illegal drug use during pregnancy, "the black women are more likely to be reported to authorities" (Olen 1991: Sec. 3: 14). Illinois is one of a number of states where medical personnel are required to report suspected prenatal drug use to authorities. However, few places in the state can care for babies born with drugs in their bloodstream, so these infants are usually sent home with their mothers and given some type of outpatient help and monitoring (Poe and Searcey 1996).

Demand Reduction: Expanding Treatment

While the core of the U.S. response to drug abuse has centered on enforcement, expanding the availability of treatment may be more productive for reducing demand. There is almost universal agreement that without reduced demand, our efforts will remain ineffective. Unfortunately,

> Not only is there a desperate lack of clinics, long-term rehabilitation centers and counselors, but there is no comprehensive system linking existing services or seeking to steer addicts toward help. Nor is there adequate follow-up to insure that addicts move from one step of treatment to the next. No major city in the country has a central referral system or clearing house for treatment services, and while many centers have long waiting lists, vacancies at others go begging. (Treaster 1990d: 16)

The cost effectiveness of *treatment versus law enforcement* is emphasized by Peter Rydell and Susan Everingham (1994: xv). They argue that $246 million dollars would have to be spent on domestic law enforcement to achieve the same reduction in drug use that could be achieved by spending $34 million on treatment. And no assumption is made about the long-range effect of treatment—abstinence—on the individual abuser: "The cost advantage is so large that even if the after-treatment effect is ignored, treatment is still more cost-effective than law enforcement."

Methadone Treatment

As noted above, methadone has proven an attractive substitute for narcotic maintenance programs in England. In an editorial ("Which War on Drugs?" 1987), the *New York Times* states (incorrectly) that methadone "effectively blocks the heroin craving" and that "nearly all heroin addicts eventually will try to quit as they weary of committing crimes or otherwise finding $100 a day to finance the habit." While this is a dubious assertion, as noted in chapter 5, methadone maintenance has proven an effective method of dealing with the drug abuse problems of certain heroin addicts. Nevertheless, there are reportedly long waiting lists of heroin addicts wanting to enter methadone treatment programs. Researchers for the General Accounting Office (GAO 1990), however, did not find any significant shortage of treatment slots, although addicts on waiting lists at one program often did not know about treatment available elsewhere or were constrained by geographic considerations.

The GAO researchers did find numerous problems with existing methadone maintenance programs (1990: 13): "At 10 of the 24 clinics, more than 20 percent of the patients continued to use heroin after 6 months of treat-

VIEW FROM THE RIGHT

Treatment is not now available for almost half of those who would benefit from it. Yet we are willing to build more and more jails in which to isolate drug users even though at one-seventh the cost of building and maintaining jail space and pursuing, detaining, and prosecuting the drug user, we could subsidize commensurately effective medical care and psychological treatment. (William F. Buckley, "War on Drugs Is Lost" 1996: 37)

ment. . . . At two clinics almost one-half the patients continued to use heroin. We also found that many of the patients used other drugs, primarily cocaine." Few comprehensive services were offered at the clinics; patients were usually referred to other agencies, but the clinics did not know if patients used the referred services. And none of the programs evaluated the effectiveness of their treatment.

Furthermore, if drug abuse is a response to social conditions, such as a lack of educational and employment opportunity and efforts to find a meaningful life,[1] then changing social conditions—as opposed to individual treatment—would be the rational response to the problem.

Mandatory Treatment

It is the possession of controlled substances that constitutes a crime—an addict is not a criminal by virtue of his or her addiction. In *Robinson v. California,* 370 U.S. 660 (1962), the Supreme Court ruled that persons cannot be prosecuted for "being under the influence" or for "internal possession" of illegal drugs. The Court, in that same decision, upheld the civil commitment of drug addicts for purposes of *treatment* (similar to commitment of the mentally ill): "A state might determine that the general health and welfare require that the victims of these and other human afflictions might be dealt with by compulsory treatment, involving quarantine, confinement, or sequestration." Some twenty-seven states have made such a determination and enacted legislation that permits the civil commitment of drug addicts (Kaplan 1983b). Only California and New York, however, have made extensive use of such statutes. As noted in chapter 5, in 1961 the California legislature passed comprehensive legislation raising the penalties for drug violations and providing for the compulsory civil commitment of narcotic addicts. In its first twelve years, the Cal-

---

1. As noted in chapter 4, the "retreat" into drugs provides a lifestyle of excitement with attainable goals—getting "high" (Waldorf 1973; Irwin 1970; Sackman et al. 1978).

ifornia Civic Addict Program admitted more than 18,000 addicts for treatment. Most of those committed to the program, however, were persons who had been convicted of felony crimes, with a much smaller number convicted of misdemeanors, and an even smaller amount committed without any criminal charges at all (Wood 1973). While the California program continues to operate, the New York program was discontinued in 1974 after an enormous expenditure of tax dollars with, at best, questionable results.

Bruce Johnson and his colleagues (1986, 1986b) argue in favor of mandatory treatment, because almost all objective evidence suggests that drug treatment has an important impact on heroin-cocaine abuser criminality. The cost of such a policy, they note, would be prohibitive unless treatment was on an outpatient basis, a method they support. Because most heroin and cocaine abusers have come into contact with the criminal justice system, all criminal defendants should be subjected to drug tests, which, if positive, should require mandatory treatment. They argue that drug treatment should be part of any sentence for convicted drug abusers and that postrelease treatment should be a condition of probation/parole supervision, with a careful monitoring of urine for at least one year. This writer has supervised heroin addicts on parole in New York, and their careful monitoring by a parole officer does ensure a high rate of abstinence, at least during the period of supervision. But, as noted by the Office of National Drug Control Policy, supervision in the community is often superficial, "so overcrowded and so loosely managed that it can barely be said to exist in any meaningful sense. Offenders who violate the condition of probation often go unpunished, remaining at liberty until they are arrested again for yet another drug offense" (1989: 26).

MEASURING THE RESULTS OF POLICY CHANGES

A major problem with instituting any changes in policy is measurement of results. Increases or decreases in the number of persons using illegal substances cannot be measured with any accuracy, and the statistics that are often presented as "data" are usually meaningless. As noted earlier in this chapter, there are no direct measures of the incidence of drug use in the general population; all estimates are derivative: "measures which infer such incidence or prevalence from various data gathered by law enforcement or medical sources" (Lidz and Walker 1980: 49).

Patrick Biernacki (1986: 189) points out:

> It cannot be determined with any degree of certainty what effect U.S. drug policy has had on the addict population. What we do know is that the indicators used to estimate the size of the addict population at any one time are unreliable. For example, if the number of hospital emergency room admissions for heroin

overdoses drops, does this indicate the effectiveness of police control methods, or the successful treatment of addicts? Or can the drop in admissions be attributed to a change in drug preference? Or to an increase in the number of natural recoveries?

Natural recovery, or the abandoning of heroin use, was discovered among returning Vietnam veterans on a relatively large scale (Robins 1973, 1974) (Robins, Helzer, Hesselbrock, and Wish 1980).[2] To the extent that we have been able to measure the effect of our drug policy, the results, but not necessarily the claims, have not been clear.

CONCLUSION

Suggesting a comprehensive policy acceptable to mainstream America does not take a great deal of imagination—but it would take a great deal of money to carry out. The level of funding required to institute most of these recommendations makes them unrealistic in the present economic-political climate. We already spend about $4 billion a year on controlling illegal drugs, with more than half going for drug-law enforcement.

Reducing the consumption of drugs by increasing law enforcement and large-scale treatment programs does not solve such significant sociological problems as lack of educational and employment opportunity and residential instability. We know that drug abuse is not randomly dispersed over the population but, rather, concentrated in areas of poverty. Insofar as drug abuse is the result of despair, frustration, hopelessness, and alienation, programs directed only at the symptom—drug abuse—cannot succeed. Elliott Currie (1993) points out that drug abuse is not an isolated problem within stricken inner city communities but part of a syndrome that includes family disintegration, child abuse/neglect, delinquency, and alcohol abuse. Successful treatment of individual drug abusers would not stem the tide of new entries generated by unchanged social conditions that serve as a fertile breeding ground. "Even the best, most comprehensive programs to help addicts transform their lives will inevitably be compromised if we do not simultaneously address the powerful social forces that are destroying the communities to which they must return" (1993: 279).

No author enjoys ending a book, particularly one designed for a college audience, on a note of pessimism. Defeatism is anathema to the American culture—Yankee ingenuity can overcome any problem, just as we have overcome the Nazis, Iraqis, Communists, and a host of diseases. But reality indicates that some problems, particularly social ones—crime and poverty, for example—can be intractable. The United States has the widest gap between rich and poor in the industrial world, and that gap is growing (Bradsher, 1995b, 1995c).

2. On natural recovery among middle-class addicts, see Granfield and Cloud (1996).

A COMPREHENSIVE PROGRAM FOR RESPONDING TO DRUG ABUSE

1. Institute educational programs at the elementary, high school, and college levels that fully present all aspects of the use of psychoactive chemicals, including moderation and controlled use. Unfortunately, to date there has been little evidence to indicate that educational efforts actually reduce the use of drugs, although they may encourage a more rational or controlled use.

2. Decriminalize marijuana for personal use to conserve valuable resources and to avoid stigmatizing persons unnecessarily. This may also help "steer young people away from hard drugs by breaking the connection between marijuana smokers and drug pushers." In many cities, notes Andrew Kupfer (1988: 40), "pushers are walking drugstores, selling marijuana and hashish, barbiturates, stimulants, cocaine, and heroin." Furthermore, notes Richard Cowan (1986), effective law enforcement against marijuana drives up the price and may move users toward more readily available crack cocaine.

3. Reduce the supply of drugs by enhancing domestic law enforcement; that is, significantly increase personnel and equipment for the Coast Guard, Customs, and DEA (the FBI should not have drug-law enforcement responsibilities, because this merely increases interagency conflict and detracts from the major law enforcement role of that agency, which includes combatting espionage and terrorism).

4. Reduce the supply of drugs at source countries; that is, provide more technical support and equipment and more financing for crop-substitution and eradication programs.

5. Reduce the consumer market by expanding local law enforcement efforts and place all convicted drug abusers on intensive probation supervision or incarceration followed by intensive parole supervision. This would require a significant increase in local law enforcement personnel assigned to drug-law enforcement, an expansion of correctional facilities (which are already overtaxed), and a significant increase in probation and parole personnel.

6. Drastically expand the availability of treatment programs, enabling every substance abuser—including those addicted to nicotine and alcohol—to have access to treatment. Continue research efforts into the causes of substance abuse and the effectiveness of various approaches to treatment. As noted in chapter 5, attempts to open additional treatment centers have often generated vigorous community opposition—the NIMBY syndrome.

7. Provide educational and vocational programs for drug abusers who have enrolled in treatment programs. In addition to the problem of financing such efforts, there is the problem of equity: Should only drug abusers be entitled to receive educational and vocational services, or should these be made available to all disadvantaged persons?

8. Enact and enforce legislation prohibiting employment discrimination against former substance abusers.

A COMPREHENSIVE PROGRAM FOR RESPONDING TO DRUG ABUSE *(con't.)*

This comprehensive program would require a significant expenditure of tax dollars at a time when governments are struggling with budget deficits. A *Newsweek* (18 September 1989) poll revealed that while Americans were in favor of increasing penalties and additional funding for treatment and law enforcement, 63 percent opposed an increase in personal income taxes to support these goals.

David Bellis (1981: xiv) states that "resolving issues like poverty, crime and addiction, especially in isolation from one another, and unmediated by economic, social and political factors may be impossible." That our current strategies in response to drug abuse have failed is obvious. As noted in chapters 6 and 7, despite the dramatic pronouncements of several administrations, we have been unable to stem the flow of heroin and cocaine into the United States and are unlikely to do so in the future, despite the continued posturing of elected officials. Our success against foreign marijuana has led to improvements in domestic cultivation, so that the homegrown crop is now preferred by pot connoisseurs. There is every reason to believe that if efforts to eradicate coca and poppy cultivation in source countries and/or to improve antismuggling techniques ever succeeded, it would simply spur the domestic production of cocaine and heroin substitutes. Furthermore, as indicated in chapter 5, there is no evidence that widespread educational efforts have the ability or the potential to significantly reduce the number of persons abusing drugs or that treatment programs will be any more successful.

Our current policy of "shared simplifications" (Gerstein and Harwood 1990) appears to reflect the popular will: allowing the majority of society to be against drug abuse while remaining free to abuse alcohol and tobacco. In other words, laws and law enforcement efforts against substances desired by a substantial minority of our citizenry provide symbolic opposition for the majority without actually impairing their own freedom to enjoy dangerous substances and activities—a policy most Americans would be pleased to "drink to."

A quote from the National Commission on Marijuana and Drug Abuse (1973: 39) provides a fitting close to this book:

> Promises which cannot be kept must not be made. The public must be apprised that disapproved drug use is part of a larger social pattern, and that all the money and effort that American society can muster will never be able to deal effectively with this behavior if the problem continues to be defined as it is now.

In short, drug abuse is a symptom whose amelioration requires greater attention to the malady.

REVIEW QUESTIONS

1. What are the differences between *scientific* and *political* knowledge?
2. Why have some psychoactive drugs been outlawed while others are legally and widely available?
3. How does the history of the British response to drug abuse differ from that of the United States?
4. Why has the British approach changed since the 1960s?
5. How does the manner of ingestion favored by the "new" British heroin addict help explain the spread of abuse?
6. What are the possible advantages of legalizing heroin in the United States?
7. What are the possible drawbacks of decriminalizing heroin in the United States?
8. If heroin use is related to a physiological condition—an endorphin deficiency, for example—what policy implications are suggested?
9. What are the arguments against a program of medically administered heroin maintenance?
10. What are the advantages of methadone maintenance over heroin maintenance?
11. What are the possible advantages of decriminalizing cocaine?
12. What are the possible disadvantages of decriminalizing cocaine?
13. What is the "harm reduction" approach to drug abuse?
14. Why can a law enforcement focus on low-level street dealers be more effective than targeting large-scale wholesalers?
15. What are the disadvantages of such an approach?
16. What is the most significant drawback of the civil/criminal commitment of drug abusers?
17. What are the drawbacks in controlling such drugs as cocaine and heroin at their source countries?
18. Why is it difficult, if not impossible, to measure the success of any change in drug policy?

REFERENCES

Abadinsky, Howard
1995   *Law and Justice: An Introduction to the American Legal System,* 3d ed. Chicago: Nelson-Hall.
1994   *Organized Crime,* 4th ed. Chicago: Nelson-Hall.
1997   *Probation and Parole: Theory and Practice,* 5th ed. Englewood Cliffs, NJ: Prentice-Hall.

Abadinsky, Howard, and L. Thomas Winfree
1992   *Crime and Justice: An Introduction,* 2d ed. Chicago: Nelson-Hall.

Abel, Ernest L., ed.
1978   *The Scientific Study of Marijuana.* Chicago: Nelson-Hall.

Adler, Patricia A.
1985   *Wheeling and Dealing: An Ethnography of an Upper-Level Drug-Dealing and Smuggling Community.* New York: Colombia University Press.

Agar, Michael
1973   *Ripping and Running: A Formal Ethnography of Urban Heroin Addicts.* New York: Seminar Press.

Aicchorn, August
1963   *Wayward Youth.* New York: Viking.

Alexander, Bruce K.
1990   "Alternatives to the War on Drugs." *Journal of Drug Issues* 20 (1): 1–27.

Alford, Geary S.
1980   "Alcoholics Anonymous: An Empirical Outcome Study." *Addictive Behaviors* 5: 359–70.

Alford, Geary S., Roger A. Koehler, and James Leonard
1991   "Alcoholics Anonymous-Narcotics Anonymous Model Inpatient Treatment of Chemically Dependent Adolescents: A 2-Year Outcome Study." *Journal of Studies on Alcohol* 52 (March): 118–26.

All About the Civil Addict Program
1994   Norco, CA: California Narcotic Addict Evaluation Authority.

Alpert, Geoffrey P., and Kenneth C. Haas
1990   "Drug Testing at Work: Balancing Reason with Presumption." *Criminal Justice Policy Review* 3: 376–90.

Altman, Lawrence K.
1990   "The Evidence Mounts on Passive Smoking." *New York Times* (May 29): B5.
1988   "Cocaine's Many Dangers: The Evidence Mounts." *New York Times* (January 26): 18.

Altschuler, David M., and Paul J. Brounstein
1991   "Patterns of Drug Trafficking, and Other Delinquency among Inner-City Adolescent Males in Washington, D.C." *Criminology* 29 (November): 589–621.

American Psychiatric Association (APA)
1994   *Diagnostic and Statistical Manual of Mental Disorders,* 4th ed. Washington, DC: APA.

American Social Health Association
1972   *Guidelines: A Comprehensive Community Program to Reduce Drug Abuse.* Overview I. NY: American Social Health Association.

Anderson, Austin A.
1992   "Transnational Crimes: A Global Approach." *FBI Law Enforcement Bulletin* (March): 26–32.

Andreas, Peter R., Eva C. Bertram, Morris J. Blackman, and Kenneth E. Sharpe
1991–92 "Dead End Drug Wars." *Foreign Policy* (Winter): 106–28.

Andrews, Edmund L.
1990   "2 Treatments for Cocaine Addiction." *New York Times* (July 21): 18.

Angier, Natalie

1995 "Variant Gene Tied to a Love of New Thrills." *New York Times* (January 2): 1, B9.

1991 "Moderate Drinking Cuts Risk of Heart Disease, Study Says." *New York Times* (August 24): 10.

Anglin, M. Douglas

1988 "The Efficacy of Civil Commitment in Treating Narcotic Addiction." Pages 8–34 in *Compulsory Treatment of Drug Abuse: Research and Clinical Practice.* Rockville, MD: National Institute on Drug Abuse.

Anglin, M. Douglas, and William McGlothlin

1985 "Methadone Maintenance in California: A Decade's Experience." Pages 219–80 in *The Year Book of Substance Use and Abuse,* edited by Leon Brill and Charles Winick. New York: Human Services Press.

Anglin, M. Douglas, and Yih-ling Hser

1990 "Legal Coercion and Drug Abuse Treatment: Research Findings and Social Policy Implications." Pages 151–76 in *Handbook of Drug Control in the United States,* edited by James A. Inciardi. Westport, CT: Greenwood.

1990b "Treatment of Drug Abuse." Pages 393–460 in *Drugs and Crime,* edited by Michael Tonry and James Q. Wilson. Chicago: University of Chicago Press.

Anglin, M. Douglas, and Thomas H. Maugh, II

1992 "Ensuring Success in Interventions with Drug-Using Offenders." *Annals* 521 (May): 66–90.

Anglin, M. Douglas, and George Speckart

1988 "Narcotics Use and Crime: A Multisample, Multimethod Analysis." *Criminology* 26 (May): 197–233.

Aniskiewicz, Rick, and Earl Wysong

1990 "Evaluating DARE Drug Education and the Multiple Meanings of Success." *Policy Studies Review* 9 (Summer): 727–47.

Anslinger, Harry J., and William F. Tompkins

1953 *The Traffic in Narcotics.* New York: Funk and Wagnalls.

Arax, Mark, and Tom Gorman

1995 "The State's Illicit Farm Belt Export." *Los Angeles Times* (March 13): 1, 16, 17.

Arlacchi. Pino

1986 *Mafia Business: The Mafia and the Spirit of Capitalism.* London: Verso.

Asbury, Herbert

1950 *The Great Illusion: An Informal History of Prohibition.* Garden City, NY: Knopf.

Ashley, Richard

1975 *Cocaine: Its History, Use and Effects.* New York: St. Martin's Press.

"Asian Drug Lord Set to Retire"

1995 *New York Times* (November 24): 8.

Associated Press

1995 "5,600 Infant Deaths Tied to Mothers' Smoking." *New York Times* (April 13): 11.

1994 "44% of College Students Are Binge Drinkers, Poll Says." *New York Times* (December 7): B8.

Atlas, Terry

1995 "Asian Heroin Dealers Expanding Routes to U.S." *Chicago Tribune* (September 14): 1, 26.

1988 "U.S. Losing Its War on Drugs Along the Afghan-Pakistani Border." *Chicago Tribune* (May 9): 6.

Auld, John, Nicholas Dorn, and Nigel Smith

1986 "Irregular Work, Irregular Pleasures: Heroin in the 1980s." Pages 166–228 in *Confronting Crime,* edited by Roger Matthews and Jock Young. London: Sage.

Austin, Gregory A., and Don J. Lettieri, eds.

1977 *Drug Users and the Criminal Justice System.* Rockville, MD: National Institute on Drug Abuse.

Ausubel, David P.

1980 "An Interactional Approach to Narcotic Addiction." Pages 4–7 in *Theories on Drug Abuse: Selected Contemporary Perspectives,* edited by Dan J. Lettieri, Mollie Sayers, and Helen Wallenstein Pearson. Rockville, MD: National Institute on Drug Abuse.

1978 *What Every Well-Informed Person Should Know about Drug Addiction.* Chicago: Nelson-Hall.

Avants, S. Kelly, Arthur Margolin, Thomas R. Kosten, and Ned L. Cooney

1995 "Differences Between Responders and Nonresponders to Cocaine Cures in the Laboratory." *Addictive Behaviors* 20 (March/April): 214–24.

Bagley, Bruce M., and William O. Walker, III, eds.

1995 *Drug Trafficking in the Americas.* New Brunswick, NJ: Transaction Books.

Bailey, Pearce

1974 "The Heroin Habit," pages 171–76 in *Yesterday's Addicts; American Society and Drug Abuse, 1865–1920,* edited by Howard Wayne Morgan. Norman: University of Oklahoma Press.

Baker, Russell

1988 "Round up the Usual Noose." *New York Times* (June 18): 15.

Ball, John C., Lawrence Rosen, Ellen G. Friedman, and David N. Nurco

1979 "The Impact of Heroin Addiction upon Criminality." Pages 163–69 in *Problems of Drug Dependence* 1979, edited by Louis S. Harris. Rockville, MD: National Institute on Drug Abuse.

Balster, Robert L.

1988 "Pharmacological Effects of Cocaine Relevant to Its Abuse." Pages 1–13 in *Mechanisms of Cocaine Abuse and Toxicity,* edited by Doris Clouet, Khursheed Asghar, and Roger Brown. Rockville, MD: National Institute on Drug Abuse.

Balter, Mitchell B.

1974 "Drug Abuse: A Conceptual Analysis and Overview of the Current Situation." Pages 3–21 in *Drug Use: Epidemiological and Sociological Approaches,* edited by Eric Josephson and Eleanor E. Carroll. New York: Wiley.

Bandura, Albert

1977 *Social Learning Theory.* Englewood Cliffs, NJ: Prentice-Hall.

1974 "Behavior Theory, and the Models of Man." *American Psychologist* 29 (December): 860–66.

1969 *Principles of Behavior Modification.* New York: Holt, Rinehart and Winston.

Barnett, Arnold

1988 "Drug Crackdowns and Crime Rates: A Comment on the Kleiman Paper." Pages 35–42 in *Street-Level Drug Enforcement: Examining the Issues,* edited by Marcia R. Chaiken. Washington, DC: U.S. Government Printing Office.

Barnett, Randy E.

1987 "Curing the Drug-Law Addiction: The Harmful Side Effects of Legal Prohibition." Pages 73–102 in *Dealing with Drugs: Consequences of Government Control,* edited by Ronald Hamowy. Lexington, MA: D. C. Heath.

Bartecchi, Carl F., Thomas MacKenzie, and Robert Schrier

1995 "The Global Tobacco Epidemic." *Scientific American* 272 (May): 44–51.

Baumgartner, Werner A., Virginia Hill, and William H. Blahd

1989 "Hair Analysis for Drugs of Abuse." *Journal of Forensic Sciences* 34 (November): 1433–53.

Baumrind, Diana

1987 "Familial Antecedents of Adolescent Drug Use: A Developmental Perspective." Pages 13–44 in *Etiology of Drug Abuse: Implications for Prevention,* edited by Coryl LaRue Jones and Robert J. Battjes. Rockville, MD: National Institute on Drug Abuse.

Beck, Jerome, and Marsha Rosenbaum

1994 *Pursuit of Ecstasy: The MDMA Experience.* Albany, NY: State University of New York Press.

Becker, Howard S.

1977 "Knowledge, Power, and Drug Effects." Pages 167–90 in *Drugs and Politics,* edited by Paul E. Rock. New Brunswick, NJ: Transaction Books.

1967 "History, Culture, and Subjective Experience: An Exploration of the Social Bases of Drug-Induced Experiences." *Journal of Health and Social Behavior* 8: 163–76.

1966 *Outsiders: Studies in the Sociology of Deviance.* New York: Free Press.

Beeching, Jack

1975 *The Chinese Opium Wars.* New York: Harcourt Brace Jovanovich.

Belenko, Steven

1993 *Crack and the Evolution of Anti-Drug Policy.* Westport, CT: Greenwood.

Belenko, Steven, and Ko-lin Chin

1989 "Typologies of Criminal Careers among Crack Arrestees." Paper presented at the annual meeting of the American Society of Criminology, Reno, NV (November).

Belkin, Lisa

1990 "Airport Anti-Drug Nets Snare Many People Fitting 'Profiles.' " *New York Times* (March 20): 1, 11.

Bellis, David J.

1981 *Heroin and Politicians: The Failure of Public Policy to Control Addiction in America.* Westport, CT: Greenwood.

Benjamin, Daniel K., and Roger Leroy Miller

1991 *Undoing Drugs: Beyond Legalization.* New York: Basic Books.

Bennett, David H.

1988 *The Party of Fear: From Nativist Movements to the New Right in American History.* Chapel Hill: University of North Carolina Press.

Bennett, William Ira

1988 "Patterns of Addiction." *New York Times Magazine* (April 10): 60–61.

Bennetts, Leslie

1989 "Mitch's Mission: When Nancy Reagan Just Said No to Phoenix House, Its New Drug Treatment Center Went up in Smoke." *Vanity Fair* (October): 80–92.

Berger, Joseph

1989 "Judgment Replaces Fear in Drug Lessons." *New York Times* (October 30): 1, 8.

Berke, Richard L.

1990 "Survey Shows Use of Drugs by Students Fell Last Year." *New York Times* (February 14): 12.

1990b "Bennett Doubts Value of Drug Education." *New York Times* (February 3): 1, 9.

1989 "Corruption in Drug Agency Called a Crippler of Inquiries and Morale." *New York Times* (December 17): 1, 22.

Berkow, Robert, ed.

1982 *The Merck Manual of Diagnosis and Therapy.* Rahway, NJ: Merck Sharp and Dohme.

Beschner, George M., and Alfred S. Friedman, eds.

1979 *Youth Drug Abuse: Problems, Issues, and Treatment.* Lexington, MA: D. C. Heath.

Biernacki, Patrick

1986 *Pathways from Heroin Addiction: Recovery without Treatment.* Philadelphia: Temple University Press.

Bigelow, George E., Robert K. Brooner, Mary E. McCaul, and Dace S. Svikis

1988 "Biological Vulnerability: Treatment Implications/Applications." Pages 165–80 in *Biological*

Vulnerability to Drug Abuse, edited by Roy W. Pickens and Dace S. Svikis. Rockville, MD: National Institute on Drug Abuse.

Binder, Arnold, and Gilbert Geis
1983   *Methods of Research in Criminology and Criminal Justice.* New York: McGraw-Hill.

Bishop, Katherine
1991   "Business Data Is Sought in Marijuana Crackdown." *New York Times* (May 24): B9.
1990   "Mandatory Sentences in Drug Cases: Is the Law Defeating Its Purpose?" *New York Times* (June 8): B10.
1990b   "Military Takes Part in Drug Sweep and Reaps Criticism and a Lawsuit." *New York Times* (August 10): 11.
1987   "Ex-Employee Wins Drug Testing Case." *New York Times* (October 31): 18.

Blackmore, John
1979   "Diagnosis: Heroin Addiction. Prescription: Methadone." *Corrections Magazine* 5 (December): 24–31.

Blakeslee, Sandra
1996   "Complex and Hidden Brain in the Gut Makes Cramps, Butterflies, and Valium." *New York Times* (January 23): B5.
1995   "Popular Drug May Damage Brain." *New York Times* (August 15): B10.
1994   "Yes, People Are Right. Caffeine Is Addictive." *New York Times* (October 5): B9.
1991   "Finding the Secrets of Caffeine, the Drug." *New York Times* (August 7): B6.
1989   "Crack's Toll among Babies: A Joyless View of Even Toys." *New York Times* (September 18): 1, 12.
1988   "New Drug Therapies Are Being Tested to Help Smokers Quit." *New York Times* (June 9): 20.
1988b   "8-Year Study Finds 2 Sides to Teen-Age Drug Use." *New York Times* (July 21): 1, 13.

Bloom, Floyd E.
1993   "Brain Research for Today and Tomorrow: Recent Advances and Research Frontiers." Pages 9–26 in *International Research Conference on Biomedical Approaches to Illicit Drug Demand Reduction,* edited by Christine R. Hartel. Washington, DC: U.S. Government Printing Office.

Bluhm, Judy
1987   *When You Face the Chemically Dependent Patient: A Practical Guide for Nurses.* St. Louis, MO: Ishiyaku EuroAmerica.

Blum, Kenneth, Ernest P. Noble, Peter J. Sheridan, Anne Montgomery, Terry Ritchie, Puduer Jagadeeswaran, Harou Nogami, Arthur H. Briggs, and Jay B. Cohn
1990   "Allec Association of Human Dopamine D2 Receptor Gene in Alcoholism." *Journal of the American Medical Association* 263 (April 18): 2055–60.

Blum, Richard H. and Associates
1969   *Society and Drugs.* San Francisco: Jossey-Bass.

Blumenthal, Ralph
1991   "Survey Finds Slots Open in Drug Treatment Centers." *New York Times* (December 5): B8.

Boaz, David, ed.
1990   *The Crisis in Drug Prohibition.* Washington, DC: Cato Institute.

Bollag, Burton
1989   "Swiss-Dutch Drug Stance: Tolerance." *New York Times* (December 1): 4.

Bonnie, Richard J.
1980   *Marijuana Use and Criminal Sanctions.* Charlottesville, VA: Michie Co.

Bonnie, Richard J., and Charles H. Whitebread II
1970   "The Forbidden Fruit and the Tree of Knowledge: An Inquiry into the Legal History of American Marijuana Prohibition." *Virginia Law Review* 56 (October): 971–1203.

Botvin, Gilbert J.
1990   "Substance Abuse Prevention: Theory, Practice, and Effectiveness." Pages 461–519 in *Drugs and Crime,* edited by Michael Tonry and James Q. Wilson. Chicago: University of Chicago Press.

Bourgois, Philippe
1995   *In Search of Respect: Selling Crack in El Barrio.* Cambridge, England: Cambridge University Press.

Bourne, Peter
1990   "Our Dubious Crusade in Colombia." *Chicago Tribune* (July 2): 11.

Bouza, Anthony
1990   *The Police Mystique: An Insider's Look at Cops, Crime, and the Criminal Justice System.* New York: Plenum.

Bowden, Charles
1991   "La Virgen and the Drug Lord." *Phoenix* (March): 96–103.

Bowden, Mark
1987   *Doctor Dealer.* New York: Warner Books.

Bradsher, Keith
1995   "Low Ranking for Poor American Children." *New York Times* (August 14): 7.
1995b   "Gap in Wealth in U.S. Called Widest in West." *New York Times* (April 17): 1, C4.
1995c   "Widest Gap in Incomes? Research Points to U.S." *New York Times* (October 27): C2.

Brecher, Edward M., and the Editors of *Consumer Reports*
1972   *Licit and Illicit Drugs.* Boston: Little, Brown.

Bresler, Fenton
1980   *The Chinese Mafia.* New York: Stein and Day.

Brewington, Vincent, Michael Smith, and Douglas Lipton
1994   "Acupuncture as a Detoxification Treatment: An Analysis of Controlled Research." *Journal of Substance Abuse Treatment* 11 (No. 4): 289–307.

Brill, Leon, and Charles Winick
1985   *The Yearbook of Substance Use and Abuse: Volume III.* New York: Human Sciences Press.

1980   *The Yearbook of Substance Use and Abuse: Volume II.* New York: Human Sciences Press.

Britt, Chester L., III, Michael R. Gottfredson, and John S. Goldkamp

1992   "Drug Testing and Pretrial Misconduct: An Experiment on the Specific Deterrent Effects of Drug Monitoring Defendants on Pretrial Release." *Journal of Research in Crime and Delinquency* 29 (February): 62–78.

Broder, Jonathan

1984   "As a Tradeoff, Soviets Let Afghan Heroin Flow." *Chicago Tribune* (September 2): 12.

Brody, Jane E.

1995   "Tourette Syndrome Can't Be Cured, But Knowledge Often Reduces Suffering." *New York Times* (March 1): B8.

1988   "Personal Health." *New York Times* (April 21): 24.

1987   "Role of Heredity in Alcoholism." *New York Times* (August 14): 14.

Brook, Robert C., and Paul C. Whitehead

1980   *Drug-Free Therapeutic Community.* New York: Human Sciences Press.

Brooke, James

1992   "Drug Seizures Up in Latin Countries." *New York Times* (January 15): 5.

1992b   "Trafficker Is Still Feared in Colombia." *New York Times* (January 21): 5.

1991   "Colombia's Tortured City: Now It's Kidnappings." *New York Times* (January 9): 8.

1991b   "Peru, Its U.S. Aid Imperiled, Plots a New Drug Strategy." *New York Times* (January 14): 2.

1991c   "Colombia's Rising Export: Fake U.S. Money." *New York Times* (April 21): 4.

1991d   "Cali, the 'Quiet' Cocaine Cartel, Profits Through Accommodation." *New York Times* (July 14): 1, 6.

1991e   "In Brazil, a Plague Hits Port." *New York Times* (July 22): 6.

1991f   "Pressed Colombian Drug Rings Force Scourge on Venezuela." *New York Times* (September 1): 9.

1991g   "Marxist Revolt Grows Strong in the Shantytowns of Peru." *New York Times* (November 11): 1, 6.

1991h   "The Cocaine War's Biggest Success: A Fungus." *New York Times* (December 22): 9.

1990   "U.S. Anti-Drug Pilots in Peru Battle Guerrillas." *New York Times* (April 12): 1, 8.

1990b   "Bogota Chief Tells of Drug War's Toll." *New York Times* (May 27): 4.

1990c   "Drug War at Stake in Colombia Vote." *New York Times* (May 26): 3.

1990d   "Bush and Colombian to Assess Drug War Today." *New York Times* (June 5): 4.

1990e   "In the Capital of Cocaine, Savagery Is the Habit." *New York Times* (June 7): 4.

1990f   "Peru Suggests U.S. Rethink Eradication in Land

Where Coca Is Still King." *New York Times* (November 18): 3.

1990g   "Was the Beautiful Agent a Cartel Spy?" *New York Times* (December 24): 7.

1990h   "Near-Acquittal of Barry Is Outraging Colombians." *New York Times* (August 27): 4.

Brotman, Richard, and Frederick Suffet

1975   "The Concept of Prevention and Its Limitations." *Annals* 417 (January): 53–65.

Brounstein, Paul J., Harry P. Hatry, David M. Alschuler, and Louis H. Blair

1990   *Substance Use and Delinquency Among Inner City Adolescent Males.* Washington, DC: Urban Institute.

Browne, Malcolm W.

1989   "Problems Loom in Effort to Control Use of Chemicals for Illicit Drugs." *New York Times* (October 24): 17, 21.

Bruvold, William H.

1990   "A Meta-Analysis of the California School-Based Risk Reduction Program." *Journal of Drug Education* 20: 139–52.

Buchanan, David R.

1992   "Social History of American Drug Use." *Journal of Drug Issues* 22 (Winter): 31–52.

Bukowski, William J.

1990   "The Federal Approach to Primary Drug Abuse Prevention and Education." Pages 94–114 in *Handbook of Drug Control in the United States,* edited by James A. Inciardi. Westport, CT: Greenwood.

Bukstein, Oscar, David A. Brent, and Yifrah Kaminer

1989   "Comorbidity of Substance Abuse and Other Psychiatric Disorders in Adolescents." *American Journal of Psychiatry* 146 (September): 1131–41.

Burgess, Robert L., and Ronald L. Akers

1969   "Differential Association-Reinforcement Theory of Criminal Behavior." Pages 291–320 in *Behavioral Sociology,* edited by Robert L. Burgess and Don Bushell, Jr. New York: Columbia University Press.

Burkholz, Herbert

1987   "Pain: Solving the Mystery." *New York Times Magazine* (September 27): 16–19, 32, 34–35.

Burns, John F.

1995   "Heroin Becomes Scourge for 1.5 Million in Pakistan." *New York Times* (April 5): 4.

1990   "Afghans: Now They Blame America." *New York Times Magazine* (February 4): 23–29, 37.

Burns, R. Stanley, and Alan Done

1980   "Special Management Procedures for Emergency Medical Staff." Pages 95–120 in *Phencyclidine Abuse Manual,* edited by Mary Tuma McAdams, Ronald L. Linder, Steven E. Lerner, and Richard Stanley Burns. Los Angeles, CA: University of California Extension.

Burros, Marian

1996   "In an About-Face, U.S. Says Alcohol Has Health Benefits." *New York Times* (January 3): 1, B6.

Burros, Marian, and Sarah Jay

1996   "Concern is Growing over an Herb That Promises a Legal High." *New York Times* (April 10): B1, 8.

Bush, Patricia J., and Ronald Iannotti

1987   "The Development of Children's Health Orientations and Behaviors: Lessons for Substance Abuse Prevention." Pages 45–74 in *Etiology of Drug Abuse: Implications for Prevention,* edited by Coryl LaRue Jones. Rockville, MD: National Institute on Drug Abuse.

Butterfield, Fox

1988   "The Upper West Side's '2 Worst Blocks' for Drugs." *New York Times* (June 18): 10.

Byck, Robert, ed.

1974   *Cocaine Papers: Sigmund Freud.* New York: Stonehill.

Carlson, Kenneth, and Peter Finn

1993   *Prosecuting Criminal Enterprises.* Washington, DC: Bureau of Justice Statistics.

Carpenter, Cheryl, Barry Glassner, Bruce D. Johnson, and Julia Loughlin

1988   *Kids, Drugs, and Crime.* Lexington, MA: D. C. Heath.

Carter, Hodding, IV

1991   "King of the Jungle." *M Inc.* (March) 84–91.

Cashman, Sean D.

1981   *Prohibition.* New York: Free Press.

Catanzarite, Anne M.

1992   *Managing the Chemically Dependent Nurse.* Chicago: American Hospital Publishing.

Cauchon, Dennis

1992   "Michigan Drug Law: No Exceptions, No Mercy." *USA Today* (April 7): 3.

Caulkins, Jonathan P.

1994   "What Is the Average Price of an Illicit Drug?" *Addiction* 89 (July): 815–19.

1992   "Thinking About Displacement in Drug Markets: Why Observing Change of Venue Isn't Enough." *Journal of Drug Issues* 22 (Winter): 17–30.

Caulkins, Jonathan P., Gordon Crawford, and Peter Reuter

1993   "Simulation of Adaptive Response: A Model of Drug Interdiction." *Mathematical and Computer Modelling* 17 (No. 2): 37–52.

Caulkins, Jonathan P., Patricia A. Ebener, and Daniel F. McCaffrey

1995   "Describing DAWN's Dominion." *Contemporary Drug Problems* 22 (Fall): 547–67.

Cawley, Janet

1990   "3% Fail Drug Tests in Transit Industries." *Chicago Tribune* (July 11): 9.

Celis, William, III

1991   "As Fewer Students Drink, Abuse of Alcohol Persists." *New York Times* (December 31): 1, 8.

Chaiken, Jan M., and Marcia R. Chaiken

1990   "Drugs and Predatory Crime." Pages 203–39 in *Drugs and Crime,* edited by Michael Tonry and James Q. Wilson. Chicago: University of Chicago Press.

Chaiken, Marcia R., and Bruce D. Johnson

1988   *Characteristics of Different Types of Drug-Involved Offenders.* Washington, DC: National Institute of Justice.

Chambers, Carl D., and Leon Brill

1973   *Methadone: Experiences and Issues.* New York: Behavioral Publications.

Chambliss, William

1973   *Functional and Conflict Theories of Crime.* New York: MSS Modular Publications.

Chapman, Stephen

1992   "The Awful Price of Fighting the War on Drugs." *Chicago Tribune* (May 21): 23.

1991   "Do We Want to Save Addicts or Kill Them?" *Chicago Tribune* (February 21): 23.

1991b   "In the Drug War, Bigger Sentences for Smaller Crimes." *Chicago Tribune* (June 9): Sec. 4: 3.

1991c   "Prohibition—From Alcohol to Drugs—Is a Costly Failure." *Chicago Tribune* (September 1): Sec. 4: 3.

Chein, Isidor, Donald L. Gerard, Robert S. Lee, and Eva Rosenfeld

1964   *The Road to H: Narcotics, Delinquency, and Social Policy.* New York: Basic Books.

Chermack, Stephen T., and Stuart P. Taylor

1995   "Alcohol and Human Physical Aggression: Pharmacological Versus Expectancy Effects." *Journal of Studies on Alcohol 56* (July): 449–56.

Cheung, Yuet W., Patricia G. Erickson, and Tammy C. Landau

1991   "Experience of Crack Use: Findings from a Community-Based Sample in Toronto." *Journal of Drug Issues* 21 (Winter): 121–40.

Childress, Ann Rose

1993   "Medications in Drug Abuse Treatment." Summary in NIDA *Second National Conference on Drug Abuse Research and Practice: An Alliance for the 21st Century.* Pages 73–75. Rockville, MD: National Institute on Drug Abuse.

Childress, Ann Rose, Anita V. Hole, Ronald N. Ehrman, Steven J. Robbins, A. Thomas McLellan, and Charles P. O'Brien

1993   "Cue Reactivity and Cue Reactivity Interventions in Drug Dependence." Pages 73–95 in *Behavioral Treatments for Drug Abuse and Dependence,* edited by Lisa Simon Onken, John D. Blaine, and John J. Boren. Rockville, MD: National Institute on Drug Abuse.

Childress, Anna Rose, A. Thomas McLellan, and Charles P. O'Brien

1985   "Behavioral Therapies for Substance Abuse." *International Journal of the Addictions* 20: 947–69.

Childress, Anna Rose, A. Thomas McLellan, Ronald
Ehrman, and Charles P. O'Brien
1988   "Classically Conditioned Responses in Opioid and
        Cocaine Dependence: A Role in Relapse?" Pages
        25–43 in *Learning Factors in Substance Abuse,*
        edited by Barbara A. Ray. Rockville, MD: National
        Institute on Drug Abuse.

Chin, Ko-lin
1990   *Chinese Subculture and Criminality: Non-tradi-
        tional Crime Groups in America.* Westport, CT:
        Greenwood.

Chin, Ko-lin, and Jeffrey Fagan
1990   "The Impact of Crack on Drug and Crime Involve-
        ment." Paper presented at the annual meeting of the
        American Society of Criminology, Baltimore, No-
        vember.

Christian, Shirley
1991   "Central America a New Drug Focus." *New York
        Times* (December 16): 6.
1988   "Drug Trafficking and Output Rising Sharply in Ar-
        gentina." *New York Times* (April 28): 4.
1988b   "Bolivian Peasants, Hard-Pressed for Cash, In-
        crease Their Production of Coca." *New York Times*
        (May 4): 6.
1988c   "Bolivian Drug Lord Reportedly in Financial
        Straits." *New York Times* (May 9): 5.
1987   "Bolivians Fight Efforts to Eradicate Coca." *New
        York Times* (July 27): 3.

Cintron, Myrna
1986   "Coca: Its History and Contemporary Parallels."
        Pages 25–51 in *Drugs in Latin America,* edited by
        Edmundo Morales. Williamsburg, VA: College of
        William and Mary.

Clayton, Richard R., and Harwin L. Voss
1981   *Young Men and Drugs in Manhattan: A Causal
        Analysis.* Rockville, MD: National Institute on
        Drug Abuse.

"Clean and Sober—And Agnostic"
1991   *Newsweek* (July 8): 62–63.

Cloward, Richard A., and Lloyd E. Ohlin
1960   *Delinquency and Opportunity.* New York: Free
        Press.

Cloyd, Jerald W.
1982   *Drugs and Information Control: The Role of Men
        and Manipulation in the Control of Drug Traffick-
        ing.* Westport, CT: Greenwood.

Clymer, Adam
1994   "Senate Told That Cigarettes Are Entry into Hard
        Drugs." *New York Times* (March 11): 12.

"Cocaine: The First Decade"
1992   *RAND Drug Research Policy Center* 1 (April): 1–4.

Cockburn, Leslie
1987   *Out of Control: The Story of the Reagan Adminis-
        tration's Secret War in Nicaragua, the Illegal
        Arms Pipeline, and the Contra Drug Connection.*

New York: Morgan Entrekin/Atlantic Monthly
Press.

Coffey, Thomas A.
1975   *The Long Thirst: Prohibition in America,
        1920–1933.* New York: Norton.

Cohen, Albert K.
1965   *Delinquent Boys.* New York: Free Press.

Cohen, Roger
1992   "Amid Growing Crime, Zurich Closes a Park It Re-
        served for Drug Addicts." *New York Times* (Febru-
        ary 11): 11.

Cohen, Sidney
1981   *The Substance Abuse Problem.* New York: Ha-
        worth.
1979   "Inhalants and Solvents." Pages 285–314 in *Youth
        Drug Abuse,* edited by George M. Breschner and
        Alfred S. Friedman. Lexington, MA: D. C. Heath.

Collins, Alan C.
1985   "Inheriting Addictions: A Genetic Perspective
        with Emphasis on Alcohol and Nicotine." Pages
        3–10 in *The Addictions; Multidisciplinary Per-
        spectives and Treatments,* edited by Harvey B.
        Milkman and Howard J. Shaffer. Lexington, MA:
        D. C. Heath.

Collins, James J., Robert L. Hubbard, and J. Valley Rachel
1985   "Expensive Drug Use and Illegal Income: A Test of
        Explanatory Hypotheses." *Criminology* 23 (No-
        vember): 743–64.

"Colombian City Basks in Terror's End"
1991   *New York Times* (December 12): 9.

"Colombian Growth Hurt by Cocaine"
1991   *New York Times* (February 19): C1.

"Colombian Heroin May Be Increasing"
1991   *New York Times* (October 27): 10.

Colorado Alcohol and Drug Abuse Division
1987   *Drug Use Trends in Colorado.* Denver, CO.

"Coming to Grips With Alcoholism"
1987   *U.S. News and World Report* (November 30):
        56–63.

Committee on Law Reform of the New York County
Lawyers Association
1987   *Advisory Reports. Part I: Why Cocaine and Heroin
        Should Be Decriminalized. Part II: Why Cocaine
        and Heroin Should Not Be Decriminalized.* New
        York: Photocopied.

Compton, Beaulah, and Burt Galaway
1979   *Social Work Processes,* 2d ed. Homewood, IL:
        Dorsey Press.

Comptroller General
1988   *Controlling Drug Abuse: A Status Report.* Washing-
        ton, DC: General Accounting Office.
1988b   *Drug Control: U.S.-Mexico Opium Poppy and Mar-
        ijuana Aerial Eradication Program.* Washington,
        DC: General Accounting Office.
1983   *Federal Drug Interdiction Efforts Need a Strong*

Central Oversight. Washington, DC: General Accounting Office.

Cook, Christopher C. H.
1988   "The Minnesota Model in the Management of Drug and Alcohol Dependency: Miracle, Method or Myth? Part I. The Philosophy and the Programme." *British Journal of Addiction* 83: 625–34.

1988b   "The Minnesota Model in the Management of Drug and Alcohol Dependency: Miracle, Method or Myth? Part II. Evidence and Conclusions." *British Journal of Addiction* 83: 735–48.

Cook, L. Foster, and Beth A. Weinman
1988   "Treatment Alternatives to Street Crime." Pages 99–105 in *Compulsory Treatment of Drug Abuse: Research and Clinical Practice,* edited by Carl G. Leukefeld and Frank M. Tims. Rockville, MD: National Institute on Drug Abuse.

Coombs, Robert H.
1981   "Drug Abuse as a Career." *Journal of Drug Issues* 11 (Fall): 369–87.

Cooper, James R., Fred Alman, Barry S. Brown, and Dorynne Czechowicz
1986   *Research on the Treatment of Narcotic Addiction.* Rockville, MD: National Institute on Drug Abuse.

Corcoran, David
1989   "Legalizing Drugs: Failures Spur Debate." *New York Times* (November 27): 9.

Courtwright, David T.
1982   *Dark Paradise: Opiate Addiction in America Before 1940.* Cambridge, MA: Harvard University Press.

Covington, Dennis
1992   "Kidnapping Rips Open a Town's Secrets and Fears." *New York Times* (January 13): 10.

Cowan, Richard C.
1986   "A War against Ourselves: How the Narcs Created Crack." *National Review* (December 5): 26–31.

Cowell, Alan
1996   "Zurich's Open Drug Policy Goes into Withdrawal." *New York Times* (March 12): 3.

Cox, W. Miles
1985   "Personality Correlates of Substance Abuse." Pages 209–46 in *Determinants of Substance Abuse: Biological, Psychological, and Environmental Factors,* edited by Mark Galizio and Stephen A. Maisto. New York: Plenum.

Craig, Robert J.
1987   "The Personality Structure of Heroin Addicts." Pages 25–36 in *Neurobiology of Behavioral Control in Drug Abuse,* edited by Stephen I. Szara. Rockville, MD: National Institute on Drug Abuse.

Crank, John P., and Lee R. Rehm
1992   "From Drug Courier Profiles to Officer Awareness: A Study of a State Drug Interdiction Program." Paper presented at the annual meeting of the Academy of Criminal Justice Sciences, March 10–14, Pittsburgh.

Crawford, William B., Jr.
1991   "Drug Conspiracy Trial of Ex-CBOT Clerk Begins." *Chicago Tribune* (August 6): Sec. 3: 2.

1991b   "Ex-CBOT Clerk Details Cocaine Distribution." *Chicago Tribune* (August 7): Sec. 3: 3.

Crossette, Barbara
1990   "U.S.-Pakistani Bone of Contention: Narcotics." *New York Times* (December 8): 7.

1988   "Addiction Rises Among Vietnamese." *New York Times* (April 20): 9.

Crowley, Geoffrey
1996   "Herbal Warning." *Newsweek* (May 6): 60–67.

Crowley, Thomas J.
1981   "The Reinforcers for Drug Abuse: Why People Take Drugs." Pages 367–81 in *Classic Contributions in the Addictions,* edited by Howard Shaffer and Milton Earl Burglass. New York: Brunner/Mazel.

Currie, Elliott
1993   *Reckoning: Drugs, the Cities, and the American Future.* New York: Hill and Wang.

Cushman, Paul, Jr.
1974   "Relationship Between Narcotic Addiction and Crime." *Federal Probation* 38 (September): 38–43.

Danaceau, Paul
1974   *Methadone Maintenance Programs: The Experience of Four Programs.* Washington, DC: Drug Abuse Council, Inc.

D'Angelo, Rocco, and Rudolph Alexander, Jr.
1991   "Compulsory Treatment of Drug-Addicted Pregnancy: Issues and Complications." Paper presented at the annual meeting of the Academy of Criminal Justice Sciences, Nashville, TN, March.

Davis, Joel
1984   *Endorphins: New Waves in Brain Chemistry.* Garden City, NY: Doubleday.

DeJong, William
1987   *Arresting the Demand for Drugs: Police and School Partnership to Prevent Drug Abuse.* Washington, DC: National Institute of Justice.

1987b   "A Short-Term Evaluation of Project DARE: Preliminary Indications of Effectiveness." *Journal of Drug Education* 17: 279–94.

1986   *Project DARE: Teaching Kids to Say "No" to Drugs and Alcohol.* Rockville, MD: National Institute of Justice.

de Kort, Marcel
1994   "A Short History of Drugs in the Netherlands." Pages 3–22 in *Between Prohibition and Legalization: The Dutch Experiment in Drug Policy,* edited by Ed. Leuw and I. Haen Marshall. Amsterdam: Kugler Publications.

De Lama, George
1989   "Most Antidrug Aid for Colombia Used Against Rebels." *Chicago Tribune* (October 31): 1, 8.

Delaney, William P.
1977   "On Capturing an Opium King: The Politics of Law Sik Han's Arrest." Pages 67–88 in *Drugs and Politics,* edited by Paul E. Rock. New Brunswick, NJ: Transaction Books.

De La Rosa, Mario, Elizabeth Y. Lambert, and Bernard Gropper, eds.
1990   *Drugs and Violence: Causes, Correlates, and Consequences.* Rockville, MD: National Institute on Drug Abuse.

Delbanco, Andrew, and Thomas Delbanco
1995   "AA at the Crossroads." *New Yorker* (March 20): 50–63.

De Leon, George
1995   "Residential Therapeutic Communities in the Mainstream: Diversity and Issues." *Journal of Psychoactive Drugs* 27 (No. 1): 3–15.

1994   "The Therapeutic Community: Toward a General Theory and Model." Pages 16–53 in *Therapeutic Community: Advances in Research and Application,* edited by Frank M. Tims, George De Leon, and Nancy Jainchill. Rockville, MD: National Institute on Drug Abuse.

1990   "Treatment Strategies." Pages 115–38 in *Handbook of Drug Control in the United States,* edited by James A. Inciardi. Westport, CT: Greenwood.

1986   "Program-Based Evaluation Research in Therapeutic Communities." Pages 69–87 in *Drug Abuse Treatment Evaluation: Strategies, Progress, and Prospects,* edited by Frank M. Tims and Jacqueline P. Ludford. Rockville, MD: National Institute on Drug Abuse.

1986b   "The Therapeutic Community for Substance Abuse: Perspective and Approach." Pages 5–18 in *Therapeutic Communities for Addictions,* edited by George De Leon and James T. Ziegenfuss, Jr. Springfield, IL: Charles C Thomas.

De Leon, George, James A. Inciardi, and Steven S. Martin
1995   "Residential Drug Abuse Treatment Research: Are Conventional Control Designs Appropriate for Assessing Treatment Effectiveness?" *Journal of Psychoactive Drugs* 27 (No. 1): 85–91.

del Olmo, Rosa
1991   "The Hidden Face of Drugs." *Social Justice* 18 (Winter): 10–48.

DeLong, James V.
1972   "Treatment and Rehabilitation." Pages 173–254 in *Dealing with Drug Abuse: A Report to the Ford Foundation.* New York: Praeger.

Dembo, Richard, Gary Grandon, Lawrence La Voie, James Schmeidler, and William Burgos
1986   "Parents and Drugs Revisited: Some Further Evidence in Support of Social Learning Theory." *Criminology* 24 (February): 85–104.

Dembo, Richard, Linda Williams, Alan Getreu, Lisa Genung, James Schmeidler, Estrellita Berry, Eric D. Wish, and Lawrence Voie
1991   "A Longitudinal Study of the Relationship Among Marijuana/Hashish Use, Cocaine Use, and Delinquency in a Cohort of High Risk Youths." *Journal of Drug Issues* 21: 271–312.

De Quincey, Thomas
1952   *The Confessions of an English Opium-Eater.* London: J.M. Dent. First published in 1821.

Dettling, Michael, Andreas Heinz, Peter Dufeu, Hans Rommelspacher, Klaus-Jürgen Gräf, and Lutz G. Schmidt
1995   "Dopaminergic Responsivity in Alcoholism: Trait, State, or Residual Marker?" *American Journal of Psychiatry* 152 (9): 1317–21.

Di Chiara, Gaetano
1995   "The Role of Dopamine in Drug Abuse Viewed from the Perspective of Its Role in Motivation." *Drug and Alcohol Dependence* 38: 95–137.

Dickson, Donald T.
1977   "Bureaucracy and Morality: An Organizational Perspective on a Moral Crusade." Pages 31–52 in *Drugs and Politics,* edited by Paul E. Rock. New Brunswick, NJ: Transaction Books.

Dillon, Sam
1995   "Speed Carries Mexican Drug Dealer to the Top." *New York Times* (December 27): 6.

DiNardo, John
1993   "Law Enforcement, the Price of Cocaine and Cocaine use." *Mathematical and Computer Modelling* 17 (No. 2): 53–64.

Dinges, John
1990   *Our Man in Panama: How General Noriega Used the United States—and Made Millions in Drugs and Arms.* New York: Random House.

Dishion, Thomas J., Gerald R. Patterson, and John R. Reid
1988   "Parent and Peer Factors Associated with Drug Sampling in Early Adolescence: Implications for Treatment." Pages 69–93 in *Adolescent Drug Abuse; Analyses of Treatment Research,* edited by Elizabeth R. Rahdert and John Grabowski. Rockville, MD: National Institute on Drug Abuse.

Dole, Vincent P.
1980   "Addictive Behavior." *Scientific American* 243: 138–54.

Dole, Vincent P., and Marie F. Nyswander
1966   "Rehabilitation of Heroin Addicts After Blockade with Methadone." *New York State Journal of Medicine* 66 (April): 2011–17.

1965   "A Medical Treatment for Diacetylmorphine (Heroin) Addiction." *Journal of the American Medical Association* 193 (August): 146–50.

Donovan, Dennis M.
1988   "Assessment of Addictive Behaviors: Implications of an Emerging Biopsychosocial Model." Pages 3–48 in *Assessment of Addictive Behaviors,* edited by Dennis M. Donovan and G. Alan Marlatt. New York: Guilford.

Dorn, Nicholas, and Nigel South
1990   "Drug Markets and Law Enforcement." *British Journal of Criminology* 30 (Spring): 171–88.
1988   "Reconciling Policy and Practice." Pages 146–69 in *A Land Fit for Heroin? Drug Policies, Prevention, and Practice,* edited by Nicholas Dorn and Nigel South. New York: St. Martin's Press.

Dotson, James W., Deborah L., Ackerman, and Louis Jolyon West
1995   "Ketamine Abuse." *Journal of Drug Issues* 25 (Fall): 751–57.

Dowd, Maureen
1987   "Wife of Dukakis Discloses Abuse of Pills." *New York Times* (July 9): 10.

Doyle, A. Conan
1899   *Memoirs of Sherlock Holmes.* New York: Harper and Brothers.

Drug Abuse and Drug Abuse Research
1991   Rockville, MD: National Institute on Drug Abuse.
1987   Rockville, MD: National Institute on Drug Abuse.

"Drug Arrests and the Courts' Pleas for Help"
1989   *New York Times* (April 9): E6.

"Drug Crackdown Said to Sap Colombia's Economy"
1995   *New York Times* (November 24): 4.

The Drug Court Movement
1995   Washington DC: National Institute of Justice.

Drug Enforcement Administration
1995   *Illegal Drug Price/Purity.* Washington, DC: DEA.
1995b   *LSD in the United States.* Washington, DC: DEA.
1995c   *Intelligence Bulletin: Colombia.* Washington, DC: DEA.
1994   *Crack Cocaine.* Washington, DC: DEA.
1994b   *Colombian Opiate Assessment.* Washington, DC: DEA.
1993   *Worldwide Cocaine Situation.* Washington, DC: DEA.
1991   *Worldwide Cocaine Situation.* Washington, DC: DEA.
1991b   *Worldwide Heroin Situation.* Washington, DC: DEA.

"The Drug Gangs"
1988   *Newsweek.* March 28, 1988: 20–27.

"Drug Smugglers Used Cuban Base for U.S. Shipment, Jury Charges"
1988   *New York Times* (February 27): 6.

Drugs of Abuse
1989   Washington, DC: Drug Enforcement Administration.

DUF: 1988 Drug Use Forecasting Annual Report
1990   Washington, DC: U.S. Government Printing Office.

DUF: Drugs and Crime 1989
1990   Washington, DC: U.S. Government Printing Office.

Duncan, David F., Thomas Nicholson, Patrick Clifford, Wesley Hawkins, and Rick Petosa
1994   "Harm Reduction: An Emerging New Paradigm for Drug Education." *Journal of Drug Education* 24 (4): 281–90.

Dunlap, Eloise
1991   "Crack Sub-cultural Norms and Sexual Behavior: Male and Female Behaviors and Interaction Patterns." Paper presented at the annual meeting of the American Society of Criminology, San Francisco, November.

Dunwiddie, Thomas V.
1988   "Mechanisms of Cocaine Abuse and Toxicity: An Overview." Pages 337–53 in *Mechanisms of Cocaine Abuse and Toxicity,* edited by Doris Clouet, Khursheed Asghar, and Roger Brown. Rockville, MD: National Institute on Drug Abuse.

DuPont, Robert L., and John P. McGovern.
1994   *A Bridge to Recovery: An Introduction to 12-Step Programs.* Washington DC: American Psychiatric Press.

Durk, David, with Ira Silverman
1975   *The Pleasant Avenue Connection.* New York: Harper & Row.

Duster, Troy
1970   *The Legislation of Morality: Law, Drugs, and Moral Judgment.* New York: Free Press.

Duzàn, Maria
1994   *Death Beat.* New York: HarperCollins.

Dworkin, Steven I., Nick E. Goeders, John Grabowski, and James E. Smit
1987   "The Effects of 12-Hour Limited Access to Cocaine; Reduction in Drug Intake and Mortality." Pages 221–25 in *Problems of Drug Dependence, 1986,* edited by Louis S. Harris. Rockville, MD: National Institute on Drug Abuse.

Dworkin, Steven I., and Raymond C. Pitts
1994   "Use of Roden Self-Administration Models to Develop Pharmaco-Therapies for Cocaine Abuse." Pages 88–112 in *Neurobiological Models for Evaluating Mechanisms Underlying Cocaine Addiction,"* edited by Lynda Erinoff and Roger M. Brown. Rockville, MD: National Institute on Drug Abuse.

Eaglin, James B.
1986   *The Impact of the Federal Drug Aftercare Program.* Washington, DC: Federal Judicial Center.

Eddy, Paul, with Hugo Sabogal and Sara Walden
1988   *The Cocaine Wars.* New York: Norton.

Egan, Jack
1991   "How BCCI Banked on Global Secrecy." *U.S. News and World Report* (August 19): 58–59.

Egan, Timothy
1988   "U.S. Agents Aid Drug Fight in Seattle." *New York Times* (July 15): 6.

Ehrenfeld, Rachel
1990   *Narco-Terrorism.* New York: Basic Books.
Eiler, Kathryn, Melodie R. Schaefer, and Daniel Salstrom
1995   "Double-Blind Comparison of Bromocriptine and Placebo in Cocaine Withdrawal." *American Journal of Drug and Alcohol Abuse* 21 (No. 1): 65–79.
Elifson, Claire Sterk, and Kirk W. Elifson
1993   "The Social Organization of Crack Cocaine Use: The Cycle in One Type of Base House." *Journal of Drug Issues* 23 (Summer): 439–41.
Ellickson, Phyllis L.
1995   "Schools." Pages 93–120 in *Handbook on Drug Prevention,* edited by Robert H. Coombs and Douglas Ziedonis. Boston: Allyn and Bacon.
Ellickson, Phyllis L., and Robert M. Bell
1990   "Drug Prevention in Junior High: A Multi-Site Longitudinal Test." *Science* 247 (March 16): 1299–1305.
Ellis, Lee
1990   "Universal Behavioral and Demographic Correlates of Criminal Behavior: Toward Common Ground in the Assessment of Criminological Theories." Pages 36–49 in *Crime in Biological, Social, and Moral Contexts,* edited by Lee Ellis and Harry Hoffman. Westport, CT: Praeger.
Elsasser, Glen
1989   "Suspicion Is Ruled Ample Basis for Drug Search." *Chicago Tribune* (April 4): 3.
Engel, Madeline H.
1974   *The Drug Scene.* Rochelle Park, NJ: Hayden Book Co.
Engelberg, Stephen
1988   "Nicaragua Rebels Tell of Drug Deal." *New York Times* (April 8): L6.
Ennett, Susan T., Nancy S. Tobler, Christopher L. Ringwalt, and Robert L. Flewelling
1994   "How Effective Is Drug Abuse Resistance Education? A Meta-Analysis of Project DARE Outcome Evaluations." *American Journal of Public Health* 84 (No. 9): 1394–1401.
Epstein, Edward Jay
1988   "The Dope Business." *Manhattan, Inc.* (July): 25–27.
1977   *Agency of Fear: Opiates and Political Power in America.* New York: G. P. Putnam's Sons.
1974   "Methadone: The Forlorn Hope." *The Public Interest* 36 (Summer): 3–24.
Erikson, Kai T.
1966   *Wayward Puritans.* New York: Wiley.
Erlanger, Steven
1989   "In Malaysia and Singapore, a Mixed Drug Picture." *New York Times* (December 15): 6.
Fact Sheet: Drug Related Crime 1994
1995   Washington, DC: National Institute of Justice.
Fagan, Jeffrey, and Ko-Lin Chin
1991   "Social Processes of Initiation into Crack." *Journal of Drug Issues* 21: 313–43.

Farber, M. A., and Don Terry
1989   "For Out-of-Towners, New York City Is a Drug Mart." *New York Times* (November 3): 1, 23.
Faupel, Charles E.
1991   *Shooting Dope: Career Patterns of Hard-Core Heroin Users.* Gainesville: University of Florida Press.
Faupel, Charles E., and Carl B. Klockars
1987   "Drugs-Crime Connections: Elaborations from the Life Histories of Hard-Core Heroin Addicts." *Social Problems* 34 (February): 316–33.
Fay, Peter Ward
1975   *The Opium War: 1840–1842.* Chapel Hill: University of North Carolina Press.
"FBI Says Los Angeles Gang Has Drug Cartel Ties"
1992   *New York Times* (January 10): 8.
Feder, Barnaby J.
1996   "A Study Finds that Teen-Agers Are Buying Cigarettes with Ease." *New York Times* (February 16)L 10.
1996b   "Increase in Teen-Age Smoking Sharpest Among Black Males." *New York Times* (May 24): 9.
Feldman, Harvey
1977   "Street Status and Drug Use." Pages 207–22 in *Drugs and Politics,* edited by Paul E. Rock. New Brunswick, NJ: Transaction Books.
Fenichel, Otto
1945   *The Psychoanalytic Theory of Neuroses.* New York: Norton.
Fiddle, Seymore
1976   "Sequences in Addiction." *Addictive Diseases* 2 (4): 553–68.
Fight Crime Committee
1986   *A Discussion Document on Options for Changes in the Law and in the Administration of the Law to Counter the Triad Problem.* Hong Kong: Central Government Offices.
Finestone, Harold
1964   "Cats, Kicks, and Color." Pages 281–97 in *The Other Side,* edited by Howard S. Becker. New York: Free Press.
Finn, Peter, and Andrea K. Newlyn
1993   *Dade County Diverts Drug Defendants to Court-Run Rehabilitation Program.* Washington, DC: National Institute of Justice.
Finnegan, Loretta
1993   "Discussant and Discussion." Pages 189–207 in *International Research Conference on Biomedical Approaches to Illicit Drug Demand Reduction,* edited by Christine R. Hartel. Washington, DC: U.S. Government Printing Office.
Finnegan, L. P., A. P. Streissguth, G. Koren, D. Neuspiel, and K. Kaltenbach
1994   "The Teratogenicity of the Drugs of Abuse: A Symposium." Pages 51–54 in *Problems of Drug Dependence, 1993. Vol. I.,* edited by Louis S. Harris. Rockville, MD: National Institute on Drug Abuse.

"Fire in Suspected Drug Factory Kills 3 Children"
1995   *Chicago Tribune* (December 28): 13.

Fishbein, Diana H., David Lozovsky, and Jerome H. Jaffe
1989   "Impulsivity, Aggression, and Neuroendocrine Responses to Serotonergic Stimulation in Substance Abusers." *Biological Psychiatry* 25: 1049–66.

Fishbein, Diana H., and Susan E. Pease
1990   "Neurological Links Between Substance Abuse and Crime." Page 218–43 in *Crime in Biological, Social, and Moral Contexts,* edited by Lee Ellis and Harry Hoffman. Westport, CT: Praeger.

Flores, Philip J.
1988   *Group Psychotherapy with Addicted Populations.* New York: Haworth.

Foderaro, Lisa W.
1995   "Can Problem Drinkers Really Just Cut Back?" *New York Times* (May 28): 15.

Foltin, Richard W., and Marian W. Fischman
1994   "Cocaine: Self-Administration Research: Treatment Implications." Pages 139–62 in *Neurobiological Models for Evaluating Mechanisms Underlying Cocaine Addiction,* edited by Lynda Erinoff and Roger M. Brown. Rockville, MD: National Institute on Drug Abuse.

Fong, Mak Lau
1981   *The Sociology of Secret Societies: A Study of Chinese Secret Societies in Singapore and Peninsular Malaysia..* Oxford, England: Oxford University Press.

Fooner, Michael
1985   *A Guide to Interpol.* Washington, DC: U.S. Government Printing Office.

Foote, Jeffrey, Michael Seligman, Stephen Magura, Leonard Handelsman, Andrew Rosenblum, Meg Lovejoy, Kim Arrington, and Barry Stimmel
1994   "An Enhanced Positive Reinforcement Model for the Severely Impaired Cocaine Abuser." *Journal of Substance Abuse Treatment* 11 (No. 6): 525–39.

Forrest, Gary G.
1985   "Psychodynamically Oriented Treatment of Alcoholism and Substance Abuse." Pages 307–36 in *Alcoholism and Substance Abuse: Strategies for Clinical Intervention,* edited by Thomas E. Bratter and Gary G. Forrest. New York: Free Press.

Frank, Blanche, Gregory Rainone, Michael Maranda, William Hopkins, Edmundo Morales, and Alan Kott
1987   "A Psycho-Social View of 'Crack' in New York City." Paper presented at the American Psychological Association Convention, New York City, August 28.

Franklin, Stephen
1987   "Detroit Wages All-Out War against Crack." *Chicago Tribune* (December 13): 29.

Frawley, P. Joseph, and James W. Smith
1990   "Chemical Aversion Therapy in the Treatment of Cocaine Dependence as Part of a Multimodal Treatment Program: Treatment Outcome." *Journal of Substance Abuse Treatment* 7: 21–29.

Frazier, Thomas L.
1962   "Treating Young Drug Abusers: A Casework Approach." *Social Work* 7 (July): 94–101.

Fredlund, Eric V., Richard T. Spence, Jane C. Maxwell, and Jennifer A. Kavinsky
1990   *Substance Abuse among Youth Entering Texas Youth Commission Facilities, 1989: Final Report.* Austin: Texas Commission on Alcohol and Drug Abuse.

French, Edward D., Stefanie Levenson, and Angelo Ceci
1990   "Characterization of the Actions of Phencyclidine Midbrain Dopamine Neurons." Pages 255–63 in *Problems of Drug Dependence 1979,* edited by Louis S. Harris. Rockville, MD: National Institute on Drug Abuse.

French, Howard W.
1992   "Violence Makes Jamaica Fear for Tourism." *New York Times* (February 25): 4.
1991   "Filthy Rich with a Drug Connection." *New York Times* (August 6): 6.

Freud, Sigmund
1961   *A General Introduction to Psychoanalysis.* New York: Washington Square Press. Originally published in 1924.

Freudenheim, Milt
1991   "The Squeeze on Psychiatric Chains." *New York Times* (October 26): 17.
1987   "Specialty Health Care Booms." *New York Times* (November 24): 25, 26.

Friedman, David P.
1993   "Introduction to the Brain: A Primer on Structure and Function of the Brain's Reward Circuitry." Pages 53–62 in *International Research Conference on Biomedical Approaches to Illicit Drug Demand Reduction,* edited by Christine R. Hartel. Washington, DC: U.S. Government Printing Office.

Gabriel, Trip
1994   "Heroin Finds a New Market Along the Cutting Edge of Style." *New York Times* (May 8): 1, 14.

Galaif, Elisha, and Steve Sussman
1995   "For Whom Does Alcoholics Anonymous Work?" *International Journal of the Addictions* 30 (No. 2): 161–84.

Galanter, Marc, and Herbert D. Kleber, eds.
1994   *The American Psychiatric Press Textbook of Substance Abuse Treatment.* Washington, DC: American Psychiatric Press.

Gandossy, Robert P., Jay R. Williams, Jo Cohen, and H. J. Harwood
1980   *Drugs and Crime: A Survey and Analysis of the Literature.* Washington, DC: U.S. Government Printing Office.

Gardner, Stephen E., ed.
1980   *National Drug/Alcohol Collaborative Project: Issues, Multiple Substance Abuse.* Rockville, MD: National Institute on Drug Abuse.

Gawin, Frank H., M. Elena Khalsa, and Everette Elinwod, Jr.
1994   "Stimulants." Pages 111–39 in *The American Psychiatric Press Textbook of Substance Abuse Treatment,* edited by Marc Galanter and Herbert D. Kleber. Washington, DC: American Psychiatric Press.

Gazzaniga, Michael S.
1995   "Legalizing Drugs: Just Say Yes." *National Review* (July): 44–51.

Geary, Nori
1987   "Cocaine: Animal Research Studies." Pages 19–47 in *Cocaine Abuse: New Directions in Treatment and Research,* edited by Henry I. Spitz and Jeffrey S. Rosecan. New York: Brunner/Mazel.

Gelernter, Joel, David Goldman, and Neil Risch
1993   "The A1 Allele at the D$_2$ Dopamine Receptor Gene and Alcoholism." *Journal of the American Medical Association* 269 (April 7): 1673–77.

General Accounting Office (GAO)
1993   *Drug Use Measurement: Strengths, Limitations, and Recommendations for Improvement.* Washington, DC: GAO.
1991   *The War on Drugs: Arrests Burdening Local Criminal Justice Systems.* Washington, DC: GAO.
1990   *Methadone Maintenance: Some Treatment Programs Are Not Effective; Greater Federal Oversight Needed.* Washington, DC: GAO.
1987   *Drug Abuse Prevention: Further Efforts Needed to Identify Programs That Work.* Washington, DC: GAO.

Gerstein, Dean R.
1994   "Outcome Research: Drug Abuse." Pages 45–64 in *The American Psychiatric Press Textbook of Substance Abuse Treatment,* edited by Marc Galanter and Herbert D. Kleber. Washington, DC: American Psychiatric   Press.

Gerstein, Dean R., and Henrick J. Harwood, editors
1990   *Treating Drug Problems, Vol. I: A Study of the Evolution, Effectiveness, and Financing of Public and Private Drug Treatment Systems.* Washington, DC: National Academy Press.

Gerth, Jeff
1991   "Report Says Mercenaries Aided Colombian Cartels." *New York Times* (February 28): 4.
1990   "2 Foreign Bank Units Plead Guilty to Money Laundering." *New York Times* (January 17): 8.

Ghazi, Katayon
1991   "Drug Trafficking Is Thriving in Iran." *New York Times* (December 4): 7.

Gilbert, R. M.
1981   "Drug Abuse as Excessive Behavior." Pages 382–95 in *Classic Contributions in the Addictions,* edited by Howard Shaffer and Milton Earl Burglass. New York: Brunner/Mazel.

Gilbert, Susan
1996   "Doctors Found to Fail in Diagnosing Addictions." *New York Times* (February 14): B4.

Gilham, Steven A., and Wayne L. Lucas
1992   "Adolescent Drug Use and Attitudes in a Midwestern Inner City Population." Paper presented at the annual meeting of the Academy of Criminal Justice Sciences, Pittsburgh, March.

Gilham, Steven A., Wayne L. Lucas, and David Siverwright
1994   "The Impact of Drug Education and Prevention Programs: Disparity Between Impressionistic and Empirical Assessments." Paper presented at the annual meeting of the Academy of Criminal Justice Sciences, Chicago, March.

Gingrich, Newt
1996   "Letter to the Editor." *New York* (March 4): 7.

Ginzburg, Harold M.
1986   *Naltrexone: Its Clinical Utility.* Rockville, MD: National Institute on Drug Abuse.

Glassman, Alexander H., and George F. Koob
1996   "Psychoactive Smoke." *Nature* 379 (February 22): 677–78.

Glassner, Barry, and Julia Loughlin
1989   *Drugs in Adolescent Worlds: Burnouts to Straights.* Houndmills, England: Macmillan.

Goddard, Donald
1978   *Easy Money.* New York: Farrar, Straus and Giroux.

Goeders, Nick E.
1988   "Intercranial Cocaine Self-Administration." Pages 199–215 in *Mechanisms of Cocaine Abuse and Toxicity,* edited by Doris Clouet, Khursheed Asghar, and Roger Brown. Rockville, MD: National Institute on Drug Abuse.

Goffman, Erving
1961   *Asylums: Essays on the Social Situation of Mental Patients and Other Inmates.* Garden City, NY: Doubleday.

Gold, Mark S.
1994   "Neurobiology of Addiction and Recovery: The Brain, the Drive for the Drug, and the 12-Step Fellowship." *Journal of Substance Abuse Treatment* 11 (No. 2): 99–97.
1984   *800-Cocaine.* New York: Bantam.

Gold, Mark S., Charles A. Dackis, A. L. C. Pottash, Irl Extin, and Arnold Washton
1986   "Cocaine Update: From Bench to Bedside." *Advances in Alcohol and Substance Abuse* 5 (Fall/Winter): 35–60.

Gold, Mark S., Arnold M. Washton, and Charles A. Dackis
1985   "Cocaine Abuse: Neurochemistry, Phenomenology, and Treatment." Pages 130–50 in *Cocaine Use in America: Epidemiologic and Clinical Perspectives,* edited by Nicholas J. Kozel and Edgar H.

Adams. Rockville, MD: National Institute on Drug Abuse.

Gold, Steven
1980   "The CAP Control Theory of Drug Abuse." Pages 8–11 in *Theories on Drug Abuse; Selected Contemporary Perspectives,* edited by Dan J. Lettieri, Mollie Sayers, and Helen Wallenstein Pearson. Rockville, MD: National Institute on Drug Abuse.

Goldberg, Jeff
1988   *Anatomy of a Scientific Discovery.* New York: Bantam.

Golden, Tim
1995   "To Help Keep Mexico Stable, U.S. Soft-Pedaled Drug War." *New York Times* (July 31): 1, 4.
1995b   "Mexican Connection Grows as Cocaine Supplier to U.S." *New York Times* (July 30): 1, 8.
1991   "Killing of 7 Mexican Drug Agents Raises Fear." *New York Times* (November 30): 5.
1991b   "Mexican Panel Faults Army in Death of Drug Agents." *New York Times* (December 7): 3.

Goldsmith, Neal M., and Rick Doblin
1995   " 'Ecstasy' Drug Tests Employed High Doses." Letter to the *New York Times* (August 24): 14.

Goldstein, Joseph
1982   "Police Discretion Not to Invoke the Criminal Process." Pages 33–42 in *The Invisible Justice System: Discretion and the Law,* 2d ed., edited by Burton Atkins and Mark Pogrebin. Cincinnati, OH: Anderson.

Goldstein, Paul J.
1985   "The Drugs/Violence Nexus: A Tripartite Conceptual Framework." *Journal of Drug Issues* 15 (Fall): 493–506.

Goldstein, Paul J., Patricia Bellucci, Barry J. Spunt, and Thomas Miller
1991   "Volume of Cocaine Use and Violence: A Comparison Between Men and Women." *Journal of Drug Issues* 21: 345–67.

Goleman, Daniel
1992   "As Addiction Medicine Gains, Experts Debate What It Should Cover." *New York Times* (March 31): B6.
1990   "Scientists Pinpoint Brain Irregularities in Drug Addicts." *New York Times* (June 26): B5.
1989   "Lasting Costs for Child Are Found from a Few Early Drinks." *New York Times* (February 16): 20.
1988   "Psychologists and Psychiatrists Clash over Hospital and Training Barriers." *New York Times* (May 17): 21.
1987   "Physicians Said to Persist in Undertreating Pain and Ignoring the Evidence." *New York Times* (December 31): 10.

Golub, Andrew, and Bruce D. Johnson
1994   "Cohort Differences in Drug-Use Pathways to Crack Among Current Crack Abusers in New York City." *Criminal Justice and Behavior* 21 (December): 403–22.

Gomez, Linda
1984   "America's 100 Years of Euphoria and Despair." *Life* (May): 57–68.

Gonzales, Laurence
1988   "When Doctors Are Addicts." *Chicago Reader* (July 29): 1, 16–18, 20, 22–23, 26–27.

Good, Dona, Richard A. Bass, Jacqui Coder, Paula Burbach, Douglas Jenks, and Kevin McKee
1986   *California Prisoners and Civil Narcotics Addicts.* Sacramento, CA: Department of Corrections.

Goode, Erich
1989   *Drugs in American Society,* 3d ed. New York: Knopf.
1972   *Drugs in American Society.* New York: Knopf.

Goodstadt, Michael S.
n.d.   *Drug Education.* Rockville, MD: National Institute of Justice.

Goplerud, Eric N., ed.
1991   *Preventing Adolescent Drug Use: From Theory to Practice.* Rockville, MD: Office for Substance Abuse Prevention.

Gorsuch, Richard L.
1980   "Interactive Models of Nonmedical Drug Use." Pages 18–23 in *Theories on Drug Abuse: Selected Contemporary Perspectives,* edited by Dan J. Lettieri, Mollie Sayers, and Helen Wallenstein Pearson. Rockville, MD: National Institute on Drug Abuse.

Gove, Walter R., Michael Geerken, and Michael Hughes
1979   "Drug Use and Mental Health Among a Representative Sample of Young Adults." *Social Forces* 58 (December): 572–90.

Grady, Denise
1996   "Engineered Mice Mimic Drug Use and Mental Illness." *New York Times* (February 20): B5, B8.

Granfield, Robert, and William Cloud
1996   "The Elephant That No One Sees: Natural Recovery Among Middle-Class Addicts." *Journal of Drug Issues* 26 (Winter): 45–61.

Greenhouse, Linda
1990   "Use of Illegal Drugs as Part of Religion Can Be Prosecuted, High Court Says." *New York Times* (April 18): 10.
1989   "High Court Backs Airport Detention Based on Profile." *New York Times* (April 4): 1, 10.

Greenspan, Stanley I.
1978   "Substance Abuse: An Understanding from Psychoanalytic Developmental and Learning Theory Perspectives." Pages 73–87 in *Psychodynamics of Drug Dependence,* edited by Jack D. Blaine and Demetrious A. Julius. Rockville, MD: National Institute on Drug Abuse.

Griffiths, Roland R.
1990   "Caffeine Abstinence Effects in Humans." Pages

129–30 in *Problems of Drug Dependence 1990,* edited by Louis S. Harris. Rockville, MD: National Institute on Drug Abuse.

Griffiths, Roland R., Suzette M. Evans, Stephen J. Heisman, Kenzie L. Preston, Christine A. Sannerud, Barbara Wolf, and Phillip P. Woodson

1990   "Low-Dose Caffeine Physical Dependence in Humans." *Journal of Pharmacology and Experimental Therapeutics* 255 (No. 3): 1123–32.

Grinspoon, Lester

1987   "Cancer Patients Should Get Marijuana." *New York Times* (July 28): 23.

1979   *Psychedelic Drugs Reconsidered.* New York: Basic Books.

Grinspoon, Lester, and James B. Bakalar

1985   *Cocaine: A Drug and Its Social Evolution: Revised Edition.* New York: Basic Books.

1976   *Cocaine; A Drug and Its Social Evolution.* New York: Basic Books.

Grinspoon, Lester, and Peter Hedblom

1975   *The Speed Culture: Amphetamine Use and Abuse in America.* Cambridge, MA: Harvard University Press.

Gross, Jane

1992   "Collapse of Inner-City Families Creates America's New Orphans." *New York Times* (March 29): 1, 15.

1988   "Speed's Gain in Use Could Rival Crack, Drug Experts Warn." *New York Times* (November 27): 1, 14.

Grosswirth, Marvin

1982   "Medical Menace: Doctors Hooked on Drugs." *Ladies Home Journal* (February): 94, 141–44.

Gruson, Lindsey

1990   "U.S. Pinning Hopes on Guatemalan Army for Stability and War Against Drugs." *New York Times* (July 5): 4.

1989   "Drug Trafficking and Poppy Growing Find a Lush Home in Guatemala." *New York Times* (October 1): 12.

Gulley, Joshua M., Cecelia McNamara, Thomas J. Barbera, Mary C. Ritz, and Frank R. George.

1995   "Selective Serotonin Reuptake Inhibitors on Ethanol-Reinforced Behavior in Mice." *Alcohol* 12 (May/June): 177–81.

Gusfield, Joseph R.

1975   "The (F)Utility of Knowledge? The Relation of Social Science to Public Policy Toward Drugs." *Annals* 417 (January): 1–15.

1963   *Symbolic Crusade: Status Politics and the American Temperance Movement.* Urbana: University of Illinois Press.

Haas, Kenneth C.

1990   "Drug Testing and the Constitution." Pages 244–66 in *Handbook of Drug Control in the United States,* edited by James A. Inciardi. Westport, CT: Greenwood.

Haden-Guest, Anthony

1990   "Medellin East." *Vanity Fair* (May): 82–92.

Haley, Bruce

1990   "Burma's Hidden Wars." *U.S. News and World Report* (December 10): 44–47.

Hall, Trish

1990   "New Way to Treat Alcoholism Discards Spiritualism of A.A." *New York Times* (December 24): 1, 10.

Halloran, Richard

1988   "In the War Against Drugs, Military Is Found Wanting." *New York Times* (May 30): 1, 20.

Hamm, Mark S.

1991   "Implementing Prison Drug War Policy: A Biopsy of the Wallet." Paper presented at the annual meeting of the Academy of Criminal Justice Sciences, Nashville, TN, March.

Hamowy, Ronald, ed.

1987   *Dealing with Drugs: Consequences of Government Control.* Lexington, MA: D. C. Heath.

Hanbauer, Ingeborg

1988   "Modulation of Cocaine Receptors." Pages 44–54 in *Mechanisms of Cocaine Abuse and Toxicity,* edited by Doris Clouet, Khursheed Asghar, and Roger Brown. Rockville, MD: National Institute on Drug Abuse.

Hanson, David J.

1980   "Drug Education: Does It Work?" Pages 251–82 in *Drugs and the Youth Culture,* edited by Frank S. Scarpitti and Susan K. Datesman. Beverly Hills, CA: Sage.

Hargreaves, William A.

1986   "Methadone Dosage and Duration for Maintenance Treatment." Pages 19–79 in *Research on the Treatment of Narcotic Addiction: State of the Art,* edited by James R. Cooper, Fred Altman, Barry S. Brown, and Dorynne Czechowicz. Rockville, MD: National Institute on Drug Abuse.

Harms, Ernest, ed.

1965   *Drug Addiction in Youth.* New York: Pergamon.

Harris, Louis S., ed.

1994   *Problems of Drug Dependence, 1993. Vol. I.* Rockville, MD: National Institute on Drug Abuse.

1987   *Problems of Drug Dependence, 1986.* Rockville, MD: National Institute on Drug Abuse.

Harris, Louis S.

1993   "Opiates: A History of Opiates and Their Use in Treatment." Pages 85–90 in *International Research Conference on Biomedical Approaches to Illicit Drug Demand Reduction,* edited by Christine R. Hartel. Washington, DC: U.S. Government Printing Office.

Hartel, Christine R., ed.

1993   *International Research Conference on Biomedical Approaches to Illicit Drug Demand Reduction.* Washington, DC: U.S. Government Printing Office.

Hawkins, J. David, Denise M. Lishner, and Richard F. Catalano
1987   "Childhood Predictors and the Prevention of Adolescent Substance Abuse." Pages 75–126 in *Etiology of Drug Abuse,* edited by Coryl LaRue Jones and Robert J. Battjes. Rockville, MD: National Institute on Drug Abuse.

Hawley, Thersa Lawton, Tamara G. Halle, Ruth E. Drasin, and Nancy G. Thomas
1995   "Children of Addicted Mothers: Effects of the 'Crack Epidemic' on the Caregiving Environment and the Development of Preschoolers." *American Journal of Orthopsychiatry* 65 (July): 364–79.

Hayes, Monte
1987   "Peru's Maoists Join Drug Lords." *Chicago Tribune* (December 21): 13.

Hays, Constance L.
1991   "Drug Lord? This Man? Impossible." *New York Times* (August 25): 15.
1989   "Chief Loses His Image, and a City Loses Hope." *New York Times* (November 8): 10.

Hedgepath, William
1989   "'Mule Skinner.'" *Atlanta* (March): 61–62; 93–101.

Helmer, John
1975   *Drugs and Minority Oppression.* New York: Seabury Press.

Henderson, Leigh A.
1994   "About LSD." Pages 37–53 in *LSD: Still with Us After All These Years,* edited by Leigh A. Henderson and William J. Glass. New York: Lexington Books.
1994b   "Adverse Reactions to LSD." Pages 55–75 in *LSD: Still with Us After All These Years,* edited by Leigh A. Henderson and William J. Glass. New York: Lexington Books.

Henderson, Leigh A., and William J. Glass, eds.
1994   *LSD: Still with Us After All These Years.* New York: Lexington Books.

Hendler, Harold I., and Richard C. Stephens
1977   "The Addict Odyssey: From Experimentation to Addiction." *International Journal of the Addictions* 12: 25–42.

Henkel, Ray
1986   "The Bolivian Cocaine Industry." Pages 53–80 in *Drugs in Latin America,* edited by Vinson H. Sutlive, Nathan Altshuler, Mario D. Zamora, and Virginia Kerns. Williamsburg, VA: College of William and Mary.

Henman, Anthony, et al.
1985   *Big Deal: The Politics of the Illicit Drug Business.* London: Plato Press.

Henningfield, Jack E.
1986   "How Tobacco Produces Drug Dependence." Pages 19–31 in *The Pharmacologic Treatment of Tobacco Dependence: Proceedings of the World Congress,* November 4–5, 1985, edited by J. K. Ockene. Cambridge, MA: John F. Kennedy School of Government.

Hepburn, John R., C. Wayne Johnston, and Scott Rogers
1994   *Do Drugs. Do Time: An Evaluation of the Maricopa County Demand Reeducation Program.* Washington, DC: National Institute of Justice.

Hester, Reid K., and William R. Miller
1988   "Empirical Guidelines for Optimal Client-Treatment Matching." Pages 27–38 in *Adolescent Drug Abuse: Analyses of Treatment Research,* edited by Elizabeth R. Rahdert and John Grabowski. Rockville, MD: National Institute on Drug Abuse.

Higgens, Stephen T., and Alan Budney
1993   "Treatment of Cocaine Dependence Through the Principles of Behavior Analysis and Behavioral Psychology." Pages 97–121 in *Behavioral Treatments for Drug Abuse and Dependence,* edited by Lisa Simon Onken, John D. Blaine, and John J. Boren. Rockville, MD: National Institute on Drug Abuse.

Higgens, Stephen T., Dawn D. Delancey, Alan J. Budney, Warren K. Bickel, John R. Hughes, Florian Foerg, and James W. Fenwick
1991   "A Behavioral Approach to Achieving Initial Cocaine Abstinence." *American Journal of Psychiatry* 148 (September): 1218–24.

Hijazi, Ihsan A.
1991   "Army in Lebanon Seizes Militias' Smuggling Ports." *New York Times* (March 12): 4.

Hills, Stuart L., and Ron Santiago.
1992   *Tragic Magic: The Life and Crimes of a Heroin Addict.* Chicago: Nelson-Hall.

Hilts, Philip J.
1995   "Survey Finds Surge in Smoking by Young." *New York Times* (July 20): C19.
1994   "Children of Smoking Mothers Show Carcinogens in Blood." *New York Times* (September 21): 16.
1990   "How the Brain Is Stimulated by Marijuana Is Discovered." *New York Times* (July 21): 1, 5.

Himmelstein, Jerome L.
1983   *The Strange Career of Marijuana: Politics and Ideology of Drug Control in America.* Westport, CT: Greenwood.

Hinds, Michael deCourcy
1989   "The Drive for a Fire-Safe Cigarette." *New York Times* (January 28): 18.

Hinson, Riley E.
1985   "Individual Differences in Tolerance and Relapse." Pages 101–24 in *Determinants of Substance Abuse: Biological, Psychological, and Environmental Factors,* edited by Mark Galizio and Stephen A. Maisto. New York: Plenum.

Hirschi, Travis
1969   *Causes of Delinquency.* Berkeley: University of California Press.

Hoffman, Roger A.
1982   *Marijuana as Medicine.* Seattle: Madrona Publishers.

Hoffmann, John P.
1991   "Exploring the Direct and Indirect Family Effects on Adolescent Drug Use." Paper presented at the annual meeting of the American Society of Criminology, San Francisco, November.

Hoffmann, Norman G., Patricia A. Harrison, and Susan G. Streed
1991   "Outcome Evaluation." Pages 137–54 in *Substance Abuse Services: A Guide to Planning and Management,* edited by Joseph Westermeyer and Ronald S. Krug. Chicago: American Hospital Association.

Holinger, Paul C.
1989   "A Developmental Perspective on Psychotherapy and Psychoanalysis." *American Journal of Psychiatry* 146 (November): 1404–12.

Holloway, Lynette
1994   "13 Deaths by Heroin Prompt Investigation in Manhattan." *New York Times* (August 31): 1, B12.

Holloway, Marguerite
1991   "Rx for Addiction." *Scientific American* (March): 94–103.

Horgan, John
1990   "Your Analysis Is Faulty: How to Lie with Drug Statistics." *New Republic* (April 2): 22–24.

Hormes, Joseph T., Christopher M. Filley, and Neil L. Rosenberg
1986   "Neurologic Sequelae of Chronic Solvent Vapor Abuse." *Neurology* 36 (May): 698–702.

Horowitz, Craig
1996   "The No-Win War." *New York* (February 5): 23–33.

Hubbard, Robert L., Mary Ellen Marsden, J. Valley, Rachel Henrick, J. Harwood, Elizabeth R. Cavanaugh, and Harold M. Ginsberg
1989   *Drug Abuse Treatment: A National Study of Effectiveness.* Chapel Hill: University of North Carolina Press.

Hughes, John R.
1990   "Nicotine Abstinence Effects." Page 123 in *Problems of Drug Dependence 1989,* edited by Louis S. Harris, Rockville, MD: National Institute on Drug Abuse.

Hughes, Patrick H.
1977   *Behind the Wall of Respect.* Chicago: University of Chicago Press.

Hughes, Patrick H., Gail A. Crawford, Noel W. Barker, Suzanne Schumann, and Jerome H. Jaffe
1971   "The Social Structure of a Heroin Copping Community." *American Journal of Psychiatry* 128 (November): 43–50.

Hughes, Richard
1979   *The Tranquilizing of America.* New York: Harcourt Brace Jovanovich.

Huizinga, David H., Scott Menard, and Delbert S. Elliott
1989   "Delinquency and Drug Use: Temporal and Developmental Patterns." *Justice Quarterly* 6 (September): 419–55.

Humphries, Drew, and David F. Greenberg
1981   "The Dialectics of Crime Control." Pages 209–54 in *Crime and Capitalism,* edited by David F. Greenberg. Palo Alto, CA: Mayfield.

Hunt, Leon Gibson
1977   *Assessment of Local Drug Abuse.* Lexington, MA: D. C. Heath.

Hunt, Walter A.
1983   "Ethanol and the Central Nervous System." Pages 133–63 in *Medical and Social Aspects of Alcohol Abuse,* edited by Boris Tabakoff, Patricia B. Sutker, and Carrie L. Randall. New York: Plenum.

Huxley, Aldous
1954   *The Doors of Perception.* New York: Harper & Row.

Hyman, Steven E., and Eric J. Nestler
1996   "Initiation and Adaptation: Paradigm for Understanding Psychotropic Drug Action." *American Journal of Psychiatry* 153 (February): 151–62.

Ibrahamim, Youssef M.
1989   "Iran Puts Addicts in Its Labor Camps." *New York Times* (July 22): 3.

Ihde, Aaron J.
1982   "Food Controls Under the 1906 Act." Pages 40–50 in *The Early Years of Federal Food and Drug Control,* edited by James Harvey Young. Madison, WI: American Institute of the History of Pharmacy.

Inciardi, James A.
1986   *The War on Drugs: Heroin, Cocaine, Crime, and Public Policy.* Palo Alto, CA: Mayfield.
1981   "Heroin Addiction and Street Crime." Pages 53–60 in *International Narcotics Trafficking,* hearings before the Permanent Subcommittee on Investigations, November 10, 11, 12, 13, 17, and 18. Washington, DC: U.S. Government Printing Office.

Inciardi, James A., and Anne E. Pottieger
1991   "Kids, Crack, and Crime." *Journal of Drug Issues* 21: 257–70.

Institute for the Study of Drug Dependence (ISDD)
1987   *Drug Abuse Briefing.* London: ISDD.

Inverarity, James M., Pat Lauderdale, and Barry Field
1983   *Law and Society: Sociological Perspectives on Criminal Law.* Boston: Little, Brown.

Irwin, John
1970   *The Felon.* Englewood Cliffs, NJ: Prentice-Hall.

Izenwasser, Sari, and Ellen M. Unterwald
1994   "Sensitization and Tolerance to Cocaine." Pages 71–73 in *Problems of Drug Dependence, 1993,* edited by Louis S. Harris. Rockville, MD: National Institute on Drug Abuse.

Jacob, Peyton, III, and Alexander Shulgin
1994   "Structure-Activity Relationships of the Classic

Hallucinogens and Their Analogs." Pages 74–91 in *Hallucinogens: An Update,* edited by Geraline C. Lin and Richard A. Glennon. Rockville, MD: National Institute on Drug Abuse.

Jacobsen, Chanoch, and Robert A. Hanneman
1992 "Illegal Drugs: Past, Present and Possible Futures." *Journal of Drug Issues* 22 (Winter): 105–20.

Jamieson, Anne, Alan Glanz, and Susanne MacGregor
1984 *Dealing with Drug Misuse: Crisis Intervention in the City.* London: Tavistock.

Jenkins, Philip
1994 " 'The Ice Age': The Social Construction of a Drug Panic." *Justice Quarterly* 11 (March): 7–31.

Johnson, Bruce D., Kevin Anderson, and Eric C. Wish
1989 "A Day in the Life of 105 Drug Addicts and Abusers: Crimes Committed and How the Money Was Spent." *Sociology and Social Research* 72: 185–91.

Johnson, Bruce D., Paul J. Goldstein, Edward Preble, James Schmeidler, Douglas S. Lipton, Barry Spunt, and Thomas Miller
1985 *Taking Care of Business: The Economics of Crime by Heroin Abusers.* Lexington, MA: D. C. Heath.

Johnson, Bruce D., Andrew Golub, and Jeffrey Fagan
1995 "Careers in Crack, Drug Use, Drug Distribution, and Nondrug Criminality." *Crime and Delinquency* 41 (July): 275–95.

Johnson, Bruce D., Douglas S. Lipton, and Eric D. Wish
1986 *Facts about the Criminality of Heroin and Cocaine Abusers and Some New Alternatives to Incarceration.* New York: Photocopied.
1986b *Facts about the Criminality of Heroin and Cocaine Abusers and Some New Alternatives to Incarceration (Research Summary).* New York: Narcotic and Drug Research, Inc.

Johnson, Bruce D., Terry Williams, Koja A. Dei, and Harry Sanabria
1990 "Drug Abuse in the Inner City: Impact on Hard-Drug Users and the Community." Pages 9–67 in *Drugs and Crime,* edited by Michael Tonry and James Q. Wilson. Chicago: University of Chicago Press.

Johnson, Bruce D., Eric C. Wish, James Schmeidler, and David Huizinga
1991 "Concentration of Delinquent Offending: Serious Drug Involvement and High Delinquency Rates." *Journal of Drug Issues* 21: 205–29.

Johnson, C. Anderson, Mary Ann Pentz, Mark D. Weber, James H. Dwyer, Neal Baer, David P. MacKinnon, William B. Hansen, and Brian R. Flay
1990 "Relative Effectiveness of Comprehensive Community Programming for Drug Abuse Prevention With High-Risk and Low-Risk Adolescents." *Journal of Consulting and Clinical Psychology* 58 (August): 447–56.

Johnson, Earl, Jr.
1963 "Organized Crime: Challenge to the American Legal System." *Criminal Law, Criminology, and Police Science* 54 (March): 1–29.

Johnson, Fenton
1989 "High in the Hollows." *New York Times* (December 17): 30, 46–51.

Johnson, Julie
1987 "Two Reagan Officials Report Limited Success in Drug War." *New York Times* (December 9): 53.

Johnston, David
1991 "Illegal Drug Sales in the U.S. Put at Over $40 Billion in '90." *New York Times* (June 20): 11.

Joint Committee on New York Drug Law Evaluation
1977 *The Nation's Toughest Drug Law: Evaluation of the New York Experience.* New York: Association of the Bar of the City of New York.

Jones, Charisse
1995 "Crack and Punishment: Is Race the Issue?" *New York Times* (October 16): 1, 9.

Jones, Coryl LaRue, and Robert J. Battjes
1987 "The Context and Caveats of Prevention Research on Drug Abuse." Pages 1–12 in *Etiology of Drug Abuse: Implications for Prevention,* edited by Coryl LaRue Jones and Robert J. Battjes. Rockville, MD: National Institute on Drug Abuse.

Jones, Kenneth L., Louis W. Shainberg, and Curtis O. Byer
1979 *Drugs and Alcohol,* 3d ed. New York: Harper & Row.

Jones, Reese T.
1980 "Marijuana, Human Effects: An Overview." Pages 54–80 in Marijuana: Research Findings, 1980. Rockville, MD: National Institute on Drug Abuse.

Jourbert, Lucien
1987 "The Oral Dose Is Safer," Letter to the *New York Times* (August 15): 14.

Judson, Barbara A., and Avram Goldstein
1986 "Uses of Naloxone in the Diagnosis and Treatment of Heroin Addiction." Pages 1–18 in *Research on the Treatment of Narcotic Addiction: State of the Art,* edited by James R. Cooper, Fred Altman, Barry S. Brown, and Dorynne Czechowicz. Rockville, MD: National Institute on Drug Abuse.

Judson, George
1995 "Study Finds AIDS Risk to Addicts Drops if Sale of Syringes Is Legal." *New York Times* (August 30): 1, 12.

Kalogerakis, George
1995 "Stoned Again." *New York* (May 1): 41–47.

Kamm, Henry
1988 "In Wild West Not Far from the Khyber Pass, Shots Ring Out." *New York Times (March 18): 7.*
1988b "More Afghan Opium: Less in Pakistan." *New York Times* (April 14): 6.

Kandel, Denise K.
1974 "Interpersonal Influences on Adolescent Illegal Drug Use." Pages 207–40 in *Drug Use: Epidemio-*

logical and Sociological Approaches, edited by Eric Josephson and Eleanor E. Carroll. New York: Wiley.

Kandel, Denise K., and Mark Davies
1991 "Friendship Networks, Intimacy, and Illicit Drug Use in Young Adulthood: A Comparison of Two Competing Theories." *Criminology* 29 (August): 441–67.

Kaplan, John
1983 "Drugs and Crime: Legal Aspects." Pages 643–52 in the *Encyclopedia of Crime and Justice,* edited by Sanford H. Kadish. New York: Free Press.
1983b *The Hardest Drug: Heroin and Public Policy.* Chicago: University of Chicago Press.

Katcher, Leo
1959 *The Big Bankroll: The Life and Times of Arnold Rothstein.* New York: Harper and Brothers.

Katel, Peter
1995 "Justice: The Trouble with Informants." *Newsweek* (January 30): 48.

Kauffman, Eda, Martha Morrison Dore, and Lani Nelson-Zlupko
1995 "The Role of Women's Therapy Groups in the Treatment of Chemical Dependence." *American Journal of Orthopsychiatry* 65 (July) 355–63.

Kaufman, Edward
1994 *Psychotherapy of Addicted Persons.* New York: Guilford Press.

Kay, David C.
1973 "Federal Civil Commitment in the Federal Medical Program for Opiate Addicts." Pages 17–35 in *Yearbook of Drug Abuse,* edited by Leon Brill and Earnest Harms. New York: Behavioral Publications.

Kelly, David
1990 "U.S.: Syrians Aid Supply of Heroin." *Chicago Tribune* (December 7): 13.

Kempe, Frederick
1990 *Divorcing the Dictator: America's Bungled Affair with Noriega.* New York: Putnam's Sons.

Kennedy, Randy
1995 "Death Highlights Drug's Lethal Allure to Doctors." *New York Times* (November 11): 1, 10.

Kerr, Peter
1991 "Tough Choice in New Jersey on Prison Overcrowding." *New York Times* (May 26): 15.
1988 "Chinese Criminals Move to Broaden Role in U.S." *New York Times* (January 4): 1, 12.
1988b "Crime Study Finds High Use of Drugs at Time of Arrest." *New York Times* (January 22): 1, 9.
1988c "U.S. Raises Firepower in Drive on Drug Sellers." *New York Times* (April 8): 12.
1988d "Bolivia, with U.S. Aid, Battles Cocaine at the Root." *New York Times* (April 17): 6.
1988e "Cocaine Ring Holding Fast in Colombia." *New York Times* (May 21): 1, 5.
1988f "Addiction's Hidden Toll: Poor Families in Turmoil." *New York Times* (June 23): 1, 13.
1988g "Cocaine Glut Puts New York in Drug Rings' Tug-of-War." *New York Times* (August 24): 14.

Kertzner, Robert M.
1987 "Individual Psychotherapy of Cocaine Abuse." Pages 138–55 in *Cocaine Abuse: New Directions in Treatment and Research,* edited by Henry I. Spitz and Jeffrey S. Rosecan. New York: Brunner/Mazel.

Kethinineni, Sesha, Diane Alexander Leamy, Lois Guyon
1991 "Evaluation of the Drug Abuse Resistence Education Program in Illinois: A Preliminary Report." Paper presented at the annual meeting of the American Society of Criminology, San Francisco, November.

Khantzian, Edward J.
1985 "The Self-Medication Hypothesis of Addictive Disorders: Focus on Heroin and Cocaine Dependence." *American Journal of Psychiatry* 142: 1259–64.
1980 "An Ego/Self Theory of Substance Dependence: A Contemporary Psychoanalytic Perspective," Pages 29–33 in *Theories on Drug Abuse: Selected Contemporary Perspectives,* edited by Dan J. Lettieri, Mollie Sayers, and Helen Wallenstein Pearson. Rockville, MD: National Institute on Drug Abuse.

Khantzian, Edward J., John E. Mack, and Alan F. Schatzberg
1974 "Heroin Use as an Attempt to Cope: Clinical Observations." *American Journal of Psychiatry* 131 (February): 160–64.

Kidorf, Michael, and Maxine L. Stitzer
1996 "Contingent Use of Take-Home and Split Dosing to Reduce Illicit Drug Use of Methadone Patients." *Behavior Therapy* 27 (Winter): 41–51.

Kim, Sehwan, Jonnie H. McLeod, and Carl Shantzis
1990 "A Short-Term Outcome Evaluation of the 'I'm Special' Drug Abuse Prevention Program: A Revisit Using SCAT Inventory." *Journal of Drug Education* 20: 127–38.

Kinder, Douglas Clark
1992 "Shutting Out the Evil: Nativism and Narcotics Control in the United States." Pages 117–42 in *Drug Control Policy: Essays in Historical and Comparative Perspective* edited by William O. Walker, III. University Park: Pennsylvania State University.

King, Rufus
1969 *Gambling and Organized Crime.* Washington, DC: Public Affairs Press.

Kinzer, Stephen
1992 "Pro-Drug Ruling in Germany Stirs the Pot and the Politics." *New York Times* (March 3): 5.
1988 "Trust in Honduran Leaders Plummets with Drug Arrest." *New York Times* (May 25): 9.

Kissin, Benjamin, Joyce H. Lowinson, and Robert B. Millman, eds.

1978   *Recent Development in Chemotherapy of Narcotic Addiction.* New York: New York Academy of Sciences.

Kleiman, Mark A. R.

1992   *Against Excess: Drug Policy for Results.* New York: Basic Books.

1989   *Marijuana: Costs of Abuse, Costs of Control.* New York: Greenwood.

1988   "Crackdowns: The Effects on Intensive Enforcement on Retail Heroin Dealing." Pages 3–18 in *Street-Level Drug Enforcement: Examining the Issues,* edited by Marcia R. Chaiken. Washington, DC: U.S. Government Printing Office.

1985   "Drug Enforcement and Organized Crime." Pages 67–87 in *The Politics and Economics of Organized Crime,* edited by Herbert E. Alexander and Gerald E. Caiden. Lexington, MA: D. C. Heath.

Kleiman, Mark A. R., and Kerry D. Smith

1990   "State and Local Drug Enforcement: In Search of a Strategy." Pages 69–108 in *Drugs and Crime,* edited by Michael Tonry and James Q. Wilson. Chicago: University of Chicago Press.

Klein, Malcolm, Cheryl L. Maxson, Lea C. Cunningham

1991   " 'Crack,' Street Gangs, and Violence." *Criminology* 29 (November): 623–50.

Kolata, Gina

1996   "The Unwholesome Tale of the Herb Market." *New York Times* (April 21): 6E.

1989   "Medications May Ease Craving for Cocaine." *New York Times* (March 7): 21, 23.

1989b   "In Cities, Poor Families Are Dying of Crack." *New York Times* (August 11): 1, 10.

1989c   "Experts Finding New Hope on Treating Crack Addicts." *New York Times* (August 24): 1, 9.

1988   "Drug Researchers Try to Treat a Nearly Unbreakable Habit." *New York Times* (June 25): 1, 9.

Kolbert, Elizabeth

1989   "Communities Halt Narcotics Clinics." *New York Times* (September 30): 89.

Koob, George F., Barak Caine, Athina Markou, Luigi Pulvirenti, and Freidbert Weiss

1994   "Role for the Mesocortical Dopamine System in the Motivating Effects of Cocaine." Pages 1–16 in *Neurobiological Models for Evaluating Mechanisms Underlying Cocaine Addiction,* edited by Lynda Erinoff and Roger M. Brown. Rockville, MD: National Institute on Drug Abuse.

Kosten, Thomas R.

1993   "Update on Drugs: Cocaine and Stimulants." Summary of comments in *NIDA Second National Conference on Drug Abuse Research and Practice: An Alliance for the 21st Century* pp. 26–29. Rockville, MD: National Institute on Drug Abuse.

1993b   "Clinical and Research Perspectives on Cocaine Abuse: The Pharmacology of Cocaine Abuse." Pages 48–56 in *Cocaine Treatment: Research and Clinical Perspectives,* edited by Frank M. Tims and Carl G. Leukefeld. Rockville, MD: National Institute on Drug Abuse.

Kotulak, Ronald

1992   "Cocaine May Unlock Brain's Mysteries." *Chicago Tribune* (March 29): 1, 14.

Kozel, Nicholas J., and Edgar H. Adams, eds.

1985   *Cocaine Use in America: Epidemiologic and Clinical Perspectives.* Rockville, MD: National Institute on Drug Abuse.

Koziol, Ronald

1988   "Foreigners Filling Vacuum Left by Mafia." *Chicago Tribune* (March 20): 4.

1988b   "Dogs Put U.S. on Drug Suspect's Trail." *Chicago Tribune* (June 29): section 2: 1, 2.

Kraar, Louis

1988   "The Drug Trade." *Fortune* (June 20): 26–29, 32–33, 36–38.

Krauss, Clifford

1995   "Colombia Arrests Raise Price of Cocaine in New York City." *New York Times* (September 15): 1, 12.

1995b   "Drug Arrests in Colombia Lead to New York Killings." *New York Times* (November 25): 1, 6.

1992   "U.S. Plans to Aid Army in Peru to Fight Cocaine." *New York Times* (January 25): 4.

1991   "U.S. Military Team to Advise Peru in War Against Drugs and Rebels." *New York Times* (August 7): 1, 6.

1991b   "U.S. Withholding Drug Aid to Peru." *New York Times* (November 11): 6.

Krauss, Melvyn B., and Edward P. Lazear, eds.

1991   *Searching for Alternatives: Drug Control Policy in the United States.* Stanford, CA: Hoover Institution.

Kreek, Mary Jeanne

1987   "Tolerance and Dependence: Implications for the Pharmacological Treatment of Addiction." Pages 53–62 in *Problems of Drug Dependence, 1986,* edited by Louis S. Harris. Rockville, MD: National Institute of Drug Abuse.

Kristof, Nicholas D.

1991   "China Metes Out Death at Drug Rally." *New York Times* (October 27): 3.

Krystal, Henry, and Herbert A. Raskin

1970   *Drug Dependence: Aspects of Ego Function.* Detroit: Wayne State University Press.

Kuhar, Michael J., Mary C. Ritz, and John Sharkey

1988   "Cocaine Receptors on Dopamine Transporters Mediate Cocaine-Reinforced Behavior." Pages 14–22 in *Mechanisms of Cocaine Abuse and Toxicity,* edited by Doris Clouet, Khursheed Asghar, and Roger Brown. Rockville, MD: National Institute on Drug Abuse.

Kupfer, Andrew

1988   "What to Do About Drugs?" *Fortune* (June 20):
        39–41.

Kurlansky, Mark

1988   "U.S. 'War on Drugs' Reignites Militancy Among
        the Maroons." *Chicago Tribune* (March 30): 18.

Kurtis. Bill

1980   "The Caviar Connection." *New York Times Maga-
        zine* (October 25): 132–41.

Kurtz, Ernest

1979   *Not God: A History of Alcoholics Anonymous.* Cen-
        ter City, MN: Hazelden Educational Services.

Labaton, Stephen

1989   "New Tactics in the War on Drugs Tilt Scales of
        Justice Off Balance." *New York Times* (December
        29): 1, 14.

Lambert, Bruce

1996   "Fears Prompting Crackdown on Legal Herbal
        Stimulant." *New York Times* (April 23): 12.

1990   "Police Charge 10 at a Protest on Needle Law."
        New York Times (March 7): 13.

1988   "Studies Support Plan to Offer Free Needles." *New
        York Times* (June 6): 15.

1988b   "Drug Addicts in Portland, Ore., to Get Free Hypo-
        dermic Needles." *New York Times* (June 10): 7.

Lamour, Catherine, and Michael R. Lamberti

1974   *The Second Opium War.* London: Allen Lane.

Lane, Charles, Douglas Waller, Brook Larmer, and Peter
Katel

1992   "The Newest War." *Newsweek* (January 6): 18–23.

Lang, Alan R.

1983   "Addicting Personality: A Viable Construct?" Pages
        157–235 in *Commonalities in Substance Abuse and
        Habitual Behavior,* edited by Peter K. Levison,
        Dean R. Gerstein, and Deborah R. Maloff. Lexing-
        ton, MA: D. C. Heath.

Larmer, Brook

1992   " 'The Gateway to Heaven': A Trip to Peru's Per-
        ilous Cocaine Valley." *Newsweek* (January 20):
        41.

Latessa, Edward J., and Melissa M. Moon

1992   "The Effectiveness of Acupuncture in an Outpatient
        Drug Treatment Program." *Journal of Contempo-
        rary Criminal Justice* 8 (December): 317–31.

Latimer, Dean, and Jeff Goldberg

1981   *Flowers in the Blood: The Story of Opium.* New
        York: Franklin Watts.

Lawson, Gary W.

1992   "A Biopsychological Model of Adolescent Sub-
        stance Abuse." Pages 3–10 in *Adolescent Substance
        Abuse,* edited by Gary W. Lawson and Ann W. Law-
        son. Gaithersburg, MD: Aspen Publications.

Lawson, Gary W., and Ann W. Lawson, eds.

1992   *Adolescent Substance Abuse.* Gaithersburg MD:
        Aspen Publications.

Leary, Warren E.

1995   "Drug for Heroin Addiction Is Being Marketed for
        Treatment of Alcoholism." *New York Times* (Janu-
        ary 18): 12.

1995b   "Report Endorses Needle Exchanges as AIDS Strat-
        egy." *New York Times* (September 20): 1, 14.

1992   "U.S. Urges Doctors to Fight Surgical Pain (and
        Myths)." *New York Times* (March 6): 1, 9.

1988   "Survey Detects Decline in the Use of Cocaine
        Among Young Adults." *New York Times* (January
        14): 1, 17.

Leccese, Arthur P.

1991   *Drugs and Society: Behavioral Medicines and
        Abusable Drugs.* Englewood Cliffs, NJ: Prentice-
        Hall.

Lee, Rensselaer, III

1995   "Drugs in Communist and Former Communist
        Countries." *Transnational Organized Crime* 1
        (Summer): 193–205.

Lemert, Edwin M.

1951   *Social Pathology.* New York: McGraw-Hill.

Lerner, Steven E.

1980   "Phencyclidine Abuse in Perspective." Pages 13–23
        in *Phencyclidine Abuse Manual,* edited by Mary
        Tuma McAdams, Ronald L. Linder, Steven E.
        Lerner, and Richard Stanley Burns. Los Angeles:
        University of California Extension.

Lettieri, Dan J., Mollie Sayers, and Helen Wallenstein
Pearson, eds.

1980   *Theories on Drug Abuse: Selected Contemporary
        Perspectives.* Rockville, MD: National Institute on
        Drug Abuse.

Leukefeld, Carl C., and Frank M. Tims, eds.

1988   *Compulsory Treatment of Drug Abuse: Research
        and Clinical Practice.* Rockville, MD: National In-
        stitute on Drug Abuse.

Levin, Jerome David

1990   *Alcoholism: A Bio-Psycho-Social Approach.* New
        York: Hemisphere Publishing Corp.

Levine, Michael

1990   *Deep Cover.* New York: Delacorte.

Le Vine, Steve

1990   "Alleged Drug Kingpin's Election Sends a Signal to
        Pakistan." *Chicago Tribune* (January 2): 6.

Levins, Hoag

1980   "The Kabul Connection." *Philadelphia* (August):
        114–20; 192–203.

Levinthal, Charles F.

1988   *Messengers of Paradise: Opiates and the Brain.*
        Garden City, NY: Doubleday.

Lewin, Tamar

1992   "Drug Verdict Over Infants Is Voided." *New York
        Times* (July 24): B6.

1991   "Guilt Upheld for Drug Delivery by Umbilical
        Cord." *New York Times* (April 20): 1, 6.

Lewis, Larry
1988   "Bad Habit Downs a Good Cop." *Chicago Tribune* (March 22): 4.

Lewis, Neil A.
1991   "How Drugs Launched, and Then Destroyed, Career of a Thornburgh Aide." *New York Times* (February 24): 15.

Li, Guohua, Gordon S. Smith, and Susan P. Baker
1994   "Drinking Behavior in Relation to Cause of Death Among U.S. Adults." *American Journal of Public Health* 84 (No. 9): 1402–06.

Lidz, Charles W., and Andrew L. Walker
1980   *Heroin, Deviance and Morality.* Beverly Hills, CA: Sage.

Lieber, Charles S.
1991   "Perspectives: Do Alcohol Calories Count?" *American Journal of Clinical Nutrition* 54: 976–82.

Light, Ivan
1977   "The Ethnic Vice Industry, 1880–1944." *American Journal of Sociology* 42 (June): 464–79.

Lin, Geraline, and Richard A. Glennon, eds.
1994   *Hallucinogens: An Update.* Rockville, MD: National Institute on Drug Abuse.

Linder, Ronald L., with Steven E. Lerner and R. Stanley Burns
1981   *PCP: The Devil's Dust.* Belmont, CA: Wadsworth.

Lindesmith, Alfred C.
1968   *Addiction and Opiates.* Chicago: Aldine.

Lindesmith, Alfred C., and John H. Gagnon
1964   "Anomie and Drug Addiction." Pages 158–88 in *Anomie and Deviant Behavior,* edited by Marshall B. Clinard. New York: Free Press.

Ling, Walter, Richard A. Rawson, and Margaret A. Compton
1994   "Substitution Pharmacotherapies for Opioid Addiction: From Methadone to LAMM and Buprenorphine." *Journal of Psychoactive Drugs* 26 (No. 2): 119–28.

Lipton, Douglas S.
1995   *The Effectiveness of Treatment for Drug Abusers under Criminal Justice Supervision.* Washington, DC: National Institute of Justice.

Liu, Liang Y.
1994   *Substance Use Among Youths at High Risk of Dropping Out: Grades 7–12 in Texas, 1992.* Austin: Texas Commission on Alcohol and Drug Abuse.

Lizarazo, Jorge Gómez
1992   "Colombian Blood, U.S. Guns." *New York Times* (January 28): 13.

Logue, A. W.
1991   *The Psychology of Eating and Drinking: An Introduction,* 2d ed. New York: W. H. Freeman.

London, Perry
1964   *The Modes and Morals of Psychotherapy.* New York: Holt, Rinehart and Winston.

Lorion, Raymond P., Danielle Bussell, and Richard Goldberg
1991   "Identification of Youth at High Risk for Alcohol or Other Drug Problems." Pages 53–89 in *Preventing Adolescent Drug Use: From Theory to Practice,* edited by Eric N. Goplerud. Rockville, Maryland: Office for Substance Abuse Prevention.

Lubasch, Arnold H.
1990   "Trial Shows the Rich Rewards of a Federal Drug Informant." *New York Times* (November 4): 23.

Luft, Kerry
1995   "For Busted Drug Lord, Terror Too Crass." *Chicago Tribune* (June 15): 3.

Lupsha, Peter A.
1995   "Transnational Narco-Corruption and Narco Investment: A Focus on Mexico." *Transnational Organized Crime* 1 (Spring): 84–101.

1991   "Drug Lords and Narco-Corruption: The Players Change but the Game Continues." *Crime, Law and Social Change* 16: 41–58.

1990   "The Geopolitics of Organized Crime: Some Comparative Models from Latin American Drug Trafficking Organizations." Paper presented at the annual meeting of the American Society of Criminology, Baltimore, November.

1988   "Coping with Transnational Crime: A Focus on Latin American Drug Trafficking Criminality." Paper presented at the United Nations International Seminar on Policies and Strategies to Combat Organized Crime, Albuquerque, NM., December 8–11.

Mabry, Donald J.
1995   "The U.S. Military and the War on Drugs." Pages 43–60 in *Drug Trafficking in the Americas,* edited by Bruce M. Bagley and William O. Walker, III. New Brunswick, NJ: Transaction Books.

MacDonald, James, and Michael Agar
1994   "What Is a Trip—and Why Take One?" Pages 9–36 in *LSD: Still with Us After All These Years,* edited by Leigh A. Henderson and William J. Glass. New York: Lexington Books.

Maddux, James F.
1988   "Clinical Experience with Civil Commitment." Pages 35–56 in *Compulsory Treatment of Drug Abuse: Research and Clinical Practice.* Rockville, MD: National Institute on Drug Abuse.

Maddux, James F., and David P. Desmond
1981   *Careers of Opioid Users.* New York: Praeger.

Magura, Stephen, Cathy Casriel, Douglas S. Goldsmith, David L. Strug, and Douglas S. Lipton
1988   "Contingency Contracting with Polydrug-Abusing Methadone Patients." *Addictive Behaviors* 13: 113–18.

Magura, Stephen, Sung-Yeon Kang, and Janet L. Shapiro
1995   "Measuring Cocaine Use by Hair Analysis among

Criminally-Involved Youth." *Journal of Drug Issues* 25 (Fall): 683–701.

Malloy, James
1987 "Bolivia's Economic Crisis." *Current History* 86 (January): 9–12, 37–38.

Maltzman, Irving
1994 "Why Alcoholism Is a Disease." *Journal of Psychoactive Drugs* 26 (January/March): 13–31.

Mansnerus, Laura
1996 "Timothy Leary, Pied Piper of Psychedelic 60's, Dies at 75." *New York Times* (June 1): 1,11.

Marcos, Anastasios C., Stephen J. Bahr, and Richard E. Johnson
1986 "Testing of a Bonding/Association Theory of Adolescent Drug Use." *Social Forces* 65 (September): 135–61.

Margolick, David
1991 "Ex-Kent Smoker Blames Filter of Past for Illness." *New York Times* (August 30): B6.
1988 "At the Bar: Court Ruling Not to Disbar Former Addict May Have Wide Impact in Drug Abuse Cases." *New York Times* (June 24): 20.

Mark, Gregory Yee
1975 "Racial, Economic and Political Factors in the Development of America's First Drug Laws." *Issues in Criminology* 10 (Spring): 49–72.

Marlatt, G. Alan, Julian M. Somers, and Susan F. Tapert
1993 "Harm Reduction: Application to Alcohol Abuse Problems." Pages 147–66 in *Behavioral Treatments for Drug Abuse and Dependence,* edited by Lisa Simon Onken, John D. Blaine, and John J. Boren. Rockville, MD: National Institute on Drug Abuse.

Marriott, Michael
1995 "Half Steps vs. 12 Steps." *Newsweek* (March 27): 62.
1989 "Struggle and Hope from the Ashes of Drugs." *New York Times* (October 22): 1, 22.

Marshall, Ineke Haen, and Chris E. Marshall
1994 "Drug Prevention in the Netherlands: A Low Key Approach." Pages 205–31 in *Between Prohibition and Legalization: The Dutch Experiment in Drug Policy,* edited by Ed. Leuw and I Haen Marshall. Amsterdam: Kugler Publications.

Martin, B. R., S. Childers, A. Howlett, R. Mechoulam, and R. Pertwee
1994 "Cannabinoid Receptors: Pharmacology, Second Messenger Systems and Endogenous Ligands." Pages 55–60 in *Problems of Drug Dependence, 1993. Vol. I.,* edited by Louis S. Harris. Rockville, MD: National Institute on Drug Abuse.

Martin, Douglas
1990 "A Big Bribe Helps Mothers Flee the Seduction of Crack." *New York Times* (March 7): 13.

Marx, Gary
1991 "Drug Money, Poverty Fuel Medellin's Cycle of Death." *Chicago Tribune* (February 18): 1, 6.

1991b "Drug Lord, or Ghost, Stalks Colombian Town." *Chicago Tribune* (July 28): 4.
1991c "Cautious Optimism in Colombia." *Chicago Tribune* (August 4): 1, 13.
1991d "Drug Trade Spreads in S. America." *Chicago Tribune* (August 18): 1, 15.
1991e "Life Sentence." *Chicago Tribune* (August 30): Sec. 5: 1, 2.
1990 "Drug War Puts Bolivian Farmers on Front Line." *Chicago Tribune* (July 16): 1, 6.

Maschke, Karen J.
1995 "Prosecutors as Crime Creators: The Case of Prenatal Drug Use." *Criminal Justice Review* 20 (Spring): 21–33.

Massing, Michael
1990 "In the Cocaine War, the Jungle Is Winning." *New York Times Magazine* (March 4): 26, 88, 90, 92.
1989 "Crack's Destructive Sprint Across America." *New York Times Magazine* (October 1): 38–41, 58–62.

Mattison, J.B.
1883 "Opium Addiction Among Medical Men." *Medical Record* 23 (June 9): 621–23. Reproduced in Morgan, 1974, pages 62–66.

May, Clifford D.
1988 "Drug Enforcement: Once-Lonely Voice Finds an Audience." *New York Times* (June 6): 12.
1988b "U.S. Secretly Grows Coca to Find Way to Destroy Cocaine's Source." *New York Times* (June 12): 1, 17.
1988c "Coca-Cola Discloses an Old Secret." *New York Times* (July 1): 25, 29.

Mayes, Linda G.
1992 "Prenatal Cocaine Exposure and Young Children's Development." *Annals* 521 (May): 11–27.

McBride, Duane C., and Clyde B. McCoy
1981 "Crime and Drug-Abusing Behavior." *Criminology* 19 (August): 281–302.

McCoy, Alfred W.
1991 *The Politics of Heroin: CIA Complicity in the Global Heroin Trade.* Brooklyn, NY: Lawrence Hill Books.
1972 *The Politics of Heroin in Southeast Asia.* New York: Harper & Row.

McCoy, H. Virginia, Christine Miles, and James A. Inciardi
1995 "Survival Sex: Inner-City Women and Crack-Cocaine." Pages 172–77 in *The American Drug Scene: An Anthology,* edited by James A. Inciardi and Karen McElrath. Los Angeles: Roxbury.

McDonald, Scott B.
1988 *Dancing on a Volcano: The Latin-American Drug Trade.* New York: Praeger.

McElrath, Karen
1995 "Alcoholics Anonymous." Pages 314–37 in *The American Drug Scene: An Anthology,* edited by

James A. Inciardi and Karen McElrath. Los Angeles: Roxbury.

McFarland, George C.
1989 *Drug Abuse Indicators Trend Report, District of Columbia.* Washington, DC: Alcohol and Drug Abuse Services Administration.

McGehee, Daniel S., Mark J. S. Heath, Shari Gelber, Piroska Devay, Lorna W. Role
1995 "Nicotine Enhancement of Fast Excitatory Synaptic Transmission in CNS by Presynaptic Receptors." *Science* 269 (September 22): 1692–96.

McGlothlin, William H., M. Douglas Anglin, and Bruce D. Wilson
1978 "Narcotic Addiction and Crime." *Criminology* 16 (November): 293–315.
1977 *An Evaluation of the California Civil Addict Program.* Rockville, MD: National Institute on Drug Abuse.
1977b "A Follow-up of Admissions to the California Civil Addict Program." *American Journal of Drug and Alcohol Abuse* 4: 179–99.
1975/76 "Outcome of the California Civil Addict Commitments: 1961–1972." *Drug and Alcohol Dependence* 1: 165–81.

McGuire, Phillip C.
1988 "Jamaican Posses: A Call for Cooperation Among Law Enforcement Agencies." *Police Chief* (January): 20–27.

McIntosh, Lee
1988 "Letter to the Editor." *New York Times* (June 39): 26.

McKim, William A.
1991 *Drugs and Behavior: An Introduction to Behavioral Pharmacology,* 2d edition. Englewood Cliffs, NJ: Prentice-Hall.

McKinley, James C., Jr.
1990 "17 Charged in Raids of Brooklyn 'Posse' Linked to 10 Deaths." *New York Times* (December 8): 1, 7.

McMahon, Colin
1995 "Mexicans Make Their Mark in Drug Game as Middlemen." *Chicago Tribune* (September 18): 1, 14.

McNeil, Donald G.
1992 "Why There's No Methadone for Crack." *New York Times* (June 14): E7.

McNulty, Timothy J.
1988 "Cocaine Use Drops 20% Among Teens, Collegians." *Chicago Tribune* (January 14): 1, 18.
1986 "From a Concern to a Crusade: How Drug War Took on a Life of Its Own One Summer." *Chicago Tribune* (September 14): 4.

McWilliams, John C.
1992 "Through the Past Darkly: The Politics and Policies of America's Drug War." Pages 5–41 in *Drug Control Policy: Essays in Historical and Comparative Perspective,* edited by William O. Walker, III. University Park: Pennsylvania State University.

Meddis, Sam
1993 "Is the Drug War Racist?" *USA Today* (July 23): 1, 2.

Medina, Samuel Doria
1990 "Bolivia Is Trying to Dismantle Its Coca Economy." Letter to the *New York Times* (May 17): 18.

Meltzer, Herbert L.
1979 *The Chemistry of Human Behavior.* Chicago: Nelson-Hall.

Melzack, Ronald
1990 "The Tragedy of Needless Pain." *Scientific American* 262 (February): 27–33.

Mendelson, Bruce D., and Linda Harrison
1989 *Drug Use in Denver and Colorado.* Denver: Colorado Alcohol and Drug Use Division.

Mendelson, Jack H., and Nancy K. Mello
1994 "Alcohol, Sex, and Aggression." Pages 50–56 in *The American Drug Scene,* edited by James A. Inciardi and Karen McElrath. Los Angeles: Roxbury.

Mendelson, Wallace B.
1980 *The Use and Misuse of Sleeping Pills: A Clinical Guide.* New York: Plenum.

Merlin, Mark David
1984 *On the Trail of the Ancient Opium Poppy.* Rutherford, NJ: Fairleigh Dickinson University Press.

Mermelstein, Max
1990 *The Man Who Made It Snow.* New York: Simon and Schuster.

Merriam, John E.
1989 "National Media Coverage of Drug Issues, 1983–1987." Pages 21–28 in *Communication Campaigns About Drugs: Government, Media, and the Public,* edited by Pamela J. Shoemaker. Hillside, NJ: Lawrence Erlbaum Associates.

Merton, Robert
1964 "Anomie, Anomia, and Social Interaction." Pages 213–42 in *Anomie and Deviant Behavior,* edited by Marshall B. Clinard. New York: Free Press.
1938 "Social Structure and Anomie." *American Sociological Review* 3: 672–82.

Messick, Hank
1979 *Of Grass and Snow: The Secret Criminal Elite.* Englewood Cliffs, NJ: Prentice-Hall.

Mexico: A Profile
1995 Washington, DC: Drug Enforcement Administration.

Meyer, Roger E.
1988 "Conditioning Phenomena and the Problems of Relapse in Opioid Addicts and Alcoholics." Pages 161–179 in *Learning Factors in Substance Abuse,* edited by Barbara A. Ray. Rockville, MD: National Institute on Drug Abuse.

Michaels, Marguerite
1980 "Where Drug Traffic Is a Way of Life." *Parade* (January 6): 4–5.

Mieczkowski, Thomas
1995   *Hair Analysis as a Drug Detector.* Washington, DC: National Institute of Justice.
1986   "Geeking Up and Throwing Down: Heroin Street Life in Detroit." *Criminology* 24 (November): 645–66.
"Military Doesn't Seek Big Role in Drug War, Pentagon Says"
1995   *New York Times* (September 10): 13.
Miller, Norman S.
1995   *Addiction Psychiatry: Current Diagnosis and Treatment.* New York: Wiley.
Miller, Norman S., and Mark S. Gold
1990   "Benzodiazepines: Reconsidered." *Advances in Alcohol and Substance Abuse* 8 (3/4): 67–81.
Miller, Richard Lawrence
1991   *The Case for Legalizing Drugs.* New York: Praeger.
Miller, Walter B.
1958   "Lower Class Culture as a Generating Milieu of Gang Delinquency." *Journal of Social Issues* 14: 5–19.
Miller, William R., and Reid K. Hester
1980   "Treating the Problem Drinker: Modern Approaches." Pages 11–141 in *The Addictive Behaviors,* edited by William R. Miller. New York: Pergamon.
Miller, William R., and Ernest Kurtz
1994   "Models of Alcoholism Used in Treatment: Contrasting AA and Other Perspectives with Which It Is Often Confused." *Journal of Studies on Alcohol* 55 (March): 159–66.
Mills, James
1986   *The Underground Empire.* New York: Dell.
Minnesota Department of Human Services
1987   *Chemical Dependency Program Division Biennial Report.* St. Paul, MN.
Mises, Ludwig Von
1949   *Human Action: A Treatise on Economics.* New Haven, CT: Yale University Press.
Moody, John
1991   "A Day with the Chess Player." *Time* (July 1): 34–36.
Moore, Mark H.
1977   *Buy and Bust: The Effective Regulation of an Illicit Market in Heroin.* Lexington, MA: D. C. Heath.
Moore, Mark H., and Mark A. R. Kleiman
1989   *The Police and Drugs.* Washington, DC: U.S. Government Printing Office.
Morales, Edmundo
1989   *Cocaine: White Gold Rush in Peru.* Tucson: University of Arizona Press.
1986   "Coca and Cocaine Economy and Social Change in the Andes of Peru." *Economic Development and Social Change* 35: 144–61.
Moras, Karla
1993   "Substance Abuse Research: Outcome Measurement Conundrums." Pages 217–48 in *Behavioral Treatments for Drug Abuse and Dependence,* edited by Lisa Simon Onken, John D. Blaine, and John J. Boren. Rockville, MD: National Institute on Drug Abuse.
Morgan, John P.
1979   "The Clinical Pharmacology of Amphetamine." Pages 3–10 in *Amphetamine Use, Misuse, and Abuse,* edited by David E. Smith. Boston: G. K. Hall and Co.
Morgan, Howard Wayne
1981   *Drugs in America: A Social History, 1800–1980.* Syracuse, NY: Syracuse University Press.
Morgan, Howard Wayne, ed.
1974   *Yesterday's Addicts: American Society and Drug Abuse, 1865–1920.* Norman: University of Oklahoma Press.
Morgenthau, Robert M.
1988   "We Are Losing the War on Drugs." *New York Times* (February 16): 27.
Moss, Andrew
1977   "Methadone's Rise and Fall." Pages 135–53 in *Drugs and Politics,* edited by Paul E. Rock. New Brunswick, NJ: Transaction Books.
Mowatt, Twig
1991   "For Killers Who Seek a New Job." *New York Times* (August 14): 4.
Musto, David
1987   "The History of Legislative Control over Opium, Cocaine, and Their Derivatives." Pages 37–71 in *Dealing with Drugs: Consequences of Government Control,* edited by Ronald Hamowy. Lexington, MA: D. C. Heath.
1987b   *The American Disease: Origins of Narcotic Control,* expanded ed. New York: Oxford.
1973   *The American Disease: Origins of Narcotic Control.* New Haven, CT: Yale University Press.
Mydans, Seth
1989   "Vast Drug Cache and $10 Million Discovered in Raid in Los Angeles." *New York Times* (September 30): 1, 9.
Myers, Linnet
1995   "Europe Finds U.S. Drug Wars Lacking in Results." *Chicago Tribune* (November 2): 1, 24, 25.
Nadelmann, Ethan A.
1993   *Cops Across Borders: The Internationalization of U.S. Criminal Law Enforcement.* University Park: Pennsylvania State University Press.
1988   "U.S. Drug Policy: A Bad Export." *Foreign Policy* 70 (Spring): 83–108.
Nahas, Gabriel, and Nicholas A. Pace
1993   "Marijuana as Chemotherapy Aid Poses Hazards." Letter to the *New York Times* (December 4): 14.
Nash, Nathaniel C.
1992   "Cocaine Invades Chile, Scorning the Land Mines." *New York Times* (January 23): 6.

1991   "10 Die a Day, or Disappear, and Peru Goes Numb." *New York Times* (July 14): 2E.

1991b   "Peru Takes Bigger Role in Production of Cocaine." *New York Times* (July 29): 2.

Nathan, Peter E.

1988   "The Addictive Personality Is the Behavior of the Addict." *Journal of Consulting and Clinical Psychology* 56 (April): 183–88.

National Commission on Marijuana and Drug Abuse

1973   *Drug Abuse in America: Problem in Perspective.* Washington, DC: U.S. Government Printing Office.

National Council on Crime and Delinquency

1974   "Drug Addiction: A Medical, Not a Law Enforcement Problem." *Crime and Delinquency* 20 (January): 4–9.

National Institute of Justice

1991   *Drugs and Crime, 1990.* Washington, DC: U.S. Government Printing Office.

National Institute on Alcohol Abuse and Alcoholism.

1990   *Alcohol and Health: Neuroscience.* Rockville, MD.

National Institute on Alcohol Abuse and Alcoholism.

1992   "NIAA's Genetic Research." *Alcohol Alert Supplement* (No. 18): 1–2.

National Institute on Drug Abuse

1986   "Cocaine Use in America." *Prevention Networks* (April): 1–10.

Navarro, Mireya

1996   "When Drug Kingpins Fall, Illicit Assets Buy a Cushion." *New York Times* (March 19): 1, C19.

1995   "Drug Sold Abroad by Prescription Becomes Widely Abused in U.S." *New York Times* (December 12): 1, 9.

1993   "New York Needle Exchange Called Unusually Effective." *New York Times* (February 18): B8.

1992   "New York City Resurrects Plan on Needle Swap." *New York Times* (May 14): 1, B8.

1991   "Yale Study Reports Clean Needle Project Reduces AIDS Cases." *New York Times* (August 1): 1, 12.

"Navy Holds 21 Sailors in Italy in Smuggling"

1996   *New York Times* (May 29): 13.

Nelson, Jack E., Helen W. Pearson, Mollie Sayers, and Thomas J. Glynn

1982   *Guide to Drug Abuse Research Terminology.* Washington, DC: Government Printing Office.

Newcomb, Michael D., and Peter M. Bentler

1989   "Substance Use and Abuse Among Children and Teenagers." *American Psychologist* 44 (February): 242–48.

1988   *Consequences of Adolescent Drug Use.* Newbury Park, CA: Sage.

1986   "Cocaine Use Among Adolescents: Longitudinal Associations with Social Context, Psychopathology, and Use of Other Substances." *Addictive Behavior* 11: 263–73.

Newcomb, Michael D., and Linda McGee

1989   "Adolescent Alcohol Use and Other Delinquent Behaviors: A One-Year Longitudinal Analysis Controlling for Sensation Seeking." *Criminal Justice and Behavior* 16 (September): 345–69.

Newcombe, Russell

1992   "The Reduction of Drug-Related Harm: A Conceptual Framework for Theory, Practice, and Research." Pages 1–14 in *The Reduction of Drug-Related Harm,* edited by P. A. O'Hare, R. Newcombe, A. Matthews, E. C. Buning, and E. Drucker. London: Routledge.

"New Drug Law Leaves No Room for Mercy"

1989   *Chicago Tribune* (October 5): 28.

"New Hazard of Drinking in Pregnancy Is Found"

1996   *New York Times* (January 3): 9.

Newman, Robert G.

1977   *Methadone Management, Findings, and Prospects for the Future.* New York: Academic Press.

New York State Division of Substance Abuse Services

1986   *Annual Report.* Albany, NY

NIAAA. See National Institute on Alcohol Abuse and Alcoholism.

Nichols, David E. and Robert Oberlender

1989   "Structure-Activity Relationships of MDMA-like Substances." Pages 1–28 in *Pharmacology and Toxicology of Amphetamine and Related Designer Drugs,* edited by Khursheed Asghar and Errol De Souza. Rockville, MD: National Institute on Drug Abuse.

Nietschmann, Bernard

1987   "Drugs-for-Guns Cycle Produces Bitter Ironies," Letter to the *New York Times* (August 28): 22.

Nieves, Evelyn

1991   "Tainted Drug's Death Toll Rises to 10, Officials Say." *New York Times* (February 4): C11.

"The Nigerian Connection"

1991   *Newsweek* (October 7): 43.

Noble, Barbara Presley

1992   "Testing Employees for Drugs." *New York Times* (April 12): F27.

Nolan, Kathleen

1990   "Protecting Fetuses from Prenatal Hazards: Whose Crimes? What Punishment?" *Criminal Justice Ethics* 9 (Winter/Spring): 13–23.

Nordheimer, Jon

1986   "Police Arrests Plague South Florida." *New York Times* (August 3): 15.

Norris, John L.

1976   "Alcoholics Anonymous and Other Self-Help Groups." Pages 735–76 in *Alcoholism: Interdisciplinary Approaches to an Enduring Problem,* edited by Ralph E. Tarter and A. Arthur Sugerman. Reading, MA: Addison-Wesley.

North, James
1988 "Meet Roberto Fernandez, a Bolivian Father and Coca User." *Chicago Tribune* (September 7): 21.

Northern, Helen
1969 *Social Work with Groups.* New York: Columbia University Press.

Nunes, Edward V., and Jeffrey S. Rosecan
1987 "Human Neurobiology of Cocaine." Pages 48–94 in *Cocaine Abuse: New Directions in Treatment and Research,* edited by Henry I. Spitz and Jeffrey S. Rosecan. New York: Brunner/Mazel.

Nurco, David N., John C. Ball, John W. Shaffer, and Thomas Hanlon
1985 "The Criminality of Narcotic Addicts." *Journal of Nervous and Mental Disorders* 173: 94–102.

Nyre, George F.
1985 *Final Evaluation Report, 1984–1985: Project DARE.* Los Angeles: Evaluation and Training Institute.

O'Brien, Charles P., Arthur Alterman, Dan Walter, Anna Rose Childress, and A. T. McLellan
1990 "Evaluation of Treatment for Cocaine Dependence." Pages 78–83 in *Problems of Drug Dependence 1989,* edited by Louis S. Harris. Rockville, MD: National Institute on Drug Abuse.

O'Brien, Charles P., Anna Rose Childress, A. Thomas McLellan, and Ronald Ehrman
1993 "Developing Treatments That Address Classical Conditioning." Pages 71–91 in *Cocaine Treatment: Research and Clinical Perspectives,* edited by Frank M. Tims and Carl G. Leukefeld. Rockville, MD: National Institute on Drug Abuse.

O'Brien, John, and Jan Crawford Greenburg
1996 "Raids Reveal How Little Guys Climb the Drug Ladder." *Chicago Tribune* (May 3): 1,21.

O'Brien, Robert, and Sidney Cohen
1984 *Encyclopedia of Drug Abuse.* New York: Facts on File.

O'Connor, Matt
1995 "Officials Seize 12, Say Heroin Ring Is Cracked." *Chicago Tribune* (September 8): Sec. 2: 2.
1990 "Drug Court a Success, But It's Not Enough." *Chicago Tribune* (February 22): 1, 2.

O'Donnell, John A.
1969 *Narcotic Addicts in Kentucky.* Washington, DC: U.S. Government Printing Office.

Oetting, E. R., and Fred Beauvais
1990 "Adolescent Drug Use: Findings of National and Local Surveys." *Journal of Consulting and Clinical Psychology* 58 (August) 385–94.

Office of National Drug Control Policy
1995 *National Drug Control Strategy.* Washington, DC: U.S. Government Printing Office.

1995b *Pulse Check: National Trends in Drug Abuse.* Washington, DC: U.S. Government Printing Office.
1994 *National Drug Control Strategy: Reclaiming Our Communities from Drugs and Violence.* Washington, DC: U.S. Government Printing Office.
1989 *National Drug Strategy.* Washington, DC: U.S. Government Printing Office.

Ogborne, Alan C., and Frederick B. Glaser
1985 "Evaluating Alcoholics Anonymous. Pages 176–92 in *Alcoholism and Substance Abuse,* edited by Thomas E. Bratter and Gary G. Forrest. New York: Free Press.

O'Hare, P. A.
1992 "Preface: A Note on the Consent of Harm Reduction." Pages xiii–xvii in *The Reduction of Drug Related Harm,* edited by P. A. O'Hare, R. Newcombe, A. Matthews, E. C. Buning, and E. Drucker. London: Routledge.

Olen, Helaine
1991 "Racial Tinge to Drug Testing of New Moms." *Chicago Tribune* (December 19): 14.

O'Malley, Pat O., and Stephen Mugford
1991 "The Demand for Intoxicating Commodities: Implications for the 'War on Drugs.'" *Social Justice* 18 (Winter): 49–75.

Onken, Lisa Simon, and Jack D. Blaine, eds.
1990 *Psychotherapy and Counseling in the Treatment of Drug Abuse.* Rockville, MD: National Institute on Drug Abuse.

Onken, Lisa Simon, Jack D. Blaine, and John J. Boren, eds.
1993 *Behavioral Treatments for Drug Abuse and Dependence.* Rockville, MD: National Institute on Drug Abuse.

Oreskes, Michael
1990 "Drug War Underlines Fickleness of Public." *New York Times* (September 6): 12.

Organized Crime Drug Enforcement Task Force Program
1985 *Annual Report.* Washington, DC: U.S. Department of Justice.

Pace, Eric
1988 "Lois Burnham Wilson, a Founder of Al-Anon Groups, Is Dead at 97." *New York Times* (October 4): 15.

Packer, Herbert L.
1968 *The Limits of the Criminal Sanction.* Stanford, CA: Stanford University Press.

Palfai, Tibor, and Henry Jankiewicz
1991 *Drugs and Human Behavior.* Dubuque, IA: Wm. C. Brown.

Passell, Peter
1991 "Coca Dreams, Cocaine Reality." *New York Times* (August 14): C2.
1990 "Cocaine Policy: Gauging Success." *New York Times* (June 6): C2.

Pavlov, Ivan P.
1927   *Conditioned Reflexes.* London: Oxford.
PCOC. See President's Commission on Organized Crime.
Peachey, J. E. and H. Lei
1988   "Assessment of Opioid Dependence with Nalox-
        one." *British Journal of Addiction* 83: 193–201.
Pear, Robert
1992   "M.D.'s Are Making Room for Others Among the
        Ranks of Psychoanalysts." *New York Times* (August
        19): B6.
1989   "Cuban General and Three Others Executed for
        Sending Drugs to U.S." *New York Times* (July 14): 2.
Pearson, Geoffrey
1987   *The New Heroin Users.* Oxford, England: Basil
        Blackwell.
Peele, Stanton
1985   *The Meaning of Addiction: Compulsive Experience
        and Its Interpretation.* Lexington, MA: D. C. Heath.
1980   "Addiction to an Experience: A Social-Psychologi-
        cal Theory of Addiction." Pages 142–46 in *Theories
        of Drug Abuse: Selected Contemporary Perspec-
        tives,* edited by Dan J. Lettieri, Mollie Sayers, and
        Helen Wallenstein Pearson. Rockville, MD: Na-
        tional Institute on Drug Abuse.
Pennsylvania Crime Commission (PCC)
1988   *Report.* Conshohken, PA: PCC.
Pentz, Mary Ann
1985   "Social Competence and Self-Efficacy as Determi-
        nants of Substance Abuse in Adolescence." Pages
        117–42 in *Coping and Substance Abuse,* edited by
        Saul Shiffman and Thomas Ashby Wills. Orlando,
        FL: Academic Press.
Permanent Subcommittee on Investigation, U.S. Senate
1983   *Crime and Secrecy: The Use of Offshore Banks and
        Companies.* Washington, DC: U.S. Government
        Printing Office.
1981   *International Narcotics Trafficking.* Washington,
        DC: U.S. Government Printing Office.
1981b   *Witness Security Program.* Washington, DC: U.S.
        Government Printing Office.
"Peruvian Plane Is Shot Down in Error; 17 Die"
1991   *Chicago Tribune* (July 11): 11.
Peterson, Robert C.
1980   *Marijuana and Health.* Rockville, MD: National
        Institute on Drug Abuse.
Peterson, Robert C., ed.
1980   *Marijuana Research Findings; 1980.* Rockville,
        MD: National Institute on Drug Abuse.
Peterson, Robert E.
1991   "Legalization: The Myth Exposed." Pages 324–55
        in *Searching for Alternatives: Drug Control Policy
        in the United States,* edited by Melvyn B. Krauss
        and Edward P. Lazear. Stanford, CA: Hoover Insti-
        tution.

Physicians' Desk Reference
1988   Oradell, NJ: Medical Economics Company.
1987   Oradell, NJ: Medical Economics Company.
Pickens, Roy W., and Dace S. Svikis
1988   "Genetic Vulnerability to Drug Abuse." Pages 1–8
        in *Biological Vulnerability to Drug Abuse,* edited
        by Roy W. Pickens and Dace S. Svikis. Rockville,
        MD: National Institute on Drug Abuse.
Pickens, Roy W., and Travis Thompson
1984   "Behavioral Treatment of Drug Dependence."
        Pages 53–67 in *Behavioral Intervention Techniques
        in Drug Dependence Treatment,* edited by John
        Grabowski, Maxine L. Stitzer, and Jack E. Hen-
        ningfield. Rockville, MD: National Institute on
        Drug Abuse.
Pileggi, Nicholas
1982   "There's No Business Like Drug Business." *New
        York* (December 13): 38–43.
Platt, Jerome J., and Christina Labate
1976   *Heroin Addiction: Theory, Research, and Treat-
        ment.* New York: Wiley.
Poethig, Margaret
1988   "Q & A: Seizing the Assets of Drug Traffickers."
        The Compiler 8 (Winter): 11–12.
Pollan, Michael
1995   "How Pot Has Grown." *New York Times Magazine*
        (February 19): 31–35, 44, 50, 56–57.
Post, Robert M., and Susan R. B. Weiss
1988   "Psychomotor Stimulant vs. Local Anesthetic Ef-
        fects of Cocaine: Role of Behavioral Sensitization
        and Kindling." Pages 217–38 in *Mechanisms of Co-
        caine Abuse and Toxicity,* edited by Doris Clouet,
        Khursheed Asghar, and Roger Brown. Rockville,
        MD: National Institute on Drug Abuse.
Potter, Gary, Larry Gaines, and Beth Holbrook
1990   "Blowing Smoke: An Evaluation of Marijuana
        Eradication In Kentucky." *American Journal of Po-
        lice* 9: 97–116.
Powis, Robert E.
1992   *The Money Launderers: Lessons from the Drug
        Wars—How Billions of Illegal Dollars Are Washed
        Through Banks and Businesses.* Chicago: Probus
        Publishing Co.
Preble, Edward, and John J. Casey.
1995   "Taking Care of Business—The Heroin Addict's
        Life on the Street." Pages 121–32 in *The American
        Drug Scene: An Anthology,* edited by James A. In-
        ciardi and Karen McElrath. Los Angeles: Roxbury.
President's Commission on Organized Crime (PCOC)
1986   *America's Habit: Drug Abuse, Drug Trafficking,
        and Organized Crime.* Washington, DC: U.S. Gov-
        ernment Printing Office.
1985   *Organized Crime and Heroin Trafficking.* Washing-
        ton, DC: U.S. Government Printing Office.

1984   *Organized Crime and Cocaine Trafficking.* Washington, DC: U.S. Government Printing Office.

1984b   *Organized Crime of Asian Origin.* Washington, DC: U.S. Government Printing Office.

1984c   *The Cash Connection: Organized Crime, Financial Institutions, and Money Laundering.* Washington, DC: U.S. Government Printing Office.

Priddy, Drew

1990   "A Social Worker's Agony: Working with Children Affected by Crack/Cocaine." *Social Work* 35 (May): 197–99.

"Prisoners in the War on Drugs"

1990   *Insight into Corrections* 1 (April): 4–6.

Purdy, Matthew

1995   "Bars Don't Stop Flow of Drugs into the Prisons." *New York Times* (July 2): 1, 12.

1995b   "New Inmates Reflect Surge in Heroin Use." *New York Times* (December 3): 24.

Quandagno, Jill S., and Robert J. Antonio

1975   "Labeling Theory as an Oversocialized Conception of Man: The Case of Mental Illness." *Sociology and Social Research* 60 (October): 30–41.

"Quitting Caffeine Can Bring on the Blahs"

1991   *Chicago Tribune* (August 18): 24.

Raab, Selwyn

1992   "Chief Seeks Action on Narcotics Unit." *New York Times* (January 9): B8.

1987   "New York Establishes Special Courts to Hasten Disposal of Drug Cases," *New York Times* (June 7): 17.

Rachlin, Howard

1991   *Introduction to Modern Behaviorism.* New York: W. H. Freeman.

Rado, Sandor

1981   "The Psychoanalysis of Pharmacothymia (Drug Addiction)." Pages 77–94 in *Classic Contributions in the Addictions,* edited by Howard Shaffer and Milton Earl Burglass. New York: Brunner/Mazel.

Rangel, Charles B.

1990   "Letter to the Editor: 'What's Wrong with Legalizing Drugs?'" *New York Times* (July 24): 14.

1988   "Letter to the Editor: 'A False Hope.'" *New York Times* (February 1): 18.

1988b   "Legalize Drugs? Not on Your Life." *New York Times* (May 17): 31.

Rawson, Richard A., Jeanne L. Obert, Michael J. McCann, and Walter Ling

1993   "Neurobehavioral Treatment for Cocaine Dependency: A Preliminary Evaluation." Pages 92–115 in *Cocaine Treatment: Research and Clinical Perspectives,* edited by Frank M. Tims and Carl G. Leukefeld. Rockville, MD: National Institute on Drug Abuse.

Ray, Barbara A., ed.

1988   *Learning Factors in Substance Abuse.* Rockville, MD: National Institute on Drug Abuse.

Ray, Oakley

1978   *Drugs, Society, and Human Behavior.* St. Louis: C. V. Mosby.

Reese, Stephen D., and Lucig H. Danielian

1989   "Intermedia Influence and the Drug Issue: Converging on Cocaine." Pages 29–45 in *Communication Campaigns About Drugs: Government, Media, and the Public,* edited by Pamela J. Shoemaker. Hillsdale, NJ: Lawrence Erlbaum Associates.

Reiff, Phillip

1963   *Freud, Therapy and Techniques.* New York: Crowell-Collier.

"Relapse and Craving"

1989   *Alcohol Alert* 6 (October): 1–4.

Rettig, Richard P., Manuel J. Torres, and Gerald R. Garrett

1977   *Manny: A Criminal Addict's Story.* New York: Houghton-Mifflin.

Reuter, Peter

1995   "Lessons from the Absence of Harm Reduction in American Drug Policy." *Tobacco Control: An International Journal* 4 Supplement S28–S32.

1993   "Prevalence Estimation and Policy Formulation." *Journal of Drug Issues* 23 (Spring): 167–84.

Reuter, Peter, and Jonathan P. Caulkins

1995   "Redefining the Goals of National Drug Policy: Recommendations from a Working Group." *American Journal of Public Health* 85 (August): 1059–63.

Reuter, Peter, Mathea Falco, and Robert MacCoun

1993   *Comparing Western European and North American Drug Policies: An International Conference Report.* Santa Monica, CA: RAND.

Reuter, Peter, Robert MacCoun, and Patrick Murphy

1990   *Money from Crime: A Study of the Economics of Drug Dealing in Washington, D.C.* Santa Monica, CA: RAND.

Rhodes, Jean E., and Leonard Jason

1990   "A Social Stress Model of Substance Abuse." *Journal of Consulting and Clinical Psychology* 58 (August): 395–401.

Rhor, Monica

1991   "Nearly Undetectable Cocaine Found." *Chicago Tribune* (June 27): 31.

Rice, Berkeley

1989   *Trafficking: The Boom and Bust of the Air America Cocaine Ring.* New York: Scribner's.

1988   "The Cocaine Express." *The Business World (New York Times* Special Magazine, March 27): 20–21, 74–76.

Richey, Warren

1991   "Prosecutors' Deal with Criminals: Testify Against

Noriega and Go Free." *Chicago Tribune* (November 27): 4.

Riding, Alan

1988 "Colombian Courts Yield to the Drug Barons." *New York Times* (January 11): 1, 3.

1988b "Dispute Impeding U.S. War on Coca." *New York Times* (June 28): 1, 6.

1988c "Gangs in Colombia Feud Over Cocaine." *New York Times* (August 23): 1, 4.

1987 "Colombia Effort Against Drugs Hits Dead End." *New York Times* (August 16): 1, 12.

1987b "Colombia's Drugs and Violent Politics Make Murder a Way of Life." *New York Times* (August 23): E3.

1986 "Drug Abuse Catches Up to Dismayed Colombia." *New York Times* (August 20): 4.

Ring, Wilson

1988 "Local Hero Can't Run from His Reputation as Drug-Dealer King." *Chicago Tribune* (March 2): 16.

Roberton, Robert J.

1986 "Designer Drugs: The Analog Game." Pages 91–96 in *Bridging Services: Drug Abuse, Human Services and the Therapeutic Community,* edited by Alfonso Acampora and Ethan Nebelkopf. New York: World Federation of Therapeutic Communities.

Roberts, Sam

1990 "Young Lives: Rising Toll from Crack." *New York Times* (July 23): 14.

Robertson, Nan

1988 "The Changing World of Alcoholics Anonymous." *New York Times Magazine* (February 21): 40–44, 47, 57, 92.

1988b *Getting Better: Inside Alcoholics Anonymous.* New York: William Morrow.

Robins, Lee N.

1974 *The Vietnam Drug User Returns.* Washington, DC: U.S. Government Printing Office.

1973 *A Followup of Vietnam Drug Users.* Washington, DC: U.S. Government Printing Office.

Robins, Lee N., John E. Helzer, Michi Hesselbrock, and Eric Wish

1980 "Vietnam Veterans Three Years After Vietnam: How Our Study Changed Our View of Heroin." Pages 213–30 in *The Yearbook of Substance Use and Abuse, Volume II,* edited by Leon Brill and Charles Winick. New York: Human Services Press.

Robinson, Linda

1991 "Still a Cocaine Crossroads." *U.S. News and World Report* (April 15): 47–48.

Rock, Paul E., ed.

1977 *Drugs and Politics.* New Brunswick, NJ: Transaction Books.

Roffman, Roger A., and William H. George

1988 "Cannabis Abuse." Pages 325–63 in *Assessment of*

Addictive Behaviors, edited by Dennis M. Donovan and G. Alan Marlatt. New York: Guilford.

Rohter, Larry

1991 "From Brazil to Peru to Jamaica, Gun Smugglers Flock to Florida." *New York Times* (August 11): 1, 13.

1991 "Drug Ring Gave Up to $10 Million to Contras, Noriega Jury Is Told." *New York Times* (November 26): 6.

1991b "Former Smuggler Ties Top Officials of Cuba and Nicaragua to Drug Ring." *New York Times* (November 21): 10.

1990 "Drug Fight Targets U.S. Chemicals." *New York Times* (May 13): 4.

1988 "U.S. Accusations on Drugs Outrage Mexicans." *New York Times* (April 29): 5.

1988b "Who Is the Enemy in Mexico Drug War?" *New York Times* (July 24): 7.

Romoli, Kathleen

1941 *Colombia.* Garden City, NY: Doubleday, Doran.

Rosecan, Jeffrey S., and Edward V. Nunes

1987 "Pharmacological Management of Cocaine Abuse." Pages 255–70 in *Cocaine Abuse: New Directions in Treatment and Research,* edited by Henry I. Spitz and Jeffrey S. Rosecan. New York: Brunner/Mazel.

Rosecan, Jeffrey S., Henry I. Spitz, and Barbara Gross

1987 "Contemporary Issues in the Treatment of Cocaine Abuse." Pages 299–323 in *Cocaine Abuse: New Directions in Treatment and Research,* edited by Henry I. Spitz and Jeffrey S. Rosecan. New York: Brunner/Mazel.

Rosenbaum, Marsha

1981 *Women on Heroin.* New Brunswick, NJ: Rutgers University Press.

Rosenbaum, Ron

1988 "High Life: The Social Rise of Timothy Leary." *Vanity Fair* (April): 132–44; 154.

Rosenthal, Elisabeth

1993 "Patients in Pain Find Relief, Not Addiction, in Narcotics." *New York Times* (March 28): 1, 11.

Rosenthal, Mitchell S.

1991 "Giving Away Needles Won't Stop AIDS." *New York Times* (August 17): 13.

1984 "Therapeutic Communities: A Treatment Alternative for Many but Not All." *Journal of Substance Abuse Treatment* 1: 55–58.

1973 "New York City Phoenix House: A Therapeutic Community for the Treatment of Drug Abusers and Drug Addicts." Pages 83–102 in *Yearbook of Drug Abuse,* edited by Leon Brill and Earnest Harms. New York: Behavioral Publications.

Rothman, Richard B.

1994 "A Review of the Effects of Dopaminergic Agents in Humans: Implications for Medication Development." Pages 67–87 in *Neurobiological Models for Evaluating Mechanisms Underlying Cocaine Addiction,* edited by Lynda Erinoff and Roger M. Brown. Rockville, MD: National Institute on Drug Abuse.

Rowell, Earle Albert, and Robert Rowell
1939   *On the Trail of Marijuana: The Weed of Madness.* Mountain View, CA: Pacific Press.

Royal College of Psychiatrists
1987   *Drug Scenes: A Report on Drug Dependence.* London: Gaskell.

Rubington, Earl
1967   "Drug Addiction as a Deviant Career." *International Journal of the Addictions* 2 (Spring): 3–20.

Russell, Francis
1975   *A City in Terror—1919—The Boston Police Strike.* New York: Viking.

Ryan, Marie Vida, Thomas W. Kelly, John C. Keith, Dale H. Margroff, Jo Ann Spaulding, and Joseph Born
1966   *Civil Commitment Program for Narcotic Addicts.* Sacramento, CA: Department of Corrections.

Rydell, C. Peter, and Susan S. Everingham
1994   *Controlling Cocaine: Supply Versus Demand Programs.* Santa Monica, CA: RAND.

Sachs, David P. L.
1986   "Cost-Benefit Analysis of Tobacco Dependency Treatment." Pages 270–80 in *The Pharmacologic Treatment of Tobacco Dependence: Proceedings of the World Congress,* November 4–5, 1985, edited by J. K. Ockene. Cambridge, MA: Harvard University School of Government.

Sackman, Bertram S., M. Maxine Sackman, and G. G. DeAngelis
1978   "Heroin Addiction as an Occupation: Traditional Addicts and Heroin-Addicted Polydrug Users." *International Journal of the Addictions* 13: 427–41.

Santana, Rosa Maria
1996   "Drinking Blamed for Death of Teenager." *Chicago Tribune* (January 3): Sec. 2: 6.

Savitt, Robert A.
1963   "Psychoanalytic Studies on Addiction: Ego Structure in Narcotic Addiction." *Psychoanalytic Quarterly* 32: 43–57.

Sawyers, June
1988   "When Opium Was Really the Opiate of the Masses." *Chicago Tribune Magazine* (January 3): 5.

Scarpitti, Frank R., and Susan K. Datesman, eds.
1980   *Drugs and the Youth Culture.* Beverly Hills, CA: Sage.

Schecter, Arnold
1980   "Long-Acting Methadone (Levo-Alpha-Acetyl-methadol) in the Treatment of Opiate Dependence." Pages 99–112 in *The Yearbook of Substance Use and Abuse: Volume II,* edited by Leon Brill and Charles Winick. New York: Human Sciences Press.

Schiffer, Frederic
1988   "Psychotherapy of Nine Successfully Treated Cocaine Abusers: Techniques and Dynamics." *Journal of Substance Abuse Treatment* 5: 131–37.

Schmalz, Jeffrey
1988   "Addicts to Get Needles in Plan to Curb AIDS." *New York Times* (January 31): 1, 12.

Schmetzer, Uli
1991   "Burmese Heroin Plagues China, U.S." *Chicago Tribune* (May 2): 1, 14.
1991b   "China Declares a 'Peoples War' on Drugs." *Chicago Tribune* (July 3): 2.
1991c   "'Nigerian Connection' Ties Chicago To Asian Drugs." *Chicago Tribune* (December 21): 1, 11.
1991d   "Slave Trade Survives, Prospers Across Asia." *Chicago Tribune* (November 15): 1, 18.
1990   "'Prince of Death' Is a Wanted Man." *Chicago Tribune* (March 21): 21.

Schmidt, William E.
1993   "To Battle AIDS, Scots Offer Drugs to Addicts." *New York Times* (February 8): 3.

Schneider, Andrew, and Mary Pat Flaherty
1991   "Drug Law Leaves Trail of Innocents." *Chicago Tribune* (August 11): 1, 13.

Schneider, Keith
1988   "Marijuana Once Reigned as the King." *New York Times* (January 26): 8.

Schnoll, Sidney H.
1979   "Pharmacological Aspects of Youth Drug Abuse." Pages 255–75 in *Youth Drug Abuse,* edited by George M. Beschner and Alfred S. Friedman. Lexington, MA: D. C. Heath.

Schottenfeld, Richard S.
1989   "Involuntary Treatment of Substance Abuse Disorders—Impediments to Success." *Psychiatry* 52 (May): 164–76.

Schroeder, Elinor P.
1990   "Legal Aspects of Urine Testing." Pages 218–24 in *Problems of Drug Dependence 1989,* edited by Louis S. Harris. Rockville, MD: National Institute on Drug Abuse.

Schuckit, Marc A.
1985   "Genetics and the Risk for Alcoholism." *Journal of the American Medical Association* 254: 2614–17.
1983   "The Genetics of Alcoholism." Pages 31–46 in *Medical and Social Aspects of Alcohol Abuse,* edited by Boris Tabakoff, Patricia B. Sutker, and Carrie L. Randall. New York: Plenum.

Schur, Edwin H.
1973   *Radical Non-Intervention: Rethinking the Delinquency Problem.* Englewood Cliffs, NJ: Prentice-Hall.
1965   *Crimes Without Victims: Deviant Behavior and Public Policy. Abortion, Homosexuality, Drug Addiction.* Englewood Cliffs, NJ: Prentice-Hall.

1962   *Narcotic Addiction in Britain and America.* Bloomington Indiana: University Press.

Schuster, Charles R.

1993   "A Natural History of Drug Abuse." Pages 37–51 in *International Research Conference on Biomedical Approaches to Illicit Drug Demand Reduction,* edited by Christine R. Hartel. Washington, DC: U.S. Government Printing Office.

Sciolino, Elaine

1988   "Diplomats Do Not Hurry to Enlist in the War on Drugs." *New York Times* (February 21): E3.

Sciolino, Elaine, and Stephen Engelberg

1988   "Narcotics Effort Foiled by U.S. Security Goals." *New York Times* (April 10): 1, 10.

Scott, Peter Dale, and Jonathan Marshall

1991   *Cocaine Politics: Drugs, Armies, and the CIA in Central America.* Berkeley: University of California Press.

Selden, Lewis W., William L. Woolverton, Stanley A.
Lorens, Joseph E. G. Williams, Rebecca L. Corwin, Norio
Hata, and Mary Olimski

1993   "Behavioral Consequences of Partial Monoamine Depletion in the CNS After Methamphetamine-Like Drugs: The Conflict Between Pharmacology and Toxicology." Pages 34–51 in *Assessing Neurotoxicity in Drugs of Abuse,* edited by Lynda Erinoff. Rockville, MD: National Institute on Drug Abuse.

Seligmann, Jean, and Patricia King

1996   " 'Roofies': The Date-Rape Drug." *Newsweek* (February 26): 54.

Senay, Edward C.

1986   "Clinical Implications of Drug Abuse Treatment Outcome." Pages 139–50 in *Drug Abuse Treatment Evaluation: Strategies, Progress, and Prospects,* edited by Frank M. Tims and Jacqueline P. Ludford. Rockville, MD: National Institute on Drug Abuse.

Seymour, Richard, David Smith, Darryl Inaba, and Mim
Landry

1989   *The New Drugs: Look Alikes, Drugs of Deception, and Designer Drugs.* Center City, MN: Hazelden Foundation.

Shabecoff, Philip

1987   "Stress and the Lure of Harmful Remedies." *New York Times* (October 14): 12.

Shannon, Elaine

1991   "New Kings of Coke." *Time* (July 1): 29–33.

Shenon, Philip

1990   "Peru Drug Fund Used in War, Aide Says." *New York Times* (June 21): 3.

1988   "Enemy Within: Drug Money Is Corrupting the Enforcers." *New York Times* (April 11): 1, 8.

Sheppard, Nathaniel Jr.

1991   "In Panama, Drug War Is Corrupted." *Chicago Tribune* (May 26): 19.

1991b   "Drug Trade Flourishing in Panama." *Chicago Tribune* (February 17): 25.

1991c   "In Panama's Drug Capital, Small Police Unit Faces Uphill Fight." *Chicago Tribune* (January 31): 23.

1990   "Drug Lords Easily Flee Panama Jails." *Chicago Tribune* (October 7): 22.

1990b   "Guatemalan Climate: Good for Poppy Fields, Drug Traffickers." *Chicago Tribune* (September 23): 12.

Sher, Kenneth J.

1991   *Children of Alcoholics: A Critical Appraisal of Theory and Research.* Chicago: University of Chicago Press.

Short, James F., Jr.

1968   *Gang Delinquency and Delinquent Subculture.* New York: Harper & Row.

Siegal, Harvey A., Richard C. Rapp, Casey W. Kelliher,
James H. Fisher, Joseph H. Wagner, and Phyllis A. Cole

1995   "The Strengths Perspective of Case Management: A Promising Inpatient Substance Abuse Treatment Enhancement." *Journal of Psychoactive Drugs* 27 (No. 1): 67–72.

Siegel, Ronald K.

1989   *Intoxication: Life in Pursuit of Artificial Paradise.* New York: E. F. Dutton.

Siegel, Shepard

1988   "Drug Anticipation and the Treatment of Dependence." Pages 1–24 in *Learning Factors in Substance Abuse,* edited by Barbara A. Ray. Rockville, MD: National Institute on Drug Abuse.

Silvas, Jos

1994   "Enforcing Drug Laws in the Netherlands." Pages 41–58 in *Between Prohibition and Legalization: The Dutch Experiment in Drug Policy,* edited by Ed. Leuw and I. Haen Marshall. Amsterdam: Kugler Publications.

Simpson, Edith E.

1989   "Adherence to Cigarette, Marijuana, and Cocaine Treatment Programs: A Survival Analysis." Paper presented at the annual meeting of the American Society of Criminology, Reno, NV, November.

Sinclair, Andrew

1962   *The Era of Excess: A Social History of the Prohibition Movement.* Boston: Little, Brown.

Sinclair, Upton

1981   *The Jungle.* New York: Bantam. Originally published 1906.

Skinner, B. F.

1974   *About Behaviorism.* New York: Knopf.

1938   *The Behavior of Organisms.* Englewood Cliffs, NJ: Prentice-Hall.

Skolnick, Jerome H., Theodore Correl, Elizabeth Navarro,
and Roger Rabb

1990   "The Social Structure of Street Drug Dealing." *American Journal of Police* 9: 1–41.

Sly, Liz
1989   "Bennett Attacks Drug Legalization." *Chicago Tribune* (December 14): 24.
Smart, Frances
1970   *Neurosis and Crime.* New York: Barnes and Noble.
Smart, Reginald G.
1980   "An Availability-Proneness Theory of Illicit Drug Abuse." Pages 46–49 in *Theories on Drug Abuse: Selected Contemporary Perspectives,* edited by Dan J. Lettieri, Mollie Sayers, and Helen Wallenstein Pearson. Rockville, MD: National Institute on Drug Abuse.
Smith, David E.
1986   "Cocaine-Alcohol Abuse: Epidemiological, Diagnostic and Treatment Considerations." *Journal of Psychoactive Drugs* 18 (April-June): 117–29.
Smith, David E., ed.
1979   *Amphetamine Use, Misuse, and Abuse.* Boston, MA: G. K. Hall and Co.
Smith, David E., and Donald R. Wesson
1994   "Benzodiazopines and Other Sedative-Hypnotics." Pages 179–90 in *The American Psychiatric Press Textbook of Substance Abuse Treatment,* edited by Marc Galanter and Herbert D. Kleber. Washington, DC: American Psychiatric Press.
Smith, Peter H.
1987   "Uneasy Neighbors: Mexico and the United States." *Current History* 86 (March): 97–100; 130–32.
"Sniffing for Drugs by Testing Vapors"
1991   *New York Times* (October 9): C7.
Snyder, Solomon H.
1989   *Brainstorming: The Science of Politics and Opiate Research.* Cambridge, MA: Harvard University Press.
1986   *Drugs and the Brain.* New York: Scientific American.
1977   "Opiate Receptors and Internal Opiates." *Scientific American* (March): 44–56.
Soble, Ronald L.
1991   "Seized Assets Underwrite the War on Drugs." *Los Angeles Times* (April 16): 3, 23.
Speart, Jessica
1995   "The New Drug Mules." *New York Times Magazine* (June 11): 44–45.
Speckart, George, and M. Douglas Anglin
1987   "Narcotics Use and Crime: An Overview of Recent Research Advances." *Contemporary Drug Problems* 16 (Winter): 741–69.
1985   "Narcotics and Crime: An Analysis of Existing Evidence for a Causal Relationship." *Behavioral Sciences and the Law* 3: 259–82.
Specter, Michael
1995   "Opium Finds Its Silk Road in Chaos of Central Asia." *New York Times* (May 2): 1, 4.
Spence, Richard T.
1989   *Current Substance Abuse Trends in Texas.* Austin: Texas Commission on Alcohol and Drug Abuse.

Spitz, Henry I.
1987   "Cocaine Abuse: Therapeutic Group Approaches." Pages 156–201 in *Cocaine Abuse: New Directions in Treatment and Research,* edited by Henry I. Spitz and Jeffrey S. Rosecan. New York: Brunner/Mazel.
Spitz, Henry I., and Jeffrey S. Rosecan
1987   "Overview of Cocaine Abuse Treatment." Pages 97–118 in *Cocaine Abuse: New Directions in Treatment and Research,* edited by Henry I. Spitz and Jeffrey S. Rosecan. New York: Brunner/Mazel.
Spotts, James V., and Franklin C. Shontz
1980   "A Life-Theme Theory of Chronic Drug Abuse." Pages 59–70 in *Theories on Drug Abuse: Selected Contemporary Perspectives,* edited by Dan J. Lettieri, Mollie Sayers, and Helen Wallenstein Pearson. Rockville, MD: National Institute on Drug Abuse.
Starkweather, C. Woodruff
1982   "Techniques of Therapy Based on Cognitive Learning Theory." Pages 37–47 in *Communication Disorders: General Principles of Therapy,* edited by William H. Perkins. New York: Thieme-Stratton.
Stellwagen, Lindsey D.
1985   *Use of Forfeiture Sanctions in Drug Cases.* Washington, DC: National Institute of Justice.
Sterling, Claire
1990   *Octopus: The Long Reach of the Sicilian Mafia.* New York: Simon and Schuster.
Stevens, Jay
1987   *Storming Heaven: LSD and the American Dream.* New York: Atlantic Monthly Press.
Stevens, William K.
1987   "Deaths from Drunken Driving Increase." *New York Times* (October 29): 12.
Stimson, Gerry V.
1988   "The War on Heroin: British Policy and the International Trade in Illicit Drugs." Pages 35–61 in *A Land Fit for Heroin? Drug Policies, Prevention, and Practice,* edited by Nicholas Dorn and Nigel South. New York: St. Martin's Press.
Stimson, Gerry V., and Edna Oppenheimer
1982   *Heroin Addiction: Treatment and Control in Britain.* London: Tavistock.
Stitzer, Maxine L., George E. Bigelow, Ira A. Liebson, and Mary E. McCaul
1984   "Contingency Management of Supplemental Drug Use During Methadone Maintenance Treatment." Pages 84–103 in *Behavioral Intervention Techniques in Drug Abuse Treatment,* edited by John Grabowski, Maxine L. Stitzer, and Jack E. Henningfield. Rockville, MD: National Institute on Drug Abuse.
Stitzer, Maxine L., George E. Bigelow, and Mary McCaul
1985   "Behavior Therapy in Drug Abuse Treatment: Review and Evaluation." Pages 31–50 in *Progress in*

the Development of Cost-Effective Treatment for Drug Abusers, edited by Rebecca S. Ashery. Rockville, MD: National Institute on Drug Abuse.

Stone, Michael
1990   "Coke, Inc.: Inside the Big Business of Drugs." *New York* (July 16): 20–29.

Strong, Simon
1992   "Peru Is Losing More Than the Drug War." *New York Times* (February 17): 11.

Stuart, Richard B.
1974   "Teaching Facts About Drugs: Pushing or Preventing?" *Journal of Educational Psychology* 66 (April): 189–201.

Stutman, Robert M., and Richard Esposito
1992   *Dead on Delivery: Inside the Drug Wars, Straight from the Street.* New York: Warner.

Sugarman, Barry
1974   *Daytop Village: A Therapeutic Community.* New York: Holt, Rinehart and Winston.

Sunderwirth, Stanley G.
1985   "Biological Mechanisms: Neurotransmission and Addiction." Pages 11–19 in *The Addictions: Multidisciplinary Perspectives and Treatments,* edited by Harvey B. Milkman and Howard J. Shaffer. Lexington, MA: D. C. Heath.

Suro, Roberto
1992   "In Bad Lands of Texas, Drug Traffickers Reopen Old Routes." *New York Times* (February 7): 9.
1987   "Italy's Heroin Addicts Face New Challenge: AIDS." *New York Times* (December 28): 10.

Sutherland, Edwin
1973   *On Analyzing Crime,* edited by Karl Schuessler. Chicago: University of Chicago Press.

Swadi, Harith, and Harry Zeitlin
1987   "Drug Education for School Children: Does It Really Work?" *British Journal of Addiction* 82: 741–46.

Sykes, Gresham M.
1967   *Crime and Society,* 2d ed. New York: Random House.

Szara, Stephen I., ed.
1986   *Neurobiology of Behavior Control in Drug Abuse.* Rockville, MD: National Institute on Drug Abuse.

Szasz, Thomas
1974   *Ceremonial Justice: The Ritual Persecution of Drugs, Addicts, and Pushers.* Garden City, NY: Doubleday.

Tackett, Michael
1990   "Drug War Chokes Federal Courts." *Chicago Tribune* (October 14): 1, 12.
1990b   "Minor Drug Players Are Paying Big Prices." *Chicago Tribune* (October 15): 1, 9.

Tarter, Ralph E.
1988   "Are There Inherited Behavioral Traits That Predispose to Substance Abuse?" *Journal of Consulting and Clinical Psychology* 56 (April): 189–96.

Tarter, Ralph E., Arthur I. Alterman, and Kathleen L. Edwards
1985   "Vulnerability to Alcoholism in Men: A Behavior-Genetic Perspective." *Journal of Studies on Alcohol* 46 (July): 329–56.

Taylor, Ian, Paul Walton, and Jock Young
1973   *The New Criminology.* New York: Harper and Row.

Terry, Charles E., and Mildred Pellens
1928   *The Opium Problem.* New York: The Committee on Drug Addictions in Collaboration with the Bureau of Social Hygiene, Inc.

Texas Commission on Alcohol and Drug Abuse
1987   *Drug Abuse Trends in Texas.* Austin, Texas.

Thompson, Hunter S.
1966   *Hell's Angels: A Strange and Terrible Saga.* New York: Random House.

Thornburgh, Dick
1989   *Drug Trafficking: A Report to the President.* Washington, DC: U.S. Government Printing Office.

Thoumi, Francisco E.
1995   "The Size of the Illegal Drug Industry." Pages 77–96 in *Drug Trafficking in the Americas,* edited by Bruce M. Bagley and William O. Walker, III, New Brunswick, NJ: Transaction Books.

Tieman, Cheryl R., William L. Tolone, and Lisa Zuelka
1991   "Drug Education and Drug Use Decline: An Assessment of Trends from 1976–1984." Paper presented at the annual meeting of the American Society of Criminology, San Francisco, November.

Tilson, Hugh A.
1993   "Neurobehavioral Methods Used in Neurotoxicology." Pages 1–33 in *Assessing Neurotoxicity in Drugs of Abuse,* edited by Lynda Erinoff. Rockville, MD: National Institute on Drug Abuse.

Tims, Frank M., Nancy Jainchill, and George De Leon
1994   "Therapeutic Communities and Treatment Research." Pages 1–15 in *Therapeutic Community: Advances in Research and Application,* edited by Frank M. Tims, George De Leon, and Nancy Jainchill. Rockville, MD: National Institute on Drug Abuse.

Tims, Frank M., and Carl G. Leukefeld, eds.
1993   *Cocaine Treatment: Research and Clinical Perspectives.* Rockville, MD: National Institute on Drug Abuse.

Tindall, George B.
1988   *America: A Narrative History. Vol. 2.* New York: Norton.

Tolchin, Martin
1988   "Surgeon General Asserts that Smoking Is an Addiction." *New York Times* (May 17): 1, 26.

Tollison, Robert D., and Richard E. Wagner
1992   *The Economics of Smoking.* Boston: Kluwer Academic Publishers.

Toloken, Steve
1991 "Martinez Calls Drug War Success; Democrats Highlight Its Failure." *Chicago Tribune* (September 6): 8.

Tomasson, Robert E.
1990 "21 States Imposing Drug Tax and Then Fining the Evaders." *New York Times* (December 24): 1, 13.

Tonry, Michael, and James Q. Wilson, eds.
1990 *Drugs and Crime.* Chicago: University of Chicago.

Tortora, Gerard J.
1983 *Principles of Human Anatomy,* 3d ed. New York: Harper and Row.

"A Town That's Addicted to Illegal Drug Money"
1991 *New York Times* (May 16): 7 .

Trends in Heroin
1994 Washington DC: Drug Enforcement Administration.

Treaster, Joseph B.
1995 "Colombian Arrest Heartens the U.S." *New York Times* (June 12): 1, 6.

1995b "Drug Therapy: Powerful Tool Reaching Few Inside Prisons." *New York Times* (July 3): 1, 9.

1992 "Nigerian Connection a New Threat in Heroin War." *New York Times* (February 15): 1, 10.

1992b "Hospital Visits Show Abuse of Drugs Is Still on the Rise." *New York Times* (May 14): 6.

1992c "20 Years of War on Drugs and No Victory Yet." *New York Times* (June 14): E7.

1991 "Inside a Crack House: How Drug Use Is Changing." *New York Times* (April 6): 1, 10.

1991b "Cocaine Is Again Surging Out of Panama." *New York Times* (August 13): 1, 4.

1991c "Plan Lets Addicted Mothers Take Their Newborns Home." *New York Times* (September 19): 1, 16.

1991d "Study Finds Drug Use Isn't Just Urban Problem." *New York Times* (October 1): 16.

1991e "Federal Agents Track Down a Cocaine Lab in Upstate New York." *New York Times* (October 5): 9.

1991f "To Avoid AIDS, Users of Heroin Shift from Injecting to Inhaling It." *New York Times* (November 17): 1, 13.

1991g "New York City's Top Cocaine Smugglers Are Arrested in Raids, Police Say." *New York Time* (December 7): 10.

1991h "Use of Cocaine and Heroin Rises Among Urban Youth." *New York Times* (December 19): 12.

1990 "Eager for Good Press, Drug Bosses Sacrifice Laboratory in Colombia." *New York Times* (February 15): 1, 6.

1990b "A Peruvian Peasant Fails to See Bush." *New York Times* (February 16): 9.

1990c "Bypassing Borders, More Drugs Flood Ports." *New York Times* (April 29): 1, 18.

1990d "Programs Find Adolescents' Use of Cocaine Can Be Curtailed." *New York Times* (June 2): 10.

1990e "In Brooklyn, Young Love Is Crushed by the Anguish of Crack and Heroin." *New York Times* (June 21): 16.

1990f "Cocaine Epidemic Has Peaked, Some Suggest." *New York Times* (July 1): 11.

1990g "Cocaine Users Adding Heroin to Their Menus." *New York Times* (July 21): 1, 10.

1990h "At City's Heart, Carnival for Haunted." *New York Times* (September 27): 4.

1990i "Bush Hails Decline in Drug Abuse, but Critics Say Survey Is Flawed." *New York Times* (December 20): 12.

1989 "Colombia Cali Drug Cartel: The Less Flamboyant Competitor of Medellin." *New York Times* (September 19): 6.

1988 "Behind Takeover in Haiti, a Struggle Over Drugs." *New York Times* (June 27): 6.

Trebach, Arnold S.
1987 *The Great Drug War: A Radical Proposal that Could Make America Safe Again.* New York: Macmillan.

1982 *The Heroin Solution.* New Haven, CT: Yale University Press.

Trebach, Arnold S., and Kevin B. Zeese, eds.
1990 *Drug Prohibition and the Conscience of Nations.* Washington, DC: Drug Policy Foundation.

Trujillo, Stephen G.
1992 "Corruption and Cocaine in Peru." *New York Times* (April 7): 19.

Tucker, Richard K.
1991 *The Dragon and the Cross: The Rise and Fall of the Ku Klux Klan in Middle America.* Hamden, CT: Archon Books.

Tullis, LaMond
1995 *Unintended Consequences: Illegal Drugs and Drug Policies in Nine Countries.* Boulder, CO: Lynne Reinner.

Turner, David
1991 "Pragmatic Incoherence: The Changing Face of British Drug Policy." Pages 175–90 in *Searching for Alternatives: Drug Control Policy in the United States,* edited by Melvyn B. Krauss and Edward P. Lazear. Stanford, CA: Hoover Institution.

"Two Studies Disclose Dangers to Brain Caused by Smoking"
1991 *New York Times* (February 25): 6.

Tyler, Patrick E.
1995 "China Battles a Spreading Scourge of Illicit Drugs." *New York Times* (November 15): 1, 7.

1995b "Heroin Influx Ignites a Growing AIDS Epidemic in China." *New York Times* (November 28): 3.

1991 "Teheran Convicts Nine in Opposition." *New York Times* (September 22): 9.

Tymoczko, Dmitri
1996 "The Nitrous Oxide Philosopher." *Atlantic Monthly* (May): 93–101.

Uelmen, Gerald F., and Victor G. Haddox, eds.
1983   *Drug Abuse and the Law.* New York: Clark Board-
        man.
Uhlig, Mark A.
1991   "Graft Sullies Mexico Drug Haul." *New York Times*
        (May 8): 8.
1991b   "Surrender Ends Mexico Prison Takeover." *New
        York Times* (May 31): 3.
1991c   "Standoff." *New York Times* (October 6): 40–48, 73.
1990   "Panama Drug Smugglers Prosper as Dictator's
        Exit Opens the Door." *New York Times* (August 21):
        1, 4.
"U.S. Plans to Resume Using Paraquat to Eradicate
Marijuana."
1988   *New York Times* (July 14): 26.
"U.S. Resists Easing Curb on Marijuana."
1989   *New York Times* (December 31): 14.
"U.S. Seizes Florida Properties Seen as Profits of Drug
Trade."
1987   *New York Times* (December 2): 18.
"U.S. Smoking at Lowest Level in 37 Years"
1992   *Chicago Tribune* (May 22): 2.
1989   "In 'Machine Gun City,' Life's Not Worth a Song."
        New York Times (July 9): 4.
"U.S. to Cut Bolivian Aid Over Drug-War Failures"
1987   *Chicago Tribune* (September 22): 12.
Vaillant, George E.
1983   *The Natural History of Alcoholism.* Cambridge,
        MA: Harvard University Press.
1970   "The Natural History of Narcotic Drug Addiction."
        Seminars in Psychiatry 2 (November): 486–98.
Van Dyke, Craig, and Robert Byck
1982   "Cocaine." *Scientific American* 246 (March):
        128–41.
Verhovek, Sam Howe
1995   "Young, Carefree and in Love with Cigarettes."
        New York Times (July 30): 1, 10.
"Victims of Botched U.S. Drug Sting Sue"
1995   *Chicago Tribune* (January 24): 7.
Vigilantes in Colombia Kill Hundreds of 'Disposables' "
1994   *New York Times* (October 31): 7.
Visher, Christy A.
1990   "Linking Criminal Sanctions, Drug Testing, and
        Drug and Drug Abuse Treatment: A Crime Control
        Strategy for the 1990s." *Criminal Justice Policy Re-
        view* 3: 329–43.
Vivanco, Jose Miguel
1995   "Letter to the New York Times: 'U.S. Aids Bolivia
        in Trampling Rights.' " *New York Times* (July 18):
        14.
Vorenberg, James, and Irving F. Lukoff
1973   "Addiction, Crime, and the Criminal Justice Sys-
        tem." *Federal Probation* 37 (December): 3–7.
Wagstaff, Adam, and Alan Maynard
1988   *Economic Aspects of the Illicit Drug Market and

Drug Enforcement Policies in the United Kingdom.*
        London: Her Majesty's Stationary Office.
Wald, Patricia M., and Annette Abrams
1972   "Drug Education." Pages 123–72 in *Dealing with
        Drug Abuse: A Report to the Ford Foundation.*
        New York: Praeger.
Wald, Patricia M., and Peter Barton Hutt
1972   "The Drug Abuse Survey Project: Summary of
        Findings, Conclusions, and Recommendations."
        Pages 3–61 in *Dealing with Drug Abuse: A Report
        to the Ford Foundation.* New York: Praeger.
Wald, Patricia M., Peter Barton Hutt, and James V. DeLong,
eds.
1972   *Dealing with Drug Abuse: A Report to the Ford
        Foundation.* New York: Praeger.
Waldorf, Dan
1983   "Natural Recovery from Opiate Addiction." *Jour-
        nal of Drug Issues* 13 (Spring): 237–80.
1973   *Careers in Dope.* Englewood Cliffs, NJ: Prentice-
        Hall.
Walker, William O., III, ed.
1992   *Drug Control Policy: Essays in Historical and
        Comparative Perspective.* University Park: Penn-
        sylvania State University.
Wallace, John
1993   "Modern Disease Models of Alcoholism and Other
        Chemical Dependencies: The New Biopsychosocial
        Models." *Drugs and Society* 8 (1): 69–87.
Wallance, Gregory
1981   *Papa's Game.* New York: Ballantine.
"War on Drugs Is Lost"
1996   *National Review* (February 12): 34–48.
Warner, Roger
1986   *Invisible Hand: The Marijuana Business.* New
        York: William Morrow.
Washton, Arnold M
1989   *Cocaine Addiction: Treatment, Recovery, and Re-
        lapse Prevention.* New York: Norton.
Washton, Arnold M., and Mark S. Gold
1987   "Recent Trends in Cocaine Abuse as Seen from the
        '800-Cocaine Hotline.' " Pages 10–22 in *Cocaine:
        A Clinicians Handbook,* edited by Washton and
        Gold. New York: Guilford.
Washton, Arnold M., Nannette S. Stone, Edward C.
Henrickson
1988   "Cocaine Abuse." Pages 364–89 in *Assessment of
        Addictive Behaviors,* edited by Dennis M. Donovan
        and G. Alan Marlatt. New York: Guilford.
Washton, Arnold M., and Nanette Stone-Washton
1993   "Outpatient Treatment of Cocaine and Crack Ad-
        diction: A Clinical Perspective." Pages 15–30 in
        *Cocaine Treatment: Research and Clinical Per-
        spectives,"* edited by Frank M. Tims and Carl G.
        Leukefeld. Rockville, MD: National Institute on
        Drug Abuse.

Waterson, Alisse
1993 *Addicts in the Political Economy.* Philadelphia: Temple University Press.

Watlington, Dennis
1987 "Between the Cracks." *Vanity Fair* (December): 146–51, 184.

Weber, Max
1949 *The Methodology of the Social Sciences.* Glencoe, IL: Free Press.

Weil, Andrew
1995 "The New Politics of Coca." *New Yorker* (May 15): 70–80.

Weiner, Eric
1989 "Mexico Shooting Down Drug Planes, Officials Say." *New York Times* (December 8): 11.

Weiner, Tim
1994 "Blowback from the Afghanistan Battlefield." *New York Times Magazine* (March 13): 52–55.

Weingarten, Paul
1989 "Profits, Perils Higher for Today's Bootleggers." *Chicago Tribune* (September 14): 1, 22.
1989b "Drug Cash Flows Over U.S. Border." *Chicago Tribune* (December 10): 25.

Weinstein, Adam K.
1988 "Prosecuting Attorneys for Money Laundering: A New and Questionable Weapon in the War on Crime." *Law and Contemporary Problems* 51 (Winter): 369–86.

Weisheit, Ralph A.
1990 "Cash Crop: A Study of Illicit Marijuana Growers." Working draft for the National Institute of Justice.
1990b "Declaring a 'Civil' War on Drugs." Pages 1–10 in *Drug, Crime and the Criminal Justice System,* edited by Ralph A. Weisheit. Cincinnati: Anderson.
1989 "Domestic Marijuana Growers: Mainstreaming Deviance." Paper presented at the annual meeting of the American Society of Criminology, Reno, NV, November.

Weisman, Alan
1989 "Dangerous Days in the Macarena." *New York Times Magazine* (April 23): 40–48.

Weiss, Roger D., and Steven M. Mirin
1987 *Cocaine.* Washington, DC: American Psychiatric Press.

Wellisch, Jean, Michael L. Prendergast, M. Douglas Anglin
1994 *Drug-Abusing Women Offenders: Results of a National Survey.* Washington, DC: National Institute of Justice.

Weppner, Robert S.
1983 *The Untherapeutic Community: Organizational Behavior in a Failed Addiction Treatment Program.* Lincoln: University of Nebraska Press.

Wesson, Donald R., and David E. Smith
1985 "Cocaine: Treatment Perspectives." Pages 193–203 in *Cocaine Use in America: Epidemiologic and Clinical Perspectives,* edited by Nicholas J. Kozel and Edgar H. Adams. Rockville, MD: National Institute on Drug Abuse.
1977 *Barbiturates: Their Use, Misuse, and Abuse.* New York: Human Sciences Press.

Westermeyer, Joseph, and Ronald S. Krug, eds.
1991 *Substance Abuse Services: A Guide to Planning and Management.* Chicago: American Hospital Association.

Westrate, David L.
1985 "Drug Trafficking and Terrorism." *Drug Enforcement* (Summer): 19–24.

Wethern, George
1978 *A Wayward Angel.* New York: Marek Publishers.

Wever, Leon
1994 "Drugs as a Public Health Problem." Pages 59–74 in *Between Prohibition and Legalization: The Dutch Experiment in Drug Policy,* edited by Ed. Leuw and I. Haen Marshall. Amsterdam: Kugler Publications.

Wexler, Harry K., Gregory P. Falkin, and Douglas S. Lipton
1990 "Outcome Evaluation of a Prison Therapeutic Community for Substance Abuse Treatment." *Criminal Justice and Behavior* 15: 71–92.

Wexler, Harry K., Douglas S. Lipton, and Kenneth Foster
1985 "Outcome Evaluation of a Prison Therapeutic Community for Substance Abuse Treatment: Preliminary Results." Paper presented at the American Society of Criminology, San Diego, CA, November.

Wexler, Harry K., and Ronald Williams
1986 "The Stay 'N Out Therapeutic Community: Prison Treatment for Substance Abusers." *Journal of Psychoactive Drugs* 18 (July-September): 221–30.

"Which War on Drugs?"
1987 *New York Times* Editorial (August 31): 18.

White House Conference for a Drug-Free America
1988 *Final Report.* Washington, DC: U.S. Government Printing Office.

White, Peter
1989 "Coca—An Ancient Herb Turns Deadly." *National Geographic* (January): 3–47.

Whitlock, Rod Van, Howard Collings, and Cathleen Burnett
1990 "Relationship Between Cocaine Use and Severity of Crime." Paper presented at the annual meeting of the American Society of Criminology, Baltimore, November.

Whitman, David, with Dorian Friedman
1990 "The Streets Are Filled with Coke." *U.S. News and World Report* (March 5): 24–26.

"Why Did Gunmen Yield in Colombia?"
1991 *New York Times* (December 10): 4.

Wicker, Tom
1987 "Drugs and Alcohol." *New York Times* (May 13): 27

"Widening Drug War"
1991 *Newsweek* (July 1): 32–43.

Wiebe, Robert H.

1967   *The Search for Order: 1877–1920.* New York: Hill and Wang.

Wieczorek, William F., John W. Welte, and Ernest L. Abel

1990   "Alcohol, Drugs and Murder: A Study of Convicted Homicide Offenders." *Journal of Criminal Justice* 18: 217–27.

Wiedrich, Bob

1988   "Airlines Taking the Rap for Drug Smugglers." *Chicago Tribune* (July 25): Sec. 4: 1, 6.

Wiegand, Ginny

1988   "Drug Killings Soar Here." *Philadelphia Inquirer* (July 24): 1, 8–10.

Wilbanks, William

1990   "The Danger in Viewing Addicts as Victims: A Critique of the Disease Model of Addiction." *Criminal Justice Policy Review* 3: 407–22.

Wilkerson, Isabel

1991   "Court Backs Woman in Pregnancy Drug Case." *New York Times* (April 3): 13.

Williams, Jay R., Lawrence J. Redlinger, and Peter K. Manning

1979   *Police Narcotics Control: Patterns and Strategies.* Washington, DC: U.S. Government Printing Office.

Williams, Terry

1989   *The Cocaine Kids: The Inside Story of a Teenage Drug Ring.* Reading, MA: Addison-Wesley.

Willoughby, Alan

1988   *The Alcohol-Troubled Person: Known and Unknown.* Chicago: Nelson-Hall.

Wilson, James Q.

1990   "Against the Legalization of Drugs." *Commentary* 89 (February): 21–28.

1978   *The Investigators: Managing FBI and Narcotics Agents.* New York: Basic Books.

1975   *Thinking About Crime.* New York: Basic Books.

Wilson, Terry

1991   "County Jail Inmate Total Now Tops 8,000." *Chicago Tribune* (September 13): Sec. 2: 3.

1990   "Up in Smoke." *Chicago Tribune* (April 2): Sec. 5: 1, 5.

Wines, Michael

1989   "Drug Ring-Profits Reported Seized." *New York Times* (December 7): 8.

1988   "Against a Tide of Drugs in New York the Police Resort to a Holding Action." *New York Times* (June 24): 12.

Winger, Gail

1988   "Pharmacological Modifications of Cocaine and Opioid Self-Administration." Pages 125–36 in *Mechanisms of Cocaine Abuse and Toxicity,* edited by Doris Clouet, Khursheed Asghar, and Roger Brown. Rockville, MD: National Institute on Drug Abuse.

Winick, Charles

1964   "Physician Narcotic Addicts." Pages 261–79 in *The Other Side: Perspectives on Deviance,* edited by Howard Becker. New York: Free Press.

Winter, Jerrold C.

1994   "The Stimulus Effects of Serotonergic Hallucinogens in Animals." Pages 157–82 in *Hallucinogens: An Update,* edited by Geraline C. Lin and Richard A. Glennon. Rockville, MD: National Institute on Drug Abuse.

Winters, Ken C., and George Henly

1988   "Assessing Adolescents Who Abuse Chemicals: The Chemical Dependency Adolescent Assessment Project." Pages 4–18 in *Adolescent Drug Abuse: Analyses of Treatment Research,* edited by Elizabeth R. Rahdert and John Grabowski. Rockville, MD: National Institute on Drug Abuse.

Wise, Roy A.

1994   "Cocaine Reward and Cocaine Craving: The Role of Dopamine in Perspective." Pages 191–206 in *Neurobiological Models for Evaluating Mechanisms Underlying Cocaine Addiction,* edited by Lynda Erinoff and Roger M. Brown. Rockville, MD: National Institute on Drug Abuse.

Wish, Eric

n.d.   *Drug Testing.* Rockville, MD: National Institute of Justice.

Wish, Eric D., and Bruce Johnson

1986   "The Impact of Substance Abuse on Criminal Careers." Pages 52–88 in *Criminal Careers and Career Criminals,* edited by Alfred Blumstein, Jacqueline Cohen, Jeffrey A. Roth, and Christy A. Visher. Washington, DC: National Academy Press.

Wishart, David

1974   "The Opium Poppy: The Forbidden Crop." *Journal of Geography* 73 (January): 14–25.

Wisotsky, Steven

1987   *Breaking the Impasse in the War on Drugs.* Westport, CT: Greenwood.

Witkin, Gordon

1991   "The Men Who Created Crack." *U.S. News and World Report* (August 19): 44–53.

Witkin, Gordon, and Jennifer Griffin

1994   "The New Opium Wars." *U.S. News and World Report* (October 10): 39–44.

Wodak, Alex

1990   "Needle Exchange Succeeding in Australia." Letter to the *New York Times* (March 26): 14.

Wolfe, Tom

1968   *The Electric Kool-Aid Acid Test.* New York: Farrar, Straus and Giroux.

Wood, Daniel

1991   "Bar Lab Challenges the Alcohol Mystique." *Chicago Tribune* (February 24): Sec. 5: 6.

Wood, Roland W.
1973   "18,000 Addicts Later: A Look at California's Civil
        Addict Program." *Federal Probation* 38 (March):
        26–31.
Woodiwiss, Michael
1988   *Crime, Crusades and Corruption: Prohibition in
        the United States, 1900–1987.* Totawa, NJ: Barnes
        and Noble.
Woods, James R., Jr.
1993   "Effects of Drugs of Abuse on Mother and Fetus."
        Pages 179–87 in *International Research Confer-
        ence on Biomedical Approaches to Illicit Drug De-
        mand Reduction,* edited by Christine R. Hartel.
        Washington, DC: U.S. Government Printing Office.
Woody, George E., Lester Lubrosky, A. Thomas McLellan,
Charles P. O'Brien, Aren T. Beck, Jack Blaine, Ira Herman,
and Anita Hole
1983   "Psychotherapy for Opiate Addicts: Does It Help?"
        Archives of General Psychiatry 40 (June): 639–45.
Wren, Christopher S.
1996a   "Mexican Role in Cocaine is Exposed in U.S.
        Seizure." *New York Times* (May 3): C19.
1996b   "New Law-Enforcement Worry: Surge in Ampheta-
        mine Use." *New York Times* (February 14): 12.
1996c   "U.S. Imposes Controls on Chemical Exports to
        Colombia." *New York Times* (March 28): 13.
Wright, Fred D., Aaron T. Beck, Cory F. Newman, and
Bruce S. Liese
1993   "Cognitive Therapy of Substance Abuse: Theoreti-
        cal Rationale." Pages 123–46 in *Behavioral Treat-
        ments for Drug Abuse and Dependence,* edited by
        Lisa Simon Onken, John D. Blaine, and John J.
        Boren. Rockville, MD: National Institute on Drug
        Abuse.
Wurmser, Leon
1978   "Mr. Pecksniff's Horse? (Psychodynamics in Com-
        pulsive Drug Use)." Pages 36–72 in *Psychodynam-
        ics of Drug Dependence,* edited by Jack D. Blaine
        and Demetrios A. Julius. Rockville, MD: National
        Institute on Drug Abuse.
Wysong, Earl, Richard Aniskiewicz, and David Wright
1994   "Truth and DARE: Drug Education to Graduation
        and as Symbolic Politics." *Social Problems* 41 (Au-
        gust): 448–72.

Yates, Ronald E.
1987   "Afghanistan Invasion Propels Pakistan to Top in
        Opium Trade." *Chicago Tribune* (February 12): 32.
Yorke, Clifford
1970   "A Critical Review of Some Psychoanalytic Litera-
        ture on Drug Addiction." *British Journal of Medical
        Psychology* 43: 141–59.
Young, James Harvey
1961   *The Toadstool Millionaires: A Social History of
        Patent Medicines in America Before Federal Regu-
        lation.* Princeton, NJ: Princeton University Press.
Yu, Jiang and William R. Willford
1994   "Alcohol, Other Drugs, and Criminality: A Struc-
        tural Analysis." *American Journal of Alcohol and
        Drug Abuse* 20 (No. 3): 373–93.
Zahniser, Nancy R., Joanna Peris, Linda P. Dwoskin,
Pamela Curella, Robert P. Yasuda, Laurie O'Keefe, and
Sally J. Boyson
1988   "Sensitization to Cocaine in the Nigrostriatal
        Dopamine System." Pages 55–77 in *Mechanisms of
        Cocaine Abuse and Toxicity,* edited by Doris
        Clouet, Khursheed Asghar, and Roger Brown.
        Rockville, MD: National Institute on Drug Abuse.
Zimmer, Lynn
1990   "Proactive Policing Against Street-Level Drug
        Trafficking." *American Journal of Police* 9:
        43–74.
Zimring, Franklin E., and Gordon Hawkins
1992   *The Search for Rational Drug Control.* New York:
        Cambridge University Press.
Zinberg, Norman E.
1984   *Drug, Set, and Setting: The Basis for Controlled In-
        toxicant Use.* New Haven, CT: Yale University
        Press.
Zinberg, Norman E., Wayne M. Harding, Shirley M.
Stelmack, and Robert A. Marblestone
1978   "Patterns of Heroin Abuse." Pages 10–24 in *Recent
        Developments in Chemotherapy of Narcotic Addic-
        tion,* edited by Benjamin Kissin, Joyce H. Lowin-
        son, and Robert B. Millman. New York: New York
        Academy of Sciences.
Zinberg, Norman E., and John A. Robertson
1972   *Drugs and the Public.* New York: Simon and
        Schuster.

AUTHOR INDEX

SUBJECT INDEX

Coca Cola, 48, 50
Cocaine
    blacks and, 48–49
    business of, 218–30
    crack, 9, 12, 49–50, 100–102,
        155–56, 254
    dangers, 104
    history of, 47–50, 67
    medical use, 103
    pharmacology, 96–105,
    psychology. *See* Drug abuse/use,
        psychological explanations of
    sociology of. *See* Drug abuse/use,
        sociological explanations of
    stages, 145
    tolerance, 102–3
    withdrawal, 102–3
Coffee. *See* Caffeine
Colombian drug dealers, 219, 220,
    221–29, 242–43
Commission on Marijuana and Drug
    Abuse, 63
Comprehensive Drug Abuse
    Prevention and Control Act of
    1970, 63–64, 276, 277,
    278–80
Conspiracy, 276, 280–81
Continuing Criminal Enterprise, 281,
    298–99
Controlled Substances Act. *See*
    Comprehensive Drug Abuse
    Prevention and Control Act of
    1970
Corruption, 240, 270–72
Crack. *See* Cocaine, crack
Crime control model, 264–67
Cuban drug dealers, 221, 222
Cure industry, 162–63
Customs Service, 274, 289–91

DARE. *See* Project DARE
Daytop Village, 191–92
Decriminalization. *See* Drug policy,
    decriminalization
Department of Defense (DOD), 64,
    295–97
Depressants, 11, 76–78. *See also*
    specific drugs
Designer drugs, 118
Detoxification, 165–66
Disease model, 70, 148
Dole, Vincent, 166, 168. *See also*
    Author Index
Dopamine, 95, 98–99, 170
Drinking. *See* Alcohol

Drug abuse/use
    characteristics of, 4–5
    crime and, 15–22
    defined, 3–8
    disease model of, 14, 196, 197
    English response to. *See* Drug
        policy Great Britain
    extent of, 1, 309–14
    history of, chapter 2,
    influences on, 11
    by medical doctors, 1n
    pharmacology of, chapter 3, 169
    policy. *See* Drug policy
    polydrug use, 12–13, 21, 71–72,
        168
    prevention, 204–15
    psychological explanations of,
        125–40
        behaviorism/learning theory,
            135–40, 153, 174
        psychoanalytic, 126–35, 169,
            172–74
    public health model, 14
    self-medication thesis. *See* Self-
        medication thesis
    sociological explanations of, 140–59
        anomie, 136, 146–49
        differential association, 149–51,
            152
        social control, 151–53
        subcultures, 153–56
        symbolic interactionism
            (labeling), 155, 156–59
    treatment for. *See* Treatment
    violence and, 15–22
Drug Abuse Control Amendments of
    1965, 61
Drug Abuse Warning Network
    (DAWN), 312–13
Drug court, 184, 186
"Drug Czar." *See* Office of National
    Drug Control Policy
Drug, defined, 2–3
Drug education. *See* Drug abuse/use,
    prevention
Drug Enforcement Administration
    (DEA), 64, 291–92
Drug law enforcement. *See* Law
    enforcement
Drug policy, 314–59
    decriminalization, 318–30
    Great Britain, 314–18
    harm reduction, 330–32
    of United States, 13–14, 18,
        333–57

Drug testing, 349–51
Drug trafficking, chapter 6
    Cali cartel, 227–29
    Golden Triangle/Southeast Asia,
        231–35
    Medellín cartel, 227–29
    Mexican, 229, 230
    street level, 251–56
Drugs. *See* specific drugs
Drugs decriminalization. *See*
    Decriminalization
Due process model, 264–67
Du Pont, Robert L., 64

Ecstasy. *See* MDMA
Endorphins, 76–78
English system. *See* Drug policy,
    Great Britain
Enkephalins. *See* Endorphins
Ephedra. *See* Herbal stimulants
Exclusionary rule, 265

Federal Bureau of Investigation
    (FBI), 64, 292
Federal Bureau of Narcotics (FBN),
    41–42, 52, 60, 61, 63
Fetal liability, 352–53
Forfeiture, 283–86
"French Connection," 239, 246
Freud, Sigmund, 48–49, 126, 172. *See
    also* Author Index

Gangs, drug trafficking by. *See* Drug
    trafficking, street level
Goddard, James, 54
Giordano, Harry, 61
Golden Crescent, 237–39
Golden Triangle, 231–37
Gompers, Samuel, 37
Grand jury, 286–87

Hague Convention, 40
Hallucinogins, 11
    dangers of, 112
    history of, 57–59
    pharmacology, 109–12
    tolerance, 112
Harm reduction. *See* Drug policy,
    harm reduction
Harrison Act, 40–42
Hashish, 116
Herbal stimulants, 119–20
Heroin
    business of, chapter 6
    dangers of, 85